WILLIAM SERRIN

HOMESTEAD

William Serrin was the labor and workplace correspondent for *The New York Times* from 1979 until 1986, when he left to write this book. He began his career as a reporter on his hometown newspaper, the *Saginaw (Michigan) News,* then he was a reporter and editor for the *Detroit Free Press.* He has written for numerous publications, among them *The Nation, The New York Times Magazine, The Village Voice,* and the *National Catholic Reporter.* He is the author of *The Company and the Union,* a study of the General Motors Corporation and the United Automobile Workers. He and his wife, Judith, have two daughters, Sara and Catherine, and reside in Glen Ridge, New Jersey. He currently is an associate professor of journalism at New York University.

ALSO BY WILLIAM SERRIN

The Company and the Union:
*The "Civilized Relationship" of the
General Motors Corporation and the
United Automobile Workers*

HOMESTEAD

Photo by Kucera International, Inc.
Reprinted with the permission of the Southwestern Regional Planning Commission.

Aerial view of Homestead, 1990.

H O M E

THE GLORY AND TRAGEDY OF

VINTAGE BOOKS · A DIVISION O

STEAD

AN AMERICAN STEEL TOWN

WILLIAM SERRIN

RANDOM HOUSE, INC. • NEW YORK

First Vintage Books Edition, September 1993

Copyright © 1992, 1993 by William Serrin

All rights reserved under International and Pan-American
Copyright Conventions. Published in the United States by
Vintage Books, a division of Random House, Inc., New York,
and simultaneously in Canada by Random House of Canada
Limited, Toronto. Originally published in hardcover by Times
Books, a division of Random House, Inc., New York, in 1992.

Grateful acknowledgment is made to the following for
permission to reprint previously published material:

HarperCollins Publishers, Inc.: Excerpt from *Right to Challenge*
by John Herling. Copyright © 1972 by John Herling. Reprinted
by permission of HarperCollins Publishers, Inc.

The New York Times: Excerpt from an article by Louis Stark,
June 15, 1934; excerpt from "Business, Too, Has Ivory
Towers" by Clarence B. Randall from *The New York Times
Magazine,* July 1963; excerpt from an editorial, November 26,
1964. Copyright 1934, © 1963, 1964 by The New York Times
Company. Reprinted by permission.

Penton Publishing: Excerpt from an article by Edgar Speer from
the June 1969 issue of *33 Metal Producing.* Reprinted by
permission of Penton Publishing.

Viking Penguin, a division of Penguin Books USA Inc.: Excerpt
from *The Roosevelt I Knew* by Frances Perkins. Copyright 1946
by Frances Perkins. Copyright © renewed 1974 by Susanna W.
Coggeshall. Reprinted by permission of Viking Penguin, a
division of Penguin Books USA Inc.

Library of Congress Cataloging-in-Publication Data
Serrin, William.
Homestead: the glory and tragedy of an American steel town/
William Serrin.—1st Vintage Books ed.
p.   cm.
Includes bibliographical references and index.
ISBN 0-679-74817-2
1. Homestead (Pa.)—History. 2. Steel industry and trade—
Pennsylvania—Homestead—History. 3. Iron and steel
workers—Pennsylvania—Homestead—History. I. Title.
[F159.H7S47 1993]
974.8'85—dc20   93-13105
CIP

Map on page x by Kristin Bearse

Manufactured in the United States of America
10 9 8 7 6 5 4 3

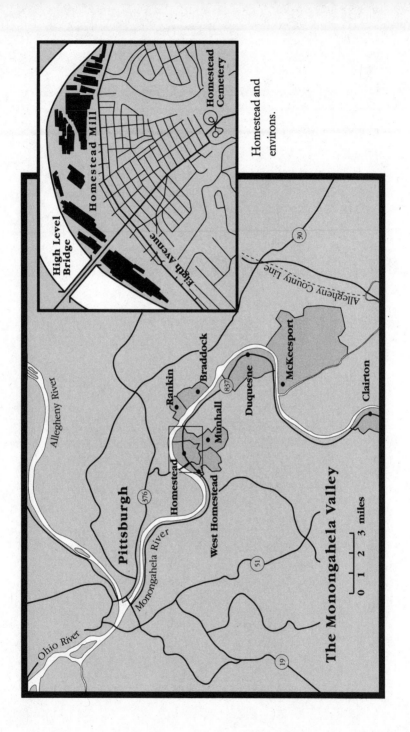

The Monongahela Valley

0 1 2 3 miles

Ohio River

Allegheny River

Monongahela River

Pittsburgh

Homestead

West Homestead

Rankin

Braddock

Munhall

Duquesne

McKeesport

Clairton

Allegheny County Line

Homestead and environs.

High Level Bridge

Homestead Mill

Eighth Avenue

Homestead Cemetery

I have always had one rule: if a workman sticks up his head, hit it.

> —A member of the executive committee of the United States Steel Corporation, early in this century

. . . the labor leaders are newly risen men; no matter how much bluster some of them may employ, they feel the social gap. They reveal their feelings in their general tendency to imitate the standard middle-class business-like mode of living, and by the resentment they show when they talk about business's lack of respect for labor. This craving for status and respect is often a strong undercurrent of their lives.

> —C. Wright Mills, *The New Men of Power: America's Labor Leaders,* 1948

I would rather see steel poured than hear a great symphony.

> —Mary Heaton Vorse, *Men and Steel,* 1919

ACKNOWLEDGMENTS

I OWE MUCH TO MANY PEOPLE in the reporting and writing of this book. In Homestead and the rest of the Pittsburgh and Monongahela Valley areas, people were gracious and helpful to me even on occasions when they knew, I suspect, I did not share their points of view.

I wish to thank these people who were of assistance to me: Anita Alverio and Eric Leif Davin, Robert Anderson and Theresa Chalich, Cheryl Bacco, Jack Bair, Eileen Barrett, William Baumgarten, Herman W. Benson, Walter N. Bielich, Bill Brennan, Mark M. Brown, William (Car Wash) Brown, Tony Buba, Steve Butala, Ed Buzinka, Father Bernard Costello, Carol and George Couvaris, Marie Coyne, Charles R. Cronin of Weirton Steel, George DeBolt, David Demarest of Carnegie-Mellon University, James Dockery, Steffi Domike, Michael Drapkin, John Duch, Betty Esper, Ed Estok, Bill Evans, Anselmo (Babe) Fernandez, Rose G. Ferraro, George A. Ferris of Wheeling-Pittsburgh Steel Corporation, Russell Gibbons, Jack Giran, Malvin R. Goode, Joseph Havrilla, Bill Holoman, Charles L. Honeywell, David Houston of the University of Pittsburgh, Robert Kosko, Bob Krovocheck, Lawrence G. Kuhn of the Iron and Steel Society, Larry Levine, Susan Lewis, Jerry Longo, Staughton and Alice Lynd, Charles McCollester, Michelle McMills, Sister Marie Margaret, Sam Marks, Jack Melvin, Walter Miller, David Montgomery of Yale University, Spanky O'Toole, Ed Palo, Kelly Park of the Park Corporation, Evelyn Patterson, Bernard R. Queneau, Mary Edna Rahuba, Ed Rappa, Larry Regan, Monsignor Charles Owen Rice, Harold J. Ruttenberg, Joel Sabadasz, Edward Sadlowski, Ronald Schatz of Wesleyan University, Bobby Schneider, Natalie Schwoeble, Dan Spillane, Ray Supak, Karen Supansic, R. P. Suto, John Tarasevich, John J. Tichon, Bob Todd, Charles Van Horn, Louis Washowich, Denny Wilcox, Earle Wittpenn of The (Monongahela) Valley Mirror, Barbara Wolfe, Jennie Yuhaschek.

A number of people were of special assistance to me, helping me time and again and on numerous occasions extending special hospitalities to me. They included Joseph and Florence Chiodo, Marty and Skip Costa, Larry Evans, Leslie Evans, William J. Gaughan, Randolph J. Harris, Ann and John Hart, John and Ann Hornak, Mark and Beth Hornak, Raymond Hornak, Christopher Kelly and Paula Kelly, John J. McLean, Jr., and Jean McLean, Steve Simko, Michael Stout, Richard J. and Noreen Terrick and Chris Terrick, Margaret Mary Vojtko, the Rev. James D. Von Dreele, Ronald and Jean Weisen and Bobby Weisen.

Joseph Chiodo introduced me to numerous people and was always pleasant to me at his friendly food and drink emporium; Ann Hart, the director of the Carnegie Library of Homestead, similarly was always gracious and helpful. Christopher Kelly was of great assistance to me on numerous occasions; one fine May night, he and his wife, Paula, took me to a Pittsburgh Pirates game. Steve Simko was always helpful and in fine spirits and was a great storyteller to boot. Margaret Mary Vojtko, a historian of the town and a scholar, was helpful to me on numerous occasions; Ronald Weisen and the Rev. Von Dreele always found time for me, and both, in an often harsh and depressing world, were also always of good humor.

I also wish to thank William J. Gaughan, steelworker and historian, who opened to me his extensive collection of photographs and other materials of the Homestead Works. His assistance was invaluable to me. In addition, I wish to thank Randolph J. Harris, who also provided Homestead photographs and historic materials to me. Both of these men were always willing to share with me their views on events that had transpired, or were transpiring, in Homestead.

To all these people, I owe more than I can say.

A number of Pittsburgh reporters assisted me at important junctures. They included Jim McKay of the *Pittsburgh Post-Gazette* and Patricia Van Horn and Mary Kane, reporters, and Madelyn Ross, managing editor, of the *Pittsburgh Press*.

I also must give special thanks to the late Rich Locher, whose story, plus my inability to get that story into print, did much to foster my interest in the workers and townspeople of Homestead following the closure of the Homestead Works.

I also owe special gratitude to Alice and George Bruhn, of Durant, Iowa.

A number of individuals helped me in gaining financial assistance for this book. Without this help, I could not have completed my task. These people included Daniel Cantor; James Dwyer and others of the Richard Goldensohn Fund; Carol and W. H. Ferry; Moe Foner of the Bread and Roses Cultural Project, Inc., of New York City; Victor Gotbaum of the

Labor Center at the City University of New York; William Kornblum of the Graduate Center at City University of New York; Les Leopold of the Labor Center of New York; Joyce Miller and Jack Sheinkman at the Sidney Hillman Foundation; Richard Severo at Vassar College; and Stanley Sheinbaum. I would also like to thank James DeGeorge and Craig Swauger and other members of the faculty of the Department of Journalism at Indiana University of Pennsylvania, which awarded me the Elizabeth Ray Sweeney visiting professorship of journalism, and members of the faculty, particularly Harley Shaiken, of the Department of Communication at the University of California, San Diego, which selected me as a regents' lecturer.

I should also like to thank Linda Lake of *The New York Times*; Tony Mazzocchi, the labor activist; Thomas Fox of the *National Catholic Reporter*; Irwin Marcus and Martin J. Morand, both faculty members at Indiana University of Pennsylvania, who befriended me on numerous occasions; Nick Salvatore and Peter Lazes, both of Cornell University; Michael P. Weber of Carnegie-Mellon University; and David Parker, director of information for the National Labor Relations Board.

I would also like to thank Earl Dotter, the splendid photographer of working-class people, for coming to Homestead to take the photographs of Homestead today and for working so diligently when he was there. This book is much better because of these handsome photographs.

I know that I have failed to mention others who assisted me, and to them I apologize.

I would also like to thank my two editors at Random House, Peter Osnos and Olga Tarnowski. At a time when it is widely reported that book editing no longer is meticulous or professional, the two again and again demonstrated highly skilled editing in the shaping of this book. I owe each an enormous debt.

I would, in addition, like to thank my dog, Zeke, a bassett, who loyally sat under my desk for many months as I was writing this book. On cold mornings, he kept my feet warm.

I also wish to express my debt to three former professors of mine, Dr. John Hepler, Dr. Arthur Waterman, and Dr. Mary Wills, all of Central Michigan University, who encouraged me to seek a career in writing. Without them, I likely would have ended up in a far less important profession than journalism.

Finally, I would like to thank my wife, Judith, a skilled journalist, who once again encouraged me to forsake the security of a major newspaper to embark upon an independent writing project and who

CONTENTS

PART FOUR

INTRODUCTION

I WROTE THIS BOOK because I came to understand that if I did not, no one would.

For several years I had been covering industrial decline in New York, Pennsylvania, West Virginia, Ohio, Michigan, and other parts of the East and Midwest for *The New York Times*. What was going on was phenomenal. Tens of thousands of men and women were losing their jobs. Many were in their forties and fifties, others in their sixties. Many would never find meaningful employment again. Industry after industry was in crisis —steel, mining, autos, rubber, textiles, the needle trades, and more. A way of life was disappearing as town after town, whole areas of America, were going down.

What was more phenomenal was that no one seemed to care. People on Wall Street or in Washington said that the economy was robust, that the 1980s were a splendid time to be alive, that there were fortunes to be made. The press ate this notion up and called the 1980s "the go-go years." It was as though the men and women in the steel towns, the mining towns, the auto towns, the farm towns, on the poultry processing lines, in the back offices—working-class people across the country—did not exist.

Then, in the spring of 1986, I heard that the Homestead Works, at Homestead, Pennsylvania, would be closed. I was stunned. The Homestead Works was the most famous steel mill in the world. In the 1880s, with the introduction of the open-hearth process, it had brought cheap steel, easily produced in large quantities, to the world. The Homestead Works turned out rails for railroads as America moved west, beams and plates for many of the emblematic structures of the American skyline, plates that transformed the American Navy from a wooden-hulled into a steel-hulled armada and made America a twentieth-century imperial power.

On July 6, 1892, the mill was the site of the epochal fight between striking workers and armed men employed by the Pinkerton Detective

Agency. The strike, which stretched on until just before Christmas, broke unionism in the American steel industry and set back unionism everywhere in America until the advent of the New Deal of Franklin Delano Roosevelt.

The town of Homestead, which grew up around the mill, was the archetype of the American mill town produced by the Industrial Revolution, a rich, vibrant community, as important in its way as the mill. It was a great American place.

I used to poke about Homestead when I was doing newspaper work —under strict deadlines, which limited what I could do—and wonder what this storied place was like—who the people were, what had gone on there.

Now the mill was closing, and the town was collapsing as well. More than that, the steel industry—the industry that had been the basis for the Industrial Revolution in America, that had led the way in the astounding transformation of America in the twentieth century—was disappearing.

So I decided to go to Homestead, and stay there for a while, to see what happens when a way of life ends, to see what happens to people and communities and their institutions when a mill closes. I wanted, too, to try to figure out what had happened in the mills, in the steel corporation, in the steelworkers' union, to bring down a once-vibrant mill and town, to bring down a once-stupendous industry. Perhaps, I thought, by reporting and writing the story I could make the Homestead workers and the people of Homestead—by extension, working-class people everywhere—important.

This decision meant leaving newspaper journalism, which I had always enjoyed immensely, and this was not easy. It meant saying goodbye to breaking stories, bylines, the camaraderie and hijinks of the newsroom; goodbye, too, to the substantial salary, the substantial expense account.

I had been to Homestead many times before I began the book. The first time was years before, when I was driving with my wife and daughters from Washington to Detroit. We had gotten off the Pennsylvania Turnpike for some reason and were lost, and soon we were driving through a land of small homes stuck into hillsides—the houses were called "clingers," I was to learn in the course of my work on this book— and onion-domed churches and mills belching fire and smoke. It was, we thought, as though we had come to another country.

Later, I passed through Homestead as the labor and workplace correspondent of *The New York Times*. The steel industry and much of the rest of industrial America were coming apart, and Homestead and the Monongahela Valley were the logical places to go to report about what was going on. But I wasn't getting the story, and nobody else was getting it, either.

Some journalists wrote good pieces, but most never went to Homestead or the other industrial towns, or if they did they came in like paratroopers, jumping in with their notebooks and tape recorders and minicameras, getting quotes on the main streets and in the bars and then getting back into their taxicabs or rented cars and going back to the airport and flying back to their offices.

Some journalists would crank out long analyses without leaving the newsroom. They would arrange interviews through public-relations officers and telephone Wall Street stock analysts or university experts for quotes; most of these analysts and university experts said the same thing, that what the steel industry was doing, "downsizing"—that is, closing mills and firing workers—made eminent sense.

This was phenomenal, too, this perverted logic. It was as if a person were ill, and every time the person went to the doctor the doctor cut off another member, a finger, a toe, an arm, a leg, and after each amputation the doctor remarked how much better the patient was looking.

This was shoddy journalism, but it was expectable. A curious phenomenon has occurred in American journalism. Journalists have become as ambitious, as career-minded, as any stockbroker or banker. And labor journalism—a simple interest in working-class people—has fallen into disrepute.

I remember standing in Homestead on a hot, muggy July day. The Homestead Works was closing that day, and I watched the last men come from the plant, the last of tens of thousands of men and women who had worked there, who had, in a substantial way, built America. After a time I realized that I was the only journalist there.

I had participated in some facile journalism myself. I had called the stock analysts and economists and gotten quotes on what was wrong with the steel industry and put them in the paper. Imports, a worldwide oversupply of steel, changing markets—that was what was wrong.

But I came to realize that these experts in their glass offices for the most part did not have the slightest idea what was wrong with the steel industry. Like the journalists, most of them had never been to steel towns, had never talked to workers, blue- and white-collar, who made up the industry; one expert confessed to me he had never been in a steel mill, had never seen steel made.

It was mandatory, I thought, to go and see for myself, over a long period of time, what was occurring. So I split my time between my home in New Jersey and whatever were the cheapest accommodations I could find in or near Homestead—a room above a bar, college dormitories in Pittsburgh during the summer, inexpensive motel chains. It was a far cry from my days in the big hotels with the unlimited expense accounts. But at times, going to Homestead was like going home, and this made my reporting and writing easier.

I was raised in a working-class family in what was an industrial town, Saginaw, Michigan. My father was a working-class man if ever there was one. He had once had higher goals, had gone for a year, perhaps two, to college, had served his country in World War II. But he had never been able to advance, for many reasons, and had ended up as a baker in a hot, demanding bakery. The work was as hard in that bakery as it was in a steel mill. I used to take his lunch to him and could see what he did.

For years, it was his responsibility to take huge, heavy trays of bread, one after the other, and place them in an oven to be baked. When the baking was completed, he would lift the huge, heavy trays of bread from the oven and return them to the carts from which he had got them.

After some years, for a few cents more an hour, he was promoted, if that was the word, to the bun department, where it was his responsibility to take huge, heavy trays of buns, one after the other, and place them in the oven to be baked, and, when the baking was completed, to remove the huge, heavy trays of buns from the oven and return them to the carts from which he had got them.

It was, bread or buns, a burdensome position, and he said to me, "Whatever you do, don't end up doing this."

My memory is that he was white. White T-shirt, white pants, white hat, white apron, and, over all this and on his face and hands, white flour. That is how I think of my father—the white man.

I would stare up at him when I took him his lunch and wonder why he did it, why he put up with this job he loathed. Later I came to understand. He did it for the same reason the Homestead steelworkers put up with making steel—for the money.

My mother worked equally hard. We had little money, and she worked diligently to get the best prices on food, to keep the house clean, to keep her children in clothes and to keep the clothes clean. She was as much like the Homestead women as my father was like the Homestead men. She gave as much attention to her curtains, for example, washing and ironing them, as the Homestead women, each Easter and Christmas, gave to their curtains, washing them and then stretching them on racks to dry.

I believed that because I grew up in a working-class part of an industrial town, that because my father and mother were working-class people,

. I could, more than some others, figure out Homestead. I greatly under-
estimated the task.

I thought I could do the book in a year and a half, maybe two.
Instead, it took more than five years to complete. It involved much pain,
for the reporting and writing was lonely, demanding work. But it was, I
believe, worth it. I know this: I never met a stock analyst or an economist
—or any other expert I have ever seen quoted in the newspapers or
speaking on television—on a street in Homestead.

Because Homestead is a suspicious town, I had to overcome suspicion of me, an outsider. It took three years or more before some people
trusted me, knew that I was in for the long haul.

I found that I had to spend far more time than I had imagined
attempting to understand Andrew Carnegie and Henry Clay Frick. Carnegie acquired the Homestead Works in 1883 and transformed it into the
nation's most productive and important steelworks. He and Frick determined to break the union at Homestead in 1892, and in achieving their
goal, they reduced labor costs for decades, enabling the Carnegie empire
to earn hundreds of millions of dollars through the rest of the 1890s.
Crushing the union helped them to establish the powerful, integrated
company that, in 1901, became the United States Steel Corporation, the
nation's first billion-dollar corporation and the model of the twentieth-
century American corporation.

The two men remain presences in Homestead, although both have
been in their graves for more than seventy years. There is the Carnegie
Library of Homestead, Frick Park, Andrew, Louise, and Margaret streets,
named after Carnegie, his wife, and his daughter, respectively. But they
remain presences for other reasons as well. The repression that Carnegie
and Frick established continues to this day. Homestead remains a frac-
tious, suspicious place, unable to organize, unable to confront its enemies.
Paradoxically, Homesteaders today are proud of Carnegie and Frick,
proud that the two men are linked to their town. The people and the
town to this day remain in awe of big people.

Similarly, I found that I had to spend far more time than I had
expected studying the Homestead strike and lockout of 1892. The confrontation was not merely an event that happened a century ago, on some
musty date in history; in a substantial way, the workers and the town
never recovered from their defeat. Forever after that fight, much of the
energy, the independence—the grit—that had characterized the town
was gone. Even today, the Homestead workers—ex-workers now—and
the townspeople have about them the atmosphere of defeat; time after
time they are put upon, but they never seem surprised.

In the course of my research I read of the English general Edward Braddock's campaign against the French in the Monongahela Valley. I was struck by his arrogance, by how he contemptuously dismissed the advice of the colonists, who told him that his traditional ways, while fine in European campaigns, would not work in America. Two miles or so east of Homestead there is a marker at the place where Braddock and his English and Colonial forces crossed the Monongahela River on July 5, 1755, to be decimated on the other side by French troops and their Indian allies. As Braddock, mortally wounded, was carried from the field, he was heard to murmur: "Can this be? Who would have thought it?"

These were phrases I was to hear again and again from steelworkers and townspeople in Homestead, two and a half centuries after Braddock's death, as they wondered what had happened to their industry, the American steel industry, this colossus that had once seemed so strong, so invincible. Who would have thought it?

Of what I learned in Homestead, nothing was more important than that, by and large, it was not macroeconomics—that is, imports, trade policy, changing markets, and the like—that brought the steel industry down. It was, indeed, the small stuff that the experts had no knowledge of, that was going on in the plants, in the corporation, in the union. I suspect—I know—that these things are the basis not only for the upheaval in the steel industry but, as the layoffs and economic changes of the 1980s continue into the 1990s, for the upheaval in most of our troubled industries and in the other troubled institutions of American life.

I learned, too, that there are many Homesteads in America. Sometimes I would take the train from my home to Homestead, altogether an eight-and-a-half-hour ride from Newark, New Jersey, to Philadelphia, and then across the flatland farms of eastern Pennsylvania, and then over the high, forested Allegheny Mountains of central and western Pennsylvania to Pittsburgh.

On those trips, I saw what amounted to the backyard of America, abandoned and littered, and it was clear to me that what has happened in Homestead was happening in many places. From that train, I saw the slums of Newark and Philadelphia, the deserted mining towns of central and western Pennsylvania, and, as the train chugged into the east end of Pittsburgh, the shuttered steel mills and electrical plants—all this the detritus of 150 years of industrialism.

A strange way to run a country, I thought—use things up, people and places, and throw them away. But that is the way America is. Homestead and the other places were yesterday and today; more Homesteads will come tomorrow.

Now the book is done, one hundred years after the epochal Homestead fight, and I think of the warm memories I have of Homestead, of the people who took me into their homes, shared information, showed me their old photographs and scrapbooks, even though many knew they would not agree with what I wrote.

They were good people all, honest and stout of heart, as strong as the steel they made. They deserved better from America, to which they gave so much. All of America, every single person, should stand and applaud them. I liked them immensely.

I remember one night, in darkest winter, after a Homestead council meeting. The meeting, acrimonious and unfruitful as usual, ended about 10:00 P.M. It was held in the old Homestead High School building, on top of the hill, and, because I was trying to save money and had no car, I left on foot. As I headed down the hill toward where I was staying, John Patrick's Pub, on Eighth Avenue, I could see the lights of the fine, forlorn town stretching far in front of me.

I had always enjoyed coming to Homestead in winter, although I did not quite know why. Perhaps it was the town's hospitality, for the town always seemed warm even in the coldest time. Always, on these nights, the twinkling lights were there, as on a Christmas card. At night, in this cold mill town, I always felt that I was in the heart of the heart of America, in the very center of this at once exhilarating and distressing country.

I hurried down the hill, bundled in a thick down coat, gloves, a scarf, a warm hat, insulated boots like the ones that explorers wear. I had no wish to retire, even at this late hour, to my room in John Patrick's Pub, with three locks on the door and no light to read by and the men's room down the hall. I decided I deserved a martini.

I walked into a bar on Eighth Avenue, a long, narrow place that, with its warmth, was inviting on this cold, black night. There were two customers at one end of the bar. I walked past them to the far end, sat down, and started reading the newspaper. The barkeep came up.

"What'll it be?" he asked. "I'll have a martini," I said. "Right," the barkeep said. I turned back to the paper.

Time went by. I looked up. No martini. I looked down the bar. The barkeep was engaged in a conversation with the two customers. "No, no," one of the customers said. "The white stuff. The white stuff." The barkeep put the sweet vermouth back and pulled out a bottle of dry vermouth. I returned to reading my paper.

More time went by. Still no martini. The barkeep was handing a drink to one of the customers. The customer took a sip. "That's it," he said.

The barkeep picked up the drink and brought it down and set it in front of me. "One martini," the barkeep said. "Thanks," I said.

I looked at the drink. I thought, "Okay, a strange guy has sampled my drink, but how many germs can there be in all that alcohol?" I also thought, at a private end of that warm bar, "This place is better than any place I know in New York."

Bottoms up. I drank the used martini.

PART ONE

1

THE DAY
THE MILL WENT DOWN

Aprocession of cars and trucks came slowly out of the main gate of the mill, crossed the railroad tracks, and began to move up the hill toward the town. Most of the cars and trucks were clunkers, rattletraps. None of the men smiled, and no one told jokes or played grab-ass, which was unusual, because horsing around was the manner of these men. They were robust, rough-edged; they loved work, loved life—beer, food, some grab-ass—and many had known each other for years, because they had gone into the mill just out of school, twenty, thirty years before, most of them, when they were kids.

It was a hot, oppressive day in July 1986. Heavy gray clouds covered the sky, and sweat stuck your shirt and pants to your skin. All day it seemed as if it would rain, but it did not. I was standing alongside the street, Amity Street, and as I watched the cars and trucks and the desolate looks on the faces of the men, I thought of how, when I was a boy in the drab factory city where I had been born and had grown up, and a funeral procession would go by and I would sit on my bicycle and watch the slow-moving cars led by a black hearse that carried the coffin banked with flowers, and I would think to myself, "There goes another chalk-faced corpse to the grave," and then I would turn my bicycle and ride away. But in this procession, the cars and pickup trucks were not washed and polished as they would be for a funeral, and there were no small flags, thoughtfully provided by the grim-faced dark-suited men from the funeral home, flapping from the radio antennas. And you could not go away.

The works, from which the men had come, stretched for several miles along both sides of the river and was a hodgepodge of many structures—monstrous black furnaces where the iron and steel were made; huge rust-colored metal sheds where the steel was rolled, great open yards where the steel was stacked, guard shacks, machine shops, a dock on the river, office buildings, miles of wire and cables and railroad tracks.

The town, Homestead, Pennsylvania, run-down and forlorn, strag-gled up the hill that rose from the plain of the river. Homestead had for decades been America's most famous steel town, one of the great steel centers of the world, a place, too, of the most immense vitality: men and women working, shopping on Eighth Avenue, coming and going all the time, particularly at shift change, three times a day, when thousands entered and came out of the at-once dark and fiery mill. Now Homestead was a gray, depressed place. The area by the works, where men with nothing to do loafed, was especially shabby. Years before, Sixth Avenue had been a roaring strip of whorehouses, bars, and gambling dens. No more. Now it was made up of dilapidated, seamy bars, mostly, and store-front businesses. There was a barbershop, the headquarters and car barn of a bus company, the union hall, some other businesses, and many abandoned stores. The main street, Eighth Avenue, three blocks up from the mill, was also run-down, and there were few people on it, although the town's major businesses were located there: Moxley's Drugs, a phar-macy and meeting place; Levine Brothers, the hardware store; Katilius, the furniture store; Modern Bride; Marks's Card Shop; Victor Shoes; the Great American Federal Savings and Loan, "the Hunkie bank," as it was known; the Mellon branch bank; the Fantasia Health Spa, a massage parlor, abhorred by many townspeople, which the chief of police had sworn to close; the Blue Bonnet Bakery; the Sweet Shoppe, a restaurant and candy store; Shupink, the jeweler; Goodwill, the thrift shop store; Lapko's Bar and Grill; Chiodo's Bar; Eat 'n' Park, a restaurant.

The homes of the town, modest places, were on the hill above the mill. Many were not being maintained. The parks—one below the library, in Munhall, the adjacent town, the other in front of Saint Mary Magdalene's Roman Catholic Church, the biggest church in town—were scruffy; the trees had not been pruned, and the grass had not been cut for some time and was thick with weeds. The streets had many bumps and chuckholes; the town had little money for road repairs—enough for some hot-patching, not much more.

For years, the mill had thrown up thick plumes of smoke that had blackened the town. The dirt could be cleaned, but cleaning was a constant chore, and despite the effort the smoke had over the years left a grime that seemed to have been absorbed into the houses and other buildings of the town, even sometimes into the skin of the townspeople. Once there had been a man who worked in the mill, and it was his task to transport the orange material left over from steelmaking at the works to a dumping site over the hill behind the town, in what was then the country.

He would clatter through town several times a day, his truck piled high with the refuse, the material sometimes rolling up in a great cloud behind him. Most labor has peculiar demands, the prices it exacts from those who perform it, and what was unusual about this man's work was that no matter what the man did, scrub, shower, soak in the tub, he could not remove the orange color from his skin. He was orange, that was that, and this even gave him his identity, for he was known not by his name but as "the orange man."

As the procession from the mill came by, and the cars and trucks stopped at the cross street, I talked to a couple of the men. I told them I was a reporter and had come to talk to them on the day the mill went down. The line stopped behind where we were, and the men in the front vehicles waved up the men who were behind, and soon there was a clutch of us talking, there on Amity Street. Then a photographer from the newspaper by which I was employed came up and said, "Why not take a last picture?" So the men pulled their cars over to a slag-covered spot by the tracks, near the old, abandoned railroad depot, which had been there almost a century ago, when the great Homestead strike and lockout had occurred, and everybody got out and posed for some pictures, and now for the first time there were a few jokes, a few smart remarks. There were about a dozen men there, all workers in the Number Two Structural Mill, which, erected in 1927, had rolled pilings and structural beams for buildings, dams, and the like.

Ed Buzinka, a craneman, was an amiable fellow of medium height, somewhat bald, who wore his glasses on top of his head. He always seemed to have a smile on his face, and all the other men liked him immensely. Like the others, he had started in the Homestead Works— gone into the mill, as the men said—years before, had worked hard there, and had enjoyed what he had done.

Bob Todd was a stout, red-haired man who, his friends said, registered on the Richter Scale when he walked. He was a crane dispatcher, meaning he gave the orders for which crane was to go where and do what, and he was also a union grievance man, meaning that he represented the men in disputes with the corporation. He often wore blue bib overalls and smoked thick, malodorous cigars, and seemed to use the word "fuck" all the time: fuck this, fuck that, fuck something else, using it as the basis for almost every part of speech—noun, verb, adverb, adjective, gerund, object of direct address.

Todd was driving a pickup truck, an old blue number, and in the back he had his locker from the mill, figuring he might have some use for it someday. Todd was a buoyant man, but he could not mask his depression about the mill's closing. He had put twenty-three years into the place, working up from laborer to roll hand to craneman to crane dispatcher. He had always been fascinated by the cranes, huge machines that rolled through the mill with great noise. Nothing moved without a craneman, you were right at the center of things, and Todd had been impressed by this. One day he saw an opening posted on the bulletin board for a craneman trainee, and he applied and got the job. That was in 1965. Then, in 1980, he became a crane dispatcher, a doubly important position, the boss of bosses. "I didn't have a job," Todd said. "I had a position."

Ray McGuire was an equipment repairman. He spent much of his time repairing cranes, from small, twenty-ton cranes to monstrous mothers weighing five hundred tons. He went into the mill in 1949, just after he graduated from high school. "Don't be ashamed about working in the mill," his mother told him. "It's good work, and the money is good, too."

McGuire first worked in the pits, then became a motor inspector's helper and then a motor inspector. He spent all his years in the mill in Number Two Structural. The men, he said, were a good bunch of guys. Everybody tried to help each other out. Why, when the union was formed, in the 1930s, one of the first things the men did was create a flower fund, a dollar apiece each payday, so the union could buy flowers when somebody, a worker, his wife, passed on. Also, everyone seemed to know a little bit of something, so that in a group of men who worked or loafed together, about every skill imaginable was represented. Once, Ray McGuire said that he was going to put in a driveway, but that he was worried because he didn't know much about cement. Saturday morning he looked out and eight men he worked with were standing in his drive-way. They made and poured the concrete, and laid the driveway in half a day. Did a nice job, too. In the mill you helped each other like that.

Denny Wilcox was a router screwman, although by the time the mill went down he had been bumped back to the hot saw. He started in the mill on October 8, 1952, a few months after he finished a four-year hitch in the Army. Wilcox began in the mill as a laborer and worked his way up, becoming a stop-setter helper, stop setter, marker, drag-over opera-tor, hot-sawman, and finally router screwman. He had been looking for-ward to getting thirty-five years in the mill, and especially forty. Thirty-five-year gifts had been discontinued, but if Wilcox had gotten forty years, he would have been given a watch. The only gift he ever received was when he got twenty-five years. The company had a catalog, and you picked out what you wanted. Wilcox picked out, for his wife, a necklace with "U.S. Steel" engraved on it.

Bill Brennan was a millwright, meaning he did maintenance work, repairing equipment, changing rolls, and so on. Brennan was a Munhall boy, born in Munhall and a graduate of Munhall High School. He went into the mill on January 2, 1948, at age twenty-two. His father was a heater in the forty-eight-inch mill, and Brennan's four brothers also worked in the mill. Two years before, Brennan had had a heart-bypass operation. He was out sick for several months. When he came back, his pals would not let him do any hard work. "Sit down, Bill, we'll do that," they said, even though he insisted he could do the work. The men would not hear of it. That was how it was in the mill, too. You took care of your buddies.

Brennan enjoyed his time in the mill, making steel, stopping for a beer or two in the beer garden near City Farm Lane, living in the Home-stead district, although he had become depressed in the last few years, when the company was not putting money into the mill, was laying people off, turning one worker against another. "We needed bearings; they wouldn't buy bearings," he said. "Hoses, clamps. We were using every-thing up. We had the best saw-sharpener there was, but they closed our sharpener down and sent the saws out to Ohio." Life in the mill and the town was good before, when the mill was humming, he said. Then, as the company laid off workers and began to let the mill go, things began to fall apart. "It was all beautiful, not like today," Brennan said. "Everybody knew each other. They talked with each other, they associated with each other. We were good working people. It was like a family. Not like today. People today don't know you. There was no cutthroat then. Today it's all cutthroat, everybody for themselves."

Bobby Schneider had been in the mill twenty-three years. He was born in Homestead and his family lived in lower Homestead, below the tracks. In 1941, when he was three, his family had to move because their home was knocked down when the government expanded the Homestead Works for war production. He grew up in the Glen Hazel projects, across the Monongahela River from Homestead, and was going to go to college, Maryland or Michigan State. In 1953, his father died, and Schneider took it hard. He dropped out of school in his senior year and at age eighteen went to work as a laborer in the structural mill. He became a shearman's helper, then a shearman, working with the hot saw, and finally a roller, his occupation the day the mill went down. Roller was an important position in the mill, Schneider said. He had a pair of calipers and determined whether beams were of proper quality. He passed what was good and sent back what was not. It was almost as if he were in charge of the mill, and he enjoyed the authority the job gave him.

Steve Butala had started as a laborer when he was sixteen, working for nine months during World War II. The workers his age were called junior commandos and were given light jobs, like sweeping, and some that were not so light, like cleaning bricks out of furnaces. They went into the furnaces with wooden shoes on to prevent their feet from being burned—remember, now, Butala was sixteen at this time—and removed the bricks with large tongs and pitched the bricks out to helpers outside the furnace. The junior commandos worked 5:30 P.M. to 9:30 P.M. during the week and eight hours on Saturday and on Sunday. After the war, Butala continued with high school, and when he graduated, in 1947, he went back into the mill. He then entered the service, serving as a tank mechanic with the Army in Korea and making sergeant. He was mustered out in 1953, and he went into the mill again and never came out.

Butala was a local guy who had grown up on Ravine Street, in Hunkie Hollow east of town, where many people still spoke Eastern European languages. His dad was a millwright in the Homestead Works, and his mother took care of the house. He never saw the mill as his life's work, but it became that. In his department, you could often work as much overtime as you wanted, and whenever his family wanted something, Butala worked overtime and got it. His kids wanted a swimming pool, so Butala worked overtime and bought them one. He put in extra hours to take his wife and kids to Florida, and he paid cash. No credit cards for Steve Butala. He put in overtime to buy a twelve-foot boat with a motor and liked to fish on the Monongahela River, carp, bass, and muskies, although he never ate any, figuring the river and the bed of the river were loaded with chemicals from the coke and steel plants. When he went to work in the mill, he was paid $5.24 a day; when he left the mill, he was getting almost three times that an hour. "Anything I wanted, I got," Butala said. "We never hurted for anything. It was a wonderful life."

Bob Krovocheck, a craneman, was a tall, bald man with a small black mustache and a soft, lumpy body, like an old davenport that might be set out at the curb. He did not get good grades in high school and did not graduate. His father worked in the Number One Machine Shop and knew an employment boss in the mill, and in 1941, at age nineteen, Krovocheck went into the mill, first in Open Hearth Number Three and then in Number Two Structural. "I worked in that rusty mother for thirty-nine and one-half years," he said. "Now it's gone. It's a goddamned shame."

II

Homestead existed because of the mill, and the shutting of the mill by its owner, the United States Steel Corporation, department by department over several years, had brought immense economic hardship to the town. For years, the mill had provided a substantial part of the town's taxes; this amount had decreased as the mill had closed, and the town showed it. The chief of police, Chris Kelly, was on patrol the day the mill went down. Kelly was a Homestead boy who had gone to Saint Mary Magdalene's School and then Homestead High School, where he was an excellent football player, a big tackle, a hard hitter, fast for his size. He used to take his bike across the High Level Bridge to watch the Pirates at Forbes Field, where he and the other kids would get seats for a dollar in the Knothole League section in right field. And he would hitchhike up to the town athletic field, on top of the hill, and play baseball or football, depending on the season, for hours each day.

The Chief and his wife, Paula, lived in a little house almost underneath the water tower. Kelly loved Homestead and wanted nothing more in life than to be chief there. He put in hundreds of extra hours, whatever it took. The decline of the town that came with the decline of the Homestead Works disturbed him intensely. "Look at the weeds," the Chief said that day in the hot patrol car. "We have no money for recreation, for ball fields. Homestead doesn't have a baseball team, no Little League, no Pony League, nothing. Look at the weeds. It didn't used to be that way. The playgrounds were immaculate."

Six months before, it had been the Chief's duty to go to the Homestead Works and hunt for a foreman, David Sapos, thirty-nine, who had not returned home the previous night after working on the night shift. His wife had called plant security, who called the police. Kelly and other officers poked around the mill for several hours—cold work, for this was

February. The cold in such a place seeps into your body and makes you cold to your bones.

After a time, the searchers found Sapos, suspended from a beam high in the open hearth. He had hanged himself. He had wrapped a steel cable around his neck and body, and, after placing his work gloves in the right back pocket of his blue dungarees, stepped off the beam. On his head was his white safety helmet, his white hat, the symbol that he was a foreman. Finally Sapos's body was brought down, and the coroner came, and the body was removed in the dead wagon. But the Chief had not forgotten what he had seen and what it was his responsibility to do that day. The idea that Sapos, after wrapping the steel cable around his neck and body, would carefully place his gloves in his right back pocket before he stepped off that high beam, as if he were going to inspect a machine —he needed the touch of bare fingers to do this—stuck in the Chief's mind.

Rumors had gone around for years that the mill would close, but few people believed them; that is, few had believed the entire mill—the vast Homestead Works, such a storied and famous place—would close. Who would have thought that? The forty-eight-inch mill, which made structural beams up to forty-eight inches wide, had closed in 1979, and that had frightened people. Then, in 1982, the company announced it would close the mill's open hearth, known as O.H. 5, because it was the fifth open hearth in the history of the mill, built during World War II. This had made people sit up, think, "Jesus, maybe the mill will go down one day." Late in 1982, Betty Esper—who had worked as a clerk in the mill since 1953, when she was just a few weeks out of high school; she had taken the summer off for a trip west, but no more—had been Christmas shopping at Kaufmann's, the big department store in downtown Pittsburgh, and had bumped into one of her old bosses in the Homestead Works, Robert Schneider. This was three years after United States Steel had closed its huge old Youngstown Works, in Youngstown, Ohio, sixty miles west of the Pittsburgh area. "What do you think?" she had asked, and Schneider had said, "I think the Homestead Works is maybe five years from Youngstown," meaning that the Homestead Works had just five years left. Schneider had it right, except that he was off by a year. The mill had four years to go.

Still, for most people, it seemed impossible that the mill would close. The Homestead Works had existed for more than a century. It had been responsible for the creation of the town, at least for the manner in which the town had developed; it had been the centerpiece of the vast iron and steel empire put together by Andrew Carnegie, the steel master who created the American steel industry. The Homestead strike and lockout of 1892, an epochal strike in American history, broke union power in the iron and steel industry, and blocked unionism and strengthened the authority of employers throughout the country for more than a half-century. It was this, the steel that the mill made, plus the strike and lockout, that gave the Homestead Works its fame.

The mill had been constructed to make steel rails for the railroads that in the last decades of the nineteenth century were crisscrossing the continent, at the rate of ten thousand miles of track a year. When Andrew Carnegie acquired the plant, he realized that the rail market was saturated and that the rail boom could not continue forever. Carnegie had his detractors, and still does. But there is no denying that he was sharp as a tack. The elevator, invented in 1851, but not recognized at first for the revolution that it was, was becoming popular, and buildings, which before the elevator had been limited to six or so stories, were becoming higher, twelve or fifteen or even more stories, so high that people coined a new word, "skyscraper." Carnegie, always a man able to see the future, had transformed the plant into a manufactory of beams for buildings and bridges, and then, as the nation began to build its naval forces, had made the works into one of the nation's great factories for armor plate, realizing, although he regarded himself as a pacifist, that there was much money to be made in armaments.

The works had produced steel for much of the nation, including many of the emblematic structures of America: beams for the first skyscraper, the Home Life Insurance Building, in Chicago; the Panama Canal; the Woolworth Building; the Flatiron Building, the Chrysler Building, the Empire State Building, and Rockefeller Center, in New York; the George Washington Bridge, across the Hudson River; the Verrazano-Narrows Bridge, across New York Harbor; the Oakland Bay Bridge, across San Francisco Bay; the United Nations Building, in New York. Steel from the Homestead Works was used in the construction of such ships as the USS *Maine* and the USS *Oregon*, when, as the nation approached the twentieth century, the government eliminated the wooden-hulled Navy and replaced it with a Navy of steel ships. Homestead had made steel beams for dams and stadiums, steel rods for highways, beams for highway bridges, steel plate for factories. During World War I, workers at the Homestead Works constructed a new plate mill in the astonishing time of six months, and the mill set production records as workers turned out plate for the U.S. armed forces and for the nation's allies. It became known as the Liberty Mill. At times during the war, when high production was needed, the men worked so hard and put in such long hours that they had to be admonished to stop working and were sent home.

During World War II, the works was one of the great industrial centers of America. Beginning in 1940, the government, as part of its military preparations, condemned a large section of Homestead, a mile-long area along the river west of the existing mill, and allocated $50 million for expansion of the Homestead Works. Some five hundred homes were razed, as were churches, businesses, and social clubs, and more than eight thousand people were uprooted. This additional land allowed the mill to be expanded by one-third, and by the war's end more than twenty thousand workers were employed at the works, compared to twelve thousand at its beginning. Homestead in the war days was a tableau of twentieth-century industrial America—the huge buildings, the pouring of the molten steel, the steel shooting along in the rolling mills; the smoke, the noise, the men and women—substantial numbers of women now joined the Homestead workforce for the first time—streaming in and out of the plant.

For all the years that the Homestead Works existed, the strike and lockout of 1892 were never forgotten. Andrew Carnegie had wanted to reduce his labor costs and install new labor-saving equipment, and, after journeying to Europe for his vacation, as was his custom, he instructed his second-in-command, Henry Clay Frick, to eliminate the workers' contract. Frick was a tough-minded fellow, as hard an egg as might be imagined, with a history of confronting unions, and he demonstrated in the Homestead fight that his reputation was deserved. The workers refused Frick's demand that they accept cuts in wages and disband their union, and went on strike. Frick then brought in three hundred Pinkerton men on two barges to secure the property so that he could bring in strikebreakers. But the workers had vedettes posted along the river, and one of them saw the barges, and the people of Homestead were alerted. A furious, day-long battle ensued, as the workers pinned down the Pinkertons in the barges at the dock of the Homestead Works with rifle and pistol fire. The fight had its bizarre elements. One of the workers killed, Silas Wain, had his head blown off by his comrades, who had dragged an old Civil War cannon, a ten-pounder, away from Grand Army of the Republic hall in Braddock, across the river, loaded it with screws and bolts and scrap steel, aimed it at the barges, and touched the cannon off. The load overshot the barge and killed poor Wain. This did not prevent his fellow workers and their supporters from transforming him into a working-class hero, a martyr to labor's fight against capitalism.

Two weeks after the fight, the governor of Pennsylvania, Robert E.

Pattison, sent in the state militia, which encamped on the hill above the mill and on the hill on the opposite side of the river at Braddock. The militiamen were not unwelcome among some elements in Homestead, for their presence meant income for local teamsters who contracted to haul supplies to the Army camps, and a number of Homesteaders, women and young boys especially, found it enjoyable to journey to the camps when the soldiers, so dashing in their blue uniforms, some with plumed helmets, staged their Sunday reviews. But the presence of the militiamen allowed Frick to bring in strikebreakers and reopen his mill, and the strike was broken. This not only ended unionization in the Homestead Works but also broke the power of the existing union in the iron and steel industry, the Amalgamated Association of Iron and Steel Workers. At the time of the Homestead strike and lockout, the union had twenty-four thousand members and was the largest union in the country. After the Homestead strike and lockout, the Amalgamated became the shell of a union, with members in only a few western iron and steel mills. It was not until the 1930s, during the Great Depression, when intense rank-and-file agitation occurred, and, later, when John L. Lewis sent in organizers from the Committee for Industrial Organization, that unionization returned to the Homestead workers and to the American steel industry.

The new union, first called the Steel Workers Organizing Committee, and then, beginning in 1942, the United Steelworkers of America, and the company, after an initial decade or so of acrimony and sometimes bitter confrontations, settled into what they regarded as a mutually advantageous relationship. With the high profits that the steel industry generated, there were often generous contracts. Pay and benefits rose, more workers were hired, and life became good, relatively speaking, in the steelmaking towns of the Monongahela Valley and in other steelmaking towns of the United States.

III

The last day of the mill was pleasant enough, in the manner that a funeral can be pleasant, when the lid of the coffin is closed and the corpse is carted to the cemetery in the long line of cars, and the mourners adjourn to someone's home or the church basement and have a get-together, and the food is brought out, potato salad and ham and Jell-O salad and the rest.

The men were all on time the last day, twenty-three men, all that was left of the vast workforce, the tens of thousands of men and women who had been employed in the Homestead Works over more than a hundred years. The workers had been a varied crew: immigrants, farm boys, women going to work for the first time, whites and blacks, people working hard, amid smoke and flame and noise, to earn a living for themselves and their families, to get a house, a car, to rise, to be somebody.

Now it was over, and on the last day the men took their personal items—a pair of gloves, extra safety shoes, orange hats—and put them in their cars or trucks.

Lunch was enjoyable. Steelwork has always been communal. Steel is made, generally, by people who work in teams, and the workers came to know each other, to depend on each other. They ate together on the job and went to the christenings of each other's children, to weddings, to funerals. Bob Todd's wife had cooked up a mess of kielbasas and sauerkraut, and Todd had brought it in. Bob Krovocheck brought in some beer. A favorite workers' tavern, Hess's, on Whitaker Avenue, up in Hunkie Hollow, in Munhall, sent down hot dogs and buns. Someone brought in a watermelon.

So the men settled down to a meal in what remained of Number Two Structural, that big, old, empty place, a mill that was once so crowded and charged with life, as the beams came down on the rollers and were cut by the hot saws, and tested and marked for shipment, a place of immense noise, now so quiet that anything—a shout, the scraping of a cabinet—would be heard throughout the mill.

John Goodwin, the superintendent, came down from his office and had a bite to eat with the men, and shook their hands and wished them well. The men appreciated the gesture, because they liked Goodwin and knew he did not have to come by. Then the men went to their cars. It was early for quitting, and the men had never left early before—when in the history of the mill had the day shift left at 2:00 P.M.?—but Goodwin said, what the hell, it's over, get out of here, and the men went to their cars and trucks and began the slow procession out of the mill, through Amity Gate and up Amity Street.

The men said that they were going up to Hess's, run by a man who used to work in the mill. "C'mon along," Ed Buzinka said, and I, believing, correctly, that the invitation was genuine, went up and joined the boys, and we had a couple of drinks, beer mostly, a few of the guys having whiskey or vodka. I put my money on the bar, but it was pushed back. "Put your money away," said Red Hrabic, another of the last workers, not so red anymore. "It's no good here." And it was not. We chatted for a time. One of the men recalled how in May the workers in the structural mill had rolled the last beam to come out of the Homestead Works. They had taken special care that the beam was perfect and then each had cut off a piece an inch or so wide to take as a souvenir. The men laughed about that because they knew somewhere in America, on a building or bridge or other structure, workers would try to put up a beam and find it a foot or so too short. Then, late in the afternoon, it was time to get going. The men had to get home, have dinner, do some things around the house, and one by one they left. Finally, just a few of us were left, Buzinka, Hrabic, Schneider, Jimmy Sherlock, and maybe a couple more, all good guys, just sitting there, shooting the breeze. Finally, Buzinka looked at me. "Well, that was that," he said. "It's over. But I'll tell you what. It was a good run while it lasted." And he was right.

2

"HOMESTEAD, USA"

Homestead, Pennsylvania, is on the south side of the Monongahela River seven miles east of the place where, dark and turbulent, the Monongahela joins the Allegheny River to form the Ohio River. The town is on a great horseshoe bend of the river. After that, the river makes one more bend, much smaller, and runs straight to its juncture with the Allegheny, and then the waters, now the Ohio, run 980 miles south and west, where, wider and more swift, the Ohio joins the Mississippi River. To reach Homestead, you take the Pittsburgh parkway, get off at the Homestead exit, and go south across the High Level Bridge. And there it will be—another place and another time.

The town is shaped like a piece of pie, the big, or crust, end on the river, the point end twenty blocks up the hill that rises some three hundred feet above the river. Homestead is 842 feet above sea level, measured at the flats along the river. The mean average temperature is 24.1° F in winter, 71.2° in summer. The soil is sand on the floodplain and loam with some clay on the hill. It is decent soil for gardens, if manured, although not many people have gardens these days. The average rainfall is 36.15 inches a year. The population in 1880, when the first census of the town was taken, was two thousand; the largest population was twenty thousand in 1940; today the population is about four thousand.

It is a town that is at once commonplace and extraordinary. Spitting on the street was prohibited by town ordinance in 1907, and the town's last two fire horses, Dick and Bill, were retired in 1916. The town police car—the Black Mariah, famous in the valley—made its last run March 2, 1941, when it was hit by a car and damaged beyond repair while being driven by a town constable chasing two bootleggers. The town had an athlete, years ago—Johnny Pearson, skilled in football, basketball, and baseball—who used to enhance his reputation by wrestling bears when the circus came through. You can see his photograph—he is highly muscled and has dark black hair—in the trophy room at the library. In February 1893, the mud was so bad that a horse drowned on Eighth Avenue and City Farm Lane. The next year, John Ringling, the circus man, was fined ten dollars for violating a town ordinance against having a horse on the sidewalk, although considering what had happened in 1893, it seemed that Ringling may have been on to something. The impresario saw no point to the matter, however, and incensed by the fine, never allowed his circus to play Homestead again. The influenza epidemic of 1919 killed hundreds of people in the Homestead district—203 between October and December 1919 alone, including six members of one family, the Frank Dunkles. For reasons that seemingly cannot be explained, Homestead has had many suicides—by hanging, by drinking carbolic acid, by jumping off the bridges over the Monongahela, by stabbing through the throat or in the breast. A most puzzling occurrence, a mystery to this day, occurred on a cold gray day, January 31, 1956, when an Air Force B-25, on a mission from the West Coast to Washington, dropped out of the sky, glided west for a time over the river—the plane had lost its engines and was not making a sound—passed fifty feet above the High Level Bridge, and crashed into the Monongahela River. Traffic stopped on the bridge and in the yards at Mesta Machine as people, awestruck, watched the plane float downstream for a time, crew members huddling on the wing, then disappear beneath the cold, black water. Two servicemen drowned, four were rescued. The plane, as far as is known, was never found. Some say it washed downstream and broke up and that the parts are there still. Others believe it was on a secret mission and that the plane was somehow removed at night by American intelligence agents. The government has always remained silent on the matter—curiously so, some say.

Homestead and the area around it is a scruffy, hilly place. The area along the river—the flats—was given over to the mill. Above the flats is the main street, Eighth Avenue, which runs roughly parallel to the Monongahela River (Monongahela is the Delaware Indian word for "sliding banks") and is known to many simply as "the Avenue." The churches are mostly along Ninth and Tenth avenues. That is generally where the houses also begin. The houses are of brick and wood, of two stories mostly, sometimes plus an attic, except for some more substantial brick homes, constructed years ago by brickmasons brought from Italy by the United States Steel Corporation, and behind the library, a handful of larger homes, also built years ago by the corporation, for mill superintendents. The handsomest building in town is the Carnegie Library of Homestead, on Tenth Avenue, a large brick structure given to Homestead by Andrew Carnegie in 1898.

The town's parks, one below the library, the other, Frick Park, four blocks west, are on Tenth Avenue and are shaded by sycamore trees. The football field is up the hill, outside town, past the water tower. The town has three elementary schools, one junior high school, and a consolidated senior high school, Steel Valley High School, also attended by students from the neighboring towns of Munhall and West Homestead. Its sports teams are the Ironmen. Homestead used to have a trade school, the gift of Charles M. Schwab, the old steel master, in 1903, but that's been closed for years. The building was occupied by a tire company for a while, but that's been closed for years, too.

The town has many mortuaries—among them Welsh's for the Irish, Anderson's for the Germans, Braszo's and Prokopovitsh's for the Slavs, and Tunie's for the blacks.

There are more than twenty churches. Homesteaders are churchgoing people and always have been. The oldest congregation is Saint John's Lutheran, founded in 1874. There are seven Roman Catholic churches, one Episcopal Church, a Lutheran church, a Presbyterian church, a Methodist church, a Hungarian Reformed church, two Russian Orthodox churches, a Byzantine Catholic church, a synagogue, although it is hardly used anymore, and three large black churches—Clark Memorial Baptist, Park Place AME, and Second Baptist. High on top of one of the churches, Saint Michael's Roman Catholic Church, is a large, handsome statue of Saint Joseph, the patron saint of workers, installed years ago, in the glory days of the mill, to ensure protection of the Homestead workers.

The town's oldest church, Saint Mark's Chapel, a German Evangelical Protestant church, built in 1892, and known as the Rooster Church because of a rooster weathervane on the steeple, was demolished in 1989. The site was made into a parking lot.

The hill in Homestead has no name today but years ago was known variously as Cow's Hill, Shanty Hill, or Carnegie Hill. It is a steep climb, but in the old days steelworkers walked it after their twelve-hour shifts, even on the hottest days of the year, to save the nickel streetcar fare. Wives and children also walked. "I'd never have had this house if I wasted nickels taking the streetcar," John Vojtko, a master grinder in the mill, used to admonish his family when one of them took the streetcar or the bus home. You can feel the hill in your legs when you start at the river and walk up through town. You breathe heavily, and if it is a warm day your clothes become wet with perspiration.

At the top of the hill are the Homestead burying grounds, Catholics on one side of the road, Protestants on the other. The oldest tombstones in the cemeteries go back to the 1790s, and some of the town's pioneers, Abdiel McClure and Lowry H. West among them, are buried there, under large, dark granite markers that fit the stature of the men in their times. Six steelworkers killed in the 1892 fight with the Pinkertons also lie in the burying grounds, as do veterans of the nation's wars, from the Revolution to Vietnam.

Tragedy visited the Vojtko family as it did many working-class families in the Monongahela Valley. John Vojtko's wife, Anna, died in 1937 when their daughter Margaret was a child, and for years Margaret and her father and her brothers would on Sundays walk up to Mrs. Vojtko's grave in the burying grounds on the hill, the father pushing a hand lawn mower and Margaret and her brothers carrying cans for water. They would trim and mow the grave and Margaret and her brothers would then be dispatched by their father back down the hill for more water, which they would carry back to water the flowers and the grass on their mother's grave.

Yet while life in Homestead had brought its tribulations, Margaret was able to see what others could not. In those years, she would often walk the family dog, Ching, in an area on the west side of town, on a ridge, high above the town and the Monongahela River, and she saw a grand mixture of colors, the blue-gray of the water, the green of the shrubs and trees, the blue of the sky, the gray of the smoke, the reds, violets, purples of the fires from the works, and to her this was a scene that should have been painted by a great artist. Margaret Vojtko became a medieval scholar, visited the great cities of Europe, saw many famous works of art in European museums. But in 1990, on this spot, called Grand View, a run-down road above a weed- and scrub-covered hillside, she recalled what she had seen as she walked her dog years before, and wondered why others had never seen the glorious colors, only the grays and blacks, and as she thought of this, her eyes filled with tears.

Homestead has always been a patriotic town and has given more than its share of men to the nation. One of the most striking features on the hill is the town monument to the Civil War dead, a bronze figure of a Union infantryman, rifle with bayonet fixed, ready to ward off any foe. The monument was dedicated on September 17, 1891, the twenty-ninth anniversary of the battle of Antietam. It cost twenty-five hundred dollars, a large sum then, but the men and women of the town were determined to raise the money, and with a concert, a fair, a pageant, "The Drummer Boy of Shiloh," and individuals giving what they could, they did.

On the hot, sunny dedication day, 1,516 people walked or rode up the hill in a solemn procession to the burying grounds, where they were joined by many others, the crowd reaching five thousand. The green of the cemetery was "a welcome change from the dusty road, and the breeze . . . cooled their brows," the historian of the event recorded. "America" was sung by Professor McClure's choir and a chorus of schoolchildren, and then a cord was pulled, and as a cannon on an opposite hill was fired, the monument was unveiled to thunderous cheers and applause.

The cemeteries hold many of the seventeen Homestead men killed in World War I and the thirty-four district men lost in World War II. Ray Hornak, an executive in the mill for many years, had seven boyhood friends killed in World War II. When the war ended, on August 11, 1945, with the Japanese surrender, the town went wild and the mill closed for three days, the longest it had ever closed, except for the strike of 1892. A Homestead man, Private First Class John D. Kelly of the First Marine Division, was posthumously awarded the Congressional Medal of Honor for his service in Korea, where he was killed on May 28, 1952. He had been a terrific basketball player at Homestead High School and was extremely well liked. A portrait of Kelly in Marine dress uniform, the Congressional Medal of Honor painted around his neck, as though he had worn it in life, is in the trophy case of Steel Valley High School.

The people of Homestead came to the town from all over. Like many in the nation's history, they left the poverty and oppression of their own lands in search of a better life. Immigration to Homestead came in three waves. In the 1870s and 1880s came English, Welsh, Irish, and Germans, including many skilled workers. Beginning in the late 1880s and lasting until the early 1920s came an even greater wave of Eastern Europeans—Poles, Slavs, Croats, Serbs, Hungarians, Russians—and Southern Europeans—Italians and Greeks. Also mixed in were Syrians, Mexicans, and Gypsies. Beginning in the 1890s and running through the 1930s came black people, mostly from the South and many brought up as strikebreakers in railroad freight cars with fares paid by the corporation.

The mill and town often divided along ethnic and religious lines. The English-speaking men, usually Protestant, took most of the skilled or supervisory jobs. For decades, to get ahead in the mill, a man had to be a Freemason, had to wear the Mason's ring. The Slavs, mostly Catholic, newcomers who were looked down upon, did much of the heaviest and dirtiest work in the mill. They worked in cinder pits, handed steel billets and bars, and loaded trains.

Homestead also divided along racial lines, although it has probably been no more and no less bigoted than most other American towns. It had a flirtation with the Ku Klux Klan in the 1920s, and crosses were burned on the hills above the towns in the Monongahela Valley. Some people say the crosses were burned in fun, but the crosses were not fun to the Negroes who saw them on the hillsides as they sat in their fetid tenements or boardinghouses on the flats along the river. For many years, Negroes could not swim in the pool at the Carnegie Library of Homestead. At the Stahl Theatre, the town's famous vaudeville and movie house, Negroes had to sit in the balcony, "nigger heaven," as it was sometimes called, although whites could join them, the balcony being the favorite necking place for young people. Cumberland Posey, for years the town's leading black sports entrepreneur, who owned the Homestead Grays, the famous Negro League baseball team, could buy a round for the men at Straka's, the bar and restaurant on Ann Street. But Posey, highly respected, a member of the school board, an educated man, could not drink at the bar even when the men at the bar were drinking on his money, and he had to come and go by the side door.

Whatever their origins, the people of Homestead were subject to the great central force of the town, the mill. The men for many years labored twelve hours a day, seven days a week, at the most backbreaking jobs. The women, too, worked hard. They scrimped and patched and made do. They did sewing and cleaning for the wealthier ladies, took in boarders, and fought relentlessly to keep their own homes clean despite the filth. Mary Heaton Vorse, a journalist who visited the town in 1919, wrote: "The women in the steel towns fly a flag of defiance against the dirt. It is their white window curtains. You cannot go into any foul courtyard without finding white lace curtains stretched on frames to dry. Wherever you go, in Braddock or in Homestead or in filthy Rankin, you will find courageous women hopefully washing their white curtains. There is no woman so driven with work that she will not attempt this decency."

The people of Homestead sought relief from their toil and worry in a number of activities, one of the most important of which was sports. Many people knew of Homestead because of the Homestead Grays. The Grays began in 1910 as a sandlot team with a number of players from the Homestead Works. It then began fielding more skilled players, and over the following decades, playing many of its games at West Field, above town, it became one of the storied teams in baseball history. Pietro Chiodo, a shoemaker from Italy—his son, Joseph, runs Chiodo's Bar, the oldest tavern in Homestead—used to repair the Grays' spikes and put on toe plates; the players would stop at Chiodo's shoe shop, on West Street, on their way up to West Field. The Grays had many outstanding players, among them Josh Gibson, Buck Leonard, Oscar Charleston, Judy Johnson, Cool Papa Bell, and Smokey Joe Williams. Gibson, Leonard, Johnson, Bell, and Charleston are in the Hall of Fame at Cooperstown, New York. Williams should be.

The great lefthanded pitcher Rube Waddell wasn't born in Homestead but grew up there and starred for the Homestead Library Athletic Club nine. He often struck out twenty men a game. One winter he lived in a livery stable there, working at the stable for fifty dollars a month and using his free pass to the swimming pool in the library. The Rube never enjoyed himself so much as when he played for the library club, and often, when he was in contract squabbles in the big leagues, the Rube would threaten to jump the club and go back and play for the Homestead nine. His lifetime major league record, from 1897 to 1910, was 196 wins and 138 losses. In 1946, Waddell was elected to the Hall of Fame.

Homestead had numerous social clubs, in part because in the old days there were few or no benefits for workers at the mill and the clubs provided relatively low-cost life insurance and sometimes health insurance plans. Also, because many of the immigrants could not speak English, they were shy and uneasy around outsiders and tended to cluster. For years there were more than fifty lodges in Homestead, and today there are still the Russian Club, the Slavic Club, the Ancient Order of Hibernians, the Moose, the Elks, and, at West Street and Eighth Avenue, the major intersection, the Owls, where, year after year, in the windows of the club are the gray or bald heads of the old-timers who sit and play card games by the hour and watch the passersby on Eighth Avenue.

There were many self-improvement clubs. The town's Women's

Club, formed in 1897, met at the library and had thirty-five members by the early part of the first decade of the twentieth century. The women met weekly and discussed numerous important subjects, such as "Gain as an Incentive to Progress," "Everyday Psychology," "The Panama Canal," "The Jewish Nation," and "If I Had a Million Dollars." In 1907, the library had twenty-two literary and study clubs with a combined member-ship of 787. The Thursday Night Supper Club, which met at the library, studied Shakespeare for seven straight years.

There were other, less salutary or edifying activities. Homestead, for years, had, along Sixth Avenue, one of the greatest, gaudiest sin strips in America, a wild, wicked place of whorehouses, taverns, and gambling houses. For decades, Homestead had more than eighty bars—it was re-ported in 1908 that Homestead had eight bars in one block of Eighth Avenue, and this did not include the numerous speakeasies—and even by the 1980s the town had more than forty bars, though the population had dropped to about five thousand. It would have been possible, in the 1980s, for every resident of Homestead to be in a Homestead bar at one time, although it should not be assumed that this was likely to have happened.

The sporting houses over the years included Pie Man's Place, Frazier and Daisy's Place, Jew McPherson's, Lena's Place, Eleanor's Place, Broad-Ass's Place, Yackkety-Yak, Crooked Billy's Place, You Can't Find It, and, of course, the house of the town's foremost madam, Miss Evelyn Marshall, which everyone called The Tabernacle. Homestead became famous for its gambling and prostitution. The *Bulletin Index,* a Pittsburgh magazine, said in March 1940, "Homestead has two big industries—Steel and Vice."

Buck Leonard, the Homestead Grays' great first baseman, said years later of Homestead, "I had never seen so much money in all my life till I went out there. That's what made me stay out there seventeen years. The United States Steel mill [the Homestead Works] was the only thing there. Fifteen to twenty thousand people working. When I got there, things were humming. You talkin' about beer taverns! Umm-umm-umm! There was some beer drunk. Slovakians and Italians—everybody was a for-eigner out there. . . . Something else they had out there—a red-light dis-trict. They had forty-five women in one block—forty-five women doin' business with men. And what was so queer about it to me, it was black women doin' business with white men. All the women were colored, but all the men were white. After all, it may have been the best thing for them. What I mean is, they were sure to get their money."

The town's reputation was widely known. A man who lived in Homestead for years, William "Car Wash" Brown—he used to wash cars for a living, including the big, fancy cars preferred by Rufus "Sonnyman" Jackson, the jukebox and music shop entrepreneur—said that during the 1940s, when he was traveling, people would ask, as people often do, "Where you from?"

Sometimes Brown might reply, in a kind of shorthand, "I'm from Pittsburgh." But when he said that, people would often look at him and smile and say, "You're from Pittsburgh? Hey, what's happening in Homestead?"

George Couvaris, who, with his wife, Carol, ran a restaurant and candy store, the Sweet Shoppe, on Eighth Avenue for years, remembers a hot summer day, around 1959, about a decade after the worst of the whorehouses and bars and gambling dens along Sixth Avenue had been put out of business. Two fellows, one in his late teens, the other maybe in his forties or fifties, came into the restaurant. They were heavily sunburned and wet with sweat and extremely tired. They sat down. Care for some coffee? Couvaris asked. No, the men said, but a couple of cold drinks would be fine. Couvaris got them some soda pop.

The men sat for a time. Then one spoke. "Is this Homestead?" the man asked.

"Yes, this is Homestead," Couvaris said.

"Great," the men said, huge smiles on their faces.

"Where you from?" Couvaris asked.

"West Virginia," the men said.

"How did you get here?" Couvaris asked.

"Walked," one of the men said.

"What brings you to Homestead?" Couvaris asked.

"The girls!" the men said.

Couvaris looked at them. There was a moment of silence. "Fellows," Couvaris said, "you are about ten years too late."

Couvaris was born in Greece and spent his childhood there but left when the Germans invaded Greece in 1940. He escaped through Turkey, and then he enlisted in Britain's Royal Air Force and flew many missions over Italy and the Mediterranean and Adriatic seas. When the war ended, he went to Brazil, where, after a time, he obtained a position as a cook aboard a merchant ship. On leave on one cruise, he journeyed to the Monongahela Valley, where he had a relative. He met Carol Fourtas, daughter of Frank Fourtas, Homestead's most famous candymaker and proprietor of the United Candy Shop, on Eighth Avenue. The two were married, and Couvaris received his American citizenship. He had seen much of the world, but it was Homestead that Couvaris loved most. "It wasn't Homestead, Pa.," Couvaris said. "It was Homestead, USA."

And why should not Couvaris and so many others feel so affectionate toward Homestead? Homestead is a place where America can be heard, felt, seen, understood. Homestead, with its ethnic traditions, its patriotism, its love of sports, the willingness of its people to work hard, the desire of many to pull themselves up, to make something of themselves, its institutions—the stores, the taverns, the library, the funeral parlors, the sporting houses, the mill, always the mill—all this combines to make Homestead an elemental American place, an American touchstone.

Much of what makes up America can be examined in Homestead: the rise of industrialization and the breaking apart of industrialization, the role that immigrants have played in American life, the migration of black people to the North, authoritarianism and the acceptance of it, contention between workers and employers, the role of unions in American life, the heroism of ordinary people in the face of the strongest adversaries, how America uses things—people, resources, cities—then discards them.

3

BEGINNINGS

Whit is now Homestead was long ago part of a thick, dark wilderness, a hardwood forest that stretched one thousand miles from the Atlantic seaboard to the prairies that begin in what is now western Indiana. The Appalachian Mountains, a soft, dreamy landscape, blue and green in summer, black and gray and white in winter, known to pioneers as the Endless Mountains, were the spine of this vast wilderness.

It was a place of almost incomprehensible beauty. In Europe, from where the pioneers or their ancestors had come, forests like these had been gone for twenty centuries. But here the long-hunters and pioneers could walk for days through forests so thick with pines, oaks, sycamores, walnuts, and more that the sun could not be seen. Deer, elk, buffalo, bears, and panthers lived in the forests, as did immense flocks of birds. The forests seemed to shake with sound. A traveler in 1758 described the area as "an immense uninhabited Wilderness, overgrown everywhere with trees and underbrush so that nowhere can anyone see twenty yards."

The first white settler in the area is believed to have been John Frazier, who had a trading post on the north bank of the Monongahela River, where Turtle Creek comes into the river, a site that today is part of the run-down industrial town of Braddock, Pennsylvania. George Washington, a young Colonial officer and land speculator, stayed with Frazier on trips into the upper Ohio Valley in the 1750s and was favorably impressed by the commercial possibilities of the Monongahela River. He wrote in his journal, printed in 1754, that the Monongahela was "without any perceptible Fall" and that it seemed "extremely well designed for Water Carriage, as it is of a deep still Nature."

The Monongahela Valley was a part of five hundred thousand acres in the upper Ohio River Valley claimed by the Ohio Company, a group of eastern land speculators, in 1747. The claim enraged the French, who considered the area part of their vast holdings between Montreal and New Orleans. In 1753, the French built a chain of forts on the Allegheny and upper Ohio rivers, including Fort Duquesne, at the point where the two rivers meet, to defend their claims, and in 1754, Governor Robert Dinwiddie of Virginia sent Washington, twenty-two, a militia captain, and 150 men to demand that the French desist. Washington and his forces were defeated at Fort Necessity at Great Meadows, seventy miles southeast of the present city of Pittsburgh, in July 1754. The British and Virginians decided to retaliate, and in early 1755 a substantial force of British and Colonials under General Edward Braddock was mustered to force the French back. Braddock was ordered to capture Fort Duquesne, the site of which is now part of downtown Pittsburgh. On June 9, 1755, in command of about twenty-three hundred troops, Braddock set out from Fort Cumberland, now Cumberland, Maryland, on the two-hundred-mile march to Fort Duquesne. "It was a thin, long, multi-colored snake," the historian Francis Parkman said of Braddock's column a century later, "red, blue, and brown, trailing slowly through the depths of leaves, creeping round inaccessible heights, crawling over ridges, moving always in dampness and shadow by rivulets and waterfalls, crags and chasms, gorges and shaggy steeps."

The atmosphere on the march was uneasy; the men were ill-equipped for the campaign, and Braddock and many of the Colonial officers and men were at odds. The uniforms of the British regulars were made of heavy wool, hot on the summer march, and their three-cornered hats and wide-skirted coats made it difficult for the soldiers to make their way through the forests. The men subsisted largely on beans and bread and salt rations: salt beef, salt pork, salt fish. For the officers' mess, Braddock transported wines, cheeses, hams, two chests of lemons, three tubs of butter, hams, and roasts.

The Colonials had suggested to Braddock that he use packhorses inside of the heavy, cumbersome King's Wagons. These wagons, with much ironwork, had been fine on the level campaign fields of Europe but were most unsuited to the forested, mountainous route on which the column was traveling. Braddock refused to give up the King's Wagons. He also was hauling a number of cannon and mortars, against the advice of the Colonials, who said the weapons would be useless in a forest campaign. Some historians believe Braddock carried in his personal baggage a breastplate and a coat of mail, armaments that had been obsolete for a hundred years.

The Colonials also were worried about the tactics Braddock intended to use. When he arrived in the colonies, in February 1755, and during the preparation for the campaign, Braddock was advised by the Colonials, including George Washington, his volunteer aide, that he must not fight the French and Indians, who now awaited him in the vicinity of Fort Duquesne, in the European manner, with troops drawn up and massed in line and firing in volleys. This was the British way of fighting, but the French and their Indian allies were not likely to fight in that manner, Braddock was repeatedly counseled. He must adopt new ways of fighting, with his troops deployed on wide fronts, almost as skirmishers, and fighting from behind rocks and trees.

Braddock refused to listen. He was a resolute man; his courage could not be questioned. But he was not a man who could change. He was a man of the Continent and its ways, not of America, a new place that demanded new methods. Braddock was a man of the past, not of the present or the future. Braddock rejected the colonists' advice contemptuously, causing grave concern and resentment among the Colonial officers and enlisted men, and among the command's Indian allies. As his column tramped through the thick forest, French and Indian scouts could see the smoke from Braddock's campfires in the otherwise uninhabited wilderness; they could also hear the blasts from Braddock's engineers as they blew boulders from the track they were building.

On the morning of July 9, Braddock's column reached a ford of the Monongahela River, two miles upriver from what is now Homestead, Pennsylvania. An advance party was sent across the river, and then, sometime after noon, the main body crossed, drums and fifes playing "The Coldstream March." First came the Forty-fourth Regiment, the soldiers in red coats, bayonets gleaming in the sun, the king's colors snapping in the wind. Then sailors—brought along for their knowledge of ropes and knots, and to help with ferrying at the fords—barefooted, pants rolled to their knees. Then the artillery teams, brass howitzers and twelve-pounders, the pieces pulled by sweating, straining horses. Then wagons, covered with white canvas, and cattle. Then Colonial soldiers, in blue, and, finally, in red, flags unfurled, the rearguard, the Forty-eighth Regiment.

All around were the sparkling blues of water and sky and the dark greens, sometimes almost black, of the forest. It was, Washington wrote years later in his autobiography, the most splendid sight he had ever seen. On the north bank of the river, the column re-formed. Commanders were confident. Some officers said they would not be surprised to hear the sound of Fort Duquesne, ten miles away, being destroyed by the French prior to a retreat.

Then, in the early afternoon, a quarter of a mile from the river, in a clearing, the advance guard saw a shocking sight: perhaps three hundred French soldiers and their Indian allies, many of the Indians almost naked, running at them down the narrow forest track. The British formed a line of battle across the trail. "God save the king!" a subaltern shouted.

British soldiers went down, wounded or dead. Some of the advance guard retreated and in so doing fell against the main column moving up. Confusion and disorder broke out. Some men fired upon their own ranks, killing or wounding many of their comrades. Some regulars took to the trees, but Braddock, his hat tied under his chin with a large white handkerchief, beat them with his broadsword. "Cowards!" he cried. The battle continued until the British and Colonials retreated. Of the fifteen hundred officers and men who had gone into battle, one thousand had been killed or wounded. Braddock himself was mortally wounded.

He was carried from the field and back across the river. "Who would have thought it?" Braddock said.

On the night of July 13, in a glade west of Fort Necessity, a place where Washington and a Colonial force of one hundred had fought the French and Indians in July 1754, the party encamped. Stragglers—some wounded, some exhausted—stretched for miles along the line of march.

It was sunset, and Braddock was dying. "Is it possible?" he asked. About nine o'clock, he murmured. "All is over," and died.

The site of the battlefield is now part of Braddock, Pennsylvania. The site where the column began to cross the river is now occupied by a McDonald's, a small, grim shopping center, and Kennywood Park, an old amusement park. In the 1890s, schoolchildren contributed pennies to purchase a picture of the Braddock's Field battle by the artist Emanuel Leutze. A hundred years later it rested, covered with sheets, behind a counter in the abandoned Carnegie Library of Braddock. For years, a rusted, crooked brass monument on the lawn of the abandoned Alexander M. Scott High School in Braddock marked the spot where "456 soldiers killed in the battle were buried in unmarked graves." In recent years, the sign has disappeared, probably stolen and sold; brass has significant cash value in the Monongahela Valley.

The battle of Braddock's Field left the American frontier undefended and brought on the French and Indian Wars. In 1758, the French abandoned Fort Duquesne, and British troops under the British general John Forbes occupied the site without firing a shot and named the place Fort Pitt. The town that grew up around it was called Pittsbourgh, later changed to Pittsburg and then Pittsburgh. When the war was ended by the Peace of Paris in 1763, the French were forced to give up most of their claims to North America.

Settlement in the area was forbidden by the British Proclamation of 1763, which held that all lands on the western watersheds of the Appalachian Mountains were an Indian reserve and closed to white settlement. But settlers paid no attention. The Battle of Bushy Run, east of modern-day Pittsburgh, on August 5, 1763, ended the Pontiac Conspiracy, an Indian revolt, and after that settlers returned and log cabins were again thrown up along the Monongahela, Allegheny, and upper Ohio rivers. Pittsburgh was transformed from a military post into a trading post. The treaty of Fort Stanwix with the Iroquois in 1768 brought peace for a time to the upper Ohio River Valley, and in 1769 a land office was opened in Pittsburgh. On the first day, 2,790 applications were made for farms of three hundred acres apiece. Within a few months, more than a million acres in the area had been dispensed.

By the 1770s, the Monongahela River was an important water route west. By 1778, Elizabeth, a small town twenty miles up the Monongahela River from the forks of the Ohio, was a major center of boat construction for pioneers heading for the western frontier. With the end of the Revolution, in 1783, settlers swarmed over the Appalachian Mountains, clambered down the rude track to Elizabeth, and bought or bartered for boats to take them down the Monongahela River to the Ohio River in what became one of the epic American migrations. The Monongahela and Ohio rivers were often thick with pirogues, arks, skiffs, bateaux, and keelboats as families with household possessions and dogs, cats, sheep, milk cows, and beef cattle moved west.

The first settler of what would become Homestead is believed to have arrived in the 1770s. Sebastian Frederick probably came from the Palatinate in Germany. The Revolution was still going on, and the area had not been surveyed. Frederick claimed a tract of 303 acres that ran from the Monongahela River to what are now the cemeteries on the hill. What is now Sarah Street in Homestead is believed to have run down the middle of his tract. Frederick appears to have been a man of energy, but he accumulated little. He hunted, fished, trapped, and probably otherwise enjoyed pioneer life. But he was a squatter, meaning he had no title to the land on which he lived, and he moved on—whether voluntarily or because he was forced is unknown. It is said that he was displeased because game was thinning out. What became of him is not known.

The first permanent settler of Homestead is believed to have been John McClure, a trader, farmer, and land speculator. McClure came across the Appalachian Mountains from Carlisle, Pennsylvania, in early 1760, two years after the French had abandoned Fort Duquesne. His father, Abdiel, and two brothers probably came with him. McClure lived for a time at Fort Pitt, the name the British had given to Fort Duquesne. It is thought that he furnished supplies for the military, which was building new fortifications at the fort. He also traded with the Indians—he was one of the few traders in the area not killed by them in the Pontiac uprising—farmed, and speculated in lands in several areas of western Pennsylvania.

On May 16, 1786, three years after the close of the Revolution, McClure obtained for fifty-four pounds and ten shillings, a deed to 329.5 acres of land along the Monongahela River, between what is now Amity Street and Munhall Hollow, and running to what are now the burying grounds. He and his wife, Martha, had seven children, and the family built a substantial farm at the site, which McClure called "Amity" or "the Amity Homestead." He became a man of prominence in the area. He took an interest in politics and was an active Federalist. He was fond of the chase and kept a pack of hounds for this purpose. An old account says McClure traveled throughout western Pennsylvania "but found no place that suited him so well as his 'Homestead.'" It was from the name of McClure's farm that Homestead later took its name.

In July 1811, McClure died at about age ninety, and a son, also named John, inherited the Amity Homestead. This McClure was also a man of ability and of fine reputation. He and his wife, Agnes, had ten children. He also was fond of the chase, and it is said that he and companions made the hills above the Monongahela River ring as they pursued foxes with their baying hounds. He was a Presbyterian and a prominent Whig.

At his death, on February 6, 1833, at age sixty-seven, his youngest son, Abdiel, was left the western quarter of the McClure estate. Abdiel McClure, who may be regarded as the founder of Homestead, was born on July 18, 1816. He had a serious look about him, and in later years a white beard that fringed his face added to this effect. He and his wife, Anna, had eight children—the McClures seem to have been prolific and long-lived. He was a man of prominence in the area. He was a Republican, an elder in the Presbyterian church, twice justice of the peace, and a temperance man.

When Abdiel McClure received his inheritance in the decades before the Civil War, the area along the lower Monongahela River boasted rather prosperous farms, including the handsome, ornate McClure homestead, at the corner of what are now McClure and Tenth streets, and some smaller farms along the river. In 1850, a home for the destitute, the City Poor Farm, was established on 150 acres purchased from Abdiel McClure, and in 1851, a fine, three-story poorhouse was constructed there to relieve the crowded almshouses of the city. This, for the most part, was all the development that came to the area, with its pleasant, prosperous ways. There were gay parties in summer on the porches of the large homes, with Chinese lanterns on the lawns. In the winter, there were skating parties and fast cutters and bonfires on the riverbanks, and the hills above the town were often covered with merry crowds of coasters.

In 1871, Abdiel McClure, allying himself with another well-to-do landowner, Lowry H. West, formed the Homestead Bank and Life Insurance Company. The two then sold 230 acres of their lands to the institution they had established. The land was surveyed in August, and on September 17, 1871, the lots were offered at a grand public sale. The promoters touted the site as a future pleasant residential suburb of smoky, industrial Pittsburgh. Music and junketing added to the pleasures of the afternoon. The festiveness was fitting not only because of the occasion, the founding of a town, but because this was an optimistic time in much of America.

The Civil War, which had brought 600,000 deaths and immense suffering and devastation to the nation, had been over for six years. Reconstruction continued and more than one hundred thousand Federal troops garrisoned the South, but the nation was embarked upon a great expansion. New farm implements and machines were being built—sewing machines, shoemaking machines, mining machines. The transcontinental railroad had been completed in 1869, and more lines were going out; between 1865 and 1873, the nation laid thirty-five thousand miles of railroad track, an amount that surpassed the nation's entire rail network in 1860.

The week that the town lots went up for sale, the Apaches drove miners back from the desert into Prescott, Arizona, killing one; an expedition led by Professor F. V. Hayden, a U.S. geologist, was exploring the Yellowstone River country; the Chicago White Stockings defeated the Philadelphia Athletics eleven to six in the fourth game of the championship series in a new professional sport, organized baseball; the Tammany Ring continued to control New York politics; and the remains of President Abraham Lincoln were removed from a temporary vault to a permanent tomb at the cemetery in Springfield, Illinois.

Ulysses S. Grant was president. That week Grant visited Titusville, Pennsylvania, a great oil center sixty miles north of Pittsburgh, and was feted by the townspeople and honored with a review of Pennsylvania militia. The infantry units were under the command of Captain George R. Snowden, who would become part of Homestead history when, as a general, he would command the state troops that occupied Homestead during the 1892 strike.

Cities were rising taller and pushing out their boundaries. Roads were being laid and macadamized. Between 1865 and 1873, three million immigrants entered the United States, their presence and their labor helping to build the new industrial world. In those eight years, the nation's industrial production rose 75 percent; by 1873, the number of the nation's industrial workers surpassed that of its farmers, and the nation's industrial production was second only to that of Great Britain. Abdiel McClure and Lowry H. West and the other boomers who had formed the Homestead Bank and Life Insurance Company were not going to miss this bonanza, no sir.

The Homestead area was an excellent location for town jobbing. It was an attractive place, with the cool river, the thick trees, the high green hills. The river offered easy access to the site, and the floodplain afforded excellent building sites. In three days of public sale in September 1871, 447 lots were purchased for a total of $385,496. By 1872, several hundred homes had been constructed, and that year a railroad, the Pittsburgh, Virginia, and Charleston, was extended along the south bank of the Monongahela River to Homestead, linking the town with Pittsburgh. In 1873, McClure, seeing a demand for lumber for construction, built a planing mill, or lumber mill, in Homestead.

But the Panic of 1873, the first major crisis of industrial capitalism, brought on by the collapse of the New York banking house of Jay Cooke and Company, stopped Homestead's growth. By 1876, most of the land, while platted, remained undeveloped. The panic did not reach bottom until 1878, a year in which some ten thousand businesses across the country failed.

Then, in 1879, a glass manufacturer, Bryce, Higbee, and Company, was established in Homestead, at the foot of West Street, on the Monongahela River. Glassmaking had been a major industry in the upper Ohio Valley for decades, and Bryce, Higbee, the first manufacturing concern to come to Homestead, made excellent glasses, vases, and the like, and was highly successful. This success brought a need for houses for working-class people, and the first rental houses, for married workmen and their families, were erected on Fifth Street. By the late 1870s, the town had a population of one thousand, although much of the land above the glassworks—including the hill—was still a place of fields, pastures, and woodlots.

Then came the development that would alter the area forever: the Homestead Works. Iron and steel manufacture had been the centerpiece of the Pittsburgh area's economy for decades. An iron foundry was first established in 1793. The first rolling mill powered by steam was constructed in the area in 1812, and from then on the number of steam-powered mills rose rapidly. Pittsburgh iron foundries supplied cannon and shot for Commodore Oliver Hazard Perry in the Battle of Lake Erie in 1812, for Andrew Jackson's army in the Battle of New Orleans in 1814, and for American forces in the Mexican War of 1846–1848.

Pittsburgh was joined to the East Coast in 1852 by the completion of the railroad between Philadelphia and Pittsburgh, and the town boomed during the Civil War, producing cannons and other arms and munitions, and coal. The expansion accelerated after the war. By 1870, Pittsburgh's blast furnaces were producing almost 40 percent of the nation's iron. Pittsburgh also had some seventy glass factories, which produced perhaps half the nation's output of glass, and massive railroad-marshaling yards. Smoke from the ironworks, the glass factories, and the stern-wheelers and side-wheelers covered Pittsburgh and gave it the reputation of America's dirtiest city.

The Monongahela Valley remained largely unspoiled, however. Then, in 1873, the great industrialist Andrew Carnegie began construction of the Edgar Thomson Works, with its immense, fiery Bessemer furnaces, at Braddock. In 1879, a group of businessmen financed the construction of the Homestead Works, and in 1887, work was begun on the Duquesne Works, three miles up the Monongahela River from Homestead. The area was forever changed. Gone the gay cotillions, gone the shimmering skating and sledding parties. From now on, the lower Monongahela Valley, with Homestead at the center, was to be a factory, a workplace.

4

"WHERE IS THERE SUCH A BUSINESS!"

In October 1883, a group of Pittsburgh merchants approached Andrew Carnegie, Pittsburgh's leading iron and steel man. The men were owners of the Homestead Works, which had opened in March 1881, a little more than two and a half years before. The men were unhappy; Carnegie knew it and had been expecting them for some time.

The Homestead mill, with a Bessemer furnace, a rail mill, and other facilities, was among the most advanced steelworks in the nation. But it had experienced one problem after another. The man who had guided its construction, Andrew Kloman, an associate of Carnegie's years before but then a foe, had died in December 1880, before the mill was opened. His partners had worked hard and had overcome his loss. But once the mill opened, severe labor and management problems developed, and they seemed intractable. Management was arbitrary and authoritarian. Five confrontations had occurred at the mill between workers and managers; in one, a strike in March 1881, a man had been killed, strikebreakers had been assaulted, and deputies had fought a pitched battle with strikers. Another, in June 1882, had precipitated a national iron and steel strike of nearly four months. In addition to this, the price of steel was falling, and the works needed more capital. It was more than the Homestead owners could stand.

The steelmen's question to Carnegie was the one he had expected: Would Carnegie take the mill off their hands? He was courteous. He said that he would purchase the mill and made what seemed a generous offer: $350,000, which was the value of the works plus an allowance for increased land values. The Homestead owners accepted. Little cash was paid. So eager were they to sell that all but one took notes in payment; these were soon liquidated out of profits from the works. The man who came out most favorably was Carnegie. Buying the Homestead Works was one of the smartest moves in his business career. For a relatively small amount of money—with almost no cash up front—he acquired the most modern Bessemer furnaces and rail mill in the country.

Carnegie almost immediately set about improving the Homestead Works, for he was a man who insisted upon the newest technologies and methods despite the cost. In 1886, Carnegie began to install the open-hearth process at the Homestead Works, the first commercially successful open-hearth process in the nation. Then came the conversion of the mill for making beams and then the expansion for making naval plates.

In less than a decade, Carnegie would transform the Homestead Works into the most advanced, versatile mill in the nation, and one of the most profitable mills as well. By 1890, it would be known around the world and looked upon with awe by steelmen.

Carnegie was a curious man—two men, really: the stern businessman and foe of unions on the one hand, the friend of the working class, the pacifist, the philanthropist on the other.

He had come from Scotland to the United States with his mother and father in 1848, at age twelve, after five years of schooling; he had none in this country. By age thirty he was a wealthy man from investments in an express company, oilfields, a telegraph system, sleeping cars, bridge construction, and iron and steel. He was fiercely ambitious in business and in his personal life; in his efforts to make something beyond a businessman of himself, he courted those who could help him, making friends with men like Matthew Arnold, the English writer and critic, and Herbert Spencer, the English philosopher.

Carnegie was short and slender, standing five feet three inches. His hair turned white at an early age, and with his square white beard he was often mistaken for Ulysses S. Grant. He was charming when he wished to be, with the born salesman's manner of identifying and ingratiating himself with people he wished to know or use. He could also be exceedingly ruthless. Yet, he detested confrontation; throughout his life, when confrontation occurred, he was absent.

Carnegie regarded himself as a stickler for honesty, but he often embellished and exaggerated the truth. He favored labor, he said, but he headed the company that, at Homestead, fought one of the epic battles against American labor. He regarded himself as an ardent believer in free enterprise, yet he engaged in extensive pooling arrangements—entering them when it benefited him, leaving them when it did not—and supported protective tariffs, even when he knew that his enterprises, past their infant stages, did not need protection.

He proclaimed himself a pacifist, yet he made the Homestead Works one of the world's great centers of armor-plate production. He never worked in an iron or steel mill or, for that matter, any industrial plant, except for his brief years as a youth in two textile mills in Pittsburgh. The lowliest furnaceman at Homestead probably knew more abut making steel than he did. He was, however, a master of organization, a man with a sharp eye for detail, and a man with a seemingly innate talent for judging people; it was these skills that allowed him to master each industry he entered.

Although he made his fortune in Pittsburgh and is still associated with it, he disliked the place, with its provincialism and its smoke and dirt—smoke and dirt that his factories had helped create. At age thirty-two, he left Pittsburgh, moved with his mother to New York, and took up residence at the handsome Saint Nicholas Hotel in lower Manhattan, New York City's finest hostelry. He maintained a retreat at Cresson, Pennsylvania, at the crest of the Allegheny Mountains, and later lived in castles in Scotland. He never resided in Pittsburgh again.

He was a man given to some contemplation, and at an early age he began musing about life and about how a rich man who regarded himself as principled should comport himself. In December 1868, at the Saint Nicholas Hotel, he wrote a memorandum to himself. Noting that he had an annual income of fifty thousand dollars, he promised to make no effort to increase his fortune and said that he should "cast aside business forever except for others." He wrote, "The amassing of wealth is one of the worst species of idolitary [*sic*]. No idol more debasing than the worship of money." And yet by the end of the century he was to build the world's leading steel company, one of the most productive and profitable enterprises the world has ever known.

Carnegie was born on November 25, 1835, a cold and wet day, in Dunfermline, Scotland, fourteen miles northwest of Edinburgh. It is said that as a boy he had a voracious appetite, ate his porridge with two spoons, and would cry, "Mair, mair." His father, William Carnegie, was a skilled weaver and worked on a handloom at home. His mother, Margaret Morrison Carnegie, daughter of a cobbler, was hardworking, like her husband, but a person not given to depression, as he was, and, far more than her husband, a person of discipline.

By the mid-1840s, because the advent of the power loom rendered handweaving obsolete, many weavers were out of work, including Carnegie's father. One evening in the winter of 1847–1848, he came home and said to his son, "Andra, I can get nae mair work." Andrew Carnegie, in his autobiography, wrote, "My father did not recognize the impending revolution, and was struggling under the old system." Andrew Carnegie would not be like that. He recognized revolutions and used them to his advantage.

Because of the staggering economic problems they were encountering, the Carnegie family—mother, father, Andrew, and his brother, Thomas, eight years younger—set out in May 1848 on a journey that millions of people would take, a journey to America.

After a ninety-day voyage across the Atlantic and an arduous journey from New York City, the family settled in Allegheny City, now part of Pittsburgh, to which two of Mrs. Carnegie's sisters had immigrated from Scotland in 1840. There, the family, nearly penniless, took two free rooms in a small frame house owned by Mrs. Carnegie's sister Annie on a muddy alley behind 336 Rebecca Street, in a poor, rough area known as Slabtown.

The family, with Carnegie's mother in charge, immediately set out to find employment. Mrs. Carnegie got work binding shoes for Henry Phipps, a cobbler near Rebecca Street. Carnegie's father worked as a weaver, making coarse tablecloths that he sold door to door, although he had few customers. Andrew, at the age of twelve, found work first in an Allegheny City cotton mill, then in a Pittsburgh mill owned by businessman John Hay, for two dollars a week.

His work consisted of running the steam engine and firing the boiler, and he detested it. Soon, however, he began to advance. He possessed fine penmanship and gained a position as a clerk in the mill, although he still did some factory tasks, including dipping bobbins in oil as a preservative. He hated the odor and feel of the oil. Many years later he recalled: "Not all the resolution I could muster, nor all the indignation I felt at my own weakness, prevented my stomach from behaving in a most perverse way. I never succeeded in overcoming the nausea produced by the smell of oil. . . . but if I had to lose breakfast or dinner, I had all the better appetite for supper, and the allotted work was done."

Carnegie, however, enjoyed his work as a clerk, sitting on a high stool, working with a ledger book. He quickly saw an opportunity to advance himself. Hay kept his books in a single entry, but Carnegie decided to learn a new system, double entry. He persuaded a number of his friends from Rebecca Street to attend classes in Pittsburgh two or three nights a week to learn the double-entry system. He was fortunate in the friends he made at that time. Many were bright young men, and they would work with him later in life, worlds away from Rebecca Street.

In the spring of 1849, Carnegie's uncle Thomas Hogan found him a job as a messenger boy at the Reilly telegraph office in Pittsburgh. Carnegie reveled in his work at the telegraph office. He remembered: "What a change an entrance to a telegraph office was to me then. My 'Good Fairy' found me in a cellar firing a boiler and a little steam engine, and carried me into the bright and sunny office surrounded with newspapers, pencils, pens and paper, and ringing in the ears, the miraculous tick, tick, tick of the tamed lightning and doing the work of a man. I was the happiest boy alive, carried from darkness to light."

He memorized faces and addresses for fast delivery. He soon began to handle simple administrative matters. When more messengers were needed, two of his friends from Allegheny City, David McCargo and Robert Pitcairn, were given positions, and then two more, Henry W. Oliver and Will Morland, were added. Soon Carnegie was placed in charge of the messenger boys. He took his responsibilities seriously. When quarrels arose over who would keep the ten-cent tips for deliveries beyond regular distances, Carnegie decreed that the dimes would be put into a pool and that the money would be divided equally among the messenger boys at the end of the month. This was, he said, his first experience in financial organization. Carnegie was opposed to the use of candy, intoxicants, and tobacco. He reprimanded Pitcairn because Pitcairn sometimes charged sweets at the local confectioner's shop. And he informed the confectioner that, as treasurer of the dime pool, he would not be responsible for debts run up by the other messenger boys.

Carnegie was a success. His wages were advanced to thirteen and a half dollars a month and then twenty dollars. He was fascinated by telegraphy and during his free time began to learn Morse code. Soon he was substituting for absent operators. Later he became one of the first operators in the country to take messages by ear, meaning that he did not have to translate messages from the tapes on which they were recorded. This ability was fascinating to others, and soon businessmen were stopping at the telegraph office to watch him. His salary was raised to twenty-five dollars a month.

Always Carnegie worked to improve himself. He organized a debating society with John Phipps, Tom Miller, and Robert Pitcairn, and the group met in Henry Phipps's cobbler shop. He read Shakespeare and sometimes, with Henry W. Oliver, stopped while on telegraph runs to watch a Shakespeare play at the Pittsburgh Theater. He read the English essayists Thomas Babington Macaulay and Charles Lamb and the American historians George Bancroft and William Hickling Prescott, and he was a frequent borrower of books at the private library of Colonel James Anderson in Allegheny City, the beginning of his love for libraries.

In December 1852, the Pennsylvania Railroad was put through from Philadelphia to Pittsburgh. A young railroad man, Thomas A. Scott, was named superintendent of the railroad's western division and made daily trips to the telegraph office in Pittsburgh. He met Carnegie there and took an instant liking to him. Carnegie, in turn, quickly came to idolize Scott, a handsome, confident man on his way to becoming one of the nation's great railroaders. Soon Scott decided he needed his own telegrapher. He offered Carnegie thirty-five dollars a month to come to work for him. Carnegie accepted, joining Scott on February 1, 1853.

Carnegie quickly became more than Scott's telegrapher. He began to learn about railroading and, ambitious and daring, sometimes made decisions in Scott's absence. It was not long before he was functioning as Scott's private secretary. When Carnegie's father died, on October 2, 1855, Carnegie's responsibilities to his family were increased, although there is evidence that he did not provide the extensive support for his family that he later claimed. Nevertheless, he made payments on the family home and paid his father's medical and funeral expenses. He continued to look to his mother for advice.

In 1856, Carnegie made his first financial investment, purchasing, at Scott's suggestion, ten shares in the Adams Express Company, a message and freight delivery service. It is likely that he borrowed the $610 for the stock from Scott. Two years later, in June 1858, he found a large white envelope on his desk, addressed to Andrew Carnegie, Esquire. It contained a ten-dollar dividend check for his Adams Express Company stock

—the first return on stock that Carnegie received. Carnegie was enthralled. "Eureka!" he exclaimed. "Here's the goose that lays the golden eggs."

In September 1858, Carnegie made another investment, one that demonstrated his lifelong ability to foresee new technologies before others saw them, and to profit from them. He acquired an interest in the Woodruff Sleeping Car Company, an early producer of sleeping cars for railroads. The investment, Carnegie biographer Burton J. Hendrick wrote in 1922, was "more than a nest-egg; it was the start of the Carnegie fortune." Carnegie said years later: "The first considerable sum I ever made was from this source. . . . Blessed be the man who invented sleep."

Meanwhile, Carnegie, his fortune tied to Scott's, continued to advance with the railroad. In 1859, Scott became vice-president of the Pennsylvania. Scott named Carnegie to replace him as superintendent of the railroad's Pittsburgh division at a salary of $1,500 a year. Carnegie was twenty-four years old and had been in America less than a dozen years, but, with his railroad salary and his income from the Woodruff company, he was becoming a wealthy man.

With the start of the Civil War in April 1861, Secretary of War Simon Cameron asked Scott to come to Washington to oversee telegraph communications and to help keep the railroads running. Carnegie followed his mentor and served on his staff for five months. But he tired of the work and with Scott's consent resumed his position as western superintendent of the Pennsylvania Railroad. Carnegie then set about his primary purpose in life, amassing a fortune.

Later that year, Carnegie invested eleven thousand dollars in the Titusville, Pennsylvania, oilfields of the Columbia Oil Company. The investment ultimately returned to him more than one million dollars. Next, and more important, Carnegie became involved in bridge-building, which he enjoyed immensely, and which led him to the business that gave him his fortune and fame, iron and steel.

Until the coming of iron, bridges had been made of wood, and they were often set on fire by the cinders and flames of locomotives. Wooden bridges were also weak and could not carry heavy engines and rolling stock as the railroads expanded. Carnegie had become interested in iron bridges as early as 1856, when a skilled young Pennsylvania engineer, John Piper, showed Carnegie an iron bridge being constructed to replace a burned wooden bridge. Carnegie, as usual, foresaw the importance of the innovation, and in April 1865, with Piper and another engineer, and others, including Scott and J. Edgar Thomson, a railroad man, he established the Keystone Bridge Company, which he became fond of calling his "pet" and which, he said later in life, was "the parent of all [my] other works."

With the end of the war, bridge-building boomed. The Pennsylvania Railroad needed iron bridges; the railroads in the South had to be rebuilt, necessitating the construction of hundreds more bridges. The Homestead Act of 1862 had given new impetus to the westward movement, and there was a need for bridges across the Mississippi and Missouri rivers, and for bridges on the transcontinental railroad, under construction, beginning in 1865, between Omaha, Nebraska, and San Francisco, California.

The Keystone Bridge Company received numerous contracts. In addition to building the Eads Bridge at St. Louis, the first bridge across the Mississippi, it built the superstructures for the Ohio River bridges at Point Pleasant, West Virginia, and Cincinnati, Ohio; the Mississippi River bridge at Keokuk, Iowa; the Missouri River bridge at Omaha; and others. Carnegie also won the contract to provide steel beams and plates for the superstructure of the Brooklyn Bridge, completed in 1883. Ultimately, Keystone produced iron and steel for ten bridges across the Allegheny and Monongahela rivers, twenty-three across the Ohio River, and thirteen across the Mississippi River.

As he would in steel, Carnegie hired the best men, let them operate, and rewarded them well. His role, for the most part, was as promoter and salesman, positions for which he was highly qualified. And he traveled frequently to New York and Europe as he and his partners sought capital.

During this time, Carnegie also entered the iron business. With Keystone Bridge prospering, he needed an additional supply of iron beams and plates. In October 1864, he and his old friend from Rebecca Street, Thomas Miller, organized the Cyclops Iron Company. Construction of a mill began in the winter of 1864–1865.

Carnegie also set out to capture a rival Pittsburgh iron company, the Kloman and Phipps Company, and to combine the firms. He wanted the iron expertise of Andrew Kloman, an important industry innovator, and the business abilities of his old friend Henry Phipps. In May 1865, the two companies, Kloman and Phipps and the Cyclops Iron Company, were combined under the name Union Iron Mills, capitalized at five hundred thousand dollars, the name signifying both the union of the companies and the reunion in April 1865 of the North and South. Kloman was opposed to the merger but did not have the strength to block Carnegie. Five years later, the Union Iron Mills were renamed Carnegie, Kloman, and Company, the first time the Carnegie name appeared in the iron industry. The company, in which Carnegie owned a controlling interest, was, with Keystone, the foundation of Carnegie's iron and steel empire.

With the boom in the demand for iron at the end of the Civil War, Carnegie set about expanding his new operations. In this he demonstrated his genius for management and for selecting highly skilled associates, and his skill as a salesman. Until this time, the American iron industry was not integrated. Separate, usually small companies made pig iron, forged and rolled pig iron into billets, bars, and slabs, and rolled or cut finished products. There was no sophisticated bookkeeping and little cost control. "I heard of men who thought their business at the end of the year would show a loss and had found a profit, and vice versa," Carnegie wrote.

Carnegie integrated his operations. He insisted that Keystone purchase iron plates and beams from Union Mills, not make them. He once scolded a Keystone executive, John Linville: "You [and the Union Iron Mills] are not competitors; on the contrary you are necessary to each other—the true policy is to work together." By 1870, Carnegie had blended Union and Keystone into a smoothly integrated operation.

The Union Iron Mills were a large consumer of pig iron, and soon Carnegie saw the necessity for producing his own. In December 1870, Carnegie, Kloman, and Company decided to build the Lucy furnaces, named for Carnegie's sister-in-law, on the north side of Pittsburgh. Construction of the furnaces began in the spring of 1871 and was completed in the summer of 1872.

They were phenomenally productive, thanks to the innovations of Kloman. When slag buildup slowed the pouring of iron, Kloman devised a slag cooler that allowed the continuous removal of slag. A production technique called hard driving was practiced—when elements wore out, they were replaced. Once, a British iron man condemned "the reckless rapid rate" of driving the Lucy furnaces "so that the interior of each furnace was wrecked and had to be replaced every three years." Carnegie's furnace superintendent replied: "What do we care about the lining? We think a lining is good for so much iron and the sooner it makes it the better." Eventually the Lucy furnaces produced one hundred thousand tons of iron a year. Kloman also invented a metal saw, an unsetting machine, and machine tools that allowed the fabrication at high speeds of iron and steel beams and plates with exact measurements, all of which assisted Keystone Bridge immensely.

Phipps—fund-raiser, cost-cutter, innovator—was also indispensable. He had an old black mare, Gypsy, which he took on banking rounds in Pittsburgh so often that, after a time, the horse on its own cut back and forth across Wood Street as Phipps traveled from one bank to another. Phipps hired a chemist, one of the first in the iron and steel industry, and guided the enlargement of the Upper Mill of the Union Mills and later the installation of the open-hearth furnaces at the Homestead Works. Carnegie himself was a superb salesman. He was acquainted with most of the top railroad men in America, and he used his relationships to sell his rails and other steel products.

By 1872, iron—first the Union Iron Mills, then the Lucy furnaces— had surpassed bridge-building in its importance to Carnegie. "No longer were the mills simply a source of supply for Keystone, rather, Keystone had become a market for the Union Mills," said Joseph Frazier Wall, Carnegie's modern biographer. But it was a Keystone project that revealed to Carnegie the metal of the future, steel. During the late 1860s and early 1870s, the Keystone Company undertook the long, difficult construction of the Eads Bridge across the Mississippi at St. Louis. The chief engineer was James B. Eads, a cantankerous, demanding man who as a captain during the Civil War had won fame by constructing iron gunboats for the Union forces on the Mississippi River.

The captain was one of the most difficult men Carnegie was ever to deal with, and as demanding as Carnegie himself. Captain Eads wanted the bridge to be a masterpiece and insisted that steel be used for its important parts, including major bolts on the piers and staves that supported the superstructure. Carnegie, Kloman, and Company obtained the contract to manufacture the iron for the bridge, and Captain Eads's insistence on steel was somewhat embarrassing to Carnegie and the other iron men, because it suggested that steel was superior to iron. Carnegie complained that steel took longer to manufacture and was more expensive than iron, but Captain Eads was adamant and had his way.

The bridge was a magnificent engineering and construction achievement, consisting of three huge arches of steel and iron, and containing the longest beams rolled in America up to that time. On July 2, 1874, General William Tecumseh Sherman, the Civil War hero, drove the last spike connecting the bridge with the railway that would pass over it. Thousands of people and fourteen locomotives were on the bridge at the time. Doubters thought that the entire affair—people, locomotives, and bridge—would tumble into the Mississippi River. But the bridge held, and it survives to this day. Carnegie was impressed by Eads's insistence on steel and proud of the part he himself had played in the bridge's construction. He wrote the New York financier Junius Morgan, "The entire works—bridge, tunnel & approaches, are magnificent—only they cost double the money that should have been expended in such an enterprise."

Carnegie found a way to reduce costs when, on a bond-selling trip to Europe, he viewed in England the great Bessemer Steel plants in Sheffield and Birmingham, and heard British steelmen discuss plans for expansion. Carnegie quickly understood the promise of the Bessemer process, in which steel was made by blowing cold air through molten pig iron. He became determined to construct a vast Bessemer works in the United States with the most modern equipment that could be obtained. Gone were the musings of the philanthropist who had once vowed to make no effort to increase his fortune beyond his income of fifty thousand dollars a year. As Carnegie wrote in his autobiography, published in 1920, a year after his death: "In England, I had seen it demonstrated, at least to my satisfaction, that the [Bessemer] process could be a grand success without undue expenditure of capital or great risk. . . . It was agreed we should enter upon the manufacture of steel rails at Pittsburgh." Joseph Frazier Wall wrote: "What was needed was not a converted plant of limited facilities, but an entirely new mill with the most up-to-date equipment available. As he watched the silver-white stream of steel pour out of the great pear-shaped [Bessemer] vessel, his plans for the future expanded with the heat that engulfed him." This period, 1872 and 1873, "marks the great transitional period of Carnegie's life," Wall wrote. "It was then that he made the decision to concentrate his business interests and specialize in the manufacture of steel."

On his return from England, Carnegie talked with relatives and business associates about building a vast steelworks using the Bessemer technology. William Coleman, the father of his sister-in-law, was an amateur historian and sometimes went to an area of scrub farms and timber on the north bank of the Monongahela River, a dozen miles east of Pittsburgh, the site of the Battle of Braddock's Field 130 years before, and tramped the site looking for arrowheads, powder horns, bayonets, swords, and other relics of the battle. Coleman suggested this would be a suitable place for the mill. It was relatively flat and had water and railroad access. The land, along an old dirt road from Pittsburgh, and just east of the new town of Homestead, was scouted and cash was secured. The land was acquired at a good price compared to what Carnegie would have had to pay for land in Pittsburgh. Carnegie hired Alexander L. Holley, the foremost authority in the nation on the Bessemer process, to design and build the works. Holley also brought to the works a man who would become perhaps the nation's top steel manager of the nineteenth century, Captain William R. Jones, a Civil War veteran of Fredericksburg and Chancellorsville who kept his military title for the rest of his life. In 1877, the works was completed and the first steel poured.

In an action typical of Carnegie, who always attempted to curry favor with people he regarded as important, he secured permission from his old mentor and employer J. Edgar Thomson, to name the plant the Edgar Thomson Works. Railroads were then the nation's main consumer of steel, and in the case of the Edgar Thomson Works, railroads would be the only purchaser of the works' steel, for steel rails were all the plant made. Railroads were also the only way the rails were sent to market, another reason why Carnegie wanted to cozy up to the old railroader.

The Edgar Thomson Works, known then and today as E.T., quickly became the nation's leading rail mill because of its advanced machines and methods, and the talent of Captain Jones and the highly skilled workforce. The workers, mostly immigrants from Great Britain, Ireland, and Germany, plus native-born Americans, worked hard—twelve-hour shifts in the cold of winter and the heat of summer, seven days a week. In 1878, when Carnegie received the first six-month report on profits from the Edgar Thomson Works, he proclaimed, in a statement that would come to emblematize the Carnegie steel enterprise and the steel industry itself, "Where is there such a business!"

In 1881, Carnegie acquired a substantial interest in the vast Pennsylvania coal and coke holdings of Henry Clay Frick. This gave Carnegie assured supplies of coke, which, with iron and limestone, is a major ingredient of steel. And it brought together two men who would build an empire and would shape the town and people of Homestead.

Like Carnegie, Frick was a self-made man. He had been born on his maternal grandfather's farm near the village of West Overton, in Westmoreland County, southwestern Pennsylvania, on December 19, 1849. His grandfather was Abraham Overholt, the wealthiest man in the county. He was the owner of a large, prosperous farm but was also a distiller. In this he was following tradition, for the area was a major producer of whiskey. Frick's grandfather's brand was Overholt, noted for its purity and strength. It is said that the supply never equaled the demand.

Frick's parents were Elizabeth and John W. Frick. His maternal grandparents were highly displeased when their daughter, in October 1847, married Frick, a man of little means. The couple needed lodging, and all that Grandpap Overholt, as he was known, would do, despite his wealth, was allow the two to live in the springhouse at the foot of the Overholt farmstead. It was there that Henry Clay Frick was born. He was a delicate child, suffering from "chronic indigestion" or "inflammatory rheumatism." His parents feared he might not survive. But Frick, as a child and an adult, was resolute. By age eight, he had regained his health. His grandfather was his idol. One day, sitting near the springhouse and gazing at the large farmhouse occupied by his grandfather but off limits to his mother and father, Frick determined what he wanted to be when he grew up—rich, like Grandfather, but even more so. It was said that his grandfather was worth half a million dollars. Frick declared, "I propose to be worth that before I die."

Frick's life in remote Pennsylvania, not many years removed from the frontier, was like that of most farm youngsters of that time. He performed chores, carrying wood and water, stacking wheat sheaves, and the like. He attended an independent school at West Overton, then went briefly to Westmoreland College, in Mount Pleasant, Pennsylvania, and Otterbein College, in Westerville, Ohio. In all, he attended school only eight terms, ending his schooling at age seventeen. He seems to have been a mediocre student; only arithmetic attracted him. He saw it as the foundation for "a good business training."

Starting at age fifteen, Frick worked in several stores and proved himself an excellent salesman and bookkeeper. He eventually became chief bookkeeper in his grandfather's distillery at the wage of one thousand dollars a year.

Frick's opportunity now came. It had long been known that there were immense quantities of coal in southwestern Pennsylvania. It lay close to the surface of the earth, sometimes right on the surface. Explorers and pioneers had seen it in outcroppings; settlers sometimes used it for heating. The coal was unsuitable for commercial use in the iron industry, however, because it was high in phosphorus and thus did not burn well in the primitive iron furnaces of the time.

The introduction of the Bessemer process beginning in the late 1860s, and the resulting growth of the steel industry, made the coal valuable. The Bessemer process could not handle high-phosphorus coal, but when the coal was baked in ovens to form coke the phosphorus was reduced and the coke was usable. Not only did the coalfields around the village of Connellsville provide huge quantities of high-quality coking coal, but the coke could be cheaply transported on barges down the Youghiogheny River and then the Monongahela River to the Pittsburgh iron and steel plants. The Connellsville coalfields would in the decades ahead turn out the finest coke in the nation.

Frick drifted into the coal and coke business, borrowing ten thousand dollars, probably from his grandfather's estate, and becoming a partner in his cousin's coal venture in 1871. Once in the business, however, he dominated it. His partners did not wish their names to be associated with the debt-mired company, but Frick had no reluctance. The company was called Frick and Company.

Frick, just twenty years of age, began to expand his coal operations, often borrowing from members of his family. He always seemed to inspire confidence, and this confidence won him the support of relatives and bankers. In late 1871, he obtained a loan of ten thousand dollars to build fifty coke ovens from Judge Thomas Mellon of Pittsburgh, who had entered the banking business a year before. In December 1871, Frick acquired 189 acres of land, part of his grandfather's estate. He received another loan of ten thousand dollars from Mellon to build fifty more ovens.

Frick took advantage of the depression of 1873, borrowing more money and buying out discouraged partners. In those years, he would rise at 6:00 A.M., look over his ovens, take the train to Pittsburgh, go from mill to mill for orders for his coke, return home at 6:00 P.M., inspect his mines, and retire. The strain of overwork nearly killed Frick in 1875. But, supported by Thomas Mellon and Mellon's son and successor, Andrew, soon Frick's close friend, he continued to prosper. By 1877, the steel plants of Pittsburgh were in full production and the price of coke was up to four dollars a ton, compared to one dollar a ton in 1873. By 1879, Frick had one thousand employees and was shipping nearly a hundred railroad cars of coke a day to the Pittsburgh mills, much of it to Andrew Carnegie.

On December 19, 1879, Frick finished a game of chess with his cousins, entered the store in Mount Pleasant where he had begun his clerking career, purchased a five-cent Havana cigar, and lit it. It was his thirtieth birthday, but there was an additional reason for celebrating. That day, he calculated, his earnings had reached one million dollars, double the goal he had set as a child.

Frick continued to expand. By the end of 1880, he owned about three thousand acres of prime coal land and had constructed more than one thousand ovens. He bought out a major rival and acquired more land and ovens. On December 15, 1881, Frick married Adelaide Childs of Pittsburgh, and the two embarked on a honeymoon on the East Coast. Carnegie had sent the couple a letter of congratulations and asked Frick to have dinner with him at the Windsor Hotel in New York. It is said that Carnegie, Frick's largest customer, was in his best form, flattering both Frick and his new wife. Then, amid toasts to Frick and his wife, Carnegie proposed a toast to the success of a Carnegie-Frick partnership. Carnegie's mother, Margaret, interrupted. "Ah, Andra, that's a vera good thing for Mr. Freek," she declared, "but what do we get out of it?" But Carnegie, as Wall wrote, knew exactly what he was to get out of it—a cheap, uninterrupted supply of the world's best coke.

The purchase of the Homestead Works in October 1883, Carnegie's most important acquisition since the construction of the Edgar Thomson Works, meant that Carnegie needed an assured, expanded coke supply. Frick could provide this. It also meant a much larger assured market for Frick's coke. The capitalization of Frick and Company was increased to three million dollars, and by December 1883 Carnegie and his partners owned more than 50 percent of Frick and Company and had assumed all of Frick's outstanding debts.

Carnegie was pleased. He had associated with Frick because Frick and Company owned "the best coal and coke property." But he quickly realized that Frick was "a man with a positive genius" for management. Accordingly, on January 31, 1887, Carnegie brought Frick into his steel operations. Each benefited enormously. Carnegie agreed to sell Frick $100,000, or 2 percent, of the capital of Carnegie Brothers and Company, as Carnegie, Kloman, and Company was called after 1873, when Kloman was forced from the company following a dispute with Carnegie. Frick was not required to put up cash. Instead, the share was held in trust until the amount was paid out of dividends. In return, Frick agreed to sign an "iron-clad agreement," which stated that if his partners requested it, he must sell his Carnegie Brothers shares to them at book value. In January 1889, Frick's interest in Carnegie Brothers and Company was increased to 11 percent, and Frick was elected chairman, replacing Henry Phipps, Jr. In April 1889, Frick was named president of the renamed Carnegie, Phipps, and Company replacing William A. Abbott. Carnegie wrote Frick: "Take supreme care of that head of yours. It is wanted. Again, expressing my thankfulness that I have found the MAN, I am always yours, A.C."

An incident concerning the Duquesne Works, at Duquesne, Pennsylvania, five miles upriver from Homestead and across from the Edgar Thomson Works at Braddock, proved Carnegie and Frick a well-matched pair. The Duquesne Works had been constructed by the Duquesne Steel Company, organized by local businessmen and manufacturers. It was finished in the late winter of 1889 and was a highly advanced works, with two Bessemer converters, a rail, a blooming house, hotbeds, and a rail mill.

Carnegie and Frick watched the Duquesne Works closely, and what particularly nettled them was an ingenious innovation that the Duquesne men had introduced, a way of running ingots from the soaking pits to the rolling mills, where they were pressed into billets and then rails, without reheating. This was a radical departure from accepted practice, for until this time the ingots had been reheated before further rolling, a lengthy and expensive process. Carnegie perceived the threat offered by the process immediately, and took steps to counter it. He had a circular sent to railroads throughout the country saying that the shortened manufacturing process at Duquesne produced inferior rails because, he said, the lack of a second heating meant the Duquesne rails lacked "homogeneity." He did not say what this meant, which was wise, for it meant nothing. The charges, while without merit, deeply hurt the Duquesne Works, for railroad purchasing agents became suspicious of Duquesne rails. The number of orders fell, and the company was in trouble.

All the time, Frick was watching Duquesne, and in the fall of 1889 he made his first move, offering six hundred thousand dollars for the works. The offer was refused. Frick waited. In the summer of 1890, he made a second offer, one million dollars in bonds. The offer was accepted. Carnegie thus acquired two seven-ton Bessemer converters, six cupolas, seven soaking pits, five trains of rolls, and boilers, engines, and other equipment to operate the blooming mill and rail mills. The bonds were not to mature for five years, and by that time the Duquesne Works had paid for itself five times over the purchase price, for which Carnegie Brothers and Company had not advanced a dollar of capital. Not only were no more charges heard against the direct rolling process, but the process was immediately put into place at the Homestead Works and the Edgar Thomson Works. It then became standard throughout the industry. One of Carnegie's partners was asked if he considered the letter Carnegie had sent to the railroads condemning the direct rolling process to be a fair form of competition. He replied that "under ordinary circumstances he would not have thought it legitimate, but the competition set up by the Duquesne people was also not legitimate, because of their use of this direct rolling process." He went on: "They [the Duquesne managers] were a thorn in our flesh and they reduced the price of rails. If they had made rails by our method, we would have recognized them as legitimate competitors; but when we were attacking their method of rolling we could not recognize them by letting them take a contract." By this, the Carnegie man said, he meant, "We could not divide business with them as we otherwise would have done." Carnegie was very pleased with Frick, saying of him after the purchase of the Duquesne Works: "Frick is a marvel. Let's get all F's."

Although business was going well, Carnegie had suffered personal tragedies. His brother, Thomas, who had taken to drink, had died in October 1886, and on November 10, 1886, his beloved mother passed away. Carnegie grieved, but at last he felt free to marry. On April 22, 1887, he wed Louise Whitfield, whom he had been courting off and on since 1880. Carnegie was fifty-one years of age; she was twenty-three. She was three inches taller than he. No matter; it was an enduring romance.

Carnegie now owned two great iron-furnace complexes, the Lucy furnaces and the newly established Carrie furnaces across from Homestead; three sprawling steelworks, Edgar Thomson, Homestead, and Duquesne; the vast Frick coal and coke fields in southwestern Pennsylvania; and dozens of rolling mills and other facilities. He had proven he was a skillful manager. The company employed many of the nation's top iron and steel executives, was installing the newest machines, and had a large, skilled workforce. The import tariff was protecting his company and the other iron and steel companies. Carnegie was a world figure and had fashioned friendships with important people, which was part of his plan.

Not everything, however, ran smoothly. There was frequent labor unrest, and Carnegie and Frick, each hardheaded, clashed on how to handle it. In 1887, while Carnegie was on his honeymoon in Great Britain, a strike broke out in the Connellsville region of the southwestern Pennsylvania coalfields. Frick, who had suppressed strikes before, moved against the miners, saying he would import strikebreakers if necessary. But the price of rails and beams was high, and the Carnegie men did not wish to lose coke for their blast furnaces at Braddock and Homestead. Carnegie instructed Frick to yield to the miners. Frick capitulated, but he was furious and said he would leave Carnegie. Carnegie cajoled him, however, and after six months Frick returned.

Another confrontation with labor soon occurred at the Edgar Thomson Works, in Braddock. Captain Jones, the superintendent, had come to believe that his workers could not stand the pace of the twelve-hour shift and instituted eight-hour shifts. When Carnegie ordered Jones to return to the twelve-hour day, the rule in most of the rest of the steel industry, the Edgar Thomson workers came out on strike. Carnegie said that the works would stay closed until the men capitulated. A group of Braddock men were sure they could talk to Carnegie and change his mind, and in April 1888 they journeyed to Carnegie's home in New York. Carnegie showed the men a fine time, inviting them to dinner and taking them around New York, including a trip to Central Park. He then said that he would come to Braddock and propose a profit-sharing plan—his "sliding scale"—that he was convinced the men would approve.

Not long after, Carnegie appeared in Braddock. Some men were distrustful, but Carnegie charmed them. At one point, Carnegie asked the men to state their grievances. One man stood up and nervously began,

"Mr. Carnegie, take my job, for instance—" It was all the quick-witted Carnegie needed. "Mr. Carnegie takes no man's job," he said. The men loved it, and broke into laughter. Carnegie had them now. He outlined his sliding scale, under which workers' wages would be pegged to the price of finished steel, and gave the men two choices: an eight-hour day with reduced wages and no sliding scale, or a twelve-hour day with a sliding scale. The men voted for a twelve-hour day with a sliding scale. The strike was broken, and so was the union.

In 1889, a third major confrontation between labor and management occurred, at the Homestead Works. Numerous mechanical innovations had been installed at Homestead, and production had been substantially increased. This meant significant wage increases for workers paid on a tonnage basis. Carnegie desired to install a sliding-scale wage policy, as he had at Edgar Thomson in 1888. Carnegie said that if the workers struck, the works would be closed. He then departed on his annual six-month trip to Scotland.

On May 18, 1889, management announced that the workers' contract would be renewed, not on a tonnage basis, but on a sliding-scale basis, and that "men desirous of employment will be required to sign an agreement" to work under a sliding scale. This was opposed by the Amalgamated Association of Iron and Steel Workers, which had represented skilled Homestead workers both before and after Carnegie bought the works. The union believed, correctly, that the management's statement implied individual contracts between workers and management. The contract expired on June 30, and on July 1 the union men came out on strike and the Homestead Works was closed. Carnegie informed William Abbott, one of his executives: "Homestead is settled. No use fighting there. If it never runs it will not start except with rates it can run upon steadily and compete with others."

Abbott panicked. In early July, he advertised for strikebreakers. A group of immigrant and black workers arrived in Homestead by train, escorted by 125 deputies. Some two thousand workers and townspeople came down to the train, and the would-be strikebreakers and the deputies retreated to Pittsburgh. It was rumored that the Edgar Thomson men might walk out. Abbott capitulated. He called in the union leaders, and a compromise was reached. The union accepted a sliding scale, and the company recognized the union as the bargaining agent for its members at the Homestead Works. The Homestead workers and townspeople were pleased. There were celebrations that night in Homestead; Carnegie, the little man "who would not take his neighbor's job," was cheered. Carnegie, in Scotland, was displeased. He wrote Abbott: "The great objection to the compromise is of course that it was made under intimidation—our men in other works now know that we will 'confer' with law breakers. At this distance one can be very brave no doubt, [but] I don't like this feature at all. Seems to me a curt refusal to have anything to do with these men would have brought matters right in less time than to you seems possible. Whenever we are compelled to make a stand we shall have to shut down and wait as at E.T. until part of the men vote to work."

Later that year, on September 26, 1889, on the night shift, Captain Jones was seriously injured. The captain was standing close to a blast furnace at the Edgar Thomson Works, giving the men orders on how to fix it. An explosion occurred. Jones jumped back. He escaped the blast but fell onto a lower level of car tracks and struck his head on an ore car. He was knocked unconscious and died, never having regained consciousness, on September 28.

The captain was given a magnificent funeral. More than ten thousand people followed the horse-drawn hearse as it was pulled up the hill toward the Braddock burial grounds, where the captain was laid to rest on a gentle slope in the lower part of the cemetery. The grave is there today, under a large obelisk that says CAPTAIN WILLIAM JONES. ANTIETAM. GETTYSBURG. MANAGER, EDGAR THOMSON STEEL WORKS. The captain's death was a major loss for the company. He had been not only one of the nation's most skilled and creative steelmen, but one of the few Carnegie executives who stood up to Carnegie.

Charles M. Schwab was named as Jones's replacement. Outgoing and likable, Schwab had come a long way in his life of twenty-seven years. The son of a Pennsylvania livery stable operator (as a child he had once been allowed to hold Andrew Carnegie's horse's reins), he had gone to Braddock in 1879, at the age of seventeen, and had obtained a job in a grocery store. He came to the attention of Captain Jones, who gave him a job at the Edgar Thomson Works. Within six years Schwab was named general superintendent of the Homestead Works. Schwab's move to Edgar Thomson as Jones's successor was perhaps unfortunate for the Carnegie enterprises, for Schwab had been a big hit with the Homestead men. Had he stayed at Homestead he might have found a way to avert the labor-management confrontation that was soon to erupt there.

Captain Jones's death, however, was an opportunity for Frick. He had never liked Jones. He had considered him a maverick who was soft on labor, because he favored an eight-hour workday. With Jones gone, Frick moved to extend his control. In late 1889, he suggested that the capitalization of the Carnegie enterprises be increased to provide a more fair representation of their true value than the ten million dollars at which they were then valued. This would allow for the establishment of partnerships and additional financial rewards for a number of the Carnegie managers. The plan was complicated, and much study was required. More than two years went by, but at last a new charter was established. A new company was formed, the Carnegie Steel Company, Limited. The company, capitalized at twenty-five million dollars, was the largest steel company in the world. The chairman was Henry Clay Frick.

One problem continued to nag Frick and Carnegie—the control exercised by the Amalgamated Association of Iron and Steel Workers at the Homestead Works. The union represented just eight hundred of Homestead's thirty-eight hundred workers, but these were the skilled workers. Moreover, the eight union lodges at the Homestead Works constituted the core of its strength in the Pittsburgh district. A Carnegie partner said, "The Amalgamated placed a tax on improvements, therefore the Amalgamated had to go."

5

THE MILL

Everything was red and hot, as close to hell, the men said, as they hoped to get.

The men who worked the tapping hole at the open hearth wore thick protective coats, dark goggles, and heavy leather boots to protect against the heat and flames. A mixture of molten iron, limestone, and steel scrap bubbled at a temperature of three thousand degrees. After the mixture had cooked, the melter ordered that a sample be taken. A helper took a long, lancelike device, stuck it through a hole in the furnace, and removed a sample. If the mixture was adjudged good, a helper cleaned away the clay that dammed the six-inch tapping hole, took another long lance with a dynamite charge on the end, and—*bam!*—blew out the tapping hole. Out from the furnace into a huge ladle, amid fire, smoke, and steam, poured a great red-orange stream. Slag, lighter than steel, a mixture of limestone and other unwanted elements, among them carbon and manganese, floated on the surface and overflowed into an adjacent pear-shaped iron pot. What was left in the ladle, bubbling like thick soup in a pot, was steel, perhaps the most useful product the world has ever seen, a product that made possible the Industrial Revolution and twentieth-century life.

Through steel technology and production processes have changed over the past hundred years, to watch steel being made today is not so very different from what you would have seen a hundred years ago. A steel mill is perhaps the most basic of industrial and business operations. In a steel works, elements of the earth—coal, limestone, and iron ore—are transformed into iron, steel scrap and other ingredients are added and the iron is cooked again to make steel, and the steel is rolled or forged into shapes—slabs, blooms, and billets—from which are made many of the products of modern civilization: hairpins, tweezers, nails, screws, scissors, pails, hoes, rakes and shovels, surgical instruments, fences, wire, rails, motors and machines, cans, refrigerators, washers and dryers, automobiles and trucks, tractors and cultivators, rivets, plates for construction and warships, axles and wheels for railroads, beams for buildings, dams and bridges.

To go to a steel mill, even the most modern mill, is to be shocked—it seems like something from the Dark Ages. It is not just the fire, the smoke, the noise, but the stuff—piles of ore, coke and limestone; piles of scrap; huge machines and cranes. All of this gives the appearance of haphazardness, of disorder on a monstrous scale. The process of making steel begins with the mining of iron ore, coal, and limestone, and then shifts to the blast furnace, where iron is made. A ton of steel requires a ton and a half of ore, a half ton of coke, and a quarter of a ton of limestone. The blast furnace, a huge tower lined with brick and jacketed with steel, is charged, or filled, at the top. The ore, coke, and limestone are carried up to the top of the two-hundred-foot furnace by hoists. Hot air, heated in stoves connected to the furnace, is fed into the bottom of the furnace in a blast, thus giving the furnace its name. The heat is intense, as high as three thousand degrees. The iron is produced through a series of chemical reactions resulting from the downward movement of the ore, coke, and limestone, and the upward movement of the hot gases. The iron is smelted, or reduced, from the ore by the combustion of the coke, which burns exceedingly hot. The limestone, acting as a flux, carries away impurities in the form of slag. The molten metal—now iron—and the residue from the heating process—slag—are run off every three or four hours.

At Homestead, the iron was made at the Carrie Furnaces, across the

Monongahela River, in the community of Rankin, a small, bleak place. The furnaces looked like something from another century, and rightfully so, for the complex dated from the 1880s. The Carrie complex, between railroad tracks and the river, consisted of four to six furnaces over the decades, monstrous, rounded, rusty steel contraptions, each more than two hundred feet high and each having the capacity to turn out sixty-five hundred tons of iron a day. Each furnace had three stoves to heat air for the furnace's hot blast. The iron was made from iron ore, or refined ore, from the Mesabi Range, Quebec, Canada, or Venezuela, or from other refined ore, called sintered iron, made at a sinter plant at Saxonburg, Pennsylvania, thirty miles north of Homestead.

In the old days of ironmaking, the iron ran from the blast furnace in channels to molds that seemed to resemble piglets suckling the nipples of their mother as she lay on her side. The molds were called pigs, and this gave the material its name, pig iron. As more modern systems were installed, the iron was poured into containers and transported to the Bessemer open-hearth furnaces in molten form, although the name pig iron continued to be used.

The molten iron was brought from the Carrie Furnaces to the Homestead Works in huge cigar-shaped cars, called torpedo cars, across what was termed the Hot Metal Bridge, constructed by Andrew Carnegie and placed in operation on New Year's Eve, 1900.

At the Homestead Works, the iron was transferred to ladles, great steel chambers two stories high, and transported by huge, movable cranes to the open-hearth furnaces. There the molten pig iron was poured into a furnace, and charging machines pushed boxes of limestone and scrap after it. The mixture cooked in intense gas heat and hot air in the open-hearth furnace for eight to ten hours, depending on what kind of steel was needed and what process was being used. Then came the tapping— the creation of steel. In the old days, a team of five or more men rammed out the plug in the taphole; then the DuPont Company invented the dynamite tapping stick.

After the steel was tapped, it was teemed, or poured, into ingot molds, where it solidified into ingots as high as a house. The ingots were stripped from their molds by cranes, which were maneuvered by skilled operators; the cranes grabbed onto lugs on the molds and pulled the molds free. The ingots were then transported to soaking pits, where they were soaked—actually, heated—with hot air from gas heaters until the ingots were malleable. Then the ingots were taken to the primary mills, the slabbing or blooming mills, where they were rolled, as a cook might roll pie-crust dough with a rolling pin, into slabs, or blooms, that is, semifinished shapes—squares, rectangles, or rounds, depending on the shapes needed. Ingots, weighing as much as 780,000 pounds, could also be taken directly to the forge division, where they were beaten in huge presses into commercial shapes, among them rings, shafts, discs, spheres, blocks, and cylinders which would be further transformed into such products as gun turrets, turbines, ship shafts, and the like.

From the slabbing and blooming mills the steel shapes were taken to the finishing mills. There the slabs were rolled into plates, and the blooms into beams or pilings or railroad wheels, and sheared to desired lengths. Blooms were also forged into axles, in the forging division.

When everything was going right, when the works were operating correctly and production was being met, when, as the men said, they were "grooving the mill," the mill was magnificent to behold: fire, noise, steam, smoke, red-hot steel shooting a mile or more on rollers at thirty miles an hour.

The novelist Hamlin Garland visited the Homestead Works in October 1893, and wrote in *McClure's* magazine in June 1894:

A roar as of a hundred lions, a thunder as of cannons, flames that made the electric light look like a twinkling blue star, jarring clang of falling iron, burst of spluttering flakes of fire, scream of terrible saws, shifting of mighty trucks with hiss of steam! This was the scene upon which I looked. . . . I saw men prodding in the deep soaking pits where the ingots glowed in white-hot chambers. I saw other men in the hot yellow glare from the furnaces. I saw men measuring the serpentine rosy beams. I saw them send the saw flying into them. I saw boys perched high in cages, their shrill voices sounding wild and animal-like in the midst of the uproar; a place into which men went like men going into war for the sake of wives and children, urged on by necessity, blinded and dulled by custom and habit; an inhuman place to spend four-fifths of one's waking hours. . . . Upon such toil rests the splendor of American civilization.

The Homestead Works always had a jerry-built appearance. A building was put up here, another there, whatever was needed and wherever there was space. What was constructed had to be fitted into the long, narrow site between the river and the hill, the sand bed laid down by the river and the only flat surface available, so it was a matter of making do with what was available. The buildings, of strange shapes and sizes, made from motley materials, in a way resembled a place that tramps might fashion. Ultimately, the works, one of America's great workshops, consisted of 450 buildings and spread over 430 acres and along three miles of the river.

At its height, from World War II into the 1970s, the works consisted of seven principal units: a sintering plant; the Carrie Furnaces; the open-hearth division; slab and plate; bloom and structural; forgings, the only unit ever operated by the Carnegie company or the corporation to make forged armor plate; and wheel and axle, which made wheels and axles for railroads.

By the 1970s the Homestead Works had 76 railroad locomotives and 150 miles of railroad track, its own police and fire departments, a hospital, food facilities, and water and waste-treatment facilities.

The Carrie Furnaces were capable of consuming three hundred railroad cars of raw materials—iron ore, coke, limestone, and other materials—a day. And each day, the plant used hundreds of millions of gallons of water, primarily for cooling.

Between the 1940s and the 1970s, the works had the capacity to produce each year 2 million tons of pig iron; 4 million tons of steel ingots; 1 million tons of blooms; 2.7 million tons of slabs; 1 million tons of beams, pilings, and other structural products; 1.75 million tons of plates; 10,000 tons of forgings; 75,000 tons of wheels and other circular sections and 50,000 tons of axles; and 40,000 tons of fabricated products.

The Homestead Works' production fame rests primarily on its vast output of beams, pilings, plates, and forgings, and on the fact that it introduced open-hearth steel to the world. But the works also, in the 1880s, made rails for the western railroads and for eighty years was a premier manufacturer of railroad wheels and axles for railroads in America and much of the rest of the world. Its products helped the nation move west, shaped its skyline, bridged and dammed its waters, helped make it a world naval power, and helped it enter the Space Age. When the mill began, the nation's population was 51.5 million, Indians and the Army warred on the Great Plains, the Industrial Revolution was in its infancy, and America was innocent and isolated; when the mill went down, the nation's population was 240 million, the Industrial Revolution—based on steel—had changed America and the rest of the world irrevocably, and America was the world's dominant nation in every imaginable way, except perhaps one—steel and industrial production.

II

The work in a steel mill is long, hard, and dangerous. For over one hundred years, men and sometimes women bore the extraordinary exactions that making steel requires, and put up with the constant demands by the company to cut costs and to achieve efficiency and production.

The mill was hot in summer, cold in winter. In the nineteenth century, the journalist James Parton said that puddlers and puddlers' helpers, the men who made iron, performed "labor so severe that they have to stop, now and then, in summer, take off their boots, and pour the perspiration out of them." Sometimes, in winter, the work was, at once, cold and hot. In January 1936, it was so cold at the Homestead Works that a steel pourer's ears became frostbitten—while he was helping tap a heat at a furnace at which the temperature at the tapping hole was recorded at 2,930 degrees.

In 1919, a Homestead open-hearth laborer decribed his work in his diary: "You lift a large sack of coal to your shoulders, run towards the white hot steel in a hundred-ton ladle, must get close enough without burning your face off to hurl the sack, using every ounce of strength, into the ladle and run, as flames leap to roof and the heat blasts everything to the roof. Then you rush out to the ladle and madly shovel manganese into it, as hot a job as can be imagined." He did this twelve hours a day, sometimes seven days a week.

Another Homestead worker wrote in his diary in the spring of the same year:

Calendar of one day from the life of a Carnegie steel worker at Homestead on the open hearth, common labor:

5:30 to 12 (midnight)—Six and one-half hours of shoveling, throwing and carrying bricks and cinder out of bottom of old furnace. Very hot.

12:30—Back to the shovel and cinder, within few feet of pneumatic shovel drilling slag, for three and one-half hours.

4 o'clock—Sleeping is pretty general, including boss.

5 o'clock—Everybody quits, sleeps, sings, swears, sighs for 6 o'clock.

6 o'clock—Start home.

6:45 o'clock—Bathed, breakfast.

7:45 o'clock—Asleep.

4 P.M.—Wake up, put on dirty clothes, go to boarding house, eat supper, get pack of lunch.

5:30 P.M.—Report for work.

Conditions in the Homestead Works improved immensely over the years, but labor in the Homestead Works—in any American steel mill— was never an easy proposition. Workers particularly remembered Open Hearth 3 as an onerous and dangerous place. It closed in 1953 after two workers there were burned to death in one week. Years later, Babe Fernandez, who worked in O.H. 3 for six months during World War II as a laborer, wheeling chrome and manganese to the furnaces to make specialty steels for the war effort, remembered,

When they got ready to tap the heat, the first helper and the second helper would go behind a fence and would knock on the beams. They got a hammer and hit the beams about four or five times and that meant that everybody in that area had to go to cover. The melter foreman would look in with his blue glasses, take a test, and they would know how much carbon to put in and it would be ready to tap. They had a quarter-inch rod, twenty feet long, attached to the gas line. They would light the one end and jam it in a tapping hole in the back of the furnace to tap the heat. Then molten metal would come out of that tapping hole into the molds. Jesus, it was hot. If there was water in the molds when they would tap it, the damn thing would explode and metal would fly all over the area. That's why they would bang on the beams—so that everyone could take cover.

Mill and town—the two were inseparable. Margaret Byington, a sociologist, described this scene at Homestead in 1911: "If you are near the mill in the late afternoon you will see a procession, an almost steady stream of men, each carrying the inevitable bucket, hurrying towards the great buildings for the night's work. A little later the tide turns and back come the day men, walking slowly and wearily towards home and supper. Thus the life of the town keeps time with the rhythm of the mill."

John Duch, who grew up in lower Homestead, below the tracks, worked in the mill during World War II, and was a barber in West Homestead for years. He recalled: "I lived on Third Avenue. One block up was the thirty-inch mill. The mill sounded just like a locomotive, real loud—choo, choo, choo. And the ground shaking under you. You could see them charging the furnaces because the place was open. Believe me, when that ground wasn't shaking you knew something was wrong. You couldn't go to sleep unless the mills shook you to sleep like a baby in a cradle."

But it was different for an outsider. After World War II, John McLean, Jr., a Homestead boy, then a young attorney, and his wife, Jean, came to live in Homestead. Their first night, as they lay in bed in their new home, Jean McLean awakened her husband and asked him what that frightful noise was. McLean listened and said he did not hear any noise. Of course there is a noise, his wife said. Listen—that heavy, throbbing noise. McLean listened again and then realized what his wife was talking about—the noise of the mill. He had never heard the noise, he realized, for it was not noise to him. It was just the mill, just Homestead.

The grueling labor in the mill hardened workers and aged them beyond their years. A Homestead worker told Hamlin Garland in 1893: "The worst part of the whole business is this. It brutalizes a man. You can't help it. You start in to be a man, but you become more and more a machine, and pleasures are few and far between. It's like any severe labor. It drags you down mentally and morally, just as it does physically."

John A. Fitch, a sociologist who studied Homestead in the early years of this century, wrote: "Often I was told by workmen of forty and forty-five that they had been at their best at thirty years of age, and that at thirty-five they had begun to feel a perceptible decline in strength. The superintendents and foremen are alert to detecting weakness of any sort, and if a man fails appreciably, he expects discharge." Fitch found no old men in the mill; there, he said, it was "old age at forty."

Turnover was often high at the Homestead Works in the early years. In 1919, for example, the corporation said that it lost 575 workers a month, or 6,800 workers a year, despite efforts to maintain a workforce of 11,500. This changed over the years as people settled in. In 1951, of ten thousand male employees at the Homestead Works, more than four thousand were father-and-son combinations. The Rushe family of Homestead amassed a total of more than seven hundred years in the Homestead Works.

The monstrous crucibles of molten iron and steel, the white-hot ingots, the great slabs and billets, the fast-moving cranes, the great cutting machines, the locomotives and railroad cars, the exploding furnaces, the splashing steel, the scalding water from bursting pipes, the high, dark walkways—all this made the mill a natural place for injury and death. Wives and children in their homes came to dread the sound of whistles, the screaming sirens that meant that an accident had occurred, the telephone call, particularly late at night, that could mean that a steelworker, "the mister," was injured or perhaps dead.

Men fell into kettles of molten steel, were knocked senseless or killed by slamming machinery or swinging beams or moving cranes, were run over by locomotives or railroad cars. They had their eyes put out, their arms or legs crushed or severed, received great cuts or contusions. Fitch wrote in 1910, "A dinkey engineer who had been running a engine for twenty-five years told me that he has killed two men in that time and smashed fingers or hands of so many hook-ons that he has no idea as to the number."

Here, from corporation records, are descriptions of three of the dozen deaths at the Homestead Works in 1918, the year between 1914 and 1980 with the highest number of deaths in the works:

6/6/18. Michael Kacsur. Check No. 19262. Crane Floorman. Crane chain broke and piece of steel (17500# gun carriage forging) fell on man— killing him instantly. Crushed head. Taken to Mikulla's Undertaking Rooms.

6/20/18. Seniyon Jackobowsky. Check No. 12943. Stocker & Chipper. Turning over bloom for Inspector and wick blew from torch held by inspector and set patient's clothes on fire. Injury: 2nd and 3rd degree burns all over face, neck, arms, and body to waist. Died: 2:30 P.M.—St. Francis Hospital—same day.

7/7/18. John Kovczun. Check No. 30250. Laborer. Crane picked up ladle of molten metal from buggy and ladle bumped ladle standing on floor. Metal splashed out on man. Injury: 2nd and 3rd degree burns of back, thigh, legs and arms, and chest. Died: 7:47 A.M.

The mill gave the town life, but it also took it away. It is impossible to say how many workers were killed or maimed or otherwise seriously injured in the mill over the decades; as far as is known, no cumulative records on this matter were kept. However, before and after the turn of the twentieth century it was not uncommon for fifteen, perhaps twenty-five workers, perhaps more, to be killed in the works each year. Moreover, according to a Homestead Works document prepared in the early 1980s, 313 workers were killed in the Homestead Works between 1914 and 1980.

In the last decades of the works, the 1950s, 1960s, and 1970s, life improved for the workers. Working conditions were better and hours were shorter. Safety improved dramatically after the 1920s, largely because of the corporation's "Safety First" campaign begun early in the century. But for decades workers were confronted with enormous demands, and the work remained as arduous as can be imagined.

Yet, extrapolating from the figures in the Homestead Works document, it seems fair to say that eight hundred to one thousand workers were killed in the Homestead Works in the more than one hundred years that it was operated. They lie in the old burying grounds now, many in unkempt or unmarked graves, under rusted iron and steel markers; these markers, cheaper than stone, often being all that the workers' survivors could afford. In addition to this, probably several thousand workers were seriously injured in the Homestead Works, and this estimate does not include the thousands of others who probably contracted diseases—cancers and the like—in the works, and died.

In a sense, the workers were artists, although neither they nor almost anyone else regarded themselves so. There were electricians, carpenters, brick masons, millwrights, welders, cranemen, blacksmiths, pipe-fitters, melters, heaters, rollers, accountants, chemists, engineers, and more. They could, had they been asked, have built a city. That would have been easy. After all, they and others like them built a nation.

William J. Gaughan, a white-collar worker in the Homestead Works, was struck by the skill of many of the men in the works, how, for example, men used to walk down finished beams and feel through their shoes with their feet for buckles in the beams. If buckles were found, the beams would be adjudged deficient and sent back for rerolling, unless, of course, quality control had lessened, and an executive said the beams must be shipped. There was no need for expensive measuring devices; the men's feet and their brains did the work. The men who worked at Homestead took tremendous pride in their mill. Gaughan said: "We knew how to make steel, boy. I mean, we knew how to make steel. We were the premier, the premier plant in the U.S.A. Nobody else could touch us."

Michael "Kentucky" Stout, a craneman in the 100-inch and 160-inch mills in the 1970s and 1980s, said: "I never in my life had seen anything as big, as spread out, had never seen equipment as big. When I started, we had this burr-headed ex–Marine sergeant giving us orientation. He sat us down in this room and said: 'Anybody in this room have intentions of just working in here in the summer or for a year or two or five years ought to hit the road right now. We're looking for career people, looking for twenty-five-, fifty-year people.' I liked that. I had worked in three or four different plants, had seen shutdowns, and I was tired of moving around. I thought, 'Holy cow, I've finally found a place I can stay.'

"One thing I liked about it was you had all these people and it didn't matter what age, sex, color, or country you were from. The mill formed the basis of a family. You went in in the morning and the first thing you did was have coffee and a safety meeting and then you went on the job. You came back for lunch, then back to work. It was a family thing. There were differences, divisions, but generally the mill eliminated those, welded people together, formed the basis for a lot of friendships.

"The other thing was the strange beauty of the place. In between the hundred- and hundred-sixty-inch mills, it was almost mystical. I'd never seen anything like that—big slabs of steel stacked up ten, fifteen, twenty feet high, pile after pile, huge cranes moving with two-hundred-pound chains, picking steel up, putting it on cars, moving faster than you could almost watch; that's how awesome it was. The hundred- and the hundred-sixty-inch were always kept clean, especially in the earlier days, when they had laborers and roll hands whose jobs it was to keep the mills clean and sweep and water them down every evening. When we rolled pipe, the pipe let off this red dust that hung in the air. It was mystical, wild, especially during daylight, when the dust was going up and the sunlight was coming through the cracks in the roof. It was like you were at a theater watching a play, and the play was industrial production."

6

REBELLION I

In the late spring of 1892, a few months before the contract between the Amalgamated Association and the Homestead Works was set to expire, Henry Clay Frick initiated an unusual construction project at the works: a fence, made of two-inch-thick wooden planks, that, eleven feet high and three miles long, ringed the works and ran down to the boat landing on the Monongahela River and then into the river so that boats could be pulled to the landing site with security. Holes were bored in the fence at intervals and at what appeared the proper height for sharpshooters. Frick kept his own counsel, but months later told a congressional committee that the holes were for observation, to look out, he said, at whoever might be looking in. On top of the fence were strung three strands of barbed wire, which some Homestead people thought were electrified, although there is no evidence that this was the case. Twelve-foot towers with searchlights were also erected. Frick, being a man who liked his operations in good order, retained Amsted Kemp, a well-liked black man, to whitewash the fence. Kemp set about his task with buckets and a long-handled brush. All of this—fence, towers, searchlights—was, the always matter-of-fact Frick later explained, "for the purpose of putting the property in a position that it could be defended against an assault." Workers knew what the fence was for: to allow the company, in the event of a strike, to guard the Homestead Works so that strikebreakers could be brought in. The workers gave the Homestead Works a new name, "Fort Frick."

II

The confrontations between labor and management that had occurred at the Homestead Works before Carnegie purchased it had not ceased, and destroying the union at the Homestead Works had been in the minds of Carnegie and Frick for some time. The union had been broken at the Edgar Thomson Works in 1887, and no union had ever existed at the Duquesne Works. Carnegie and Frick strongly wished to eliminate the last union holdout in the Monongahela Valley.

The issues were the same, by and large, as those at the center of thousands of confrontations between American labor and management before and since—wages, manning levels, and who, employees or employers, should benefit from the introduction of new manufacturing technologies.

The company said that wages at Homestead were excessive and that it wanted a reduction. Another important though largely hidden issue was technology. The company had for some time, at great cost, been installing the most modern steelmaking processes and machines at the Homestead Works: automatic rolling tables, hydraulic jacks, furnace jacks, and the like. In some cases, one man could now do the work that four or five, even nine or ten, men had done. The company wanted to secure the profits that came about through the reduced costs brought by the new technologies.

Just as important, the introduction of the new machines and methods represented an attack on the union, because many of the jobs that were being eliminated were skilled jobs, and thus union jobs. Charles M. Schwab, a chief Carnegie assistant, said that with the new technologies he could take an untrained man with only minimal knowledge of machinery and make a skilled melter of him in six weeks, implying that there was no need for experienced workers.

Finally, there was the matter of unionism itself. Carnegie and Frick opposed it. Carnegie might have accepted unionism had it been pliant or company-dominated, but Frick detested unions and wanted nothing to do with unionized workers or union leaders. Both believed that running a company was the province of its managers, that workers should do what they were told and, if dissatisfied, leave. The *Homestead Local News* said that the 1892 confrontation at Homestead "was not so much a question of disagreement as to wages, but a design upon labor organization."

The union men at the Homestead Works were the most important and most skilled workers and earned the highest wages. They were mostly Anglo-Saxons—English, Scottish, Irish, Welsh, and Germans. The unskilled men did the worst jobs in the mill and earned far less money. They were mostly Slavs and Hungarians, plus a few blacks.

The Amalgamated Association had been formed in August 1876 by the merger of three existing unions: the United Sons of Vulcan, an organization of iron puddlers; the Associated Brotherhood of Iron and Steel Heaters, Rollers, and Roughers; and the Iron and Steel Roll Hands of the United States. At its formation, the Amalgamated had 3,775 members, almost all of them in the iron industry. The 1881 strike, which the union lost, brought a drop in membership. But the Amalgamated began to grow again, and in 1891 it had 290 lodges and twenty-four thousand members, almost a quarter of the roughly one hundred thousand eligible workers in the iron and steel industry. It was the most powerful union in the country. Its major strongholds were in the iron mills of western Pennsylvania and Ohio, but it never made substantial inroads in steel.

The Amalgamated was an elitist, conservative organization that had much in common with management. Over the years, a number of union executives left the union to obtain better-paying jobs in industry or government. The union favored the twelve-hour day, saying that an eight-hour day would mean wage reductions and would bring new workers into the industry. It also favored the seven-day week. It opposed strikes "for little frivolous purposes" and did not attempt to block new technologies or the formation of large business combinations. "The Association never objects to improvement," said William Weihe, who served nine terms as the union's president. If workplace changes "do away with certain jobs they make no objection. They believe in the American idea that the genius of the country should not be retarded."

The union was clannish, with the original membership, English, Scottish, Irish, Welsh, and native-born Americans, looking suspiciously at workers of other nationalities, and different classes of workers quarreling with one another. "When the puddlers ruled, the finishers sulked, and when the finishers got control the puddlers were disgruntled," wrote John

A. Fitch. The union, for the most part, did not admit unskilled foreign-born or black workers. When the two lodges at the Edgar Thomson Works were dissolved, the union did not complain. The 1889 settlement at Homestead, while a victory for the union, included substantial set-backs. Wages were reduced through the introduction of the sliding scale, and the union allowed Homestead managers to hire and pay heating and rolling crews; previously, unionized roll hands had performed this work.

Whenever possible, the union cooperated with management. In the 1880s, the president of the union wrote to the companies that "as the annual reunion of the association was to take place June 7, he would feel obliged to the employers if they would shut down the mills in Pittsburgh, Wheeling, Youngstown, and Sharon districts on that day." The manufac-turers cordially consented. In April 1888, at the Edgar Thomson Works, when Captain Jones was upset over whether the union would have a say in the use of new machines and was making one of his periodic threats to quit, Carnegie asked union officers to see Jones, in order to assure him that the union would be reasonable and to implore him to stay on. The union men obediently went to see Jones and convinced him that the union would be fair.

But Carnegie and Frick believed that the union had acquired exces-sive power. The memorandum of agreement at the Homestead Works between the union and management was so elaborate that it contained fifty-eight pages of footnotes defining work rules for the union men.

Carnegie liked to portray himself as a friend of the workingman, but this was an illusion. In April 1886, Carnegie had written an essay in the *Forum,* a popular magazine, in which he said that sometimes "collision where there should be combination" occurred between labor and capital. But he could see a time when confrontation between working people and their bosses would be as rare as international war appeared to be at that time. He declared: "The right of working men to combine and to form trade unions is no less sacred than the right of the manufacturer to enter into associations and conferences with his fellows. . . . My experience has been that trade unions upon the whole are beneficial both to labor and capital."

In May, during a labor rally at Haymarket Square, in Chicago, eleven persons, including seven policemen, were killed and more than a hundred injured when a bomb exploded and the police began shooting wildly. Antilabor sentiment among businessmen grew, but Carnegie, later in 1886, published a second *Forum* article more favorable to labor than the first. In it, he said that much of the blame for labor-management unrest lay with management:

It is not asking too much of men [entrusted] with the management of great properties that they should devote some part of their attention to searching out the causes of dissatisfaction among their employees, and where they exist, that they should meet the men more than half way in the endeavor to allay them.

I would have the public give due consideration to the terrible temptation to which the workingman on a strike is sometimes subjected. To expect that one dependent upon his daily wage for the necessaries of life will stand peaceably and see a new man employed in his stead is to expect much. . . . In all but a very few departments of labor it is unnecessary and I think improper to subject men to such an ordeal. . . . The employer of labor will find it much more to his interest, wherever possible, to allow his works to remain idle and await the result of a dispute than to employ a class of men that can be induced to take the place of other men who have stopped work. Neither the best men as men, nor the best men as workers, are thus to be obtained. There is an unwritten law among the best workmen: "Thou shalt not take thy neighbor's job."

Late in life, in his autobiography, Carnegie said that he had never employed strikebreakers, and that until 1892 his companies had never had a serious labor problem. He spoke of "the reward that comes from feeling that you and your employees are friends," and said, "I believe that higher wages to men who respect their employers and are happy and content is a good investment, yielding, indeed, big dividends."

But this was Carnegie talking, not acting. He had fought unionism on a number of occasions. In 1867, at the Union Iron Mills in Pittsburgh, he joined with other iron manufacturers to bring in foreign workers to take the jobs of striking iron puddlers; in 1884, he used strikebreakers to defeat Amalgamated Association strikers at his Beaver Falls, Pennsylvania, mill. In addition to fighting the Amalgamated at the Edgar Thomson Works in 1885, Carnegie used strikebreakers there in a dispute in 1886–1887.

Frick was as fearsome an opponent of unions but not so duplicitous. In 1884, he used Pinkerton detectives to protect Hungarians and Slavs whom he had brought in as strikebreakers in the coalfields, and in 1891 he used Pinkertons to protect Italians he had brought in as strikebreakers against the Hungarians and Slavs. He also used Pinkertons and strikebreakers in a major strike in the Connellsville coal and coke district in 1887.

As the June 30, 1892, contract deadline at the Homestead Works approached, Carnegie and Frick were determined not to be weak, as they believed Abbott had been three years before. They intended to destroy the union. In January 1892, Frick had asked the Homestead union leaders to submit their proposals for a new contract. In response, the union, in March, submitted modest demands, asking only for a renewal of the 1889 contract. For men paid on a sliding scale, varying with the market price of steel billets, the minimum rate below which wages would not be reduced would be kept at twenty-five dollars a ton. Men paid on a tonnage basis would be paid at the same rate as required by the 1889 agreement.* The union men were confident. They believed what Carnegie had written in the press. In addition, the Homestead Works had contracts with the government to produce armor plate—plate for the Navy ships USS *Monterey* and USS *New York* was being produced at Homestead in the spring of 1892—and the men believed that the company would not want a strike, which would cause a delay in meeting the deadline for the Navy contracts.

On April 4, 1892, Carnegie, in New York, sent Frick a message that he suggested Frick post in the Homestead Works. It read: "As the vast majority of our employees are Non-Union, the Firm has decided that the minority must give place to the majority. These works therefore will be necessarily Non-Union after the expiration of the present agreement." Carnegie added: "This action is not taken in any spirit of hostility to labor organizations, but every man will see that the firm cannot run Union and Non-Union. It must be either one or the other." Frick did not post the letter, but he understood what Carnegie wanted done.

Later, from abroad, Carnegie sent another message to Frick saying that the company would not have to make a decision to run the Homestead Works as union or nonunion, but that the Homestead workers must accept the terms that existed at Edgar Thomson and Duquesne. He then told Frick to do what he, Frick, wanted to do, saying: "We all approve of anything you do, not stopping short of approval of a contest. We are with you to the end." Carnegie then set off with his wife for their lodge in a remote part of the Scottish Highlands, miles from the nearest railroad and unreachable by public transportation.

---

* Henry Clay Frick and other executives and pro-company writers have said that some Homestead workers earned as much as $12.00 to $15.00 a day. J. H. Bridge wrote in 1903 that Homestead was "familiar with the sight of steel-workers being driven to the mill in their carriages." *The New York Times* also wrote, at the time of the strike, of highly paid Homestead workers. The stories of numerous Homestead workers earning exorbitant wages are untrue. Of the 3,800 Homestead workers employed at the works at the time of the strike, 113 earned an average of $4.00 to $7.60 a day in 1891, according to Edward Bemis, writing in the *Journal of Political Economy* in June 1894. Bemis computed that 1,177 workers averaged $1.68 to $2.50 a day, and that 1,625 averaged $1.40 a day or less.

More communications followed. Carnegie wrote Frick from Scotland on June 10, 1892: "As I understand matters at Homestead, it is not only the wages paid, but the number of men required by Amalgamated rules, which make our labor rate so much higher than those in the East. Of course you will be asked to confer, and I know you will decline all conferences, as you have taken your stand and have nothing more to say. . . . Provided you have plenty of plates rolled, I suppose you can keep on with armor." On June 28, Carnegie sent Frick this dispatch: "Cables do not seem favorable to a settlement at Homestead. If those be correct, this is your chance to reorganize the whole affair. Exact good reasons for employing every man. Far too many men required by Amalgamated rules."

In May, Frick rejected the union's proposal and submitted his own. He demanded that the minimum wage of the sliding scale be set at twenty-two dollars a ton, not twenty-five dollars, as the union had requested. He asked that the tonnage rate be cut 15 percent, so that management could receive a greater share of the production increases made possible by the new processes and machines. He demanded, finally, that the new contract expire on December 31, 1895, not the end of June. The company claimed this would allow it to forecast its costs more accurately: the prices for the steel that it sold were generally set at the beginning of the year, and therefore labor costs should also be fixed then. The union knew that Frick had another goal in mind: if every contract expired at the end of a year, and the workers had to strike, they would have to strike in the dead of winter.

When it received Frick's counterproposal, the union was accommodating. It called Frick's proposal "a proposition by the firm that they knew we would not accept." But, wanting to keep negotiations open, the union said that it would accept wage reductions if management could show that they were necessary. "We want to settle it without trouble," William T. Roberts, a union man, said. "We don't want a strike."

But on May 30, Frick sent a letter to John A. Potter, general superintendent of the Homestead Works, stating, "You can say to the committee that these scales are in all respects the most liberal that can be afforded." The mill also began to roll as much armor plate as possible; it was stacked, unfinished, in the mill yards. In case of a strike, the company planned to finish the plates at Edgar Thomson or Duquesne. Then Potter, on Frick's instructions, told the union that unless the union accepted the company's offer by June 24, the company would begin bargaining with the workers as individuals and no longer bargain with the union. "Do you think this is fair, Mr. Potter?" Roberts asked. "I cannot help it," Potter said. "It is Mr. Frick's ultimatum."

On June 19, a union meeting was held at the Homestead opera house. Hundreds of workers attended. John McLuckie, the burgess of Homestead, a mill worker and strong union man, made a stirring address. The workers had been betrayed, said McLuckie, known as "Honest John." Many had voted Republican in 1888, believing that a high tariff would ensure American steel production and thus maintain high wages. Now, the company wanted to cut wages. "You men who voted the Republican ticket voted for high tariff and you get high fences, Pinkerton detectives, thugs, and militia," McLuckie proclaimed.

The meeting was adjourned, and the union attempted to continue negotiations. Frick agreed to meet with the men on June 23. At that meeting, attended by William Weihe, the Amalgamated's president, and about two dozen Homestead union men, the union said it would accept a sliding-scale minimum of twenty-four dollars. Frick rejected this, although Potter told the men, when Frick had left the room, that he believed the company might accept a minimum of twenty-three dollars. That was the first and last suggestion of compromise. Frick was determined to close the Homestead Works on July 1 and reopen on July 6 with a non-union workforce. On June 25, notices were posted in Homestead that henceforth the company would bargain only with individual workers, not with the union. Many union men continued to believe that Carnegie— labor's friend, they believed—would intervene.

III

The solidarity and organization achieved by the Homestead workers and townspeople in preparing for and then enduring the strike were unsurpassed in American history. In late June, a workers' advisory committee was organized, with forty members—five representatives from each of the eight Amalgamated Association lodges at the Homestead Works. A popular worker, Hugh O'Donnell, a roller, was elected chairman, and in a plan announced by O'Donnell the mill workforce was organized on what he called "a truly military basis." Some four thousand men, both workers and townspeople, were divided into three divisions, or watches, each on duty eight hours a day, with pickets posted at the roads leading into Homestead, at the two railway stations, at the plant gates, and along both sides of the Monongahela River, to watch for attempts by the corporation to bring in strikebreakers by boat or train. A steamboat, the *Edna,* was chartered to patrol the Monongahela, about fifty skiffs were sent out onto the river, and scouts were sent downriver to watch for invaders from the bridges at Pittsburgh. A large steam whistle was purchased and installed at the electric light works in Homestead and a code of whistle blasts established, so that the workers and townspeople would know instantly where their commanders wished them to assemble. "A brigade of foreigners"—eight hundred Slavs and Hungarians—was organized as a reserve under the command of two Hungarians and two interpreters. In 1928, Frick's sympathetic biographer, George Harvey, wrote of O'Donnell's plan, "So audacious a manifesto as this had never before and, to our knowledge, has never since been put forth."

The townspeople were solidly behind the workers. Not only was Burgess McLuckie a member of the strike committee, but other town officials and businessmen supported the strike. Strike leaders were determined to preserve order. Taverns were ordered to curtail sales of beer and liquor, in order to prevent excessive drinking. When, on the night of June 29, effigies of Frick and Potter were hung on telegraph poles, they were quickly removed, on the orders of the advisory committee. The leaders were determined to prevent rowdyism.

Sensing an important confrontation brewing, reporters began to arrive from around the country. Rumors began to sweep Homestead—strikebreakers were coming, deputies were coming, Pinkerton detectives were coming. Payday was June 25, but there was little spending in the stores along Sixth and Eighth avenues. People were uncertain about what was going to happen and were hanging on to their money.

On June 28, the company ordered the closing of the open-hearth department and the armor-plate mill, locking out eight hundred men. By June 30, all four heating and rolling departments were shut down, locking out three hundred more. On July 1, the remaining men in the Homestead Works—twenty-four hundred workers—refused to report to work. The strike was on.

Not a wheel turned nor a furnace burned. Men congregated about the plant fence and peered through the loopholes at the company guards inside. *The New York Times* reported on July 1: "It is evident that there is no 'bluffing' at Homestead. The fight there is to be to the death between the Carnegie Steel Company, Limited, with its $25,000,000 capital, and the workmen." On Saturday, July 2, the Homestead Works employees were served with notices of discharge. "There will be no further conferences with the Amalgamated Association," Francis T. F. Lovejoy, the company's secretary, announced. Some workers seemed to relish being at the center of attention. On July 2, the Homestead newspaper said, "The workers are pretty much all dressed in their best clothes and are enjoying themselves, conversing and smoking good cigars."

On Sunday, July 3, Father John J. Bullion of Saint Mary Magdalene's Roman Catholic Church preached to his congregation, which included many mill workers: "Whatever the circumstances should be, you men should preserve order. To keep the peace should be your first endeavor. You must do so if you desire to retain public opinion on your side in this fight. You will lose nothing by remaining quiet. . . . Disorder could result only in harm to you."

The Reverend John J. McIlyar of the Fourth Avenue Methodist Episcopal Church delivered a more pointed sermon, entitled "The Master and the Man." He said the question was often asked, "Where would Homestead be without the mills?" Why not ask, he suggested, "Where would Andrew Carnegie be without the millions he has made from the mills?"

On the Fourth of July, about one thousand workers attended the town's traditional holiday picnic. The Homestead newspaper discounted stories in the Pittsburgh papers that Pinkertons could be effective strikebreakers. It said a Pinkerton man could not last five minutes in town.

On July 5, William H. McCleary, the Allegheny County sheriff, accompanied by a number of deputies, arrived in Homestead, saying he wished to provide protection for the Carnegie properties. A week before, the company's attorney, Philander C. Knox, had asked the sheriff whether he would deputize Pinkerton men if they were marshaled to guard strikebreakers and the plant. The sheriff had refused to commit himself. Now, the advisory committee gave the sheriff a tour of the Homestead Works, said the workers were providing ample protection to the property, and escorted him out of town. He then sent twelve deputies to Homestead; the union men sent them back with one union man, saying, "No deputy will ever go in there alive." On July 5, *The New York Times* conjectured, "The strike will be fought to the bitter end, and few who know Mr. Frick's methods and resources can hope that the end will be otherwise than the defeat of the workmen."

About 1:00 A.M. on Wednesday, July 6, pickets posted on the Smithfield Street Bridge at Pittsburgh made out in the darkness two large barges being pulled slowly up the river. Word was flashed to Homestead by telegraph or horseback or both. The record on this is unclear, but Arthur G. Burgoyne, a Pittsburgh journalist, wrote that at about 3:00 A.M. a "horseman riding at breakneck speed dashed into the streets of Homestead giving the alarm as he sped along." The barges, the *Monongahela* and the *Iron Mountain,* under tow of a small steamboat, the *Little Bill,* proceeded upstream, and were sighted again at Lock Number 1, three miles below Homestead. About 4:00 A.M., the steam whistle was sounded, and hundreds of Homestead workers and residents burst from their homes and rushed toward the Homestead Works; other workers and union supporters hurried down to the bank on the north side of the Monongahela River. The Homesteaders—men, women, children—carried whatever weapons they could find—rifles, shotguns, pistols, sticks, rocks, fence staves.

The barges were filled with three hundred Pinkertons who had been brought from a staging area at Bellevue, Pa., on the Ohio River, twenty-five miles below Pittsburgh. This was Frick's work. On June 25, one day after the deadline by which he had told the workers they had to accept the company's proposals, Frick had written Robert A. Pinkerton, head of the Pinkerton National Detective Agency, to ask that three hundred Pinkerton men

be assembled at Ashtabula, Ohio, not later than the morning of July 5th, when they may be taken by train to McKees Rocks, or some other point upon the Ohio River below Pittsburgh, where they can be transferred to boats and landed within the enclosures of our premises at Homestead. We think absolute secrecy essential in the movement of these men so that no demonstration can be made while they are en route. . . . As soon as your men are upon the premises, we will notify the Sheriff and ask that they be deputized either at once or immediately upon an outbreak of such a character as to render such a step desirable.

The Pinkerton National Detective Agency of Chicago and New York had been founded in 1850 by Allan Pinkerton, like Carnegie an immigrant from Scotland, and, like Carnegie, most ambitious. The organization's symbol was a single open eye, which gave rise to the term "private eye." The company's slogan was "We Never Sleep." The Pinkertons, in their distinctive blue coats with brass buttons, were used in numerous labor-management confrontations during the last decades of the nineteenth century, from the anthracite coalfields of eastern Pennsylvania in the 1860s to the Colorado coalfields in the 1870s.

The men aboard the barges, except for the officers, were not Pinkerton "regulars." Rather, they were "specials," part-timers of varied backgrounds—vagrants, working-class men, college students who wanted to make some money, petty criminals. *Harper's Weekly,* no friend of the strikers, said the Pinkerton agency had "a distinctly medieval flavor" reminiscent "of the *condottieri* in Italy, and of the *Landsknechte* in Germany, who hired themselves out, and fought more or less bravely on whatever side of a contest they found the best pay and the most tempting booty, without taking the slightest interest in the merits or demerits of the cause they fought for or against." The pay was fifteen dollars a week. Also on board the tug was John A. Potter, general superintendent of the Homestead Works.

Until the morning of July 6, when they heard the warning blasts of the new steam whistle, no workers had trespassed on the company's property. Now hundreds of workers and townspeople stormed the works. Parts of the wooden fence that Frick had ordered built were pulled down, and the Homesteaders erected barricades and took up positions. Amsted Kemp, hired by the company to whitewash the fence, came to work early that morning, saw what was occurring, and left town.

It had been planned that the Pinkertons would land secretly and occupy the mill, so that strikebreakers could be brought in. Now the workers were in the mill. If the Pinkertons were to occupy it, they would have to do it by force.

About 4:00 A.M., as the sky was beginning to grow light, the barges were pulled to the landing site, the *Iron Mountain* next to the shore, the *Monongahela* next to the *Iron Mountain*. A gangplank was thrown out, and a number of Pinkerton men, armed with Winchesters and pistols, started coming down the gangplank to shore. A shot was fired, then more.

No one can say who began the firing. There were guns everywhere— the Pinkertons had them, as did the strikers in their assorted craft on the water and on both banks of the river. It does not matter; fire came from both sides. A number of Pinkertons were hit, and one, J. W. Kline, was mortally wounded. On shore, a number of Homesteaders were also struck down and carried from the field. The battle of Homestead, like no other confrontation in American history, was on.

Both sides took up positions, the Pinkertons inside the barges, the workers and townspeople behind breastworks of scrap iron and beams and plates or in mill buildings. At the advisory committee's headquarters, a hotel on Eighth Avenue, rifles and shotguns and ammunition were distributed. Soon more than five thousand people were at the site, fighters and observers alike, many of the latter sitting on the hill above the mill and town, as if Homestead were an amphitheater and the fight at the mill a melodrama being staged for them. More armed men, workers and supporters, continued to gather by the Carrie Furnaces, on the north shore across the river from Homestead. The Pinkertons, some huddling, frightened, others firing from windows or holes they had knocked in the sides of the barges, were under fire from both sides of the Monongahela.

Myron R. Stowell, a Pittsburgh journalist and eyewitness to the fight, wrote in 1894:

Many a battle has gone down in history where less shooting was done and fewer people were killed. There were hundreds of men, well armed, thirsting for the lives of others in the boats, while thousands of men and women stood just out of range and cheered them on. Each crack of a rifle made them more bloodthirsty and each boom of the cannon more eager for the blood of the [Pinkerton] officers. One of the strikers remarked: "There are but two weeks between civilization and barbarism, and I believe it will take only two days of this work to make the change." Indeed, it looked as if the veneering of gentility had already been cracked.

J. H. Bridge, a steel industry historian, wrote in 1903, "American workmen seemed inspired with the spirit of the French Reign of Terror."

The *Little Bill*, with a number of wounded Pinkerton men aboard, chugged off across the river, where the Pinkertons were placed on a train for Pittsburgh.

About 9:00 A.M., a great noise was heard—artillery! Workers across the river had obtained a cannon, loaded it with steel scrap, aimed it at the barges, and touched the piece off. A shot struck one of the barges, tearing a hole in the roof, but that was the best cannon round of the day. It was this shot, wide and long, that struck the worker Silas Wain in the mill yard and blew off his head. He was the first worker to die on the field. Another cannon was obtained from the Homestead lodge of the Grand Army of the Republic, on Sixth Avenue, and put in place, but it was too high on the hill and the muzzle could not be sufficiently lowered to be targeted on the barges. The artillery pieces were abandoned.

The firing continued. Whenever anyone, worker or Pinkerton, exposed himself, he was fired upon. At one point, it was believed, more than a thousand shots were fired within ten minutes. Three more union men went down. George Rutter, a Civil War veteran and member of the Grand Army of the Republic, was shot in the thigh and carried from the field, mortally wounded. John E. Morris was shot in the forehead and killed instantly. Henry Striegel, nineteen, was shot and fell dead. It was believed that Striegel had shot himself accidentally with his own gun and was then shot by the Pinkertons as he lay in the mill yard.

The temperature rose, and soon the heat in the barges was almost unbearable. Just after 11:00 A.M., the *Little Bill* steamed back toward the landing site, apparently in an effort to release the barges so that they could float downstream. The tug was flying the Stars and Stripes at bow and stern. "We determined to fight under the colors," Captain Rodgers of the Pinkertons said. He thought the workers would not fire on the American flag. But volley after volley struck the ship, smashing the glass in the pilot house and wounding the watchman. The captain saved himself by throwing himself to the deck. The *Little Bill*, pilotless, circled about, then drifted back out of range.

At midday, a second Pinkerton, Thomas J. Connors, twenty-four, a regular, was killed when a bullet went through an open door on the barge and struck him in the arm, severing an artery. A third Pinkerton, Edward A. R. Speer, was shot in the leg. He died in a Pittsburgh hospital on July 17. Three more strikers were killed. Joseph Sotak, thirty, was shot in the knee. He was carried from the field and taken to a Pittsburgh hospital, where he died that day from loss of blood. Thomas Weldon, thirty, was shot dead. Peter Farris, in his early twenties, was shot in the head and fell to the ground dead.

The workers attempted several stratagems to roust the Pinkertons. A raft was soaked with oil, fired, and sent drifting downriver toward the barges. But the flames were extinguished by the water, and by the time the raft reached the barges it was a smoking, blackened mass that did no damage. A railroad freight car was run down onto a track near the barges, loaded with oil, timber, and mill refuse, and set afire. Flames rose high in the air, and the car was sent rolling down the track toward the barges. Everyone—strikers, Pinkertons, townspeople—watched in suspense. The car jumped the track and came to a stop in the dirt by the water's edge. The fire burned out. No damage was done.

As the day wore on, the streets of Homestead filled with men, women, and children. The sounds of the battle could be heard throughout town. About 1:00 P.M., men with baskets of food were sent into the mill yard. They dodged from one barricade or building to another, with the people behind them on the hill cheering as the fighters were handed lunch. In the afternoon, the men attempted another tactic. A number of sticks of dynamite were obtained—dynamite is used in steel mills to blow out tap holes—and distributed to a dozen or so workers. The men worked their way as close as they could to the barges, and hurled the sticks. Some sticks struck the barges but did little damage. Most fell wide of the mark.

The barges were also bombarded with skyrockets and Roman candles left over from Homestead's Fourth of July celebration. This had no effect, so the men obtained a town fire engine, pumped oil onto the water, and set it afire. The fire burned out with no damage to the *Iron Mountain* or the *Monongahela*. The situation settled into a stalemate, although the workers had the upper hand because the Pinkertons were confined to their barges. Moreover, armed reinforcements for the strikers were coming up from Braddock and Pittsburgh.

At 3:00 P.M., William Weihe, the Amalgamated Association's president, and other union leaders arrived in town. A meeting of strikers and sympathizers was hastily convened in a mill building. Weihe—seven feet tall, called "The Giant Puddler" by the union men—and the other leaders pleaded with the strikers to allow the Pinkertons to leave. The men refused. "Kill them," the strikers cried. "Burn them." But the union leaders were able to calm the strikers, and now Hugh O'Donnell grabbed a small American flag, mounted a barricade of iron, and begged the men to allow a truce. The men agreed—providing that the Pinkertons, not the strikers, hoisted the first white flag.

The Pinkerton men had also been parlaying, and occasionally white flags had been stuck up from the barges but had been shot away. Now, in midafternoon, another white flag went up from the *Iron Mountain,* and this time it was not shot at. Cries of triumph went up from the workers: "Victory! We have them now. They surrender." O'Donnell and two other advisory committee members went down to the riverbank and negotiated with one of the Pinkerton detectives. If the Pinkertons surrendered, the union men said, they would not be harmed. The Pinkertons said that they would come out.

By now, thousands more people had arrived in Homestead and were milling about the streets or on the hill above the works. A motley gang it was, too—millhands from other ironworks and steelworks along the Monongahela, toughs looking for fun, anarchists from Pittsburgh. Hundreds of women—wives of workers and townspeople—were also on the scene. It was 4:00 P.M. The fight had lasted twelve hours. The Pinkertons were weary and frightened. None wanted to be among the first to leave the barges. Then a few Pinkerton men hesitatingly began to come out. Others cowered inside. Most of the Pinkertons had accepted the assignment because they were looking for work; except for a few of the leaders, most of the men had signed on not only without knowing that they were to help break a strike, but without knowing what town they were headed for. Now, hundreds of workers stormed the barges and pulled the Pinkertons out and sent them trudging up the hill with their comrades.

Workers and townspeople pressed in toward the battle site. As the Pinkertons, disarmed and under guard, began clambering up the bank, their wounded carried on litters, the strikers and onlookers formed two lines stretching some six hundred yards up from the barges. The route of the Pinkertons was between the lines. As the Pinkertons, hungry, thirsty, some wounded, all scared, were made to walk, many of them stumbling, they were mercilessly beaten by strikers and sympathizers—including many workers' wives—armed with sticks, fence staves, umbrellas. Some women gathered stones in their aprons and stoned the Pinkertons. Children threw rocks and clods of mud. Many of the Pinkerton men had their blue uniforms torn from their bodies. A number were beaten to the ground. It was like the gantlets that Indian fighters or pioneers might have been made to run by Indians a century and more before. "We were clubbed at every step," a Pinkerton said. "Sticks, stones, and dirt were thrown at us. The women pulled us down, spat in our faces, kicked us, and tore our clothing off while the crowd jeered and cheered." A number of strikers, including Hugh O'Donnell and other members of the advisory committee, attempted to shield the Pinkerton men but had little success. It is said that some workers pointed their rifles at the Pinkertons' tormentors, saying they would shoot them—their fellow townspeople—if they did not stop. Some workers were struck down in the melee.

With great difficulty, the guards herded the Pinkertons into town, to the Homestead opera house and the skating rink, on Sixth Avenue. The Pinkertons were forced inside and the mob surged forward. A dozen guards leveled their rifles at the persecutors. Burgess John McLuckie stepped forward and ordered the crowd to desist. Finally, they began to disperse. The Pinkertons huddled in the opera house, under guard. It was about 5:00 P.M. The Pinkertons, about half of them seriously injured, remained in the opera house through the evening. Members of the advisory committee met with the town's elected officials, and it was agreed to allow the Allegheny County sheriff to come to Homestead to pick up the Pinkertons. At about 11:00 P.M., Sheriff McCleary arrived on a special train with national officers of the Amalgamated Association, and the Pinkertons were herded aboard the train and taken to Pittsburgh. About twenty of them, the severely wounded, were placed in hospitals. The train containing the rest was shuttled to a side track, while Sheriff McCleary and Pittsburgh municipal and business officials conferred. It was decided that the wisest course of action was to get the Pinkertons out of town as fast as could be arranged, and the men were placed on trains. One group was sent to New York, a second to Chicago. One Pinkerton, James O'Day, delirious from wounds suffered in the fight, committed suicide on July 10 at Chesterton, Indiana, by jumping from the train carrying him and other Pinkertons to Chicago.

At 3:00 A.M., July 7, union men searched the Homestead Works to ensure that no Pinkertons had fled there and that the property was secure. Remnants of the fight—cartridge cases, discarded weapons—were everywhere. It was said that even the rats had abandoned the works. Company watchmen who had fled when the fight began were now directed to return and to resume guarding the company's property. After the sun came up, the barges were ransacked. The Homesteaders took provisions, bedding, and the Pinkertons' personal gear. Winchesters and ammunition were taken as souvenirs. Some weapons remain today in Homestead, including a Winchester in firing condition, although owners are reluctant to say they possess the weapons. Oil was spread on the barges, and they were fired and set adrift. The flames climbed high in the air, and two columns of smoke rose lazily in the sky as the barges drifted slowly downriver to the cheers of the Homestead people. After a time, the barges, still burning, seemed to settle into the water. Then they slowly disappeared beneath the surface.

On July 7, Carnegie cabled Frick from Scotland: "Cable received. All anxiety gone since you stand firm. Never employ one of these rioters. Let grass grow over works. Must not fail now. You will win easily next trial."

IV

That day, Homestead began to bury its dead. John E. Morris was buried from the Fourth Avenue Methodist Episcopal Church. The Reverend John J. McIlyar, who on July 3 had attacked the company from his pulpit, was far angrier now. "The mill men were organized in an association that enabled them to obtain just and adequate remuneration for their services," he said. "The existence of this union of men was threatened by a body of Pinkertons, employed by somebody for the purpose. This is what has put this blessed man in his coffin today: a perfect citizen; an intelligent man; a good husband who was never lacking in his duty; a brother who was devoted and loyal and who will surely find his reward."

Reverend McIlyar said that the dispute might have been adjudicated through arbitration but that the company had refused. One man was responsible, McIlyar said—Frick. "This town is bathed in tears today and it is all brought about by one man, who is less respected by the laboring people than any other employer in the country. There is no more sensibility in that man than in a toad." Morris's body was borne in a hearse up the hill to the Homestead burying grounds. On the way, another hearse fell into the procession. It bore Peter Farris's body. The men were buried, and the mourners started back down the hill. Now another funeral procession formed, and the body of Silas Wain was borne up the hill and buried. The next day, Friday, July 8, Henry Striegel, Joseph Sotak, and Thomas Weldon were buried. George Rutter died July 17. He was buried in Verona, Pennsylvania.

The strikers and the other residents of Homestead were confident that their losses had not been in vain. They believed they had acted in defense of their jobs and their town and that they would get their jobs at the mill back at fair terms. On the night of July 7, when a band of anarchists arrived in Homestead and began to distribute circulars saying that the mill was the property of the workers and that the workers should seize it, the townspeople arrested two of the anarchists and placed them in the town lockup, and shipped the rest out of town.

When Carnegie, on vacation in Scotland, first heard of the battle, his reaction was to return, in order to take charge of the situation. He cabled Frick that he was returning, but the other owners feared that if he did, he would undermine Frick and Frick's hard line. They convinced Carnegie to remain where he was. He was distressed that the situation had become so messy. He wrote his cousin Dod Lauder: "Matters at home bad—such a fiasco trying to send guards by Boat and then leaving space between River & fences for the men to get opposite landing and fire. Still we must keep quiet & do all we can to support Frick & those at Seat of War. I have been besieged by interviewing Cables from N York but have not said a word. Silence is best. We shall win, of course, but may have to shut down for months."

A representative of the Associated Press reached Carnegie at Rannoch Lodge and made repeated efforts to interview him, but each time he was rebuffed. At last, one morning, Carnegie told him: "I authorize you to make the following statement: I have not attended to business for the past three years, but I have implicit confidence in those who are managing the mills. Further than that I have nothing to say."

On July 7, John A. Potter, the general superintendent, returned to Homestead. He walked through town and toward the works. "You cannot visit them," a picket said. "You know who I am?" Potter asked. "Yes, but we have orders not to allow anyone to enter the works," the union man replied.

On July 8, Sheriff McCleary returned to Homestead, but Homestead citizens, including businessmen, refused to be deputized, and the workers refused to surrender the mill to him. He took the train back to Pittsburgh. The situation—watched throughout the nation and in Europe—was unprecedented. The strikers held the Homestead Works and the town. Persons the workers did not trust, including some reporters, were made to leave. The union men were guarding the mill but also ensuring that it could not be retaken. The fence around the mill had been repaired, and arms and ammunition had been distributed to pickets, who were posted to watch for company forces sent to recapture the mill. Even when the Amalgamated Association's attorney urged the strikers to allow the sheriff to take possession, the strikers refused.

Across the country, newspapers began writing editorials on the sanctity of property and calling for an end to workers' rule. Frick said, "The country is certainly reaching a commendable point when a man is debarred from using his property by an organized band of strikers."

There had been talk since the fight that Governor Robert E. Pattison would send in the Pennsylvania National Guard, the state militia. On July 8, a delegation from Homestead, including Hugh O'Donnell, journeyed to Harrisburg, the state capital, conferred with the governor for over an hour, and left with the conviction that the militia would not be mobilized. On the morning of Sunday, July 10, Sheriff McCleary informed the governor that he could not establish authority in Homestead: "The strikers are in control, and openly express to me and to the public their determination that the works shall not be operated unless by themselves." At 10:00 P.M., the governor acted, ordering the mobilization of the eight-thousand-man Pennsylvania militia and dispatching it, with arms and ammunition, to Homestead. Within twelve hours, it was on the march.

Monday, July 11, was a day of excitement. The townspeople knew that the militia was on its way, but they continued to believe that they had done nothing illegal. At 2:00 P.M. that day, strikers and townspeople met in the Homestead opera house and discussed the situation. The workers saw the militia as their friends and protectors. "We don't want Pinkertons here," McLuckie said, addressing the gathering. "We want the militia." A reception committee headed by McLuckie and Hugh O'Donnell was designated to meet the soldiers, and it was decided that the town's four brass bands would be mustered to play for the troops. A discussion ensued over what selection should be played, and a decision was finally reached: the favorite, "Ta Ra Ra, Boom De Ay."

A millworker, well dressed and sporting a large corkscrew mustache, took the floor and said, "I move that any man who insults the troops be ducked in the Monongahela." "Good, duck 'em," came the response. The motion was adopted by a large majority.

The town waited. McLuckie went to a grocery store, where he practiced a welcoming speech. But no soldiers appeared. Night fell, and after a time most townspeople went to bed. Then, at 8:45 A.M., Tuesday, July 12, two trains chuffed across the Pittsburgh, Virginia, and Charleston Railroad Bridge and pulled into the Munhall station, at the eastern end of Homestead. One train, with two cars, carried Major General George R. Snowden, commander of the Pennsylvania militia, and his staff, and Sheriff McCleary; the second, with ten cars, carried hundreds of troops, bayoneted rifles protruding from the windows. Behind came more trains carrying hundreds more troops. The troops dismounted and formed in column. Skirmishers were sent down the tracks toward Homestead, and the troops marched behind them. The troops, seven regiments in all, seized the hill, known at the time as Shanty Hill, owned by the Carnegie company and today the site of the Free Carnegie Library of Homestead; artillery pieces were unlimbered and trained on the mill and town below. Gatling guns also were deployed. Within half an hour, four thousand troops were formed in line of battle, facing down on the town. Across the

Monongahela River, Homesteaders saw the glistening of the sun on metal; the metal was rifles and bayonets and field pieces—another four thousand troops with artillery had been deployed across the river.

These were efficient troops, militiamen, yes, but highly trained and well-officered soldiers, armed with new forty-five-caliber Springfield rifles. The Pennsylvania militia had performed poorly in the labor riots of 1877, and General William Tecumseh Sherman, the U.S. Army's commander, had ordered that the training and arms of the militias be improved as protection against more civil disorder; it was said that the Pennsylvania militia was now among the best in the country. Militiamen had encamped at Homestead on their way home following service in Pittsburgh during the railroad riots of 1877, but the town had seen nothing like this. The advance upon Homestead had been carried out with the utmost precision. Snowden, a Civil War veteran, had gone so far as to make public incorrect times and places for marshaling areas, for he wished to take the town by surprise. The workers and townspeople had been foolishly naive.

On the morning of July 12, O'Donnell and a group of townspeople journeyed up the hill to meet with General Snowden, who had established his headquarters at the Carnegie schoolhouse. "We come as representing the citizens of Homestead as well as the Amalgamated strikers," O'Donnell said. "I am always glad to meet the citizens, the good citizens, of any community," the general said. "We have been peaceful and law-abiding citizens," O'Donnell said. "No, you have not," Snowden said. "You have not been peaceful and law-abiding citizens." O'Donnell and the other union men stood silent. Their cheeks were flushed, their faces downcast. O'Donnell spoke again. "General," he said, "we've got four brass bands, and we would like to have them and a parade of our friends pass in review before the camp." "I don't want any brass-band business while I'm here," Snowden said. "I want you to distinctly understand that I am master of this situation." Homestead was occupied.

V

It was the purpose of the militia to prevent violence and to protect the property rights of the Carnegie company. This meant breaking the strike.

Troops garrisoned the mill yards and sentries were posted outside Frick's fence. The *Little Bill* was chartered by the militia to haul supplies, an act galling to the workmen, who saw the tugboat as a symbol of Frick and the Pinkertons and the effort to oppress them. Another tug brought over what the workers most dreaded, strikebreakers, whom company recruiting agents were signing up in eastern and midwestern cities. Food and cots were brought into the Homestead Works, and within a week a hundred strikebreakers were quartered inside.

Some residents enjoyed having the troops in town, and some profited by it. Boys loved hanging around the cantonment and watching the soldiers at their drills and fatigue duty; some girls and townspeople delighted in coming up to the camp area on Sundays, when formal drills were sometimes held; even the militia's Sheridan Cavalry performed maneuvers, despite the limits of the confined parade areas. The sounds of bugles and of the guns fired at sunset each day were exciting. A number of townspeople were hired as teamsters to bring supplies up to the troops, and thus they made money during the occupation.

But the troops accomplished their mission—securing the Carnegie company's property for its owners.

On July 15, three days after the troops' arrival, smoke rose from the works for the first time since the strike had begun. Workers gathered and rushed the works, but the soldiers held them back by leveling rifles with fixed bayonets at them.

On July 16, notices were posted in Homestead that applications for work would be accepted from old employees until 6:00 P.M. July 21. The company, the notices said, intended to retain those workers who had not taken part in the disturbances; those workers who did not apply would be replaced. On July 19, seven days after the arrival of the militia, work resumed in the open hearth and the armor-plate mill.

Most of the workers refused to submit applications. A leaflet circulated on July 22 made a remarkable claim, that the workers and the public had earned an interest in the mill through the labor of the workers and through the tariffs that had been supported by the public. But on that day a large force of strikebreakers was transported from Pittsburgh to the Homestead Works by the tugboat *Tide,* and more trips were made every day thereafter. "There is always an army of unemployed in the United States, and upon these as well as underpaid workers in various lines— clerks, struggling young professional men and others—who were tempted by the high wages said to be paid at Homestead the firm could and did draw freely," Arthur G. Burgoyne wrote in 1893.

The government and local law-enforcement officials were also moving against the strikers in court. On July 18, Burgess McLuckie was arrested on charges of the murder of the Pinkerton guard Edward Connors. Six other workers, including Hugh O'Donnell, were also charged in the death. Deputies and guardsmen assisted in other arrests. More arrests came in September. Four strikers, including Hugh O'Donnell, were arrested for the murder of Pinkerton detective J. W. Klein. Other workers were arrested for conspiracy. On September 21, 167 strikers were indicted on various charges, including riot, conspiracy, and murder. Later that month the Pennsylvania Supreme Court indicted thirty-four strikers, including McLuckie and Hugh O'Donnell, for treason against the state of Pennsylvania under an obscure 1860 state law.

On two occasions, however, juries refused to return murder convictions, and some prosecutions were called off because the prosecutors and the Carnegie company realized they could not obtain convictions. Four union supporters were convicted of poisoning nonunion workers and were sentenced to three to seven years in the state penitentiary.

On Saturday, July 23, a startling event occurred. That day, as was his custom, Henry Clay Frick had taken lunch at 1:00 P.M. at the Duquesne Club. He apparently had not noticed, but he had been followed on his return to his office by a thin, pale, nervous man, Alexander Berkman, an anarchist. Frick went to his office and, sitting at his desk, talked with J. G. A. Leishman, a company vice-president. For several days, Berkman, posing as an agent of a New York employment agency and claiming he could supply nonunion labor for the Homestead Works, had tried to see Frick. Frick had put him off, but that day Berkman suddenly burst through the door and made a rapid movement toward his back pocket. Frick sprang to his feet, but he was too late. Berkman had a revolver in his hand, and he fired a shot that struck Frick in the lobe of his left ear and then in the neck, penetrating to the middle of his back. As Frick lay on the floor, Berkman fired a second time and struck Frick again in the neck. Berkman would probably have gone on pumping shots into Frick, but Leishman jumped from his chair, ran around the desk and attacked Berkman, reaching him just as he fired a third time. This shot went wild, striking the wall near the ceiling. Berkman and Leishman grappled, and Frick picked himself from the floor and grabbed Berkman from behind. The three men struggled and then all fell in a heap on the floor, Berkman on the bottom. Berkman pulled a dagger from his pocket and stabbed Frick three times, in one hip, the right side, and the left leg. Frick could not be stopped, however. He again threw himself on Berkman and pinned him to the floor. By now clerks had rushed in, and they helped to subdue Berkman. Shortly, a deputy sheriff arrived, and he raised his revolver as if to shoot Berkman. Frick, on his feet, cried: "Don't shoot. Leave him to the law, but raise his head and let me see his face." Frick pointed to Berkman's jaw. Berkman was chewing something. The deputy forced Berkman's mouth open and extracted a capsule of fulminate of mercury, often used by anarchists. A bite or two and Berkman would have blown them all, including himself, to bits. Frick was standing at his desk, blood streaming from his wounds. Leishman and Berkman were also covered with blood. More policemen arrived, and Berkman was taken from the room. Leishman collapsed and was carried from the office.

Frick was helped onto a chaise lounge, and physicians were summoned. As the men waited, Frick commented favorably upon his assailant's strength. The doctors arrived and had some doubts about whether Frick would survive. But Frick was indomitable. He sat for two hours as a surgeon probed his neck and back for the bullets, refusing chloroform so that he could tell the doctor when the probe was nearing the bullets.

The bullets extracted, and his wounds sutured and dressed, Frick turned to work. He completed arrangements for a loan and signed a number of letters he had already dictated. He sent his mother a telegram: "Was shot twice but not dangerously." He dispatched a similar message to Carnegie, in Scotland, adding: "There is no necessity for you to come home. I am still in shape to fight the battle out." He then completed his paperwork and prepared a statement for the press that said: "This incident will not change the attitude of the Carnegie Steel Company toward the Amalgamated Association. I do not think I shall die, but whether I do or not, the Company will pursue the same policy and it will win."

Berkman's assassination attempt cost the strikers much sympathy in Pittsburgh and across the nation, although Berkman had no connection with the strikers. In August 1892, Berkman was convicted of carrying a concealed weapon and assault with intent to kill. He was sentenced to twenty-one years in prison. He was not a workingman or a union member; he was an anarchist, and a crazed anarchist at that. He was, in addition, atrociously incompetent in the practice of professional violence on behalf of the working class. But Berkman became identified in people's minds with working people and the Homestead strikers. Hugh O'Donnell, the strike's leader, said, "It would seem that the bullet from Berkman's pistol, failing in its foul intent, went straight through the heart of the Homestead strike."

The workers were losing the strike. Under the protection of the state militia, the company continued to bring in strikebreakers and to lure back former workers who agreed to renounce the union. Many Homestead merchants had allowed strikers to purchase groceries and other necessities on credit, but they could no longer afford to do this, and strikers had little money.

Efforts by political leaders and strikers to bring the company into negotiations failed. The Republican Party was worried that the strike would cost its ticket—Benjamin Harrison for president and Whitelaw Reid for vice-president—the votes of working people by demonstrating that the Republicans were the party of big business and the high tariff. On July 18, Hugh O'Donnell had taken the train to New York, where he met with Reid. O'Donnell agreed to write Carnegie a letter asking Carnegie to intervene in the strike, and Reid forwarded the letter to Carnegie with an appeal of his own. Carnegie received these communications on July 28. That day, he telegraphed Pittsburgh that he believed the proposal for settling the strike was "worthy of consideration." He immediately reconsidered, however, and the next day, July 29, he sent Pittsburgh a second cablegram saying that O'Donnell's proposition was "not worthy of consideration." He told Frick, "Use your own discretion about terms and starting [the mill]. George Lauder, Henry Phipps Jr., Andrew Carnegie solid. H. C. Frick forever." Carnegie then cabled Reid that he would not compromise.

On July 31, four hundred new workers—strikebreakers—attended a church service in the Homestead Works, with 150 company guards watching over them, and one thousand National Guardsmen nearby. A Sixteenth Regiment chaplain preached the sermon. By early August, fifteen hundred men were at work in the mill.

On August 31, still recovering from his wounds, Frick visited the Homestead Works for the first time since the strike had begun. He pronounced the mill in working order and informed reporters that the strike was a thing of the past. The last of the militiamen were recalled from Homestead on October 13.

The town became split over the strike as it dragged on. Businesses were experiencing hard times and tax revenues were down. The borough council was unable to function, because members who sympathized with the strikers refused to sit with members who opposed the strike. On October 15, the *Homestead Local News* said that more than two thousand men were at work in the mill, including one hundred former workers, and that more workers were being brought in every day. Two conclusions were inescapable, the newspaper said: "First, the Carnegie Company is gradually succeeding. Second, the great Homestead strike is gradually dying out." The paper said that businessmen and intelligent union leaders knew that the strike was lost. The Carnegie company was building over a hundred new homes for the new workers, and on November 5, the paper said that "the new workmen are beginning to spend their money" and that "our most enterprising merchants are putting in a large stock of goods [in] anticipation of a good fall and winter trade." On November 12, the newspaper said it was time for the town to seek a "business revival." A strike leader, William T. Roberts, said the "Carnegie firm has bought the *News*." The paper denied this. But on November 19, with money borrowed from mill executives, the *Local News* went from being a weekly to a daily paper.

On October 17, four strikers openly applied for work and were given employment. On October 21, Samuel Gompers, president of the American Federation of Labor, came to Homestead. Almost the entire population turned out to hear him speak. He talked of a boycott of Carnegie products, but nothing came of it. Schwab had been brought back by Carnegie from Edgar Thomson to be Homestead's general superintendent, and he courted the former workers, particularly the skilled workers, whom the company needed. By mid-November, twenty-seven hundred men were at work in the mill, and on November 18 some two thousand laborers and mechanics, nonunion men, met in Homestead and drafted a proposition that the strike be declared over, and that the laborers and mechanics be released from their obligation to continue striking. The union men met that evening and voted 224 to 129 to continue the strike. But the next day the laborers and mechanics went to the mill and submitted applications for employment. The laborers were hired, as were half of the mechanics. The rest of the mechanics were turned away because their positions already had been filled by strikebreakers. Frick was there to watch the men come in.

On November 21, a group of strikers met at the opera house. Some workers argued passionately against giving in, but the arguments were of no use. The men voted 101 to 91 to return to work. The decision caused almost no excitement in town. The spirit of the workers and townspeople had been broken. And, too, the holidays were approaching, making being on strike harder to bear. Hundreds of strikers now walked down to the mill and besieged the company with applications for reemployment. Schwab himself was present on Monday, November 22, to receive applications. Workers whose names were not on the company's blacklist were authorized to file applications with department superintendents. Men stood in line all day, but so many strikebreakers and former workers already had been given employment that the number of vacancies was small. At least twenty-five hundred strikers were unemployed.

On November 22, Frick sent Carnegie a cablegram saying: "Strike officially called off yesterday. Our victory is now complete and most gratifying. Do not think we will ever have any serious labor trouble again." Carnegie, in Rome, replied: "I am well and able to take an interest in the wonders we see. . . . Shall see you all early after the New Year. Think I'm about ten years older than when with you last. Europe has run with Homestead, Homestead, until we are sick of the name, but it is all over now— So once again Happy New Year to all. I wish someone would write me about your good self. I cannot believe you can be so well. Ever your Pard. A.C."

By December thirty-one hundred men were at work in the mill, but of the twenty-two hundred strikers who applied for reinstatement, only four hundred were rehired, and most of these were laborers, that is, unskilled workers. Many Homestead families were destitute. To help the children, Kaufmann Brothers, a Pittsburgh department store, sent each one a book and a box of candy for the holidays. The workers of McKeesport sent the Homestead workers a thousand turkeys. Just before Christmas, Homestead schoolchildren were asked to write letters to Santa Claus saying what they wanted for Christmas. Almost all of them asked for shoes and other practical items.

VI

The defeat of the Homestead strike devastated the town. When Hamlin Garland visited Homestead in 1893, he wrote: "The town was as squalid and unlovely as could well be imagined, and the people were mainly of the discouraged and sullen type to be found everywhere where labor passes into the brutalizing stage of severity. . . . Such towns are sown thickly over the hill-lands of Pennsylvania. . . . They are American only in the sense in which they represent the American idea of business."

Another writer, Charles Spahr, lived in Homestead for a number of weeks in 1900, and wrote in *America's Working People* that Homesteaders "were cheerless almost to the point of sullenness," adding: "The atmosphere was at times heavy with disappointment and hopelessness. Some of the men were afraid to talk; even the Catholic priest—to whose class I am accustomed to go for fair statements of the relations of men to their employers—was unwilling to make any statement."

Lives were ruined. Honest John McLuckie was blacklisted. His wife died. His money ran out. In November 1892, he resigned as burgess and left town. He drifted to the Southwest and then to Mexico. In 1900, a professor at Rutgers University and a friend of Carnegie's, John C. Van Dyke, happened upon McLuckie while Van Dyke was on a hunting trip in the Sonora Mountains, in northern Mexico. McLuckie was unemployed and "down to his last copper." Van Dyke wrote Carnegie that he had met McLuckie and that he was down and out. Carnegie replied, "Give McLuckie all the money he wants, but don't mention my name." Van Dyke wrote McLuckie and, without mentioning Carnegie, offered him enough money to get on his feet. McLuckie refused the offer. He said he would make his own way.

A year or so later, Van Dyke happened upon McLuckie again while on another vacation. By now McLuckie had obtained a position as a repair superintendent with the Sonora railway in Mexico. Van Dyke said: "McLuckie, I want you to know now that the money I offered you was not mine. That was Andrew Carnegie's money. It was his offer, made through me." McLuckie was stunned. "Well, that was damned white of Andy, wasn't it?" he said.

Hugh O'Donnell, though cleared of murder charges, was blacklisted by the Carnegie companies and the rest of the iron and steel industry. Workers also were suspicious of him for his dealings with Whitelaw Reid. "I am now shunned by both labor and capital, a modern Ishmael, doomed to wander in the desert of ingratitude," he wrote in 1894 to a political scientist preparing an article on the Homestead strike. The Amalgamated Association never regained its prestige and strength, although it hung on for decades.

The Homestead fight also cost Carnegie and his companies much prestige. Newspapers, church leaders, and politicians condemned him, in America and Great Britain. Perhaps the most bitter statement, widely reprinted, was carried by the *St. Louis Post-Dispatch:*

Count no man happy until he is dead. Three months ago Andrew Carnegie was a man to be envied. Today he is an object of mingled pity and contempt. In the estimation of nine-tenths of the thinking people on both sides of the ocean he had not given the lie to all his antecedents, but confessed himself a moral coward. One would naturally suppose that if he had a grain of consistency, not to say decency, in his composition, he would favor rather than oppose the organization of trades-union among his own working people at Homestead. One would naturally suppose that if he had a grain of manhood, not to say courage, in his composition, he would at least have been willing to face the consequences of his inconsistency. But what does Carnegie do? Runs off to Scotland out of harm's way to await the issue of the battle he was too pusillanimous to share. A single word from him might have saved the bloodshed—but the word was never spoken. Nor has he, from that bloody day until this, said anything except that he had "implicit confidence in the managers of the mills." The correspondent who finally obtained this valuable information expresses the opinion that "Mr. Carnegie has no intention of returning to America at present." He might have added that America can well spare Mr. Carnegie. Ten thousand "Carnegie Public Libraries" would not compensate the country for the direct and indirect evils resulting from the Homestead lockout. Say what you will of Frick, he is a brave man. Say what you will of Carnegie, he is a coward. And gods and men hate cowards.

In his autobiography, Carnegie wrote: "Nothing I have ever had to meet in all my life, before or since, wounded me so deeply. No pangs remain of any wound received in my business career save that of Homestead. It was so unnecessary."

The Homestead fight also played a part in a presidential election. In November 1892 it may have helped defeat President Benjamin Harrison, a Republican and a high-tariff man, who lost to Grover Cleveland, a Democrat. Some historians have disputed this, but Harrison and his vice-presidential candidate, Whitelaw Reid, did not. Harrison said that he was defeated by "the discontent and passion of the working men growing out of wages or other labor disturbances." And after the election, Reid wrote a friend, "It was Homestead more than all other agencies combined that defeated us in 1892."

But none of this mattered. The workers and townspeople had engaged in a confrontation with authority unequaled in America. It was, as Samuel Gompers said years later, "the big struggle" in America between labor and a modern industrial corporation; the confrontation was also, in a substantial way, the beginning of American labor history. Today, the Homestead fight remains one of the most important and compelling confrontations between labor and capital: men, women, children, an entire town, rising to confront their employers—not their masters, in the view of the workers and townspeople. Such assurance, such audacity!

General Snowden, in his official report, wrote: "Philadelphians can hardly appreciate the actual communism of these people. They believe the works are theirs quite as much as Carnegie's." But the workers and the townspeople were confronted by forces far too formidable for them: Carnegie and Frick and the power of the Carnegie enterprises; deputies; the state militia. Time was another factor. The workers and the townspeople could hold out only so long. Their money ran out and then their resistance. When their children needed shoes, the strike was lost; a thousand free turkeys could not keep it going.

The company's authority was established. Carnegie and his men had gotten what they wanted, control of the mill and the town and the breaking of the union.

Periodic revolts by workers, some of them intense and large, would occur, but they would be suppressed. The company continued the introduction of new machines and methods, and at the same time attacked labor costs. Within a year after the strike, wages for many skilled workers at Homestead, including rollers, shearmen, tablemen, and heaters, were reduced by half. The minimum for the sliding scale was abolished in 1892, and the sliding scale was ended in 1894. The price of steel billets in the next years rose 40 percent, but wages at Homestead increased only 10 percent. The twelve-hour day and the seven-day week continued.

Even the defeat of President Harrison was of little consequence to Carnegie. As Carnegie wrote to Frick after the election: "Cleveland! Landslide! Well, we have nothing to fear and perhaps it is best. People will now think the Protected Manfrs. will be attended to and quit agitating. Cleveland is [a] pretty good fellow. Off for Venice tomorrow."

On February 1, 1893, Carnegie visited Homestead for part of the day, chatting with some of the older workers. It was a private affair. He did not talk to reporters. He was tired; he had taken a long train ride after attending services for his friend James G. Blaine, the longtime congressman, a high-tariff man, and Republican candidate for president in 1884. Carnegie arrived at the works by carriage, visited some mills, and then, after his conversations with the men, was driven back to his private train and returned to Pittsburgh. From there, he issued this statement:

I have not come to Pittsburgh to rake up but to bury the past. . . . When employer and employed become antagonistic, either antagonism can only be described as a contest between twin brothers. No genuine victory is possible for either side, only the defeat of both. . . . I made my first dollar in Pittsburgh and expect to make my last dollar here also. . . . Unless the Pittsburgh works are prosperous, I shall have nothing. I have put all my eggs in one basket right here, and I have the satisfaction of knowing that the first charge upon every dollar of my capital is the payment of the highest earnings paid for labor in any part of the world for similar services. Upon that record I could stand.

Of Frick, Carnegie said:

I am not mistaken in the man, as the future will show. Of his ability, fairness, and pluck no one has the slightest question. His four years' management stamps him as one of the foremost managers of the world— I would not exchange him for any manager I know. . . . His are the qualities that wear; he never disappoints; what he promises he more than fulfills.

I hope after this statement that the public will understand that the officials of the Carnegie Steel Company, Limited, with Mr. Frick at their head, are not dependent upon me, or upon anyone, in any way for their positions, and that I have neither power nor disposition to interfere with them in the management of the business. And further, that I have the most implicit faith in them.

Then, as was so usual for Carnegie, he adopted an optimistic view. In April 1893, writing John Morley about his Homestead visit, Carnegie said: "I went to Homestead & shook hands with the old men, tears in their eyes & mine. Oh, that Homestead blunder—but it's fading as all events do & we are at work selling steel one pound for a half penny."

7

"ALL HAIL,
KING STEEL"

In August 1892, Henry Clay Frick, still recovering from his wounds, and still struggling to bring the Homestead Works to full production, was approached by a Pittsburgh iron and steel man, Henry W. Oliver, with a proposition. In July, Oliver had gone to the Republican National Convention in Minneapolis. There he had heard stories of the discovery of vast amounts of iron ore in the pine forests one hundred miles north of Duluth. Oliver had immediately lost interest in the convention and had taken a train to Duluth, where, unable to find a room because the hotels were crowded with prospectors, he slept on a billiard table. The next day he purchased a horse and rode up to the wilderness known as the Mesabi Range. He toured the diggings, saw ore so loose it could be shoveled like sand, and met Leonidas Merritt, the woodsman and iron prospector who, with his sons and nephews, six others in all, had discovered the vast quantity of ore on the Mesabi. When the Merritts began to bring ore back to Duluth for shipment down the Great Lakes to the steel furnaces in Pittsburgh and Chicago, they caused an iron-ore rush like the California gold rush half a century before. By the time of Oliver's trip, some fifty mining companies were staking claims on what became known as the Iron Range.

Oliver was regarded as one of the cleverest businessmen in Pittsburgh but was something of a sharpster; he had made and lost several fortunes in iron and steel. He was financially embarrassed now, but he convinced Merritt that he represented substantial iron and steel interests in Pittsburgh, wrote him a check for $5,000, and returned to Pittsburgh, first to cover the check and then to attempt to convince the Carnegie Steel Company to join him in his Mesabi investment. Oliver proposed to Frick that the company lend him $500,000, to be secured by a mortgage on ore properties that Oliver and Merritt planned to develop. In return, Oliver promised the company a half-interest in the company Oliver and Merritt were to form, the Oliver Mining Company.

Frick had met Leonidas Merritt. In 1890, Merritt had come to Pittsburgh to attempt to convince Frick to invest in his Mesabi holdings. Frick had refused. "Frick did not use me like a gentleman, and cut me off short and bulldozed me," Merritt later complained.* Now Frick reversed himself. The iron rush was on, and he wanted to be part of it. He also recognized that Oliver was offering him an attractive proposition. The $500,000 would be a loan; the Carnegie Steel Company would be investing nothing. The obstacle to proceeding was Carnegie.

When Carnegie, in Scotland, was apprised of Oliver's proposals, he wrote Frick, "Oliver's ore bargain is just like him—nothing in it." Oliver had been one of the ragamuffins in Carnegie's boyhood neighborhood on Rebecca Street in Allegheny City. Carnegie had obtained a position for

---

* The saga of the Merritts—the "Seven Iron Men," the writer Paul de Kruif called them—is one of the great stories in American business history and one that has never received its due. The Merritts were sons of the wilderness, able woodsmen all. They hacked out trails, poled up wild rivers, battled mosquitoes and blackflies, clambered about on snowshoes at fifty below zero. Their first strike on the Mesabi was made in November 1890, and soon they had invested all their savings in efforts to find and bring out Mesabi ore. By 1892, some five thousand miners were ranging about the Mesabi. A railroad was built to Iron Mountain on the Mesabi, and extraction was begun. Once the Merritts were offered $8 million for the stake, but they refused it. The panic of 1893 struck the Merritts hard. They borrowed $350,000 from John D. Rockefeller and went further into debt, and soon found they had lost title to their mines and railroad. There was litigation against the Rockefeller interests, and an out-of-court settlement, with Rockefeller paying the Merritts $500,000, which the Merritts turned over to creditors. All the Merritts died with almost no money. Lon Merritt, for example, who died in 1926, left an estate consisting of $1,500 in household goods, $800 worth of miscellaneous items, and $150 in cash.

him as a messenger boy in the telegraph office, and like Carnegie, Oliver had entered the iron and steel business. But Carnegie viewed Oliver, a handsome, charming man with a twinkle in his eye, as a "speculator," meaning, in Carnegie's view, that he was a man who could not be relied upon. Oliver was no more of a plunger than most other businessmen of the Gilded Age. Carnegie himself had been a speculator for years and had amassed his first fortune that way. But he was past that now and chose to forget it.

Frick, however, was extremely desirous of going ahead with the deal. He pointed out its merits to Carnegie, won the approval of other company associates, and in November 1892, in his capacity as president of the Carnegie Steel Company, accepted Oliver's proposition. Frick's action was one of the most important in the history of the Carnegie enterprise. With other steps that Carnegie and Frick would take—continuing to reduce labor costs, the constant introduction of new machines, exerting control in the steel towns, the establishment of an export trade—it began the making of a colossus, a company that would be horizontally and vertically integrated, with holdings in natural resources, ship and rail transportation, and iron and steel manufacturing, all that was necessary to make and market steel. It would be a company the likes of which the world had not seen nor likely will see again. It was the company that set the pace for the rise of American business and the establishment of American economic power as the nation entered the twentieth century.

II

The richness of the Mesabi ore and the advantages in its lying so close to the surface quickly became apparent. Eight men working a steam shovel could mine more in an hour than several hundred miners in an underground mine in a day. The ore could be brought out at a few cents per ton, compared with three dollars or more per ton for ore in deep mines.

None of this, at first, could change Carnegie's mind. Through 1893 and 1894, he continued to disparage Oliver and his ore claims, not only because he distrusted Oliver, but also because he had lost substantially before on an ore investment. "The Oliver bargain I do not regard as very valuable," he told associates in April 1894. "You will find that this ore venture, like all our other ventures in ore, will result in more trouble and less profit than almost any branch of our business. I hope you will make a note of this prophecy."

But by early 1896, Carnegie was beginning to accept the fact that the

Minnesota iron range offered an abundance of rich ore that could be cheaply mined. "The Mesabi ore field, with mines each containing from thirty to fifty millions of tons of proved ore, which has only to be shovelled into cars, renders competition from other fields almost impossible," he wrote an associate in November 1896. He told the Stanley Committee in 1912: "The truth of the matter is until I went to Lake Superior and saw and studied the question, I was averse to buying ores at all. [Then] I went to Lake Superior myself, because at that time I had thought we would not engage in the risk of mining, but I went up myself and looked over the whole question of ore there, and I saw those immense steam shovels shoveling up this ore at 15 or 20 cents a ton—and changed. 'We will go and own our own ore.' "

For a time, however, Frick's action in allying the Carnegie company with Oliver looked questionable. Almost immediately upon the conclusion of the agreement between Oliver and Frick, the depression of 1893 occurred. The Merritts were vastly overextended; while stouthearted visionaries, they were not businessmen. Oliver kept his interest in the Oliver Iron Mining Company. But the Merritts, in distress, turned to John D. Rockefeller, the oil magnate, and in 1894, in negotiations conducted between the Merritts and Rockefeller's associate Frederick T. Gates, Rockefeller assumed almost complete control of a separate Merritt operation, the Lake Superior Iron Mines Company, which included six mines, the Merritt railroad to Duluth, and shipping facilities. Now two millionaires, Carnegie and Rockefeller, had holdings on the iron range, and there were rumors that Rockefeller intended to enter the steel industry. The industry was abuzz with stories that Carnegie and the Rockefellers were preparing for combat.

The two were far too canny for that, however. Neither wanted competition. Carnegie wanted to lock up the iron range's ore and also outflank Rockefeller. Rockefeller—whom Carnegie insisted on calling Reckafellor or Rockafellow—was interested in ensuring ore shipments for the extensive Great Lakes shipping fleet he had acquired. The two interests entered into negotiations, and in December 1896 an agreement was reached in which the Oliver Mining Company and the Carnegie Steel Company would lease all the Rockefeller ore holdings and pay a royalty of twenty-five cents for each ton extracted from the Rockefeller lands. The Oliver and Carnegie companies agreed to extract at least 1.2 million tons of ore a year from the Rockefeller holdings and to ship the ore on the Rockefeller railroad to Duluth and on Rockefeller's ships and railroads to the new Lake Erie harbor at Conneaut, Ohio, east of Cleveland, near the New York State border. Rockefeller agreed not to enter the steel business and Carnegie and Oliver agreed not to purchase or lease other Mesabi ore lands without Rockefeller's approval. The agreement was to last fifty years.

The agreement sent shock waves through the iron and steel industry, for its terms were highly favorable to the Carnegie forces: the twenty-five-cent-a-ton ore royalty that Carnegie was to pay was far below the conventional royalty of sixty-five cents, and the shipping prices, eighty cents a ton by rail and sixty-five cents a ton by the Great Lakes, undercut rates paid by other steel companies. The trade paper *Iron Age* said that the agreement "completes the last link in a chain which gives the Carnegie Steel Company a position unequalled by any steel producer in the world."

The agreement set off a panic among other ore holders, and many rushed to sell, fearing Carnegie would reduce prices and destroy them. Ore markets were demoralized, and prices for ore and ore lands fell dramatically. Carnegie was prohibited by his agreement with Rockefeller from acquiring more Mesabi mines. But by July 1897 Oliver had reported that he could lease or purchase mines on other Great Lakes ranges—the Norrie and Tilden mines, on the Gogebic Range, and the Pioneer, on the Vermillion Range—at favorable prices. Carnegie was again hesitant, saying that the company should lease, not purchase, mines. Oliver leased the Tilden and Pioneer mines and, after a personal appeal to Carnegie—"Do not allow my hard summer's work to go for naught"—obtained the approval of the Carnegie board of managers in September 1897 to purchase the Norrie mine. He later purchased the Pioneer mine. Joseph Frazier Wall said of Oliver, "Never did a man have to work as hard to present a fortune to others."

Now the Carnegie company controlled the Mesabi, Gogebic, and Vermillion ranges. It would no longer have to buy ore on the open market and, *Iron Age* said, was "largely independent of any wide fluctuations in the cost of raw materials." Thus was the north country opened for development. Towns were thrown up, roads built, immigrants brought in to work the mines. Production was enormous. At one Mesabi mine obtained by Oliver, one steam shovel loaded fifty-eight hundred tons of ore in ten hours. In 1900, three giant shovels, operating on one shift a day, mined 915,000 tons of ore. A twenty-five-ton railroad car could be filled in two and a half minutes. As Carnegie said of his Mesabi holdings, "Pretty good, I think."

III

As the Carnegie Steel Company established control of the Great Lakes ore lands, Carnegie began efforts to gain superiority in transportation, an area that had vexed him for years.

Although Carnegie had risen in business largely through the railroads, he regarded them as his bitter enemies, convinced that he had long been forced to pay higher freight rates than his competitors. "No other item on the cost sheets upset him as much as transportation costs," Wall said. As an old railroad man, Carnegie knew all about railroad rebates, a widespread practice of the time, and about how often great differences existed between the published rates and what railroad customers actually paid. He was an expert at finding out the rates that his competitors paid, and he often used these figures against the company that was his chief tormentor, his old employer, the Pennsylvania Railroad.

In 1884, Carnegie joined in a major campaign that William K. Vanderbilt of the New York Central Railroad was waging against the Pennsylvania. It was usually the policy of railroads in those days to respect each other's territories, but in 1884 the Pennsylvania invaded the territory of the New York Central by backing a new railroad, the New York, West Shore, and Buffalo. In response, Vanderbilt purchased the long-dormant charter of another railroad, the South Pennsylvania, which years before had acquired the authority to purchase the right-of-way for a railroad between Harrisburg, Pennsylvania, and Pittsburgh.

Vanderbilt asked Carnegie to come in on his side, and Carnegie did so eagerly, enlisting as supporters a number of Pittsburgh businessmen who, like Carnegie, were excited about the prospect of a second railroad through southern Pennsylvania to rival the Pennsylvania, and about the lower freight rates they believed would result. The businessmen put up five million dollars, and construction of a new route by the South Pennsylvania began that summer. But the plan was scuttled when the banker and investor J. Pierpont Morgan intervened. Morgan thought competition was unnecessary and wasteful, and in July 1885 he gathered representatives of the two parties on his yacht, the *Corsair,* off the New Jersey coast, to settle the matter. Under Morgan's mediation, the two sides exchanged properties and agreed that each could do with them what it wished. The New York Central used the West Shore property it acquired to run a line up the Hudson River to Albany. The Pennsylvania abandoned the southern Pennsylvania route it received, despite the enormous amount of money that Vanderbilt and others had invested and the efforts that had been made—the construction of piers over the Susquehanna

River, the grading of the roadbed, the blasting of tunnels through the Allegheny Mountains, all of which had taken the lives of more than two thousand workers.*

Carnegie was angry about the settlement and the loss of the money he and his associates had advanced, and he fumed for years. In 1895, he again moved against the Pennsylvania. Frick opposed attacking the railroad, saying that it was the Carnegie Steel Company's best rail customer and that it transported Carnegie shipments at reasonable cost and provided extensive rebates to the Frick Coke Company. Carnegie was not swayed. Now that he controlled the ore fields, he was determined to have his own railroad between the ore port of Conneaut, Ohio, and his unloading facilities at Bessemer, Pennsylvania, next to Braddock. In 1895, he entered into negotiations to purchase an almost defunct railroad, the Pittsburgh, Shenango, and Lake Erie, which ran from Conneaut, Ohio, to Butler, Pennsylvania, thirty miles north of Pittsburgh. The railroad was "little more than a right of way and two streaks of rust," according to J. H. Bridge, an early Carnegie biographer. In April 1896, three million dollars was assembled to connect the line from Butler to Bessemer, with Carnegie putting up two million.

In May, Carnegie went on the offensive. He wrote to Frank Thomson, a vice-president of the Pennsylvania and a nephew of Carnegie's mentor J. Edgar Thomson, that he had purchased the Pittsburgh, Shenango, and Lake Erie. He noted that it crossed four main railroad lines and that he could thus easily divert his freight to those lines at favorable rates. Carnegie and Thomson met. "What are you fighting the Pennsylvania Railroad for?" Thomson asked. "You were brought up in its service. We were boys together."

"Well, Frank, I knew you would ask that, and here is your answer," Carnegie said. He handed Thomson a list of the freight rates that his competition paid, which were in many cases lower than the rates that the Pennsylvania charged the Carnegie Steel Company. The Pennsylvania capitulated. It could not afford to fight, for Carnegie Steel was the largest freight-shipper in the world. Rates were reduced on ore, coke, and limestone, and Thomson pledged to ship Carnegie's steel products at rates equal to those of his competitors. Carnegie promised to prohibit the Pennsylvania's competitors from running lines into his plants. The agree-

---

* The right-of-way sat abandoned for half a century, until the 1930s, when it was taken over by the state of Pennsylvania and used as the route of the Pennsylvania Turnpike between Pittsburgh and Philadelphia. Drivers today travel through tunnels blasted for the railroad.

ment saved Carnegie $1.5 million a year on shipments of raw materials in the next few years and more after that. The parties to the agreement also pledged "to bring the PRR and the CS CO. [Carnegie Steel Company] into close alliance." The agreement was "never to be referred to." Carnegie wrote Thomson to thank "the dear old Pennsylvania Railroad" and said that he hoped the railroad would get "a great deal more traffic than ever."

Carnegie now set out to rejuvenate the Pittsburgh, Shenango, and Lake Erie, the line that would connect his ore-unloading facilities with his furnaces in the Monongahela Valley. He brought in new engines, including two of the largest locomotives ever constructed, each of which could pull twenty-five fully loaded steel freight cars. It was said at the time that these were the heaviest freight trains ever pulled by one engine. The Pittsburgh, Shenango, and Lake Erie quickly became the most efficient freight road in the world. Then, in early 1898, Carnegie purchased the entire Conneaut harbor area and spent $250,000 to install the most up-to-date unloading equipment. When the harbor was finished, a sixteen-thousand-ton ore vessel could be unloaded in fourteen hours, and twenty freight cars an hour could be loaded. The ore was then transported south on the railroad, renamed the Pittsburgh, Bessemer, and Lake Erie, to Bessemer, where the ore was unloaded and shipped to furnaces by Carnegie's highly efficient Union Railroad. The Union was the railroad, put together by Frick, that transported materials between the company's Monongahela Valley plants. Carnegie had broken the power of the Pennsylvania as it applied to his national shipments and now owned the most efficient private industrial railroad in the country.

Only one final stroke was needed to complete Carnegie's transportation monopoly. By 1897, he was shipping more than 3 million tons of ore down the Great Lakes from Duluth, Minnesota, to Conneaut, Ohio, far more than the 1.2 million tons he had pledged in his agreement with Rockefeller to ship on Rockefeller's ore vessels. Carnegie was shipping the excess ore on other shipping lines, but they often charged far higher rates than Rockefeller. In 1899, Carnegie arranged for the purchase of six ore vessels from the Lake Superior Iron Company, and established the Pittsburgh Steamship Company to carry the excess ores of the Carnegie Steel Company and the Oliver enterprises. Carnegie now controlled all shipping of his iron ores, except for the fifty-mile run from the Mesabi Range to Duluth on Rockefeller's railroad. On the day that the first Carnegie ore vessel left Duluth for the fifteen-hundred-mile journey to Conneaut, Ohio, Carnegie wrote Frick, "Today Pittsburgh becomes a lake port."

IV

As the Carnegie Steel Company solidified its control of raw materials and transport, it also worked hard to establish control in Homestead and the other steel towns following the Homestead strike. Paying particular attention to the Homestead Works, it continued to watch labor costs and to block efforts at unionization.

Carnegie kept his mills running during the depression of 1893, and some praised him for it. But what he was doing was following his old principle of "running full" to capture markets even if it meant reducing prices. In 1893, wages were reduced as much as 60 percent, and the *Pittsburgh Press* said, "These are the lowest scales of any in this section, union or non-union.... The men at Homestead are disgruntled." W. M. Garland, president of the Amalgamated Association of Iron and Steel Workers, said: "Mr. Carnegie seems to think that what the workmen want is work and not money. He coincides with [President] Cleveland's statement that it is better for men to work steadier for less wages than intermittently for higher pay ... but intelligent workmen do not see it [that way] nor will they.... It's the money not the work we are striving for." But the workers and the townspeople could do little. They had been beaten and were demoralized, and the company's efforts to strengthen its control of all the mills and steel towns added to this demoralization.

In 1894, the company established a Bureau of Information—a spy department. Operatives were placed throughout the mills and were on the lookout for loafers, union organizers, and others whom the company regarded as troublemakers. "We are advised and on pretty good authority that there is a move on foot to organize the Structural and Shop men in all the Bridge Works in this district," the director of the Bureau of Information, J. R. Mack, wrote to an operative in 1896. "Please keep your eyes and ears open and the minute you get onto anything of this kind, advise us at once. Be especially particular to give the names of anyone connected with this movement." For a time, the Carnegie Steel Company sent its spies a turkey each Christmas, but this practice was abolished when the Homestead workers realized that the company's agents could be identified by observing who received turkeys, which arrived by express, the week before the holiday.

A disturbing development for the company occurred early in 1899, when a number of workers at the Homestead Works, despite the savage defeat suffered seven years before, attempted again to organize a lodge of the Amalgamated Association.

W. E. Corey, general superintendent at Homestead, quickly picked up word from his spies that workers were trying to organize. Company executives were notified, and in May 1899 Charles M. Schwab, president of the Carnegie Steel Company, informed Carnegie: "Labor seems to be giving us some little trouble in all directions. This week at Homestead there was an effort on the part of some men to reorganize a union. We promptly took action and discharged a half dozen of them yesterday and will do the same today. I feel this will nip the move in the bud."

Yet the Homestead workers continued their efforts to unionize. By mid-June, the matter was brought up at a meeting of the company's board of managers, chaired by Schwab.

SCHWAB: The labor problem is one I want the Board to be familiar with and clear upon. The Amalgamated Association is making a very strong effort to get into our Homestead Steel Works. They are able to make a better effort in this direction just now because of the large percentage advances in tonnage rates they have been able to obtain from other Iron and Steel Companies, and because of the misleading ways in which these advances in rates are spoken of in the newspapers. There is no question of wages or earnings involved, but the Amalgamated officials are working on the organized labor basis. They have had organizers at Homestead for several months, and John Jarrett [an official of the Amalgamated Association] tells me he is informed that nine hundred of our men at Homestead Steel Works have obligated themselves to join any movement toward organization. I do not believe anything like this number are implicated. We have agents in the Mills, and as fast as we learn the names of any men taking active parts we discharge them. We should not permit the Amalgamated association to get into Homestead again—we should keep them out at any cost, even if it should result in a strike. . . . I would like to know what the board thinks of the situation.

ALEXANDER PEACOCK: I would certainly do everything possible to keep them out.

WILLIAM H. SINGER: I would not let them get a foothold under any circumstances—not under any condition—stop it at once. It would mean not only Homestead but the rest of the Works. We have gone through that condition of affairs, and it cost us a good deal of money to get our works back again; but it was money well spent.

COREY: Every man we discharged, excepting one, on being asked if he was satisfied with the wages, replied that he was, but that he preferred to work in a union mill.

FRANCIS T. F. LOVEJOY: I would rather see the works blown up with dynamite than turned over to the control of those scoundrels.

The eleven board members were unanimous in their opposition to the union. Before the end of June, Carnegie and Frick, in Scotland, sent this message to Schwab: "We heartily endorse views of Board of Managers with regard to Amalgamated Association. Stop Works if necessary to hold present position." Carnegie sent a cable, in code, to Schwab, that said: "Seems to me best plan you strike first blow, post notice understand efforts organize union. Desire notify men we never will recognize Amalgamated because it broke agreement. Men can decide stop or run just as they please. Every member firm determined never recognize Amalgamated."

Schwab ordered that a notice be posted in the Homestead Works stating that the Carnegie Steel Company would under no circumstances recognize a union at Homestead. Then forty workers believed to be active in the effort to revive the Amalgamated Association were discharged. A committee of workmen called upon Corey and demanded that the discharged workers be reinstated. If they were not rehired, the union men said, the works would be struck.

Corey fired the men who had come to see him. The union then placed pickets at plant gates to meet with workers as they came off their shifts, but only a few dozen men on each shift, according to Corey, stayed off the job. One Sunday night, a scuffle occurred, and some workers who stayed on the job had their lunch buckets kicked from their hands. But the workers would not come out on strike.

Schwab was elated. "I think Mr. Corey should have the congratulations of the Board for the way in which he has handled this matter," he said. "Any other course of action would have caused us a great deal of trouble." Corey professed modesty, saying that credit for the victory belonged to others—the company's spies. He said: "Thank you; but I think our thanks are also due M. M. Lindsay and Milton for the manner in which they have kept us posted. They covered every meeting, and gave us most thorough reports from inside on all that was going on."

The next day, Schwab wrote Carnegie in Europe: "We have completely knocked out any attempt to organize Homestead workmen. . . . I now feel satisfied no further attempt will be made for some time at least."

V

A final matter remained for Carnegie to resolve—his relationship with Henry Clay Frick.

The two had gotten on famously in the first years of their association, but over time their relationship had cooled. The two men were unalike, except that they were both strong-willed and were in business together. Though he had supported him at the time, Carnegie was convinced that Frick had mishandled the Homestead strike by fighting with the workers rather than keeping the works closed until the workers capitulated; the two men had also disagreed over the purchase of the ore lands and Carnegie's campaign against the Pennsylvania Railroad.

Frick for his part regarded Carnegie as a hypocrite. Frick knew that Carnegie, despite how he portrayed himself in his articles and on the world stage, was no more a tribune of the working classes than was Frick himself. Moreover, Frick had never been one of Carnegie's "boys," like Schwab, Phipps, and others. He had made himself what he was on his own and had joined Carnegie when he was already a wealthy man. He was no bootlicker.

A major confrontation between Carnegie and Frick flared in late 1894, when Carnegie tried to absorb another coke firm, the W. J. Rainey Company, into the Frick Coke Company and to change the name of the combined firm to the Frick-Rainey Coke Company—all without informing Frick. Rainey had been a rival of Frick's since the beginning of the coke industry in the early 1870s and was Frick's largest competitor. Frick disliked him and wanted nothing to do with him. When he learned of Carnegie's plan, Frick was enraged. He resigned as president of the Carnegie Steel Company and the Frick Coke Company, and asked Carnegie to buy out his interest in the former. Carnegie accepted the resignations and offered some patronizing advice: "You are not well, my friend. . . . Go to Egypt . . . take the cure." Frick, seething, replied that unless Carnegie stopped making statements about his health, "I will take such measures as will convince you that I am fully able to take care of myself." More exchanges ensued and finally Carnegie dispatched this note: "It is simply ridiculous, my dear Mr. Frick, that any full-grown man is not to make the acquaintance of Mr. Rainey, or anybody else, without your august permission—really laughable. . . . You are determined to resign. All right."

Phipps and Schwab stepped in as peacemakers, however, and Frick was persuaded to reconsider his resignations. Carnegie, to help make peace, agreed to have Frick appointed chairman of the Carnegie Steel Company's board. Carnegie regarded the position as honorary. Frick did not.

In 1898, another dispute arose. At that time the Carnegie Steel Company dominated the world's steel industry. Profits for 1898 were $10 million, an increase of $3 million over 1897. For more than a year, Carnegie, in Scotland in the summer and at Cannes in the winter, had made vague statements about selling out in order to devote more time to leisure and philanthropy. Frick and Phipps were interested in arranging for the purchase of the company, and in December 1898 Carnegie informed Frick that he was free to go ahead.

In April 1899, Frick and Phipps believed that they had located three potential buyers—two brothers, William and James H. Moore, and John W. "Bet-a-Million" Gates. Frick told Carnegie that he had to keep the names of the men secret for a time but that he and Phipps had received a proposal. The Carnegie Steel Company would be purchased for $250 million and the Frick Coke Company for $70 million. For his holdings, Carnegie would receive $57 million in cash and $100 million in 5-percent bonds. Carnegie said that he would accept the offer, but he was suspicious because the names of the investors were not revealed and because they wanted ninety days to raise the capital. He demanded $1.7 million in cash, as a deposit for an option on his holdings. Frick and Phipps agreed. The syndicate advanced $1 million and Frick and Phipps put up $700,000 of their own money.

In May, in Scotland, Carnegie learned the names of the proposed buyers. He was furious. Both the Moores and Gates were notorious speculators, the Moores with such companies as Diamond Match and National Biscuit, Gates in the steel industry and on Wall Street. At the same time, the investors found themselves unable to raise the cash for the purchase. The banker J. P. Morgan, sharing Carnegie's views of the Moores and of Gates, said that no sound investor would lend to such dubious speculators. In June, it became apparent that the money could not be obtained within the ninety-day period. Frick and Phipps journeyed to Carnegie's Skibo Castle, in Scotland, to seek an extension from him. "Not an hour!" he said. The sale collapsed. Frick and Phipps were then informed that Carnegie refused to refund the $1.7 million deposit. As it happened, Carnegie was then making additions to Skibo costing about a million dollars, and in later years, when he gave guests tours of the residence, atop the hills overlooking the Dornoch Firth, he took joy in saying that the additions were "just a nice little present from Mr. Frick."

Later in 1899, the final collision between Carnegie and Frick occurred. In late 1888, the two had made an oral agreement, to commence January 1, 1899, under which the Frick Coke Company agreed to sell coke to the Carnegie Steel Company for $1.35 a ton, fifteen cents below the market rate. Both men soon became unhappy with the agreement. Carnegie was disturbed because if the coke market fell below $1.35, he would still have to pay that price. Frick was disturbed because the coke market had gone up and he was taking a beating. He began to bill

Carnegie Steel at higher rates—$1.45, then $1.60, then $1.75. The company refused to pay the higher rates, and Frick said that he would ship it no more coke, even though he was still chairman of the board. Schwab, the president and chief operating officer of Carnegie Steel, was befuddled; he instructed his treasurer to pay the bills submitted by Frick but to mark the amounts over $1.35 as "payments on advances only."

In October 1899, Carnegie returned from Scotland and demanded that Frick stand by the $1.35 agreement. Frick refused, saying that no contract existed. Carnegie fumed. "No, sir," he said. "Frick can't repudiate contracts for any company which myself and friends control. We are not that kind of cats."

A complicating matter arose. Frick had recently acquired a piece of land, known as the Wiley Farm, at Peters Creek, Pennsylvania, and was contemplating placing it on the market. Schwab said that Carnegie Steel might need the land at some time in the future. Frick offered it to the company at thirty-five hundred dollars an acre, and in November 1899, the board, including Carnegie, accepted. Not long after, however, Carnegie began making remarks to his associates critical of Frick for selling land to his partners at a profit. Carnegie said that Frick had committed "an improper act." Frick heard of Carnegie's remarks, and the matter—the coke rates and the land sale—broke into the open at the next board meeting.

Frick said: "I learn that Mr. Carnegie, while here, stated that I showed cowardice in not bringing up the question of the price of coke. . . . He also stated that he had his doubts as to whether I had any right, while Chairman of the Board of Managers of the Carnegie Steel Company, to make such a purchase [of the Peters Creek site]. . . . Why was he not manly enough to say to my face what he said behind my back? . . . Harmony is so essential for the success of any organization that I have stood a great many insults from Mr. Carnegie in the past, but I will submit to no further insults in the future."

Carnegie, enraged, wrote board member George Lauder, Jr., in reply: "Frick goes out. . . . He's too old, too infirm in health and mind. . . . I have nothing but pity for Frick. . . . His recent exhibition is childish." Schwab respected Frick but sided with Carnegie, writing him: "I am always with you. Aside from deep personal regard and feeling for you, you have heaped honors and riches upon me and I would indeed be an ingrate to do otherwise. . . . Believe me, my dear Mr. Carnegie, I am always with you and yours to command."

Carnegie demanded Frick's resignation as chairman of the board of managers of Carnegie Steel, and on December 5 Frick resigned his chairmanship, although he retained his interest in the company.

The matter of the coke prices remained, however. Carnegie moved to depose Frick from the Frick Coke Company. To do this, he packed the board with his allies, and at a meeting on January 8 a contract was approved requiring the Frick Coke Company to sell coke to the Carnegie Steel Company at $1.35 a ton and ordering a refund of charges in excess of that amount. Frick stalked from the meeting, declaring, "You will find there are two sides to this matter."

The next morning, January 9, 1900, Carnegie called upon Frick at his office. Carnegie did most of the talking, Frick most of the listening. Carnegie demanded that Frick accept the terms of the new coke contract and bring no lawsuits against Carnegie Steel. Frick asked, "And if I don't accept this contract and am successful in enjoining the Frick Coke Company from making any deliveries to Carnegie Steel, what then?"

Carnegie now chose to invoke the company's "iron-clad agreement" of 1883. Under its provisions, Carnegie informed Frick, Frick would, by a two-thirds vote of his colleagues, be forced to sell his interest in Carnegie Steel back to the company at book value. Both men knew there was a tremendous disparity between the company's real value and its book value. In 1899, the real value of the company was calculated at $250 million, while the book value was $50 million.

Frick leaped from his chair. He shouted: "For years I have been convinced that there is not an honest bone in your body. Now I know that you are a goddamned thief. We will have a judge and jury of Allegheny County decide what you are to pay me."

Carnegie hurried to the boardroom of the Carnegie Steel Company. The board of managers was assembled. He described what had occurred at Frick's office and demanded that the iron-clad agreement be invoked and that Frick be directed to sell his interest in Carnegie Steel to the company. The members agreed. Within the next two days, thirty-two of the company's thirty-six associates had approved the action.

Frick kept his promise, too. In February 1900, he filed suit in the Allegheny County Court of Common Pleas. The suit made public, for the first time, the profits of the Carnegie Steel Company—twenty million dollars in 1899, forty million expected for 1900. The nation was fascinated. *The New York Times* made it clear that the company's immense profits had been made while the steel industry was protected by high tariffs—the same issue that had come to the fore during the Homestead strike, almost a decade before. *Iron Age* said: "The part of the Frick-Carnegie conflict that has caused the most talk is the revealed profits of the Company. It has roused all the old anger against trusts. There is much free trade talk in the newspapers." Republican leaders were frightened, believing that antibusiness talk and stories would harm the party in the 1900 election, as the Homestead strike had in 1892.

The matter was too messy to be allowed to continue. Associates and friends of Carnegie and Frick, plus leading businessmen, brought pressure on the two men to settle. On March 22, 1890, representatives of Carnegie and Frick met in Atlantic City, New Jersey. Carnegie refused to attend or to allow partners who had stuck with him to attend. Frick was represented by Phipps and Francis T. F. Lovejoy, the company secretary. A new company was created, the Carnegie Company, with Carnegie Steel and Frick Coke as separate divisions. The company was capitalized at $320 million with $160 million in common stock and $160 million in 5-percent first-mortgage bonds. Carnegie's interest was established at $174,526,000, with $86,379,000 in stock and $88,147,000 in bonds. Frick was accorded $15,484,000 in stock and $15.8 million in bonds, far in excess of the $4.9 million he would have received if he had been bought out under the iron-clad agreement.

That was that. Although he retained his stock, Frick was forced out of the company. After their stormy meeting in Frick's office in Pittsburgh in January 1900, Carnegie and Frick never saw or talked to each other again, even though for years the two maintained New York residences twenty-one blocks apart, Carnegie at Fifth Avenue and Ninety-first Street, Frick in a mansion he constructed for $5.4 million on Fifth Avenue at Seventieth Street. It was said that Carnegie, not long before his death in 1919, sent a message to Frick saying that they both were getting on in years and that perhaps it would be pleasant if they could meet and forget the past. Frick said to Carnegie's messenger, "Tell Mr. Carnegie I'll meet him in hell, where we are both going."

Carnegie was in command. He had created an industrial empire of iron ore, coke, iron and steel furnaces, rolling mills, ships, railroads. He had money beyond comprehension. The Carnegie Company was the largest capitalized company in United States history, a private company, controlled by Carnegie. No aggregation of such industrial power had ever been so under the domination of a single man. This company had led the way in the establishment of the American steel industry. The American steel industry dominated the world's steel industry. Steel was society's basic metal—for railroad tracks, engines, and railroad cars; for buildings, bridges, and dams; for the naval fleet that had enabled the United States to defeat the Spanish in the Spanish-American War and to begin its century as a world power; for a new contraption, the automobile, already in the experimental stage. As Carnegie wrote in January 1901 in the *New York Evening Post,* in a piece that was part of the newspaper's turn-of-the-century edition, "Farewell, then, Age of Iron; all hail, King Steel, and success to the republic, the future seat and centre of his empire, where he is to sit enthroned and work his wonders upon the earth."

8

"THE COMBINATION
OF COMBINATIONS"

On the evening of December 12, 1900, Charles M. Schwab was in New York, and he had brought with him his dress clothes. The man who had started as a Braddock stake-pounder and who as a child had held Andrew Carnegie's horses was going to a dinner in his own honor, a fancy stag affair given by the cream of the New York financial community at the University Club.

The dinner was partly a gesture of politeness. Some weeks before, two New York financiers, J. Edward Simmons and Charles Stewart Smith, had visited Pittsburgh, and Schwab, ever the ebullient host, had entertained them in splendid fashion. He had shown them the new armor-plate vault that the Carnegie enterprise was manufacturing for the Union Trust Company in Pittsburgh and had led them on a tour of the Carnegie Company's iron and steel plants in the Monongahela Valley. Now, with Schwab in New York, the financiers were reciprocating his cordiality and were placing such importance on the dinner that it was becoming a topic of much discussion in the New York business community. A few days before the affair, Andrew Carnegie wrote an associate, "Everyone invited has accepted, and [they are] really the biggest men in New York."

There were other reasons for the dinner. One was to introduce Schwab to the New York financial community. Schwab was important in Pittsburgh but like many western manufacturing men was little known in the East. Among the eighty business and financial leaders invited to the dinner were E. H. Harriman, the railroad man; August Belmont and Jacob H. Schiff, investment bankers; H. H. Rogers, president of Standard Oil and a leading associate of John D. Rockefeller; and perhaps the most well known and important guest, J. Pierpont Morgan, the financier, who that evening was seated to Schwab's right. Andrew Carnegie made an appearance but left early to give an address elsewhere. Finally, and most important, the dinner was planned to provide a forum at which Schwab could spell out his vision of the American steel industry in the twentieth century.

Schwab was an excellent speaker. He had charmed the Homestead and Braddock workers for years, and he would charm the New York crowd, too. It was said years afterward that he had never been in finer form than on this night. His moment came when, after dinner, as guest of honor, he was called upon to speak. Rising from the table and saying that he had no text (Schwab rarely spoke from a text), he began with the best of his stock openings, one he had used for years and would use for years more. Looking at the men before him, he said he would talk about steel because he knew nothing else to talk about. (Years later, J. H. Reid, a businessman present at the dinner, recalled Schwab's opening remarks. "Mr. Schwab started out by saying that he could not talk about anything but steel. I remember that because he always starts every speech that way.")

Schwab spoke for about half an hour on the themes of integration and economy of operations, which were necessary, he said, for the American steel industry to reduce prices, increase its authority in the United States, and capture the world steel market. The demand for steel was growing and would continue to grow, he claimed. He said that the Carnegie Company had managed to reduce production costs to the lowest possible level but that no additional major reductions could be made. Only a company even larger than that enterprise could achieve the integration and savings necessary to capture the world market.

Substantial savings could be made in organization and distribution,

Schwab said. To realize them, not only the Carnegie Company but the entire steel industry had to reorganize to provide for maximum efficiency: obsolete mills or mills in poor locations had to be abandoned; new plants had to be constructed in locations where markets could best be served; wasteful competition had to be ended. He said that only a single steel corporation, fully integrated, with iron-ore, limestone, and coke holdings, blast furnaces, steel mills, and rolling and finishing mills, could achieve what he was proposing. Such an enterprise would be a giant trust, organized for rational production, with each mill and other facility playing its part in the whole. If such an enterprise were to be created, he stated, it could manufacture the best steel and steel products and, because of its efficiency, sell its products in the United States and abroad at such low prices that competitors would be eliminated. It was clear that what Schwab had in mind was the greatest steel company the world had ever seen.

All the guests were fascinated, but none more than Morgan, the shrewd, stern financier at Schwab's elbow. Morgan had picked up a cigar for an after-dinner smoke, but it remained unlit throughout Schwab's address. When Schwab finished, Morgan asked him to step aside for a private conversation. Burton J. Hendrick, author of a biography of Carnegie, wrote in 1922: "After the cheers had subsided, [Morgan] took Schwab by the arm and led him to a corner. For half an hour the two men engaged in intimate conversation. The banker had a hundred questions to ask, to which Schwab replied with terseness and rapidity." Morgan told Schwab that he looked forward to a longer session to discuss Schwab's views on the steel industry, and then the two men departed, Morgan for his New York home, Schwab for Pennsylvania Station and the night train to Pittsburgh. Schwab, then living in the magnificent superintendent's mansion next to the Carnegie Library in Homestead, wished to be home for the holidays and for the celebrations to mark the turning of the century.

The dinner was "one of those informal parliaments" at which "without the interference of police or senators the issues of heavy industry could be faced peacefully and a balance of power effected," the critic and economic historian Matthew Josephson wrote in 1934. In 1935, the social historian Frederick Lewis Allen called the dinner "one of those events which direct the destiny of a nation." It began a series of events that culminated three months later—as the new century began—in the establishment of the United States Steel Corporation, "the combination of combinations," in the phrase of the time, the corporation that would come to stand for the American steel industry and, in many ways, American manufacturing and the nation's industrial might in the twentieth century.

II

The effort to form an enterprise of the kind Schwab envisioned began a few weeks after the dinner. In January 1901, Morgan asked Schwab to come east to meet with him. Without informing Carnegie of the meeting, Schwab took the train for New York and then went down by hansom cab to Morgan's mansion at 219 Madison Avenue, at Thirty-sixth Street.

Also summoned to the gathering were Robert Bacon, a young associate of Morgan's who was a Harvard graduate and would later be secretary of state and ambassador to Britain, and John W. "Bet-a-Million" Gates, the man whose association with the two other plungers, the Moore brothers, had turned Andrew Carnegie against the sale of the Carnegie holdings that Henry Clay Frick had attempted to arrange in 1899. Morgan shared Carnegie's distrust of Gates but knew that Gates was knowledgeable about the steel industry, particularly in the West, and about Wall Street.

The gathering, in Morgan's high-ceilinged, mahogany-paneled library, lasted throughout the night, as the men laid plans for the consolidation of steel companies that Schwab had outlined in December. Morgan was fearful that Carnegie, by entering the manufacture of steel products, would destabilize the iron and steel industry, in which Morgan now had substantial investments. Of course, to be significant, any consolidation would have to include the Carnegie Company. At length, Morgan asked whether Carnegie would sell. Schwab said he did not know; Carnegie was unpredictable. "Well, if Andy wants to sell, I'll buy," Morgan replied. "Go and find [out] his price." Schwab said he would try. The sun was streaming through the windows of Morgan's library when Schwab left the Morgan mansion and took a horse-drawn cab to his hotel.

A number of actions had set the stage for the December dinner and the January meeting. Despite the dominance and profitability of the Carnegie empire, a new order was emerging in the American steel industry. The Carnegie empire was the largest industrial operation in the world, with twenty thousand employees. Deflation of labor costs, begun with the Homestead lockout, plus sales generated by the Spanish-American War and the Boer War, had meant dramatically increased profits. In 1900, the company had earned forty million dollars, as expected. But beginning in 1898, a vast combination movement had struck the steel industry, part of a larger consolidation movement that was sweeping through American manufacturing. Dozens of independent iron and steel companies, including steel-product companies, were combined. One consolidation alone, the Tin Plate Trust, a promotion of the Moore brothers, brought together 265 mills, practically all the tin-plate mills in the United States.

Some of these combinations were shaky and speculative, with antiquated machines and mills and watered stock. Others were modern and well organized, among them enterprises brought together with Morgan financing—Federal Steel, National Tube, and American Bridge. The formidable Federal Steel Company—created in 1898 by the merger of Illinois Steel, long the largest western producer, with a number of other western companies—had been put together, with the financial support of Morgan, by Elbert H. Gary, a Chicago attorney. When it was completed, Morgan asked Gary to become its chairman.

Carnegie was contemptuous when Federal Steel was put together, as he had been two decades before, in 1879, when Andrew Kloman and the six other Pittsburgh steel manufacturers had begun construction of the Homestead Works. "I think Federal the greatest concern the world ever saw for manufacturing stock certificates—we are not in it—but they will fail sadly in steel," Carnegie said. But Carnegie was wrong, as he had been about the Homestead Works. Federal Steel, located in McKeesport, just ten miles from Homestead, quickly emerged, under Gary's steady hand, as one of the Carnegie Company's most formidable competitors. By 1900, production at Federal Steel had increased to 1.225 million tons, still far below that of Carnegie, with 2.97 million tons, but an astonishing achievement.

By 1900, adventuresome companies like Federal Steel, which specialized in finishing, were expanding backward, that is, constructing or planning to construct their own iron- and steelmaking facilities, and canceling or preparing to cancel their steel orders from the Carnegie Company. With Frick having been forced out of the company early in the year, Carnegie was again running it directly. He and his associates, notably Schwab, knew that they had to meet the challenge posed by the consolidated companies.

Carnegie was sixty-five years old and rich almost beyond comprehension, but he was still a combative businessman. He determined to strike, and strike hard, against his competitors. If the companies that made finished articles were to have the impudence to integrate backward into the manufacture of iron and steel, Carnegie would integrate forward into the manufacture of steel products. "Our policy should be to make finished articles," he wrote Schwab.

A number of Carnegie partners, among them Henry Phipps, Jr., and

George Lauder, Jr., were frightened by the notion of renewed industrial warfare. Some of them, Phipps in particular, had been complaining for years of Carnegie's practice of reinvesting profits. They were not young men anymore, and they felt like Jay Gould, the railroad man, who had said, in one of the representative utterances of the Gilded Age, that he was rich and it was time he had some fun.

But Carnegie and Schwab were excited by the notion of renewed conflict. Carnegie wrote Schwab: "We should go into making their products at once. . . . Lose not a day. . . . Crisis has arrived, start at once, hoop, rod, wire, nails mills. . . . Spend freely for finishing mills, railroads, boat lines. . . . Our safety lies in being independent and running our business in our own way. Whenever we do so we have the big trusts at our mercy."

He wrote to the Carnegie Company board of managers: "A struggle is inevitable, and it is a question of the survival of the fittest . . . but no half measures. If you are not going to cross the stream, do not enter at all and be content to dwindle into second place."

The Carnegie board had no choice but to accede to Carnegie's dictums, and, accordingly, in July 1900, the managers voted to build a $1.4 million rod, wire, and nail mill at Duquesne, upriver from Homestead.

Then came an even more stunning decision by Carnegie. He announced that he planned to build a new, $12 million steel works at the forty-five-hundred-acre site that the company owned at Conneaut, Ohio, on Lake Erie.

Conneaut seemed an ideal site for a steel plant. Ore shipped from the Lake Superior mines could be unloaded directly into the iron furnaces, eliminating the need for costly shipment by railroad to the furnaces in the Monongahela Valley. In addition, Carnegie freight cars that hauled ore from Conneaut to Bessemer, on the north shore of the Monongahela River, now returned empty to Conneaut; with a mill at Conneaut, the cars could haul coke north to Conneaut on their return trips at almost no cost. The site also offered other transportation advantages. Steel products manufactured at Conneaut could be shipped on a number of railroad lines that served the area, by the Great Lakes, or possibly on a reconstructed Erie Canal, then under consideration. Carnegie also made it known that the new plant would make steel tubes, a slap at Morgan and his McKeesport National Tube plant.

This was not all that Carnegie was up to. He was back to fighting the railroads, specifically his old bête noire, the Pennsylvania Railroad, which he again was accusing of charging him inflated shipping rates. Frank Thomson, the Pennsylvania Railroad executive with whom Carnegie had arranged the truce in 1896 that provided for the Carnegie enterprises to receive rebates and reduced rates, had died in 1899, and Thomson's successor, Alexander J. Cassatt, was an ardent opponent of rebates. Cassatt united in cooperative relationships with other railroad men, and later in 1899 it was announced that the rebate system was being abolished. Carnegie was furious.

He started his campaign by trying to convince the Pennsylvania Railroad to reduce the rates it charged the Carnegie Company. He was unsuccessful. At the same time, he began an attempt to assume control of other railroads, principally the Western Maryland, that he could tie in with his Pittsburgh, Bessemer, and Lake Erie line and thus gain his own routes to ship his products east. Carnegie also began cooperating with George Gould, son of the railroad buccaneer Jay Gould, who had plans to put together a new transcontinental line from Baltimore through Pittsburgh and St. Louis to the West Coast.

All of this—Carnegie's decision to enter the manufacture of finished products, his decision to build a works at Conneaut, his willingness to face off with the railroads—was closely watched by Morgan, and Morgan was disturbed.

Although regarded as the archetype of the American capitalist, Morgan was in many ways not a capitalist. His holdings were substantial and included railroads, oil, banking, and his two major steel investments, the Federal Steel Company and the National Tube Company, but as Joseph Frazier Wall wrote: "[Morgan] did not really believe in the free enterprise system. . . . Like the most ardent socialists, he hated the waste, duplication, and clutter of unrestricted competition." It was for this reason that he had been so intoxicated by Schwab's portrayal of a combined, efficient steel industry.

Morgan, hearing of Carnegie's plans, declared, "Carnegie is going to demoralize railroads just as he demoralized steel." Morgan had another worry. Federal Steel was not developing into the "rounded proposition" that Morgan and Gary had envisioned. For example, it lacked access to Lake Superior mines. It was these concerns which had led to the Schwab dinner and the January meeting after the Schwab dinner, to Morgan's dream of an enormous, consolidated steel company, and to his assignment of Schwab to find out whether Carnegie wished to sell.

In late January 1901, a week after the meeting with Morgan in his library, Schwab returned to New York to put the matter before Carnegie. Schwab was apprehensive and decided to first approach Carnegie's wife, Louise, to make private inquiries. He called on her at the Carnegies' New York home, told her of his meetings with Morgan, and solicited her views. Would Mr. Carnegie wish to sell? How should Schwab approach him?

Mrs. Carnegie was open to Schwab's suggestions. Her husband, although in robust health, was getting on in years, and Mrs. Carnegie knew that he retained his desire, set down on paper in 1868, thirty-three years before, to retire from business and devote his life to philanthropy. He had already been involved for years in extensive philanthropic efforts, making substantial donations for organs; libraries; a swimming pool at his birthplace, Dunfermline, Scotland; and other projects. But Mrs. Carnegie knew that he wished to pursue his philanthropy on a far grander scale.

She suggested that Schwab approach Carnegie with the utmost tact. Carnegie, two years before, had taken up golf, a growing American craze, and had become fascinated with the game. He was often in his best mood while playing golf or just after playing, particularly if he had won, and Mrs. Carnegie suggested to Schwab that the best place to discuss the possible sale would be at Carnegie's club, St. Andrews, in Westchester County, north of New York City.

The next day, Schwab went up to St. Andrews and the two men set out on the links. The thermometer that day reached only thirty-one degrees, an indication of Carnegie's zest for the game and of Schwab's desire to talk with him in a convivial setting. Carnegie won handily and was in an effervescent mood. They adjourned for lunch to the pleasant stone cottage that Carnegie maintained at the edge of the course. There, while they ate, Schwab disclosed his meeting with Morgan and Morgan's interest in purchasing the Carnegie enterprises. Carnegie was amiable but said little. When lunch was over, Carnegie said he would think matters over. He asked that Schwab call upon him the next morning.

It was a momentous time for the men involved and, it turned out, for the nation. Though Carnegie had talked of retirement and wanted to get on with dispensing his fortune, he had immensely enjoyed the combat of recent months with the heads of the steel trusts, in particular with Morgan. Moreover, he was being asked to sell operations that he had spent much of his life creating. But he had to make a decision, and he always had been a man who could do that. One night was all he needed.

The next morning, Schwab called on Carnegie, who handed him a single piece of paper on which he had scribbled with a blunt lead pencil two columns of figures, one listing his holdings, the other what he thought their worth to be. At the bottom of the paper was a figure that Carnegie adjudged to be the total value of the holdings—$480 million. There would be no haggling. This was what he would accept. Schwab went down to Wall Street, where he met with Morgan. Morgan looked at the statement. He would not haggle, either. "I accept this price," he said. The deal for what would be the largest transaction in American business history at that time had been made.*

Morgan had a few small but ticklish matters to take care of before the massive consolidation he envisioned was complete. John W. "Bet-a-Million" Gates demanded what Morgan, Gary, and others thought to be an exorbitant sum for the American Steel and Wire Company, a company that was to be part of the merger. Hours of haggling were conducted at Morgan's offices at 23 Wall Street until Morgan threatened to build his own plant, and Gates capitulated. On March 2, 1901, a circular announced the establishment of the new corporation. Shortly after the announcement, Gary came to the conclusion that the corporation needed ore lands beyond those being acquired from Carnegie, and this meant acquisition of the vast Rockefeller ore holdings, the Lake Superior Consolidated Iron Mines, which Rockefeller still maintained in Minnesota.

Gary had first to convince Morgan of the necessity of acquiring the mines and then of the necessity of Morgan's going to speak to Rockefeller, whom Morgan disliked intensely. After two awkward meetings, one with Rockefeller and one with his son, Morgan brought in Henry Clay Frick as mediator. Rockefeller admired Frick greatly for the way he had handled the Homestead strike, and he asked him to determine a fair price for the ore lands. Frick did and presented it to Morgan, who accepted it despite Gary's protestations that it was too high. On April 1, 1901, the establishment of the corporation was formally announced, and on April 3 the corporation began to conduct business. The name selected illus-

* Not long after the sale, Morgan realized that he had not personally talked to Carnegie for some time, and he called up Carnegie and asked if he would be so kind as to come meet with him at his office at 23 Wall Street. Carnegie replied that it was the same distance from 23 Wall Street to Carnegie's home at Fifth Avenue and Fifty-first Street (he had built a home further downtown) as it was from Fifty-first Street to 23 Wall Street; since he was the senior of the two men, Carnegie said, perhaps it would be polite for Morgan to journey to see him.

Such matters made little difference to Morgan, and he went to Carnegie's home, where the two men talked for fifteen minutes. When Morgan departed, he said to Carnegie, "Mr. Carnegie, I want to congratulate you on being the richest man in the world!"

A year or so later, they met again, this time aboard ship as they sailed for Europe. "I made one mistake, Pierpont, when I sold out to you," Carnegie said (Morgan was always piqued that Carnegie called him "Pierpont").

"What was that?" Morgan asked.

"I should have asked you for a hundred million more than I did," Carnegie said.

There are two versions of Morgan's reply. In one, he says, "Well, you would have gotten it if you had." In the other, he says, "If you had, I would have paid it to you—if only to be rid of you."

trated its size and power—the United States Steel Corporation. Gary was named chairman, Schwab president.

It was a stupendous achievement. This was America's largest corporation, bringing together in one institution under one management 65 percent of the American steel industry, with a capitalization of $1,402,846,817. It employed 168,000 workers. With the Carnegie and Federal empires, United States Steel controlled what had been the largest and the second-largest iron and steel companies in the nation, Carnegie and Federal. It owned the Lucy and Carrie iron furnaces, and the Braddock, Homestead, and Duquesne works. It owned the Carnegie mines of the Mesabi Range and the other ranges along Lake Superior, and the Rockefeller ore lands—in all, about half of the nation's known iron-ore reserves. It owned the Frick empire, which consisted of fifty-seven thousand acres of coal lands in the Connellsville region of southwestern Pennsylvania, the most valuable coking fields in the world, and twenty-five coke ovens.

Through Federal Steel (itself a combination of the Minnesota Mining Company and the Illinois Steel Company), United States Steel gained ownership of the vast South Works, in Chicago, and the Worcester, Massachusetts, ironworks, which dated from 1833. In John Gates's American Steel and Wire Company, it possessed the mills that had brought barbed wire to the West and helped end the open range and the cattle empires. It owned the trusts that William and James H. Moore had established, the American Tin Plate Company, the American Steel Hoop Company, and the National Steel Company. It owned Morgan companies, among them the American Bridge Company, the American Sheet Steel Company, and the National Tube Company, with its advanced tube mill at McKeesport, Pennsylvania.

In all, the new corporation owned 41 iron mines, 78 blast furnaces, 213 steel mills, 1,000 miles of railroad lines, and 112 Great Lakes ore boats, plus coal and coke barges and towboats. It could make almost anything that could be made from steel: rails; armor plate; beams for buildings, bridges, and dams; sheet metal for home appliances and automobiles; tubes for oil pipe; buckets and drums; wire for fences and the telephone and telegraph industries; nails, screws, needles, pins.

This was a time of trusts, and the nation was used to massive business consolidations, but no one had ever seen anything like this. The new corporation immediately became a matter of controversy, bringing "such a cry of alarm as has never greeted any business enterprise in this country," wrote Ida M. Tarbell, Gary's biographer in the 1920s.

The *Philadelphia Evening Telegraph* predicted that if "a grasping and unrelenting monopoly" resulted from the trend toward concentration represented by the creation of the United States Steel Corporation, then it might bring about "one of the greatest social and political upheavals that has been witnessed in recent history."

The president of Yale University, A. T. Hadley, said that unless trusts were regulated, there would be "an emperor in Washington within twenty-five years." The *London Chronicle* said the establishment of the corporation was "little less than a menace to the commerce of the civilized world. . . . It sets the seal to the triumph of the millionaire." William Jennings Bryan's newspaper, the *Commoner,* jested: " 'America is good enough for me,' remarked J. Pierpont Morgan a few days ago. Whenever he doesn't like it, he can give it back to us." John Brisben Walker wrote in *Cosmopolitan* magazine that, with the creation of the corporation, the world "ceased to be ruled by . . . so-called statesmen" and became ruled by "those who control the concentrated portion of the money supply." Almost immediately the corporation became known as "the Steel Trust." Later, it was called "Big Steel" or "the Corporation."

III

The sale made millionaires of many men, including Carnegie's associates, who seemed to become crazed with their riches. What a fine time it was in Pittsburgh that spring and summer, as the men began to behave in the fashion of millionaires, or in the fashion they believed millionaires should behave. Their behavior gave rise to a new term in America, "Pittsburgh millionaire," meaning people of wealth who act in an ostentatious or vulgar manner.

At least ten former Carnegie partners set sail for Europe with their families. One went alone, except for his mistress. According to Herbert N. Casson, a historian of the steel industry, one new millionaire "ordered a special brand of half-dollar cigars made in Cuba, each with his name and coat of arms on the wrapper," and another "had his wife's portrait painted by every obtainable foreign and American artist." The men, upgrading their wardrobes, for a time brought the silk top hat back into use, and their consumption of Scotch whiskey, which was Carnegie's favorite drink and thus theirs, made it a major import into the United States.

Most of the men stayed in or around Pittsburgh, homebodies despite their wealth. The fashionable place to build large homes at that time was in the suburb of Sewickly, on the north bank of the Ohio River about ten miles west of downtown Pittsburgh, far from the smoke and grime of the mills of the Monongahela Valley.

There, on a high, wooded bluff, the millionaires built stupendous mansions, many of them copied from English country homes or Norman castles. One old Carnegie man, Alexander Peacock, remained on Highland Avenue in Pittsburgh, but he would not be outdone in ostentation. He built a mansion, Rowanlea, and constructed a nine-foot fence with gates so massive they had to be on wheels so that they could be opened and closed. Peacock had greenhouses covering two acres constructed, and it is reported that when he heard of a former colleague who had purchased two gold-plated pianos for his Sewickly home, Peacock purchased four gold-plated pianos for his. At the Duquesne Club, a prestigious club in downtown Pittsburgh, a steward once came upon a former Carnegie partner, sprawled in a chair, covering page after page of the club's embossed stationery with figures. "I am trying," the man said, "to find whether I am worth six million or if it is eight million." He then ordered another drink.

In 1935, David Garrett Kerr, a Carnegie executive who had retired in 1932, said:

Many of them [the Carnegie millionaires] didn't know what to do with their money after they got it. There was a reason. They had been making steel all their lives. They hadn't much time or inclination to go in for outside interests. They hadn't even been counting the money they were piling up for themselves. As a consequence, they were amazed when the Corporation was founded. They found themselves in possession of millions. There was a letdown. All they could do was try to devise ways to spend the money that, after all, meant nothing to them. As a consequence, many of them died comparatively poor. The stock market got some of them, for they were babes in Wall Street. Poor business ventures took away some of their fortunes. Reckless spending and jovial adventures accounted for many more millions.

Carnegie, in New York or, if on vacation, in Europe, disapproved most deeply of this undisciplined spending. But he could do nothing except complain, and that in private. At the Hudson Trust Company, in Hoboken, New Jersey, a special vault—of steel—was constructed to house the nearly $3 million in gold bonds that Carnegie received. Carnegie—the "industrial Napoleon," his friend John Morley called him—never entered the vault to look at the bonds. On March 16, 1901, Carnegie, his wife, and their daughter boarded a steamship for the Mediterranean and the sun. It was fifty-two years, nine months, and thirty days since the young Carnegie, he and his family penniless, had arrived in America on the sailing ship *Wiscasset*.

IV

The United States Steel Corporation—"Morgan's masterpiece," said Morgan biographer John K. Winkler—was created at an optimistic time. The recession that lasted through much of the 1890s had ended. New industrial processes were ready for development; the electrical age and the age of mass production were at hand. America was emerging as a world power. Now an industrial power had been established to dominate the American and world steel industry. Its management was composed of some of the most influential men in American business. The twenty-four-member board contained "every name famous in the industrial annals of the period," Winkler said, with some exaggeration. Among them were John D. Rockefeller, H. H. Rogers of Standard Oil, Marshall Field, W. E. Dodge, P. A. B. Widener, G. A. Griscom, George W. Perkins, Abram S. Hewitt, and four Carnegie men—Frick, Schwab, Phipps, and James Gayley. Gary was chairman of the executive committee. Robert Bacon, the Morgan man, was chairman of the finance committee. Schwab, the president, was regarded as a perfect choice. He was one of the most skilled steelmen in the United States and, in addition, was an excellent publicist for the corporation and the steel industry, always ready with a quote or an anecdote for the representatives of the newspapers and magazines.

Despite his immense riches, Schwab never forgot his simpler days, although, of course, he had no desire to return to them. Not long after the creation of the corporation, he made a nostalgic visit to Homestead and Braddock before leaving for Wall Street and a new life in New York. He spent the day in Homestead and Braddock, poking about the mills and the towns, chatting with workmen and townspeople in the towns where he had gotten his start, learned his trade, and risen to prominence in American business. A newspaperman who spent the day with Schwab reported a number of acts of courtesy by Schwab toward the workmen.

But a new time was at hand. Though Gary knew little about iron or steel, he was regarded as a most capable administrator, one of the first examples of the rise of an attorney to the top ranks of an American business, a pattern that would later be repeated many times. He was, an admirer said, "a statesman rather than a man of affairs."

A number of union leaders also seemed hopeful about the new corporation. The president of the Pittsburgh district of the United Mine Workers of America, Patrick Dolan, said, "If there is a disposition on the part of the men at the head of this new trust to be fair, it will last and flourish." Theodore J. Shaffer, president of the Amalgamated Association of Iron, Steel, and Tin Workers (the tin workers had been added to the union in 1898), said that he thought the new steel combination, under Gary, would help labor achieve its goals. It was possible, Shaffer said, that now the union could secure recognition from the steel industry, the recognition it had lost in the Homestead strike of 1892.

PART TWO

9

THE JUDGE:
A MAN OF PRINCIPLES

Sometime after Elbert H. Gary assumed command of the United States Steel Corporation, he ordered installed in his office at the corporation's headquarters at 71 Broadway an electric sign that he could activate with a button on his desk. The sign was one of his favorite and most useful devices. When he wanted something done and sensed that his subordinates disagreed, he pushed the button and the electric sign flashed IT CAN BE DONE. This was the signal that the meeting was over, that Gary had decided what should be done, and that the men should go and do it.

The use of such a device was typical of Gary and typical of how he operated the United States Steel Corporation. He knew how he wanted things done and insisted that they be done that way. He always had been fastidious—of the four Gary children, only Elbert had let his mother scrub his ears without a fuss. And even as a child he had a fierce belief in the rectitude of his views. Once, a teacher attempted to beat him for a transgression that she believed he had committed. He took the ruler from the teacher's hand and broke it into pieces. "I never allowed a teacher to punish me if I didn't think I deserved it," Gary later said.

Gary was an ardent Methodist. He did not drink, smoke, chew, use vulgar language, or permit off-color stories in his presence. When he was a young lawyer, he led the fight to make Wheaton, Illinois, where he was practicing law, a temperance town. The Judge, as he was called because of the two short terms he had served as judge of the DuPage County court, almost never lost his temper. He believed that in any dispute, one had only to ascertain the facts and then work matters out on the basis of these facts. *Fortune* magazine was to call him "a cold-eyed Methodist lawyer." H. L. Mencken called him "the Christian hired man."

Early in the corporation's existence, it was the custom that each board member receive a twenty-dollar gold piece for attending directors' meetings. Usually, some board members were absent, and the board members who were present would match coins for the leftover gold pieces. Gary put up with this for a time but was annoyed. At length his patience was exhausted, and he declared that the practice was not becoming to the board and thus to the corporation. "I told them that I was not brought up to believe in gambling and I thought the board of directors of the United States Steel Corporation should set a good example," he explained. He told his biographer, Ida M. Tarbell, that he believed Sunday-school teachings should be applied to business.

Gary, however, was a clever man. There was a pragmatic reason for his staunch principles and moralistic tone—to ensure the survival of the corporation with as much strength as possible. Gary believed that his principles, if practiced, would produce a smoothly running enterprise and save the company from criticism and perhaps dissolution by the government.

Gary had hinted at his principles and their purpose before the corporation was established. Morgan had called in a group of lawyers, including Gary, "to inquire if it is the unanimous opinion that the organization is legal and not opposed to any of the existing laws." The lawyers, except one, said that they believed the corporation was legal and would be approved in any court action. The exception was Gary. He said:

I believe, Mr. Morgan, that if there should be a direct attack by the Attorney General against the new corporation at the beginning of its business career, the attack would probably be successful for the reason that so large a percentage of the iron and steel business is included in the new company . . . [that] the Corporation is liable to be held to be a monopoly in opposition to the Sherman [antitrust] law. But I also think that if the Corporation . . . is properly managed and it is allowed to continue in business until it has been proven that the intentions of the managers are good, that there is no disposition to exercise a monopoly or to restrain legitimate trade, that in that case, if there is a contest, the company will be held to be legal.

This was perhaps Gary's first enunciation of what was to become his dictum—that there were good and bad trusts. The corporation, he said, must be a good trust. "The essence of the Gary policy was to avoid the appearance of monopoly while keeping as much as possible the reality," *Fortune* said. On prices, Gary was "apparently able to do a good deal of shrewd underbidding without losing his reputation in the public eye as a benevolent uncle to the whole steel industry." A veteran steelman said of him with admiration, "Gary made a wonderful thing out of principles."

II

As chairman, Gary was confronted with numerous difficulties. He battled Schwab over which one of them would run the company. More companies had to be acquired to round out the corporation, and Gary had to bring a measure of control over the corporation's far-flung operations, which comprised more than two hundred subdivisions with several hundred plants and stretched from New England through Pittsburgh to Chicago and then to the ore fields of Minnesota. Gary was confronted with demands from the Amalgamated Association of Iron, Steel, and Tin Workers and from other labor organizations. He believed that he had to end what he regarded as the ruinous price competition that had been going on for decades between steel companies, in order to bring stability to the industry. This, after all, had been a primary reason for forming the corporation. Finally, the corporation had to contend with a poor image, complaints about its size and strength, and intense press and government scrutiny.

Always, Gary faced these matters with confidence, bolstered by his conviction that his principles could be applied to all the actions of the corporation. He began to practice his principles almost immediately upon assuming the chairmanship. He not only allowed stockholders to ask questions at annual meetings but answered them. He began to publish quarterly and annual reports, a practice largely unknown at the time. He published price lists and order backlogs. He gave out corporation information at 3:00 P.M., at the closing bell of the stock exchange, thus ending the common practice of providing advance information on company matters—profits, losses, acquisitions, and the like—to board members so that they could make personal market decisions on the basis of the information. The move particularly irritated Henry Clay Frick, a man of the old school who questioned what the point of being on a board was if you could not make money at it. It was some time before Gary and Frick reconciled, though when they did they became close associates. Most important, Gary understood the value of favorable press attention. He granted numerous interviews to journalists—who treated him with much deference—and, in doing this and making other corporation information available, he helped establish the concept of business public relations, also almost unknown then.

Gary, however, quickly learned that it was one thing to have a position of authority and to outline principles of conduct, and quite another to get others to accept his authority and to conduct themselves in accordance with the tenets he laid down. As Percival Roberts, Jr., a member of the corporation's executive committee and its board of directors, said, "The crowd [the board of directors] naturally had different ideas of running the Corporation. Gary had to handle a basket of cats and dogs. . . ."

What to do with Schwab was the first vexing matter for Gary. When the corporation was formed and Schwab was named president, he was far more well known than Gary and the object of much more attention. He was a favorite of the press and was always ready with quotes for reporters. Gary could tolerate Schwab's receiving most of the attention, at least for a time. What was important was who would run things. Under Carnegie, Schwab's position as president had been supreme, next to that of Carnegie, and Carnegie had usually been in Europe half the year anyway. Schwab was a strong-willed man who was used to running things his way. As Schwab once told Carnegie, "I am no good at carrying out another man's orders."

And Schwab was not used to functioning under the corporation's executive-committee system, which Gary and Morgan had borrowed from the Standard Oil Corporation. Some members of the board, including many of the steelmen, made it clear they agreed with Schwab in his opposition to the committee system. On July 1, 1901, Schwab brought to the corporation's executive committee a plan that would give him supreme power and eliminate the executive committee. Gary, always understated, remarked that Schwab's plan seemed the opposite of what Morgan had had in mind when he created the corporation, and what was spelled out in the corporation's bylaws. The discussion became heated. Schwab said that the business of the company could not be conducted under the bylaws and that he must ignore them. Finally, the committee adopted a resolution that unless the board of directors altered the bylaws, Schwab must continue to report to the executive committee. Gary won this battle, but the board members had taken sides, and the situation festered.

Gary and Schwab then confronted each other on two other matters: Schwab's salary and his desire, like the other Pittsburgh millionaires', to have a little fun. At the Carnegie Steel Company, in 1900, Carnegie had rewarded Schwab for siding with him against Frick with a contract that provided a substantial income, perhaps as much as one million dollars a year for five years. When the Carnegie Company was merged into the United States Steel Corporation, Schwab went to Gary with his contract. "What are you going to do about this, Judge?" he asked.

"Nothing. Get rid of it—that is Mr. Carnegie's affair," Gary replied. The matter was apparently taken care of by Carnegie, although this is not known for sure. But the information went out that Schwab was being paid a salary of as much as one million dollars a year, and Schwab reveled in the attention, bantering with the press about the salary without saying precisely how much it was. Gary was vexed. He wished to protect the reputation of the corporation, and talk of million-dollar salaries—even though the corporation apparently was not paying the money—was not good for the company's reputation.

In January 1902, another incident caused an even more serious rupture between Gary and Schwab. Schwab had worked hard, helping establish the corporation and assisting it through its first months. He believed he had earned a vacation, and in December 1901 he and his wife set out for a combined business and pleasure trip to Europe. In Paris Schwab purchased a "large, fast automobile" and then joined a wealthy, fun-loving crowd that included Baron Henri de Rothschild and Dr. Greiz Wittgenstein, an Austrian steelman, to drive to the Côte d'Azur and the Grand Corniche. One can imagine them—Schwab as Mr. Toad in *The Wind in the Willows,* the others as his courtiers, none of them counting the costs—tearing in a madcap manner through the French countryside, dust billowing behind them, heading for the sun and the sea and the Monte Carlo gaming tables.

In Monte Carlo, on the night of January 12, Schwab and his companions played a few spins of roulette, then had a nightcap and went to bed. A newspaperman from the *New York Sun* was in Monte Carlo, however, and overnight a story was cabled to New York. On the morning of

January 13, under a headline that blared SCHWAB BREAKS THE BANK, the *Sun* reported that the president of the United States Steel Corporation had won fifty thousand francs in Monte Carlo. On January 14, the *Sun* ran a second story, saying that Schwab had played roulette a second night and again broken the bank, winning fifty-four thousand francs. The *Times,* the *World,* and other papers picked up the story.

Most observers who have studied the matter say that Schwab was traduced by the press; he had winnings but nothing substantial, and he had not broken the bank. But the affair caused a sensation. The *Times* said in an editorial: "A man who is the head of a corporation with more than a billion dollars of capital stock, which controls a great part of one of the chief industries of a great Nation, and of which the securities are offered to the public as a safe and profitable investment, is under obligation to take some thought of his responsibilities. We should suppose that the friends of Mr. Schwab would call these strange stories to his attention in order that he may deny them if he is in a position to say that they are untrue."

Carnegie, although out of the corporation, was furious. He already had been angered by the vulgar, high-spending displays of the Pittsburgh millionaires. Now this, from a man he had treated as a son. He cabled Schwab: "Public sentiment shocked. *Times* demands statement gambling charges false. Probably have [to] resign. Serves you right." Carnegie then dispatched to Morgan a clipping of the *Times* editorial condemning Schwab, with a letter in which he said Schwab should be made to resign.

Schwab was dumbfounded by what was happening. On January 15, he cabled George W. Perkins, J. Pierpont Morgan's chief assistant: "Am advised that there have been sensational publications regarding gambling. . . . Did play but sensational statements of great winnings and losses absolutely false." On January 16, Perkins cabled Schwab: "Everything all right. Andrew Carnegie and several others were very much excited but they did not make the slightest impression on Mr. Morgan. Do not give the matter any further thought or consideration. Go ahead and have bully good time."

But Schwab was distressed, and he cabled his resignation to Morgan. Morgan, a man who liked to have a little fun himself, refused to accept it. On February 16, Schwab returned to the United States and went to see Morgan. Schwab explained, "I did gamble at Monte Carlo, but I didn't do it behind closed doors." Morgan replied, "That's what doors are for." Schwab could not get over the affair, especially what he saw as betrayal by his patron, Carnegie. He had spells of nervous irritability and insomnia. He lost weight.

Gary, particularly disturbed by Schwab's indiscretions, determined to use the incident to see who possessed authority at the corporation. Gary laid his case before Morgan. He said that he was meeting constant opposition from the directors. If the corporation was to succeed, it must be run in the manner he had laid out to Morgan, for the good of the corporation and the stockholders, not the officers and the directors. If he could not run it that way, he would resign.

Morgan listened, then replied: "I didn't know that you felt this way, Judge Gary. Now, you remain where you are [as chairman], and, from this time on, when you want me to do anything or say anything, all you have to do is to tell me. You needn't explain. Just say, 'Do so and so,' and I will do it."

Schwab could not last. In late 1902, still not well, he took a leave of absence. With Schwab out of the picture, Gary asserted his control. The duties of the chairman of the executive committee and the president were described precisely, with the chairman, Gary, being the head of the corporation. Gary was also made chairman of the board of directors, a new position.

In August 1903, Schwab, who in December 1900 had first put forth the idea of the corporation, was forced to resign, although for a time he remained a member of the board and the finance committee. A newspaperman wrote of him about that time: "Although he was apparently in a cheerful mood, a slight quivering about the mouth and an indefinable lack of physical poise plainly showed that he was suffering from nervousness. His manner was restless and his eyes lacked their usual brilliancy."

III

In 1902, Gary set about acquiring the companies needed to round out the corporation. Its first acquisitions were the Troy Steel Works, in Troy, New York, and the Trenton Iron Company, in Trenton, New Jersey. In May 1904, the corporation acquired the Clairton Steel Company, in Clairton, Pennsylvania, ten miles up the Monongahela River from Homestead. Clairton, tied in with Edgar Thomson, Homestead, and Duquesne, made the corporation's dominance in the Monongahela Valley even more overwhelming.

These were a prelude to larger expansions. In 1905, the corporation announced that it would build a huge iron- and steel-manufacturing complex and an accompanying city on a nine-thousand-acre area of sand dunes that it had acquired on the shore of Lake Michigan, east of Chicago. The mill, Gary said, would incorporate the newest steel-manufacturing technologies, and the city would be constructed in accordance with the newest philosophies of American city planning, with homes for employees, schools, and playgrounds. Gary allowed the works and the city to be named after him. Thus was born one of the nation's most famous steelworks and one of its most important manufacturing cities—the Gary works, and Gary, Indiana. Construction began in August 1906, and in 1911 the plant and city and vast port and railroad terminals were finished, and the first steel was tapped. The plant had the capacity to produce six million tons of steel a year.

In 1906, the corporation purchased the Universal Portland Cement Company to expand its cement-making operations, which utilized slag that otherwise would have been discarded. In that year, the corporation leased more iron-ore lands on the Mesabi Range, negotiating what became known as the Hill Lease from the railroad magnate James J. Hill. This added to the corporation's monopoly on the nation's ore deposits. Later, the corporation also acquired large ore reserves in Cuba.

In 1907, the corporation purchased the Tennessee Coal and Iron Company, which dated from the late 1860s, when a group of Alabama businessmen believed that the South, then beginning its recovery from the Civil War, would need an iron and steel industry. But though T.C.& I., as it was known, was the largest iron and steel company in the South, it was ill managed and never found financial success.

Still, it was an enticing property, and in 1906 a new syndicate took over the operation, among the investors being Grant B. Schley and his New York brokerage house, Moore and Schley. In October 1907, a financial panic struck the nation. Several banks failed, and the stock market was demoralized. Moore & Schley was in danger of collapse, and it was feared that if it fell, other brokerage houses also would fall. It was now proposed to Morgan that the United States Steel Corporation purchase Tennessee Coal and Iron. This would cause the company's stock to go up, and Moore & Schley would be saved.

Morgan agreed, but Gary balked. He feared that such a purchase might make the corporation subject to antitrust prosecution. Morgan talked with Gary and won him over, but Gary insisted that President Theodore Roosevelt be informed of the situation; unless the president agreed, Gary said, he himself would not approve the purchase.

Gary and Henry Clay Frick, a corporation board member still useful in a crisis, boarded a night train for Washington. At 8:00 A.M., they went to the White House, where the president was having breakfast. Roosevelt detested being interrupted at breakfast, but he was persuaded to leave his table, and the matter was discussed. Roosevelt said that he would make no objection, and he dictated a letter to the attorney general affirming this view. Gary telephoned Morgan on an open line to New York to say that the purchase would not be opposed by the government. It was announced on November 1, 1907. The corporation paid thirty-five million dollars, mostly in bonds, and acquired vast natural resources and manufacturing outlets in the South. Julian Kennedy, the old Homestead steelman and now a noted consulting engineer in the steel industry, estimated that the acquisition was worth ninety to one hundred million dollars.

IV

Gary liked to maintain that his views on labor were far different from those of most other industrialists of the time, men like Carnegie, Frick, Schwab, John D. Rockefeller, or George F. Baer, the Pennsylvania coal magnate who, during the anthracite strike of 1902, said that working-class people would be "protected and cared for—not by the labor agitators, but by the Christian men to whom God has given control of the property rights of the country." To the corporation executive who said, "If a workman sticks up his head, hit it," Gary professed abhorrence of such a philosophy. "So long as I am here," he testily replied, "no workman's head shall be hit! You can get another chairman, but I shall never recognize that policy." The Judge said that in his dealings with labor he preferred to determine facts and then decide what was fair for both sides. He maintained that labor relations were simply a matter of common sense. Yet Gary's views on labor were, at bottom, little different from those of most other businessmen, and the corporation's labor practices were little different from the practices of many other corporations, including those of the Carnegie Company, whose reputation had been so soiled by the Homestead strike.

In April 1901, when the United States Steel Corporation was formed, the Amalgamated Association of Iron, Steel, and Tin Workers represented only 13,800 of the nation's 434,000 iron and steel workers, compared to the 24,000 workers it had represented at the time of the Homestead strike. Most of these workers were employed in the corporation's tin division, which had been organized for some time and had come into the corporation at its founding, through the acquisition of the American Tin Plate Company. Moreover, the union remained the same moderate organization it had always been. It did not complain when the corporation was founded; it still represented only skilled men; and its president, an ordained minister, Theodore J. Shaffer, was a milquetoast, as other presidents had been and would be. Shaffer thought he should act quickly, before the corporation gained strength. Being new and concerned with consolidating its position, the corporation was relatively weak, he reasoned. Morgan, Gary, and the other executives did not want a strike, and the corporation was generally conciliatory toward the union. But when Shaffer demanded increased wages at a number of key mills, even some that were nonunion, the corporation refused. On July 15, 1901, Shaffer ordered the union men out of the tin-plate mills, and the strike began.

Two weeks later, Shaffer and the union secretary, John Williams, traveled to New York for negotiations with Morgan. Morgan charmed the union men. He said that he was sympathetic to unions and that it was acceptable to him if the corporation's mills were organized, but that the situation was complicated and events must proceed slowly. The labor leaders were thrown off guard by Morgan's amiable manner, so different from his reputation for abruptness and authoritarianism. Williams called the meeting with Morgan "one of the pleasantest I ever attended." They accepted a proposal by Morgan for a wage scale in the mills that the union had had under contract as of July 1.

The union's executive board met on July 30, but after two days of meetings, to the dismay of the union leaders, the board rejected the agreement. Morgan was incensed. He had reached an agreement with the union, and the union had repudiated it. This was not how gentlemen conducted themselves, he said, and he declared that he would have no more dealings with men such as these.

On August 10, the Amalgamated Association, seeing no option, called for a general strike against the corporation. But many western workers, including some Amalgamated men, refused to come out. Meantime, the company began bringing in strikebreakers, and plants that had been struck were reopened. Shaffer asked Samuel Gompers, president of the American Federation of Labor, to transform the strike against the corporation into "a central fight for unionism." Gompers said no. On September 14, the union capitulated, accepting a settlement inferior to the one it already had rejected, and losing contracts in fifteen mills that had been reopened by strikebreakers.

The corporation established two points: it would be an "open shop" —that is, it would allow no union representation except in plants already under union contract when the corporation was formed—and it would be resolute in its dealings with labor. Moreover, the corporation, because of its size and importance, and the militant stand it had taken, emerged as the leader in American business's opposition to unionism, just as the Carnegie company had previously been.

The Amalgamated Association became more submissive. Now it was no more a union than was the Rotary Club. In 1903, the union was forced to surrender its charters in the few steel mills in which it still represented workers. In 1904, the corporation reduced wages in union mills; the union briefly struck but lost and was forced to surrender its charters in the western hoop mills. The union also was forced to eliminate rules that restricted production as a means of protecting workers from overwork and rate-cutting. President Shaffer told the union convention in 1905 that militant actions by the union would make the union "unreflecting, jejune, and vicious." He went on, "I enter my most vigorous protest against any strike which does not emanate from the employer." In 1907 and 1908, the union lost its members at the last tube mills in which it still represented workers. It now represented workers in just a few of the corporation's sheet and tin mills.

Gary, meantime, to counter unionism and foster loyalty to the corporation among the workers and towns, began to institute a new industrial-relations policy. It was a broad program that included a stock-purchase program for employees, increased safety measures, employees' housing, and other benefits. It became known as "Garyism" or "welfare capitalism." Speaking to a group of fellow steelmen, Gary explained his program this way: "If cooperation—friendship and fairness—is a good doctrine for us, it is equally as good for others. . . . We should have it in mind in dealing with other employees."

On December 31, 1902, the Judge instituted the stock program—"a New Year's gift" to the workers, Ida M. Tarbell wrote—which allowed workers to purchase corporation stock at below-market prices. More than twenty-six thousand workers signed up in January 1903 alone. Gary said that with such programs "the interests of capital and labor will be drawn more closely and permanently together." He reminded his fellow steel executives that "the employers, the capitalists, those having the highest education, the greatest power and influence," had the responsibility to see that "the workmen and their families are appropriately and efficiently cared for, drawing the line so that you are just and generous and yet at the same time . . . keeping the whole affair in your own hands."

In 1906, a safety program, one of the most advanced in American industry, was established, in which the corporation, borrowing from a program that Henry Clay Frick had introduced in the coal and coke industry, began using the motto "Safety First." An accident-insurance and pension program followed. Plant sanitation was improved, and the corporation began a housing program in some steel towns. A substantial sports program was established, as the corporation began to sponsor teams and build baseball and football fields.

The welfare program, however, was the company's, not the workers' program; the company ran it for the workers. It was paternalism of the highest order and was also a subtle way to counter unionism.

Gary soon made a direct move to end unionism in the mills altogether. On June 1, 1909, the corporation posted a notice at the twelve mills where the Amalgamated Association still had members. The notice said: "After a careful consideration of the interests of both the company and its employees, the American Sheet and Tin Plate Company has decided that all its plants after June 30, 1909, will be operated as 'open' plants." The notice also said that wages would be reduced by 2 to 8 percent.

The Amalgamated Association leaders were stunned. The union had been malleable, Shaffer said, "giving way to every request" that the corporation had made. Now the union leaders again believed that there was no choice but to strike. On July 1, 1909, the Amalgamated Association's members laid down their tools. Another strike was on.

The company would not yield. It brought in strikebreakers and kept its operations running. By September 1909, the company claimed that its struck mills were operating at 70 percent of capacity. Many workers continued to strike, but the cause was hopeless, and in August 1910, after fourteen months on strike, the union capitulated, ending what remains the longest strike in the American steel industry. The union retained members in some independent mills, but the corporation was free of unionism, as the Carnegie Steel Company had been after the Homestead strike.

V

The financial panic of 1907 left a great feeling of unease at the corporation and in the rest of the steel industry. Gary, as the head of the largest company, settled on a solution: the men who ran the steel industry would get together to determine what the problems were and what should be done to solve them. This decision led to what became known as "Gary dinners," meetings that would prove the truth of Adam Smith's dictum "People of the same trade seldom meet together, even for merriment and diversion, but the conversation ends in a conspiracy against the public or in some contrivance to raise prices." The first dinner was held on November 20, 1907, at the Waldorf-Astoria Hotel, in New York, and others followed throughout 1908. These gatherings were nothing less than price-fixing sessions. Rumblings about restraint of trade were heard in the government and elsewhere, but the dinners continued.

On October 9, 1909, the steel masters of the United States and Canada gathered at a Gary dinner in Gary's honor. Charles M. Schwab, still a spellbinding after-dinner speaker, was designated as spokesman for the executives. Six years before, Schwab had been forced out of the company in disgrace. But he was not a man to hold a grudge. More than that, Schwab, now the president of the Bethlehem Steel Corporation, had been won over by Gary's principles and was practicing many of them himself. He spoke in a most adulatory manner of the man who had forced him out of the company, and his words illustrated how the Gary principles had been accepted throughout the steel industry:

I am thankful for this opportunity of saying one thing, Judge. The broad principles that you brought into this business were new to all of us who had been trained in a somewhat different school. Their effect was marvelous, their success unquestioned. It was a renaissance and a newness of things in this business that were necessary and invigorating. Judge, we feel that your position in the steel industry is unique. I have been present at many gatherings where men have been honored for scientific attainments in steel; but, sir, this is the first time in the history of the industry when the great heads of all the big concerns in the United States and Canada have gathered to do honor to a man who has introduced a new and successful principle in our great industry.

VI

Some executives, among them William E. Corey, Schwab's successor as president, continued to complain that Gary's power was too immense. Corey had not proven as malleable as Gary had expected. Gary and the other top corporation men lived with this, but not happily, until they were ready to make their move.

Corey was an engaging fellow and a self-made man, one of the many American steel masters who got their starts in the Homestead Works. The workers liked him, and so did many fellow executives. He had been born and raised in Braddock. At age sixteen, he went to work as a messenger in the Edgar Thomson Works. In the evenings, he attended business school in Pittsburgh, and also studied chemistry and metallurgy. He was a husky man who worked as a furnace man, roller, and puddler. Seeking the widest experience, he worked in every department of the works.

In 1887, Corey went to work at the Homestead Works and rose rapidly. In 1893, he was made superintendent of the armor-plate department, a capacity in which he served until 1897, when he succeeded Schwab as general superintendent of the Homestead Works. Corey replaced Schwab as president of Carnegie Steel in 1901, when Schwab was made corporation president, and in 1903 Corey replaced Schwab as corporation president. But Corey made two errors, almost the same errors Schwab had made: he confronted Gary, and he violated what Gary and others regarded as proper social conduct for a corporation man. He did not go to the gaming tables, as Schwab had done. He did something even more shocking: after twenty-three years of marriage, he deserted his wife, the plump daughter of a Braddock miner, for a showgirl, one who was said to be a floozy.

Corey met Maybelle Gilman when she played in Pittsburgh with a traveling troupe in *Mocking Bird,* a popular stage show. He sought a divorce from his wife and declared his intention to marry Miss Gilman. The announcement shocked Corey's associates in the steel industry. He was, after all, president of the United States Steel Corporation, a premier position in American business. The Pittsburgh steelmen were men of the world, to be sure, and they could put up with a man's peccadilloes, but such carryings-on had to be kept quiet. They urged Corey to think about what he was doing. But he could not be dissuaded.

The wedding took place at the Hotel Gotham, in New York, in May 1907 and was such an expensive, splashy affair that it caused a sensation. Corey trumpeted his wedding expenses to the press—$5,000 for flowers, $6,000 for an intimate wedding supper, $200,000 set aside for the honeymoon, on the Continent, of course. It was thought that Corey's divorce and remarriage might bring his immediate ouster from the corporation, but Gary waited until Corey made his second mistake—that of demonstrating independence in business matters.

Early in 1910, Gary asked an executive of a western mining company that was part of the corporation to obtain some information for him. This came to the attention of the president of the mining company, and he fired the man, saying that in obtaining the information and providing it to Gary he had gone behind his—the president's—back. The fired executive, caught in the middle and outraged, complained to Gary, and Gary reinstated him. Corey objected, as did a number of subsidiary presidents, saying that the chairman had no authority to bypass the president of the mining company. The presidents of the subsidiaries had been accustomed to autonomy. More incidents like this, Corey and the presidents said, and discipline would be destroyed. A number of subsidiary presidents threatened to resign if Gary's authority was not curbed, and they so informed Morgan. This was a mistake. Gary was Morgan's man, and Morgan let the executives know it. "Tell them," Morgan said, "that their resignations will be accepted."

George W. Perkins, Morgan's right-hand man, asked Gary whether there were any other actions that he wanted the committee members to take. "Yes," Gary said. "I would like a resolution more definitely fixing my status in this corporation." On March 1, 1910, the directors adopted a resolution stating that the chairman of the board would be the chief executive officer of the corporation and "in general charge of the affairs of the corporation." Gary was now chairman of the finance committee, chairman of the board of directors, and chief operating officer. His power was supreme. On January 1, 1911, Corey resigned and was replaced by James A. Farrell, a corporation man who had started out as a wire-drawer in the Worcester, Massachusetts, works. Farrell was a skilled steelman but, unlike Schwab and Corey, was pleased to defer to Gary and to stay out of the public eye—no gaming tables or showgirls for him.

VII

From the moment it was formed in 1901, the corporation was confronted with almost constant scrutiny—from journalists, sociologists, Congress, and the government. The journalist Ida M. Tarbell said that it seemed to be under attack by "every agency that was seeking a hearing, unionists, the single taxer, the Socialist, the tariff reformer." The first government inquiry began in January 1905, when President Roosevelt ordered a probe of the corporation by the commissioner of the Federal Bureau of Corporations, James R. Garfield. The corporation men, particularly Morgan, were taken aback.

Morgan had had an intense dislike of Roosevelt ever since February 1902, when he had learned that Roosevelt's attorney general, Philander C. Knox, who had been a lawyer for the Carnegie Steel Company during the 1892 Homestead lockout, was preparing to prosecute the Northern Securities Corporation, a gigantic holding company created by Morgan and James J. Hill to control the Northern Pacific and other railroads, for violation of the Sherman Antitrust Act of 1890. Morgan had gone to the White House and had told the president, "If we have done anything wrong, send your man to my man and they can fix it up." Morgan had been incensed when Roosevelt had refused and when Attorney General Knox had had the gall to say, "We don't want to fix it up; we want to stop it."

Gary, on the other hand, had established a friendly relationship with Roosevelt, beginning in December 1902, when at the suggestion of Perkins, a college chum of Roosevelt's, Roosevelt had invited Gary to the White House. Gary and the president took an immediate liking to each other. Both men believed in self-reliance and self-restraint and in the notion that hard work will overcome handicaps. They began to meet regularly. Now, in 1905, Roosevelt had authorized an investigation of the corporation that would drag on for several years.

Another critical year for the corporation was 1911. In May, Representative Augustus O. Stanley of Kentucky, concerned about the corporation's strength, called for an investigation. Congress established what became known as "the Stanley Committee." The committee began taking testimony in the summer of 1911, and hearings went on for months, making front-page news, with the committee ultimately calling more than four hundred witnesses, among them Carnegie, Gary, Schwab, and numerous other executives.

In July 1911, six years after Roosevelt had set it in motion, the report of the Federal Bureau on Corporations was released. It said that the corporation dominated the steel industry, and that much of this domination was due to its monopoly on the Mesabi iron-ore reserves. It charged that the Hill ore lease had been acquired at such high rents that the corporation clearly intended to monopolize the ore lands.

Pressure to dissolve the corporation mounted. Finally, on October 26, 1911, President William Howard Taft's attorney general, George W. Wickersham, filed suit in Trenton, New Jersey, to dissolve the corporation as a monopoly in restraint of trade. That day, to placate public opinion, the corporation's directors voted to cancel the Hill lease. This deprived the corporation of vast, rich ore deposits, which were then acquired by a number of the corporation's competitors.

Also in 1911, *The Pittsburgh Survey,* a six-volume study of the steel industry and steelworkers, began to be published. Since 1908, a group of writers and sociologists, sponsored by the Russell Sage Foundation, had been investigating conditions in the Pittsburgh steel mills and in the area's communities. Their study, a masterpiece of American sociology, described the difficult conditions under which steelworkers labored—the long hours and arduous, hazardous work, the smoke and dirt of life in the steel towns.

The Stanley Committee's report was released in August 1912. It, too, was a strong attack, criticizing the corporation for its overcapitalization, bond conversion, Hill ore lease, interlocking directorships, Gary dinners, purchase of the Tennessee Coal and Iron Company, and attitude toward workers and labor unions. For the corporation, there seemed no end of criticism.

There was a reprieve on June 3, 1915, when a United States Court of Appeals ruled in the corporation's favor and against the government's effort to dissolve it. Roosevelt, who had testified in defense of the corporation, was pleased. He wrote Gary that he regarded the decision as "a great personal victory" for Gary. But on October 28, 1915, the government appealed, and in March 1917 the case went before the United States Supreme Court. Then, on April 8, 1917, the United States entered World War I. The government again needed the corporation. The case was postponed.

10

WARS

The war brought immense prosperity to the corporation. The corporation had, largely through the work of James A. Farrell, Corey's successor as president, built a substantial export business, one of Gary's goals in forming the corporation. By 1911, the corporation had offices in major cities throughout much of the world and was selling products, ranging from nails to rails to structural beams to plates, in dozens of countries. That year, the corporation had ninety million dollars in foreign sales. The war, beginning in 1914, increased sales and profits dramatically. By the middle of 1915, the corporation was operating at 90 percent of capacity and exporting a third of its production. In 1916, the corporation's earnings were $333.5 million, twice the previous high.

With America's entry into the war, production and profits increased even more. During the war, the corporation manufactured thousands of miles of barbed wire, 75,000 kegs of horseshoes, 500,000 kegs of iron nails, 20,000 tons of book wire to bind government publications. The Clairton Works, on the Monongahela River, was by now, with substantial expansions, the largest coke by-product plant in the world; benzol by-products from the works were made into explosives and poison gases.

At the request of the government, the corporation entered shipbuilding. It constructed two shipbuilding plants, one at Kearny, New Jersey, at the mouth of the Hackensack River, the other at Mobile, Alabama, on Mobile Bay. By the war's end, the plants could turn out a steel ship every ten days. The corporation also began construction of a huge ordnance and munitions plant at Neville Island, in the Ohio River, below Pittsburgh, although the war ended before the plant could be put into operation. In 1916, 1917, and 1918, the corporation's production averaged twenty million tons of steel a year, and profits were 160 percent higher than in 1913, the year before the war in Europe began. The government controlled steel prices, and war taxes were high, but the corporation's wartime earnings totaled $709 million. "The corporation's patriotism did not go unrewarded," *Fortune* said.

II

In December 1917, meat-packers in the Chicago stockyards won a remarkable victory over the packinghouses—a 10-percent wage increase, the right to organize, and seniority and grievance systems. In March 1918, the unionized workers, now numbering more than two hundred thousand, gained another victory when a federal judge awarded them an additional wage increase of 10 to 25 percent, an eight-hour day with ten hours of pay, overtime pay, and equal pay for men and women.

These triumphs were the result of an aggressive, six-month-long union-organizing campaign led by two dedicated Chicago unionists, John Fitzpatrick and William Z. Foster. Immediately after these successes, Fitzpatrick and Foster decided to take on a larger, more powerful adversary—the United States Steel Corporation and the rest of the nation's iron and steel industry. Foster, particularly, saw an iron and steel drive as the beginning of a campaign to organize American industry. "To organize the steel industry would be like putting the backbone in the labor movement," he said.

Fitzpatrick, president of the Chicago Federation of Labor, was amiable and respected. He was an idealist and a friend of immigrants and working people. "When I think of those [steel] trust magnates and the conditions their workers live in and work in and die in—why, their hearts must be black as the ace of spades," Fitzpatrick once said.

Foster was a methodical, soft-spoken man with radical views. He was born in Taunton, Massachusetts, and grew up in the slums of Philadelphia. He went to school for only three years and participated in his first strike at age fourteen. Between 1897 and 1917, he worked as a sculptor's assistant, fertilizer mixer, fruit-picker, timber-cutter, camp cook, miner, circus-canvas painter, railroad brakeman, meat-packer, and trolley-car motorman on the Third Avenue Line in New York City. He also went to sea and spent three years circling the globe, a journey that "helped very much to steel me in my growing revolutionary convictions," he wrote later. In 1909, he joined the Industrial Workers of the World (IWW). Becoming convinced that dual unionism—that is, more than one national labor organization—could not succeed, in 1912 he left the "Wobblies," as the IWW was called, and came to Chicago, where he joined the Brotherhood of Railway Car Men. Foster was a brilliant tactician and organizer. The radical journalist Mary Heaton Vorse called him "probably the ablest labor organizer this country has ever known."

The need for unionism in the steel industry was clear. Conditions in the mills and the steel towns had remained essentially unchanged in the nearly three decades since the Homestead fight. Wages rose 10 percent during the war, but living costs increased 70 percent. Most steelworkers did not earn what the government said was a living wage, and living conditions deteriorated dramatically. The average workweek in the industry was sixty-nine hours, and the twelve-hour day was more widespread in 1919 than a decade before. Half of the industry's 500,000 employees worked a twelve-hour day. Because workers rotated weekly from morning to afternoon to night shifts, every three weeks they worked twenty-four hours straight, "the long-turn." Many steelworkers worked a seven-day week.

In the first decades of the twentieth century, there had been numerous clashes between labor and management in the steel industry and related industries. But the United States Steel Corporation, having defeated the Amalgamated Association in 1901 and 1909–1910, for the most part had escaped agitation in its iron and steel mills. Almost all of the many strikes in this period ended in defeat for the workers, and strikes ended altogether with the nation's entry into World War I. Workers were patriotic; strikes were regarded as unpatriotic. Moreover, with many workers joining the military and the immigration of European workers shut off, steel companies faced a severe labor shortage. To retain workers, wages were increased and other workplace improvements were made; the corporation, for example, tripled its welfare expenditures during the war.

Yet the war created new vigor in the labor movement. The notion of fighting a war for democracy abroad made workers and union leaders hopeful about achieving democracy in the American workplace, and they believed that the government would assist them. The government—like business, desirous of an acquiescent workforce and continued production —was reaching out to the labor movement. "I am for the laboring man," President Wilson declared. In March 1918, the War Labor Conference Board, going further than the government ever had in support of unions, endorsed "the right of workmen to organize in trade unions" without hindrance "by the employers in any manner."

Fitzpatrick, Foster, and other militant unionists had sensed the surge in support for unionization. The two men had wanted to begin an iron and steel organizing drive as early as 1917, but the national unions had not supported them. Finally in June 1918, Foster won approval for an iron and steel organizing campaign from the American Federation of Labor. A planning meeting was set for August 1–2 in Chicago. There, representatives of fifteen unions established the National Committee for Organizing Iron and Steel Workers. Samuel Gompers, president of the American Federation of Labor, was named chairman, but since Gompers would be traveling in Europe and Mexico in the following months on government and labor missions, Fitzpatrick was given the chairman's duties. Foster was named secretary-treasurer. In the first week of September 1918, with the number of unions supporting the campaign now twenty-four and a treasury established, the drive began.

The drive at first was limited to the mills of the Chicago district. The unions were not united, and money from them was slow in coming, but the organizers achieved some success: by the end of September, thousands of workers had signed union cards. On October 1, Foster, who had assumed the campaign's leadership because of his skills, and others moved their headquarters to Pittsburgh to take on the mills there and in the Monongahela Valley, the citadel of the steel industry.

The corporation was prepared for a vigorous fight, and the end of the war, on November 11, 1918, freed its hands. Continued high steel production was no longer necessary. Wartime restrictions prohibiting discrimination against unions were ended as government agencies that had supported labor were disbanded. With war profits, the corporation had enormous amounts of money at its disposal. Finally, the corporation exercised strong control in the steel towns. It did this in subtle ways, as enumerated by Gary in a warning to his subsidiary presidents to stay ahead of trouble and "make the Steel Corporation a good place for [workers] to work and live. Don't let the families go hungry or cold; give them playgrounds and parks and schools and churches, pure water to drink, every opportunity to keep clean, places of enjoyment, rest, and recreation." And there were less subtle ways. It was clear who possessed power. Late in 1918, as union organizers began efforts to organize the steel industry, an organizer, J. G. Brown, rented a hall in Homestead for a union meeting, then talked with P. H. McGuire, the Homestead burgess, who had been a union activist during the 1892 strike and for a number of years after that but then had gone over to the company side. As William Z. Foster was to say of him, he had "fully recovered from his unionism" and "made peace with the enemy." Brown recalled the conversation.

MCGUIRE: Well, you cannot hold any meetings at Homestead.

BROWN: Why not?

MCGUIRE: In the first place, you cannot get a hall.

BROWN: Well, we have a hall. We have got a hall, all right.

MCGUIRE: Then what do you want of me?

BROWN: We want to arrange to have a band play on the street and distribute some advertisements.

MCGUIRE: There will be no bands playing on the streets of Homestead and no advertising done.

BROWN: Well, now, could not we pass cards around to the houses or something of that sort?

MCGUIRE: No, sir, you cannot pass anything in any way.

BROWN: Could we not advertise in the papers?

MCGUIRE: Oh, yes, if you want to; if you can get the space. I don't think you can get the space.

The next morning, Brown said, he was informed that the hall had been rented to the union by mistake, that it had already been rented to someone else, and that the lease with the union would have to be canceled.

The union organizers persevered. Prohibitions against meetings were ignored. In the spring of 1919, organizers began conducting mass meetings on the Homestead streets. McGuire, as Burgess, ordered the arrest of Foster and another organizer, J. L. Beaghen. Then McGuire, who was also the Homestead magistrate, tried them. Foster and Beaghen asserted that the Homestead ordinance did not mention street meetings. "But it's the best we've got, and it will have to do," McGuire said. He fined Foster and Beaghen and a day or so later had a new ordinance enacted that covered street meetings.

Union meetings were held in McKeesport, Rankin, Clairton, Monessen, and Donora. In the spring of 1919, the National Committee said that it had enlisted one hundred thousand workers and that a union organization existed in every important steel community in the country. Now the workers demanded action. On May 25, 1919, some six hundred workers from steel towns throughout the East and Middle West gathered in Pittsburgh. The union leaders had planned the meeting as a way to allow the workers to let off steam, but the workers were tired of delay. They passed a resolution demanding that the unions in the organizing drive enter into negotiations with the companies for "better wages, shorter hours, improved working conditions, and the trade-union system of collective bargaining."

On June 20, Samuel Gompers wrote Gary and asked for a conference to discuss conditions in the steel industry. Gary did not reply. On July 20, the committee increased pressure on the corporation and other companies. It sent out strike ballots to steelworkers across the country and issued these demands: the establishment of collective bargaining in the industry; the reinstatement of men discharged for union activities, with pay for time lost; the eight-hour day; one day's rest every seven days; the abolition of the twenty-four-hour shift; an "American living wage," with double-time pay for overtime work; a standard wage system; the checkoff (deduction) of union dues from employees' paychecks; a seniority system for advancement and layoffs; the abolition of company unions; and the ending of physical examinations for employment. On August 20, the committee said that 98 percent of the workers had voted to strike if their demands were not met (the committee never released the number of workers who had voted). The workers' battle cry was "Eight Hours and the Union."

On August 26, Foster and Fitzpatrick appeared at Gary's office on Wall Street to ask for a conference at which differences between the workers and the corporation could be arbitrated. Gary refused to meet with the union men. A secretary said that if the men desired, they could state their business in a letter. The men did so, and Gary informed them that the corporation had a no-union policy, and that therefore "the officers of the corporation respectfully decline to discuss with you, as representatives of a labor union, any matters relating to employees." Foster and Fitzpatrick asked Gary to reconsider. He refused.

The situation was explosive. Unemployment had risen after the armistice; real wages were down. Repression of workers was being stepped up.

On August 15, Joe Mayor, a Homestead worker, was called into the office of a Homestead superintendent, William Munle.

MUNLE: Were you at the meeting Tuesday night?

MAYOR: I was. How do you know?

MUNLE: Somebody turned your name in, and I am going to discharge you.

MAYOR: What's the matter? What did I do, rob the company of a couple of dollars?

MUNLE: We don't want you to attend union meetings. I don't want union men to work for me.

Munle then asked who had been present at the meeting and what had been said. Mayor refused to answer. The superintendent fired him and called in a plant guard to escort him from the works.

On August 20, the famous labor agitator Mother Jones, then eighty-nine years old, came to talk to the workers. She declared: "We are to see whether Pennsylvania belongs to Kaiser Gary or Uncle Sam. Our kaisers sit up and smoke seventy-five-cent cigars and have lackeys with knee pants bring them champagne while you starve, while you grow old at forty, stoking their furnaces. You pull in your belts while they banquet. They have stomachs two miles long and two miles wide, and you fill them. . . . If Gary wants to work twelve hours a day let him go in the blooming mill and work. What we want is a little leisure, time for music, playgrounds, a decent home, books, and the things that make life worthwhile."

She was pulled from the speakers' platform and taken to the lockup in the Homestead Borough Hall. Later she was released on fifteen dollars' bond, once she agreed to tell the workers grouped around the jail to disperse.

On August 29, Gompers asked President Wilson to arrange a meeting between Gary and the strikers. Wilson asked the financier Bernard M. Baruch, who had been director of the War Labor Conference Board during the war, to make the request. Gary again refused to meet with the union men. Baruch asked a second time. Gary refused again.

Wilson had opposed a strike all along, and in his Labor Day message on August 31 he said that he would call an industrial conference to "discuss fundamental means of bettering the whole relationship of capital and labor." On September 11, Wilson asked the committee to postpone a strike until after the conference, to begin October 6. Gompers, who also opposed a strike, asked the committee to agree to the president's request.

The committee leaders refused. Any "vague, indefinite postponement would mean absolute demoralization and utter ruin for our movement,"

Fitzpatrick said. "Our only hope is the strike." On September 12, the committee voted to strike on September 22. Two hundred thousand copies of the strike call, in seven languages, went out.

The cautious Gompers was confounded by such militancy. He complained to Fitzpatrick that "the unorganized, the newly organized recruits," were acting "against the best judgment of the experienced men," and he predicted that no significant number of workers would strike.

But on September 22, tens of thousands of steelworkers struck. Foster said that 175,000 workers came out on the first day of the strike and that by the second week 365,000 workers were out, although that number no doubt is high. Probably, at the strike's height, the second week, 250,000 workers in ten states were out, half of the nation's steelworkers. It was the largest strike the nation had ever seen.

The strikers fought valiantly. Wives joined picket lines. In Braddock, Father Adelbert Kazinscy, pastor of Saint Michael's Roman Catholic Church, held strike meetings in his church; the steel corporation tried to foreclose on his church, but his Slovak parishioners paid off the debt. Almost no strikers received strike benefits. A fund-raising drive yielded $418,000, including $150,000 from a mass rally at Madison Square Garden, in New York City. Relief committees for strikers were established all over.

But the corporation and the other steel companies conducted a brutal campaign against the strikers, setting in motion one of the great mass violations of civil liberties in the nation's history. For the union and the workers it was as if time had turned back to Homestead in 1892. The Allegheny County sheriff, W. S. Haddock, prohibited gatherings of three or more persons in any outdoor public place in the county. Indoor meetings were authorized if no foreign languages were spoken. At the request of the steel companies, Haddock deputized five thousand citizens; all were selected, armed, and paid by the companies. Company spies infiltrated local unions and the national strike committee; one of Foster's top lieutenants, it turned out, was a company man. The corporations spent heavily on munitions, arming their guards with rifles, riot guns, and machine guns. Some 150 members of the Coal and Iron Police—the state constabulary of Pennsylvania, used by operators and the state as a strike-breaking force since 1894, when the Pennsylvania legislature, reacting to the Homestead strike, had outlawed the use of Pinkertons in industrial disputes—were called to western Pennsylvania to repress strikers. The policemen, in high helmets, carrying truncheons, and mounted on black horses, broke up workers' meetings in North Clairton and Donora; accosted workers on the streets of Homestead and Braddock; went on their horses into homes and businesses; rode up the steps of Father Kazinscy's church in Braddock. In one example of violence, two members of the Coal and Iron Police entered the home of Trachn Yenchenke, who lived on Third Avenue in Homestead, woke him up, punched and kicked him, dragged him half-clothed to their automobile, and hauled him to the lockup. There he was informed that the authorities were looking for someone who had fired a gun at a man and that the corporation had posted a thousand-dollar reward. Yenchenke said that he knew nothing about the incident, but he was held in jail from Sunday afternoon until Tuesday evening, when Burgess McGuire fined him $15.50 and released him.

Despite such abuses, much of the American press was against the workers from the beginning, urging the strikers to return to work, saying that those who did not were un-American, and exaggerating violence by workers and the number who had already returned to work. (The strike leaders counted up the number of workers the newspapers claimed had returned to work and said that if the numbers were true, the industry's workforce would total 4.8 million.)

Events now turned against the strikers. On October 4, rioting broke out against strikebreakers in Gary, Indiana. On October 6, federal troops entered the city, and Gary—the nation's model working-class city—was placed under martial law. Two strikers were killed. Union men were arrested and put to work chopping wood. The troops made raids on union offices and seized what the military said were radical pamphlets.

On October 6, President Wilson's National Industrial Conference, composed of business, labor, and public representatives, including Gary and Gompers, met in Washington. The union men wanted to use the conference to gain support for the strike, but on October 21 the conference rejected Gompers's resolution supporting "the right of wage earners . . . to bargain collectively . . . in respect to wages, hours of labor, and relations and conditions of employment." Furious, Gompers walked out. Steel executives used his leaving against the strikers, saying that the labor movement was opposed to compromise.

By this time, too, strikebreakers were being imported by the corporation and other companies, including, in the following weeks, some thirty thousand black workers, many brought by bus and railroad from the South. By late October, the nation's steel production was 60 percent of what it had been before the strike, and it was clear that the industry was winning.

It was also the misfortune of the strikers that the walkout occurred in 1919, a year full of strikes and radical activities. In January, thirty-five thousand Seattle shipyard workers struck for higher wages and reduced hours. In February, a general strike was called in Seattle and sixty thousand more workers left their jobs, paralyzing the city. In May, a series of bombings across the country occurred and were attributed to radicals. There were more strikes—by wool workers and silk workers in New Jersey, telephone operators in New England, carpenters and machinists in Ohio, tobacco workers in Pennsylvania, shirtmakers in New York City. In September, 1,120 of Boston's 1,540 policemen went on strike. The policemen were defeated, but the strike shook the nation. Then, as the steel strike began, there was talk of a nationwide coal strike in the late fall, when people would begin needing coal for heating. The country was fearful.

The corporation seized on this fear and branded the strike as radical. Communists were the instigators, the companies and the press said. Foster's radical past and membership in the IWW were unearthed. He was branded as a revolutionary who had engineered the strike to nationalize American industry.

That many strikers were immigrants also was used in the anti-Communist campaign. The strike was called "a Hunkie strike" and a strike of Bolsheviks. (The derogatory term "Hunkie," derived from "Hungarian," was often applied to all foreign-born workers indiscriminately. Since radicalism was considered a foreign importation, labor militancy was routinely blamed on followers of the Bolsheviks, who had led the 1917 Russian Revolution.) The American-born workers were urged to split off from the immigrants and return to work. *The New York Times* said that the strike was "an industrial war in which the leaders are radicals, social and industrial revolutionaries, while their followers are chiefly the foreign element among the steel workers, steeped in the doctrine of the class struggle and social overthrow, ignorant and easily misled." The *Chicago Tribune* called the strike "a choice between the American system and . . . the dictatorship of the proletariat." The *Wall Street Journal* said, "Judge Gary is fighting the battle of the American constitution."

The strikers, in addition, were betrayed by the union movement. The railroad unions refused to call out their men, and so the steel companies were able to continue rail transport. Gompers gave only lukewarm support to the strike, in part because he had never been a friend of immigrant workers, believing that they were radicals and that they took Americans' jobs. In November, the Amalgamated Association of Iron, Steel, and Tin Workers, headed by Michael F. Tighe, another in the union's long list of conservative presidents, ordered its members employed in mills that had contracts with the union to return to work. The Amalgamated Association had never been in favor of the strike; it generally opposed strikes. Moreover, its members, skilled workers, were largely native-born Americans who disliked immigrants. The companies needed the skilled workers, and the decision helped break the strike. Also that month, another disastrous blow came. The national strike of 394,000 coal miners that had been talked of began on November 1 but was called off after only ten days by the United Mine Workers of America. Its president, John L. Lewis, still in his conservative phase, said, "We are Americans. We cannot fight our government."

Finally, winter—always an enemy of strikes—was coming on, and many strikers, with no victory in sight, began to return to work. The corporation and other steel companies took advertisements in numerous languages saying that the strike was broken and the workers should return to their jobs. By January 1, steel production was 70 percent of normal, and 125,000 workers had returned to work. On January 8, 1920, the committee ended the strike. It had been broken by "the arbitrary and ruthless misuse of power," the committee said. "All steel workers are now at liberty to return to work pending preparations for the next big organization movement."

Twenty lives had been lost, and the workers had made no gains. Foster's dream of organizing steel and of using the campaign as a wedge to organize all of American industry was ended. Bitter, he resigned from the committee. In 1920, he was among the founders of the American Communist Party. He was the party's candidate for president in 1924, 1928, and 1932, and for years he served as its national chairman. The domination of the steel towns by the companies continued, and the corporation's role as the leader of the fight against unionism was solidified.

Almost immediately, the corporation gained another victory. On March 1, 1920, the United States Supreme Court, in the antitrust case brought by the government against the corporation in 1911 and postponed in 1917 because of the war, ruled in the corporation's favor. In a four-to-three decision, the Court said, "We are unable to see that the public interest will be served by yielding to the contention of the Government . . . and we do see, in a contrary conclusion, a risk of injury to the public interest, including a material disturbance of, and it may be a serious detriment to, the foreign trade." The decision easily could have gone against the corporation. Two justices could not vote, one because of his previous involvement in the case as a government attorney, the other because he had spoken out against the corporation. Had they voted, it is likely that the corporation would have been dismembered. The court did not address the issue of whether the corporation was a monopoly but concluded only that the public would not be served by dismembering it. What Gary regarded as among his prime tasks, preventing unionism and the corporation's dissolution by the government, had been accomplished.

III

Despite its victories, the corporation was in vulnerable condition, although Gary, other corporation men, Wall Street, newspapers, and magazines did not realize it. The corporation, large and triumphant, the symbol of twentieth-century industry, was rotting from inside. It remained the world's largest steel company and produced almost all its own raw materials. The Frick operations were still the world's largest coal company. The corporation owned the world's largest tube and pipe company. It controlled half of the nation's known iron-ore deposits. It owned some seventy-five ships, and its forty thousand miles of railroad tracks, if laid in a straight line, would have extended from New York to Hawaii. It employed, at the beginning of the 1920s, 267,000 workers, the largest workforce in the country, 70,000 more men than in the armed forces.

Its power established, the corporation coasted through the 1920s. Its share of the steel market, 64 percent when the corporation was created, was falling dramatically. By the mid-1920s, it was 35 percent.

The corporation continued to run in the grooves that its immense size had scoured for it, demonstrating almost no creativity. For example, it made no effort to construct a works at Detroit to serve the automobile industry. Founded and dominated by financial men, the corporation was interested primarily in protecting its investment, in stability. In 1936, *Fortune* said, "The chief energies of the men who guided the Corporation were directed to preventing deterioration in the investment value of the enormous properties confided to their care."

Carnegie had said, "Pioneering don't pay," but he did not practice this. Gary and his men did not say this, but they practiced it. For years, Gary avoided large dividends and invested substantial portions of corporation earnings into plants, but the corporation continued to install old technologies and methods. The more it invested in this manner, the more rigid it became and the more eager to protect the status quo. Finally, because the corporation dominated the industry, other steel companies mimicked its actions. The nation's steel companies "have preferred to take no risks, to content themselves with modest but safe objectives," *Fortune* said.

The corporation was late in expanding into continuous-strip mills and alloy steels, and in adopting combustion and other advancements in open-hearth furnaces. By the mid-1930s, Germany, ruined by war a decade and a half before, was the leader in steel technology, and American steelmen were learning from Europeans how to make stainless steel. In 1935, Charles Ramseyer, a respected engineer, told the American Institute of Mining and Metallurgical Engineers: "Actually the operation of . . . basic processes [in the iron and steel industry] has not changed significantly in either theory or fundamental design of equipment in the past seventy-five years. While automobiles were being made better and cheaper with ever newer processes . . . tonnage steel, as distinguished from the special and alloy steels, grew neither cheaper nor better."

As the 1919 strike showed, Gary's labor policies also were bankrupt, but he continued to repeat "the same worn phrases of his welfare philosophy," wrote the labor historian David Brody. In 1923, under pressure from the Interchurch World Movement, a Protestant organization, and the administration of President Warren G. Harding, Gary finally replaced the twelve-hour day with an eight-hour day. But the corporation went on running its steel towns with a firm hand, beating down any moves toward unionism. Other steel companies took it as a model. Said *Fortune* in 1936:

It is charged with . . . spying upon its workmen both inside the plants and in their homes, with debauching unions, corrupting union leaders, and, with imperturbable aplomb, grinding down its workers day and night. The influence of its open-shop policy is thought of as extending far beyond the confines of the steel industry itself into secondary and tertiary zones, constantly menacing labor organizations in communities and industries where they are well established. Its welfare work is dismissed as mere publicity given to measures that are taken for granted by other companies, or it is analyzed as a benevolent-appearing policy for which the steel workers themselves are charged. Above all, the corporation is attacked for suppressing any measure of democracy, not only in its plants but in the communities that it dominates—for denying free speech and the right of assembly to its employees, for intimidating workmen who are dissatisfied with their working conditions and attempt to change them, for preventing, in a thousand devious ways, that free expression of political belief that is a fundamental part of the American tradition.

IV

Then Gary was gone, and gone with him was a singular period in the history of the corporation and American business. The Judge had suffered from a heart problem for years, but the seriousness of the ailment had been minimized and Gary had soldiered on, though he suffered from spells of bad health throughout the early 1920s.

Early in 1927, while in a chair at his desk, he leaned back and fell, striking his head against the radiator. On April 25, 1927, after the corporation's annual stockholders' meeting, Gary talked with reporters. He seemed to have a premonition that his time had come: "I would not blame the members of the corporation if they should decide to say, 'It is time for that old gentleman to lay himself on the shelf.' My age is such that I must expect such a thing to happen."

On June 16, in a ceremony at his office in New York, Gary pulled a switch that put on the electricity at the gigantic new structural mill at the Homestead Works. This was his last public act. On June 18, he left his office and never returned. At 3:40 A.M. on August 15, 1927, at the age of eighty, he died at his home at 1130 Fifth Avenue in New York.

Gary's body lay in state at his home for a day, then was taken by motor hearse to Grand Central Station, where it was placed in a special section of the Twentieth Century Limited for the eighteen-hour trip to Chicago. Floral pieces were carried to the terminal in thirty-five motor cars. A dozen leading steelmen were aboard the train, including Schwab, whose unfortunate task it had become, with the passage of time, to stand at the biers of many of the giants of the steel industry. When the train arrived in Chicago, the mourners were driven to the Drake Hotel, and the body was taken by motor hearse, moving slowly because of the weight of the coffin, to Wheaton, Illinois. On August 18, the funeral was conducted at the Gary Memorial Methodist Episcopal Church in Wheaton, a handsome stone structure that had been a gift of the Judge to the congregation. The body was to be buried in a crypt in a $250,000 mausoleum that the Judge had directed be constructed.

The nation's leaders praised Gary. President Coolidge said that he had "stood foremost among those who find in the great private enterprise of our country an opportunity for public service as well as a medium for financial profit." Thomas Alva Edison saw Gary as practical, like one of Edison's inventions. "He was one of America's most useful men," Edison said. G. H. Jones, chairman of the board of the Standard Oil Company of New Jersey, said, "More than any other one man, perhaps, he shaped policies which have done so much to improve the efficiency of large-scale operations." Charles M. Schwab said, "Judge Gary will go down in industrial history as one of the greatest figures in America." The businessman Owen D. Young went further, calling Gary "one of the greatest figures of the world." Alva C. Dinkey, president of the Midvale Steel

Corporation and an old Carnegie man, said of the Judge, "The United States Steel Corporation is his monument."

Because of the weight of the coffin, ten young men—members of the Northwestern University football team, including the brother of the football star Red Grange—were enlisted to carry the coffin. The coffin was so heavy because it was made of steel.

11

"THE BEST SNOWBALL FIGHT I WAS EVER IN"

It was cold and raining heavily in Homestead on November 5, 1898, but the weather seemed to bother no one. This was one of the important days in Homestead's life, the day of the dedication of the town library, formally known as the Carnegie Library of Homestead. Construction of the massive building, at the east end of town, on the hill where soldiers of the Pennsylvania National Guard had encamped during the strike in 1892 and had conducted their spirited drills, had been in process for three years. Up it had gone, three stories and more, the handsome building of tan-colored brick with turrets and chimneys and a massive slate roof. At last it was finished.

The crowd began to gather in the late morning, coming by foot, wagon, and train, and by early afternoon more than six thousand people were on hand. Finally, at 2:20 P.M., a special train from Pittsburgh arrived at the Homestead station. Aboard was the official party—Andrew Carnegie and his wife, Louise; leading company executives, including Charles M. Schwab, smiling and voluble, as usual; and Henry Clay Frick, unsmiling and taciturn, as was usual for him. The members of the party were escorted from the train to a covered carriage and driven along Eighth Avenue and then up the hill to the imposing building.

With the official party in place, a parade began, moving from Eighth Avenue up McClure Street and then east on Tenth Avenue to the library. The parade was one of the finest in the history of the Homestead district, this in a town that loved parades and could always find a reason for one. Leading the parade were over fifteen hundred schoolchildren, each carrying a miniature American flag. (The Spanish-American War was going on, and patriotic spirit was running high.) Then came several thousand steelworkers and townspeople, followed by a contingent from the General Griffin Post of the Grand Army of the Republic, headed by the Old Steel Workers Band.

After them came men from the beam mill of the Homestead Works, on a large float with a tall flagpole from which the American flag snapped in the wind. Then came the Whittaker Drum Corps, then a delegation from Saint Michael's Roman Catholic Church, the Slovak church, headed by the Slavonic Society Band. Then came four companies of firemen from Homestead and East Pittsburgh; "the brave fire laddies," as the men were known, marched to the music of the Duquesne Greys Military Band. Town leaders, among them Reid Kennedy, the burgess, and C. F. Williams, the police chief, brought up the rear.

The official party came out to the front of the library, and it was agreed that Andrew Carnegie and his wife had never looked happier. When the marchers reached the library, the dignitaries and as many of the paraders and townspeople as could fit squeezed into the music hall, where the Carnegies, Schwab, Frick, and William E. Corey, the works' general superintendent, and his wife, Mary Cook Corey, the daughter of a Braddock miner, were presented with bouquets of red, white, and yellow chrysanthemums by steelworkers from the Homestead Works. The Ladies' Choir of Homestead sang a number of appropriate airs.

Schwab, always popular in Homestead, introduced Carnegie, his friend and mentor: "Mr. and Mrs. Carnegie have evidenced a deeper personal interest in the establishment of your library than in any public benefaction with which they have been identified." Carnegie had "suggested many of the detailed plans of the building and insisted upon being fully advised as to the progress of the work," Schwab said.

Carnegie then took the speakers' stand. This was the first time he had been to Homestead since February 1893, when he had come to smooth relations with the workers after the Homestead fight. The workers and townspeople, so often impressed by authority, were in a forgiving mood. There was a storm of applause, then silence, and Carnegie began his address: "Few events in my life have filled me with such pleasure as I have in appearing before you to hand over this building, with its library rightly in the center, the hall upon the right, and the Workingmen's Club upon the left—three foundations from which healing waters are to flow for the instruction, entertainment, and happiness of the people, the great mass of whom find useful and, I am happy to say, well-paid employment in these works which have become famous throughout the world."

It was clear that Carnegie's trip to Homestead had dredged up painful memories for him, not only of the Homestead strike of 1892, six years before, but of the many years before the strike, when, in his view, the Homestead workers had not demonstrated proper deference to the corporation. Nine years earlier, in 1889, at the dedication of the Carnegie Library in Braddock, across the Monongahela River, Carnegie had said of Homestead: "I should like to see a library [in Homestead, but] . . . our men there are not partners. They are not interested with [*sic*] us."

Carnegie had held to his word, and Homestead had not gotten a library. But then, sometime after the Homestead strike, a delegation of town leaders had gone to Carnegie and asked him to donate a library. Carnegie had agreed. He knew the union was crushed at Homestead. The town was in his control; building a library was a sign of this. Now, in the packed music hall, facing the damp workers and townspeople, the rain beating on the roof, Carnegie talked of the Pinkerton fight and of the distress he said the strike had caused him. "The one great pain of our united lives," he said, speaking for himself and his wife, "arising from business and which has haunted us for years, came from the deplorable event here, which startled us when far away, and which even yet has not lost its power at intervals to sadden our lives."

Then Carnegie, as was his habit, turned blame from himself. The Homestead Works, he said, "were probably the most difficult we ever had anything to do with. Many of you remember that we did not build these works; we did not man them; on the contrary we purchased them as a running concern from some of our neighbors, who had been compelled to employ any kind of men, such was the scarcity of labor at the time they started. If I may be allowed to say so, they were not such men as we have been blessed with at our works, and such as we now rejoice in having here. It was under great difficulty we labored to improve the town of Homestead. Many good men were sent from our other works, only to return, giving as their reasons that it was no place for their wives and children, nor even for themselves. How bravely is all this changed now."

The library, Carnegie said, represented a new beginning: "By this meeting, by your welcome, by these smiling faces, all the regretful thoughts, all the unpleasant memories, are henceforth and forever in the deep bosom of the ocean buried. Henceforth, we are to think of Homestead as we see it today."

The Carnegie Library was a magnificent building, a library but much more. The reading rooms and stacks were in the center of the building. In the west wing was the natatorium, with athletic facilities, a swimming pool, eight showers and twenty bathtubs, a billiard room with ten tables, four bowling alleys, an exercise room, and a basketball court with a running track above it. In the east wing was the auditorium, or music hall, into which the townspeople were now crowded. It resembled Carnegie Hall, in New York City, but was built on a much smaller scale. The auditorium had seats for 1,071. Carnegie had spared no expense. It was estimated that the library had cost $350,000, a significant sum at that time.

Carnegie concluded his speech, "Take . . . this building as the gift of one workman to other workmen." A blacksmith from the Homestead Works, a Scot, John Bell, Jr., now rose. Bell had been selected to deliver the response to Carnegie because he was a strong company man. He felt awkward, he said, a mere blacksmith on the podium with such important people: "I would feel more at home standing behind an anvil." But he understood his responsibilities: "I am here . . . as a representative of the workingman. And now, Mr. Carnegie, permit me on behalf of myself and fellow workmen to tender you our sincere and earnest thanks for, and appreciation of, this magnificent gift."

After a reception, Carnegie and his wife, Schwab, Frick (who as far as is known made no remarks during the dedication—no false modesty, no false humility, for him), and the rest of the official party returned to the covered carriage and were transported through the rain down the hill to the special train, which took them back to Pittsburgh.

II

The gift of the library was representative of the ways in which, after the 1892 strike, the Carnegie Company worked to establish control in Homestead and the other steel towns. The company men knew that it was not enough to break the union; the towns themselves had to be broken. The company strove diligently to seize the institutions of community life—newspapers, churches, schools, social clubs, police, municipal government. Only by doing this could they ensure that unionism would not rise again.

When the Carnegie operations were purchased and combined with others to form the United States Steel Corporation in March 1901, the corporation men saw what Carnegie had done and went further, for Gary and his crew were experts at control. The Gary welfare system—the stock plan, the housing program, the sports program, and more—was one set of instruments used to gain control over workers and the steel towns. Other instruments included spies, blacklisting, suppression of wages, pay-offs for jobs and advancement, corruption of priests and ministers, gifts to communities, control of borough governments, exploitation of ethnic and racial differences, and countenancing corruption.

Homesteaders were bitter about the authority that the Carnegie company and then the corporation exerted over almost every facet of their lives. The sociologist Margaret Byington found clear antipathy toward the corporation when she lived in the town for six months in 1908 as part of her research into Homestead working-class life. But given the power of the employers, there was little the townspeople could do.

The mill had created the town and was itself a major instrument of repression. The men worked long hours at backbreaking labor, and at the end of a day's work they had little time or energy left for pursuits such as union activity or community improvement. One Homestead worker kept a record of his working hours in a notebook for eight months prior to the strike of 1919. He recorded that in 244 days he had seventeen days off (less than one day off every two weeks) and worked 2,930 hours (more than twelve hours a day on average), including eighteen twenty-four-hour shifts. Another worker, a Slav employed as a laborer, worked twelve hours a day with a twenty-four-hour shift every other Sunday. He earned forty-two cents an hour, or sixty dollars every two weeks.

"Men weary from long hours of work, men who have been refused any share in determining the conditions under which they work, are not prompted to seize opportunities for improving the conditions under which they live," Margaret Byington wrote in 1911. "Their habitual suppression industrially has meant a loss of initiative. Somehow it is easier to pay a neighbor fifty cents a month for the privilege of bringing drinking water three times a day from his well, than to insist that the borough provide a wholesome supply."

At the same time, the mill had its lures for the men of the steel towns. Because the mill was there, people knew that jobs were there. Boys refused to continue their education because they knew they could get work in the mill. Fathers said that if the mill was good enough for them, it was good enough for their sons. Parents expected their daughters to marry mill workers and thus be taken care of. There was also, as Margaret Byington said, a fascination about the mill: "Men wanted to show they could meet its challenge, that they could do the hard, hazardous work." The work defined the men, gave them an identity—they were *steelworkers*.

The myth of the steel millionaire also seduced the people of the steel towns. Carnegie, Frick, Schwab, Julian Kennedy, Alva Dinkey, William E. Corey and his brother A. A. Corey, William B. Dickson, A. R. Hunt— they and others had started poor and become rich, important men. They were regarded as representatives of that quintessential American hero, the self-made man, and were much honored by the townspeople. Many a mill-town boy, especially in the early days, went into the mill with the hope of making himself rich, a big man in steel, even though it was impossible in most cases to rise from the rank and file. Finally, the sheer size of the mill, the gigantic machines, the vast sheds, the high cauldrons of bubbling steel, overwhelmed the men who worked there. Men could not work in such a setting and regard themselves as important.

But it was not just the mill itself that controlled the men. The corporation's espionage system was substantial, well beyond what had existed in the days of Frick and Carnegie. In 1919, in testimony before a Senate committee investigating the 1919 steel strike, this exchange between Senator David I. Walsh and Judge Gary occurred.

WALSH: Have you a secret service organization among your employees at any of the subsidiary plants of the Steel Corporation?

GARY: Well, Senator, I cannot be very specific about that, but I am quite sure that at times some of our people have used secret service men to ascertain facts and conditions.

Such espionage had its effect. The sociologist John A. Fitch said, "If you want to talk in Homestead, you must talk to yourself."

The corporation also utilized blacklisting. They kept lists of workers whom they regarded as union men or troublemakers and refused to hire them. In 1907, Margaret Byington found men who still could not obtain work in any corporation mill because of their participation in the strike a decade and a half before. Corruption in the mill also fostered the corporation's power. Favoritism, nepotism, and abuse of power by foremen was rampant in the Homestead Works and other mills. It was traditional for men to make payoffs to foremen and other supervisors in order to get jobs for themselves or for their sons, relatives, friends, and to get promotions.

In the steel towns, the corporation established close ties with priests and ministers so that they would be beholden to the corporation and assist them in controlling the workers and the townspeople. In the 1892 strike, a number of Homestead ministers had spoken out against the corporation, notably Father Bullion of Saint Mary Magdalene's Roman Catholic Church and the Reverend McIlyar of the Fourth Avenue Methodist Episcopal Church. But in the 1919 strike, almost no ministers in Homestead and the other steel towns in the Monongahela Valley supported the workers. Only Father Adelbert Kazinscy, in Braddock, was known as a solid union man, and he was ultimately driven from town. Early in the twentieth century, Homestead ministers defended the twelve-hour day, saying that hard work helped develop steadiness among the workers, and Pittsburgh ministers attacked Sunday work in drug and confectionery stores but not steel mills. As Judge Gary said to the president of the corporation's subsidiaries in 1919: "It's a great thing to keep in touch with the priests and the clergy. The pastors are in contact with the families and the workmen themselves."

Other institutions were also corrupted by the corporation. Early in the twentieth century, an investigator from the magazine *Survey* suggested to the secretary of a branch of the Young Men's Christian Association in the Pittsburgh district that the association campaign for a shorter workday. The secretary replied: "Oh, no, we could not do that. In the first place, the association is the child, you might say, of the steel company. They are the heaviest contributors. . . . Probably [the state association] couldn't touch it either. You see, we are backed up everywhere by the substantial businessmen of the various localities; they would not stand for any such movement."

After the 1892 strike, employers throughout the iron and steel industry worked hard to control the instruments of government of the towns. The corporation encouraged its executives to become active in community affairs—to run for burgess, borough councils, school boards. The Homestead burgess in 1907, Thomas L. Davis, was a superintendent at Jones and Laughlin, and in 1919 the president of the Homestead borough council was a mill executive, as were the burgesses of Munhall and Clairton. The burgess of Duquesne and the Allegheny County sheriff were brothers of important steel executives. "Homestead has no leaders," Margaret Byington said.

Control not only meant docile workers and townspeople but brought financial returns to the corporation. The borough councils kept taxes on the corporation low and permitted the existence of the most wretched living conditions, with workers penned into crowded flats and shabby row houses. The Homestead borough council refused for years to enact modern sanitary regulations, in a community whose mill was one of the most profitable in the nation. Even by 1910, a large percentage of Homestead homes had neither toilets nor running water. The stream that ran down Munhall Hollow, just west of Homestead, was for years an open sewer, tumbling human excrement and other filth and debris down the hollow from settled areas up the hill. In the hot summer months, the stench in Munhall Hollow, or Hunkie Hollow, was almost unbearable; wagonloads of lime had to be hauled in and dumped in the creek bed. Local physicians forbade residents to drink borough water unless it had been boiled and filtered, but many residents "seemed to accept such a situation as a matter of course," Margaret Byington said. For years, there were no building codes in Homestead, except one provision, enacted after a terrible fire in 1886, that required buildings in the business district to be fireproof.

The practice of gerrymandering for corporate tax gains and municipal control was rampant in the Monongahela Valley. For example, in 1900, the Homestead town government, under pressure from the corporation, established the borough of Munhall, adjacent to Homestead. At the time, three-quarters of the Homestead Works was in what was established as Munhall, which meant a major decrease in corporate tax revenues for Homestead. But it meant tax advantages for the corporation, so it was done. The corporation also worked to keep other businesses out of towns, thus denying the towns a more diversified economic base and ensuring its own power.

It was widely known that the corporation men were engaging in underhanded practices, but borough councils and state legislators found it to their advantage not to confront the corporation. The Republican Party controlled the borough governments in the steel towns and the Pennsylvania state legislature, and the corporation dominated the Republican Party. The Pennsylvania custom of aldermanic courts, in which squires, or justices of the peace, heard most local court cases, also was used to the corporation's advantage. In Homestead, as in many towns, the burgess was also the squire. Thus, a single man under the thumb of the corporation not only was in charge of municipal affairs and ran the police force but, as squire, possessed judicial authority as well.

The corporation and the other steel companies also used gifts as a means of control. If a borough wanted a street paved, light posts at the athletic field, refuse picked up, help with downed trees, assistance in emergencies such as fires or accidents, the mill provided it. Tom Girdler, chairman of Republic Steel during the violent Little Steel Strike of 1937, said that when he was general superintendent of the Aliquippa, Pennsylvania, works of Jones and Laughlin in the 1920s, it was "the habit of everyone to look to the company for anything the community needed. . . . The most anybody ever did was to make a suggestion and immediately bracket it with a fulfillment by saying, 'We'll ask the company.' "

Homestead received the Carnegie Library, and later Charles M. Schwab donated the Charles M. Schwab School for the Manual Arts to Homestead, and Henry Clay Frick donated a park, Frick Park. With each gift, in Homestead and elsewhere, the corporation's control was strengthened.

Margaret Byington said of Homestead: "These generous gifts beautify Homestead and provide something toward its recreation and intellectual stimulus. Yet, though the people are very proud of them, many a man said to me, 'We'd rather they hadn't cut our wages and let us spend the money for ourselves.' " The workers "resent a philanthropy which provides opportunities for intellectual and social advancement while it withholds conditions which make it possible to take advantage of them." Finally, these gifts and other practices were highly paternalistic and robbed the workers and the communities in which they lived of the ability to make decisions themselves, that is, to live democratically.

The corporation made sure the workers did not unite by exploiting differences between ethnic groups and races. When the first group of workers—English, Scottish, and Germans—became demanding, the corporation brought in "Slavs"—a catchall term for the various nationalities of Eastern and Southern Europe—to replace them. By 1910, Slavs made up more than half of the workforce of the Homestead Works, and immigrants made up more than six to seven thousand of Homestead's population of twenty thousand. They were easy to control. Few of the Slavs were citizens, and many—60 percent of the Homestead workers in 1907 —were illiterate. The Slavs, moreover, in many cases had come from authoritarian societies; even the church to which many belonged, the Roman Catholic Church, was authoritarian and hierarchical. Authoritarianism and obedience were the norm for them.

When the Slavs acted independently, as they did during the steel strike of 1919, the corporation began to bring in black workers to replace them. Blacks were useful: they worked for less money and were as undemanding as the English, Irish, Welsh, Scottish, and Germans, and later the Eastern and Southern Europeans, had once been. The Amalgamated Association of Iron, Steel, and Tin Workers denied membership to black workers throughout most of its existence and did little for them; thus many blacks had little concern about breaking strikes. Strikes were an opportunity—to obtain a job, to rise at least a bit in life.

In 1935, the labor writer Harvey O'Connor, said:

Since the turn of the century, the Steel Corporation . . . has held the political and social life of Pennsylvania in the hollow of its hands. . . . The dark flower of Steel's dictatorship bloomed in the black towns of Duquesne, Homestead, Braddock, Birmingham, Gary, and a score more, bearing fruit in wretched slums, debased politics, and tyranny. These were regarded by the corporation's financiers in New York as inevitable by-products of steel manufacture, like the black pall of smoke that smudged the towns. Steel-making, as Schwab repeatedly insisted, was merely incidental to the making of money. No time was wasted in sentimental reflection of the human costs.

III

What is remarkable, given what they were up against, is that the people of Homestead fashioned for themselves a full and often rewarding life. Despite the smoke and dirt, the grinding exactions of the mill, and the corporation's stranglehold, the people of Homestead built a splendid American community, with richness, texture, and grit.

Homestead loved holidays, particularly Memorial Day, the Fourth of July, and Christmas; the last two were, for decades, the only two days of the year when the mill was closed. All American towns celebrate these holidays, but in Homestead they seemed to take on special importance. Perhaps it was because steelwork offered so little that the men and women turned to their families and their community; perhaps it was because the town was largely isolated. Whatever the reason, there was a special sense of community in Homestead, which was reflected in holiday celebrations.

Each Memorial Day, the townspeople, including the old soldiers, would trudge up the hill to the Civil War monument, sweating profusely but determined not to be stragglers. General John A. Logan's General Order Eleven would be read. Logan was a founder of the Grand Army of the Republic, and Order Eleven directed that celebrations be held each Memorial Day to honor the Northern dead. Then the old boys in blue and other townsmen would conduct a retrograde movement down the hill to some tavern or place like the Opera Hall for refreshments and a hearty repast. The Fourth of July was something people looked forward to for weeks. There were picnics and baseball games and fireworks at night. In 1919 there was a magnificent balloon ascension by the daring Reno Brothers.

Christmas was a splendid affair. Beginning shortly after Thanksgiving, the merchants along Eighth Avenue filled their windows with items that residents might find suitable for presents; the churches put up trees and other decorations; and in mid-December people began to decorate their houses. It was a town custom to provide sweets for the children on Christmas Eve. Then came the splendid day itself, with gifts and drinks and songs, and plump turkeys or geese purchased from the fine butcher's shops on Eighth Avenue.

In December 1900, this letter was written by a Homestead child to Santa Claus:

Dear Santa Claus,
    I am a little boy eight years old, and I want a gun and an express wagon & a wheel barrow & a new suit & pair of kid gloves & some candy. This is all. Your little friend, George Rudly. Don't burn your whiskers when you come down the chimney.
    Kisses

And this:

Dear Santa—
    I just write & tell you I am still living at Munhall 34 Harrison St.
    Please bring me a drum and grinding organ Sambo doll & lots of things.
    I remain your good little boy.

There were other celebrations. In 1903, the Charles M. Schwab School for the Manual Arts, on Ninth Avenue, was dedicated. More than ten thousand workers and townspeople, and eighteen bands, marched in a gigantic parade to celebrate the opening of the school. Genial old Charlie was there himself. He was stouter then ever, with the passage of time and the accumulation of riches, and had not long before undergone the trying public disclosure of his madcap gambling on the Riviera. But he was smiling as always, and waving. He had helped break the 1892 strike and twice after that had helped thwart unionism at Homestead. But he was still immensely popular; the workers showed him great deference, as they did to so many steel executives.

Boys took classes in woodworking and metal-turning, girls in cooking and sewing. Many parents regarded the cooking classes at the Schwab School as putting on airs, complaining that far too much attention was given to fancy dishes. But one girl's family, after she had learned to make waffles at the Schwab School, was so pleased with the delicacy that having waffles every Sunday morning became a tradition in their home.

In 1905, the town received another gift—Frick Park, the gift of Henry Clay Frick. Frick had sent Pinkertons to Homestead. He had been responsible for the deaths of seven Homestead workers and of at least three Pinkertons, and there were still many men and women in town who had participated in the fight with the Pinkertons, had spat on them, thrown stones at them, or beaten them with umbrellas or fence staves as they were marched to the opera house. But the residents of Homestead were not about to turn down a free park, and so the park was built, a block in size, between Ninth and Tenth avenues, with play areas and a water fountain and handsome sycamore trees to provide surcease from the sun and a splash of green in the otherwise black city.

In 1925, a momentous event in Homestead's history occurred when the magnificent, four-story Stahl Theatre opened on Eighth Avenue. The creation of a former Braddock mailman, John E. Stahl, the theater was a vaudeville house and it brought in a number of top stars, among them Sophie Tucker, Fred Allen, and George Burns and Gracie Allen. The famed striptease artist Peaches Browning appeared there. She was a hit with many of the men, but she shocked the town's ministers.

Stahl, who did not finish high school, started his career as a showman about 1907, when he began building movie houses in Homestead; by 1925, he had put together a string of them in the Homestead business district, including the Elite—pronounced E-lite—the Tiffany, the Crescent, and the Grand. Then Stahl made the stunning announcement that he would tear down the Grand to build a theater equal to any in America. People laughed, but construction began, and on November 11, 1925, Armistice Day, the Stahl was opened. Ticket-holders waited in line on Eighth Avenue trying to get a glimpse inside, where there was a large Kimball organ, a ten-piece orchestra, and seats for 1,828 people. It was said that the theater had cost one million dollars. It was the first million-dollar theater in America, Homesteaders always said, although whether this is true cannot be verified. The first night's bill featured ten vaudeville acts and a silent comedy. Two orchestras played, and ticket-holders danced much of the night on the theater's ballroom-sized dance floor.

Stahl was a sharp operator and a tremendous promoter. When the Charlie Chaplin movie *The Gold Rush* opened at the theater in 1925, Stahl hired a man who looked like Chaplin to impersonate him on Eighth

Avenue, and from time to time other characters were hired to walk along Eighth Avenue and drum up interest in movies that were playing at the Stahl—Indians, Confederate soldiers, and the like. The theater was often the site for marathon dances; in 1928, twenty-four couples finished a marathon at the Stahl that lasted 144 hours and 55 minutes.

In July 1917, the Buffalo Bill Wild West Show and Circus—"The Big Show with the Big Punch"—played at the circus grounds in Rankin, across the Monongahela River from Homestead. A special attraction was the heavyweight champion Jess Willard, "the Great White Hope," who had defeated Jack Johnson, a black man, in April 1915. He was now touring between fights to pick up a few dollars. Two years later, on July 4, 1919, a torrid day, with the temperature reaching ninety-six, several thousand Homesteaders gathered on Eighth Avenue, in front of the office of the *Homestead Messenger,* to watch bulletins posted there on the magnificent fight between Willard and the challenger, Jack Dempsey. It was a vicious fight that Dempsey won when Willard could not answer the bell for the fourth round.

Homesteaders not only followed sports avidly but loved to play them. The millhands, after all, were tough people, and the rough and tumble and the competition of sports appealed to them. There were baseball and basketball leagues sponsored by the Homestead Works, and the Homestead Athletic Department was always a busy place, attracting hundreds of children and adults every day. Boxing was always a favorite sport, as were wrestling and swimming. People reveled in these sports, and those who had special skills became town heroes; years later people still remembered their names and feats. The Homestead Athletic Department's swimming club was widely known. In 1928, Susan Laird, a member of the Carnegie Library swimming team, placed second in the freestyle in the Olympic Games.

Pleasures in Homestead came with the seasons: swimming in the Monongahela River in summer, corn roasts in the fall, and, in winter, bean suppers, fort-building and snowball fights, and coasting down the sleek borough streets, despite police admonishments.

In the winter of 1919, the morning after a heavy snowfall, two rival groups of youths, Irish and black, decided to have a snowball fight and set out up the hill toward Westfield. One of the black youths was Jester Hairston, the first black quarterback on the Homestead High School football team. He was so poor that in the 1919 Thanksgiving game he had to wait until the other players took the field so he could poke around the locker room and find a pair of cleats that fitted him. He went on to a highly successful acting career, playing LeRoy, the Kingfish's brother-in-law on the radio program *Amos 'n' Andy* and appearing in musical-comedy films, and on Johnny Carson's *Tonight* show on television.

That day in 1919, the two gangs took opposite sides of the snow-blanketed football field. The next couple of hours were given over to fort-building, and each side went about its task with utmost diligence. The black kids seemed to have particular zest, or knowledge of snow architecture, for they finished first and, having ensured that a goodly supply of snowballs had been made, Hairston waited.

But then a detachment of Irish kids came walking across the field under a white flag. The Irish kids said that their fort was not finished and it would take too much effort to finish it. They wanted to call off the snowball fight. The black kids held a council of war. This was not fair, they felt. They had worked hard on their fort and wanted to have the fight. They returned to the center of the field and made an offer: "We will help you build your fort."

The Irish kids accepted the offer, and the fort was finished. The Irish kids were impressed by the generosity of the black kids. "It was awfully nice of you to help us with our fort," the Irish kids said. "Let's not fight." "Yeah," one Irish kid said, "you niggers aren't so bad."

"YOU NIGGERS AREN'T SO BAD!" The words hung in the air like icicles. A furious snowball fight ensued. Boom! Boom! Boom! Boom! The snowballs flew across the field. "It was," Hairston said seventy years later, "the best snowball fight I was ever in."

IV

Yet life in Homestead and the other steel towns was a life within limits. A small circle of businessmen, professional people, and mill executives ruled the town. The symbols of the corporation's power were everywhere—the mill on the river, the library on the hill, the general superintendent's mansion next to the library, the Schwab School and Frick Park on the west end of town, the churches that the corporation often helped fund, even street names like Andrew and Louise streets, named for Andrew and Louise Carnegie. Fundamental American rights —free speech, freedom of assembly, the right to run their towns and their lives themselves—were denied to the people of Homestead.

In 1922, the perfect tool of the corporation took office as burgess of Homestead. John Cavanaugh, a coroner by trade, was also employed as a Homestead policeman and later a county detective. Like all politicians in the steel towns of that time, he was a Republican. Cavanaugh, who for many years lived in a large house on the corner of Eighth Avenue and

West Street, was to rule Homestead for almost two decades, using intimidation and strong-arm methods and violence against voters who opposed him. A determined man, he had met his wife when he was twenty and she was nine. He waited until she was twenty and he was thirty-one before he proposed. An ally was a young dentist, John McLean.

Cavanaugh's diligence in the service of the corporation was evidenced in July 1933, when Frances Perkins, President Franklin D. Roosevelt's newly appointed secretary of labor, visited Homestead as part of a tour of steel-producing communities to build support for the steel code that was part of the National Industrial Recovery Act of June 1933. The Depression was three and a half years old, and the steel industry was in disarray. The code, it was envisioned, would set wages, hours, working conditions, and prices for the steel industry.

Burgess Cavanaugh had agreed to allow Miss Perkins to hold a meeting in the borough building on Ninth Avenue. She spoke to a crowded hall and found the workers spirited but inarticulate. At the end of the meeting, as she was saying goodbye to Cavanaugh, she heard a disturbance downstairs. A newspaperman whispered to her that a number of people had not been allowed to attend the meeting and were clustered in the lower hall and on the sidewalk on Ninth Avenue. She turned to Cavanaugh and asked if she could meet in the hall with the demonstrators for a few moments.

Cavanaugh's face turned red. He blustered: "No, no, you've had enough. These men are not any good. They're undesirable reds. I know them well. They just want to make trouble."

But Miss Perkins wanted to see the workers and went downstairs. There she encountered perhaps two hundred people, many of them angry. They had been pushed out of the borough building by the Homestead constabulary. She stood on the steps of the hall and began to make a short speech. By this time, Cavanaugh had arrived with two secretaries and the police. "You can't talk here!" he cried. "You are not permitted to make a speech here—there is a rule against making a speech here."

The people on the sidewalk were tense. Miss Perkins spied Frick Park, a block away, at Tenth Avenue and Amity Street. "All right. I am sorry," she said. "We will go to the public park."

Burgess Cavanaugh and the policemen were at her side, saying: "You can't do that. There is an ordinance against holding meetings in a public park."

"This is just a hearing, not a meeting," Miss Perkins said. "It would not be long, only a few minutes."

The burgess repeated that the men were "undesirable reds."

Now Miss Perkins saw the American flag flying from the staff of a building diagonally across from the borough building. "Ah, the post office, she thought—"federal property." "We will go to the post office. There is the American flag," she said.

She and the irate townspeople filed across the street and then up the steps into the post office. Miss Perkins climbed onto a chair and made a short speech about the steel code. Twenty or thirty of the men in the crowd spoke. They said that they wished the government would free the workers from the domination of the corporation. The meeting ended with Miss Perkins and the townspeople shaking hands and agreeing that the leaders of the New Deal were not afraid of the corporation.

When Miss Perkins returned to Washington, she found members of the press at her door. What happened in Homestead? the reporters wanted to know. Why did the burgess act as he did?

Miss Perkins thought this over. "Why, he seemed a little nervous," she said. "The Nervous Burgess." My, how the press loved it. So did President Roosevelt. He telephoned Miss Perkins. "You did just the right thing, and you gave the post office free advertising," the president laughed. "That's priceless."

Cavanaugh had another view. The burgess said that the borough should regard itself as fortunate that he had put together such a keen intelligence operation. "The entire lower Monongahela Valley and Pittsburgh has been resting on a smoldering volcano, which has been ready to burst out at any moment, due to a widespread communistic movement which has been gaining momentum for months past," he said. "Luckily, I have known practically every move they have been making lately, and I have been able to break up the organization in Homestead, but other districts are not so fortunate."

1 2

"THE MAN NOBODY KNOWS"

The Judge was dead, and as his body was being transported across the Midwest for burial in the black prairie from which he had come, talk already had begun about who would succeed him. The names of several men were bandied about. Some thought the chairman would be Nathan L. Miller, the corporation's general counsel and a former New York governor. Others talked of James A. Farrell, the old wire-drawer and expert on foreign markets, and now the corporation's president. Others spoke of Dwight Morrow, the lawyer, and J. Pierpont Morgan, Jr., the son of J. Pierpont, Sr. It was even suggested that President Calvin Coolidge might succeed Gary, at the end of Coolidge's term, in March 1929, but this was just a rumor. The truth was, the successor would have to be one of the members of the corporation's inner circle, that is, the eight men of the corporation's finance committee, who, in addition to Gary, Miller, Farrell, and Morgan, Sr., included Percival Roberts, Jr., an old steelman from Philadelphia; William J. Filbert, the corporation's secretary-treasurer and an accountant with the company since it was founded; George F. Baker, another Morgan man; and Myron C. Taylor, a New York lawyer and financier.

There was no doubt who had the final say in the matter—Morgan and Baker. They and Gary had functioned as the corporation's "big three," and, it was said, had never had a serious disagreement. In September 1927, the decision was announced, and a strange decision it was. The authority that Gary had possessed would be divided among three men: Morgan, who would be chairman of the board, Farrell, who would be chief executive officer, and Taylor, who would be chairman of the finance committee. In agreeing to the decision, the younger Morgan broke the longstanding practice of the house of Morgan that Morgan men did not hold offices in corporations.

Morgan was well known, a premier American banker, like his father. Farrell had been a steelman for years and was respected for his knowledge of the industry. Taylor, while important on Wall Street, was something of a mystery. He had a reputation as a sharp investor in the textile industry but was a newcomer to steel, and not many people knew much about him. The press called him "the Man Nobody Knows."

But what did it matter who ran the corporation? It was huge and powerful—slow-moving and ponderous, yes, but a great force that, it seemed, could not be stopped. The corporation had prospered immensely during World War I. Attempts by the government to break it up had been beaten back, and the workers' latest effort at unionism had been defeated in the strike of 1919. The 1920s, the last years of Gary's reign, had been uneventful and highly prosperous. That the corporation would be run by three men was most unusual, but it was believed that no matter who ran it, it would remain what it had been since its establishment—the world's largest business enterprise, the supreme symbol of American manufacturing.

II

The triumvirate was a failure. Morgan's presence provided the corporation with a prestigious name but little more. He was a banker, not a steelman, and put little time into the corporation. Farrell concerned himself almost solely with day-to-day operations. He was good at that, but the role, by definition, was limited. Taylor spent most of his time working to improve the company's financial position, which he did splendidly, but he did little more. No one, it seemed, was running the corporation.

Then, in October 1929, came the Great Depression, a turning point for the corporation and for America. Steel executives, like most other businessmen, had not foreseen the Depression, nor, even long after it had begun, did they realize the deep, wrenching effect it was having, or that it would last so long. "Steel leaders express unanimous satisfaction with the conditions of the industry" at the 1929 meeting of the American Iron and Steel Institute, the *Wall Street Journal* said. Myron C. Taylor, at the corporation's April 1930 stockholders' meeting, seven months after the Depression began, said: "The foundation on which we stand today is basically sound. . . . There is gold in the cargo."

But the Depression devastated the corporation and the steel towns and the workers and townspeople in them. Depressions had struck the iron and steel industry in the past—in 1873, 1893, and 1921, for example —but this one was different. In 1932, the corporation operated at 17 percent of capacity, and that year it lost $71.2 million, the first loss in its history. In 1933, American steel production reached its lowest point in the twentieth century. Blast-furnace production for the week of March 31, 1933, was the lowest ever recorded; rail production that year was the lowest since 1865; and iron-ore shipments on the Great Lakes were at the level of 1880 to 1885, before the opening of the Mesabi Range.

The steel towns were in misery. Fifty percent of Homestead workers were unemployed. Nationwide, full-time steel employment in 1932 dropped to 18,000 of the 158,000 listed on industry employment rolls. Many corporation workers were employed as part-time workers under a spread-the-work formula that Myron Taylor and his associates devised. Wages dropped from an all-time high of $469 million in 1923 to $133 million in 1932. In that year, wages for laborers dropped to thirty-three cents an hour.

The optimism of the corporation's leadership finally gave way, in the face of plummeting steel markets, layoffs, and the workers' hardships. In 1931, a despondent Taylor was forced to confess, "We have been forced by events beginning in the summer of 1929 to retreat from one position to another, always hoping to entrench ourselves in a position that would mark the culmination of the depression."

Something had to be done. Taylor was one of the few bright stars in the corporation. He had gradually begun to expand his duties from finance, and by the spring of 1931 it was an open secret in the American business community that he was the chief authority in corporation policy. It was time to formalize the situation and reenergize the corporation. In March 1932, the corporation announced that Morgan was resigning as chairman of the board and Taylor would replace him, and that Taylor would keep the chairmanship of the finance committee and take from Farrell, who was forced from the corporation, the title of chief executive officer. *Fortune* said, "After five years of interregnum, Gary's imperial power found an inheritor."

III

Taylor was an imperious-appearing man who traced his patrician ancestry to Colonial days. He was tall and handsome, with deep-set, piercing eyes, a thin slit of a mouth, and a determined, even pugnacious face. He preferred high, stiff collars, and for reading he donned tortoiseshell pince-nez glasses. He often carried a cane, although he had no impairment that demanded one, and often wore gloves, even if it was not cold. He was formal and reserved. The journalist Dwight MacDonald described Taylor's voice as "soothingly cadenced, gently authoritative and reassuring, like that of a great psychiatrist who specializes in treating nervous women."

Taylor had few close relationships with associates and seemed to have few emotional attachments—to business or his hobbies. He had married at the age of thirty-two; he and his wife, Anabel, had no children. Though he belonged to many clubs, he rarely visited any. He gave liberally to charity and served on fund-raising committees for the Salvation Army, the American Red Cross, Cornell University, and other institutions, but there is no hint of any special zeal in his charitable work. He collected art, but desultorily.

As chairman of the corporation, he was in essence the head of a government, and his manner was suited to the part. His communications, the historian Irving Bernstein said, would have done honor to the British Foreign Service; they were characterized by "meticulous drafting, exhaustive treatment, smooth phrasing." After President Franklin D. Roosevelt had been in office for a time, he and Taylor became close friends. When Taylor had business with the government, he did not bother with members of the cabinet or any other subordinates but telephoned or stopped by the White House to talk to the president directly. He once said, "Our difficulty is to find men who will leave private business and devote themselves to the Corporation," as if the corporation were not a private enterprise but a government entity.

Myron Charles Taylor was born on January 18, 1874, in Lyons, New York, the son of William Deiling Taylor, who made a fortune in textiles and leather, and Mary Morgan Underhill Taylor. He attended the Lyons Union School and the National Law School, both in Washington, D.C., and took his final year in law at Cornell University, where he was a pupil of Charles Evans Hughes, later a Supreme Court justice. Taylor was something of a child prodigy, graduating from Cornell in 1894, at the age of twenty, having gone directly to law school from secondary school. He was admitted to the New York bar on his twenty-first birthday, January 18, 1895.

Despite his age, Taylor was able and ambitious. He immediately set up an office at 71 Broadway, later the address of the United States Steel Corporation, and declared himself available "for the practice of corporation law." But it quickly became apparent that he had a flair for corporate finance and reorganization, and it was not long before he abandoned the law. He had become familiar with the textile industry through his father, and it was there that he made his first fortune.

He developed what became known as "the Taylor formula" for salvaging textile businesses. He would analyze the financial situation of a company, and its production and sales methods, and then offer his recommendations on how the company should be restructured. If money was needed, he would obtain it—usually privately, for he disliked the stock market—and would simplify the company's financial arrangements. He made sure that the latest equipment was purchased for each mill and stressed continuous operation—three shifts a day. Then, with the company on solid ground, he would turn his attention to sales, encouraging aggressive salesmanship and attention to detail; always he used his connections in the rest of the textile industry to further the company he was assisting. Finally, he would receive a substantial fee or, if he had acquired control, a profit from selling the company.

Taylor employed this formula for more than twenty-five years throughout the textile belt—from Massachusetts through New Jersey and Pennsylvania to the coastal South—and probably earned more than $20 million. By 1923, seeking new challenges and greater profits, Taylor had largely abandoned the textile industry and was concentrating on banking and on several railroad directorships, where he again achieved remarkable success. He had, by this time, the perfect reputation for the business world, as a man who was at once conservative and progressive, conservative in that he was disciplined and made money, progressive in that he was skilled at analyzing and reorganizing financial and production methods.

All this time, Taylor was being watched by the leading financial men, including J. Pierpont Morgan, Jr., and his associates. Taylor had become a close friend of George F. Baker, Morgan's aide and the largest individual stockholder in the corporation. In 1927, Taylor was appointed by

Morgan to the United States Steel Corporation's finance committee and its board of directors. He had no intention of making steel a career. But when he was named chairman of the finance committee upon Gary's death, later in 1927, he pitched in and did his job well. In fewer than two years, helped significantly by a bull market, Taylor retired $265 million of the corporation's $400 million bond debt, cutting the corporation's interest charges from $24 million in 1928 to $5 million in 1934. Then, in March 1932, when the triumvirate seemed not to be working, Morgan and Baker, seeking "the finest flower of sound business judgment and statesmanship," asked Taylor to accept the chairmanship. Taylor, age fifty-eight, still not seeing steel as a career, accepted. He believed it was his responsibility to put the corporation in order.

IV

It was clear to Taylor upon his ascendancy to chairman that the corporation faced major obstacles. It had obsolete plants in uneconomical locations and had made little effort to seek new markets or develop new products. It concentrated excessively on the manufacture of heavy steel products for railroads and construction, and far too little on the manufacture of light steel for automobiles and home appliances. As late as 1934, only 9 percent of the corporation's sales were in the automobile industry, compared to 21 percent for the rest of the industry.

Efficient new competitors, like National Steel, Republic Steel, and Inland Steel, created or consolidated from older companies, often were more innovative in sales and manufacturing. Bethlehem Steel had patented the Gray beam, and United States Steel, after attempting to pirate it by building a beam plant at the Homestead Works in 1927, had lost a court suit and was now forced to pay royalties on the beam to Bethlehem. The American Rolling Mill had developed the continuous-strip process, but by the early 1930s the corporation had constructed only one continuous-strip mill. Only in low-alloy steel—high-tensile steel with small percentages of costly chromium, manganese, vanadium, and other alloy metals—had the corporation pioneered.

The corporation had been run by one man—Gary—far too long and had become highly bureaucratic, with too much power centralized at the corporate headquarters in New York. Under Gary, every expenditure of more than twenty-five thousand dollars had to be approved by the finance committee in New York. When the presidents of subsidiaries came to New York, they were forced to wait hours or even days to see Gary. The corporation's archaic, unaggressive sales operations were an object of ridicule throughout the steel industry. Other steel companies often had sales systems in which one salesman would sell a variety of steel products. Automobile-company buyers, for example, who needed sheets, bars, wires, tubes, and more, could make their purchases from one salesman or sales department. At the corporation, subsidiaries had separate sales offices on different floors of the same building, and customers might have to see several salesmen to buy the steel they needed.

The corporation's idea of public relations—making pronouncements to favored reporters and touting the corporation's welfare programs—had had some success in Gary's day but was now outmoded. For 1935, the corporation's advertising budget was $700,000—this for the nation's largest industrial enterprise. Finally, the corporation's reputation in the steel communities was appalling, despite the welfare program's expenditures of millions of dollars over three decades. Gary and his subordinates had thought that the corporation could buy subservience. It could not.

Taylor quickly began to implement the principles he had employed in the textile industry. One of the first things he did upon taking command of the corporation was to ask for an outside report on its condition. The report, prepared by the management-consulting firm of Ford, Bacon, and Davis in the 1930s, was highly critical and was kept private. But its findings were summarized by George Stocking, an expert on the steel industry, in hearings before the Subcommittee on the Study of Monopoly Power in 1950. The report, said Stocking, portrayed the corporation thus:

A big, sprawling, inert giant, whose production operations were inadequately coordinated; suffering from a lack of a long-run planning agency; relying on an antiquated system of cost accounting; with an inadequate knowledge of the costs or of the relative profitability of the many thousands of items it sold; with production and cost standards generally below those considered everyday practice in other industries; with inadequate knowledge of its domestic markets and no clear appreciation of its opportunities in foreign markets; with less efficient production facilities than its rivals had; slow in introducing new processes and new products . . . slow to grasp the remarkable business opportunities that a dynamic America offered it. The corporation was apparently a follower, not a leader, in industrial efficiency.

By the time Taylor became chairman, the corporation had begun an expansion program. Three major acquisitions were made in 1930. The Columbia Steel Company, an independent firm based in San Francisco and Los Angeles, gave the corporation a West Coast iron- and steelmaking operation. The Oil Well Supply Company, a pipeline company with extensive sales and warehouses, was purchased. Finally, the Atlas Portland Cement Company was added to the corporation's Universal Cement Company, creating the world's largest cement company and a profitable outlet for the slag left over from steelmaking.

Then Taylor moved to address other flaws holding the company back. He worked to improve the corporation's unaggressive sales operations and attempted to upgrade the company's advertising and its price system. To improve operations, on August 29, 1935, the two original steelmaking companies, Carnegie Steel, purchased from Andrew Carnegie when the corporation was formed in 1901, and Illinois Steel, were merged. This made for production and sales efficiencies. To reduce centralization, Taylor began to allow decision-making by subsidiaries in Pittsburgh, Chicago, Youngstown, and Birmingham. A research division was initiated, new alloys were developed, continuous mills were ordered, and large expenditures were ordered to modernize the Chicago and Youngstown mills.

Taylor also addressed the corporation's weaknesses in management. Unlike its predecessor, the Carnegie Company, the corporation suffered from a lack of good steelmen. Executives like Schwab and Corey had been forced out or had left; others had retired or died. Moreover, under Gary's autocratic management, the corporation had stopped being an attractive place for talented and ambitious executives.

In 1931, Taylor had the directors set sixty-five as the age at which executives could retire on pensions and seventy as the maximum age to which executives could work. He began to bring in new, younger men. On September 17, 1935, the corporation announced that Benjamin F. Fairless, an executive of Republic Steel, was being brought into the corporation with strong powers to direct the corporation's steelmaking operations as president of the Carnegie-Illinois Steel Corporation.

Fairless, who had grown up in Ohio and had gone to work in the steel industry at the age of sixteen, was highly regarded. To bring in an outsider was a surprising move for the corporation, but as *Fortune* said, "It looks as if the depression had taught Mr. Taylor something that Gary never learned: that a steel company should be run by steel men as well as lawyers and bankers."

In December 1935, Taylor made another surprising move, bringing in Edward R. Stettinius, Jr., thirty-five, the son of a Morgan partner, and a highly regarded vice-president of the General Motors Corporation, to replace William J. Filbert, seventy, as chairman of the finance committee. Stettinius, a handsome man, already silver-haired, with a flair for dealing with the public and the press, was regarded as one of the bright young men of American business.

Despite Taylor's reforms, the corporation's share of American steel production continued to fall, dropping to 38.4 percent of the market by 1936 from the 65 percent it had represented when the corporation was created in 1901. One problem was not so tractable—the workers. Taylor, like Gary and Carnegie before him, refused to concede that the corporation, the largest employer in any of the nation's basic industries, faced difficulties with its blue-collar workers.

Until the mid-1930s, the corporation continued to rely on its welfare programs, instituted by Gary three decades before, as its primary method of employee relations. In 1935, the corporation said, it spent more than $295 million on its welfare programs. In 1936, it had on its payroll 406 doctors and 199 nurses and maintained 244 emergency first-aid stations and nine hospitals. It had established 24 churches, 17 schools, 34 clubhouses, 53 restaurants and lunchrooms, 176 restrooms and waiting rooms, 120 playgrounds, and 96 athletic fields. It was particularly proud of its activities in the area around Birmingham, Alabama. Since acquiring the Tennessee Coal and Iron Company in 1907, the corporation had drained the swamps in twenty-two towns, reducing malaria cases from six thousand a year to two hundred; built homes and schools; sent visiting nurses to educate the wives of workers in housekeeping and domestic hygiene; built a library in every community; built bathhouses; and established a hospital in Fairfield, Alabama.

But the corporation's welfare programs were hardly as extensive or successful as the corporation claimed. As had long been its practice, the corporation included everything it could when listing welfare expenditures. For example, the corporation counted as part of its safety programs money spent on sanitation, lighting, heating, and ventilation in its plants, such as the construction costs of twenty-five hundred plant restrooms and thirty-eight hundred urinals. Secondly, the programs were seen by many workers as what they were—charity meant to keep them in line.

Now change was forced on the corporation. On June 16, 1933, President Roosevelt signed the National Industrial Recovery Act (NIRA), an early piece of New Deal legislation. It authorized the establishment of price codes in steel and other major industries, and for the first time gave American workers the right under the law to organize unions and to bargain with their employers through representatives elected by the workers.

The corporation favored the price-code section of the law, under which the steel industry, like other industries covered by the act, was essentially made immune from antitrust attack and could for the first time legally set prices. Prices would have to be approved by the Code Authority for the Steel Industry, but this group consisted of the board of directors of the American Iron and Steel Institute, the industry trade association established in 1911 to take over the price-setting functions of the Gary dinners. Charles M. Schwab said that this was the first time in his more than half a century in the steel industry that "the business of the industry could be conducted on a commonsense basis."

In the summer of 1933, the heads of the major steel companies were invited to Washington to meet with Secretary of Labor Frances Perkins and to prepare a statement on the steel code of the National Industrial Recovery Act. All of them came—Myron C. Taylor, chairman, and William A. Irvin, president, of United States Steel; Eugene Grace of Bethlehem Steel; Ernest Weir of Weirton Steel; and Tom Girdler of Republic Steel. When they entered Miss Perkins's office, they found, sitting in a chair, William Green, president of the American Federation of Labor. Miss Perkins began to introduce the steelmen to Green, but most of them, she later recalled, "backed away into a corner, like frightened boys." It was "the most embarrassing social experience of my life."

I had never met people who did not know how, with hypocrisy perhaps but with an outward surface of correct politeness, to say how-do-you-do even to people they detested. I had been engaged in conversation with Green and went right back to him, thinking perhaps he would not notice the coldness. After a while, at the invitation of the steel executives' lawyers, I went over to the corner where they were having their huddle to see what ailed them. I found that they had expected to see only me and economists of the Department of Labor. They did not see how they could meet with the president of the A. F. of L. I was a little shocked, unable to believe that grown men could be so timid. But their faces were long, their eyes were solemn, and they were the picture of men with no self-assurance whatsoever.

Only Irvin, always amiable, refused to retreat. He pulled up a chair next to Green and in an almost jolly manner engaged the union leader in a conversation ranging from politics to the weather. Later, the executives privately explained to Miss Perkins that had they known they would be in the same room with Green, they would not have come. They protested that if they talked with Green, it would destroy their longstanding position against dealing with representatives of the labor movement, even though Green, a mild-mannered former Methodist minister, was one of the most conservative labor leaders. Miss Perkins pointed out that Green represented no steelworkers—none at that time belonged to any union—

and that his only purpose in being in Washington was to make a statement approving the steel code. Still the steelmen refused to talk to him, and finally Green stalked from the room. When the steelmen left, Miss Perkins remembered, "I could not resist the temptation to tell them that their behavior had surprised me and that I felt as though I had entertained eleven-year-old boys at their first party rather than men to whom the most important industry in the United States had been committed."

Whether or not they would talk to Green, the steel executives could not fail to see that a drive for unionism had been unleashed by the passage of the NIRA. Throughout the summer of 1933, there was a clamor for organization in many industries—coal, rubber, automobiles, and steel. In February 1933, three months before the NIRA was passed, an organizer for the United Mine Workers of America had glumly reported from the Appalachian coalfields, "As far as western Kentucky is concerned there is no sign of organization." On June 23, just one week after passage of the act, Van A. Bittner, another organizer, reported from West Virginia, "We expect to be practically through with every mine in the state and have every miner under the jurisdiction of our union by the first of next week." Much of the organizing was completed by August 1, and much of it was done by the miners themselves, who flocked to the union. Often all the organizers had to do was hand out union cards. Even the Amalgamated Association of Iron, Steel, and Tin Workers, moribund but still in existence, found new growth. The number of lodges jumped to more than two hundred and by early 1934 membership was estimated at fifty thousand.

Taylor thought he saw a way to head off unionism—"employee representation." The corporation would set up organizations of workers in every plant. The concept of employee representation—"company unions"—was decades old. The most famous plan had been established at John D. Rockefeller's Colorado Fuel and Iron Company following the massacre in Ludlow, Colorado, in April 1914, of twenty coal miners and members of their families during a strike. The tents in which they were living, after being evicted from their company-owned houses, were set on fire by state militiamen. The killings, much like those at Homestead, had created a national furor, and Rockefeller, to quell it, had retained two public-relations experts, Ivy Ledbetter Lee and W. L. MacKenzie King. In 1917, Colorado Fuel and Iron established an employee-representation plan under which workers and managers met regularly to exchange ideas and grievances. The workers had no power, but the plan received much favorable press attention for Rockefeller and allowed the company to avoid real unionism. In late 1918, a similar plan was instituted by Lee, by now the nation's leading public-relations man, at the request of Charles

M. Schwab of the Bethlehem Steel Corporation. The plan was credited with keeping unionism out of Bethlehem's plants during the 1919 steel strike. It was widely praised by the press and by such figures as Dr. Charles W. Eliot, president of Harvard University, who said that it was an answer to Communism and had "won a place in the esteem of the employees in every plant." But workers had no more power at Bethlehem than at Colorado Fuel and Iron. Schwab, on board ship for Europe in 1923, discussed the plan with the journalist Clarence W. Barron, explaining that his antipathy toward independent unionism had originated with the Homestead strike of 1892: "Since that day I have never had labor unions in any of my concerns. We make our own labor unions. We organize our labor into units of three hundred and then the representatives of these three hundred meet together every week. Then every fortnight they meet with the head men. Although we are only twenty or thirty and they are all elected as representatives of groups of three hundred behind them, we never allow dictation. We discuss matters but we never vote. I will not permit myself to be in the position of having labor dictate to the management."

Some steelmen had suggested to Gary when he was chairman that the corporation should institute an employee-representation plan. Gary preferred to rely on the welfare program. Now, with the NIRA, the corporation knew that it had to do something, and the law, broadly interpreted, seemed to allow company unionism. In December 1933, Taylor hired Arthur H. Young, who had worked under Ivy Ledbetter Lee at Colorado Fuel and Iron, as the corporation's vice-president of industrial relations. The Industrial Relations Department replaced the Bureau of Safety, Sanitation, and Welfare, which Gary had originated in 1911. Young guided the establishment of the employee-representation plan at the corporation and assisted other steel companies in setting up their own plans.

Young was regarded as the nation's leading authority on company unions. He said that "the sound and harmonious relationships between men and management" that were provided by employee-representation plans were like "the sound and harmonious relationships between a man and his wife"—a remark said to have occasioned many ribald remarks in the steel towns. According to industry figures, by the beginning of 1935 ninety-three plans were in existence, covering 90 to 95 percent of the nation's steelworkers. The corporation rejected the term "company union." But it was Carnegieism, or Garyism, under another name. Even the corporation admitted that. I. Lamont Hughes, a corporation vice-president, said in 1933, "The employee-representation plan isn't a 'company union'—it isn't a union at all."

13

"TELL JOHN L. LEWIS TO STOP WINDBAGGING"

On Sunday afternoon, July 5, 1936, four thousand steelworkers, coal miners, members of their families, and union supporters gathered at the Seventeenth Avenue Playground in Homestead to mark two occurrences: the deaths, forty-four years before, of seven steelworkers in the Pinkerton fight, and the beginning of the campaign by the Committee for Industrial Organization, led by John L. Lewis and several other labor leaders, to organize the nation's industrial workers.

The Committee for Industrial Organization had begun its campaign on June 17. Immediately, the steel companies, led by the United States Steel Corporation, had taken advertisements in newspapers across the country, including the *Homestead Messenger,* proclaiming that, consistent with "fundamental American principles," the industry would oppose any attempt "to compel its employees to join a union or to pay tribute for the right to work." The advertisements said that outsiders threatened to undermine the choice of "the overwhelming majority of the employees in the Steel Industry" to participate in industry-sponsored employee-representation plans. "The Steel Industry will use its resources to the best of its ability to protect its employees and their families from intimidation, coercion, and violence and to aid them in maintaining collective bargaining free from interference from any source." Then the steel companies fired workers suspected of harboring union sympathies.

Union organizers in the Monongahela Valley cast about for a way to counter the corporations' threats and to raise the militancy of the workers. Steve Bordich, a West Homestead steelworker, sitting in his kitchen with other rank-and-file activists, conceived the idea of a gathering in Homestead to mark the 1892 strike and the beginning of the organizing campaign. Over the next several days, workers from the Monongahela Valley and organizers Lewis had dispatched to the steel towns from Washington, D.C., were enlisted to help plan the event. The union men decided to call it "Steel Workers' Independence Day," and Tom Shane, an organizer from Swissvale, near Braddock, was put in charge of drafting "The Steel Workers' Declaration of Independence," to be read at the rally.

Although the rally was a stupendous success, there were some dark notes—the stern-eyed Homestead policemen dispatched by Burgess Cavanaugh and stationed around the playground; a beefy-faced patrolman who glowered from the window of the borough's notorious patrol car, the Black Maria; and the arrival of William J. Unger, an assistant general superintendent of the Homestead Works, who strolled by the rally to gather intelligence. Still, the workers' enthusiasm could not be dampened. The day was clear and hot, the playground was packed, and the speakers were superb. The new lieutenant governor of Pennsylvania, Thomas Kennedy, who was also secretary-treasurer of the United Mine Workers of America, guaranteed the workers the protection of the state authorities if they were harassed during their efforts to organize a union. No Pinkertons in blue suits with brass buttons, no Coal and Iron Police in high helmets on coal-black horses this time, Kennedy promised. Michael Angelo Musmanno, a young lawyer and writer, waved his arms and shouted to the sky like a piney-woods preacher that the workers had the right to organize and must not be intimidated.*

---

* Musmanno was one of those remarkable characters America produces. The son of Italian immigrants, he was born in McKees Rocks, Pennsylvania, and named after the Italian artist and sculptor. While in high school he worked as a coal miner and as a

Then Charles Scharbo, a rank-and-file organizer and president of the Amalgamated Association's Lodge 184, at Rankin, across the Monongahela River from Homestead, walked to the makeshift podium to read "The Steel Workers' Declaration of Independence":

They have interfered in every way with our right to organize in independent unions, discharging many who have joined them. They have set up company unions, forcing employees to vote in their so-called elections. They have sent among us swarms of stool pigeons, even in our homes. They have kept among us armies of company gunmen with stores of machine guns, gas bombs, and other weapons of warfare.

We steelworkers today solemnly publish and declare our independence. We say to the world: We are Americans. We shall exercise our inalienable right to organize into a great industrial union, banded together with all our fellow steelworkers.

Through this union we shall win higher wages, shorter hours, and a better standard of living. We shall win leisure for ourselves and opportunity for our children. We shall abolish industrial despotism. We shall make real the dreams of the pioneers who pictured America as a land where all might live in comfort and happiness.

In support of this declaration we mutually pledge to each other our steadfast purpose as union men, our honor, and our very lives.

The meeting then ended, and the crowd trudged the five blocks up the hill to the Homestead burying grounds, where six of the seven workers killed in the Pinkerton fight were buried, to lay wreaths. Some graves had not been marked; on others the stones were weathered or overturned, so the graves could not be easily located. But one union organizer, Emmet Patrick Cush, knew where the graves were. His father, Dennis M. Cush, had been a member of the union advisory committee during the strike

---

waterboy in a steel mill, and then went on to earn seven degrees from five universities. He was one of the defense attorneys in the Sacco-Vanzetti case, during the 1920s, and wrote a book about the case, *After Twelve Years,* in 1939. He also wrote the novel *Black Fury,* an indictment of the Coal and Iron Police in Pennsylvania, which was made into a movie and helped bring about the abolishment of that constabulary. In the 1940s he was elected to a judgeship on the Pennsylvania Supreme Court. At the Nuremberg war crimes trials, following World War II, he was one of the judges. He discarded his liberalism and became an ardent anti-Communist, at times leading raids on Communist Party offices in Pittsburgh during the 1950s. He also campaigned against what he regarded as flag-desecration and obscene movies and literature, and championed Christopher Columbus as the true discoverer of America. Musmanno died on October 12, 1973—Columbus Day.

and lockout of 1892, and years before he had told his son where the workers were buried. Emmet Patrick Cush had not forgotten.

At the cemetery, the men took off their hats and the men and the women and the children stood solemnly while Patrick T. Fagan—son of another 1892 strike leader and now president of District 5 of the United Mine Workers of America, handpicked by John L. Lewis to help organize the steelworkers—delivered a homily for the slain workers whose bodies lay beneath their feet. "We have come to renew the struggle for which you gave your lives," Fagan said. "We pledge all our efforts to bring a better life for the steelworkers. We hope you have found peace and happiness. God rest your souls."

II

The success of the 1936 rally had been a long time in coming. It was preceded by the failure of three organizing drives, in 1933, 1934, and 1935, years of increasing labor agitation in steel and other industries. The men and women in Homestead and other American steel towns had been quiescent through the 1920s. The defeat of the 1919 strike, like the defeat in 1892, had crushed the grit and independence out of them. Then came the Great Depression, and nowhere—not in the auto towns, the coal camps, the slums of big cities, or the farm communities on the High Plains—was its impact greater than in the steel towns. By 1933, 56 percent of the steelworkers were unemployed. Wages were the lowest in fifteen years. The average annual wage among steelworkers was $560; the government said that $1,500 a year was the minimum necessary for a decent standard of living. Homestead and other Monongahela Valley towns could not have gotten by had it not been for relief efforts organized by workers and members of their families to provide food and other assistance for the unemployed. The Homestead town government established a soup kitchen, and children from the schools often took home Mason jars of soup.

American labor leaders seemed to lack the will or even the desire to respond to the workers' crisis. The American labor organization remained as cautious and conservative as ever, concerned with preserving its prerogatives as the representative of mostly skilled workers and uninterested in organizing unskilled workers. The American Federation of Labor (AFL), a confederation of some seventy unions, was regarded as the main voice of labor, yet it had refused to support workers in numerous important confrontations—the Homestead strike, the Pullman strike of 1894, the steel strike of 1919, the textile strike of the late 1920s, and others.

The AFL had been formed in 1886, and for years its president had been the conservative, cautious Samuel Gompers. When Gompers died in 1924, he was succeeded by the conservative, cautious William Green. In December 1933, *Fortune*—which, although a business magazine, did some of the finest reporting on labor in those years—said that the AFL "has been suffering from pernicious anaemia, sociological myopia, and hardening of the arteries for many years." Labor leaders, by and large, were "machine bosses who are as inept at directing a militant labor movement as they are skillful in keeping their jobs." *Fortune* said of the typical union executive, "No proletarian, the A.F. of L. leader is blood brother to George Folansbee Babbitt [in his] white-collar, business-suited, baldheaded, horn-rimmed bourgeois glory."

The Amalgamated Association of Iron, Steel, and Tin Workers was still run by Michael F. "Grandmother" Tighe, eighty-four years of age and as timid and confused as he had been during the 1919 steel strike, when, as he later explained, the union had maintained its existence "by giving way to every request made by the subsidiary companies when they insisted on it." Even an up-and-coming labor leader like John L. Lewis, president of the United Mine Workers of America, was an ambitious schemer, a fierce red-baiter, a supporter of violence when it suited his purposes, and a longtime conservative.

Yet, amid the workers' despair and the lack of leadership, the election of President Roosevelt in November 1932 brought hope to the steel towns, coal camps, and other manufacturing centers. Then, with the passage of the National Industrial Recovery Act three months after Roosevelt had taken office, the hope increased. On June 16, 1933, the day the act was passed, a sound truck appeared in the streets of Homestead blaring the announcement that a union meeting would be held that night at Turner Hall, in lower Homestead, below the tracks. More than one thousand workers and union supporters attended the meeting and formed a "Spirit of 1892" Lodge of the Amalgamated Association. Even the *Homestead Daily Messenger,* long an organ of the corporation, put the blue eagle, the symbol of the National Recovery Administration, on its masthead. Unionism was returning to Homestead.

What was happening was remarkable. The workers and townspeople of the Monongahela Valley had been beaten back time after time, before the Homestead strike and since, and they had faced the most formidable obstacles—dismissal; blacklisting; yellow-dog contracts, under which workers agreed not to join unions; opposition in the courts; and the use of sheriffs' deputies, state militia, and federal troops by employers and the state. But the flame of resistance had not been extinguished.

The Amalgamated Association, though only the shell of a union (in 1933 it had just five thousand members, all in independent iron, sheet, and tin-plate mills), under the AFL constitution had organizing jurisdiction in the steel industry. But Tighe and the other Amalgamated Association leaders were blind to the opportunities that the NIRA presented, and so the workers began to organize themselves. Soon Tighe was deluged by demands from Amalgamated Association lodges for a steel-organizing drive. Many mill men demanded recognition of their lodges and called for a strike if necessary. Tighe did not know what to do. He confessed, "We are puzzled where such organizations as ours come in" under the new law.

The rank-and-file steelworkers saw, in protests that had arisen in the coal and coke fields, an opportunity to push for union recognition. The mines of southwestern Pennsylvania were known as "captive mines," because they were owned by steel companies, principally the corporation. Since the days of Henry Clay Frick, unionization had been outlawed and ruthlessly suppressed in the fields. The mine owners and iron and steel executives were fearful that unionization of the captive mines would lead to unionization of the iron and steel industry.

On June 1, 1933, to thwart the NIRA, which it knew was coming, the Frick Coal Company announced that it was establishing an employee-representation plan at its mines. The workers recognized this for what it was—a company union intended to subvert the NIRA—and rebelled. In July, coal miners at the Frick Coal Company struck, demanding recognition of the United Mine Workers of America and the right to elect their own check-weigh men, the men who double-checked the weights of coal that the miners had dug, which determined the miners' pay. The strike spread to other counties, and by August 2 thirty thousand miners were out and all of the Frick mines were closed. Violence occurred, and two men were killed. President Roosevelt opposed the strike, believing that it would upset the fragile recovery. John L. Lewis urged the miners to return to work and to let a government board resolve their grievances. The men refused.

In September, a settlement was reached between the union and non-captive-mine operators in Pennsylvania and West Virginia, providing for a minimum wage of $3.40 a day and guarantees of an eight-hour day and a five-day week, a dues checkoff, and the right of the workers to choose their check-weigh men. Soon after, the corporation and the other captive-mine operators approved the wages and hours that the other operators had accepted, but they continued to refuse to establish a dues checkoff or to recognize the union. The strike continued. Soon seventy thousand miners were on strike, and in late September what the steel executives had most feared happened—steelworkers went on strike.

On September 26, striking coal miners drove in a motley caravan of cars and trucks to the corporation's coke plant at Clairton, Pennsylvania, on the Monongahela River, twenty-five miles upstream from Pittsburgh, where coke was processed for the corporation's Monongahela Valley blast furnaces. Clairton was the largest coke works in the United States, and half of the Clairton workers came out to march with the miners. The unrest spread, and the unionists believed that the Homestead, McKeesport, Braddock, and Duquesne works might be closed by strikes or by lack of coke and gas.

Meantime, at Weirton, West Virginia, on the Ohio River, fifty miles west, twelve thousand steelworkers left the mills of the Weirton Steel Company, which was run by the skilled, tough steelman E. T. Weir. The workers demanded recognition of the Amalgamated Association lodges they had formed. Weir refused. Tighe declared the Clairton and Weirton strikes "outlawed."

At Ambridge, Pennsylvania, on the Ohio River, twenty miles west of Pittsburgh, thousands more steelworkers left their jobs at the corporation's American Bridge Company, successor to Andrew Carnegie's Keystone Bridge Company. The strikes in the coal fields and then at Clairton, Weirton, and Ambridge stunned the corporation and the other steel companies. The industry magazine *Steel* warned, "The rattlesnake of labor strife has struck once and today its poisonous head sways menacingly over . . . strategic points in the iron and steel industry."

On Lewis's orders, Philip Murray, vice-president of the miners' union, stepped in. Murray was practiced at doing Lewis's bidding; he had helped Lewis call off the coal miners' strike of 1919. Now he ordered the miners' leaders to Pittsburgh and there implored them to return to work. One of the insurgent leaders, Martin F. Ryan, a burly, forty-four-year-old immigrant from Ireland, a leftist, and an elected check-weigh man, demanded of Murray, "Why do you ask seventy-five thousand men to go back to work instead of telling one man [Tom Moses, president of the Frick Coal Company] to sign the contract?" The miners ignored Murray's plea and stayed out.

The steel companies ordered munitions and tear gas, and steel-town officials who were allied with the companies promised retribution. Some of the mayors who had viciously fought the workers in the 1919 steel strike were still in office, among them George H. Lysle in McKeesport and James "Toad" Crawford in Duquesne. "We're not going to stand for any goddamned hoodlums coming into town," Crawford said. "We're going to meet them at the bridge and break their goddamned heads. They're only a bunch of Hunkies and Communists." The *Duquesne Times* suggested that a few lynchings might take the starch out of the unionists: "There are plenty of vacant trees, and hemp can easily be procured."

On October 5, two hundred deputies armed with shotguns and machine guns and carrying tear gas marched upon Ambridge; a merchant was killed and twenty people were wounded. Violent encounters also occurred between state troopers and strikers in Weirton. "It may be necessary to shoot a few strikers," Weir said. The strikers' only leaders were inexperienced local men. Officials of the United Mine Workers of America and the Amalgamated Association denounced what they called "outlaw" and "wildcat" strikes. Dismay spread among the strikers.

Now Roosevelt intervened. On October 7, he met with Myron C. Taylor at the White House. On October 10, the corporation and the other captive-mine operators agreed to a voluntary checkoff but still refused to recognize the union. Roosevelt said that the companies were not bargaining in good faith. "I beg you to remember," he wrote Taylor, "that the old doctrine of 'pigs is pigs' applies. Coal mining is coal mining. . . . Therefore, as a matter of public policy, I must hold that the conditions of work in the captive coal mines must conform to the conditions of work in the average run of commercial coal mines."

Finally, on October 30, a compromise was reached, the captive-mine companies and the union signing separate agreements. The companies accepted the wages, hours, and working conditions that the other companies had accepted earlier. The companies also agreed to a dues checkoff and to government-run elections in which workers selected their representatives. In return, the union pledged to call off the strike. On November 6, the captive miners in Fayette County, without jubilation, returned to work. They formed into columns, headed by workers carrying the American flag, and marched in silence to the mines. The election in Fayette County was held on November 23. The corporation won nine mines, the union six. The corporation refused to deal with the union, however, only with miners' representatives as individuals. In January 1934, the government ordered the corporation and the other steel companies to sign contracts with Lewis and other individuals selected by the miners, but said that they need not do so with the union. The corporation's open-shop principles were preserved. The miners had made some gains, particularly the dues checkoff, as a result of their stubbornness. The steelworkers had achieved nothing.

At Clairton, the picket lines dwindled and then the strike there was called off. At Weirton, Weir made good use of the weeks between the settlement and the December 15 government-supervised election at his works. The company conducted dances and liquor parties at its handsome country club overlooking the Ohio River. A worker said: "It really makes you sick. Clothes baskets full of pork and cheese sandwiches and lots of beer. They [the workers] got to fighting, throwing sandwiches. And you think of the hungry kids at home. Sunday, exactly when the union mass meeting was scheduled, they told us to come in to the forty-eight-inch cold mill to a meeting. 'We will have lots of beer, and you'll be paid for three hours,' the foreman said. 'Better be here, or you may find you have no job.' "

After the election, Weir said that the company union had been approved by the workers, but some workers said that the votes had been miscounted. Strike activists were fired, and the militancy of the Weirton workers was broken. At Ambridge, the workers, no match for the heavily armed deputies, also returned to work.

The 1933 campaign to organize the captive mines and the steel industry was defeated, but the leaders of the rank-and-file movement were determined to try again. They soon began to plan for a second campaign. On March 25, 1934, some 350 delegates from fifty newly formed Amalgamated Association lodges across the country met in Pittsburgh to plan tactics for the annual convention, to be held there in a few days.

These delegates formed the nucleus of what became known as the rank-and-file movement. They decided to present a simple, militant program of "concerted action" at the convention: all union lodges would simultaneously request recognition from the companies; if recognition was denied, a strike date would be set. Other unions, including those in coal mining and automobile manufacturing, would be asked to support the steelworkers.

The convention was a raucous affair, with fierce arguments between the moderates and the radicals. The concerted-action program was adopted. All lodges would request recognition from employers on May 21. If it was denied, a strike date would be set. The delegates also demanded that a committee of ten rank-and-file leaders be included in all negotiations and oversee a strike if one occurred. Tighe was distraught. "The rank-and-file men don't know what they are doing," he said. "What they did was caused by the indignities they have suffered from 'small men' in management, not by Weir, Taylor, and their kind."

The organizing immediately ran into difficulties. When union men visited mills on May 21 and requested recognition, they were treated haughtily by company men. At the Duquesne Works, the general superintendent returned unopened a registered letter requesting a conference. At the Edgar Thomson Works, the general superintendent ejected the committee. Production at Monongahela Valley mills was increased as the corporation rolled extra steel in case of a strike. On May 22, five rank-and-file leaders met with Tighe at the union's headquarters in Pittsburgh and asked for $100,000 to conduct a strike and for use of the building as a strike headquarters. He refused.

The rank-and-file leaders faced another dilemma. They had almost no experience in leadership. "Most of us were capable local or district leaders," one of the insurgents, Clarence Irwin, said, "but we had very little idea what the national picture was like. . . . We were completely unprepared for a strike. We had no funds, no central leadership, no national organization except the Amalgamated's officers, and they were opposed to strike action."

The rank-and-file men turned for assistance to four intellectuals known to be sympathetic toward workers—Heber Blankenhorn, Harold J. Ruttenberg, Harvey O'Connor, and Stephen Rauschenbusch. Blankenhorn had been field secretary for the Interchurch World Movement's report on the 1919 steel strike, which had put pressure on the corporation and the other steel companies to adopt an eight-hour day. He had close ties with John L. Lewis and Senator Robert F. Wagner, Sr., Democrat of New York, who was strongly sympathetic to labor. Ruttenberg was a college student doing research on the steel industry under a government grant, and he could type. O'Connor was a labor journalist. Rauschenbusch had worked for the committee, headed by Senator Gerald P. Nye, which investigated the role of the munitions industry in America's involvement in World War I; later he was an aide to Governor Gifford Pinchot of Pennsylvania. These advisers, known as "the Big Four," worked secretly, for they did not want their association with the union to become public. They suggested that the rank-and-file men take their campaign to Washington in order to generate publicity and to seek the assistance of the government, a longstanding tactic in the labor movement.

The union men got publicity but no help. For two weeks, they were "passed like hot stones" between the National Labor Board (which became the National Labor Relations Board in 1935), the Labor Department, the National Recovery Administration (NRA), and the White House, the historian Irving Bernstein later wrote. The union leaders also

© The Bettmann Archive.

Andrew Carnegie

© UPI/Bettmann.

Henry Clay Frick

The William J. Gaughan Collection.

"Fort Frick": The Homestead Works General Office Building surrounded by a fence at the time of the strike.

Courtesy of the Library of Congress.

Pay line at the Homestead Works around 1908.

A Pinkerton barge in flames.

The William J. Gaughan Collection.

Courtesy of the Library of Congress.

The Pennsylvania militia parades in Homestead during its occupation.

The main entrance to the Homestead Works, 1894.

Courtesy of the Carnegie Library of Homestead.

Courtesy of the Carnegie Library of Homestead.

The Homestead Works Beam Yard.

Homestead children in 1907.

Courtesy of the Library of Congress.

Courtesy of the Carnegie Library of Homestead.

Homestead workers at the turn of the century.

The William J. Gaughan Collection.

Black teamsters making a delivery of steel in the Homestead area. Local steel shipments and hauling were by horse and wagon until the advent of heavy hauling trucks.

Courtesy of the Library of Congress.

Water boys, Homestead Works, circa 1905.

The William J. Gaughan Collection.

A nurse visits a Slavic millworker and his wife, circa 1910. The visiting nurse program was part of the social welfare program established by the company.

The William J. Gaughan Collection.

Blast furnace laborers sitting on an excavated concrete foundation pier
during repairs at the blast furnaces, 1934.

The William J. Gaughan Collection.

Workers forging an axle to size at the Howard Axle Works, part of the Homestead Steel Works.

Courtesy Duquesne Light Company.

Eighth Avenue in the 1940s.

Alfred Eisenstaedt, Life Magazine, © Time Warner, Inc.

Judge Michael Angelo Musmanno addressing the Homestead rally,
July 5, 1936.

The William J. Gaughan Collection.

The 12,000-ton forging press, 1944. The forging press was purchased in 1903 to manufacture armor plate for President Theodore Roosevelt's expanding navy. After being rebuilt in 1944, it helped produce armor plate for the great shipbuilding program of World War II.

United States Steel Corporation photo.

Workers leaving the Homestead Works by the Amity Street Gate, circa 1950.

© *New York Times* pictures.

Kenneth Jackey holds up the watch and emblem given him by Nikita Khrushchev during the Soviet premier's visit to the Mesta Machine Company on September 24, 1959.

Leaders of the Steelworkers Union:

© The Bettmann Archive.

John L. Lewis, president of the Congress of Industrial Organizations, 1936–1940.

© UPI/Bettmann.

© UPI/Bettmann.

David M. MacDonald, president of the Steelworkers Union, 1952–1965.

Philip Murray, president of the Steelworkers Union, 1942–1952.

© Earl Dotter.

A Homestead Street, 1991.

© Earl Dotter.

Seventh Avenue in Homestead.

© Earl Dotter.

Mayor Betty Esper with young constituents in Frick Park.

© Earl Dotter.

Leslie Evans teaching a class at Steel Valley High School.

Jimmie Sherlock, Red Hrabic, and Bobby Schneider at the Slovak Club.

Ronnie Weisen and the Reverend James Von Dreele in front of
Saint Matthew's Episcopal Church.

© Earl Dotter.

© Earl Dotter.

© Margaret Vojtko.

Signs of change.

"ReMAKING CITIES"
PROPOSAL 342:

PLANT FLOWERS, HOLD INTERNATIONAL
GARDEN SHOW, MAKE WOODEN SHOES.
AND KEEP A MILL OR TWO RUNNING

HOMESTEAD
TULIP CAPITAL
OF WESTERN PA!

© Tim Menees. Reprinted with permission of the
Pittsburgh Post-Gazette.

© Earl Dotter.

The 12,000-ton press, 1991.

© Earl Dotter.

Ray Hornack and
Marty Costa.

© Earl Dotter.

Former Mayor Simko in front of the Homestead "Big Shop."

© Earl Dotter.

spent much time attempting to get Secretary of Labor Frances Perkins and General Hugh Johnson, head of the National Recovery Administration, to assist them. Neither did. Johnson sneered at the men, saying that they were "green" and "inexperienced." They in turn said that Johnson was "a big windbag" and that "NRA" stood for "National Run-Around."

The union leaders also were red-baited, a traditional tactic of those who opposed unions. The men had refused to work with a Communist-led union, the Steel and Metal Workers' Industrial Union, which had been founded in 1932 and now had ten to fifteen thousand members. Yet General Johnson—he had been a cavalryman on the Great Plains—claimed that the rank-and-file leaders were "activated by motives of communistic politics . . . when [they] demand . . . a dollar an hour" for steelworkers.

Tighe also carried on about "Communists." He declared: "The Amalgamated Association is an American institution—loyal to the core to its government and its traditions. Communism, and all such isms, had no part in its makeup. We warn our members to shun these vipers who are trying to poison the minds of our membership. The very presence of Communists contaminates the atmosphere of pure trade unionism. 'Keep away from it' is not only our advice, but our command."

Still, by the first week of June 1934, there was talk across the nation of a nationwide steel strike. The companies began stringing barbed wire around their mills and purchasing munitions—in June alone the steel companies' purchases from one arms merchant totaled $100,000. The companies had the employee-representation organizations conduct elections that, they claimed, showed that the workers were against unionization. The rank-and-filers again went to Washington and tried to meet with Roosevelt, but the president was on his yacht and did not see them. Tighe now called a special convention of the Amalgamated Association at Elks Lodge 11 in Pittsburgh on June 14. A strike date was to be set, probably June 16, if recognition was refused by the companies. The nation closely watched what was happening, fearing a strike.

Louis Stark of *The New York Times* said of the rank-and-file leaders:

They are aware that the extent of their union organization is not a secret to the steel corporations. They know that they are in danger of having their union crushed for another decade by a combination of company unions, strikebreakers, deputy sheriffs, and bullets.

They know that "money can wait" and that hungry men and their families cannot. They know that lack of cohesive organization works against them. Nevertheless, they are strongly of the conviction that once the strike begins it will rise like a wave, sweeping hesitant workers before it, rolling up in a mass movement that will engulf the industry. On the crest of this tide the rank-and-file leaders hope they may carry through their movement to success.

There are young, determined steelworkers in and around Pittsburgh, Duquesne, Braddock, Youngstown, and Gary who are willing to die, if necessary, for the right to organize independent unions.

However, Roosevelt and labor leaders like Lewis, Tighe, and Green continued to oppose a strike. On the morning of June 15, Green addressed the convention, after an all-night train ride from Washington, D.C., where he had met with Roosevelt the day before.

Green demanded that the delegates rescind the strike call and adopted one of the time-honored ploys often used by labor leaders when making such a plea—he dredged up his working-class background, specifically his twenty years, long before, as a miner: "I come as a miner speaking to steelworkers. . . . It is my firm opinion, based on my own interest in the workers and my own experience, that the time will come when your wrongs will be righted, but I do not believe the time is here at this moment."

He then presented Roosevelt's plan to settle the situation. A three-man government board would be established by the president to receive complaints, mediate disputes, and hold elections. "I believe that if this is done it will cause consternation to the steel corporations and mobilize public opinion behind you," Green said. At noon, the convention was adjourned until evening.

The workers were confused and divided. There was a bar on the second floor of the Elks lodge, and delegates gathered there throughout the afternoon. Some of the rank-and-file leaders had a few drinks as well and by the evening session had difficulty expressing their views coherently. That night, the delegates revoked the strike call and accepted Roosevelt and Green's proposal. The threat of a steel strike, a strike that—given the resolve in the steel towns, the workers could possibly have won—was ended.

The next year, 1935, brought a third attempt to organize the steel industry. On February 3, four hundred steelworkers and one hundred coal miners met in Pittsburgh. It was clear to them that neither the Amalgamated Association nor the American Federation of Labor nor the federal government was going to help. They adopted a resolution that said,

"Steelworkers know from their own experience that they can secure no help in their struggles from the labor boards or other federal agencies, but that their only defense . . . is the power of their own organization, exercised by the calling of strikes if and when necessary."

Tighe now acted—against his own union's members. He ordered the expulsion of the twenty-six lodges that had been represented at the Pittsburgh meeting in February. He also disbanded the union's first and sixth districts, which represented Pennsylvania and Ohio, where activism was high, even though these districts contained a large majority of the union's membership.

The activists, rather than forming an independent union, which would have been the militant course, appealed for reinstatement through the courts. The fight dragged on through much of the summer, eliminating the possibility of any action against the corporation or the other steel companies. On August 1, 1935, a federal court ordered that the twenty-six lodges be reinstated, but the momentum of the organizing drive had been lost. The Amalgamated Association dropped to ten thousand members, and that year the union chartered only four lodges and disbanded eighty-four. Tighe and the conservatives had bested the rank-and-file movement, a development that pleased Lewis and his men in the miners' union.

Were steelworkers ever to be organized? And if so, who would do it?

III

In October 1935, delegates of the American Federation of Labor gathered for their annual convention at the Chelsea Hotel in Atlantic City, a favorite convention site and watering hole of the nation's labor leaders. There were many items of business, but the major discussion centered on the old question, long answered in the negative by the leadership, of whether the AFL should lead a campaign to organize steelworkers and other mass-production workers.

The campaign for industrial unionism was led by John L. Lewis; Sidney Hillman, president of the Amalgamated Clothing Workers; and David Dubinsky, president of the International Ladies' Garment Workers Union. Each had used the recovery act to revive his union and each, with a large treasury, was now pressing for an aggressive, broad campaign to organize industrial workers. It was Lewis, a genius at timing and public relations, who was the guiding force. Except for a time early in his career, Lewis had shown little nerve in standing up to company bosses or government leaders. He had worked for only the briefest time as a coal miner and then, having enough of that, began the far more comfortable life of the union bureaucrat. The miners' union headquarters was in Indianapolis, a quiet, conservative midwestern town that suited Lewis and the union well. David J. McDonald, a member of Lewis's entourage at that time and later president of the United Steelworkers of America, later remembered, "Indianapolis was incredibly dull . . . a wild evening consisted of a movie and a lobster dinner at the Claypool Hotel . . . most evenings were spent with other UMW staff members in the lobby of the Claypool, sitting in a discreet semicircle around Lewis and listening to his talk. Usually, his topic was the union, but once in a while he would venture into politics or foreign affairs. Lewis was a staunch Republican, and his political views—which he expressed forcefully—would be considered reactionary today and almost were then."

Besides calling off the coal strike of 1919—just at the point at which it might have benefited the striking steelworkers—Lewis had sent the men back into the pits during the great coalfield wars in West Virginia in 1922, ending a rank-and-file movement to establish unionization. He was a ferocious red-baiter, using the label "Communist" to force radicals and others who disagreed with him out of the miners' union in the 1920s and the early 1930s. He had stopped red-baiting only when he realized that he could use radicals to help him in his quest—and a mighty quest it was—to organize industrial workers, principally steelworkers.

The man at the 1935 convention, however, was a new Lewis. He, with only a few other top labor leaders, recognized the opportunity that was at hand. On October 16, at the Chelsea, a relic of the past and thus a perfect place for an AFL gathering, the convention took up the matter of industrial organization, debating it from 2:30 P.M. to 11:45 P.M., with Lewis as the primary speaker for industrial unionism. The labor movement, Lewis said, existed on the principle that "the strong shall help the weak." He implored the strong craft workers to give help to the weak industrial workers, to "heed this cry from Macedonia that comes from the hearts of men." But Lewis could not prevail. The vote (delegates' votes were weighted to reflect their membership) was 18,024 to 10,933 against organizing industrial workers.

The day after the convention, October 20, Lewis met for breakfast at the President Hotel with eight other labor leaders. He did most of the talking, portraying a huge, powerful labor movement embracing almost all of America's working-class people. The men agreed that the time for organizing industrial workers had come. On November 9, Lewis, the eight leaders, and two others gathered in Washington, D.C., and formed the Committee for Industrial Organization (CIO). Lewis was elected chairman.

Lewis spent much of the rest of 1935 and the first half of 1936 working on the campaign to organize steelworkers. In February 1936, Lewis sent a letter to William Green calling for a massive steel-organizing drive. Lewis offered to supply trained organizers and said that he would contribute $500,000 as part of a $1 million fund. He asked the AFL to put up the rest. Green agreed to discuss the matter but refused to contribute the $1 million. The AFL executive council told Lewis that steelworkers organized by such a drive would have to be placed in existing craft unions.

On April 15, Lewis wrote to Michael F. Tighe, repeating the offer made to Green for a massive organizing campaign and promising that the CIO would respect the Amalgamated Association's jurisdiction. Tighe was afraid to cooperate with the CIO and thus earn Green's enmity. He also feared cooperating with Lewis, because Lewis was an audacious man. In his letter, Lewis had said that an independent organizing committee would be established, under a "responsible and energetic" person. Tighe knew that person would be an outsider. He had to be, because there was no one at the Amalgamated Association's headquarters who fitted that description. Tighe replied, "Under no circumstances, while I am President, will I surrender to any other organization the right to direct the affairs of our organization."

The issue came to a head at the Amalgamated Association's convention, beginning April 28, at the Alhambra Theatre, in the mining community of Canonsburg, in southwestern Pennsylvania. The lobby was filled with steelworkers, officials of the AFL and the CIO, newspapermen, and photographers. Expectations of action soon died, however, as the convention, typical of an Amalgamated Association gathering, dragged on without excitement. Much of the day was taken up by Tighe's reading of his annual report. On May 8, Lewis wired the convention that the AFL plan to organize the steel industry into craft unions would "preserve . . . leadership . . . in the hands of men who have through the years demonstrated their utter incapacity to establish stable organization and modern collective bargaining in the mass-production industries. . . . The policy . . . is inadequate, futile, and conceived in a mood of humiliated desperation." He reiterated his offer to establish a steel-organizing committee.

The activists had been spreading their views. Feeling the pressure, Amalgamated Association leaders met with Lewis in Washington on June 3, 1936. Tighe was ill and was absent. Lewis said that the miners would contribute a large amount of money and would organize steelworkers on an industrial basis, provided the Amalgamated Association would accept CIO leadership. He gave the union leaders twenty-four hours to make up their minds. "If you don't want it, we want to find out as soon as we can," Lewis said. "We're tired—want action. . . . If you spurn it, we'll announce to the country and you can do your own explaining. If you accept, you stand to have great power."

The union men knew that Lewis was bluffing. They knew they would have no power. But they had no choice, for they were certain that the CIO would conduct a drive regardless of what they did. On June 4, they signed an agreement affiliating with the CIO and agreeing to have representatives serve on the Steel Workers Organizing Committee (SWOC), which Lewis would create. It was understood that all decisions would be made by the CIO and by the SWOC. The Amalgamated Association, a charter member, since 1886, of the American Federation of Labor, and at the time of the Homestead strike the largest and most powerful union in America, was at an end. Tighe had belonged to the Amalgamated Association since it was formed in 1876. He had once been known as an aggressive, ambitious puddler. Now he was old, and his union had been swallowed up (it would be officially dissolved in 1942). A few years later, he died, at the age of eighty-nine.

On the day of the agreement, Lewis announced the formation of the Steel Workers Organizing Committee to organize the United States Steel Corporation and the other steel companies, and on June 17 the SWOC established its headquarters on the twelfth floor of the Commonwealth Building, in downtown Pittsburgh, a building where several steel companies had their headquarters. Lewis named Philip Murray, his longtime vice-president, as chairman. Murray appointed his assistant, David J. McDonald, as secretary-treasurer.

Murray, forty-nine years of age, a bald, rumpled man, and an ardent Roman Catholic, had come to America from Scotland at sixteen, arriving barefoot in the snow at a relative's house on Christmas Day, and gone to work in the southwestern Pennsylvania mines. Four years later, in 1905, he was elected president of a miners' local union, and in 1912 he was appointed to the union's executive board. He had allied himself with Lewis, and in 1920 Lewis had appointed him as the union's vice-president. For the next two decades, Murray was Lewis's right-hand man. He made himself an expert on the coal industry, testified before congressional committees, and did what Lewis told him.

McDonald was a handsome, ambitious man, thirty-four years of age, who had been hired by Murray in 1924 as his secretary. Murray and his wife, Liz, had no children, and Murray had come to look on McDonald as a son. McDonald had worked briefly in a steel mill but had not liked it, and having taken commercial courses in school, including typing and shorthand, he had seen a chance for advancement in office work and had thus joined Murray and the union movement. He was now performing many important tasks for Murray. He also was a schemer and infighter.

Now Murray and McDonald "would step out on our own," to use McDonald's words. With a twenty-five-thousand-dollar check from Lewis, they set up their operation in Pittsburgh, but almost immediately they sought a new headquarters. Murray complained that the Commonwealth Building was rather shabby and asked McDonald to search for something better. "Nothing but the best, Dave," Murray said. McDonald found a suite on the thirty-sixth floor of the Grant Building, then Pittsburgh's tallest structure. McDonald liked the building not only because it was rather plush but also because, on the thirty-sixth floor, the union was several stories above the offices of a number of steel companies that also occupied the building. "Psychology, I had learned at Lewis's knee, is nine points of negotiating," McDonald said.

On Sunday, June 21, a large SWOC rally was held in McKeesport. Mayor George Lysle grudgingly issued a permit for the rally—on the bank of the Monongahela River, next to the town dump. The Homestead rally followed on July 5, and on July 6, continuing the campaign, Lewis went on NBC radio—he was as adept at using the radio as was President Roosevelt—with a nationwide address.

"I salute the hosts of labor who listen," he said. "My voice tonight will be the voice of millions of men and women unemployed in America's industries, heretofore unorganized, economically exploited, and inarticulate." A great struggle was coming, he said, that would determine "whether the working population of this country shall have a voice in determining their destiny or whether they shall serve as indentured servants for a financial and economic dictatorship which would shamelessly exploit our natural resources and debase the soul . . . and . . . pride of a free people. On such an issue there can be no compromise." The campaign to organize the corporation and the rest of the steel industry was on.

IV

The Democratic administration, the New Deal, and the upsurge in unionism were changing life in Homestead. The national ascendancy of the Democratic Party was bringing upheaval in Homestead politics. The fall of the Republican Party in Homestead began in March 1934, when Doc McLean, the town controller, broke with the town burgess, John Cavanaugh, whom he had served as chief lieutenant since 1920. McLean and a number of other politicians and town leaders established a new political organization, which became the Homestead Democratic Party. At the meeting at which the party was formed, McLean said that the domination of Homestead by bootleggers and gamblers had gone on long enough. He said that the clean-living people had to have a say, and that he would refuse to take direction from the racketeers. The leftist Steel and Metal Workers' Industrial Union called Cavanaugh "a ward-heeling politician, policeman, private detective, deputy coroner, and super stool pigeon" for the corporation.

Municipal elections were held in November 1935. The Democrats charged that there were many phantom voters on the voting lists; the Republicans sent in police and broke up a musical show sponsored by the Democrats, ousting some one thousand people. The president of the Democratic organization called this "a brazen attempt to prevent any concentrated opposition to the vicious reactionary reign of John Cavanaugh, Police Captain Cup Jenkins, and his other henchmen."

The Democrats appealed to Governor Earle for police protection, and two detachments of state police arrived in Homestead the night before the election. The *Homestead Daily Messenger* said that it would be one of the most torrid election nights in Homestead's history. The paper was correct. So much violence occurred on election day that the *Messenger* put out an extra to chronicle it. Gangs of thugs roamed the streets attacking Democrats. The fire chief, Herman Samuels, a former Republican who had gone over to the Democrats, was arrested twice by the police; his face was bruised and his nose bloodied. But when the fury ended, the Democrats had won, taking four of seven seats on the borough council and all three seats up for election on the school board. It was, the *Messenger* said, "a sweeping victory for the Democrats."

The last act for the Cavanaugh regime came two years later, in November 1937, when McLean opposed Cavanaugh in a spirited campaign for the mayoralty and won by a three-to-one margin. Eight borough-council seats were won by the Democrats, as well as two more seats on the school board. "The strongest political power ever to dominate Homestead" was dead, the *Messenger* proclaimed. More than one thousand Democrats paraded through the streets in a hundred-car procession. A black coffin was carried by pallbearers to symbolize the end of Cavanaugh and his machine. "Mourners" used onions to make themselves cry. Everyone then repaired to Doc's home on Tenth Street for a grand party.

V

In the early summer of 1936, the SWOC dispatched some two hundred organizers into the steel towns. Murray was in charge, and he was aided by McDonald and three regional directors with long experience in the labor movement—Clinton S. Golden, a labor intellectual, and Van A. Bittner and William A. Mitch, activists in the miners' union. Murray also hired Lee Pressman, a leftist lawyer and a Harvard man, as general counsel; Harold J. Ruttenberg, the young economist who had been one of the four secret advisers to the steelworkers' rank-and-file movement in 1934–1935, as research director; and Vincent Sweeney, a Pittsburgh reporter, as editor of the SWOC newspaper, *Steel Labor.* The drive was backed by $500,000 from the miners' union.

The goal of organizing the steel industry's 500,000 workers—222,000 of them at the corporation—was formidable. But the organizers were optimistic. The National Industrial Recovery Act had been declared unconstitutional by the Supreme Court in May 1935, but in July 1935 the National Labor Relations Act—the Wagner Act—was passed, guaranteeing workers the same right to organize and to bargain with their employers that the recovery act had provided. The law was now on the side of unions.

The labor organizers were also aided by a Senate investigating committee established on June 6, 1936, as the organizing drive was beginning, and headed by Senator Robert M. La Follette, Jr., the Progressive from Wisconsin. Like his father, he was known for his liberalism. The committee's staff members were also liberals and union supporters, among them the chief investigator, Heber Blankenhorn, who had been one of the advisers to the steelworkers' rank-and-file movement and was close to Lewis and to Golden, Ruttenberg, and others on the SWOC staff. It had been Blankenhorn who had in large part convinced La Follette to form the investigating committee, and now he pushed continuously for a spirited investigation while keeping in close communication with his friends on the steelworkers' organizing committee.

The committee turned up much damaging information about the corporation and the other steel companies, finding, for example, that the nation's corporations were spending $80 million a year in the mid-1930s to fight unions. Murray used this information to criticize the anti–SWOC advertisements taken out by the steel companies on June 29, saying that the millions of dollars spent on the advertisements illustrated the vast sums of money that the steel corporations had at their disposal to use against the unions and what Murray called "the little people."

Despite these favorable circumstances, the SWOC campaign did not go very well at first. On January 1, 1937, Murray claimed that the SWOC had enrolled 125,000 members, but years later, in his autobiography, McDonald admitted that at the beginning of 1937 only 82,000 steelworkers—15,000 from the corporation—had signed up. The total membership was not much more than the 80,000 to 100,000 workers that the moribund Amalgamated Association had signed up in the summer of 1933 with almost no effort.

In his autobiography, McDonald said, "The biggest problems we had were with the workers. . . . Contrary to union propaganda—some of which I helped to write—the steelworkers did not fall all over themselves to sign a pledge card with the SWOC." McDonald said that some workers feared a dictatorship of the union as much as one of the company. Workers, having seen union organizers beaten so many times, also feared they might lose their jobs if they joined the union.

To enroll members, the organizers went to plant gates or union meetings and distributed union cards. The organizers would praise unionism, saying that a union would mean more money for workers, improved working conditions, and the right to file grievances—that immemorial workers' wish, the right to talk back to the boss. But many workers remained unconvinced.

McDonald, in his autobiography, wrote:

What we hoped would be a torrent turned out, instead, to be a trickle. . . . Oftentimes the locals consisted of the half-dozen men daring enough to sign the charter application. When these skeleton requests straggled in, we assigned impressively high lodge numbers in the hope that outsiders would think we had that many locals. Only Murray and I knew how thin the tally was, although Lewis would insist on the truth whenever I visited Washington, then would shake his head in wonderment at the lack of progress.

Another problem was collecting dues, which had been established at one dollar a month. Some workers would pay their initial dollar but never send in more money. In 1970, after he had left the union, McDonald told interviewers from Pennsylvania State University that at the time of the Little Steel Strike in 1937, only 7 percent of the corporation's blue-collar workforce had signed with the union and only 3.5 percent were paying dues. Homestead—with many workers still wary of challenging management—was, McDonald recalled, among the worst plants in terms of workers joining the union and paying dues. In 1941, McDonald said, he decided the only solution to raising membership and dues money was a little hardball: "I was a young, mean son-of-a-bitch, and I said, 'We're going to get these guys,' and we got them. Rough, slam-bam tactics, we even paid guys a buck to sign a union card. . . . I just went ahead. . . .

You had your choice: join the union if you don't want to get hit in the face with a baseball bat."

During the Depression organizing was not the romantic occupation it is often portrayed as having been. McDonald recalled:

On a typical day, I would meet with the local organizers at 5 A.M. to pass out handbills for distribution at the plant gates. The handbills would urge the steelworker to "join the SWOC for better hours, pay, and working conditions." We would arrive at the plant about 6 A.M., usually to a reception as cold as the raw morning wind. While our sound truck made a union pitch nearby, we would pass out handbills and try to collect a group of workers to listen to our arguments and ask us questions. In a discouragingly few minutes the gate would be deserted and the ground littered with our handbills. . . .

Towns began to look the same to me. There was Warren, Ohio, where the local charter signers had promised me a big audience and four people showed up in a hall that seated five hundred. In Birmingham, there were more people on the stage than in the audience. In Weirton, we promoted a "mass meeting" of twelve people. . . .

The only thing that saved us during this period was the overreaction of the steel companies to our modest efforts. In spite of their extensive spy system, they apparently believed the figures we were putting out and had no idea how really badly we were doing. . . .

Then a strange development occurred. The corporation, for so long the leading anti-union company in the nation, voluntarily signed a union contract. A union was given to the workers.

VI

On Saturday, January 9, 1937, John L. Lewis and Senator Joseph F. Guffey, Democrat of Pennsylvania, elected the previous November as part of the 1936 Roosevelt landslide, were having lunch in the dining room of the Mayflower Hotel in Washington, D.C., a popular spot with government people.

Shortly after 1:00 P.M., Myron C. Taylor and his wife, Anabel, entered the dining room, and as they were being escorted in, they passed Lewis and Guffey's table. Taylor bowed to the two men, conducted his wife to a table, and seated her. Then, unexpectedly, he returned and offered his hand, first to Guffey, then to Lewis. They chatted briefly, and then Taylor went back to his table. It was a remarkable scene—the corporation chairman and the CIO president and prime architect of the SWOC shaking hands and chatting. Diners' heads turned. Even waiters stopped and stared.

Then something even more astonishing occurred. When Lewis and Guffey had completed their meal, they walked to the Taylors' table, where Taylor introduced Lewis to his wife. The two men took chairs and remained with the Taylors for twenty minutes. Lewis could be a charming man when he wished to be, and he wished to be this day. Mrs. Taylor found him most amusing, and occasionally laughter bubbled up from the table. Lewis said that he would enjoy meeting with Taylor sometime. Taylor suggested the following day, Sunday, and Lewis agreed.

The Saturday encounter in the Mayflower dining room was one of as many as a dozen meetings that Lewis and Taylor conducted over the next two months, and it was the only one that was not secret. Most took place at Taylor's residence—three townhouses made into one—at 16 East Seventieth Street, in New York. Taylor had agreed to the meetings because he had made a decision. He wanted to come to terms with Lewis.

The previous summer, Taylor, like a number of leading businessmen of the time, had sailed for Europe to vacation at his villa in Florence, to explore the museums and the ruins, and to sail the Mediterranean Sea. The journey had not been one solely for pleasure, however. Taylor did much thinking. The Depression was continuing, and much of the nation was in distress. A number of the nation's industrial cities, including many steel communities, were in ferment because of confrontations between labor and management. Officially, the company's policy was to continue with Arthur H. Young's employee-representation program, but in view of the labor agitation that was going on, Taylor was unsure that the program was working.

There were other considerations. Despite the Depression, the steel industry was experiencing something of an upswing, and Taylor did not want this resurgence, for which he had worked so hard for much of a decade, endangered by labor strife. Finally, there was the political situation. President Roosevelt had handily defeated his Republican opponent, Alfred M. Landon, in November 1936, and Democrats had swept many other elections; candidates supported by the CIO had won numerous local and state elections in Pennsylvania. Taylor pondered these changes and wondered whether it was not time for the corporation to alter its policies.

He remained in Europe until the late fall and during his months there worked diligently on a new statement of the corporation's labor policy. The statement read:

The Company recognizes the right of its employees to bargain collectively through representatives freely chosen by themselves without dictation, coercion, or intimidation in any form or from any source. It will negotiate and contract with the representatives of any group of its employees so chosen and with any organization as the representative of its members, subject to the recognition of the principle that the right to work is not dependent on membership or non-membership in any organization and subject to the right of every employee to bargain in such manner and through such representatives, if any, as he chooses.

On his return, Taylor kept the statement a secret, showing it to only a few corporation executives. He still opposed unions and believed that most workers did, too, but he was not Carnegie or Gary—he was willing to talk with union men; he was willing to change.

For a time the meetings between Taylor and Lewis were prevented by Lewis's involvement in the bitter sitdown strike that had begun at Flint, Michigan, in December 1936, when auto workers, in one of the seminal moments in American labor history, occupied plants of the General Motors Corporation. On February 11, 1937, the Flint sitdowns ended after forty-four days, with General Motors recognizing the new United Automobile Workers. This was an astounding victory for Lewis and the American labor movement, and, it is likely, made Taylor even more desirous of meeting with Lewis and working out a peaceful settlement with the union men attempting to organize the corporation. Now, too, the corporation was negotiating for war contracts with the British government, contracts the corporation badly wanted. It was also clear that, in the event of a national steel strike, state law-enforcement agencies and the federal government could not be used to assist the corporation, as in the past.

On February 17, the day that the General Motors agreement was ratified by the workers, Lewis and Taylor, again secretly, resumed their meetings. During the last week in February, Murray, McDonald, SWOC general counsel Lee Pressman, and Sidney Hillman were summoned by Lewis to the Essex House Hotel, on Central Park South, in New York. Murray, although president of the SWOC, had not known of the negotiations between Lewis and Taylor, nor had any of his assistants. Lewis entered the room in which the other labor men had gathered. He told Murray that he had just returned from Taylor's home and that he and Taylor had reached an agreement. The corporation would recognize the SWOC as the bargaining agent for its members—the first time an assertive union would represent workers in the steel industry since the Homestead strike of 1892.

Lewis explained the terms of the agreement. There would be a wage increase of ten cents an hour, raising the basic wage in northern mills to sixty-two and a half cents an hour and five dollars a day; an eight-hour day and a forty-hour week, with time and a half for overtime; a form of seniority for promotions and layoffs; the beginning of a grievance procedure. These terms were much like the demands made by the workers during the 1919 steel strike. He then instructed the men to return to Pittsburgh, where, he said, Benjamin F. Fairless, the corporation's president, would sign the agreement for the corporation. Fairless, like Murray, had not known of the negotiations. On February 27, Taylor summoned him to New York and informed him of the agreement.

The union and corporation men met on Tuesday, March 2, 1937, and Fairless and Murray signed a preliminary agreement. On the afternoon of March 17, the two men met with their assistants in the conference room of the Carnegie-Illinois Steel Company to sign the final agreement, which was to last a year. As they passed the pen, it is said that one of the signatories to the agreement noticed that the portraits of corporation executives hanging on the wall had been changed since the previous meeting.

"Who is that in the oil painting behind you?" one man asked. A second man replied, "He wasn't there yesterday." "Is that so?" the first man said. "Whose picture was there yesterday?" "Old H. C. Frick," the second man said. "They took him out. Didn't think he could stand it."

VII

On Labor Day, 1937, in Pittsburgh, John L. Lewis addressed an assembly of two hundred thousand workers and members of their families, probably the largest labor assembly ever held up to that time. "The workers of the nation have organized a new labor movement within the principles of the Bill of Rights and committed to the proposition that the workers are free to assemble in their own way, voice their own grievances," Lewis declared, his words transmitted by radio across the nation. "Labor seeks peace. The voice of labor, insistent upon its rights, should not be annoying to the ears of justice or offensive to the conscience of the American people."

What had occurred in the labor movement since June 1933, four years and a summer before, was remarkable. The CIO now had four million members. Workers in steel, autos, meatpacking, rubber, radio, and other mass-production industries had been organized. The SWOC claimed 500,000 members, and although that number was inflated, it probably had at least 250,000 members. The corporation and its subsidiaries had been organized, as had numerous independent companies. Even the AFL had found a resurgence and now had 4.5 million members. Abandoning its craft-union tradition, the AFL had organized aircraft workers, electrical workers, lumber workers, machinists, construction workers, truckers, and others.

There had been some setbacks. The SWOC had been unable to organize the "Little Steel" companies, little only in comparison with the corporation—Republic Steel, Bethlehem Steel, Youngstown Sheet and Tube, Inland Steel, National Steel, American Rolling Mill, and Jones and Laughlin. In May and June 1937, Murray ordered the seventy thousand workers at these companies to strike, but the SWOC's resources were too limited. And the union had no experience in fighting—it had never had to strike to gain its victories.

On Memorial Day, 1937, Chicago police attacked demonstrating steelworkers at Republic's South Chicago works. Ten workers were killed and some one hundred were injured; most of the dead and injured were shot in the back. The union and the CIO looked to Roosevelt for help against the industry. He refused. "A plague on both your houses," the president said. The strike was lost, and in July 1937 the SWOC called it off.

Nevertheless, it was a time of victory for the union. But Myron C. Taylor and others, including labor's supporters in government, had gotten what they wanted, too—orderly, predictable labor relations and unions led by moderate men. Already the CIO was showing signs of weakness. Lewis was reverting to what he had always been, an authoritarian with a massive ego and an uncontrollable desire for power. Of Lewis's speech on Labor Day, 1937, the journalist James Wechsler wrote: "It may be that it was at this meeting that he reached the pinnacle of his power, the grand climax of his glory. . . . It is said that at this point his hallucinations of grandeur began seriously to impair his judgment, that he was now to pay the price for having lost all perspective in viewing himself and the movement he led."

The steelworkers were organized, but they had not organized themselves. The organizing had been done for them, from above, from outside —by emissaries from Lewis and his union, who brought with them the mine workers' authoritarian tradition and deep distrust of democracy in unions. There were no steelworkers in the SWOC leadership. Murray was a former coal miner and had been one only briefly. McDonald had worked in a steel mill for a few months early in the 1920s. He was a union bureaucrat. Of the other leaders, three were officials of the miners' union, two were officials from needle-trades unions, and two were longtime officials of the Amalgamated Association of Iron, Steel, and Tin Workers who had not worked in the iron mills for decades and who hardly participated in SWOC affairs. Some men from the rank-and-file movement who had joined the SWOC were given secondary jobs; others were not given jobs and disappeared.

"The Steelworkers' Organizing Committee is a Democracy," Thomas R. R. Brooks wrote in "As Steel Goes . . . Unionism in a Basic Industry," in 1940. "It is a democracy *of* steel workers and *for* steel workers but not *by* steel workers. The problem of satisfying the third of Lincoln's conditions of democracy is one of the major tasks facing the union as it moves into a crucial period in the history of democratic institutions."

14

VICTORY VALLEY

The news came on the radio at 2:25 Sunday afternoon, December 7, 1941. The Japanese had attacked Pearl Harbor. The next day, the headline in the *Homestead Daily Messenger* read U.S. DECLARES WAR ON JAPS. 3,000 CASUALTIES IN HAWAII.

Like many Americans, the people of the Homestead district had expected war for some time. The nation's first peacetime conscription had begun in September 1940, and Homestead had initially provided thirty-four selectees, as draftees were known. Homestead men had always been red-blooded, and dozens more Homestead young men had soon volunteered and gone off to the training camps. Some had volunteered for the adventure because they wanted to get out of the Monongahela Valley and see the world. Others had volunteered because they knew they would probably be drafted anyway, and they wanted to get in and get it over with while winning the honor of being volunteers. At the time of the attack on Pearl Harbor, many Homestead men had already finished basic training, and some had participated in maneuvers in South Carolina or Louisiana. Some had already come home on leave and had loafed on Eighth Avenue in their uniforms and caught the eyes of the girls, which was one of the reasons for volunteering in the first place.

The summer of 1941 had been dry and sunny. The Fourth of July celebration at West Field had been especially festive, for patriotism was in the air. Rain forced the cancellation of the morning and afternoon events, but the skies had cleared and the show had gone on. More than twenty thousand people had gone up to the field to see what remained of the day's events, a comedy team and a trapeze act. That night, an especially fine fireworks display had been presented; rockets, pinwheels, and Roman candles burst high and bright above the town.

The fall had been lovely too, crisp and clear. The season's highlight had come on a cold Saturday in early November, when seven thousand people went up to West Field to watch Homestead and Munhall play each other in football for the twenty-seventh time in a rivalry that went back to 1908. Both teams had suffered through lackluster seasons. Homestead had a record of three-to-four going into the encounter, and Munhall's was five-to-four. But records never meant anything when these fierce rivals played. It turned out to be a glorious day for Homestead; the stouthearted Homestead men prevailed, fourteen to nothing.

No one, of course, knew for sure that war was coming, but people could sense that America probably would go in. In October 1941, the *Reuben James,* an American destroyer, had been torpedoed off the Irish coast by a German submarine, and the war spirit had risen. Homestead was getting a lesson in what war would mean on the home front, for in the flats along the river a huge construction project was under way: Lower Homestead was being demolished to make way for an expansion of the Homestead Works that had been ordered by the federal government, and people were preparing to move. Even Evelyn Marshall, the town's noted madam, had to move, and by early December she was building a new place, at 545 Heisel Street. It was larger and more elaborate than the old, because with the expansion of the mill Miss Marshall expected an expanded clientele, and she wanted to serve the customers well. The new house had oak floors, plastered walls and ceilings, twenty rooms, and air conditioning. Folks called it "the Tabernacle," because it looked a bit like a house of worship, though, as the *Homestead Daily Messenger* pointed out, "Evelyn Marshall doesn't build churches." The Tabernacle was scheduled to open at Christmas.

Now, with Pearl Harbor, the war had arrived. A number of people missed the announcement. Some were downtown, on Eighth Avenue, at the movies. *Smilin' Through,* with Jeanette MacDonald, Gene Raymond, and Brian Aherne, was at the Leona Theatre; *Week-End in Havana,* with Alice Faye, John Payne, Carmen Miranda, and Cesar Romero, was at the Elite Theatre; and *Unfinished Business,* with Irene Dunne, Preston Foster, and Robert Montgomery, was at the Park Theatre. But the moviegoers heard the news from other townspeople when they spilled out into the streets late in the afternoon, and then they went home and talked late into the night about what the war might mean. In an editorial on Monday, December 8, the day that the United States declared war, the *Homestead Daily Messenger* summed up what most people were thinking and saying: "It had to come. Most Americans were astounded by the word that hostilities had started but the general feeling was that it had to come and now that it has we want to do the job before us with the greatest dispatch and bring reason to the yellow men by force of arms. Let every patriot do the job assigned to him without flinching."

In response to America's entry into the war, an air-raid warden was appointed, and the *Messenger* published this advice on what to do in the event of a raid:

1. Keep cool.
2. Stay home.
3. Put out the lights.
4. Lie down.
5. Stay away from windows.

Policemen were dispatched to guard the reservoir on the hill above town in case Japanese or German saboteurs infiltrated the area. The authorities also gave thought to how to provide protection against sabotage at the Homestead Works or the Mesta Machine Company. But no sabotage occurred, and the worry that it would occur was soon forgotten. The Homestead steelworkers' union, Local 1397, did its part. It purchased sixty-six hundred dollars in defense bonds and pledged to purchase more.

The Christmas of 1941 was a pleasant one, people agreed, although the weather was unusually warm. The payroll at the Homestead Works was at a record high. Over ten thousand men were employed at the works, the greatest number since the Depression had begun twelve years before. Eighth Avenue was busy with Christmas shoppers, and many spent heavily, making the holiday the most prosperous in years for the merchants.

On Christmas Eve, the *Messenger* said, "Things are going to be different next year, and so most of us are planning to make the most of tomorrow."

II

To the people of Homestead, the war was tragic or exhilarating, depending on what they did. For many, the war years were the best years of their lives. For workers, the war meant long hours, and often they "doubled out"—worked two eight-hour shifts in a row. But the money was good, and this was a heady change after more than ten years of the Depression. Workers had not only money to spend but money to put away. For the first time, many could start thinking about buying a house and a car.

For soldiers who came home in pretty much one piece, with ribbons and medals, and discharge buttons—"ruptured ducks"—in their lapels, the war was an exciting experience. It gave a lot of young fellows from Homestead a chance to see the world—North Africa, England, France, Italy, Germany, China, Japan, places no one had ever heard of, even those who had paid attention in geography class at Homestead High School, instead of mooning over girls or working on their cars or playing football and basketball. For others, the war meant injury or death. And Homestead paid a heavy price. Thirty-four Homestead district men gave their lives for their country.

For the corporation, the war meant a rebirth—expanded production, a great contribution to the war effort, and enormous profits. For the union, it meant not only legitimacy but also the solidification of certain traits—authoritarianism, a strict hierarchy—that continue to mark it today.

For the town of Homestead, the war meant economic revitalization. Money flowed like water. The mill ran flat out during the war; the lights of the mill literally never went out. The sin strip on Sixth Avenue ran unchecked. But the war also brought substantial change, for with the federal government's order to expand the Homestead Works, almost the entire lower section of Homestead, a fourth of the town, had to be demolished. More than eight thousand residents, 40 percent of Homestead's population, were relocated, and 1,262 buildings were torn down —1,225 homes, 2 convents, 5 schools, 12 churches, 28 saloons, a dozen social clubs, confectionery shops, and grocery stores. It was the largest expansion of a steelworks during the war, but Homestead gave of itself almost without protest. The demolition was necessary to win the war, it was said, but Homestead was never the same again.

The expansion of the Homestead Works had been rumored for months. The official word came on June 28, 1941, with this headline in the *Messenger*: $75,000,000 TO BE SPENT HERE ON NEW MILLS. LIFTING OPTIONS. NAVY BACKING RESULTS IN PROJECT GOING THROUGH. ALL LAND BELOW TRACKS TO BE USED FOR EXPANSION. The government selected the Homestead Works for expansion primarily because, since the days of Carnegie, it had been a manufacturer of armor plate, and more armor plate was now needed for shipbuilding and tank construction. The purchase and demolition of the old facilities and the construction of the new ones was directed by the Defense Plant Corporation, a federal agency established in August 1940 to finance and direct industrial expansion for war production. Under the government's plan, five new complexes were to be installed at the Homestead Works—an open-hearth facility with eleven furnaces, Open Hearth 5 or O.H.5, as it would become known; a 45-inch slab mill; a 160-inch plate mill; a forging and heat-treating shop; and a machine shop. Additional construction at the Edgar Thomson Works in Braddock and at the Duquesne Works was ordered by the government, with the new facilities to be tied in with the Homestead Works.

The area purchased by the government, roughly six blocks long and six blocks wide, was known as "the Ward," although it was composed of two wards and parts of two others. Early in Homestead's history, the riverfront had been a fine neighborhood of substantial homes with lawns running to the river. Some of the town's wealthier citizens had lived there, and it was there where they had gay parties, dancing under Chinese lanterns in the summer, skating and sledding on the river in the winter.

In the 1880s, when the first employees of the mill, primarily English and German immigrants, began coming to Homestead, the area by the river started to change. The wealthy families abandoned the mansions, which were then divided and rented to workers. Additional new houses, much smaller than the old ones, were constructed for workers. In the 1890s, Homestead's second wave of immigrants, Eastern and Southern Europeans, began to move into the neighborhood, and it became more run-down. Finally, starting in the 1890s and reaching a high at the time of the 1919 steel strike, black workers came to Homestead and were quartered below the tracks. The Ward was flat and thus suitable for home-building, the reason that the town was built there in the first place. In addition, people who lived there did not have to climb the hill at the end of their shifts at the mill, or pay a nickel to ride the streetcar.

By the beginning of the twentieth century, Homestead was composed of two basic areas—the Ward, the area below the railroad tracks, and "the Hill," above the tracks. The more skilled workers and many of Homestead's merchants—except for the Jews, who tended to move across the river to the largely Jewish area of Squirrel Hill—generally lived on the Hill. The unskilled lived in the Ward. The area above the tracks was largely Protestant, while the one below was mostly Catholic. The last Protestant church in the ward closed in 1914, and the building became a Russian Orthodox church.

In the Ward there were slum neighborhoods with dilapidated frame houses, boardinghouses, and "immigrant courts"—L- or U-shaped tenements, often without sewers or water. Many of the courts had privies and one central faucet outside, to serve all the residents. The sociologists who studied Homestead for the Pittsburgh Survey early in the century saw the overcrowding of the Ward as one of the evils of American industrialization. And parts of the Ward were seamy; there were not only filthy residences but saloons and whorehouses.

But the area, also known to Homesteaders as Down Below, in some ways was not what it seemed. Many residents wanted a good life and worked hard on their small homes and yards to make them attractive, despite the dirty, noisy mill close by. Lawns were tidy, and many were fenced; trees had been planted. Numerous clubs existed—the Lithuanian Club, the Turner Hall, the Sokol Hall, the Rusin Hall, and others. There were also many confectioneries and grocery stores. In 1913, the corporation built a playground in the Ward, on Second Avenue, and during the summer movies were shown there, projected onto sheets hung from clotheslines. It was not a slum for those who lived there. Now this life came to an end.

At first, most people were enthusiastic about the project. The expansion of the mill would mean more jobs and more money for Homestead. Soon, however, they discovered that, as with most government projects, work would not proceed as quickly and smoothly as had been predicted. Defense Plant Corporation officials appeared in Homestead in July 1941 and said that the Ward would be razed within two or three weeks. This, of course, was absurd—property appraisals had to be done, payments to owners made, disputes adjudicated—and the deadline was pushed back. Demolition did not begin until October 24, 1941. The Defense Plant Corporation said that it must be completed by November 5, but when that deadline went by, a new one was established for late December. After Pearl Harbor, the pressure increased to get on with the project. Some residents went to see their priests to ask whether the government's price for their home or business was sufficient. Take it, the priests usually said. Some families are still angry about that advice.

The first to sell was the Baruska family, who lived on Fourth Avenue. On July 30, 1941, Mr. Baruska, who had been employed at the Homestead Works since 1904, accepted a fifty-five-hundred-dollar check for his home, a six-room frame house that he had purchased in 1914 and where he and his wife had raised three children.

Some people forced to move found homes in Homestead. Others went to the Munhall Homesteads, a public-housing project in Munhall, up the hill, and others scattered among three other public-housing projects, one in West Mifflin and two across the Monongahela River. But no black families were allowed in the projects. In September, Eleanor Roosevelt—the president's wife, who was much loved in Homestead, as she was elsewhere—came to dedicate one of the new housing projects, the Riverview Homes.

The pastor of Saint Anne's Roman Catholic Church, Father Clement R. Hrtanek, was one of the few town leaders who cautioned that the expansion plans should go slowly. Saint Anne's, the largest church below the tracks, had been founded in 1908. That year, Saint Michael's Roman Catholic Church acquired property in Munhall, near the Carnegie Library. It was a fine location, open and green, high above the smoke and dirt and overcrowding of the Ward. But many parishioners were disturbed. They felt that Saint Michael's should remain in the Ward, and they split off to found Saint Anne's. They met in various locations until, in 1915, they purchased a Protestant church on Fourth Avenue from the Methodists, who were moving up to the Hill. The parishioners of Saint Anne's worshipped there until the building was destroyed by fire in 1920. In 1921, they began construction of a splendid new church with altars of marble imported from Italy; expensive frescoes, some donated by Slovak merchants who had become prosperous in the good times that came with World War I and the years thereafter; and an elaborate rose window.

Father Hrtanek was one of the few clergymen who had supported the Homestead workers during the 1919 steel strike, and now he again did what he could to assist his parishioners. When the appraisers pressured them to sell, he advised them not to panic and to wait for a fair price. But finally the homes were sold, as was Saint Anne's, and the parishioners gathered to dismantle the ornate window and store the stained glass so that it could be used whenever another church was built.

By mid-December 1941, the government had purchased all but eighty-five properties. Even this small number of holdouts angered those who favored expansion. They were "absolutely unpatriotic," said a local housing official, A. H. Mercer. "By such an attitude, they delay and hinder the war effort of the nation." By the early spring of 1942, the

Ward was almost gone, and the expansion of the works had begun. All that was left of the Ward were basements and a few houses, and they were soon to go. Only one building was allowed to remain, the Rusin Hall, a favorite place for christenings and weddings. It was turned into an office building for the works.

Later, during the war, a Homestead man, Corporal Joseph Raschak, hailed a cab in Pittsburgh to take him to Homestead, to which he was returning for a furlough. He paid little attention to the route, and when his cab arrived in Homestead, Raschak berated the driver for taking him to the wrong town. He had not recognized Homestead, and why should he have? A third of it was gone.

III

World War II was a war of steel, and if, as some authorities said, steel won the war, then the workers and the corporation played a major role in the victory. During the war, the United States produced 414 million ingot tons of steel, turning out as much steel in one year as the Germans could in three and Japan in nine. The corporation alone produced as much steel during the war as the Germans.

The corporation manufactured almost every conceivable item that could be made from steel. It made a steel wire nineteen ten-thousandths of an inch in diameter for blood-plasma strainers. It manufactured 31.4 million kegs of nails—enough kegs to fill a freight train 687 miles long, roughly the distance from New York to Chicago. It manufactured enough fencing to stretch from New York to San Francisco. It manufactured 90,500 tons of barbed wire, which John W. "Bet-a-Million" Gates had first sold to ranchers in San Antonio, Texas, in the 1870s, and which now was an important weapon of war. It produced 79 million barrels of cement for military construction. It manufactured 3 million "Blitz" or "Jerry" cans, olive-drab cans, a foot high, still found in many Army and Navy stores, for water and gasoline. It made steel tubes for 11 million bazookas. It manufactured 290 portable and easily assembled Bailey bridges. It manufactured 1.4 million springs, 316,815 tons of wire ropes and cables, and 2.8 million bombs. It became a major shipbuilder, converting sheet mills into plate mills in five weeks, to build plate for ships. It constructed 77 destroyers, 522 destroyer escorts, 200 landing craft, 11 troopships, 475 barges and derrick hulls, and 33 cargo vessels.

At its Lorain, Ohio, works the corporation made all but 100 miles of the 1,250 miles of pipe that went into the "Big Inch" pipeline constructed from Texas to New York, to overcome a shortage of gasoline and oil on the Atlantic seaboard brought on by the diversion of oil tankers to military use and the blockade by German submarines of the Atlantic Coast and the Gulf of Mexico. It made pumps that sent gasoline, aviation fuel, and diesel oil through military pipelines in Europe and the Pacific; strapping wire for air-cargo containers that could be dropped without parachutes from planes; noncorrosible stainless-steel tubing for amphibious vehicles; 2 million feet of traction mats that were laid down on beaches to provide traction in sand and mud for amphibious-assault vehicles. It mined 259.3 million tons of iron ore, 168.9 million tons of coal, and 105.8 million tons of limestone, and shipped 109.7 million tons of finished steel.

It had what amounted to its own navy, not just its Great Lakes fleet but the Isthmian Steamship Company, the largest merchant fleet under the U.S. flag, which hauled military supplies to North Africa, Sicily, Italy, France, the Soviet Union, Guam, Alaska, and the Philippines. The ships transported 60 percent of the crude rubber and half of the tin imported into this country during the war, as well as materials for steel alloys. The corporation also suffered battle losses; twenty-two of its ships were sunk by enemy torpedoes.

To accomplish all this required enormous expansion by the corporation and the rest of the nation's steel industry. In addition to the Homestead Works, the Gary Works, at Gary, Indiana, underwent a $12 million expansion. The corporation also constructed and ran for the government an entire new works, the Geneva Works, outside Provo, Utah, which provided steel for the western shipbuilding industry. The corporation employed 254,393 men and women in 1940, and 340,498 by 1943.

IV

The head of the corporation during the war was the engaging Benjamin F. Fairless. Fairless had been brought into the corporation in September 1935 by Myron C. Taylor to be president of the two steelmaking units that had been merged into a single new unit, the Carnegie-Illinois Steel Corporation. When it was announced that Fairless, an outsider, was going to head Carnegie-Illinois, the industry was impressed by the choice. Fairless was called "an inspired salesman" and "a crack steel executive, . . . one of the outstanding figures in the industry."

It seemed that Fairless could not have joined the corporation at a less propitious time. With the downturn in steel production caused by the Great Depression, the corporation had lost about $130 million from 1932 to 1934 and was only a bit out of the red in 1935. But Fairless persevered, and on January 1, 1938, he was named president of the corporation. On

April 5, 1938, when Taylor resigned as chairman, believing that his work was done, Edward R. Stettinius, Jr., who had been brought into the corporation from General Motors as chairman of the finance committee on January 1, 1936, was named chairman of the corporation. But in 1940 Stettinius abruptly resigned to enter government service.*

On paper, the corporation was now to be run by a triumvirate that consisted of Fairless, the president; Irving S. Olds, chairman of the board of directors; and Enders M. Voorhees, chairman of the finance committee. But this triumvirate worked no better than the triumvirate of Morgan, Baker, and Taylor had after the death of Gary ten years before. Fairless was the only top man at the corporation who knew much about making steel, and it was clear that he was the only one with real authority and responsibility. By early in World War II, Fairless was not only the chief executive officer at the corporation but for all practical purposes the head of the American steel industry.

Handsome, burly, with black hair, Fairless was a man who got on easily with people. He liked cigars, baseball, and fishing. Corporation executives, government officials, union leaders, workers—everybody liked him. He believed in the American dream. In 1957, not long after he retired, he published a short memoir, a reprint from a *Life* magazine story on him from 1956. He entitled it *It Could Happen Only in the U.S.: A Coal Miner's Son Describes His Remarkable Career That Led from Pigeon Run, Ohio, to the Summit of American Industry.*

Fairless's real name was Benjamin F. Williams. He had taken the surname of an aunt and uncle who had adopted and raised him after his mother was injured in a buggy accident and it was clear that she would never recover fully. Fairless's adoptive home was a white frame house in the town of Justus, four miles from Pigeon Run. His uncle ran a small grocery store in the front of the house, "the kind," Fairless said in his autobiography, "with a stalk of bananas hanging in the window."

He remained close to his mother and father. She taught him "that everybody should work, that everybody should be honest, that no one should expect something for nothing." Some years later, when he had become one of the area's finest baseball players, his father would come to see him play whenever he could, even if this meant walking ten miles or more.

---

* Stettinius never reached the heights expected of him in business or government. After serving in a number of government posts, he was secretary of state from 1944 to 1945, then worked to help create the United Nations. He died, still a relatively young man, at the age of forty-nine, in 1949.

Fairless worked hard as a boy, taking care of the lawn and horses of his aunt and uncle's neighbor Clark McClintock and delivering the *Cleveland Press.* The papers were brought to town each afternoon on the Baltimore and Ohio train. Fairless bought them for half a cent apiece and sold them for a cent apiece. "In many ways it was the best business I ever had," he wrote. "My profit was 100 percent and I had no overhead at all. Unfortunately I lacked volume. I had only a dozen customers and made six cents a day." He also had a third job, as the janitor at the local high school. He would rise at 6:00 A.M. to fire the coal furnace and dust the desks and chairs in the four classrooms. After school, he would sweep the floor and, in winter, shovel the walk.

Encouraged by a teacher he liked, he worked hard in school, despite his extra activities. He was valedictorian, in a class of eight, and at the age of seventeen, after just three years in his country high school, he obtained a position as a teacher, hoping to earn enough money to go on to college. He was paid forty-eight dollars a month. He did the school's janitorial work, so as not to have to pay a janitor out of his salary, and boarded with a farm family for ten dollars a month.

He loved baseball and was a good-hitting catcher for the tank-town teams in the area. But he wanted desperately to get ahead. Hard work, not sports, was what he cared about. He finished his fourth year of high school by taking classes at Wooster College, twenty miles from his home, and then enrolled at Ohio Northern University, one hundred miles away. He worked summers, borrowed two hundred dollars from McClintock, and got an engineering degree.

He obtained a position on a railroad construction gang but disliked it, believing that it would lead nowhere. Then, one day in 1913, he took the inter-urban train to Massillon, Ohio. He had heard that a second Coxey's Army was gathering there, preparing to march on Washington to demand, as the first Coxey's Army had in 1894, that the government issue bonds to build roads to provide jobs for the unemployed. He had no plans to join the march; he only wanted to see what was going on.

On the way to Massillon, he happened to gaze out the window and saw a group of men in khaki doing surveying work. The conductor told him that they were laying out a new steel plant. Forgetting about Coxey's Army, Fairless got off at the next stop, walked back, and found the man in charge of the work crew. "I'm a good engineer, and I'm looking for a job," Fairless said. He was hired at seventy-five dollars a month and went to work building the plant, which was being constructed by the new Central Steel Company. Soon he was promoted to boss the crew. As the plant neared completion, he expected to move with the engineering gang to a construction project in Chicago, but he was called in one day by the head of the steel company, Frederick J. Griffiths, and asked if he would like to stay with Central Steel. Fairless said yes. He thus became a steelman.

Central Steel was a small, almost primitive operation, but the men who ran it had plenty of spunk. The automobile age was coming on, and the company concentrated on the light alloy steels that the auto companies demanded. The expanded production of World War I helped the company grow. Fairless rose rapidly in Central Steel, becoming mill superintendent, then general superintendent, then vice-president in charge of operations. When the company merged with another firm in the area, the United Alloy Steel Corporation, Fairless was made vice-president and general manager of the merged companies. Two years later, he was named president. In 1930, the firm was one of a number of companies that were merged into a new, large enterprise, the Republic Steel Corporation, that a Cleveland industrialist, Cyrus Eaton, was organizing. Fairless was named executive vice-president under the president, Tom Girdler.

Fairless did his work well. When Central merged with Republic, it possessed one of the industry's greatest concentrations of electric furnaces, which made stainless steel, just coming onto the market, as well as a noted research staff and a highly skilled workforce. With the merger, he was joining one of the most advanced American steel companies, and the third-largest steel producer in the country, behind the United States Steel Corporation and the Bethlehem Steel Corporation. But when Myron C. Taylor asked him to come to the United States Steel Corporation, Fairless could not refuse. "I wanted to play in the big leagues," he later said.

Under Fairless, the corporation performed admirably, demonstrating astonishing creativity and diligence. Four products of the war years illustrate the corporation's creativity and production abilities—razor-blade steel, tin cans, steel helmets, and perforated landing pads.

Shortly before the United States entered the war, it became clear that razor-blade steel, which for years had come from Sweden, would no longer be available. Corporation metallurgists developed an excellent razor-blade steel, and the American Steel and Wire Company, a corporation subsidiary, captured the market. By the war's end, it had become the world's largest supplier of razor-blade steel, shipping as many as three hundred tons a month.

Tin cans are actually made of steel coated with a layer of tin thinner than a human hair. Before the war, most of the tin for cans came from Southeast Asia. For some years, the corporation had been experimenting with new ways of making tin plate for cans. The traditional method consisted of dipping steel sheet into molten tin. Researchers devised a method of attaching tin to the steel electrolytically. In 1937, a mill with an electrolytic-tinning line was constructed at the corporation's Gary Works. The new method used 60 percent less tin than the traditional one. When, in 1942, the government said that all canned goods would go to the military, and thus that there would be little or no tin left for the home front, the corporation constructed nine electrolytic-tinning lines and also shared the process with other steel manufacturers. By the war's end, twenty-seven electrolytic-tinning lines had been constructed, and so much tin was saved through the process that there was tin both for the military and for civilians. This new tin plate also went into bread boxes, pails, dippers, dairy equipment, and bottle caps. The tin cans were used not only for foods but for paint, petroleum products, varnish, tobacco, beer, and coffee.

When the United States entered the war, the helmets issued to the troops were still the flat ones that American soldiers had worn in World War I. The government said that a new helmet was needed, one that would offer greater protection by extending farther over the head and having greater ability to withstand bullets and shrapnel. But the helmet also had to have give, so that when it was hit it would not shatter. The government asked the corporation for assistance, and its technicians developed a manganese alloy steel that could withstand a forty-five-caliber bullet fired at pointblank range. The corporation then went into helmet production. The steel for the helmets, made at the corporation's South Works plant, in Chicago, was rolled into sheets and then cut into discs that were shaped into the famous "steel pots," standard government issue until the 1980s and still used widely around the world. Ultimately, the corporation produced steel for 21 million helmets, 90 percent of all the helmets made in the United States during the war.

As air power was expanded and the military pushed into new areas, new airfields were needed, and often needed quickly. The corporation set to work and developed perforated landing pads—ingenious devices ten feet long and sixteen inches wide, joined together through hooks and slots, that could be laid down on graded fields. The pads could be transported to the most remote locations, laid down, and hooked together, thus creating airfields for fighters, bombers, or medical-evacuation planes. The corporation shared the invention and at one time during the war the pads were being made by twenty-eight companies.

V

When it was recognized by the corporation in 1937, the steelworkers' union had promised to bring democracy to the steel mills and the steel towns, and to give the men and women there a say in their lives. But though it did give people a greater voice in the workplace, the union did not bring democracy. Even early in the war, several years after it had been formed, the Steel Workers Organizing Committee had no elected officers. Moreover, Philip Murray, chairman of the SWOC, relished his authority and ran the union "from the outset as though full powers resided in its chief executive," the historian Irving Bernstein has written.

Today, Murray is described as saintly and is praised for his human touch and unpretentiousness. "It was Murray's special quality," the journalist Murray Kempton said, "to touch the love and not the fear of men." But Murray was a limited man, under the influence of Lewis for years and of the Roman Catholic Church all his life. He was not well read, and though he was unpretentious he displayed almost no keen thinking or creative intellectualism. He had no social vision beyond believing that workers should have better lives. He was also—and this is not characteristic of a saint—shrewd and ambitious. He saw conspiracies where none existed. He was, no less than Lewis and perhaps more, an ardent red-baiter. He distrusted experts and intellectuals, and when he thought they were becoming too uppity, he harried them out of the union. He trusted the union's lawyers, however, and often seemed to be in their control. In this he established a pattern that exists even today, when lawyers still have immense authority in the union.

Murray seemed compelled to keep all power in his own hands. The historian Nelson Lichtenstein said that Murray had "none of the inner calm of one comfortable with great power. Although he cultivated a dignified and fatherly demeanor, he could not tolerate opposition within the CIO. He took it personally, thought it threatened his manhood, and felt humiliated when other union leaders contradicted him in public or private." Bernstein wrote: "Murray felt that organizational survival depended on tight control and internal discipline. Moreover, the oligopolized steel industry required that a union, to be effective, must also be centralized. Democracy could wait." What had happened was that the union had created itself in the image of the corporation. The corporation was the only model that Murray and the other leaders knew, other than the miners' union, which was highly autocratic itself.

Murray did not face an easy task as he and his staff tried to build a steelworkers' union. After the deal to provide recognition for the union was made by Lewis and the corporation, the campaign to organize the rest of the steel industry was impeded by the failed Little Steel drive. The Great Depression seemed to be subsiding, but a recession struck the nation between 1937 and 1939, bringing unemployment again to the steel industry.

Murray faced internal problems, too. In early 1940, at a SWOC wage and policy convention, the first such gathering since Lewis had created the SWOC four years before, some members complained about the lack of democracy. Murray finally promised that the next convention, set for 1942, would be a constitutional convention. The delegates accepted this, and the complaining stopped.

Finally, Murray faced an agonizing rupture in his relationship with his mentor, John L. Lewis. Lewis, a lifelong Republican, had supported Herbert Hoover in 1928 and 1932, Roosevelt in 1936. But in 1940 he and Roosevelt were at odds, and in a radio address on October 25 Lewis made this astonishing announcement: "It is obvious that President Roosevelt will not be reelected for a third term unless he has the overwhelming support of the men and women of labor. If he is, therefore, reelected it will mean that the members of the Congress of Industrial Organizations have rejected my advice and recommendation. I will accept the result as being the equivalent of a vote of no confidence, and will retire as president of the Congress of Industrial Organizations* at its convention in November."

On election day, November 5, 1940, Roosevelt defeated Wendell L. Willkie by 4.5 million votes, receiving 449 electoral-college votes to Willkie's 82. Shortly afterward, the CIO convention was held at the Chelsea Hotel in Atlantic City. Lewis resigned. It was assumed that Murray would be his successor, but many, including Murray himself, had doubts about his leadership ability. It is said that he paced the boardwalk during the convention and that he sought the counsel of his priest and of others. "I don't want the job," he told a union official. "I'm afraid I'd make a horse's ass of myself in it."

At the convention, Lewis nominated Murray, praising "his great mind, his brilliant talents, and his constant, untiring energy." Murray was unanimously elected CIO president, while remaining president of the SWOC and the miners' union. Murray had always been number two to Lewis. Now he was being asked to become a leader. He gave a halting, self-deprecating acceptance speech. Lewis, in his speech opening the con-

---

* In 1938 the Committee for Industrial Organization had become the Congress of Industrial Organizations.

vention, had said, "I've lived my life among men. . . . I am myself a man." Murray echoed that theme: "I think I am a man. I think I have convictions. I think I have a soul and a heart and a mind. . . . With the exception, of course, of my soul, they all belong to me, every one of them."

The SWOC's first constitutional convention, the one that Murray had promised two years earlier, opened on May 19, 1942, in Cleveland, with seventeen hundred delegates. The corporation and the other steel companies had said for decades that union people were radicals, but here the union people were, hundreds of them, in white shirts, ties, and dark suits, many with vests—the picture of middle-class Americanism. The union, Murray said, now had 660,000 members and had established collective-bargaining agreements with more than nine hundred companies in steel manufacturing and fabricating. He reported that the SWOC had made the final payment, of $250,000, on the $600,000 it had owed the United Mine Workers of America since the founding of the SWOC. He also said that he expected no shenanigans from the delegates, no criticism of the leadership, no rump movements: "I do not want this convention to waste a single, solitary moment of its time discussing, by resolution or otherwise, internal differences of any description." The constitution that he wanted the delegates to approve would establish an autocracy.

Under Murray's plan the organization would have a president but no vice-presidents. Instead, there would be three international-union officers —two assistants to the president, and a secretary-treasurer. The executive board would consist of the president, the assistants, and the secretary-treasurer, plus the organization's thirty-nine district directors, all of whom would be appointed by the president. Dues and initiation fees collected by the local unions would be forwarded to the international union, which would retain three-quarters of the dues and two-thirds of the fees and return the remainder to the locals. Collective bargaining would be centralized, and "no strike shall be called without the approval of the international president." The president would have "the authority to appoint, direct, suspend, or remove such organizers, representatives, agents, and employees as he may deem necessary."

Some delegates were disturbed by the undemocratic structure that Murray proposed. They said that organizers and representatives should be elected, but Murray replied that elected men could defy the president and thus create "internal strife," which, he contended, the steelworkers' union was "not old enough to survive." Justifying the proposed allocation of dues and initiation fees, he said, "The only thing the employer fears in this nation is . . . a big union with a big treasury."

Murray easily carried the day. On May 22, he was elected president by acclamation, and all of his nominees for subordinate positions were elected—Van A. Bittner, the dedicated organizer from the miners' union, and Clinton S. Golden, the rumpled, pipe-smoking labor intellectual, were elected as assistants to the president, and David J. McDonald, Murray's right-hand man, became secretary-treasurer. Until now, Murray had accepted as recompense for leading the SWOC his salary as a vice-president of the miners' union. But the new constitution stipulated that the president would receive a salary of twenty thousand dollars a year, and Murray accepted this as well. There was one other matter—choosing a name for the organization. The delegates agreed to call it the United Steel Workers of America. It was then realized that if the words "steel workers" were combined into one, the initials of the union would be "USA," a perfect way for the union to show its patriotism in wartime. The words were merged.

This was a moment of glory for Murray: three days later came a moment of humiliation. On May 25, a year and a half after Lewis had praised Murray and brought about his election as CIO president, he put Murray on trial within the miners' union for "treasonable activities" against the union. Embittered by his loss of power, Lewis was looking for a way to humiliate Murray. He questioned the propriety of loans that the miners' union had made to the CIO—loans that he himself had approved. He claimed that Murray had challenged his patriotism by referring to him as a "Jap"—which Murray had not done—and that Murray had criticized the miners' union. He made an issue of the fact that Murray had accepted a salary as president of the steelworkers' union even though he continued to draw a salary as a vice-president of the miners' union. Murray was summoned to a basement room of the union's headquarters in Washington, and one by one, officials of the union, doing what Lewis wanted, denounced Murray, their union brother for forty years. Lewis's biographer Saul Alinsky described the scene: "It is Lewis's personal trophy room, and . . . here the spirit of Lewis leaps at one from every part of the room and paralyzes any resistance." The contemptible charade continued for three days, and Murray accepted the humiliation. On May 28, Lewis stripped Murray of his miners' union vice-presidency. "Thus did John L. Lewis, the great labor leader of the thirties, demean himself," wrote Irving Bernstein.

Murray had lost his mentor, but his power was growing. He concentrated on running the steelworkers' union and the CIO. Running the union was still difficult. There was trouble collecting dues, as McDonald admitted years later: "So with all our wind and with all our puffing and blowing we had increased our dues-paying membership by about 500,000 in five years, or perhaps 600,000 members. Steelworkers will go out and die for the union in the excitement of the picket line, but they'll be damned if they'll give another dollar to that 'lousy shop steward.' " Moreover, the union claimed eligibility for all workers, not counting supervisors, "in and around iron and steel manufacturing, processing, and fabricating mills and factories on the American continent." But it was still not recognized by some steel companies. The war allowed the union to solve these two problems. When the war broke out, Murray immediately pledged that the steelworkers and the other industrial workers who belonged to the CIO would not strike for the duration. In return, Roosevelt created the War Labor Board to handle labor-management disputes. The War Labor Board then drafted contracts for the Little Steel companies that included maintenance of membership and, most important, dues checkoff. Inland signed on August 5, 1942, Youngstown Sheet and Tube on August 12, and Bethlehem and Republic on August 13. The government had provided the steelworkers' union with what the Little Steel strike five years before had failed to produce—recognition.

During the war, the union was becoming much like any institution. Soon it had little use for mavericks. Two union officials, Clinton S. Golden and Harold Ruttenberg, in their book *The Dynamics of Industrial Democracy,* published in 1942, wrote, "The most militant local union leaders, who rise to the surface in the organizing stage of unions, fall by the side when the union moves into the stage of constructive relations with management." The task was to convert "an organizing staff into contract administrators."

As an illustration, Golden and Ruttenberg told the story of Stanley Orlosky, a steelworker expelled from the SWOC in 1940 after a trial on charges of "violation of obligation to the Steel Workers Organizing Committee." The union officials who tried Orlosky were men whom he had convinced to join the organization in the 1930s. Orlosky came to Golden and Ruttenberg's office to appeal his expulsion. "Being a good union man is agitating—that's what I always knew as a union man—and I got fired for agitating," he told them. "The union was organized to have freedom, and not to be fired for talking. The men that tried me in the local, I had a hard time getting to join the union a few years ago. Now they're big union shots. The company has had it in for me since 1933. I'm a thorn in the flesh to it. Now the union sides with the company, and I'm out. That ain't justice. The national office should give me another hearing, and give me back my membership card."

Golden and Ruttenberg investigated the case and discovered that the remarks that Orlosky had been expelled for making consisted of charges that union officials were "selling the men down the river" because they had settled grievances to his dissatisfaction. Golden and Ruttenberg concluded that Orlosky had been properly expelled, because union officials had settled grievances "on their merits." They wrote, "Stanley's leadership was essential to the establishment of the union against bitter resistance, but after it had been fully accepted by management such leadership was a handicap to the development of cooperative union-management relations."

Near the war's end, the union was in as favorable a position as the companies. It had a number of intelligent, skilled staff members. The steelworkers were the nation's largest union, representing 90 percent of the five hundred thousand American steelworkers; with workers in related fields, it had, by 1945, eight hundred thousand members, who, with the members of their families, represented "nineteen out of every one thousand persons in the U.S.—enough people to more than populate the states of South Carolina, Wyoming, and Vermont," *Life* magazine said. It had close links to the government. It had its fine headquarters in the Grant Building, in Pittsburgh, and handsome offices on Jackson Place, in Washington, in which it rented extra space to the CIO.

Life for most steelworkers had improved dramatically. Wages had increased from $29.30 a week, on average, in 1939, to $56.93, on average, in 1944. Increases approved by the government late in the war raised wages even more. The absence of militancy and democracy may have been felt by some workers, but the union's moderate, businesslike approach appealed to the nation's press. *Fortune* said:

The USA [United Steel Workers of America] is, in the best sense of the word, a business union. Since it is designed to live in a business world, USA, unlike the almost anarchistically democratic United Automobile Workers, is formed into a compact, hard-hitting phalanx ready to face employers with no sabotaging or ideological sass from the rear ranks. . . . The offices of the USA are usually in the better office buildings; its officers and organizers are as carefully dressed as the company executives with whom they deal. . . . The union now has $1 million in its treasury and its scrupulously audited accounts show revenues of about $1 million a year.

The press, the union, and the steel industry were pleased by the prospects that lay ahead. "It's industrial peace for the Postwar period," the *CIO News* said.

VI

At the war's end, money was pouring into Homestead. The mill was running flat out, and workers were earning more than they ever had.

Yet there was a melancholy quality to those months. Almost every day, by the beginning of 1945, another story appeared on the front page of the *Homestead Daily Messenger* about the death in combat of another Homestead boy. That was all they were, most of them, boys—smiling young fellows in uniform. They had walked the streets of Homestead a few years before, performed with distinction on the athletic fields and in the gymnasiums, taken their dates to Eighth Avenue on Saturday night. Then they had left from the Homestead station, and now, one after the other, they were gone. Small flags with gold stars were going up in front windows, and there were many gold-star mothers in Homestead. Among those who died were: Private First-Class Mike Skoap, killed in action; Corporal Ernest Katona, killed in action January 9, 1945, Luzon, Philippines; Lieutenant Wiley Hawkins, fighter pilot, killed in action January 15, 1945, China; Lieutenant Clair E. Jones, glider pilot, killed in action January 20, 1945, Belgium; First Lieutenant Edward F. Wilfinger, killed in action February 1, 1945, Burma; Sergeant Walter Gudenburr, infantry-man, killed in action February 12, 1945, Luzon, Philippines; Lieutenant Louis Hays, killed in action April 8, 1945, Italy; Private Michael Ondo, killed in action April 15, 1945, Okinawa.

Katona, Gudenburr, and Hays had been employed at the Homestead Works. Just before Katona had been killed, he had sent his parents a Japanese flag as a souvenir and said he would be home soon. Skoap had been "one of the best blockers ever to carry the gold and blue of Homestead," the *Homestead Daily Messenger* said. He had played three years of hard, clean football. Hawkins had flown seventy-nine missions over the Mediterranean and had shot down four enemy planes. He had returned to the United States for four months before being shipped to the China-Burma-India theater. Wilfinger had played the violin in the Homestead High School orchestra. Ondo had been a delivery boy for Wohlfarth Brothers, a bakery on Eighth Avenue.

Jones had arrived in Europe in May 1944 and met up with an old friend from Homestead, Private John Hart, another member of the Eighty-second Airborne Division. They were at the front, and Jones had volunteered to go on a patrol. Experienced men never volunteered, but Jones had said he was going to capture a German tank and have it taken to Homestead and placed in front of the Carnegie Library. Artillery rounds started coming. Experienced men knew by the sound when incoming artillery was coming toward them, and they hit the dirt. Jones remained standing and was blown apart. His wife had just given birth to a son, but Jones would never see him.

For a time, Burgess John McLean had made it a practice to go down to the train station to say goodbye to the soldiers. Then he began to realize that he would never see many of them again, only their obituaries in the *Messenger*. After a close friend's son—a young man whom McLean had seen off at the station—was killed, McLean would no longer go down there to say goodbye. It was too painful.

On April 12, 1945, a Thursday, more saddening news came on the radio. Franklin D. Roosevelt was dead. He had been a great hero in Homestead; he had done much for Homestead and communities like it. Because of Roosevelt, the union had been formed, and Democrats had come to power in Homestead's local government. Now men and women were benumbed by the news of the president's death. Most stores closed at 3:00 P.M.

Near the end of the war, after four years of anxiety and sacrifice, four years of hard work and grief, the spirits of some were flagging. The weather that spring had been wet, and some people had given up on their victory gardens because it was hard to get anything going. There also was slackening on rationing. People were paying small bribes at gasoline stations to obtain extra gasoline, and meat was being purchased on the black market. The *Messenger* said that it was despicable when "we expect the other fellow to do without meat and then we patronize the black market ourselves. We are a pretty contemptible lot."

Then, suddenly, the war was over. V-E Day, victory in Europe, came on May 8, and on August 14 the Japanese laid down their arms. Homestead erupted in joy. After the victory over Japan, the Homestead Works and Mesta Machine closed for three days, which was unheard of; even after World War I, the mills had not closed. People went to garages and barns and brought out cars not driven since the war began because of gasoline rationing. They crowded into the cars and drove through town, horns blaring, tin cans rattling on back bumpers. Bells clanged on the fire trucks. It seemed that the driving skills of some residents had atrophied during the war years; there were numerous minor accidents. Many people stayed up and celebrated until dawn.

Not everyone celebrated, however. On the day that the war with Japan ended, Evelyn Patterson, a librarian, was at work in the Carnegie Library. She had worked there since 1941. Her husband, James, a Navy man, had been killed in the European theater in February 1944. She had two brothers in the Pacific, Harold, with the Army, and Russell, with the Navy, and she feared that they might be killed, too.

The children's room had closed at 6:00 P.M. that day, and Mrs.

Patterson was alone in the library. It was hot and quiet. Suddenly she heard the mill whistle go off. Then the most curious thing happened: The whistle kept sounding. Minutes went by. Still the whistle kept sounding. She looked up. A boy stuck his head in a window of the reading room. "The war is over," he cried. Mrs. Patterson locked up the library as fast as she could and hurried down to the Avenue. Only a few moments had elapsed, but already the street was filling with people. Cars were whizzing by. Horns and whistles were blowing. Church bells were ringing.

Mrs. Patterson met her mother and a neighbor, Mrs. Clark, who had two sons, Ray and James, in the service. They watched the crowd for a while, mostly younger people. Neither Mrs. Patterson nor her mother nor Mrs. Clark said much. They were glad that the war was over, but they did not feel like celebrating. They went home.

It was not long before everyone—town, corporation, union, workers— began to look ahead. The local brewery, Hofbrau, began taking advertisements in the paper again, having with understandable tact—considering the beer's German name—cut advertising during the war. Canned fruits and vegetables came off the rationed list. Gasoline rationing was ended. New models of irons and washing machines began to appear in store windows on Eighth Avenue—a good sign for the steel industry—and orders were placed for fall delivery. A Homestead merchant got in a big shipment of nylons, and there was almost a riot as women queued up to buy them, one pair apiece.

At the war's end, the United States had about as much steel capacity as the rest of the world combined, one-third more than in 1929, the year that the Great Depression began. The corporation made almost one-third of the nation's steel. It had the world's largest steel plant, at Gary, Indiana; the world's largest soft-coal company; and the world's largest cement company. It owned half of the nation's iron ore and had its own limestone quarries, railroads, ships, and barges.

Yet there were disturbing signs. Though employment had expanded substantially because of war production, new steel-production methods and machines meant that it had not expanded as much as might have been expected. It is an immutable rule of industrialism that advanced methods mean fewer people. This, after all, is one of the main reasons for advanced technologies. It was also clear that the high-grade ores of the Mesabi Range, mined for some sixty years by now, and mined especially heavily during the war, were becoming depleted. The industry had substantial excess capacity, but its leaders believed that in the long run the use of steel would catch up to the capacity. Moreover, new products—plastics and aluminum—were replacing steel.

Still, the markets for steel were substantial. The steel-appliance industry was ready to boom, producing washers, dryers, refrigerators, and air conditioners. The automobile market was poised to take off, following five years of war production, when almost no cars had been manufactured for the civilian market. Farming was increasingly mechanized, meaning a greater demand for steel tractors, combines, and other machines. New chemicals were being developed, many from materials created during the war; this meant a substantial increase in the products—and profits—made from coke by-products produced at plants like the massive Clairton Works. There was talk of vast irrigation projects in the West, of colored steel for the automobile industry that would make it no longer necessary to paint cars, of women's stockings made from fine steel threads. The company looked forward to the period ahead.

The union was also looking forward to good times. It had been a valued partner of the government and the industry in war production. The dues checkoff was "manna from heaven," a union executive said, and the union announced that it would use its expanded income and power to organize workers in the South and West. It expected to grow with expanded employment from new production.

On Sunday, August 26, Philip Murray motored to Homestead to speak before a union rally at West Field. It was a hot, bright day, and more than four thousand people attended. Murray was popular and important, no more the frightened Scottish immigrant who walked to his relatives' home in the snow on Christmas Day after his arrival in America, no longer a factotum for John L. Lewis. He hobnobbed with presidents and other big men in government now; he was always getting on the train or the plane for Washington. He was a big man. He did not come to Homestead every day.

Murray made a fiery speech. It had not been just the men and women in the armed services who had won the war. They might have won the war on the battlefield, but the men and women on the homefront, union brothers and sisters, had "won the battle of production," which was as important for victory as anything done by the troops. Now the war was over, and for what they had done the nation's fifty-eight million industrial workers deserved higher wages. He pledged to demand for steelworkers "an immediate and substantial wage increase." Goddamned right, Phil, the steelworkers shouted.

PART THREE

15

"NO LONGER
A CLASS WAR"

At 12:01 A.M. on January 21, 1946, 750,000 steelworkers went on strike. It was the largest strike in American history up to that time. The strike was about money. Steelworkers had received two wage increases during the war, totaling fifteen and a half cents an hour, but throughout 1945 they and union executives complained that this increase was inadequate, considering the industry's huge wartime profits and the end of the overtime wages that workers had earned during the war. In bargaining that began in 1945, the steelworkers demanded an increase of twenty-five cents an hour, and the steel companies offered twelve and a half cents. After several months, the union dropped its demand to twenty cents, and the companies increased their offer to fifteen cents, but that was as close as the two sides could come. President Harry S. Truman, trying to stem inflation, intervened, suggesting a compromise of eighteen and a half cents. On January 18, the union agreed, but the corporation and the other steel companies refused. Three days later, the steelworkers went on strike.

They were not the only workers on the picket line. More than 320,000 automobile workers at the General Motors Corporation had been on strike since November 21, 1945, and the steelworkers were soon followed by workers in coal, electrical equipment, meatpacking, trucking, maritime, and other industries. By early 1946, more than two million workers were on strike, and at one time during that year more than four and a half million were out. For some other striking unions, notably the United Automobile Workers (UAW), more than money was involved. The leader of the UAW strike, Walter P. Reuther, a blusterer but a creative man with social vision, was taking an unusual approach. He not only demanded a substantial wage increase but argued that General Motors should open its books to the public because, he believed, they would show that the company could increase wages without having to raise prices. On January 10, 1946, a government fact-finding board recommended that General Motors and the auto workers settle at nineteen and a half cents an hour. Reuther accepted, but the company refused.

Philip Murray dismissed Reuther's proposals. Profit margins were not the province of unions, he said: "Unlike the union in the General Motors case, the steel union . . . has not coupled its demand for wage increase with a flat demand that present basic steel prices be maintained." The steelworkers' strike was about wages alone.

In mid-February, Murray and Benjamin F. Fairless met privately and worked out an agreement. The steelworkers settled for an increase of eighteen and a half cents an hour and returned to work, undercutting the auto workers. In return, the steel companies were granted price increases of five dollars a ton by the government, as Fairless had earlier requested. Reuther complained, "The torch we lit during the General Motors strike was not picked up by the steelworkers." On March 13, Reuther, with no other choice, capitulated, settling for eighteen and a half cents and no agreement on prices. The settlements destroyed efforts at price stabilization. Price controls were lifted; prices—and profits—rose dramatically throughout much of American business.

The leaders of the steelworkers' union were pleased with the settlement and pleased that the union's members were back at work. Let someone else be creative, they thought. They had never cared for Reuther, who, like his union, always got more favorable press attention than did the steelworkers. Besides, the strike had not been the radical confrontation between laborers and capitalists that most of the press portrayed it as. There had often been a holiday air on the picket line, and there was almost no violence. A strike was a way to let off steam.

Years later, David J. McDonald, secretary-treasurer of the steelwork-ers' union, recalled:

There was an undercurrent to this strike I'd never sensed before. No one was really very angry, and I had the feeling from the beginning that the steel industry was conditioned to the eighteen and a half cents and simply wanted a breather it could blame on us while its customers used up some swollen inventories. That feeling was by no means one-sided. Steelwork-ers who had been at it seven days a week for almost four years and had accumulated overtime savings they couldn't use during the war didn't object to a few weeks away from the mills. So the 1946 showdown was more a vacation than a strike.

II

The corporation was, *Life* said in 1946, "the most fabulous giant yet produced by the industrial revolution." Steel was the basic metal on which the development of America, and the building and rebuilding of the postwar world, depended. The steelmaking facilities in Germany and Japan had been destroyed in the war and those in Great Britain substan-tially damaged. Since no other countries had had a sizable steel industry, the corporation and the rest of the American steel industry faced almost no competition. There were no steel imports to America, and American companies dominated the export trade.

Production and employment had dropped a bit with the end of the war but then rebounded. In 1950, the corporation produced 31.4 million tons of steel, surpassing its wartime high of 30.8 million tons a year. Its workforce in 1950 reached 288,265, the highest level in its history, except for the war years. Profits were immense. In 1950, the corporation made $215.5 million, three times 1946 earnings and the largest amount since 1917, during World War I, when earnings were $224.2 million.

The corporation, more than other companies, was also able to make astute purchases after the war, acquiring at remarkably cheap prices three steel mills constructed at the government's order and expense during the war—the Geneva Works in Provo, Utah, forty miles south of Salt Lake City, new mills that had been added at the corporation's South Works, in Chicago, and the new Homestead facilities, constructed at a cost of $124 million, and purchased for $12 million. There was controversy about whether the corporation should be permitted to acquire the immense Geneva Works and thus add to its already formidable market position. But President Truman's attorney general, Tom C. Clark, ruled that the acquisition would not violate antitrust laws. On June 19, 1946, the sale was formalized, with the corporation paying $40 million—less than a quarter of its cost—and pledging to spend at least $18.6 million to convert it to peacetime construction.

The corporation won another legal victory in 1948, when it acquired a second western operation, the Consolidated Western Steel Corporation, a beam, plate, pipe, and shipbuilding company formed in 1854 to manufacture the iron pipe used by California gold miners to wash gravel deposits. The corporation's purchase of Consolidated Western was challenged in a case that went to the Supreme Court. While the majority ruled in the corporation's favor, the minority held that it constituted "a purchase for control of a market for which U.S. Steel has in the past had to compete but which it no longer wants left to the uncertainties that competition in the West may engender."

During the early postwar years, the industry as a whole was also doing well. Since 1900, the nation's population had doubled, but the nation's steel capacity had increased four times and steel production had increased four times. In 1900, the industry produced 300 pounds of steel per person a year; by 1950 it produced 1,276 pounds per person. In 1953, the industry employed 544,330 hourly workers, 650,200 total workers, the highest figures in industry history.

New markets were emerging. Leisure activities and spectator sports were increasing, and steel was being used for tow ropes and towers at ski resorts, and in football stadiums. The automobile market was surging. Although some anticipated markets, like colored steel for cars, had not panned out, the automobile industry, which in 1910 had used eleven kinds of steels, was by 1950 using 162 kinds in more than one thousand combinations of sizes and shapes.

The housing market was booming, the suburbs were expanding, and the corporation had entered the housing market in 1944 with its purchase of a promising new enterprise, Gunnison Homes, a maker of prefabricated houses located in New Albany, Indiana, on the Ohio River. It had been established in 1935 by the imaginative Foster Gunnison, who believed in the longstanding American dream of a nice house at a price that an average family could afford. After the war, with servicemen coming home and starting families—there were a record 2.3 million marriages in 1946 alone—it seemed the perfect time for such a house.

By 1951, Gunnison had built thousands of houses and achieved a production speed of one house every sixteen minutes. They were being produced in five sizes, with two to three bedrooms, the largest house selling for ten thousand dollars. One of the low-cost models could be erected in five hours. The key to the Gunnison house was steel. The exterior was made of wooden panels, but each house contained steel kitchen cabinets with double steel sinks, steel bathroom facilities, steel hot-water heaters, and steel furnaces. The corporation's acquisition of Gunnison meant that Gunnison was assured of a supply of steel at predictable prices and that the corporation had its own purchaser of steel.

In the immediate postwar years, there was some criticism of the corporation and the industry. Despite its innovativeness during the war, after the war—as before it—the American steel industry ceded the development of new steelmaking technologies to other nations. For instance, it was Austria that developed the basic oxygen furnace in 1950. The corporation's share of the U.S. steel market continued to fall. In 1950, it was 33 percent, half of the 65 percent that the corporation had enjoyed when it was founded.

In 1950, in hearings before the House Subcommittee on the Study of Monopoly, an expert on steel, George Stocking, testified that the corporation "has lagged, not led," in innovation and that it "was neither big because it was efficient, nor efficient because it was big." Other economists testified that the corporation could be broken into at least three separate, integrated units and that this would improve efficiency. Another expert, Professor George Stigler, noted that "all the largest steel firms . . . are the product of mergers" and that "not one steel company has been able to add to its relative size as much as 4 percent of the ingot capacity of the industry in fifty years by attracting customers."

But critics always were around, the corporation countered. No one need worry about it or about the rest of the industry. In April 1951, as the corporation observed the fiftieth anniversary of its founding, Irving S. Olds, who had become the corporation's chairman in 1940, declared: "There has been a ceaseless effort on the part of United States Steel to improve efficiency and to secure a better product at every stage of its operations. . . . United States Steel has helped substantially to build America and make it the powerful nation it is today." And the success of the corporation, he said, held true for the industry. In one week alone, in January 1951, spurred by the production demands of the Korean War, the industry's weekly production had surpassed two million tons for the first time. "The industry has placed no limit upon its eventual size," Olds said.

III

The union was as optimistic and as well off as the corporation and the other companies. Wages and benefits were increased during each contract negotiation. In early 1947, for example, the union reached new agreements that provided for substantial wage increases and the formation of a joint labor-management committee to study accident-prevention and health plans.

There were problems, however. The labor movement was becoming bureaucratized, and its image was changing from that of a dedicated social movement to that of a selfish, small-minded, ossified institution. The strikes of 1946 had led in June 1947, over President Harry Truman's veto, to the passage of the Labor-Management Relations Act, known as the Taft-Hartley Act. This law severely limited the power of unions by banning closed shops, allowing states to ban union shops, and enabling Congress to issue injunctions against strikes with national impact.

The steelworkers' union and the rest of the labor movement paid no more attention to their shortcomings and critics than did the corporation and the rest of the steel industry to theirs. After just a decade of the union's existence, membership stood at one million. The union dominated the CIO. The unions were important elements in the Democratic Party and played a key role in the 1948 election of President Truman. Truman was asked how he had defeated the Republican candidate, Thomas E. Dewey. "Labor did it," he replied.

Furthermore, during these Cold War years, the labor movement, led by the steelworkers, was strengthening its position in society by attempting to end an old, nagging problem—Communism. It was no secret that Communists and other radicals had been active in the steelworkers' union and numerous others for years. They could be rude and exasperatingly self-righteous. They dominated union meetings, so that often no official business could be transacted. They had their own agenda, which often meant that of the Communist Party in the Soviet Union, and thus their position on any issue could change abruptly, even during a caucus at a convention.

Yet the Communists and other radicals were fiercely dedicated. They would work for almost nothing. They would accept the most wretched conditions—cheap hotels, broken-down cars—without complaint. It is likely that the steelworkers could not have been organized without the Communists. Of the two hundred organizers sent out by the SWOC in 1936, sixty were Communists. John L. Lewis didn't like their politics, but he admired the Communists' skill and dedication. He was convinced that he could control them as well as he did everyone else. Once, asked if he felt uncomfortable using Communists as organizers, he replied, "Who gets the bird, the hunter or the dog?"

The labor movement had both fought and used Communists and

other radicals since its inception. The American Federation of Labor, at its founding convention in 1886, had declared that its goal was the protection of "the toiling millions" in the struggle "between the oppressors and the oppressed, . . . between the capitalist and the laborer," but the AFL leaders had always been bourgeois men interested mostly in maintaining their jobs. Attacking Communists and other radicals was a surefire way to combat opponents within the labor movement and to curry favor with business and government leaders. Samuel Gompers's dislike of William Z. Foster, the leader of the 1919 steel strike and later head of the Communist Party, was a major reason for the defeat of the 1919 strike. John L. Lewis had red-baited opponents in the miners' union throughout the 1920s. The AFL had fought against the government's recognition of the Soviet Union for years. Such AFL leaders as Matthew Woll of the photoengravers' union and John P. Frey of the moulders' union made careers out of attacking those in the labor movement whom they regarded as radicals. Woll had been called by *Fortune,* in December 1933, an "arch-conservative, red-baiter, rock-bound Republican." Frey "frequently concentrated his fire on radicals within labor more readily than upon employers," *The New York Times* once said.

Murray was part of this tradition. At the miners' union convention in 1924, he had condemned what he called "Russianized revolution." In 1929, he had arranged for Pittsburgh police to look the other way as thugs hired by the union smashed a "Save the Union" convention of left-wing miners; one radical was killed and five were wounded. At the steelworkers' constitutional convention, in Cleveland in 1942, he had refused to add the words "or political affiliation" to a clause being inserted into the organization's constitution to prohibit discrimination in the union on the basis of "race, creed, color, or nationality." He also refused to allow his wife to wear a fur coat presented to her by Ben Gold, president of the Communist-dominated fur workers' union.

Murray had made common cause with Communists during World War II, in support of President Roosevelt's wartime policies. In 1946 and 1947, perceiving President Truman as antilabor, he had allied himself with liberals and leftists searching for an alternative Democratic presidential candidate in 1948.

Now, times had changed. With the Cold War, there was almost unbearable pressure to oppose Communism. One of the provisions of the Taft-Hartley Act made it illegal for Communists to serve as union officials. But even earlier, Murray and the steelworkers' union had taken the lead in declaring their opposition to Communism, and in ferreting out Communists and those perceived as Communists first from leadership positions and then from the rank and file of the labor movement. "We must be pro-American in these trade-union activities of ours," he had declared.

Murray—supported by his Roman Catholic advisers, notably his friend Father Charles Owen Rice of Pittsburgh—slowly at first, then with increasing speed and ferocity, moved to destroy labor's left wing. The steelworkers convention in Portland, Oregon, in November 1946 had passed a resolution stating, "This union will not tolerate efforts by outsiders—individuals, organizations, or groups, be they Communist, Socialist, or any other group—to infiltrate, dictate, or meddle in our affairs." The union's general counsel, Lee Pressman, a leftist, added the phrase "As a democratic institution we engage in no purges, no witch-hunts." But no attention was paid to these words. Murray then made support for the Marshall Plan a loyalty test for CIO leaders. The CIO convention in 1947 adopted a resolution supporting the Marshall Plan over the objections of left-wingers, who criticized the plan's extension of American capitalism to Europe.

During the 1948 presidential campaign, Murray increased the war against the Communists. In August, the CIO endorsed Truman. Although Murray had sharply criticized him two years earlier, he now campaigned vigorously for the president and demanded that all CIO union leaders do likewise. Those who did not, he regarded as disloyal—as Communists. He was particularly disturbed by the formation of the Progressive Party, whose candidate for President was Henry A. Wallace. Murray insisted that an evil scheme had been concocted by the Communist Party—William Z. Foster was now the Party's general secretary—to defeat labor's choice for president and to ensure the election of the Republican candidate, Thomas E. Dewey. Early in 1948, Lee Pressman left the union and the CIO to campaign for Wallace.* He was replaced by an ambitious young Chicago attorney, Arthur Goldberg.

In October 1948, at the steelworkers' convention in Boston, the union barred Communists or anyone opposing "democratic principles" from holding office. In November, at the CIO convention in Portland, Murray, Reuther (once a Socialist but now also an anti-Communist), and others in the CIO leadership, buoyant after Truman's victory, routed left-wing unionists. The leftists were chastised in speech after speech by CIO

---

* Pressman was alleged by Whittaker Chambers in 1948 to have led a Communist cell before the war. When Pressman refused to answer the questions of the House Committee on Un-American Activities, Murray fired him. In 1950, Pressman acknowledged that he had belonged to a Communist group in Washington in 1934, when he worked in the Department of Agriculture under Wallace.

regulars, and left-wing resolutions were rejected. The way was open for the final move against the Communists. Murray was at the height of his popularity, having won breakthroughs on pensions and insurance in bargaining with the Bethlehem Steel Corporation. He selected as his first target the United Electrical Workers (UE), which, with five hundred thousand members, was one of the nation's largest unions. The UE had opposed the Marshall Plan, and its leaders had supported Wallace in the 1948 election. Early in 1949, the UE said it would boycott the CIO convention. Murray expelled the UE and another left-wing union, the Farm Equipment Workers. At the convention in Cleveland, more than a dozen other unions were charged with being Communist-dominated. Arthur Goldberg, the CIO's new general counsel, accused the unions of possessing a loyalty to a foreign ideology not in keeping with the purposes of the CIO. The convention also passed a constitutional amendment barring Communists from CIO office. Murray then set up a new union, the International Union of Electrical Workers (IUE), as a rival to the UE; doubled the dues of CIO members to organize a war against the left-wing unions; and established committees to try the unions. All were ultimately expelled from the CIO. McDonald later wrote:

I sat on five of these panels, and they were quite honestly kangaroo courts. . . . We heard the heads of the indicted unions, but our decisions were preordained. . . .

We could tolerate this [the Communists'] sort of attitude and behavior to a limited degree when much of management was acting almost the same way—as it did in the coalfields of the 1920s or during the Little Steel strike. But that era was behind us now. We were no longer fighting a class war with management. Labor's purposes and function had generally been accepted by the American business community, and we were ready to go on to bigger and better things for the American workingman —things that would be delayed and perhaps lost completely if we were to tolerate any longer the hate tactics of the Communists.

The Communists were expelled from the labor movement, and the movement lost the fierce dedication that the Communists had brought to it. The purge also cost the CIO one-quarter of its membership. More than that, the anti-Communism practiced by American labor leaders allowed the purging not only of Communists and those suspected of being Communists, but of any who were considered enemies by the leaders—people who were mavericks or idealists, who did not demonstrate the total loyalty that the labor leaders demanded.

One by one, the union's impressive core of intellectuals left the union. They were an interesting group of men—firm believers in unionism; adherents of "social planning," a fashionable liberal idea in the 1930s and 1940s; and apostles of what they called "cooperative relationships between labor and capital." But they had always been on uneasy terms with Murray and other union leaders, McDonald among them. Some of the intellectuals detested the infighting that characterized the union and came to believe that their views were not appreciated by the leadership.

These political problems only compounded the general awkwardness that characterizes the relationships in American unions between elected union officers—the union establishment—and research men, lawyers, and other staff members, particularly those regarded as intellectuals. The elected officers run the union. In most cases, the staff members can never aspire to high office. Still, the officers are generally suspicious of the staff and disdain them for not having worked their way up through the union. They enjoy humiliating them occasionally, keeping them under their thumb always.

Clinton S. Golden was the first intellectual to leave the steelworkers' union. In 1942, Golden had gone to Washington to work for the War Production Board, and he and Murray, who spent substantial time together in the capital during the war, had become rather close. But upon his return from Washington in 1945, Golden faced increasing difficulties in the union. He and Murray also differed philosophically. Golden believed that Murray was too quick to resort to strikes or threats of strikes and that Murray did not support his ideas on cooperation between labor and capital. He also did not get along with McDonald, whom he regarded as smarmy and opportunistically ambitious.

Golden was a rare kind of person in the labor movement of this century. He was kindly, intelligent, and principled. He had almost no interest in personal power and was one of the few union staff members who would stand up to Murray. But, as the labor writer John Herling said, "to stand up to Murray was also to run the risk of being considered a troublemaker."

Once, Averell Harriman, impressed by the quality of the research staff Golden had assembled, asked him, "Where do you find these young people?"

"Averell, they are in the mills," Golden said. "[A]ll you do is comb them out."

Another time, taking questions at a university, Golden was asked sharply, "How can anyone believe that there is such a thing as an honest labor leader?" Golden pointed a finger at his questioner. "Brother," he said, speaking just as sharply, "you're looking at one now." Golden resigned on July 1, 1946, citing ill health as the cause. But he was, he said privately, "tired and frustrated." That fall, he joined the Harvard Graduate School of Business as a visiting lecturer on labor.

Harold S. Ruttenberg, bright and brash, was a twenty-two-year-old student at the University of Pittsburgh in 1933 when he was asked by an economics professor to participate in a Brookings Institution study on the effects of the National Recovery Administration's iron and steel code. In this capacity, he began to attend gatherings of the activities associated with the Amalgamated Association of Iron, Steel, and Tin Workers. When the union men found out that he could type, he was drafted to type press releases. He joined the SWOC staff in 1936, and Golden then made him research director. Ten years later, tiring of the union wars and wanting to make some money, Ruttenberg left the union to become an executive with the Portsmouth Steel Corporation of Portsmouth, Ohio.

Joseph Scanlon was from Mansfield, Ohio. He was president of the SWOC local there when he and Golden met in 1937. Empire Steel, the company where Scanlon worked, was experiencing difficulties. Scanlon and Golden advised Empire executives that the workers had ideas on how money could be saved and productivity increased. The ideas were accepted, and soon Empire was making money again and gave the workers a wage increase. In 1938, Golden brought Scanlon to the SWOC as its first industrial engineer.

Scanlon soon became an expert on cost-cutting and on worker-participation programs. He advised union locals and companies on how to install participation programs; often, the union granted wage reductions in exchange for union-shop agreements. Now, in September 1946, seeing no future at the union for participation programs, Scanlon left to become a lecturer at the Massachusetts Institute of Technology. There he devised what became known as "the Scanlon Plan," which called for worker participation in production decisions and bonuses for workers who helped to increase production and profits. Ultimately, several hundred of the plans were adopted across the nation.

These three men were idealists, and were somewhat naive. The executives at the steel companies, for the most part, had no interest in cooperating with the union and the workers, although they occasionally made statements that suggested they did. Union executives like Murray and McDonald also had no real interest in such programs, although they, too, would sometimes advocate them. Union leaders like to run their unions just as companies are run, with line and staff organization and top-down decision-making. They want no impediments such as legitimate workplace-cooperation committees. But Golden, Ruttenberg, and Scanlon were intelligent and creative. They were not locked into old ways of doing things. After they were gone, other creative people left as well. The men were not replaced by similarly dedicated people with ideas.

Both of these losses—of the energy of the Communists and the creativity of the intellectuals—was evident in the failure of Operation Dixie, a CIO campaign to organize southern industrial workers. Murray had no special interest in the drive, and the CIO did not aggressively pursue black workers, who made up the bulk of workers in many industries. Often, black workers who were recruited were placed in segregated locals.

IV

The steelworkers' union stuck with what it did well—bargaining. Assisted by the government, which abhorred steel strikes, the union almost always delivered. The 1952 negotiations were among the most tumultuous in history. They had begun in November 1951. The union presented a thirty-two-point program, including a demand for an industrywide union shop. The corporation and the other companies rejected it and made a series of counterproposals designed to give management the right to eliminate and combine jobs and to increase workloads without additional compensation or the use of grievance procedures.

Hearings were conducted before the Wage Stabilization Board for more than three months. In April 1952, the board issued its report, accepting a number of the union's proposals. Spokesmen for the industry said that the report was "pro-labor and inflationary" and refused to comply with it.

The Korean War had been going on for almost two years. And President Truman was angered at the industry's actions. On April 8, 1952, in a radio and television address that astonished the nation, he said that because of the need for military production it was imperative that the nation's steel industry operate without interruption. To ensure this, he said, the government would seize and operate the steel mills. Murray and McDonald watched the address in a New York hotel suite. Murray was delighted. "Attaboy, Harry," he shouted. The mills remained open, with employees reporting to work as usual.

The industry challenged Truman's actions in court, and a federal district court ruled that Truman's actions were illegal. Congress stripped the Wage Stabilization Board of its powers. The plants reverted to the management of the steel companies, and the union ordered its members out on strike. Three days later, a federal appeals court reversed the district court's ruling and restored government control of the mills. The union sent its members back to work.

On June 2, the U.S. Supreme Court reversed the appeals court's decision, declaring the president's seizure of the mills unconstitutional. The union ordered its members out on strike again. Eight hundred thousand workers walked out, a new record in American history. Clarence Randall, president of Inland Steel Corporation and a major figure in the steel industry, condemned Truman and said that Murray, in ordering the strike, was guilty of "subversive actions" that were aiding Communists and "threatening the safety of American soldiers in Korea."

In July, Truman convened a White House meeting of union and industry executives. In the Cabinet Room, the atmosphere was tense and acrimonious. Truman entered. Each man called him "Mr. President," except Randall, who called him "Mr. Truman." The industry suggested that it would accept a union shop in every mill if provision was made to allow older workers who opposed unionism not to join. The union accepted this, but still the strike continued.

The strike was now settled as strikes often are, privately and without the drama attributed to them. On July 24, Truman called Benjamin F. Fairless and Murray to the White House. They entered Truman's office and took seats. He stared at them across his desk. "Ben," he said, "can you settle this strike?" Fairless replied, "Alone?" Truman looked at Murray. He asked, "Phil, can you settle this strike?" Murray did not answer. Truman then had Fairless and Murray ushered into the Fish Room and left them by themselves. They began chatting. In five minutes they had reached an agreement. Fairless was pleased. "Let's go tell the president," he said. "Oh, no," Murray said. "Think of all those newspapermen out there. We've got to make this look more difficult."

They sat and talked about baseball. Murray told a joke about a priest —a fight fan—who went to a fight with a Protestant minister who had never seen a boxing match. Before the fight, one of the fighters crossed himself. The minister was confused. "Father, will that help him?" he asked. "It will if he can fight," the priest said. The joke so pleased Fairless that he used it in after-dinner speeches for years.

Fairless and Murray continued to chat. At last, after three hours, Murray said, "All right, let's go," and they walked out and announced to the newspapermen that they had reached a settlement. In return for a partial union shop, the federal government granted the companies a price increase.

The Union's Wage Policy Committee, composed of union presidents (the union had never made provision for its members to ratify contracts), was summoned and approved the agreement. Toward the end of the meeting Murray introduced a surprise guest—Fairless. Fairless said that strikes such as the 1892 Homestead strike and the 1919 steel strike were anachronisms that were injurious to workers, companies, and the nation. A better way must be found to settle labor-management disputes. He then made an unusual proposal. He asked that Murray accompany him on a nationwide tour of the corporation's mills and talk to workers and managers to explain that each side had an equal stake in a harmonious, efficient industry. As the union men cheered, Fairless and Murray shook hands to signify their agreement to make the tour.

With the bargaining ended, Murray turned his attention to the 1952 presidential race. His strategy for decades had been to use the government as an ally against the corporation and the other steel companies, and so the outcome of the race was crucial to labor. In early 1948, despairing of Truman, Murray had attempted to persuade General Dwight D. Eisenhower to run for the Democratic nomination. Now that Eisenhower was the leading candidate for the Republican nomination, Murray saw him as a foe of labor. The pollster Samuel Lubell wrote at the time:

Many labor leaders are painfully aware that much of their following was recruited under the patronage of a friendly government rather than through labor's own strength. What if an unsympathetic administration came to power? What if that coincided with a recession? The still unexploded dynamite of the Taft-Hartley law lies in those fears. . . . The real threat in the act lies in its union-busting potential during a period of unemployment, when labor's bargaining power is weak, and when a government hostile to labor might be in power.

Murray and the CIO gave their support to Adlai E. Stevenson, governor of Illinois. On July 24, 1952, the day the steel strike ended, Stevenson, to Murray's immense satisfaction, was nominated.

Murray was getting on in years—he was now sixty-six. His health was bad, and he was exhausted from the recent months of difficult bargaining with the steel companies. He had been forbidden by his doctor to travel by air, but this did not stop him from campaigning for Stevenson. He spent weeks on trains, barnstorming across the country. He warned workers of "a raw deal" if Stevenson was not elected. But Eisenhower could not be stopped. He was elected by 6.5 million votes, and both houses of Congress also went Republican. Murray was acutely depressed.

Throughout the campaign and election another problem had been eating away at Murray—McDonald. After Lee Pressman had left the union in 1948, Murray had begun to depend more heavily on McDonald. This dependence increased as Murray suffered from continued health problems—several heart attacks, most of them mild, over the years—and was occupied with his many periodic negotiating activities and the demands on him as CIO president.

Murray had come to believe that McDonald was creating an apparatus to seize control of the union. Murray was a suspicious man, and some of his feelings about McDonald were part of his paranoia. But there is no doubt that McDonald, always a schemer, had arrogated to himself major responsibilities in the union, including the dispensing of funds and the appointment of many staff members. He had created his own machine. Murray, raised in the rough school of union politics, in which rivals were not tolerated, decided that McDonald must go.

In January 1952, at a union gathering in Atlantic City to drum up support for the 1952 bargaining, Murray lashed out at his protégé. It was a rambling speech, in Murray's typical manner. He did not mention McDonald by name, but everyone, including McDonald, knew who he was talking about. Murray declared:

There are going to be no little dictatorships in this union, no connivances, no bribery. There is going to be no money used out of the treasury of this organization to buy the friendship of anybody in this union to promote any man to any office in this organization, and you are going to help the officers of your union, when a convention comes around, to see to it that you have the kind of a constitution that will permit you, the owners of this organization, to play a part in the operation of its affairs. That is a principle to which we adhere, and the bigger you get and the more responsibilities you assume, the closer you must live with the people who pay the taxes.

At the convention, in May, the union members—at Murray's request —unanimously approved changes in the constitution that decreased the power of the secretary-treasurer, McDonald, and increased the power of the president, Murray. The hiring of staff members in the secretary-treasurer's office was made subject to the approval of the international president. The vice-president, a position the union had recently added, would be required to sign convention reports, in addition to the president and the secretary-treasurer. No paid representative of the international union—that is, no one appointed by McDonald—would be eligible to serve as an "international teller"—a person who counted votes during union elections. Other changes in election procedures were also made, all to reduce McDonald's power.

Some men in the union believed that Murray was going too far and that his power had become absolute. They saw similarities between McDonald's humiliation and the humiliation that Murray had suffered eleven years before, when John L. Lewis had forced him out of the miners' union. But they said nothing. Neither did McDonald.

One night during the convention, in a scene recorded by John Herling, McDonald came down in the elevator at the hotel. Usually, he had a large retinue with him, but now, his power diminished, his retainers had fled. As he emerged into the lobby, not one person went up to shake his hand or talk with him. A few faint hellos were all he received. At length, McDonald spotted Emery Bacon, the union's educational director, and asked if he would take a walk with him. They set off down the street, and after a time they began to talk.

MCDONALD: Wasn't that quite a show this afternoon?

BACON: It really was. Why in the world did you stand there and take it? It would have been better if you had stood up and fought this. At least you would have the respect of the group, and at the end you would have been a bigger man.

MCDONALD: You've got it all wrong. Murray's not going to live.

BACON: You're kidding.

MCDONALD: No. I know. He won't live. The chances are he won't live the year out. That's the reason why I took it. I'll inherit everything.

On November 4, 1952, the morning after the presidential election, Murray—tired, pale, dispirited—boarded a train in Pittsburgh bound for California with his wife, Liz. He planned to attend a conference of the union's western district directors in San Francisco over the weekend and then travel to the CIO convention, which was to begin on Monday in Los Angeles. McDonald had offered to chair the conference in San Francisco, so that Murray could go directly to Los Angeles and rest before the convention. But Murray was accepting no assistance from McDonald. He would run both gatherings.

Murray arrived in San Francisco late on Saturday, November 8, after the meeting had begun but in time to speak to a dinner meeting of some six hundred people. Murray appeared tired and drawn, and when Mc-Donald arrived, midway through the dinner—he had flown out, arriving before Murray—he found that Murray had already been speaking for two hours. The speech was disjointed—mostly recollections of his years in the labor movement and visions of the future—and his diction was difficult to understand. The audience was restless and uneasy. Murray continued for another half an hour. There was only a brief mention of the Eisenhower-Stevenson presidential campaign. The labor movement was not seeking just "garages or chickens or pots" for its members anymore, Murray said: "The changes labor looks forward to are slum clearance, more homes, more television sets, more schools, more and better medicines, more of the better things of life." He made a small joke: "I want to tell you again how glad I am as a Scotsman to be able to come here and enjoy a free plate of roast beef." Then he was finished.

He lingered at the dais, chatting with union members. McDonald went up to say hello. Murray's eyes were glazed. Walter Burke, a district director, shook hands with Murray and felt Murray's hand trembling. Murray smiled at Burke. "I'll see you down in Los Angeles sometime tomorrow, Walter," he said. "Good night. Have a good rest." He left the auditorium with his wife. Murray's gait was wobbly. McDonald thought of helping Murray across the street but realized that his mentor would resent it.

16

THE DAVE
AND BEN SHOW

McDonald spent the rest of the evening having drinks with the district directors and then went to bed. Late the next morning, he was sleeping soundly in his room at the Mark Hopkins Hotel when he was awakened by a telephone call from his gofer, Frank N. "Nordy" Hoffman, at the Huntington Hotel. Murray was dead. He had not responded to a wake-up call at 6:30 A.M., and Liz Murray had not heard the telephone because she wore a hearing aid and always turned it off when she retired for the night. The desk clerk had sent a bellboy to their room. He had unlocked the door with a passkey, had found Murray on the floor, and had then awakened Liz Murray. The hotel physician had been summoned. Hoffman, hearing the commotion, had followed him into the room and listened to him pronounce Murray dead. He had suffered a massive heart attack. Hoffman, good gofer that he was, had immediately called McDonald.

McDonald sat on the edge of his bed, staring out of the window. In the distance, the sun reflected off the Golden Gate Bridge. "A thousand thoughts tumbled over one another" in his mind, he later wrote in his autobiography. He had known Murray for three decades. Murray had plucked him from nowhere and made him what he was. Had it not been for Murray, McDonald might never have gotten away from the dirty mills, the slag heaps, the wooden frame houses, covered with grime, of his childhood in the Hazelwood section of Pittsburgh. No sense in living in the past; the sentimental thoughts lasted "a second or two," and then his mind turned to what was always most important to him—McDonald. For Christ's sake, he thought. He was ready for the presidency. He had performed the job when Murray had been sick, in 1941 and 1948, and had stood in for the old man at other times and made many important decisions. "Only the title and the authority had been lacking," McDonald said, "and now these would be mine, too."

He swung out of bed, dressed quickly, and hurried to the Huntington. Liz Murray seemed to be in shock. She was sitting in a straight chair between Murray's secretary and Hoffman, and staring straight ahead, her eyes frightened and bewildered. McDonald took her hand, expressed his sympathy, then asked the key question: Would she like him to make arrangements for the funeral? Why, yes, David, she said.

This was what McDonald wanted, and he bolted into action. He spent much of the day working the telephone, an activity at which he was very skilled. He chartered a TWA plane to fly himself and the rest of the union leaders back to Pittsburgh and made sure that a large union crowd would be on hand to meet them. He also arranged for the Flying Tigers, a freight airline, to transport Murray's body to Chicago; from there it would go by train to Pittsburgh.

By coincidence, McDonald and the other union men and Murray's body arrived in Pittsburgh at about the same time, and this presented a prickly dilemma for the union executives in Pittsburgh. Emery Bacon, the educational director, said, "This question worked away in most everybody's mind: Where do we go, do we go out and meet McDonald, or do we go and meet the coffin?" The union men thought the matter over and most of them, being no fools, went to the airport to wait for McDonald and his entourage, and the former Murray men who wanted to become part of McDonald's entourage. Bacon recalled:

I, myself, was terribly devoted to Murray but I did go to the airport to meet the chartered flight. I took my wife out . . . I suppose, mainly for the spectacle that was involved in seeing the flight come in—all of us sitting in the Ambassadors Club and getting reports on the progress of the chartered McDonald flight across the continent. Also, seeing all the people who would gather out there to welcome the new emperor and the retinue that would get off the plane and get into the limousines that were lined up. . . . Tom Murray [a union staff member not related to Philip Murray], on the other hand, went to the railroad station and met the body. He did not go out to meet McDonald. Very few accompanied Tom. The king was dead.

Murray's funeral was, as McDonald described it, "a state funeral." McDonald deserved much of the credit: he was good at putting on anything that required a lot of show. The funeral was at Saint Paul's Roman Catholic Cathedral, on Forbes Avenue, and just about anyone who was anyone came, union man, government man, businessman. McDonald worked the crowd and even helped to "soothe the ruffled feelings of pseudo big shots who hadn't been selected as pallbearers." Then the funeral procession set out, going through downtown Pittsburgh, across the Monongahela River, and out on state Route 88 to Saint Anne's Roman Catholic Church in Castle Shannon, an old coal-mining town already becoming a substantial upper-middle-class suburb. There, in the grave-yard, Father Charles Owen Rice of Saint Anne's, one of Murray's advisers during the purge of Communists in the late 1940s, said a final prayer as the body was lowered into the grave.

After waiting two days, McDonald convened a meeting of the union's executive board. As he later explained, "The king was dead, but the kingdom had to function." He had worked hard over the years—lining up people to be on "Dave's team," as his group was known; scheming to oust possible contenders; dispensing patronage; doling out union funds and other perquisites to those who demonstrated loyalty to him. Now he called in his markers. The executive board unanimously named him act-ing president, to serve until the regularly scheduled election of union officers in 1953. But that election would be a formality, and everyone knew it. His appointment assured his ascension to the presidency.

His one possible rival was James G. Thimmes, who had replaced Clinton S. Golden as vice-president, and who was the first steelworker to rise to a position of authority in the union in its sixteen years of existence. McDonald offered Thimmes a deal: Thimmes would retain his union vice-presidency and also be named a vice-president of the CIO. There were thirty-five CIO vice-presidents, and he would be lowly among them, but he accepted the offer.

Another matter facing McDonald was the selection of his replacement as secretary-treasurer. Various factions within the union put their choices forward. McDonald settled on a compromise candidate, a quiet, deliberate man, little known within the union and almost unknown outside it, I. W. Abel. Abe, as he was known, was a district director from Canton, Ohio. McDonald did not know much about him, and there was no reason why he should have. Abel seldom spoke at executive board meetings and always voted the administration line. His Canton operation was clean, to McDonald's knowledge, and no one had a bad thing to say about him. McDonald passed the word that he wanted Abel as secretary-treasurer, and the appointment was made.

In February 1953, at the regularly scheduled union election, McDonald and Abel, both unopposed, were named to four-year terms. As McDonald put it, "The members of the United Steelworkers confirmed by ballot the appointments made by the executive board." Years later, McDonald told a reporter: "I know how to run elections. I stole four elections for Joe Germano as director of District 31 [the Chicago-Gary area]."

II

The men who ran the steel industry considered McDonald a buffoon and a blowhard. They spoke contemptuously of him behind his back and were astonished by the favorable press he received. But for them he was the perfect union president. First, he kept the workers under his thumb, which is what employers want most from union presidents. Second, if he cut a deal, the deal was done, pure and simple. Murray had been subject to moods. In his later years, particularly, he had been crotchety and unpredictable. Companies want stability and predictability in unions. Otherwise, why go through all the trouble of dealing with them? Companies also detest men who appeal to the masses, who talk in radical terms. Murray had been no radical, but there was often just enough talk, enough threat in his talk, to make them uneasy. One moment he would mutter something about cooperation—which businessmen always interpret as meaning that the union was going to ease up on the company— and the next moment something about the class struggle. McDonald had an ego a mile long, and it had to be stroked, but he was harmless. The company men laughed at his self-importance, his retainers, his love of the high life. But if they had to put up with his hijinks, his posturing, his press coverage, it was a small price to pay. Dave, they said, was an ass, but he delivered.

This sort of attitude exemplified the steel industry as a whole. This was a period of "get along and go along," of high production and easy profitability. The postwar demand for consumer goods was continuing, as was the boom in apartment and home construction. The expansion of the suburbs was on, and it was clear that it could only increase. Soon, construction would begin on the nation's forty-thousand-mile expressway system, which would consume enormous amounts of steel. Exports of American steel, pioneered by the corporation years before, remained high, exceeding imports by five to one. The Korean War had provided an immense boost to production and profits. Production during the war rose to 103 percent of capacity, and steel production was regarded as an important factor in keeping the United States strong militarily and a bulwark of the free world.

New technologies were being bandied about or experimented with—processes for coating steel, basic oxygen furnaces, continuous casters, vacuum degassing. But most executives of the corporation believed that there was little need to invest in these technologies, or, at the least, no need to rush into investing in them. Better to let others—the Europeans or the Japanese, or other American companies—make the experiments. Then, if the technologies were proven, the corporation could decide whether to adopt them.

Both union and corporation took the easy path. The union wanted continuing increases in wages and benefits and continuing expansion of the union as an institution. The company wanted tonnage and sales at the highest possible prices. No one wanted to upset things. Why would they? The future was bright.

An example of the views prevailing in the steel industry was provided in May 1955, when the leaders of the industry gathered at the Waldorf-Astoria Hotel, on Park Avenue in New York, for the annual meeting of the American Iron and Steel Institute, founded by steel executives in 1911 to take over the functions of the Gary dinners, which had been terminated that year when the government began to investigate possible antitrust violations. The institute had grown into a major research, propaganda, lobbying, and social organization. At the Waldorf, the steelmen could not have been in a more ebullient, optimistic mood. The industry was having the finest year in its history and would produce by year's end 117 million tons, one-third more steel than ever before. Mills in 1955 were running at almost 100 percent of capacity, and many order books were full for a year or more.

Arthur Homer, president of the Bethlehem Steel Company, said, "If the projections for the economy as a whole are realized, the steel industry will need an ingot capacity of about 180 million tons in fifteen years to handle peak requirements." The many representatives of the press covering the gathering shared his optimism. "The steel industry has burst through its own built-in sonic barrier and assured itself that the future is probably as good as it looks," *Business Week* wrote.

III

McDonald, forty-nine years old when he assumed the presidency, established control over the union almost immediately. He had coveted the job for years, and he was going to operate in the manner he saw fit. His style was that of the tyrant king. He almost always had a claque of retainers with him. When he walked down the corridor of a hotel, he was usually surrounded by a phalanx of assistants and bodyguards. Since neither he nor they looked left or right, regular hotel patrons were swept to the side and left to huddle against the wall. He generally refused to use an elevator unless it had been specially set aside for him and his entourage. Hotels were alerted to this demand and complied. And, of course, no more taxis or—God forbid—buses, which Murray had often taken from his simple brick home to the union's offices in Pittsburgh. Chauffeured limousines were McDonald's style, with a high-paid plug-ugly as his driver. There was no longer a simple working-class bungalow either, but instead a nice spread in Mount Lebanon, a prosperous suburb, and a second home in Palm Springs, California.

From the beginning of his tenure it was clear that McDonald intended to continue to follow his extracurricular pursuits, making a name for himself nationally—lounging at a cabana in Miami Beach when the labor leaders came together for their winter conclaves, hobnobbing with big shots and show girls at New York nightclubs like "21" or Jack Dempsey's or the Stork. The role of Arthur Goldberg, the union's general counsel, was thus made more important, because someone had to watch the store. When Goldberg replaced Lee Pressman as general counsel, he harbored doubts about McDonald, wondering whether he was smart enough to have a high position in the union. When Murray died, Goldberg still did not trust McDonald to be union president, doubting his intellectual capabilities and disdaining his after-hours shenanigans. But Goldberg was ambitious and welcomed the extra responsibilities McDonald gave him, and soon he was an ardent McDonald man. The position of union counsel was an important step in Goldberg's career, and after a time he was as powerful in the union as McDonald, perhaps more so.

Others in McDonald's coterie included Howard Hague, his office manager, whose responsibilities included gathering information on union staffers and officials; Phil Regan, singer and public relations man; the former gofer Nordy Hoffman, a burly former Notre Dame football player with a flat-top haircut, who functioned as the union's legislative and political director in Washington, D.C.; and Phil Weiss, a somewhat unsavory fellow whose responsibilities most people never ascertained. Regan was always on hand at union conventions to sing "God Bless America" or some Irish ballad, and he often sang in Pittsburgh nightclubs. Typically, he would look around the room to see which notables were on hand and then bring them into his act. John Herling, in *Right to Challenge: People and Power in the Steelworkers Union,* one of the finest books on American unionism, described how Regan would spot someone, say Benjamin F. Fairless, and burst out, "And this song is dedicated to Ben Fairless, that great industrial statesman. Hello there, Mr. Fairless." Of Hoffman, Herling said: "Thanks to an unlimited expense account, Hoffman's well-tailored bulk made an impressive splash on Capitol Hill and in restaurants around town. He was an expansive host, and no one was faster in picking up the tab. He gave luncheons and dinners at the Touchdown Club, where he entertained those whom he and McDonald delighted to honor or sought to impress." Weiss was a similarly colorful character. He was reportedly intimate with racketeers. In 1959 he was summoned before the Senate Select Committee to Investigate Improper Practices in Labor and Management to explain these reported connections. He took the Fifth.

McDonald worked out a way of running the union that accommodated his style and work habits. The district directors were allowed to function almost independently; he did not bother them. In return, they allowed him to function as he pleased. This was traditional in many American unions. There were no rules outlining such an arrangement, but it existed as though it had been codified, and because everyone benefited, everyone was happy.

McDonald was not a worker and essentially had never been one. Making steel was one of the farthest things from his mind. He had gotten into unionism by chance, but it became for him what it had been for many others—a way out of the shop and the grim factory town, a way to get ahead.

McDonald worked briefly in two steel mills, as a messenger boy in the first, as a clerk in the second. For the better part of two decades, he held a high position in the miners' union, but because he had never worked in a coal mine—an elected official was required to have been a miner for five years—he never could be a union member or be elected to office. (The SWOC and the steelworkers' union had similar requirements and McDonald, like Murray and a number of others, technically was ineligible for membership in either.) He was a union businessman, as even two Pittsburgh journalists hired by him in 1954 to write his biography, *Man of Steel,* said: "Getting right down to it, McDonald is a businessman. . . . He has to be, to run things right. Because the steelworkers' union is big business." Once, on a golf outing, McDonald was asked by a reporter whether he would ever resign from the presidency of the union. "Now look, let's be realistic, fellows," he replied. "Where the fuck would I be able to get another job at fifty thousand dollars a year and all expenses?"

McDonald wore Brooks Brothers suits, as he liked to point out. He was invited to a number of President Dwight D. Eisenhower's black-tie dinners at the White House and became an important figure in the Democratic Party. He liked to brag that he was close to seven presidents— Harding, Roosevelt, Truman, Eisenhower, Kennedy, Johnson, and Nixon. While this is an exaggeration—he hardly knew Harding, Roosevelt, Truman, or Eisenhower—he was close to Kennedy and Johnson while they were president, and he knew Nixon well before he became president.* McDonald loved seeing his name in the papers. Who would have believed, he said, after he had achieved prominence, "that one day my picture would appear in Pittsburgh newspapers more often than any other living American."

McDonald seems a cartoon character today, a burlesque caricature of a union boss. Yet in his day he was never portrayed this way in the press. Rather, he was described as a hardworking, farsighted labor man, "a labor statesman," by the labor press, which was always willing to curry a little favor. He is not much remembered today, yet he ran the steelworkers' union for thirteen years, just three years fewer than Murray. More than that, his authority in the union stretched over more than a quarter of a century, longer than that of any other man.

McDonald was born on November 22, 1902, in the Hazelwood section of Pittsburgh, a dirty, gritty steel community on the north bank of the Monongahela River. His father, an immigrant from Wales, was a steel-

---

* Although he was a longtime Democrat, McDonald came to detest Hubert H. Humphrey, the 1968 Democratic nominee, who he believed had stabbed him in the back by not supporting him for reelection in 1965, and he endorsed Nixon, the Republican nominee, for President.

worker and a union man. He had been an organizer for the Amalgamated Association of Iron, Steel, and Tin Workers in Springfield, Illinois, and had ridden the rails to Pittsburgh to escape retribution from the iron masters and the Pinkertons for his role in labor agitation there. He tried running a hotel for a time but failed. McDonald's grandfather on his mother's side, Patrick Kelly, was financial secretary of the Sons of Vulcan, one of the three predecessors of the Amalgamated Association, and an uncle, Jack Kelly, had had a leg broken by a club-swinging Pinkerton in the Homestead strike.

McDonald grew up on what he called "an undersized block just long enough for three brick houses set neatly in a row. The street was cobble-stoned and the air laden with smoke and soot." From the small, fenced backyard of the home, or the window of the second-floor bedroom, the family could "feel the waves [of heat] and look into the inferno of the steel-rolling mill where my father worked."

In 1912, his father was burned by a runaway billet in the mill and was in the hospital for six months. During that time, his mother rented out rooms, and he and his brother, Joe, worked at odd jobs. He did not want to go into the mills and realized there were two ways out—getting involved in politics or acquiring the skills to get a white-collar job. He chose the latter and enrolled at Holy Cross High School, which offered what were then called commercial courses—typing, shorthand, and bookkeeping. The school was on the south bank of the Monongahela River, so his father secured a pass that allowed him to cross the river on the Jones and Laughlin hot-metal bridge. "There were many winter mornings I would cross that bridge in a darkness thickened by smoke and perforated by the fires from the mill that would light occasional patches of the muddy waters below me," he said. "It always made me think that I was getting a preview glimpse into hell. . . ."

While in high school, he obtained a position as a messenger boy at Jones and Laughlin, working eleven hours a day at twenty-two cents an hour. He attended classes at night and on Sundays, graduating with a commercial diploma in June 1918. He then obtained a position working in the tool room of the National Tube Company's Continental Works, a subsidiary of the United States Steel Corporation, working sixty-six hours and earning $23.76 a week. He also enrolled in evening courses at the Carnegie Technical School, a forerunner of the Carnegie Institute of Technology, attending classes three nights a week. The family had by now moved to Greenfield, a mill town just south of downtown Pittsburgh. He played football—left tackle—on a tough sandlot team and also joined a dramatic club, which, being a born ham, he enjoyed immensely.

Then came the break that changed his life. He had just obtained a

new job, as a typist at the Wheeling Steel Corporation. He loved the
hours and the fact that he could wear a white collar, but he disliked the
salary, eighty dollars a month. One day, in 1923, as he passed the time
with friends at McMillan's Drug Store in Greenfield, someone said that
Philip Murray, then vice-president of the United Mine Workers of America, was looking for a secretary—a young man, as was then customary.
McDonald sought out a local politician who knew Murray, and an interview was arranged. Murray, then thirty-eight, was reserved and handsome, with shiny black hair and impeccable clothes. Murray took an
immediate liking to McDonald, already a personable fellow. He was impressed that McDonald was active in Catholic activities, and, besides,
McDonald could type and take shorthand. He was hired at $225 a month,
a large salary for the time, especially for such a young man.

McDonald went to work immediately, for Murray had a trip planned.
On September 10, 1923, Murray, with McDonald in tow, set off by train
for New York. McDonald had spent the weekend brushing up on his
shorthand by having his sister and friends give him practice dictation. In
New York McDonald met John L. Lewis, president of the union since
1920. Lewis, surrounded by retainers, was sitting deep in an overstuffed
chair behind palm trees in the lobby of the Hotel Pennsylvania, imposing
and heavyset, his hair then brown, cascading over his forehead, almost
touching his bushy eyebrows. McDonald never lost "the feeling of school-
boy awe" that he felt on meeting Lewis that September morning.

He was then off on a round of more union trips, going in October
1923, for example, to his first labor meeting, the American Federation of
Labor convention, in Portland, Oregon, where he saw Samuel Gompers
preside over what would be Gompers's last AFL convention—he died in
1924—and heard his first labor tirades against Communism, first by William Green, secretary of the convention's resolutions committee, and then
by Lewis and Murray. McDonald was struck by the appearance and
manner of the labor men. They did not look like radicals but wore high
collars and dark suits. They were prone to long, boring orations and were
as conservative as businessmen.

Murray and his wife had no children of their own. They had adopted
a boy, Joe, from a Pittsburgh orphanage and also took in a niece. But Joe
was "a willful, difficult kid," in McDonald's words, and Murray seemed
to see in McDonald the son he had hoped to have. Soon, McDonald, also
liked by Lewis, was an accepted union functionary—though he, along
with other handsome young men of his time, had to put up with being
called "The Sheik," after the title character in Rudolph Valentino's 1921
silent film.

For the next thirteen years, McDonald was Murray's trusted assistant in the miners' union, a job he found alternately boring and exhilarating. On the one hand, McDonald, much younger than most of the other men and wanting a little action, abhorred what seemed one of the others' prime pastimes—sitting around musty hotel lobbies redolent of cigar smoke, talking baseball or politics, or listening to the always self-important Lewis muse about unionism or politics or whatever else was on his mind. Still, he had the opportunity to get to know Lewis well, which McDonald was glad of, and he enjoyed observing the intrigues and she-nanigans that characterized the union. For example, the plush union headquarters in Indianapolis was divided into two sections, with Lewis and Murray on one side, the secretary-treasurer on the other. McDonald inquired about this arrangement, and it was explained to him that Lewis and Murray were opposed to the secretary-treasurer and that neither side wanted the other to listen to its telephone calls. This kind of suspicion and distrust would sometimes characterize the steelworkers' union during Murray's and McDonald's years as president.

McDonald observed the violent Appalachian coal wars of the 1920s. And he continued to hobnob with important people. He visited the White House with Lewis in 1930 to meet with President Herbert Hoover. This, as McDonald described it, was "my first visit to the Oval Office, which in later years would become a familiar place to me."

McDonald retained in these years his fondness for dramatics and was not sure whether he should become an actor or stay with the union. In the late 1920s, he went back to school, enrolling in an evening drama course at the Carnegie Technical School, and in 1932, through a friend, he was offered a position as an assistant film director at Warner Brothers in Hollywood. He almost accepted the offer, but that summer he jour-neyed with Murray and other union men up the Hudson River to meet Franklin Delano Roosevelt, the Democratic candidate for president, at the governor's mansion in Albany (Lewis supported Hoover in 1932 and did not make the trip). Murray endorsed Roosevelt, and McDonald, also excited by Roosevelt, spent that summer and fall campaigning for him. In 1933 and 1934, he helped oversee the drive to organize miners that was part of the frenzy of labor organizing that followed the passage of the National Industrial Recovery Act, in June 1933, and that in less than a year saw the miners' union increase its membership from one hundred thousand to four hundred thousand. He also did political work for Lewis —for example, he helped repress the strike in the captive mines of south-western Pennsylvania during the summer and fall of 1933. By the mid-1930s, his salary had increased to $350 a month.

Then, in February 1936, Lewis selected Murray to direct the Steel Workers Organizing Committee. One cold, bleak day that month, as

Murray and McDonald were returning to Pittsburgh by train through the grim and dirty steel towns along the Monongahela River east of Pittsburgh, Murray informed McDonald of his new position and said that he had a new job for McDonald—he would be the SWOC's secretary-treasurer. McDonald's main responsibility was to watch over the treasury. He did his best to collect dues until the union won the dues checkoff in 1942. When Murray suffered a heart attack in June 1941, McDonald ran the SWOC for much of the year, although it might have been expected that the responsibility would have been given to one of the other, older leaders.

He enjoyed the importance that unionism afforded him. During World War II, he was ecstatic when he was sent to South America on a trade mission for the Rockefellers. He was also part of a delegation of labor leaders who visited Europe. They were outfitted with fatigues and steel helmets—helmets that the United States Steel Corporation had devised—and were shown staging areas. Later, they dined with Generals Dwight D. Eisenhower and George S. Patton. McDonald liked to recount how close he and the other labor leaders had been to the front, but it can be assumed that they were not taken anywhere near it, since the military never jeopardized the safety of visiting dignitaries.

In 1954, after he had been president of the union for less than two years, a union-sponsored biography of McDonald called *Man of Steel* was published. The book was so adulatory that it embarrassed the union and even McDonald, and it had to be recalled. Today it occasionally turns up in out-of-print bookshops. It portrayed McDonald as representing a new kind of labor leader. Here are some excerpts:

Nearing his fifty-first birthday (November 22, 1953), McDonald resembled anything but the popular conception of a labor leader. He looked more like a college football coach, big, broad-shouldered, blue-eyed, handsome, with wavy silver-white hair.

Unlike the old-style labor leaders, who thought the members wanted them to put up "a poor front," this man of steel dresses to fit the occasion and in keeping with the growing prestige of labor. While seeking the best possible in life for the steelworkers, he believes their officers should set the pace by putting their best foot forward. He goes first class everywhere.

Although favoring sports outfits and tweeds with bow ties, he wears Brooks Brothers business suits when conservative clothes are in order.

His strenuous, unending round of union business, civic, social, and sports activities has kept his figure to a solid two hundred pounds-plus.

However, the heavy strain of the steelworkers' presidency, unceasing demands on the banquet circuit, and more worries than a big-league baseball manager are exacting their toll. Deep lines are etched on his Irish face and an occasional nervous twitch of the head shows the constant pressure under which he lives.

Still a striking figure, he is equally at home and welcomed in millionaire clubs like Pittsburgh's austere Duquesne Club, as well as in union halls. Some snipers object to his crossing the lines, but it has helped promote understanding in the big picture of labor-management relations.

In preparing the work, the authors—two Pittsburgh writers—interviewed McDonald in his first-class suite aboard the SS *United States,* bound for Scotland, in October 1953. McDonald was by now referring to himself in the third person, as megalomaniacs sometimes do, and the writers transcribed the scene.

Summing up his own career, the Man of Steel gazed out a porthole and said:

"The greatest influence on McDonald has been McDonald. You have to believe things and feel things for yourself. My mother and father were greater influences on me than Lewis, Murray, Green, Gompers, and all the others in the labor movement put together. Why do I have to believe in anybody except Christ? I have a mind of my own. I think for myself. My mother and my father, they believed in this thing. They believed in unionism. Lewis and Murray influenced my mind, of course. But they didn't change it one bit."

There isn't much more a man of destiny can say.

IV

As McDonald's high living and high jinks characterized the union, continued unflagging optimism characterized the corporation. That optimism was evident one morning in June 1953, when seven-year-old Nancy Fairless, one of Benjamin F. Fairless's granddaughters, ignited a blast furnace —named Nancy, after her—at the United States Steel Corporation's Fairless Works, in Morrisville, Pennsylvania, on the Delaware River, above Philadelphia. The ceremony marked the opening of the huge new plant, a showcase of the American iron and steel industry and of American manufacturing. Fairless, still the corporation's president, looked on, beaming. A second furnace at the works was named Hazel, after his wife.

Planning for the plant had begun in 1944. It was in many ways a visionary project for the corporation, which had not built a new plant since the Gary Works, in 1907. What made it feasible was that the corporation had recently obtained a significant new ore supply from Venezuela on the advice of a noted mining engineer, Mack Lake. Lake had gone to see Fairless at Fairless's office in Pittsburgh and said: "My story's very simple. I think there's iron ore in Venezuela, south of the Orinoco River and west of the Caroni River. Nobody's ever gone in to find out, or at least the Venezuelan government has no record of it. So I'm interested in finding somebody who'll put up the money to prove whether I'm right or wrong."

It was reminiscent of Henry W. Oliver's determination in 1892 to open the Mesabi Range. Fairless, however, was not as hesitant as Andrew Carnegie had been. "How much?" he asked. "Say fifty thousand dollars right off the bat. That'll pay for the aerial photography," Lake replied. "Go ahead. We'll pay for it," Fairless said. Some weeks later, Lake returned. "The pictures show there's ore there, all right," he reported. "The question is: How much, and how good is it? We ought to go in there now with a diamond drill and take some samples." "What will you need?" Fairless asked. "Well, that's really going to run into some money," Lake told him. "Maybe half a million." "Go ahead," Fairless said.

Lake's optimism proved well founded, and the corporation acquired the vast area of wilderness known as Cerro Bolívar. Quickly a mine, housing for the workers, and airstrips were constructed. The Orinoco, which had been choked with sand and gravel bars, was dredged, and soon oceangoing ships were picking up the ore. When full production was reached, the mine produced nearly eight million tons of ore a year, all of it shipped to the Fairless Works.

With the acquisition of the Venezuelan ore lands, the corporation decided to go ahead with a new plant—in essence, what Carnegie had proposed for Conneaut, Ohio, a half century before. It purchased four thousand acres of farmland along the Delaware River and in May 1950 announced that construction would begin in the spring of 1951. Docks were built so that the ships carrying the Venezuelan ore could be unloaded at the plant. Even before it opened, it was described as the most modern steel plant in the world, and once production began, it was soon setting records. Everything was on site—the world's most modern sintering plant, where ore was compressed; the huge Nancy and Hazel blast furnaces (the Hazel soon had set a world's record for pig-iron production); coke batteries that could produce three thousand tons a day; monstrous open-hearth furnaces that could produce 290 tons of steel at a time; and a continuous-hot-strip mill more than half a mile long that also set world production records. Eight miles away, the corporation constructed a new community of twenty-two hundred homes, Fairless Hills, bringing in William Levitt, the innovative builder of suburban housing, to design and construct it.

Fairless loved the works, loved to walk around "a brand-new integrated plant" built from scratch, "the finest of all modern steel plants." It reminded him, he said, that "the size and the complexity of the steel business . . . are such as to stagger the imagination." It also made him believe that Carnegie, Frick, Schwab, and the others had operated on "the most modest of scales" compared to men in the steel industry of the 1950s. It wasn't just the old-timers who "took all the risks and made all the exciting decisions."

V

In the early 1950s, the two institutions, corporation and union, were coming together in "a mature relationship." McDonald and Fairless liked each other enormously. Moreover, amity was the rule not only between the two men but between the corporation and the union, as was demonstrated by two curious events in the fall of 1953. The first was one of the more unusual odysseys in the history of American labor-management relations—a joint tour by McDonald and Fairless of the corporation's steel plants to attempt to make the corporation's workers understand that both blue-collar workers and white-collar workers had a stake in how the corporation performed. The second was a gala "Day for Dave," a joint tribute to McDonald by the union and the corporation.

The idea of the plant tour originated during the negotiations that settled the fifty-four-day strike of 1952. After Murray's death, McDonald agreed to make the tour. In November 1953, Fairless and McDonald set out, each surrounded by his own entourage, and over the next five months they visited all of the corporation's thirty-eight major plants, from the East Coast to the West. Fairless traveled in a private railroad car, McDonald by Pullman and commercial aircraft.

Each visit was essentially the same. McDonald and Fairless, with a group of a dozen or so whose members usually changed from mill to mill, would pull up at a mill in a bus (originally McDonald had arrived by limousine, but a union public-relations man told him that this made a bad impression). Inside, they would talk with local union officials, shop stewards, plant managers, and foremen about the need for cooperation. Then, with their retainers in tow, they would walk at a leisurely pace through the plant, stopping to chat with workers. Often Fairless would hand out

cigars. In the evening, they would host a dinner with union and management leaders, have some drinks with them, and preach the doctrine of
cooperation. Fairless stressed that the corporation had accepted the
union as a partner; McDonald inveighed against wildcat strikes.

The two leaders, each at home with people, got on well with workers
and managers. Once, at the Edgar Thomson Works at Braddock, at the
change of shifts in the open hearth, McDonald and Fairless chanced upon
a great raw-boned man, six feet tall and 230 pounds, as he was putting
on his undershirt. "No shit, are you Ben Fairless?" the worker asked.
Fairless said he was. "Well, you son of a bitch," the open hearth worker
said. "I always figured I could lick you; now I know I can." The men all
laughed, and the worker and Fairless shook hands. At the Geneva Works
at Provo, Utah, a local union official advised McDonald and Fairless to
stay away from one of the rollers because he was a real hardhead, a guy
who hated everybody. But Fairless did not hear the advice, and he approached the roller, offering his hand. The roller refused to shake. Fairless was taken aback, but later McDonald told Fairless that the roller had
the reputation of being the most miserable man in the mill. "Thank
God," Fairless said. "I thought he was probably the chairman of the
grievance committee."

The press loved the tour. "The ranking chieftains of management and
labor in the nation's most vital industry proposed to break through the
wall that separates the top hierarchy, both company and union, from the
men who do the industry's physical work," *Collier's* said. "His [Fairless's]
relations with David J. McDonald of the United Steelworkers have blos-
somed into a 'Ben' and 'Dave' friendship," wrote *Iron Age*.

Fairless said in 1954: "We . . . had the opportunity to look beyond
the issues that divide us and to see in much better perspective the over-
shadowing task that confronts all of us today: the task of finding a road
to industrial peace. This can be accomplished simply if we can rid ourselves of the utterly false idea that our economic interests are in conflict
and that, therefore, we must always try to take something away from each
other."

Years later, reflecting on the tour, McDonald said:

What did all this accomplish? Most important of all, I suppose, it demonstrated to hundreds of thousands of union members that Fairless didn't
have horns and to management people across the nation that I could talk
in complete sentences and didn't carry bombs in my suitcase. . . .

I've been criticized on this count, for figuratively going to bed with
management. There are those who still believe that labor contracts should

be negotiated at arm's length, in enmity. I contend that only the results are important, and if better results can be obtained through closer relationships and increased understanding, then that's the best way to proceed. I can think of no instance where my demands on behalf of the steelworkers were watered down or I was softer in seeking those demands because I knew the people with whom I was negotiating.

The companionability demonstrated by the Dave and Ben tour was surpassed by the Day for Dave, conducted by the union, the corporation, and the Pittsburgh community on November 28, 1953, just a year after Murray had been buried and McDonald had assumed the presidency. Pittsburgh's streets, airport, railroad stations, and hotels were all decorated with banners and bunting and with pictures of McDonald. Downtown buildings were specially lit, and McDonald and those who came to honor him ascended Mount Washington and gazed at the splendid sight of the dazzling city below them, the lights of downtown and of the mills reflecting on the rivers. More than three thousand union people, corporation executives, government and community leaders, and foreign labor attachés attended the evening's gathering. Two hotels were set aside for the festivities—the William Penn, where the main dinner was held, and the Roosevelt, several blocks away, where lesser personages went, all to honor the man whom his supporters were calling, and who was calling himself, "the Man of Steel." Tickets were twenty dollars a plate, which included a floor show. Some steel companies bought tables for ten at two hundred dollars a table. The chairman of the evening was William J. Hart, director of the union's District Nineteen, the Pittsburgh district. He called the event "the most important labor-management undertaking ever planned."

The evening's speakers were Fairless and Robert F. Wagner, Jr., mayor-elect of New York. Fairless urged that labor and management eliminate "the endless and senseless succession of strikes" and replace "recrimination, suspicion, and distrust of each other's motives" with "mutual respect, understanding, and confidence in one another." "Our interests are identical," said Fairless, as smooth an after-dinner speaker as Charles M. Schwab. "For better or worse, we are inseparably bound together in a state of economic matrimony. We live in the same industrial household, and the individual welfare of each of us depends entirely on the strength and security of the household itself."

Wagner, son of Senator Robert F. Wagner, Sr., Democrat of New York and principal author of the National Labor Relations Act of 1935, said that the old days of harsh confrontation between labor and management were gone:

The very proof that labor achieved a partnership with industry that it had never had before is in this room, with the presence of Mr. Fairless on the dais. . . . Now Mr. Fairless and Mr. McDonald are touring the steel plants together, discussing conditions, talking to the men and the plant super-intendents, doing everything they can to see that the United States Steel Company and the United Steelworkers of America are partners in the task of building a greater and stronger and more prosperous America. If they succeed, they will also be building a greater, and more peaceful world, and for that they will have earned the thanks of every responsible citizen and every responsible nation.

Some union officials were privately displeased by the unctuousness, the lavishness, of this breaking of bread with the enemy. Murray never would have allowed such a thing, they said. Hart rejected this notion. "Look," he said of McDonald, "we're going to give this guy everything he wants. If you call this brown-nosing, all right. I'm brown-nosing all the way."

When not touring or being feted, McDonald attended to labor-management relations, but usually only the public aspects. He saw nego-tiations as a matter of slogans, of raising wages and benefits, and he concerned himself no more than Murray had with company practices. These, he said, were none of his business. He conducted his negotiations pretty much out of his hip pocket, for there had been no real research operation at the union since Murray had forced the intellectuals out in the late 1940s.

For most of this period, labor-management relations were little trou-ble. In 1954, there was a twelve-hour strike. In 1956, after a four-week strike, the union negotiated its first cost-of-living agreement. McDonald had always opposed the concept, in part because the United Automobile Workers had pioneered it at the General Motors Corporation in 1948. "That's that Reuther bullshit, and we're going to have none of that in our union," he had said, until Arthur Goldberg convinced him to change his mind. McDonald and Goldberg exaggerated the value of the agreement, an old trick of union leaders, and it was approved by the membership. Decades later, the authority wielded by Goldberg and the other union attorneys was seen as having been excessive. "The Goldberg role was wrong," Lloyd McBride, then union president, said in 1982. "In negotia-tions he began to call the shots. The relationship was out of balance. You had a weak president and a dominant general counsel."

Good relations with the steel companies allowed McDonald to turn to issues within the labor movement—leading the CIO back into the AFL and beating back internal dissent in the steelworkers' union. Combining the AFL and the CIO had been talked of for years, particularly after the passage of the Taft-Hartley Act of 1947, but the way to a merger was cleared with the deaths, within three weeks in November 1952, of both Philip Murray, president of the CIO, and William Green, president of the AFL. Green was replaced by George Meany, president of the New York State Federation of Labor and secretary-treasurer of the AFL, a crusty labor bureaucrat and former plumber who boasted that he had never once called or participated in a strike. Murray was succeeded by Walter P. Reuther, president of the United Auto Workers. Meany was elected with only ceremonial opposition, Reuther after a bitter confrontation. McDonald wanted a steelworkers' union leader, Allan Heywood, a well-liked former Yorkshire coal miner who had given his life to the labor movement, to replace Murray, and he was angered when Reuther was chosen. Reuther returned the antipathy. After Reuther's election, McDonald told him that, as a result of the contest, "at least we have come to like each other better." Reuther replied, "I would say that we have come to *know* each other better, Dave."

Both the AFL and the CIO were by now rather lackluster institutions. The AFL was characterized by lassitude of purpose and lavish winter retreats in Florida. Early in its existence, the CIO had begun to ape the AFL, and by now it had lost much of its own unity and spirit. Reuther spent little time running the CIO. "The real sickness," Daniel Bell wrote in *Fortune* in 1953, "lies in the decline of unionism as a moral vocation. . . . Where there has not been outright spoliation, one finds among union leaders an appalling arrogance and high-handedness in their relation to the rank and file, which derives from the corruption of power."

The 1953 and 1954 discussions of the merger of the two organizations produced no results. Then McDonald, taking a swipe at Reuther, began suggesting that he might take the steelworkers' union out of the CIO and back into the AFL. In late 1954, a joint AFL-CIO committee that included Meany and Reuther was formed to discuss a merger. Goldberg did much of the behind-the-scenes work, and on December 5, 1955, in New York, the organizations merged.

After the AFL-CIO merger, things seemed to quiet down. The year 1956 was a good one for McDonald. He believed, correctly, that the 1956 contract was excellent and that the union membership was happy and firmly in his grasp. He was, however, in for a surprise.

At the convention in Los Angeles in September 1956, the leaders recommended that officials' salaries be increased, the president's from forty to fifty thousand dollars and those of the two other international officials from thirty-five to fifty thousand dollars. One speaker told the convention delegates that the leaders did not want the increases—an old ploy in unions—but said, "We feel the dignity of the office must be maintained and that the international officers could only maintain that dignity if they accepted that which we think is fair and just."

The delegates voted for the salary increases, as delegates to union conventions generally do, but someone asked whether they were linked to a dues increase scheduled to come before the convention at a later session. McDonald was infuriated. He had yielded the gavel while the question was being discussed, but he now moved back to the rostrum and stared at the questioner. "It has nothing to do with the dues increase, and I don't want a wage increase," he cried. "Is that clear?"

At the afternoon session, it was proposed that dues be increased from three to five dollars a month. I. W. Abel, the secretary-treasurer, reported that the union's net worth was now more than $21 million, double that of four years before. But the cost of running the union was high, he said. The increase in dues was necessary so that the union could "maintain our place of leadership among the important unions of the world" and was "the minimum support we owe our great president if we expect him to lead us effectively."

The convention turned acrimonious. McDonald called for a division of the house on the dues question. The members stood, aye and nay. McDonald declared the dues increase adopted. Some delegates demanded a roll call. The union, however, had never had a roll call in its entire history and was not going to have one now. McDonald slammed down the gavel, and the matter was closed.

But emotions remained high. Ushers had to take knives and guns away from a number of delegates. Back in the steel towns, particularly in the Monongahela Valley, an uprising broke out. A dues-protest committee was formed, with Donald C. Rarick, from the Irvin Works, as chairman.

The movement grew, and in February 1957 Rarick ran against McDonald for the union presidency. McDonald won, 404,172 to 223,516. Nevertheless, what had happened was astonishing: a rank-and-file worker, with little money or leadership experience and no access to the union's propaganda apparatus, had challenged the president and won almost a quarter of a million votes. The insurgents, alleging that McDonald's forces had tampered with the vote-counting, appealed to the AFL-CIO's ethical practices committee. The committee, whose counsel was Arthur J. Goldberg, refused to intervene.

Daniel Bell, in an August 1958 *Fortune* article called "Decline of Dave McDonald," wrote: "In the last year or so, McDonald has paid less and less attention to union affairs. When he has paid attention, he ignored the union's executive board. His actions have turned a majority of the board against him.... The district directors ... are convinced that McDonald, psychologically, will be unable to control the union convention and that only a statement by him that this will be his last term will stave off disaster." The article angered McDonald and goaded him to action. He went on a tour of the steel towns, pledging to "root out this cancerous growth of treachery before it is too late."

The showdown came at the 1958 convention, in Atlantic City. McDonald resorted to an anti-Communist attack on the insurgents—which was absurd, for they had not even the slightest leftist leanings—and simultaneously accused them of being agents of management. He told the delegates that the insurgents would "use every iniquitous means that they can command here—the Communists, the Trotskyites, NAM [National Association of Manufacturers] agents, company agents.... They are going to fall back on the old Communist Party line which I first heard expressed in the United Mine Workers convention in the year 1924 [actually it was 1923]—the old Communist line that staff representatives must be elected."

Then came the climax of his address: "Rise up, you strong men of steel, rise up united, strong men of steel, and show America, show those who hate you and show all the people of the world the real tough metal of which you are made." The regulars loved it. McDonald was cheered.

It was a rigged convention. When the insurgents spoke, they were shouted down. A McDonald man, Paul Rusen, urged the delegates to "go back to your districts and local unions, and anywhere they [the insurgents] raise their ugly heads, file charges and let's kick them the hell out of this union." The convention voted to do that, passing a resolution that the union should "take prompt and vigorous action to eliminate from our ranks those guilty of serious constitutional violations." The convention closed with McDonald's old crony Phil Regan leading the delegates in singing "God Bless America." A *New York Times* editorial called the convention "a model of democracy."

The insurgency beaten back, McDonald and the other union men turned their attention toward bargaining, and once again he was in the national spotlight. In the summer of 1959, the union struck the steel industry. The 116-day strike would be the longest one in the industry since the Amalgamated Association of Iron, Steel, and Tin Workers had struck the United States Steel Corporation in 1909–1910.

It was a curious strike. During the negotiations preceding it, the workers were quiescent. Thousands had been laid off during the 1958 recession and did not want now, a year later, to lose more income. McDonald knew this. Then, on June 10, 1959, the negotiating committee for the corporation and the other steel companies presented McDonald with a letter demanding radical changes in the industry's labor-management relations, including giving the management the unilateral right to make widespread workplace operating changes in order to end "featherbedding and loafing." McDonald in 1970 told interviewers from Pennsylvania State University, "It was stupid. . . . I had nothing. What the hell [were] we going to fight about? How [were] we going to get an agreement? And all of a sudden, Coop [R. Conrad Cooper, a corporation negotiator], demands changes in workrules and the grievance machinery. . . . Wow! I bit my lip, and I said, 'Let's have an adjournment.' And we went into the other room and laughed our heads off. Now we had something to fight about. . . ."

The union issued a statement saying that the companies were "determined to destroy the individual rights so carefully and painstakingly developed over the years," and at 12:01 A.M. on July 14, 1959, the strike began.

McDonald was at his theatrical best during the strike. On its first day, he was in Trenton, New Jersey, when a television reporter asked him, "Do you feel that your career hangs in the balance of this strike?" McDonald was annoyed by what he regarded as the impudence of the question. People weren't going to see him challenged by a question like that, he decided. He demanded the reporter's film. The reporter refused to give it to him, but two of McDonald's goons walked up, knocked the camera off its tripod, ripped the film from it, and smashed the camera.

At the Roosevelt Hotel in New York the next day, Goldberg, summoned to smooth things over, read a statement drafted for McDonald that seemed to be an apology: "I deeply regret the incident, but I was outraged at a question which seemed to imply that I would consider selfish personal interests at a time when my only concern is the destinies and welfare of five hundred thousand members of the United Steelworkers of America and their families. My consuming interest, first, last and always, is the welfare of human beings who have been forced on strike."

In September, the union broke off negotiations, which were being conducted in New York. "We are going home," the posturing McDonald said. "This farcical filibuster that has been going on since May 5 has ended." The chief mediator, Joseph F. Finnegan, said, "We don't intend to let this drift." But mediators always say things like that. The strike did drift.

On October 1, negotiations were moved to Pittsburgh, and the next day, the companies made their first wage offer. The union rejected it three days later. On October 9, President Eisenhower invoked the Taft-Hartley Act. He ordered a three-man fact-finding team to investigate the strike and report to him by October 16. Negotiations resumed on October 15, but the companies and the union rejected each other's proposals on October 17. On October 19, Eisenhower instructed the Department of Justice to ask the federal district court in Pittsburgh to order the strikers back to work. The court issued an injunction against the strike on October 21. The union filed an appeal on October 27, but it was rejected by the federal circuit court. The union then appealed to the Supreme Court, and again the appeal was rejected. The injunction stood. The strikers went back to work under an eighty-day cooling-off period.

On October 26, Kaiser Steel had broken with the other companies and signed an agreement with the union. On January 4, 1960, an agreement was reached in Washington between the rest of the companies and the union. The industry put the value of the agreement at forty-one cents an hour over thirty months. The demand that the companies have a say in local work practices was referred to a committee. The agreement also called for the establishment of a human relations committee, composed of union and company executives, to examine inefficient and archaic work practices and change them by mutual agreement. Vice-President Nixon and Secretary of Labor James P. Mitchell played active roles in working out the agreement, and it was suggested in the press that this was an important step for Nixon, who was seeking the Republican presidential nomination.

VI

Life was good for both sides, if the company and the union, ever more alike, can be called sides. Fairless retired in May 1955, and the impersonal, stern Roger Blough, a longtime corporation lawyer, took his place. McDonald called these years "the happiest of my life." He was being invited regularly to the White House; steelworkers were relatively high-paid and, they believed, secure; and, McDonald said, "relations with the steel industry seemed on a firm and friendly footing of mutual respect."

In January 1956, *Fortune,* so critical of the corporation two decades before, praised what it saw as new thinking:

Although the corporation still has some way to go, it has transformed itself into something it never was before—a fairly well coordinated commercial enterprise, almost if not quite rid of the curse of *noblesse oblige,* run by buoyant, ambitious men, expanding in a national market under a much freer price system than once prevailed, pursuing efficiency with a single-mindedness that almost amounts to an obsession, behaving, in short, more and more as a competitor should behave. . . . It stands today as an excellent example of how industrial progress occurs in the American economy.

The problem was that all this was untrue. The corporation and the union were stuck in their traditional ways of doing things and could not see the need for change. The Fairless Works, for example, using open hearths, was obsolete the moment it opened. And the union, along with most other observers, missed one of the striking aspects of the plant—that it employed relatively few workers. An old steelman like Fairless could see this, though. "The absence of all mass operations involving manual labor" meant that the plant employed "fewer than two thousand workers on any given shift," he said, noting that the works "sometimes look almost deserted."

Between 1957 and 1962, some one hundred thousand jobs in the steel industry were lost, but no one paid attention. A new soda and beer container, a can made from aluminum, was becoming popular, replacing the steel soda and beer can, a major use for steel since the 1920s. In 1958, Esso began using aluminum cans for motor oil, and in January 1960 orange juice began appearing in aluminum cans. New plastics also were coming into use, and between 1958 and 1963 their sales tripled. The men who ran the companies and the union paid no attention to this, either.

The 1959 strike had established the notion that imports were rising. They had, in fact, begun to rise before the strike, but now they became a bogeyman, something to take the industry and the union's attention away from the real problem—ineffective management and production.

Most of the traditional measurements, however, said that the industry was in excellent shape. Tonnage remained up. Employment was high, despite the losses in recent years. Wages and benefits were increasing. In 1962, Arthur Homer, president of the Bethlehem Steel Corporation, spoke for the industry when he said he saw no necessity to introduce new technologies: "We have a nice business as it is."

McDonald had a similar view of the union. In fact, there was almost no need for a union anymore, he said. American steelworkers "had achieved just about everything a union could provide them."

KHRUSHCHEV'S
WRISTWATCH

In October 1952, the Homestead
Works had the biggest payday in its history up to that time. More than
$2,700,000 was paid out to fourteen thousand workers, an average check
of $192.70 for a worker. The town knew that it would be a record payroll
and brought in extra police on overtime. The Homestead Branch of the
People's First National Bank and Trust Company and the First Federal
Savings and Loan Association of Homestead put on more tellers and
brought in additional private guards.

The 1950s in Homestead were a golden time. The mill was running
at full capacity. In 1952, the one-millionth ton of steel was poured at the
Homestead Works. The union, Local 1397, had more than ten thousand
members, more people than in many towns in the United States. "Everybody was making a good buck," said Betty Esper, who had just gone to
work as a clerk in the mill. "No doubt about it—the fifties were the big

years, the glory years," said Ray Hornak, also a white-collar worker in the mill.

"Homestead was like when you went to Coney Island," said Steve Simko, who first worked in the mill in 1940, served in the Navy in World War II, then returned to the mill in 1946 and stayed there until 1984, ending up as supervisor of the Homestead Works' Valley Machine Shop. "A lot of fun, a lot of money around, a lot of music, a lot of noise. Everybody was just having a good time. Eighth Avenue was like a little Broadway. You could go there at three o'clock in the morning, and it would be full. . . . People were loaded into the ice cream stores, the saloons. Christ, when I used to go to work midnight to eight A.M., I'd go an hour early just to watch, see what was going on, see the saloons, particularly in the black sections, down by the mill. There was a lot of noise, a lot of fun. Just like in a park. Money was no problem. . . . Everybody had cars, everybody was doing everything, buying everything. Oh, Christ, on payday—payday and the day after—the bars were going and there was music all over the place, loud so you could hear it outside. There was credit in the bars. Steelworkers had bills. They'd go in and drink until payday and put it on the book. There was gambling, prostitution. It was one of them real towns."

It seemed that nothing could stop the good times. In 1953, the corporation closed Open Hearth Number Three, "the Grand Old Lady of Victory Valley," as it had become known during World War II. Planned by Andrew Carnegie and Charles M. Schwab, and opened in 1901, OH Three consisted of twenty-four furnaces—until World War II, more furnaces under one roof than at any steelworks in the world—with a capacity of seventy-five to one hundred tons apiece. In its fifty-two years of operation, OH Three turned out 148,000 tons of steel, including steel that the Homestead structural mills rolled into beams for the Empire State Building, the United Nations Building, the Delaware River Bridge, and the San Francisco–Oakland Bay Bridge. But production was not hampered by its closing. Open Hearth Four and Open Hearth Five remained open, and the works, after its vast wartime expansion, was larger than ever, numbering 450 buildings spread over 130 acres.

"The skies were red and blue from the steel production," said Richard Holoman, who went into the mill in July 1955 at $1.97 an hour. "Everybody was working. At Christmastime, everybody had a couple of bucks in their pocket. Christmas was good. Easter was good. The Avenue was booming, the town was booming. I'm telling you, it was a big, booming time."

Since steelmaking was done in teams, the men and women in the mill

—most women had left the mill at the end of the war but some now held clerical jobs—often established a rich communal life. Betty Esper recalled: "We cooked many a meal on our hot plates. Instead of bringing in our lunch or dinner, we would bring in barbecue, hot dogs, sauerkraut, and cook in an electric frying pan." After work, the men and women might go to Buffington's, on Eighth Avenue, even though there was an unwritten rule in Homestead that Buffington's was a high-class place, a place for the bosses. Or they might go to the Hollywood Bar, in West Homestead, or the Green Gables, in Duquesne. "You had your places," Betty Esper said, meaning that you knew where your group was welcome.

The town was small enough for people to know one another, yet large enough and—because of the mill—rich enough to offer benefits usually associated with far larger towns. Teachers' salaries, for example, were as high as forty-eight hundred dollars a year, among the best in the nation. Almost everything one wanted could be obtained in Homestead. There were many small meat markets and grocery stores. Running a store had been a way out of the mill for many workers, and if you had a store you were regarded as an important person. There was a quality about the stores that now seems largely absent from American life: Customers knew store owners and store owners knew their customers. Many stores took phone orders and delivered. They extended credit, and accounts were settled twice a month, on payday.

On Saturdays, thousands of people thronged Eighth Avenue, a major shopping area for the lower Monongahela Valley. People shopped most of the day, at Friedlander's clothing store, Sol's clothing store, Solomon's men's clothing store, Harry's clothing store, Zaine's women's clothing store, Half Brothers' department store, Moxley's drugstore, Katilius's furniture store, Wolfson's jewelry store, Post's shoes, Levine Brothers' hardware store, Climer's cigar store, Ewing's meat market, Morris Grinberg's ladies' and children's clothing store, Meyer I. Grinberg's housewares and electrical store, Wohlfarth's bakery. Often it was almost impossible to get into Wohlfarth's because the store was so packed with people seeking out the breads and pastries regarded as the best in southwestern Pennsylvania.

Then people went home, and they often got dolled up and came back to the Avenue for a movie or a restaurant dinner, or to hit some of the night spots. "You took baths on Saturday night whether you were dirty or not, and then you went down to the Avenue," said Babe Fernandez, a worker in the mill. "On Saturday nights in Homestead, you couldn't even walk on Eighth Avenue, couldn't even get on the sidewalks, there were so many people." Barbara Wolfe, a longtime Homestead resident, said, "If you weren't dressed to kill, you were a bum."

Teenagers took their dates to the H and H Restaurant or to the United Candy Shop, or perhaps up to the cemeteries on the hill to neck. Often people came over from other towns in the valley to attend a movie or go to a bar. The numbers parlors and sporting houses along Sixth Avenue continued to flourish—three dollars an assignation.

Borough policemen directed traffic along Sixth and Eighth avenues three times a day, at shift change. A fixture on Eighth Avenue was Hunkie Steve Pachuta, the policeman. He rode a motorcycle and wore black chaps that came up over his calves, and many people in town, certainly the children and teenagers, respected his authority. "You didn't mess with Hunkie Steve, because you'd get your head broke," said Ray Mc-Guire, a worker in the mill.

The general superintendent of the mill still lived in the mansion next to the library. The house now had two putting greens with bent grass—golf was popular among mill executives—and the mansion lawns were carefully maintained, the grass cut first by sickle and scythe if it was high, and then by hand mowers. Mill policemen, some mounted on horses kept in the mansion's stables, guarded the superintendent's house and drove him back and forth to work. The most important man in town, he seemed like a character out of a Charles Dickens or George Eliot novel from a century before.

Sports flourished. Ten thousand people would attend high school football games between Homestead and Munhall at West Field, and when sellouts occurred a young Homestead disk jockey called Porky Chedwick would sometimes broadcast the games over loudspeakers set up on Eighth Avenue.

There was, among many people, immense pride in working at the Homestead Works. When Dan Spillane, a plate-smoother in the armor-plate mill, took his family on vacation, he often tried to stop at a shipyard and see ships like the USS *Massachusetts* and *North Carolina,* so that he could show his wife and children the armor plate for gun turrets that he and his fellow workers had made.

Homestead in these years was an especially pleasant place for children. The movie theaters changed their programs three times a week and showed serials, called "chapters," every Saturday afternoon—Tom Tyler in *The Phantom,* Buster Crabbe in *Flash Gordon,* Buck Jones in *The Rough Rider,* and many others. The children would reenact scenes from the serials as they made their way home up the hill. They also rode their bicycles across the High Level Bridge to see the Pirates at Forbes Field for a dollar a seat, in right field, if you played in the Knothole League.

At six each evening, Saint Mary Magdalene's Roman Catholic Church sounded the angelus, and this was a signal to the children playing in Frick

Park across from the church, in the alleys (boys often nailed butter tubs to telephone poles in the alleys to serve as baskets for basketball games), and in other places around town that it was time to go home for dinner. After dinner, the children reemerged and played until the streetlights went on, the second signal that it was time to go home.

The town was sometimes not a very pleasant place for black people. The color barriers had eased, but only somewhat. In the mill, they continued to hold the worst jobs and generally could not rise higher than second helper. There were no black foremen or supervisors.

One summer in the 1950s, Candy Esper, who then worked in the forty-five-inch mill (he found the mill so onerous that he soon quit to sell numbers, becoming known as an honest numbers dealer), said to a fellow black worker, "You've been working in hell all these years." His friend looked at him and replied, "Don't you think I know that?"

Black people could now swim in the pool at the Carnegie Library, but they still had to sit in the balcony at the Stahl Theatre and in special sections in the other movie houses, even though whites could sit in the black sections when the white sections were full. There were no black teachers at Homestead High School, and in a traditionally white area like Hunkie Hollow, above the mill in Munhall, or in Homestead Park, also in Munhall, up the hill beyond the cemeteries, the only black people were the garbage collectors.

Some black people were doing well in Homestead, like Rufus "Son-nyman" Jackson, proprietor of the Skyrocket Lounge and the Manhattan Music Shop, which were both housed in a two-story brick building on the corner of Amity Street and Second Avenue. Many famous performers appeared at the Skyrocket during the 1930s, 1940s, and 1950s, among them Lena Horne and Earl "Fatha" Hines. Jackson had established himself in the jukebox business in Allegheny County, and from the Manhattan Music Shop he also ran a nationwide mail-order record business.

In the late 1940s and the early 1950s, Porky Chedwick, the white disc jockey, still in his teens, began to come in and poke around in the basement for records that had not been sold—78s and later 33s—and take them back to Homestead's radio station, WHOD, and play them on his show. Soon all kinds of music that many people, black and white, had never heard before—rhythm and blues, and then rock and roll—was coming out of WHOD and being heard up and down the Monongahela Valley, to the delight of black and white teenagers and the consternation of their parents. Among the performers Chedwick broadcast were the Ravens, the Orioles, Bo Diddley, Chuck Berry, Little Anthony and the Imperials, the Platters, the Drifters, Little Richard, Little Willie John, and Hank Ballard and the Midnighters.

Another star at WHOD was a young black man, Malvin Goode, who broadcast news and sports. He had been born and raised in Homestead, the son of a first helper in the open hearth. Billy Goode, one of the best men in the works, was barred because of his race from rising to boss melter. Once a white supervisor said to him, "Bill, it's too bad you are a colored man." He replied, "I know."

Malvin Goode graduated from Homestead High School in January 1936. For twelve years he worked in the Homestead Works, including the years he was in high school. After graduation, he worked as a porter and in the Pittsburgh juvenile court. His sister, Mary, who went by the name Mary Dee, had a four-hour music show on WHOD that featured performers like Diahann Carroll, Nat "King" Cole, Joe Williams, and many others. Goode was a good talker, glib, a man who could talk to time, and in 1952 he got a job at WHOD. Jackie Robinson of the Brooklyn Dodgers had broken the color bar in the major leagues in 1947, and there were now four or five black baseball players on many teams. When they were in Pittsburgh to play the Pirates, they would come to Homestead just to appear on Goode's show. He would take a tape recorder to the hotels where they stayed and interview them. Most of the black players came through at one time or another, including Jackie Robinson, Roy Campanella, Junior Gilliam, Monte Irvin, Hank Aaron, and Willie Mays. Children, black and white, came down to Eighth Avenue on their bicycles and crowded around WHOD waiting for autographs.

II

Homestead and the mill rode the prosperity boom. It was as though the workers and the town had concocted a magic formula for riches, had become alchemists who somehow turned steel into gold. Not only was the money rolling in, but every time there was a negotiation between the union and the corporation, wages and benefits were increased. "Everybody was working, everybody was having a good time," Betty Esper said.

But there were other, less positive products of the golden times. Not much of the money being earned was invested in developing the town and improving its services. It was still the mill that took care of the boroughs of Homestead, Munhall, and West Homestead. The mill would send out crews to salt the streets in winter. When the bridge washed out on Ravine Street, in Munhall, the mill sent out steel beams on a truck and the bridge was immediately rebuilt.

Steve Simko said: "We took care of the library. All the maintenance of the library. You sent men up there. Somebody had to pay those men.

My shop paid them. That shouldn't be, but that's the way it was. I don't think there's a church in the valley that we didn't do something for. A church in Oakland—I fabricated bearings for their bells. Saint Mary's Church, Saint John's, Saint Vincent's, we helped them all—church bells, church towers, church doors. Pumps for the steel-valley schools, for Munhall High School. We took care of the laundry in the hospital. Anytime the *Homestead Messenger* equipment broke, we took care of that. We made them gears, we made them shafts. When somebody needed a crane on the outside, when a catastrophe happened, we took care of that. When a guy was pinned in the junkyard, I sent a crane. We saved his life. Lifted another crane off him. A guy fell through the floor with a forklift in a beer distributorship. We went down there with a crane and lifted him out. The borough would have a break in the main line, we'd lend them equipment, lend them manpower. We did a lot for everybody. The Boy Scouts—they wanted help and my boss said to me, 'Steve, use your head. You're from here.' We built cottages, training buildings for the Boy Scouts. I had two machinists up there all summer. I took care of the payroll."

Homestead and the other towns reveled in this system, for everyone benefited—the politicians, who claimed credit for the projects; the corporation executives, because by providing these services the corporation perpetuated its control of the towns; and the people, because they could get a newly graded and seeded playground, a new flagpole, an improved road, a new bell in the church tower, new lights at the football field. And it was free, or so it seemed.

Also growing was nepotism and an accompanying evil—overmanning. People depended on the mill to provide not only jobs for regular workers but also summer jobs for high school and college students, and for teachers in the Homestead school system, particularly the coaches, like the basketball coach, Chick Davies, who needed the extra money. "I doubled my teacher's salary by working in the mill in summers," said Ray Supak, then a teacher at Homestead High School and later the principal of Steel Valley High School.

Often, personnel people had little say over who was hired in the mill. They hired whoever the plant managers and other supervisors told them to hire. "It helped if you had somebody in there, if you knew the employment boss," said Bob Krovocheck, who started in the mill in 1949, at age nineteen, after dropping out of high school. "That's how I got in there." Marty Costa, who went into the mill in 1953, at age twenty-eight, and later became superintendent of the open-hearth division, said: "Everybody had a shot at making money to go to school. We were just loaded with people, far too many people. Grandfather, father, son—everybody worked in the mill."

The corruption that existed in the mill was also part of the life of the town. Vice and corruption were an important source of money for Homestead and for many Homestead families. The numbers game, in 1950 alone, took in an estimated $4.5 million. Burgess McLean and other Democrats had gotten elected during the 1930s in part by saying that they would clean up the town, but vice and corruption were too profitable, and, just as important, too ingrained in Homestead life. Raids were made, but the fix was always in. People were arrested and bail set, but bail would be forfeited and court costs paid, and nobody would do big time.

Vice had rewards for little people and big shots—prostitutes, madams, pimps, numbers men, businessmen, policemen, and political leaders. It was easier work than the work in the mill and often much more lucrative. For some, including a few black people, who would have been blocked from advancement in the mill, it was a way up the ladder. "Some of those black families are spending that money still," Spanky O'Toole, a Homestead policeman, said one day years later. "White folks, too." Politicians benefited by adding to their income and using the vice and the corrupt system to increase their authority. "They could damn near fix anything, up to murder," Spanky O'Toole said. "And they could even help you there." Others who did not directly participate in crime, such as priests and ministers, also profited from it. "Father wanted that five percent in the collection plate each Sunday," Police Chief Chris Kelly said. Father did not care where the five percent came from.

The corporation could have stopped the vice and corruption at any time by putting pressure on the local officials, but it did nothing. The prostitution, the numbers game and other kinds of gambling, and the after-hours drinking were all just fine with the executives; boys will be boys, they thought, especially mill hunkies. To the executives, Sixth Avenue provided harmless recreation and another means of control. People knew that the corporation could put an end to this lucrative source of income and power, and thus they were doubly subservient.

By the early 1950s, however, the vice and corruption in Homestead and the other steel towns had become embarrassing in some quarters. It seemed too open, and, at the same time, a remnant of the past. This kind of thing had been okay in the rowdy old days of steelmaking, but now Pittsburgh was changing its image from the smoky steel town it had been for more than a hundred years. A new office and hotel complex was rising downtown, at the confluence of the Monongahela and the Allegheny.

Pittsburgh politicians and business leaders had careers to make, and the vice and corruption were a godsend to them.

In Homestead, a simple burglary made the police chief a laughing-stock and set in motion the forces that were to bring down the brothels, the illegal liquor joints, and the gambling. On September 19, 1949, two thieves broke into the home of Police Chief Muck Conlin and his wife. From a safe behind the fireplace they stole some money. The amount would become a matter of intense controversy and would never be deter-mined. At first, the Conlins said that it was $100,000. This set tongues wagging. How had Muck Conlin accumulated $100,000 on his salary of $3,000 a year? The incident became the talk of the town, and people laughed uproariously.

The Conlins gave some thought to the matter and decided that only $31,941.90 had been stolen, though they immediately added that this represented their entire life savings. If they had thought that the gossip would now die down, they were mistaken. Whether it was $100,000 or $31,941.90, the question was the same: How had Muck gotten the dough?

Early in 1950, a Pittsburgh grand jury started investigating corruption in Homestead and other steel towns of the Monongahela Valley. On May 2, 1951, Burgess McLean, the town's beloved mayor, was indicted—as Burgess Cavanaugh had been twelve years before—along with twenty-eight others, including Police Chief Conlin, the fire chief, and three po-licemen.

The indictment stated that for years the Homestead council had passed pious resolutions condemning vice, but that McLean and other town leaders, including borough council members, had in fact cham-pioned "said practices." As a result of the rise to power of the McLean-Conlin team over the last decade and a half, vice now appeared to be more effectively and rewardingly organized.

The chief responsibility of the Homestead constabulary seemed not to be to enforce the law but to keep order among the patrons of the dives along Sixth Avenue. Why else were Homestead policemen not only refus-ing to enforce laws against prostitution, after-hours drinking, and gam-bling, but directing traffic on Sixth Avenue to make access to the place more convenient? And why else was one Homestead policeman, a plain-clothesman named Benny Buford, known as "the Boss of Sixth Avenue"? Everything was done in the open, as if there were no laws: "Colored girls catered to white men exclusively" in some brothels. "Gambling and liquor-selling were brazenly and openly conducted under the eye of the police of said borough." The grand jury stated that Homestead represented "the poorest and the weakest example of public responsibility that has come to our notice."

If all this weren't enough, there was the matter of contributions to McLean's athletic-club boxing program. Involvement in sports by politicians was an old story in Homestead. It was a way of winning votes, and it helped produce some outstanding athletic programs. But the grand jury said that McLean, "under the fraudulent guise of helping the community's youth," had diverted to personal use ten thousand dollars that had been given to the boxing program. He was charged with three counts of fraud, all misdemeanors.

None of this mattered a great deal in Homestead. Most people supported McLean, saying that he was a Democrat, a great man who cared about them, and asking why the do-gooders didn't pick on some other town and leave Homestead alone.

Conlin, charged with taking payoffs, went on trial first. How, the prosecutor inquired, had he accumulated such wealth, whether $100,000 or $31,941.90, on a salary of $3,000? Indignantly Conlin replied, "I worked hard all my life and saved my money." He claimed that to augment his income he had secured a part ownership in a pinball machine company. And why was the money in a safe behind the fireplace? Because he distrusted banks. And why not? Didn't anybody remember the Great Depression? If any individual was at fault for letting the rackets run wild, Conlin said, it was McLean, the highest public official in Homestead.

None of this convinced the judge, who asked, "If suppression of crime isn't his [the police chief's] duty, then just what is the use of having a police chief in our government?" In October 1952, Conlin was convicted.

McLean did not live to be tried. On a cold, gray day, December 13, 1951, he was working at his office. Late in the afternoon, he left for home but found his automobile blocked by one that had stalled. He and some other men pushed the stalled vehicle out of the way. Suddenly he felt fatigued and had difficulty breathing. He was taken to his home, 329 East Tenth Avenue, where he had held so many political gatherings in the basement and the politicians had drank beer and supped on Mrs. McLean's baked beans and sandwiches. At about 6:00 P.M. he died. He was young, just fifty-four. His pastor, Father Vincent Burke of Saint Mary Magdalene's Roman Catholic Church, recorded his last words: "I've never done any harm to anyone I can think of."

McLean was laid out, and hundreds of people—friends, political cronies, people he had helped in one way or another—came to view the body. Then it was taken to a cemetery in Pittsburgh, which some Homestead residents thought odd, seeing that the town had cemeteries of its own, and Homestead had been as good to McLean as McLean had been to Homestead. But no matter. McLean went out an esteemed man and remains so today.

A year later, in December 1952, a memorial service for McLean was held at Saint Mary's. An estimated three hundred people attended, and Judge Michael A. Musmanno, the old firebrand who had spoken at the rally in Homestead on July 5, 1936, to mark the beginning of the drive by the Committee for Industrial Organization to organize the steel industry, was enlisted to deliver the eulogy. He was a noted orator, but now he outdid himself. For an hour he recalled the highlights of McLean's life— his football-playing, his exploits as an aviator in World War I, his political career in Homestead and in the Pennsylvania Democratic Party. You know this of Doc McLean, Musmanno said: If your son or daughter wanted a job working at the mill or on the borough, you saw Doc, and he took care of it. If your sewers backed up, you saw Doc. If you fell behind in your taxes, you saw Doc. If you needed a little something to tide you over the holidays, you saw Doc.

Now it was time to say goodbye. As to the indictment, wasn't it clear what had happened? Had not God, by taking Doc when he did, absolved him of any sins that he might have committed? It was as clear as lightning on a summer night that this had been an example of divine decision-making. God had sat as judge and jury: "I can see how last December 13 the great judge of all looked down from the heavens and ruled, 'There need be no trial. I acquit this man. He is innocent.'"

III

The crackdown on crime did not reduce the town's spirits, not in those flush times. It was now seventy-five years since, in October 1880, Homestead had been chartered, and in August 1955, in a week-long ceremony, the town celebrated its diamond jubilee. The *Messenger* declared:

The town is bursting with civic spirit. A larger than usual number of citizens own homes. All the streets and alleys are well paved. We have not only a fine police force, but also an efficient full-time fire-fighting organization. Our schools and churches are broad in scope. Frick Park, a gift of Henry C. Frick, offers a place of rest and solitude away from the hustle and noise of the city's industrial center.

Eighth Avenue, one of the busiest commercial thoroughfares in the

Monongahela Valley, is lined with more than three hundred stores, count-less business offices, a daily newspaper office, and two large, progressive banks. These serve us, our friends and neighbors: a trading population of over fifty-three thousand citizens.

Amity Homestead, the little plot of farmland which was sold to John McClure for $272 in 1786, has in seventy-five years become one of our nation's most vital industrial communities.

Homestead was on the map, and if ever there was a demonstration of that, it occurred in the midst of the 1959 steel strike, when, like many famous people before him, Nikita S. Khrushchev, premier of the Soviet Union, came to Homestead as part of the American tour that he and his wife, Nina, made. The Cold War was at its height, but some Americans and Russians were working to break down barriers between the two nations. Khrushchev's trip had been planned for months. He would arrive in Washington to confer with President Eisenhower and other govern-ment officials. Then he would see something of America. But Khru-shchev, always feisty, had his own idea of what America was, and he wanted to see three things that to him represented the country—Holly-wood, a farm, and a steel mill. Given his irascibility and unpredictability —and the almost constant badgering he took from anti-Communists, including a number of labor leaders, all bent on riling him and making a name for themselves—the trip was hectic from the moment he stepped off the plane.

In Washington, he attended to ceremonial matters. Then he flew to Los Angeles, where he learned that his visit to Disneyland had been canceled with no acceptable explanation. His dour spirits throughout the rest of his time in California were not improved by the fact that almost everyone, rather than being a genial host or hostess, seemed to want to debate or otherwise confront him. The mayor of Los Angeles, Norman Poulson, tried his best to goad him at a dinner, in his honor, attended by seven hundred persons—actors and actresses, political figures, and other West Coast personalities. "You shall not bury us, and we shall not bury you," Poulson said. "The nature of man in your own society will force you to pattern new freedoms along the line already enjoyed here." Khrushchev was clearly irritated. In Hollywood, after watching a number of dancers—among them Juliet Prowse and Shirley MacLaine—filming a scene for the movie *Can-Can,* he pronounced the dance immoral. The can-can was a French dance, but the Americans took offense.

Khrushchev's mood was not improved at his next stop, San Fran-cisco. He enjoyed chatting with Harry Bridges, the longtime president of the International Longshoremen and Warehousemen's Union, leader of the 1934 general strike in San Francisco, and a noted American leftist. But he was incensed when, at the AFL-CIO convention, the fiercely anti-Communist AFL-CIO president, George Meany, refused to meet with him, saying that he would rather be dead. Khrushchev then had to put up with a harangue from a group of labor leaders led by Walter P. Reuther, president of the auto workers' union.

When Khrushchev left the West Coast, things began to improve. First he visited the large farm of Roswell Garst, near Coon Rapids, in central Iowa. Garst was an important figure in American agriculture who had become wealthy in the 1930s, when he began to produce and sell hybrid seed corn. He had sold some of it to the Soviet Union and other Eastern Bloc countries, had met and become friendly with Khrushchev, and was now a bridge-builder between the American and Soviet people. Khrushchev immensely enjoyed his day on the farm, especially when photographers and reporters—several hundred were on hand—swarmed over fences and onto stacks of feed corn and silage, prompting Garst to throw ears of corn at them. Khrushchev thought that Garst had a grand idea and joined in with the utmost glee.

Then it was on to Pittsburgh. He arrived at the airport on the night of September 23 and was driven the twenty-five miles to his hotel. But first he stopped at a place that for two centuries had been visited by everyone who came to the three rivers, whether frontiersman or travel writer or politician—Mount Washington, on the south bank of the Monongahela River across from downtown Pittsburgh, from which can be viewed the lights of the city shimmering in the black river. The steel mills along the river, including the Homestead Works, were dark, because of the steel strike that had begun more than two months before. But Khrushchev was going to visit a place just as interesting and important as a steel mill—the Mesta Machine plant.

The next morning, he emerged from his hotel, stepped into his limousine, and was driven east, to Homestead. It was a lovely autumn day, and he enjoyed the drive along the south bank of the Monongahela. The hills, the immense factories, the piles of steel, coal, and coke—this vast industrial landscape, bleak yet compelling—called up sharp and bittersweet images of his youth in the coal mines and steel plants of the Ukrainian industrial region known as the Donets Basin.

Just after 11:30 A.M. Khrushchev's caravan came off the southern end of the High Level Bridge and entered Homestead. It turned right on Eighth Avenue, at Chiodo's Tavern, and headed west. Several thousand people, Homesteaders and others, had come down to Eighth Avenue to see him and were stationed along both sides of the Avenue. He was in an ebullient mood as he waved to the crowds on the Avenue and went up State Road 837 to the Mesta Machine plant. He was delighted by the turnout there.

The workers had been instructed on security and protocol: Don't talk to Khrushchev. Don't try to shake his hand. Stay at a distance. Show respect. Federal agents and police swarmed over the plant. But one worker, a janitor named Dmitri Zastupenevich, was a native of the Soviet Union, and when he saw Khrushchev he became so excited that he suddenly called out to him in Russian. For a moment, Khrushchev was taken aback. Then he quickly walked up to Zastupenevich, who was standing with other workers behind ropes that the security officers had erected. "Where are you from?" Khrushchev asked in Russian. "Minsk," Zastupenevich replied.

Khrushchev was flabbergasted. What a small world! He was in a steel town in the middle of the United States, and here was a man from the Byelorussian city of Minsk. He grabbed the Soviet foreign minister, Andrei A. Gromyko, and pulled him toward Zastupenevich. "Here's another Byelorussian," Khrushchev said to Zastupenevich, referring to Gromyko. "Hello and good luck," said the always dour Gromyko, showing no enthusiasm.

Now another worker, Kenneth Jackey, a clerk, ignoring security, stuck out his hand and presented Khrushchev with a cigar, for which he had paid eight cents. Khrushchev was again startled. What a splendid gesture! He wanted to give Jackey something in return. Stripping off his wristwatch, he handed it to Jackey. "It's yours," he said in Russian.

Jackey looked at the watch, a silver Pobeda—the Russian word for "victory." It had probably cost five hundred rubles, the equivalent of fifty dollars. He was thrilled. He put it on and looked at it. He held his arm high in the air, the sun shining on the watch. He lit a cigar of his own. He said he would keep the watch as long as he lived.

18

"THE CREATIVE ENERGIES OF PRIVATE ENTERPRISE"

No one who could obtain an invitation and who enjoyed a good time on somebody else's money would, in the 1950s and 1960s, miss the gala Christmas party that the United States Steel Corporation put on for reporters.

The party was usually held in the William Penn Hotel, on Grant Street, in Pittsburgh, a gracious old hostelry built largely with Henry Clay Frick's money early in the century. The top executives were there, senior men from the corporation's headquarters a block away, as well as executives from the major mills in the Pittsburgh district. And, of course, there were the honored guests—journalists from newspapers in the steel towns of western Pennsylvania, from the Pittsburgh papers, and from the national papers and magazines that maintained bureaus in Pittsburgh.

Journalists have long been wooed by free drinks and food. But the corporation's Christmas party was a particularly sumptuous affair, even by the standards of the 1950s and 1960s, when parties for the press were the norm in numerous industries. Press people and corporation people looked forward to the party. There were turkeys, sides of roast beef, platters of oysters, and beer, wine, and liquor in such amounts that one's glass never had to be empty, if one had the sobriety to make one's way back to the bar or the patience to wait for a roaming waiter or waitress. Men and women danced far into the night, some well into the hours of the next day. What was more, the executives were in high spirits, from the endless rounds of drinks and the giddiness of the holiday season, and reporters could get on-the-record answers to their questions as well as interesting, high-placed scuttlebutt on the steel industry, with the unstated rule that a reporter would not make an executive look silly, would not put a man's name on something that might get him into trouble.

Off the record or on, what the reporters got was optimism. Production was high. The industry was making record profits. This year had been good. Next year would be even better.

II

Everyone involved with steel was optimistic about its future. The corporation and the other companies was doing excellently. Steelworkers were making good money and spending it. The union had been accepted into the mainstream of American life. In the 1960s, David J. McDonald was still considered important. Arthur Goldberg, the union's general counsel, was named secretary of labor by President John F. Kennedy in 1961 and appointed to the United States Supreme Court in 1962. In 1965, President Lyndon B. Johnson persuaded Goldberg to become ambassador to the United Nations. (Johnson was convinced that Goldberg could help him win acceptance for the Vietnam War. But he could not, and leaving the Supreme Court was a decision that he regretted for the rest of his life.)

The importance of steel in American life was highlighted in April 1962, when a major political confrontation resulted after the steel industry first said that it would not raise prices, then did. Roger Blough, chairman of the corporation, was pitted against President Kennedy. Kennedy was distressed at the effect that the price increase would have on the economy, or at least on the perception of his control of the economy. "My father always told me that all businessmen were sons-of-bitches," he muttered to his aides, "but I never believed it until now." Kennedy summoned Blough to Washington and forced him to back down. The confrontation was front-page news across America for days, so central was steel to the economy.

It became fashionable for the corporation and the other steel companies to admit errors that in the 1950s they had denied existed. It is typical of many business enterprises that each generation of executives criticizes the generation that has gone before, even though the older men helped the younger ones to advance. Elbert H. Gary had tactfully observed that the methods of Carnegie, while perhaps correct for his day, were no longer suitable. Myron C. Taylor and his associates had complained that Gary had assumed too much power, had arrogated too many decisions to himself, and had centralized too much control in New York. Benjamin F. Fairless had said that Carnegie, Frick, Schwab, and the rest had been strong men, but that their ways had become obsolete, and that his generation faced equally demanding problems, and was just as bold.

Now the leaders of the 1960s accused Fairless and the other executives of the 1940s and 1950s of not having recognized new technologies and not having invested wisely. They had put too much capital into new capacity and not enough into research and new products. Much of the expansion in the Fairless era "was in effect obsolete when it was built," *Fortune* wrote in 1966. William H. Johnstone, chief financial officer of the Bethlehem Steel Corporation, was even more emphatic. He said: "Those years are ancient history, the dodo period. We are in a whole new era." C. William Verity, Jr., president of the Armco Steel Corporation, said: "Never has our industry experienced so much change as it is experiencing now. There is an awakening in every phase of the business—in management, marketing, research, and reconstruction."

Now the industry would spend billions of dollars on new technologies and new processes to make steel stronger and more versatile—oxygen furnaces, vacuum degassing, continuous casters, computer-controlled production, sophisticated hot-strip mills. The goal was to regain markets lost to aluminum, reinforced concrete, and plastics, and to counter competition from imports.

The industry had the money for investment thanks to the 7 percent accelerated-tax-depreciation allowance, which President Kennedy had approved just one year after his apparent show of toughness with Blough and other leaders of the corporation. Between 1961 and 1966, retained cash flow—the money available to corporations after taxes and dividends —increased from $900 million to $1.7 billion, "a dramatic illustration of what enlightened public policy can do to unleash the creative energies of private enterprise," *Fortune* said. In 1956, when the American steel industry had a capacity of 126 million tons a year, it had been predicted that by 1980 the annual demand for steel would reach 226 million or even 250 million tons.

III

Optimism, however, had brought lax ways of doing things that could only lead to destruction. Many people at the Homestead Works, as at other plants, were stealing, and almost no one cared, including the security guards, who sometimes stole themselves. Superintendents would occasionally say that they were going to crack down, and for a time there would be checks of lunch pails and of foremen's cars. It was foremen and executives, for the most part, who were allowed to drive their cars into the mill, and it was thus they who—while castigating the blue-collar workers for stealing—were in many cases the biggest thieves, because one needed a car to make off with large items. But soon the guards would return to their normal lassitude.

The notion of "getting it at the mill" was now a way of life—pencils; toilet paper; hammers, wrenches, pliers, and screwdrivers; nickel, brass, and other metals, which could be sold to scrap dealers; copper piping, electrical wiring, and lumber for remodeling homes and summer cabins; almost whatever people wanted, they took, blue-collar and white-collar workers alike. The practice had gone on for decades, an outgrowth of the system of graft and payoffs that had long existed. It was now so far advanced that it was considered normal behavior. Steve Simko said: "Let me put it this way: I don't think that anybody in the valley ever bought a bolt. If they needed a bolt, they took a bolt."

There were ingenious schemes to remove items from the mill. If such creativity had been applied to steelmaking, the industry would have benefited immensely. Men would pitch materials over the fence and come back for them at night, or disassemble large items and smuggle them out piece by piece. For a time, in the 1960s, bulk nickel—used in the manufacture of steel—was being stolen by the truckload. In the early 1980s, six hundred gallons of paint suddenly disappeared. Ray Hornak, superintendent of the structural department, had to order three air conditioners in 1982 before he could install one. The first two were stolen—huge, industrial-size units large enough to cool much of an office building. "I hope they're freezing their asses off somewhere today," he said.

"The amount of stuff taken was tremendous," said Ed Salaj, a welder in the central maintenance department from 1964 to 1984. "Some people stole burning hoses for torches—Siamese hoses, we called them. I watched a fellow walk out one day who had just wrapped around his midsection, under his clothes, twenty-five feet of brand-new Siamese hoses. But he wrapped it too tight. When he got to the guard shanty, which was about two city blocks away, he was having trouble breathing, and we had to escort him, two guys on each side, past the guard shanty and down a little ways, and then we had to take his clothes off and help him take off the hoses.

"I knew one guy who would take brass bearings and throw them in the garbage dumpster. They'd go maybe twenty pounds apiece, solid brass. When nobody was looking, he'd throw some more in the dumpster. Management kept wondering: 'What the hell's going on? We're losing all these brass bearings.' He had an arrangement made with the guy who would take the garbage out. The dumpster would be dumped into a big truck. They would take it out of the plant, separate the garbage, and get the brass bearings out. He eventually got caught and got fired."

There were other forms of "getting it at the mill." One was to use materials, equipment, and labor for personal purposes. Carpenters, plumbers, or electricians would be dispatched on company time by executives to work on projects at their homes. Such assignments were called "home orders." New cabinets in an executive's wife's kitchen, new plumbing, new wiring, a new driveway, a new room, a new breezeway, a new garage—all this and more was done for executives by workers. In the 1960s, one executive had workers install a golf green at his home. He needed some work on his putting, he said. No one questioned these actions or the thinking that was behind them. The mill was there, so you used it.

Another form of corruption was taking time off from the job. Blue-collar workers sometimes slept during their shifts. White-collar workers had their own ways of escaping, the most important of which was golf. Since the days when Carnegie had enjoyed it so much, golf had become a way of life for executives. They would often come to the mill with their clubs in the trunks of their cars, do a morning's work, and then, by noon or one, slip over the hill to the Duquesne Golf Club or another of the six golf clubs in the Monongahela Valley, have lunch and a drink or two, put their golf shoes on, get onto the course for eighteen holes. Then they would head back to the clubhouse for drinks and perhaps dinner, and finally they would go home.

They were expected to do this if they wanted to get ahead, particularly if the boss was a golfer, like Dick Smith, a general superintendent at the Homestead Works in the 1960s. "I golfed until I retired, and then I quit," Ray Hornak said. "The only reason I golfed was that if they had a golf party and I didn't golf, I had to stay at work and cover for those other guys who went golfing. I said, 'Well, shit, I'm going with them.' I golfed for one reason—so I could get some time off, too. Golf was the most important thing in Dick Smith's life. You'd have a meeting, and the world could be falling apart, and he would talk about golf. And God help the guy who said, 'Well, who gives a shit about golf?' " Another executive, Jack Melvin, said, "Golf was sometimes more important than making steel."

Ray Hornak explained: "If you look at the 1950s and 1960s, they were heydays. The corporation was making money faster than it could count; it had more than it knew what to do with. So who cared if somebody stole some wrenches? People would say, 'What the hell. We'll buy some new stuff. We're doing all right. Let's take the day off and golf. It'll be all right.' People lost the understanding of what they were there for. People forgot that the only reason U.S. Steel was in business was to make money. That's the only reason US Steel was there. People got to the point where they thought, 'Well, hey, they're here for me.' It was just waste after waste after waste. If you bought something that didn't work, you'd say: 'To hell with it. Buy something else. We have the money.' And they did have the money at that time. I think everybody, including the hourly workers, the management, the higher-ups, became complacent. They said, 'We're going to be here forever. We're making money like there's no tomorrow.' "

Another problem that became apparent to both the corporation and the union was that the labor-management cooperation program, represented by the human relations committee, was not working well. In January 1960, after the 116-day strike of 1959, the union and the corporation announced the establishment of a human-relations research committee and a number of subcommittees "to study and recommend solutions of mutual problems" to establish "guides for the determination of equitable wage and benefit adjustments."

Everybody—the top union and company officials, the labor-relations experts, and the press—loved the idea. It was a blueprint for labor-management relations in the future.

Over time, however, workers and union leaders came to feel that the committee was undercutting the power of local and regional union officials and thus weakening the union. Foremen and supervisors, on the other hand, thought that the committee made it harder to make steel efficiently. There had developed a system of labor relations that was nothing short of Byzantine. Highly codified work rules and a complicated grievance system required the introduction of corporation lawyers at the plant level. It became practically impossible to fire a worker.

To avoid trouble, management adhered strictly to the contract, often at the expense of common sense. One day, a Homestead white-collar worker, William J. Gaughan, saw a foreman get into his car, drive half a mile through the plant, pick up two men working on a locomotive, and drive them to his office so the men could have lunch. The contract stipulated that the men must have lunch at an off-work site. The executives had their own practices to observe. To keep insurance costs down, for example, they would often send a guard in a car to the home of a worker who had been injured at work and bring him to the mill. He would sit for eight hours, reading newspapers or a book, then be taken home again. The corporation would pay his wages and get no work, but the injury would not be recorded as causing time off the job. Since there were many such cases, the amount saved was substantial.

After the passage of the Occupational Safety and Health Act of 1973, the corporation began to place more emphasis on safety. The law was designed to decrease the number of accidents and health hazards, yet it was corrupted by the way it was administered. Foremen would use real or imagined safety violations to write up—give discipline slips—to workers who had angered them. At the same time, the corporation insisted that every supervisor charged with overseeing safety matters write up a designated number of workers over a given period of time. If the quota was not reached, the supervisor's superiors assumed that he was not satisfactorily performing his job. As a result, a supervisor who had not achieved his write-up quota would ask workers with whom he was friendly for permission to write them up. Nothing of consequence would happen to the workers, and it was understood that the supervisor would then owe them something in return. This practice was known as "slipping people."

The safety issue was also used by workers to their own advantage. Ed Salaj said: "In some cases, when production got high and safety got a little lax, the men used safety in self-defense. You'd say: 'I can't do this job until we have a scaffold built, and I want it built out of the proper lumber according to the safety book—specially treated lumber painted green on the end, with a metal tag identifying the plank, and so on.' Or: 'I've got a ladder that's got a crack in the side rail. I can't use it. I've got to have another ladder.' Or: 'Get a motor inspector. We've got to have all these signal lights hooked up. Everybody sit down and, Smith, you go get the coffee.' And the foreman's mind would be blown, because he needed you to get that job done in a hurry, and you are sitting on your ass, but you are justified in sitting on your ass. We used that many times in retaliation for the management people having to give us a slip because of their quota system. In most cases, the bottom line of the safety program was keeping the employees safe, and it did do that. But each side used safety for their own purposes."

Extensive overmanning continued. "It's to your advantage to have a lot of guys under you. That moves your job class up," William J. Gaughan said. The overmanning occurred in both white-collar and blue-collar work, but it was always the union and the blue-collar workers whom the corporation singled out when it talked about the problem. "We over-hired, we overmanned," Ray Hornak said. "If it looked like you needed another man, you hired him. That was the thing that really started the steel business on the downslide, even though it was still the 1960s, the glory years." Marty Costa, a top executive for years, agreed. "We were loaded with people, too many people," he said. In fact, too many plants had been built. "It seemed like all they wanted to do was build plants, and it got to the point where it seemed like they didn't know what to do with them, really."

Despite its much-touted investment in new technologies, to achieve high profits the corporation emphasized the highest possible production, which led to poor quality and tremendous waste. "It didn't really matter how you got what you shipped," Marty Costa said. "We wasted millions of dollars just to produce the right numbers. You could sell whatever you made, regardless of the quality. A saying evolved: 'As long as it is hard and gray, ship it.' " Ray Hornak agreed: "Quality was never a big thing with US Steel, because US Steel had a lock on the market."

More and more, decision-making was taken from the mills and cen-tralized at the corporation's headquarters in Pittsburgh. "We started to lose control at the plant," said Jack Melvin, an executive in the structural mill in the 1970s and early 1980s and a supervisor at the works for thirty-seven years. "Everything had to be purchased through downtown. Down-town ran the show. When we lost that, lost doing things ourselves, we lost everything. You can't run a steel mill from a boardroom." General superintendents, under the thumb of "downtown," were fearful of dis-playing initiative. Decades before, the Homestead Works had been known for its bold, creative executives, but no more. And why should the executives be bold? As Melvin explained, "The general superintendent was never more than a phone call away from an ass-chewing."

The union was as undisciplined and uncreative, as locked into the corrupted system, as the corporation. It was a practice in many locals, including Homestead Local 1397, for shop stewards—the men who dealt with workers' grievances—to avoid work by taking "lost time"—they would report not to their jobs in the mill but to the union hall. Important union work could be performed on lost time, but often the time was spent sitting around the union hall, feet on the desk, shooting the breeze, or slipping off to a bar on Eighth Avenue, like Straka's or Lapko's, for beers. Men on lost time were paid from union funds at the same rate as if they had been paid at their jobs in the mill.

The national union, in downtown Pittsburgh, often had little connection with the people it was supposed to represent. Through the years, the presidents of the union, many of the regional directors, and the people with the most power, the lawyers, knew little about the steel business. None, after Murray, the first president, had any real interest in the steel towns. After he had left the union, McDonald had no hesitancy in expressing his disdain for the members of the union's executive board. Often, he said, union district directors failed to show up for meetings of the Human Relations Committee: "We had district directors involved who never showed up, not for one meeting." And when they did show up, they were often no help. McDonald rhetorically asked an interviewer, "Ever go to a steelworkers' executive board meeting with six drunken directors? Try to preside [with] . . . six guys blind drunk?" Furthermore he criticized the directors for lacking expertise on complicated matters. "Most of these directors did not have the technical ability, say in pensions and insurance and so forth. They were in water too deep for them." For that matter, he admitted, he also lacked knowledge in such areas. In fact the leaders were concerned almost exclusively with union politics and collective bargaining—keeping their jobs and providing more money and benefits for the men. "The benefits really got crazy," Marty Costa said. "They'd buy your shoes, glasses, teeth, all that stuff. And that stuff cost money."

The 1963 contract contained a new item—an extended-vacation plan that gave every employee with more than five years of service a thirteen-week vacation, with pay, every five years. The plan was extremely costly, and no other American industry had ever had anything like it. But it was, for the most part, not questioned; rather, it was widely praised. McDonald said that the plan would create twenty to twenty-five thousand new jobs, because new workers would have to be hired to replace workers who were on extended vacations. It did not turn out that way, however. The workforce was already bloated, so the plants needed no replacements for workers on vacation, while they were being paid for three months without working.

The plan was enormously wasteful, but it was hard to convince the workers of this. "We paid for that [the extended-vacation plan] by giving up something else or by not taking something else," Jack Bair, a strong union man, said late one frozen winter night in December 1986, during a strike against the corporation. He was sitting in a small trailer, thick with cigarette smoke, that Local 1397 had obtained to keep its picketers warm. But no industry can afford such a system, it was suggested. "Bullshit," Bair said. "We paid for it." The dozen other men in the trailer agreed with him.

When the corporation tried to address problems, the solutions were often poor ones. A striking example occurred early in the 1960s, when there was an effort to rectify the overmanning that had begun at the end of World War II and was steadily worsening. On November 2, 1962, a day that forever after would be called "Black Friday" in Homestead and the rest of the Monongahela Valley, several thousand technicians and middle-level managers who worked throughout the corporation were fired. At the Homestead Works alone, several hundred people, about 20 percent of the white-collar workforce, were fired. No warning had been given. There had not even been rumors.

It was payday, and the weekend was coming. People were in a cheerful mood. A number of white-collar workers were in the executive dining room of the general office building. Suddenly, several executives came in and began walking around the room, going up to one man after another and saying, "You—come with me." The men were taken to the office of a senior executive and told that they had been fired. They did not even get the chance to finish their lunch but were ordered to get their personal items and leave the works. Back pay and severance pay would be sent to them.

There were reasons for what the corporation did. The number of managers had expanded substantially, and now there were simply too many. But rather than warning people that reductions had to come, giving them time to find new work, seeing who might want to retire early and who might not, acting in a civilized fashion toward men who in many cases had given much of their working lives to the corporation, the men at the top simply put together lists of the people they wanted to eliminate and told them that they were through. And Black Friday was not the last time that the corporation acted in this manner.

Among those dismissed that day were some of the corporation's most capable and experienced people. Many of the executives had not gone to college but had worked their way up, learning steel the best way, by making it. The most senior men were earning as much as thirty-six thousand dollars a year. They were replaced by young college graduates, many of whom knew almost nothing about steelmaking. But they could be paid eighteen thousand dollars a year. The men who were dismissed were devastated, as were their families. Those who had not lost their jobs became fearful and suspicious. Trust began to erode. "That was the beginning of the breakup of the social compact, as far as I was concerned," said William J. Gaughan. Ray Hornak agreed: "It was horrendous. It never sat right." Said Marty Costa: "It was a son-of-a-bitching blow, boy. The valley never recovered."

19

OUT OF TOUCH

The ability to exude optimism and to ignore what was happening in the steel industry was embodied in Edgar B. Speer, who became president of the corporation in 1969. In June 1969, Speer, a handsome, black-haired man, a good talker, a back-patter, said that the corporation's share of the market, since 1968 down to 24.5 percent, would rise. He would see that the corporation expanded dramatically in domestic and international production. He conceded that the corporation had a poor reputation for servicing its customers and that it had shown no real interest in exports. All of this was changing, he claimed. The corporation would exploit its vast landholdings to maximize income—would engage in timber ventures, for example—and would enter joint ventures worldwide, particularly in minerals and other natural resources. Speer said:

US Steel has not been too aggressive about promoting offshore business. But that's changed now. I think that our performance over the last year shows we're damn well interested in the export business. . . . [T]he corporation now has a much tougher posture than before in competing in the world steel market. Some of the steel that we shipped offshore certainly has rattled the timbers of some of the traditional exporters of steel worldwide. . . . If there's money to be made in it, you can believe the corporation will get in the business.

The Vietnam War, like the Korean War, increased production and domestic and overseas profits, as had every previous war, beginning with the Civil War. Foreign companies continued to send substantial amounts of steel to the United States, but domestic production was rising dramatically, from 70.6 million tons in 1961 to 91 million tons in 1966.

Dissenting views were rare. One of them came from Clarence B. Randall, a crotchety but honest fellow who, in July 1963, seven years after he had retired as chairman of the Inland Steel Company, wrote a piece for *The New York Times Magazine* called "Business, Too, Has Its Ivory Towers." American industrial leaders, Randall said, were isolated, and the consequence of this was that when a crisis came—as crises inevitably did—the leaders were not prepared to confront it: "As a man's authority increases, so do the barriers that cut him off from direct contact with the world about him. After he reaches the very top, he is seldom seen in public and seldom heard. He becomes a myth . . . which is unwholesome both for the man and for his company."

First came special cars "chartered by the year for the exclusive use of a smug little well-heeled group." Then, once he became chief executive officer of his corporation, came the chauffeured limousine to "conserve his time and effort," and "gone forever was the boisterous elbow-rubbing with friends who might hold contrary opinions." Then came the executive plane, which "intensified his withdrawal":

Wherever he traveled, he spent the entire period closeted with his staff and upon arrival plunged with them into a waiting limousine. Gone were the chance encounters. No more taunts from the taxi driver about how bad things were, no more chatter with the man ahead of him at the gate, no more locked-in sessions with a seatmate on the plane who forced him to listen whether he wanted to or not. He was never to be anonymous again. Never really one of the people. Just always the big shot whether he wanted to be or not.

As chief officer, he does almost nothing on his own. All day, every day, he is looked after by a highly competent staff. . . . Only the seniors in his organization get through to him. Lacking time to read the newspapers thoroughly, he comes to rely upon digests prepared for him by his public-relations staff and unconsciously he is likely to absorb their opinions, too.

In the meetings of his board of directors, it is difficult for him to develop genuine independent thinking from the members, no matter how hard he tries. Many of those present are company officers, and it is doubtful that they will deliberately antagonize him. Others are what might be called professional directors. They are on many boards, and their opinions tend to become orthodox. Were he to propose a real outsider for board membership, such as a university president, who could be counted upon to scrutinize sharply the social implications of corporate decisions, there would be a general lifting of eyebrows.

Here are men of unusual ability. They have reached their high position through the most rigorous competitive tests and possess proven qualities of leadership. Yet their talents are devoted almost exclusively to the advancement of self-interest as distinguished from participation in solving the broad questions that currently challenge the United States.

Randall's views made no impact.

II

In the mid-1960s, the union faced a problem—politics. David J. McDonald, a founder of the union, union president for more than a decade, friend of presidents and frequent visitor to the White House, was challenged for the union presidency. More than that, this time the challenge was not by a nobody, an outsider, like Donald C. Rarick, who had opposed McDonald in 1957, but by one of the union's top officers, I. W. Abel, the secretary-treasurer, whom McDonald had selected in 1952, in part because he was a quiet fellow who, McDonald felt, would not stab him in the back. Abel was, as McDonald wrote years later, "a humorless man of medium stature and diffident manner." He "looked at the world solemnly from behind a pair of heavy eyeglasses. I had chosen him—as a compromise candidate because he was both inoffensive and unknown—as my secretary-treasurer when I had been elected president of the United Steelworkers of America. . . . He had served quietly, and without any particular distinction, all those years."

In the early 1960s, after Rarick's defeat, McDonald felt politically secure. Then, in 1964, McDonald's secretary brought him a copy of the

Golden Lodge News, a newspaper published by the union local at the Timken Roller Bearing plant in Canton, Ohio, Abel's home district. The paper was folded open to an editorial that said that McDonald had lost touch with the rank and file and that the steelworkers must return to the philosophy of Philip Murray. There was one man who could bring that about, the editorial said, and that was I. W. Abel. McDonald was not worried. He had gotten the boys everything they had said they wanted —high wages, company-paid pensions and insurance, a form of guaranteed annual wage, an extended-vacation plan. America's steelworkers were the highest-paid industrial workers in world history.

McDonald called Abel into his office and asked whether he had seen the editorial. Abel said that he had seen it and had been shocked. He had no idea why these people were putting his name forth like this. They hadn't talked to him. Abel told McDonald that he did not want McDonald's job. "That's what I thought, Abe," McDonald said, and flew off to his vacation home in Palm Springs. The vacation was interrupted when Secretary of Labor Willard Wirtz telephoned. President Johnson would be campaigning in the Pittsburgh area, and McDonald was needed to ensure a big turnout. McDonald chartered a plane to Pittsburgh, worked hard, and helped produce a crowd of twenty-five thousand people at the airport to greet the president. Johnson and McDonald then motored downtown in an open car. Johnson made a speech and then the two men walked the streets on the South Side, McDonald's home district, shaking hands with steelworkers. They then stopped at David J. McDonald Hall, Local 1272, where the president was warmly greeted by more steelworkers and made a brief speech. It was said that more than 750,000 people turned out to greet Johnson that day, a turnout due in large part to the authority that McDonald possessed as union president. Yet, though McDonald had a high reputation in national labor and political circles, the view of him was beginning to change in the steel towns. There were rumblings that he was not paying attention to union matters, that he had gone high-hat, that he was hobnobbing with the upper crust.

McDonald continued to hear rumors that Abel was considering running. The vice-president of the union, Howard Hague, an old hand at office intrigue, a man who recognized a conspiracy when he saw one, began to drop off copies of speeches that Abel was making at district conferences. A number of times Hague dropped into McDonald's office after the business day to say that he believed Abel was building a campaign operation and planned to run. McDonald laughed the warnings off. Abel, he thought, had no time for or interest in anything but narrow issues, bread-and-butter union matters, whereas he himself was concerned with broad issues like international trade and national politics.

The truth, of course, was that Abel was seriously considering running for president. He was supposed to be the number-two man in the union, but he was unimportant, fenced off from key decisions, and he knew it. His office was a few feet from McDonald's, but the two men hardly ever talked. He was disturbed by many aspects of the way the union was run, including the influence wielded by the general counsel, first Arthur Goldberg and then his successor, David E. Feller. Abel and some other union leaders also criticized the human-relations approach to bargaining. This was not collective bargaining, they said, but negotiation by a union elite. They were concerned about allegedly inferior wage and benefit settlements, and about the erosion of what they saw as the union's only authentic weapon—the right to strike.

McDonald went on the offensive. At the union's convention in September 1964, in Atlantic City, he announced a new bargaining goal—"total job security" for all steelworkers. Under this plan, steelworkers would never be unemployed. The plan was achievable, McDonald said. And it could be destroyed only from within, by petty internal politics. President Johnson also spoke, praising McDonald. "Your human-relations committee has established a fruitful pattern of day-in, day-out relations between employer and union," he told the convention. "You have moved steel toward an era of creative, constructive bargaining, recognizing that labor and management have a common stake in each other's welfare, and in the health of the entire economy." There was more praise for McDonald, including two staged standing ovations. Abel was allowed to play no role in the convention. He was even prevented from reading the annual financial report.

By early October 1964, Abel had made up his mind that he would run. Later that month, Joseph Molony, a district director in Buffalo, New York, who was angry at McDonald because of his frequent private negotiations with R. Conrad Cooper, the corporation's labor-relations director, agreed to run for vice-president. Another union official, Walter J. Burke, agreed to run for secretary-treasurer. On November 5, Abel sent letters to the more than thirty-two hundred local unions saying that he intended to run for president. On November 6, he announced to the press that he would oppose McDonald. The nomination process then began, and on December 21, 1964, the official returns were announced. Abel had received the nominations of 1,310 locals, McDonald 904. Each was nominated, and it was clear that McDonald was in for a tough race. The question was whether he recognized it.

The campaign began in earnest in January 1965, and it was one of the most spirited election campaigns in American labor history. Even today, when union people get together for a drink or two, and the talk turns to the steelworkers' union, they sometimes tell stories of the McDonald-Abel campaign. The main tactic of the Abel forces was to denigrate McDonald's "tuxedo unionism"—his penchant for high living, his hanging around with big shots, his home in Palm Springs. McDonald, they said, had lost touch with the members, always a sin in trade unionism and an excellent charge for an insurgent to make against an incumbent whether it is true or not—although the truth is that most union leaders, regulars or reformers, have little contact with the rank and file once they get into office.

McDonald and those who supported him countered that Abel was strike-happy, that if he was elected the industry would be beset with strikes. Beyond that, McDonald did little hard campaigning. He remained an effective campaigner when he wanted to campaign. He was still a big, handsome man and a terrific speechmaker when he was on. But he seemed to believe that he could not lose. He had never been tough, and he had been made soft by the high life. An assistant once said that when McDonald began to read a newspaper, he always turned first to the amusement section and the gossip columns to see what was going on among his Broadway and Hollywood acquaintances. He continued to party and put away the sauce. Many people knew this, although it never got into the press. It was said in the union that McDonald had two enemies—I. W. Abel and I. W. Harper.

Late in the campaign, attempting to refute the charge of "tuxedo unionism," the McDonald forces distributed leaflets showing Abel wearing a tuxedo. The photograph had been taken at a party given by the union at the Touchdown Club in 1958 by Nordy Hoffman, McDonald's legislative and political director. It had originally shown some thirty men in tuxedos, McDonald and Abel among them, but McDonald had been cropped out.

Like many unions, the steelworkers had almost no history of contested elections. Murray had ruled uncontested for sixteen years, McDonald for thirteen. Even the Rarick campaign had not been a contested election in the true sense. The 35 percent of the vote that Rarick received was regarded as a fluke. The McDonald-Abel campaign was different. It was the major topic of conversation in Pittsburgh and the steel towns, and in the other unions. It was also consuming the union. The beginning of the 1965 negotiations with the corporation and the other steel companies was postponed until February 9.

Almost everyone seemed to oppose Abel—the industry, the government, the press. The corporation liked McDonald, and so did President Johnson. You knew where Dave was coming from. The last thing the industry or the government wanted was upheaval in the steel industry, particularly with the expansion of the Vietnam War. The press loved McDonald, saying that he had brought maturity and stability to the union. Abel was branded a radical and his call for democracy within the union and for vigilant unionism were portrayed as extreme, as harking to the 1930s. *The New York Times* said in a 1964 editorial:

In the last four years, the establishment of a human-relations committee representing the union and eleven major companies has taken the crisis element out of bargaining in steel. Top leaders on both sides have met on a year-round basis to discuss the complex problems of changing technology, foreign competition, and worker needs. Agreements have been made without the pressure of strike deadlines at levels well within the administration's guideposts for curbing wage-price inflation.

Now there are indications that the HRC will be pushed out of any role of consequence in the wage talks scheduled to begin. . . . A reversion to the old wage-price spiral and the climate of the perpetual strike would damage the steelworkers as much as it would the industry and the national economy.

On February 7, 1965, McDonald and Abel appeared on the television program *Meet the Press,* which was broadcast from Washington and moderated by Lawrence E. Spivak. John Herling, the labor journalist, later recounted what happened. McDonald by now had retained public-relations specialists, and while he was rehearsing he suggested using a light touch: "I'll say to Spivak when he introduces me as 'Mr. McDonald,' 'If I knew that we were going to be formal, Larry (I'll call him Larry), I would have worn my tuxedo." There were no laughs. An assistant said, "That stinks. Don't do it." The show began this way.

SPIVAK: Mr. McDonald, you have charged your opponent Mr. Abel with being strike-happy. Since 1952, during the term of your presidency, you have had two strikes. Why do you think he is more likely to start a strike than you are?

MCDONALD: You know, you kind of amuse me, calling me Mr. McDonald, Larry, because if I knew you were going to be so formal, I would have worn my tux.

SPIVAK: Do you mind answering the question now?

McDonald's handlers, in the control room, were grim-faced.

It was an exceedingly close election. On April 30, the international tellers made the official results known—Abel, 308,910, McDonald 298,768. Abel was the victor by 10,142 votes, a margin no larger than the number of workers in a single good-sized steel mill. After the returns were in, McDonald appeared before the press. John Herling described the scene in his book *Right to Challenge*: McDonald entered the room at the William Penn Hotel in Pittsburgh, tight-lipped and surrounded by retainers. Suddenly he saw Joe Murray, Philip Murray's adopted son, whom McDonald considered an enemy. McDonald's face turned a deep red. "You, out!" he yelled at Murray. He gestured toward his bodyguard and driver, Charlie Barranco. "Charlie—out!" he said. Murray challenged Barranco to try to throw him out.

McDonald seemed to realize that a brawl would benefit Abel, not himself. "All right, Charlie, forget it," he said. He explained to the reporters that he was merely standing up for the First Amendment, that he wanted only press people at his press conference. He then smiled at the television people. "Ready to roll?" he asked. "One, two, three . . . ten." Then, once again the smooth professional, he read a statement in which he said that he would challenge the election results.

A few days went by, and McDonald changed his mind. He said that for the good of the union he would not challenge the election. But Herling suggests that he was trying to negotiate a profitable exit. He demanded the title of president emeritus plus full salary and expenses and an automobile. But Abel said that the pension of twenty-five thousand dollars a year provided for ex-presidents was sufficient. McDonald gave up. In June, in a change-of-command ceremony, McDonald, silver-haired, handsomely suited, elegant in manner, gave to Abel the president's gavel and the keys to the president's desk. "May I say to my beloved steelworkers goodbye and God bless you," McDonald said. "I officially declare my term of office ended."

Not long afterward, Abel decided to open his desk. He took out the key that McDonald had given him. It did not fit. Finally, someone got the desk open. It was empty. It was estimated that together the candidates had spent $500,000 to $750,000, raised within the union, on the campaign. It is likely that McDonald outspent Abel six to one.

McDonald was crushed by his defeat, but after a time he got over it. His cynicism and self-importance helped. Calm down, he told himself. What can you expect from people, from politicians, from a bunch of steelworkers? The executives sympathized with him. Poor Dave, they said. The bastards treated him rough.

McDonald and his wife left Pittsburgh and took up residence in their home in Palm Springs. His autobiography, *Union Man,* published in

1969, was one-sided but blunt and engaging. He went to the Vatican on a mission for President Johnson, but it was a second-echelon assignment, and he felt humiliated. In 1966, he was invited by some delegates to address the steelworkers' convention. He thought of going but stayed away. The hell with them, he said. In 1968, returning to the Republicanism of his youth, four decades before, he supported Nixon for president.

He died on August 8, 1979. His obituary made the front page of *The New York Times* (Eugene V. Debs's obituary had been on page 25 when he died on October 20, 1926) and was featured prominently in other papers, all of which described him as a labor statesman. McDonald would have been pleased.

III

Upon taking office, Abel began to institute some of the reforms he had talked of during the campaign. He canceled the twenty-thousand-dollar-a-year suite that the union under McDonald had maintained at the plush Madison Hotel in Washington; eliminated McDonald's two Cadillacs; reassigned—at a drastically reduced salary—Charlie Barranco, McDonald's doorman, chauffeur, and bodyguard; fired other bodyguards; and eliminated three secretaries from the president's staff. He invited Walter P. Reuther, president of the United Automobile Workers, whom Philip Murray and McDonald had detested, to speak at the 1966 convention.

Slowly, however, a strange phenomenon occurred. Abel was not an autocrat and a lover of the high life, as McDonald had been. He did not have McDonald's Hollywood style. But it was not long before he was being seduced by his position, by being close to big people. What Clarence Randall had said of his fellow steel executives was true for Abel, and for many union executives at any time. He was becoming increasingly remote from the union members and from the mills. He was becoming a big man, and being a big man, he realized, was a lot of fun. He was becoming like McDonald.

In December 1965, Abel was elected, in a pro-forma vote, to an AFL-CIO vice-presidency and thus became a member of its executive council, replacing McDonald. George Meany, the AFL-CIO president, had spoken warmly of McDonald during the election campaign. Now he saw that Abel could be useful to him and to the AFL-CIO, and he began to appoint Abel to key positions. Meany was feuding with Reuther, and he began to confer with Abel on important matters, often in advance of decisions, thus undercutting Reuther. Abel was flattered. Here he was, good old Abe, the district director from Canton, Ohio, the secretary-treasurer who hardly ever spoke, being sought out for advice by Meany, the top man in American labor. In February 1967, Reuther resigned as an AFL-CIO vice-president, in part because he coveted Meany's position but also because he regarded Meany as too conservative. Meany appointed Abel to replace Reuther as chairman of the economic-policy committee.

Meany began to take Abel on trips to the White House to chat with President Johnson, and Abel began to be invited to White House dinners. In 1967, at Meany's suggestion, Abel was appointed by Johnson to the prestigious Kerner Commission, charged with investigating the racial violence that had erupted in American cities. Then, also at Meany's suggestion, Johnson made him a member of the American delegation to the United Nations, headed by the former general counsel of the steelworkers' union, Arthur Goldberg.

Abel began to speak warmly of the doctrine of workplace cooperation, despite his call for militant and democratic unionism during his campaign against McDonald. On Labor Day, 1967, Abel declared that unions and companies must explore "the causes of industrial peace." The Associated Press reported, "The leadership of the steelworkers is considering a plan to surrender its right to strike in the 1968 contract talks. . . . I. W. Abel is pictured as the chief architect of the plan." Abel denied this, but then he made the same misstep that McDonald had made. He pushed through an increase in dues from five dollars a month to ten dollars. It was not long before some union leaders began to doubt him. Abel was often absent from his union duties. He was getting cozy with the bosses. What was going on? Early in 1968, Donald C. Rarick, who had run unsuccessfully against McDonald in 1957, said that he would run against Abel in 1969. But not long afterward, he died. Then Abel was challenged by another candidate, Emil E. Narick, a staff lawyer in the union's Pittsburgh office. Abel won the election, in February 1969, receiving 257,000 votes to 181,000 for Narick. But 181,000 votes was a substantial show of support for a largely unknown union lawyer.

Meanwhile, a committee of union and industry representatives continued meeting secretly, to work out a new kind of labor-management arrangement—a no-strike agreement. Three officials and two lawyers from the union, two executives of United States Steel, and one executive each from Bethlehem Steel and Republic Steel met twenty times between June 1972 and March 1973. At no time were union members informed that the meetings were occurring or that a no-strike agreement was being discussed.

There was, however, much public talk at this time about the old issue of imports, which had been simmering since the 1959 strike. Jobs were declining in the steel industry, and imports were an easy scapegoat. The industry and the union produced a movie called *Where's Joe?* It was shown on company time to all unionized employees. In Homestead, it was shown in the auditorium of the Carnegie Library. The corporation provided buses to take the workers there.

The movie hammered home the theme that the loss of jobs was caused by imports. In addition, Edwin H. Gott, then the corporation's chairman, appeared in it. He said that "hedge-buying" by companies that used steel—the stockpiling of imported steel in anticipation of strikes—was harming the industry. Unless imports could be curtailed, more workers—represented by a character named Joe—would lose their jobs. Abel also had a role in the movie. He said, "In my judgment, we must find a way to bargain our contractual differences peacefully and satisfactorily."

In late March 1973, the union's six hundred local presidents were directed to report to Pittsburgh but given no reason why. They met on March 28. The speculation had been correct. The union—an organization forged in violent confrontation—was giving up its most precious right, the right to strike. The union's executive board first saw the document detailing the agreement that same day. Quick meetings in which inadequate materials must be hastily studied are an old trick in American unions. The meeting lasted a day and a half. On March 29, the local presidents were directed to vote without asking for instructions from their members. The agreement was approved.

Later that day, "the experimental negotiating agreement" was announced. It prohibited strikes and lockouts. In exchange, the 350,000 steelworkers were guaranteed a 3 percent wage increase each year, as well as cost-of-living increases and incentive wages. Wages could be increased above 3 percent but not below. Differences between the industry and the union that could not be otherwise resolved would be submitted to binding arbitration. The agreement also called for a bonus payment of $150 to each worker. Some said that the payment was, in effect, a bribe. To help get the approval of the local presidents, Abel had inserted a clause that authorized local unions to strike over local issues. But this right, it would be made clear in the coming years, was so limited that it essentially did not exist. There was no vote by the union's members, because the union's constitution did not permit them to vote on labor-management agreements.

The agreement was praised across the country. R. Heath Larry, a vice-chairman of United States Steel and the chief negotiator for the industry, said that it "should work for the benefit of the employees, the company, its customers, and the nation." Abel called it "an unprecedented experiment that we think will prove there is a better way for labor and management to negotiate contracts." Both men said that the agreement would mean a reduction in steel imports, because, with a guarantee against strikes and lockouts, steel purchasers would not import as much steel in anticipation of shutdowns. They claimed that imports had eliminated 150,000 jobs and layoffs had totaled about 100,000 following the 1971 agreement. Now, they said, all that would stop.

The New York Times declared in an editorial that "the pioneering agreement" was "a breakthrough toward rationality in collective bargaining that could benefit the entire American economy," and that other companies and unions should follow the lead of the steel companies and the steelworkers' union: "The security of American jobs, the stability of the dollar, and the competitiveness of American products in world markets will all gain if labor and management follow steel's lead in substituting reason for economic force in industrial relations."

In 1973, the union, its treasury full and the future of the steel industry bright, purchased a new headquarters in downtown Pittsburgh, a tall, handsome building in the Gateway Center, an area revitalized by business and philanthropic interests. The old offices, in the Commonwealth Building, were no longer good enough.

Three years later, the union made another purchase, buying what became known as Linden Hall, a 785-acre estate with a thirty-five-room mansion, southeast of Pittsburgh. It had been the residence of the widow of a coal and coke magnate, and after she died it had been turned into a country club, with a swimming pool, tennis courts, and a golf course. The union now constructed a seventy-five-room motel and a number of classrooms, and converted the estate into a vacation retreat and training center. Critics called it a playground for Abel and his associates. A decade before, he and his campaign had condemned McDonald for engaging in tuxedo unionism. Now they had their own club and were enjoying some tuxedo unionism of their own.

Abel would turn sixty-five in 1977, and the union constitution required the president to step aside at that age. History now repeated itself, for Abel's reign ended with an election that was at least as raucous as the one in 1965.

Abel and his associates began looking for a successor, as is the custom in American unions, and in mid-1976 they picked Lloyd McBride, a district leader from St. Louis. A lackluster, soft-spoken, mild-looking man of sixty, he was a lifelong union bureaucrat who, he admitted, would have been "content to be a journeyman labor leader." McBride told those who asked him to run that he did not believe he was qualified to be president. They replied that he was more qualified than Abel had been, and they probably were correct.

The Abel forces faced one major difficulty, however. McBride was going to be challenged—by an ambitious, charismatic, thirty-seven-year-old district director from Chicago, Edward Sadlowski. Already a legend in the union, Sadlowski was an insurgent who had grown up studying the labor movement and dreaming of becoming not only president of the steelworkers' union but perhaps the new John L. Lewis. He had gone to work at the United States Steel Corporation's South Works at the age of eighteen. Seven years later, at age twenty-five, he had been elected president of Local 65, the South Works local, which had a long history of fractiousness. He was the youngest local president in the union. Next, he ran for director of District 31, accusing the top leadership of being unimaginative, conservative, and out of touch with the members. By winning the election he became the youngest district director and director of the largest district. Sadlowski and his "Fight Back" movement fast gained a following within the union, and in 1976 he announced that he would challenge McBride.

Sadlowski was new, smart, creative, and aggressive, and his campaign attracted a substantial group of younger skilled workers and liberal activists who saw in him a way to reform their moribund union and perhaps the entire American labor movement. But Sadlowski, who had an immense ego and a short temper, often refused to listen to his staff. Instead, he would bark out what he wanted done, and expect them to do it. Many of those men and women today speak only lukewarmly of him.

Sadlowski was a charmer when he wanted to be. He had a splendid routine with newspaper people. A reporter would go to his home, a modest frame house—a typical worker's house—in South Chicago, near the South Works. Sadlowski would give an interview and then take the reporter on a tour of the South Works and of Local 65's Hilding Anderson Hall, named after one of the workers killed by police in the Memorial Day Massacre at Republic Steel, in 1937. He would drive the reporter to the site of the massacre. They would stop at a restaurant or tavern for a glass or two of the best with some real steelworkers. Back at his home, he would show the reporter his library of books and articles on labor and working-class history, and maybe play some Paul Robeson or Pete Seeger records.

Reporters had never seen anything like this—a real working-class stiff who read books and listened to Robeson and Seeger records. They would return to their offices and bang out the most adulatory stories, complete with quotes from Sadlowski's admirers, like Studs Terkel, the Chicago radio personality and writer; Joseph Rauh, Jr., the Washington attorney and civil libertarian; and Arthur Schlesinger, Jr., the historian. The labor journalist John Herling, who had so capably profiled David J. McDonald in his book *Right to Challenge* in 1973, wrote in the *Washington Post* in 1974, "A new labor star has been born. He is Edward Sadlowski, thirty-six, a rangy steelworker with the gift of hard-hitting eloquence." This of a man who through much of his life had had to struggle with a belly that one might expect to see on a bear entering a cave to begin hibernating.

The Sadlowski-McBride contest attracted extensive attention. Sadlowski frightened the corporation, the other steel companies, and the government, as Abel had a decade before, but Sadlowski was not strike-happy. He merely wanted to reinvigorate the union. He condemned the no-strike agreement and accused Abel and McBride—who, he said, was Abel's surrogate—of having collaborated with management. In reply, McBride, egged on by his staff, engaged in some old-fashioned red-baiting, calling Sadlowski a tool of the left. Of course, in the traditional manner of red-baiters, he did this obliquely. "The only thing I've said about Ed is that he has not repudiated the support he's getting from *The Daily World* and other left-wing groups," McBride said. "I've never said that he's a Communist."

Another issue was the financial support Sadlowski was receiving from outside the union, mostly from liberal individuals and institutions. This was a spurious criticism. McBride was putting the arm on the union's staff people and local and national officials, who knew that they had to contribute to the campaign if they wanted to keep their jobs, and he was raising far more money than Sadlowski. Since Sadlowski could get little money from inside the union, he had to go outside.

Insurgents are generally detested in the labor movement, and the leaders of many other unions rallied to McBride, even though it was the custom, going back to Samuel Gompers and the creation of the American Federation of Labor in the 1880s, that one union did not intervene in another union's elections. Lane Kirkland, then secretary-treasurer and later president of the AFL-CIO, made a remark to the effect that you would think, if you believed what the press said about Sadlowski, that if you wanted to run a union, all you had to do was sit around your basement and play Robeson records. Many editorial-writers also supported McBride, saying of Sadlowski, as they had of Abel when he had run against McDonald, that he was a radical who wanted to return to an old-fashioned, outdated, wasteful kind of unionism.

A turning point came when Sadlowski gave an interview to *Penthouse* magazine. Perhaps he never should have given it, but he was a democratic man who believed that one newspaper or magazine was as good as the next, and that a lot more steelworkers probably looked at *Penthouse* than at *The New York Times.* On a campaign swing through the upper Midwest, he sat in a hotel room in Lansing, Michigan, and chatted at length with a *Penthouse* reporter. He said nothing particularly radical. What he said was thoughtful and was in the interest of steelworkers faced with a changing world economy. But his words created a firestorm.

Sadlowski was a true working-class intellectual, and thus he was also a romantic. He had once asked a reporter from *The New York Times,* "How many Mozarts are working in steel mills?" It was a legitimate question. There are many men and women in steel mills who might have been Mozarts, and Marie Curies, and James Baldwins, and Jonas Salks, too. But this kind of romanticism, this notion that workers had the potential to do whatever their talents allowed them, got Sadlowski into trouble.

The *Penthouse* interview appeared in January 1977, a month before the end of the voting. Sadlowski was quoted as saying that a substantial number of American steelworkers had already lost their jobs, and that jobs in the industry might be reduced further by new technologies and world market conditions. This would be acceptable if the men and women who lost their jobs were retrained at the industry's expense to perform work that was cleaner, safer, and perhaps more interesting than their work in steel mills.

"Working forty hours a week in a steel mill drains the lifeblood of a man," Sadlowski said. "Nothing is to be gotten from that. Society has nothing to show for it but waste." There were workers in steel mills "who are full of poems," open-hearth men, crane operators, rollers, clerks who had the ability to become writers, lawyers, doctors. They had not had the necessary opportunity, or had not recognized it, as young people. All that was needed now was to give them the opportunity. They and the nation would benefit. In fact, he said, the ultimate goal of the labor movement should be that no one ought to have to do work of the kind required by furnaces and open hearths. The number of American steelworkers had been reduced from 520,000 to 400,000 between 1962 and 1977 and could be reduced further, perhaps to 100,000, as long as those who were displaced were given access to training that would allow them to perform meaningful work.

The publication of the interview rocked the campaign. Neither

McBride nor most of his staff would have been capable of expressing such thoughts. The minute they saw the interview, they started making copies of it and sending them to locals across the country. Sadlowski wanted to take away workers' jobs, they said. Many union members accepted this interpretation. Sadlowski's campaign manager in the Youngstown, Ohio, district, John Barbero, said that when the interview came out, "the Sadlowski stickers came off the hardhats."

The election was conducted on February 8, 1977, and the votes were tabulated that day and the next. The final vote was 328,861 for McBride, 249,281 for Sadlowski. The defeat was devastating for Sadlowski. His supporters drifted off to other pursuits, and his movement eventually fell apart. It was a major setback in efforts to reform the steelworkers' union and the American labor movement. Many blamed Sadlowski—his ego, his temper, his informal style of campaigning, his dislike of organization. But though he could be vexing, he was more intelligent, in closer contact with working people, and better informed about the steel industry than McBride, or anyone else the union establishment could have put up.

Sadlowski's funk continued. His weight problem grew worse. He accepted the position of sub-district director of District 31, working for a man who held the job that he had once held. He went to law school for a time but then dropped out. I saw him at the steelworkers' convention in August 1982. He was lumbering down the boardwalk in Atlantic City, a number of pals trailing in his wake. I walked up, said hello, and told him that I would like to talk to him about what he was doing and write a piece on him. "Fuck you," he said, and stalked off.

IV

Everyone continued to say that the steel industry faced a prosperous future. In April 1977, the steel companies, led by the corporation, and the union negotiated a contract that made what McBride called "a start" toward the goal of lifetime job security. The contract provided nothing of the sort, but it sounded good, and it was played up in the press. What it did provide, in addition to a ninety-cent wage increase over three years, was increased unemployment-insurance benefits, pensions, and other benefits that, it was said, would cushion the impact of layoffs on workers.

Initially, the local presidents, led by the still-active Sadlowski forces, rejected the contract by 148 to 43. Then Abel, still president until Mc-Bride's inauguration on June 1, called for another vote, and it was approved by 193 to 99. Many of the six hundred presidents did not vote even once, because they had left Washington, D.C., the site of the voting, to be with their families for the Easter holiday. They left, too, because they believed that they had no real say on the issue. If they rejected the contract, which covered 340,000 workers, the two sides, under the experimental negotiating agreement, would have had it implemented through binding arbitration. There was, of course, no vote by the members.

J. Bruce Johnston, the corporation's director of employee relations, shook hands with Abel. Both men were ebullient and smiling broadly. McBride, the president-elect, said that the agreement guaranteed security to all steelworkers with more than twenty years of service.

A hundred years of American industrialism were coming apart, but almost no one could see it. The money was pouring into the companies. The pay was good, for white-collar and blue-collar men alike, and so were the benefits and other perquisites. But if you looked, what was happening was frightening.

The corporation had not invested in the Homestead Works since the completion, in 1969, of a stainless steel facility. Plans for electric furnaces were drawn up, but nothing came of them. Repairs were made instead of purchasing new equipment like bearings, hoses, and clamps. Maintenance workers were let go. "We were in 'the harvest mode' at Homestead," Ray Hornak said. "Take everything out of it you can get and abandon the rest. And when you just take out, and don't put anything in, well, pretty soon you're holding things together with baling wire.

"It really dawned on me about 1972, when the new U.S. Steel Building was built. I was assistant division superintendent of slab and plate. The 160-inch mill, which was of 1937 design, was a good plate mill, but we didn't have enough power or enough strength, so we submitted a plan to beef up the finishing mill. It would have cost fifty-nine million dollars and made us competitive with anybody in the world; fifty-nine million dollars is a lot of money, but it was worth it. But when they put that U.S. Steel Building up instead, I said, 'Uh-oh, we're finished,' because we would not be competitive with the likes of Gary [Indiana] and Sparrows Point [Maryland]. They were putting money in, and we weren't. We were being told, 'Do the best with what you have.' "

Ed Salaj said: "You'd have a broken drive shaft and you'd weld it, then weld it a second, third, fourth, and fifth time. You shouldn't weld things a second, third, fourth, and fifth time. We did, routinely. They didn't buy a lot of good spare parts. I saw shafts run without bearings and grease. They just kept them going and let the next turn worry about them.

"I saw a situation in a gag press—a beam straightener. They put two new rolls in the middle of it so that the beam would come up on the rolls and move back and forth. But the two rolls were new, and everything else was bad, and the beam got up on the two new rolls and couldn't move off them because the other parts of the table had all sunk. They had to take the two new rolls out and put the old two rolls back in that had worn down. They had to rebuild the whole table to do it right. They did that at a later stage, rebuilt the whole table. But they were in such a hurry that they threw the concrete foundations together and they crumbled. They started up the gag press too soon, didn't give the concrete a chance to cure, and the foundation crumbled.

"I did a lot of buildup work, like putting teeth on gears that had been worn away. You sat there for hours building up little pads of weld higher and higher, and you formed a tooth. It wasn't a nice tooth and not perfect. It was just a pile of weld, and it met the next pile of weld in the tooth, tooth touching tooth, until the shaft rotated and allowed the table roll to move. I did much of that, on top of cranes, in gag presses, in mill sections—things that should not have been done, but we did them. As things got bad, nobody could get any money. You stole parts from different parts of the mill."

Homestead was not the only mill having trouble. In July 1977, the Alan Wood Company, a small, distinguished old steel manufacturer near Philadelphia, went into bankruptcy and was compelled to auction off its plant piece by piece because a single buyer could not be located.

In August 1977, the Bethlehem Steel Corporation said that it would lay off thirty-five hundred workers at its famous Lackawanna Works, just below Buffalo, New York, and another thirty-five hundred at the Johnstown Works in Pennsylvania, both dating from the earliest days of the American steel industry. At about the same time, the Armco Steel Corporation announced the elimination of several hundred jobs at its Middletown, Ohio, plant. Another four thousand workers were laid off at the United States Steel Corporation's South Works, in Chicago, and at the Inland Steel plant near Chicago.

In September 1977, Youngstown Sheet and Tube said that it would eliminate five thousand jobs at its Campbell Works, in Youngstown, Ohio, built in 1900. United States Steel announced plans to consolidate operations at its Youngstown Works, in Ohio, eliminating hundreds of jobs there. The corporation denied speculation that it would close the Youngstown Works and also the McDonald Mills, in McDonald, Ohio, ten miles up the Mahoning Valley from Youngstown.

The reasons advanced for the closings varied. Some companies blamed the federal government's new antipollution regulations and traditional challenges to proposed price increases. Others said that plants had to be closed because they were antiquated. Lloyd McBride, the union's president, agreed with industry executives who blamed imports, which, he told Congress, had caused the loss of sixty thousand jobs in recent years.

Edgar B. Speer, the corporation's president, remained upbeat. He said in 1978 that plants should be built overseas, and that the corporation planned to begin construction of a $3.5 billion facility, incorporating the latest in iron and steel technologies, in Conneaut, Ohio. And in May 1979, industry analysts predicted a steel shortage by the mid-1980s.

Union officials saw the same bright future. One day, some years later, I was sitting in the office of Ronnie Weisen, president of Homestead Local 1397. I happened to glance at an open closet where there were several boxes overflowing with brochures. "What's that stuff?" I asked.

"It's nothing. Bullshit from the international," Weisen said. He told me to take what I wanted, so I gathered up twenty or twenty-five pieces, all I had room for in my briefcase. The materials had been prepared by the union for locals to distribute to workers during the 1980 bargaining. The workers were told of all the gains that the union claimed it had won in the 1977 bargaining, including lifetime job security, and they were assured that the union would be relentless in pursuing even more for them in 1980—bigger pensions, more job security, enhanced benefits. Weisen was right. It was the same old garbage.

PART FOUR

2 0

THE COMBINATION
COMES APART

On Tuesday, November 27, 1979, five days after Thanksgiving, David M. Roderick, chairman of the United States Steel Corporation, made a stunning announcement at a news conference in Pittsburgh. The corporation was closing its Youngstown Works and fourteen other plants across the country, including two Homestead plants that had been operating since the turn of the century. The Youngstown closing was particularly shocking, because six months earlier Roderick had said: "We have no plans for shutting down our Youngstown operation.... We're operating in the black there." The workers had been given no warning, even though some union officials, whose responsibility it was to represent them, had known about the corporation's plans for several months.

This was one of many plant closings and layoffs by the nation's steel companies since the late 1970s. Between 1974 and 1979, for example, the corporation had closed some forty facilities. But because the plants that were closed were comparatively small and scattered, few people had paid attention. The latest cutbacks, shutting some of the nation's most famous plants and eliminating 13,500 jobs, were the largest in the more than hundred-year history of the American steel industry. Others were soon to follow. The dismemberment of the United States Steel Corporation—the greatest industrial conglomerate in world history—had begun.

The corporation was suffering unprecedented losses. It had earned a profit of $242 million in 1978, but in 1979, Roderick's first year as chairman, it lost $293 million. In the fourth quarter of 1980, it lost $561.7 million, then the largest quarterly loss in American corporate history. To stanch the hemorrhaging, the corporation initiated a four-point program —close plants and eliminate blue-collar and white-collar jobs; sell assets; demand concessions from the local unions and then use these concessions to play one local against another; and diversify.

In closing plants and terminating workers, the corporation acted in a most arrogant and imperious manner. It made announcements around holidays. Executives never went into the communities to attempt to explain decisions. Often union officials would receive no official notification but instead would receive a telephone call just before an announcement, or read rumors in a newspaper or hear them on the radio or television.

This was an absurd manner in which to act. The workers knew that change was coming. They understood profit and loss. They had dealt with financial problems in their families for years. Dialogue with the workers might have provided an alternative to mass closings and layoffs. But the corporation could not change its imperious ways. From all their actions, it was evident that neither Roderick nor his associates in any significant way accepted blame themselves, or on behalf of previous management, for what had happened.

Many of the corporation's problems were the result of decades of arrogance and shortsightedness. Management was inbred, centralized, uncreative, and autocratic. The corporation had maximized short-term profits and for decades, despite its grand pronouncements, had neglected investment in new technologies. It had never taken research seriously. It had wasted vast sums of money on equipment and mills that were never used and had dramatically overhired. But the corporation always said that its problems were caused by imports, government meddling in pricing, environmental regulations, and high labor costs.

In fact, the corporation, like many other steel companies, had been fortunate. Had it not been for military production in World War II, the

Korean War, and Vietnam, and guaranteed production from such projects as the expressway system and airports, the corporation, like the other companies, likely would have fallen years before.

On November 28, 1979, the day after he had announced massive cutbacks, Roderick vigorously denied that inept management had anything to do with them. "We became perhaps too fat," he once told interviewers, but that was about all he ever said that suggested responsibility. Roderick was the principal architect of the vast changes to be made, and he established the style in which they were carried out. Though he never became known to most Americans, he would do more to transform the corporation than any chairman since Elbert H. Gary. Then, still almost unknown, he would retire and disappear from the scene.

Roderick had taken over as chairman somewhat unexpectedly. Rumors that Edgar B. Speer was seriously ill had been circulating for months in 1978 but had been denied. By early 1979, however, Speer's illness—he was suffering from cancer—was obvious. On April 24, 1979, he retired, and Roderick replaced him. Roderick was as tough-minded as they come. He was short and stocky, and he invariably wore a dark-blue suit with the jacket buttoned. With his thick body, largely bald head, and pale face, he resembled a Civil War minié ball. Like the corporation he was to run, he was abrasive, arrogant, and combative. But he was also shrewd. He understood power. For the most part, he ignored his adversaries and their criticism. When a group of religious and union activists from the Monongahela Valley condemned him for the plant-closings, he was unfazed. "I learned a long time ago not to flinch when someone says they're going to hit you," he told them.

Once, when Congressman Peter Kostmayer, Democrat of Pennsylvania, suggested that a committee be formed to explore ways to improve competitiveness at the Fairless Hills Works, north of Philadelphia, Roderick said: "Look, I don't want one of those goddamned committees coming in here—a priest, a Boy Scout, and a housewife—telling us what to do. We're here to make money. You guys can't get that through your heads." Roderick had little sense of humor, and his appearance and mannerisms, coupled with his high position, often intimidated people, even his strongest adversaries. Like Henry Clay Frick, he despised reporters as pests, regarded their stories as shallow and inaccurate, and saw little need to talk to them. When he did, it was mostly at quarterly press conferences in the auditorium at the corporation's headquarters on Grant Street, in Pittsburgh.

Congressman Kostmayer said:

People in private and public life seem to be . . . frightened of [the corporation]. Frightened at the prospect that they [the corporation] will close up. That's what they made clear in Bucks County [site of the corporation's Fairless Hills Works]. They were going to leave if they didn't get their way. . . . They have more and more leverage. That's why they intimidate the [Congressional] Steel Caucus. Nobody talks back to Roderick. You know how members of Congress often berate witnesses. That doesn't happen when Roderick comes up [to testify]. Nobody gives him a hard time. He's too powerful. Or there is a perception that he's too powerful.

Roderick was born and grew up on Pittsburgh's North Side, in a family of moderate means. His father was a postman, his mother a housewife. He attended Oliver High School (named for the iron and steel magnate Henry W. Oliver), where he was a mediocre student, and from which he graduated in June 1942. That fall, he joined the Marine Corps, serving until the war's end.

Back home, he entered the University of Pittsburgh, where he spent several years, at night, obtaining a degree in finance and economics. He worked for the Gulf Oil Company, then in 1953 became an accountant in the United States Steel Corporation's railroad subsidiary. In 1959, he was appointed to the corporate staff as assistant to the director of statistics. His responsibilities included gathering information for the corporation's annual report and annual meeting, and thus he came to know members of the finance committee and its chairman, Roger Blough. In 1962, he was transferred to Paris as an accounting consultant for international operations, and when he returned to Pittsburgh in 1965 he was appointed vice-president for international accounting. He was named chairman of the finance committee in 1973 and president in August 1975, in which capacity he served until he became chairman of the corporation in 1979.

Roderick was immensely proud of his Marine service in World War II. He had served on Midway and Iwo Jima and had risen to the rank of sergeant. When he returned to civilian life, he was one of those men, encountered so often in American business and government, who are professional ex-Marines; that is, when they enter business or government, they take with them their military manner and what they regard as their military toughness and superiority. Roderick attributed to his service in the Marine Corps the discipline and ability to confront challenges and to make decisions. These characteristics, he felt, were necessary for effective functioning in the business world. But Roderick had been a mopup man in the Marines, not a combat man. His unit would land several days after an invasion, when combat had moved inland, watch over prisoners, and do other rear-echelon chores. Now, as chairman, he was making decisions that, in large part, had been ordained by the failures of his predecessors. He was a mopup man again.

II

In February 1980, the corporation and the other steel companies entered into negotiations, conducted every three years, with the union. On April 14, 1980, agreement was reached on a new three-year contract. The contract provided for wage and benefit increases, but its most important provision was given little attention by negotiators and thus was accorded little public attention. The experimental negotiating agreement was eliminated. Long trumpeted as a model of American labor-management relations, it had instead been a monstrous failure. It was supposed to provide for gradual, automatic wage and benefit increases and bring rationality to labor-management bargaining by preventing strikes, thus eliminating the need for stockpiling and, in turn, reducing imports. Instead, wages and benefits rose astronomically, and imports also rose. High inflation, which the union and the companies had not anticipated, had wreaked particular havoc because automatic wage increases were tied to the increase in the cost of living. By 1980, employment costs in the steel industry were 85 percent higher than the average employment costs in American manufacturing. This was not the fault of the workers—not completely. They had accepted the raises, buying the bill of goods that the union had sold them. But they had never voted on the experimental negotiating agreement or on any of the contracts negotiated under it because the union's constitution did not allow such voting. The only goal that had been achieved was the elimination of stockpiling, which in itself had never been a major problem anyway, and the elimination of which had no effect on imports.

What was also significant about the 1980 negotiations was that they were conducted with little understanding that a crisis was at hand in the American steel industry. In refusing to extend the experimental negotiating agreement, the companies had taken cognizance of their soaring wage and benefit costs, but the union did not address the issue of plant closings. For the most part, the negotiations were conducted as though life in the steel industry were going on as usual. It was a dialogue between two defunct institutions.

Yet, for many, the signs of trouble were unmistakable, and there began to emerge in the Monongahela Valley the most important effort at working-class and community organizing that was to occur in the 1980s, probably the most important since the union-organizing of the 1930s. Some of the activists were steelworkers. Others had been activists in the antiwar movement of the 1960s, men and women who had looked about in the 1970s for a place to get a job and to organize and had become attracted to the steel industry. Finally, there were others who came out of the tradition of militancy that went back decades in the Monongahela Valley. There had been the Homestead strike of 1892, the 1919 steel strike, the Committee for Industrial Organization, and the unemployed movement of the 1930s. Pittsburgh and other parts of the valley had experienced ferocious labor and ideological wars in the 1930s, 1940s, and 1950s. There were a number of people around who still thought that conflict was the natural relationship between labor and management, the only way that the workers could make headway.

Among the colorful mavericks and reformers emerging in the Pittsburgh area were the leaders of the Homestead local of the steelworkers' union, Local 1397—Ronnie Weisen, president; Michelle McMills, editor of the local's irreverent newspaper, *1397 Rank and File*; Michael "Kentucky" Stout, a craneman in slab and plate; John Ingersoll; and Jay Weinberg. Elsewhere in the valley there were others—Mike Bonn, president of the steelworkers' Local 2227, in nearby Irwin; Darrell Becker, president of the Marine and Shipbuilding Workers Local 61, which represented shipbuilders and repairmen at the Dravo Company's shipyard on Neville Island, on the upper Ohio River; Larry Evans, who had worked in the Edgar Thomson Works and, with his wife, Leslie, an English teacher at the Steel Valley High School, had founded the *Mill Hunk Herald,* a journal of workers' prose and poems; and Staughton Lynd, an attorney in Youngstown, Ohio, and the son of the sociologists Robert S. Lynd and Helen Merrell Lynd, authors of the classic work *Middletown: A Study in American Culture* (1929), about working-class and middle-class life in Muncie, Indiana. Staughton Lynd had taught at Yale, but in the wake of his opposition to the Vietnam War, university officials advised him that it was unlikely he would be granted tenure, so he left. He had taught at Spelman College, a black school in Atlanta, then gone to law school, and was now practicing public-interest law. From the beginning, he gave advice to Weisen and the other activists.

There was Charles McCollester, a shop steward for the United Electrical Workers at the Westinghouse plant in Turtle Creek, Pennsylvania, who had been brought up in the tradition of Catholic activism and was a student of Marxism. There was Steffi Domike, one of a group of young women steelworkers, who worked at a coke battery in the Clairton Works and was also a television producer. There were Bob Anderson and Theresa Chalich, who founded the Rainbow Kitchen on Eighth Avenue in Homestead to feed laid-off workers and poor people. It became a favorite place for politicians and other celebrities to be photographed with the poor or unemployed. There was Barney Ossler, who helped establish committees to aid the unemployed.

Clergymen in the Monongahela Valley got involved, more of them than at any previous time. Among them was the Reverend James Von Dreele, a recent graduate of Drew University, who was pastor of Saint Matthew's Episcopal Church, in Homestead, and Father Charles Owen Rice, pastor of Saint Anne's Roman Catholic Church, in Castle Shannon, who had given the eulogy there when his disciple Philip Murray was buried. Fiercely anti-Communist from the 1930s through the 1950s, Father Rice had repented in the 1960s and become an opponent of the Vietnam War. His long association with the labor movement gave the activists added legitimacy.*

The activists began to coalesce in March 1979, when they attended a conference called by the Episcopal synod in Pittsburgh to discuss the implications of the corporation's plan to construct a huge, modern mill in Conneaut, Ohio. They opposed the Conneaut plant because they believed its construction would mean the closing of other plants. It was better to upgrade old plants, they said, than to construct new ones.

At the conference, corporation executives and union officials paid lip service to the activists' concerns about Conneaut and about the plant shutdowns that were already beginning. Weisen and McCollester denounced the corporation. McCollester threw an eighteen-inch section of steel rail onto the floor, declaring that if the new plant was built such products as steel rails could be put into a museum, because there would be no more steelmaking of any importance in the Monongahela Valley.

After the conference, Weisen, McCollester, Lynd, and others decided to form an organization, the Tri-State Conference on Steel, to push for modernization of the Monongahela Valley mills. The name—Tri-State referred to Pennsylvania, Ohio, and West Virginia—was somewhat grandiose, given that almost everybody involved was from Pittsburgh. But the

---

* Anti-Communist or not, Father Rice was always an ardent union man. Once, in the 1950s, during a gravediggers' strike in New York City, Francis Cardinal Spellman used seminarians to dig graves, thus helping to break the strike. Father Rice wrote angrily in his *Pittsburgh Catholic* column, "A scab is a scab is a scab, whether he wears cardinal red or denim blue." The church authorities were outraged, and he was exiled to Natrona, Pennsylvania, where he was forced to stay as a parish priest, essentially in isolation, for nine years.

activists were smart and aggressive. In July 1979, they filed suit in federal court to block construction of the Conneaut plant, charging that the United States Corps of Engineers had wrongfully approved environmental permits. Most of the legal work was done by Lynd, although Weisen, as union president, received the attention. The night that the suit was filed, a rally was held at Local 1397. Father Rice declared, "If you have no guts, you are going to be wiped out." Weisen said: "We know U.S. Steel plans to phase out the Homestead plant. It will be hard to beat Roderick, but we will do it."

III

Weisen was the elemental force behind the protest movement in the Monongahela Valley. He was not the key tactician, because that role changed according to what was going on. He was not a philosopher or an intellectual, but he was something many of the others were not—a genuine article. Weisen was a Homestead man. He had grown up in Homestead, at the top of the hill, and had gone into the mill right after high school. He was first a laborer, then a craneman, then a welder in the central maintenance department.

He had never been active in the union. Like many others, he had been occupied in making money, taking care of his family, having a good time. Then, in 1976, he was suspended for refusing to do work outside of his job description and then suspended again for calling a foreman an "imbecile," not normally a major offense in a rough-and-tumble place like a steel mill. But the foreman had it in for him, and because foremen are important people in steel mills, Weisen was in trouble.

He complained to the local union and was informed that he could file a grievance, but that if he did, he would be out of work for as much as a year while it was processed. With a wife and four children, he could not afford the loss of a year's income. It would be better to accept the punishment and return to work, he thought. But he wondered why, under the grievance system, a man was automatically judged guilty, at least punished as if he were. And he wondered why he was in trouble when nothing was being done about others, both workers and managers, who engaged in far worse abuses. He decided that he had one choice—to become active in the union and change the situation. That year he campaigned for the position of grievance man—"grievers," as they are called. He lost, but he was hooked on union politics and started hanging around with other Homestead workers he had met at meetings, among them Michelle McMills and John Ingersoll, who were talking of reforming the union.

McMills had gone to work in the mill in October 1974, at the age of twenty-two, on a labor gang in the forge division. She had graduated from Denison University and attended law school at the University of Pittsburgh for a year, but she was attracted to working in the steel industry. After studying to be a motor inspector and learning to repair cranes and machines, she was hired to work in the forge division. The mill, she decided, was the place for her and she became active in union politics. She understood the issues that were important to workers—a fair grievance system and a clean place to have lunch, for example—and she had day-to-day experience of conditions in the mill, such as the two-mile walk to the only women's restroom. In 1976, she ran for the post of local union trustee. The men liked the idea of a woman running for union office—a woman like that had spunk—and she won easily.

Ingersoll, a rigger, had been at the Homestead Works since 1967, after sixteen years at the National Works, in McKeesport. He had become involved in the rank-and-file-movement in 1976, and that summer he, McMills, and Weisen ran as delegates to the union's national convention in Las Vegas, Nevada, pledging that if they were elected, they would report back to the workers on what had taken place there. This hardly sounds earth-shattering, but it was a radical notion in the steelworkers' union or almost any other American union at that time. All three were elected, with Weisen receiving the largest number of votes. At the convention they met Edward Sadlowski, who had already begun his campaign to challenge Lloyd McBride. Sadlowski's ideas and enthusiasm impressed them, and they enlisted in his cause.

The way that the Homestead group used its expense money for the convention was significant. The delegates' expenses for travel, hotel rooms, and food were paid by the union on a per-diem basis, a typical practice in American unions. What was not typical was that the mavericks stayed at a cheap motel and ate at inexpensive places. They didn't go near the casinos, so they spent nothing on gambling, shows, or drinks. When they returned from Las Vegas, they had saved several hundred dollars. They used the money to start a fund to take over the Homestead local and began publishing a newspaper, *1397 Rank and File,* an irreverent, often profane journal that in stories and cartoons attacked not only plant managers and the corporation but union officials as well. The January 1977 issue declared: "This paper is dedicated to members who can't find their grievance men, who can't be heard at union meetings because they are 'out of order,' who have things to say about local mill conditions. . . . We ask that you join us to build a strong and democratic union that represents all of us and not just a few." It was a delicious irony. The mavericks were attacking the union with the union's money. "They gave us per diem, and we used it," McMills said. "It was just like they teach you in business school: Reinvest your money in the operation."

The movement began to grow, tied to the Sadlowski campaign. Although Sadlowski lost to McBride in February 1977, and his movement fell apart in the following months, the Local 1397 insurgents stayed together and expanded their organization. They got attention with their newspaper's attacks on the local and international union and on the corporation. Downtown, in their high-rise offices, union leaders and corporation executives watched the reformers, and neither group liked what it saw.

In the summer of 1978, Weisen announced that he would run for president of the local union. Run by hacks for years, it was a shell of a union. The glory days of steel production—the 1950s, 1960s, and 1970s —had brought complacency and corruption to the union, as they had to the corporation. In the mill, the restrooms and canteens were dirty; the food was poor and high-priced; the medical staff was mediocre; the equipment was run-down and antiquated. The local union did nothing about these problems.

Although grievance men were taking enormous amounts of "lost time," many grievances were going unattended because of laziness or because the grievers were trying to curry favor with the corporation by not pursuing grievances. Usually, only a handful of people showed up at local meetings, and often workers opposed to the local officers were not allowed to speak.

The president of Local 1397 was Anselmo "Babe" Fernandez, a round, friendly fellow, one of the few Spaniards in Homestead. Fernandez had been president since 1973, but with the insurgents demonstrating such strength, and having no heart for a knock-out campaign, he retired, and the presidency went to the vice-president, Milan "Mike" Bekich, a Slav. Weisen and the other insurgent candidates ran a vigorous campaign against "Bekich and the Forty-six Thieves." With their headquarters in a storefront one block from the Amity Gate of the Homestead Works and campaign-literature tables at all of the gates, the insurgents gained hundreds of new supporters. In April 1979, Weisen beat Bekich with thirty-six hundred votes to twelve hundred. Every other insurgent candidate except one was also elected. The forty-eight hundred ballots cast— there were now six thousand union members employed in the Homestead Works—represented the largest number of votes in a union election there since World War II. The insurgents had pulled off what is almost impossible in typically undemocratic American unions. They had captured the local.

Weisen, forty-four at this time, was tough and compact, a bulldog of a man. He'd been a tough kid growing up in Homestead, something of a bully when he was in a bad mood. As a kid, he would sometimes take a buddy and roam the neighborhood below Eighth Avenue looking for people to beat up. Not many people messed with Weisen.

After high school, Weisen, like many Homestead boys, thought about becoming a professional boxer. In 1958, he was amateur middleweight Golden Gloves champion of Pennsylvania, and he might have turned pro had he not gotten married to Jean Stevens, a Homestead girl. But there was also the matter of his boxing style. He did not dance around the ring jabbing at his opponent. That was for sissies, he thought. He bored in. He could hit and take a punch, but he never developed the discipline to stay with his plan for a match. He never was knocked out, but when his opponent started hitting him he would often fly into a rage and begin punching as hard and furiously as he could, and continue until he was exhausted. When this happened, his opponent would gain the advantage over him.

Two months after finishing high school, Weisen went into the mill. He worked hard and after a while was earning good money. Once he took his wife and children to California for a month and paid for everything in cash—he used no credit cards. "I always made a lot of money and was used to a lot of money," he said. He refused to take anything from anybody. When his foreman began leaning on him, he leaned back. Although he knew that, with a family, he could not punch out a foreman as he would have when he was younger and single, curious things began happening to foremen. The ones who stole gas—this was a common practice—suddenly found sugar in their gas tanks. Someone had put sugar in the gas cans that the foremen were using to fill their cars and trucks, and several had to get new engines. Another foreman was found at 10:30 one morning vomiting violently. Someone had placed a purgative in the coffee in his Thermos.

When Weisen and the other insurgents took office, reforms began immediately. Lost time for grievance men was reduced from two hundred hours a week for each plant zone to seventy. A lawyer was hired to come to the local twice a week and instruct grievance men in labor law. The corporation, years before, had initiated the practice of having lawyers handle even low-level grievances. Now, with a lawyer, though he was expensive, the local began to equal the corporation's skill in handling grievances.

The reformers also stopped allowing local union delegates who went to national meetings to claim reimbursement for inflated travel, food, and lodging expenses. These were still called "Pullman rates," though no one in the union had traveled by Pullman car for years.

The new local leaders demanded the same quality of food for the workers' canteens as foremen and supervisors received in the executive cafeteria on the fifth floor of the General Office Building. They demanded the cleaning of dirty showers, sinks, urinals, and toilets. They attacked the practice of contracting out work, the use of safety rules by foremen to impose discipline, and what they said was overmanagement—at one point in the late 1970s, the Homestead Works had seven hundred managers for six thousand workers. In what seemed a comprehensive indictment, *1397 Rank and File* denounced "management's stupidity, incompetence, arrogance, egotism, cruelty, etc." Weisen understood how the press works and how to get its attention. For reporters he became a perfect counterweight to what the corporation and the international union were saying. This made the people running the corporation and the union furious, but there was nothing they could do.

The insurgents were having a wonderful time. "On cold mornings in February, we would go out to the mill gate just because we loved it," Michelle McMills said. "We believed we were changing the world, and we wanted to be out there, at the mill gate, shaking hands. Everybody knew Ronnie, and everybody liked him. You get respect through your job and everybody knew he was a hard worker and a good welder. Also, he told it like it was, and people respected that. They didn't want another ass-kisser. They wanted someone who would say what he thought." Richard Holoman, a Homestead worker, said: "Weisen was for the steelworker, no two ways about it. He wouldn't take any guff from the big shots. He'd say: 'I'm a steelworker, and I'm just a high school graduate. But that doesn't mean that because you've got a degree from, say, Syracuse University, you're better than me.' And he couldn't be bullshitted, because he knew the union. He was around the big wheels, but he was a regular guy." Allied against two formidable adversaries, the corporation and the international union, Weisen was in for a hard fight. But the man who had once roamed the streets below Eighth Avenue looking for a fight, the former boxer who had lashed out furiously at his opponents, was not daunted. The truth was that he enjoyed this. He had never had a better time in his life.

IV

Life in Homestead was changing for the worse, and the corporation's announcement about the plant closings added to the unease of the workers and townspeople. In the 1950s, Eighth Avenue had been a bustling shopping district that attracted customers from throughout the Monongahela Valley. George Ewing and Brothers was a favorite place for meat and groceries, as was the Amos Supermarket, which did a particularly fine business on Sunday mornings, when it was the habit of many people to stop by after church to pick up a roast for Sunday dinner. One of the valley's finest candy stores was United Candy.

The Grinberg brothers, Morris and Meyer, ran excellent stores. Meyer Grinberg, in business since 1893, sold housewares and electrical appliances, and Morris Grinberg had offered fine ladies' and children's clothes since 1895. Harry's Men's Clothes sold high-quality suits—Hart, Shaffner, and Marx; Kuppenheimer; and other labels. Bosses got their suits at Harry's—that's how good it was. Marks's Card Shop was the place for greeting cards. The proprietor, Sam Marks, had introduced Hallmark Cards, then the nation's finest cards, to Homestead in 1940. Almost from the time that the motor car had come to Homestead, at the turn of the century, auto dealers had lined Eighth Avenue—Clark Chevrolet, Homestead Lincoln-Mercury, Homestead Buick, Homestead Pontiac-Cadillac, Toohey Ford, Bretsynder DeSoto-Plymouth, Tri-Boro Dodge-Plymouth. You did not have to go to Pittsburgh to get a car. You got it in Homestead.

But by the 1970s, Eighth Avenue was becoming run-down, and one after the other businesses began to close. As Betty Esper, a worker, said, "The politicians did not put any money into this town." The auto dealers began to disappear in the early 1970s—some went out of business; others moved to the suburbs—and by 1974 not one was left. The furniture stores, like Half Brothers, which had been in business in Homestead for ninety years, began to close in the mid-1970s. Both of the Grinbergs closed their stores. On December 19, 1979, a month after Roderick's announcement, the *Homestead Daily Messenger,* the town's newspaper, ceased publication. The closing of businesses had meant a reduction in advertising in the paper. One day, staff members came in and began reading the papers, making calls, pulling clips—the normal activities of a newsroom. Suddenly they were told to leave. For the first time since 1881, Homestead had no newspaper.

The collapse was not just the result of what was going on in the steel industry. Homestead had installed parking meters in 1951, and some people had begun to shop elsewhere, where parking was free. The trolleys had been eliminated in the summer of 1965 and replaced by buses. Though some considered it old-fashioned, the trolley system had been an excellent means of transportation. It had run along Eighth Avenue and other major streets, and passengers could get off at the corners or anywhere in between. With the trolleys gone, Eighth Avenue suffered. The town was also struck, inexplicably, by a large number of fires. A lumber and building-supply business and two furniture stores were destroyed by fire in the 1970s. None were rebuilt. The new Century III shopping mall, built over the hill behind the town, where the mill used to dump slag, drained business away from Eighth Avenue. Then another shopping center opened in Monroeville, just ten miles away, near the Pennsylvania Turnpike.

It was, however, principally the layoffs at the mill that devastated the town. As the journalist and sociologist John A. Fitch had understood decades before, the mill had made the town. Take away the mill, and the town would disappear. As the layoffs came, foot traffic along Eighth Avenue began to fall off. In the early 1970s, Marks's Card Shop had employed five clerks, and not only Sam Marks but his three brothers had also worked there. By the early 1980s, there were three clerks and two brothers; by 1984, one clerk and Sam.

The cutbacks in business meant that tax revenues were reduced and assessments fell. By 1980, Homestead was $286,000 in debt. And slowly the town's population was decreasing. In 1960, it had been 6,459. By 1980, it had fallen to 5,092. Homestead had always had a rough edge to it. A business could close, a store become vacant, a fire destroy a building, and the loss would not be particularly noticeable. Moreover, the town was used to closings. Mills became antiquated and were closed. Life was like that. Open Hearth Number Four, declared obsolete, had been closed in 1974. A sinter plant at the Carrie furnaces had closed in 1977. The difference was that in the old days, a new store replaced an old store, a new furnace replaced an old furnace, a new mill replaced an old mill. Now nothing came except promises.

In May 1979, the corporation and the federal government reached a pollution-reduction agreement that, the corporation said, would clean up the mills and save the steel industry in the Monongahela Valley. Iron, steel, and coke plants had been polluting the air and water of the valley for more than one hundred years. But for the workers and townspeople the fire and smoke meant that the mills were running and providing jobs. In announcing the agreement, Roderick said: "Although this is a demanding package, it clearly demonstrates that U.S. Steel is committed to remaining in the steel business in the Monongahela Valley. . . . U.S. Steel can now act aggressively to revitalize our Pittsburgh-area operations, moving ahead to develop further the valley's economic potential and that of its people." On May 23, 1979, he stated the matter even more strongly: "We have assured the future production of our Monongahela plants." People believed what Roderick said.

In early 1980, a $2.5 million redevelopment project was announced for the Leona Theatre, the former vaudeville house, movie theater, and dance hall. The Leona had closed in 1966 and had sat empty, except for occasional magic shows, plays, and rock-and-roll concerts. Now it was to be converted into "a mini-mall" of ten "exclusive shops" and "an exclusive restaurant and health club," and "forty deluxe apartments in a climate-controlled environment." The project, to be called Leona Shops and Apartments of Homestead Village, Pennsylvania, would, the developer said, be a catalyst for "the Homestead revitalization." People believed that, too.

In 1979, the Homestead Economic Revitalization Corporation, organized by community businessmen, was awarded $500,000 in federal grants, under the Community Development Block Grant Program, to improve sidewalks and curbs, put in new streetlamps, and plant trees along Eighth Avenue. In 1980, the Revitalization Corporation received an additional $345,000 to continue to encourage businessmen to improve their properties under "the already successful financial-incentive program." People believed in this, too.

Despite what was happening, most people trusted that the mill would stay open and that the town would be revitalized. And why not? The Carrie furnaces, Open Hearth Number Five, the plate mills, the structural mills, the forge, the Big Shop were all operating. In 1978, the Homestead Works still employed six thousand workers, and the local union had seven thousand members, making it the third-largest steelworkers' local in the country. Sister Marie Margaret, who came to Homestead in 1979 to teach at Saint Mary Magdalene's School, was stunned by the bustle and the noise. When she went to the bank on Eighth Avenue, and it was payday at the mill, she would race down Amity Street, her habit flapping, to get to the bank before the workers so that she would not have to stand in line.

In August 1980, almost as if to demonstrate its optimism, Homestead held its centennial celebration to mark the incorporation of the town on September 19, 1880. There were bands from Steel Valley High School and Bishop Boyle High School, a parade, folk dancing, open houses at the churches, a fashion show, fireworks, and a dinner-dance at Saint Michael's School. Malvin Goode, who had worked in the mill and then at WHOD, the 250-watt radio station at Eighth Avenue and West Street, and had gone on to be a correspondent for ABC News, was the guest speaker. President Jimmy Carter and his wife, Rosalynn, sent a letter to the citizens of Homestead saying: "We share your joy and pride as you commemorate this historical milestone. The values and ideals which have made your community grow and prosper have also contributed to the growth and prosperity of our entire nation."

The Mesta Machine Company, which made equipment for the steel industry, was also celebrating its one-hundredth anniversary. Mesta took out a half-page advertisement in the centennial guidebook sending congratulations from "an industrial citizen of the steel valley." The United States Steel Corporation purchased a full-page advertisement saying: "Congratulations, Homestead, on one hundred Years of Achievement! Your neighbors at U.S. Steel's Homestead Works are pleased to join in observing this milestone. We are proud to be a part of Homestead's history and heritage. It has been a rewarding, productive relationship, and we look forward to many more years of working together in one of America's great communities."

Eight months later, on April 24, 1981, the Homestead Works celebrated a century of steelmaking and commemorated the tapping of the first heat of steel on March 9, 1881. The corporation marked the occasion by dedicating a new $24 million water-recycling plant at the works, "a signal of our future commitment to a second century of operation."

V

The corporation continued its restructuring. In 1980, the forty-eight-inch plate mill at the Homestead Works, its oldest mill, was closed. It was among the forty-seven mills and other facilities closed that year in the American steel industry. On November 6, 1980, Roderick said that the corporation was abandoning plans to construct the plant at Conneaut, Ohio—a plan proposed by Carnegie and Schwab eighty years before, as a way of challenging J. Pierpont Morgan, and revived periodically over the decades, most recently by Edgar Speer. The decision was not a reaction to the opposition voiced in the Monongahela Valley. "We can't afford it," Roderick said.

As part of the effort to diversify, there came a more surprising announcement, in December 1981. The corporation was purchasing Marathon Oil for $6.4 billion, an incredible sum even for the 1980s. This was a year in which forty-five more steelmaking facilities were closed. The purchase of Marathon infuriated the workers. Why did the corporation have money to invest in the oil industry but not in the steel industry? Roderick and other corporate men said with substantial truth that they could not obtain money to invest in steel but could obtain money to diversify into oil and other sectors of the economy.

Meanwhile, the corporation had begun trying to convince the union to negotiate a new contract, though the current one, only a year old, was not scheduled to expire until August 1, 1983. In the spring of 1981, J. Bruce Johnston, executive vice-president for employee relations, had authorized the gathering of information by company researchers and outside auditors to convince the union that the industry was facing unprecedented conditions. In the summer of 1981, he had begun showing this information to Lloyd McBride, the union's president. McBride, in turn, shared it with his associates, including the union's chief economist, Edward Ayoub.

On April 6, 1982, Johnston and other top industry executives met with the union's leaders and district directors at Linden Hall, the union's estate in the old coal and coke area south of Pittsburgh. Johnston presented the statistics documenting the industry's weak position, putting particular emphasis on the cost of labor. On May 28, Johnston, at McBride's suggestion, sent an eight-page letter to the presidents of the local unions, asking that the union enter into negotiations on a new contract. He pointed out that 205 steel plants had been closed since 1974, and that since 1965 the industry had lost more than two hundred thousand jobs. The local presidents voted 263 to 79 to authorize negotiations.

Though the corporation claimed that wages were too high, and many Americans accepted the notion that it was the steelworkers who were responsible for the problems facing the industry, most workers and their families were living from paycheck to paycheck. Expenses in the steel towns were not as high as in the nation's metropolitan areas, but every family had to budget carefully, particularly if they had extraordinary expenses such as medical bills or college tuition. For example, a typical worker such as Rich Locher, a rigger at the Number Two Structural Mill, earned about $12 an hour in wages and an additional $10.50 in benefits. The average cost of labor in the nation's major steel companies was $22.69. This was 85 percent higher than in American industry as a whole, but it should be noted that for many years steel had been a highly profitable industry. Prices were high, and, like the workers' wages, they rose with increases in the cost of living.

But whatever the numbers might suggest, Locher and his family, like many others, were not living the high life. The Lochers' two cars had both been bought used, one from the proceeds of an insurance settlement. They had been on two vacations in eleven years of marriage. Each time, they and their children had gone to a trailer park in Virginia where a relative lived, and they had spent much of the time sitting in the sun on lawn chairs.

They had a comfortable home in Apollo, just east of Pittsburgh, a twenty-five-minute drive from the Homestead Works. But they had put almost every cent into building the house, and Locher, a skilled carpenter and builder, had done much of the work himself. The family ate out no more than twice a month, at McDonald's or Long John Silver's. They watched what they spent on groceries, and sometimes they received extra groceries from their parents or were invited to dinner at their homes. Finally, Mrs. Locher worked at a nearby plant, making rubberized dishes for refrigerators at $3.45 an hour.

"I'm not living high off the hog," Locher said.

Negotiations opened on July 5, 1982. The industry asked for a three-year wage freeze, the elimination of cost-of-living payments for one year and a limit of fifty cents per hour in each of the next two years, and the elimination of the fifteen-week vacation plan.

McBride and some of the other union leaders knew that the industry was facing enormous difficulties, and they wanted to grant concessions, but McBride, an uninspiring, uncreative man who had little rapport with the local presidents and rank-and-file members, had done almost nothing to prepare them. He committed an error, too, by not demanding anything in exchange—an end to plant closings and a promise to reinvest in the steel industry, for example. If concessions by the union were not made palatable to the local presidents, he feared, they would not approve the new contract. He informed Johnston on July 29 that he could not accept the proposal and on July 30 the presidents, many cheering wildly, rejected it. Johnston was furious. He believed that McBride had run out of guts and knuckled under to the union militants.

In October, following the convention, at which McBride admitted that the union's bargaining successes over the years had "created some problems," the two sides entered into a second series of negotiations. On November 16, they agreed on a contract that included a wage reduction of $1.50 an hour, with an additional seventy-five cents an hour to be deducted from paychecks to finance benefits for unemployed workers. But a number of local presidents complained that without a plan to save jobs, plants would continue to close. On November 19, the presidents rejected the proposed contract, 231 to 141.

Then, in December 1981, came devastating news for Homestead and the Monongahela Valley. The corporation announced the closing of the last two Carrie furnaces, Numbers Three and Four. The Carrie furnaces had been making iron since 1884 and had once included as many as seven massive furnaces. As recently as 1970, four had been operating. The corporation said also that it would close Open Hearth Number Five, built in 1943 as part of the defense expansion. It was the center of the Homestead Works, which, without it, would be dependent for its steel on the Edgar Thomson Works and the Duquesne Works. The decisions were protested, but nothing could be done to change them.

In February 1983, the corporation and the union entered into a third series of contract negotiations. The union, finally adopting the local presidents' suggestion, asked the corporation to promise to reinvest the money it would be saving on wages and benefits. The corporation agreed, and on March 1 the presidents ratified the contract, 169 to 63.

It had been a curious, long-drawn-out affair. The corporation had wanted $5 billion or more in concessions but had gotten only $2 billion. It didn't matter, however, because the negotiations were a sham. The damage to the corporation and the rest of the American steel industry had been done long before, for the past twenty-five years, perhaps more. Whether or not it got wage and benefit concessions, and despite its promise to reinvest the money saved, the corporation was going to pursue its primary goals—eliminating jobs, closing plants, and restructuring through diversification and the sale of assets.

Even in Homestead, a handful of people—Weisen, Staughton Lynd, Michael Stout, numerous workers—were beginning to see that what many people believed would never happen, would, that the Homestead Works would close. Some, Weisen and Lynd in particular, were sure of this, but they said Homestead would not go easily. "Homestead is going to go down," Lynd said, in his office in Youngstown one afternoon in January 1982. "And there will be a hell of a fuss when it does."

As it became clear that more mills would close, the resistance among activists in the Monongahela Valley grew, and new groups were formed. The Mon Valley Unemployed Committee was founded in December 1981. The Homestead Food Bank, which operated out of Local 1397 and provided bags of food to unemployed workers, was organized by Michael Stout and others in May 1982. By August 1982, it was the largest of the food banks, providing three bags of groceries twice a month to twelve hundred families through seven union halls in the valley. Soon there were food banks as far as the Ohio Valley, all the way to Aliquippa. In April 1982, Local 1397 sponsored a rock concert to benefit the food banks, featuring the Iron City House-Rockers, a local band. Fifteen thousand dollars was raised, and in 1984 Bruce Springsteen contributed another ten thousand dollars. Bob Anderson and Theresa Chalich's Rainbow Kitchen was now feeding five hundred people a day, although most were from the poor population that had begun to drift into the area and were not laid-off steelworkers. But the Rainbow Kitchen was performing a valuable service and was getting all kinds of publicity. Anderson was always willing to be quoted and was easy to reach, since the Rainbow Kitchen was on Eighth Avenue, just off the High Level Bridge, in an old restaurant.

Now, too, there emerged a group of young Protestant ministers with churches in the Monongahela Valley and other steel regions. As early as 1979, several ministers, among them the Reverend James Von Dreele, of Saint Matthew's Episcopal Church in Homestead, had been convinced that churches were not adequately assisting parishioners caught up in the plant shutdowns and did not understand the economic problems confronting the country. With the closing of Open Hearth Number Five at the Homestead Works and the reduction of operations at the Clairton Works, up the river from Homestead, they became increasingly concerned. In 1982, they formed the Denominational Ministry Strategy. Toward the end of the year, one of its members, the Reverend D. Douglas Roth, pastor of the Trinity Lutheran Church, in Clairton, made a public statement asking the governor of Pennsylvania, Dick Thornburgh, to declare Clairton a disaster area, just as he would if it had been struck by a natural disaster. Thornburgh refused. At Thanksgiving, the group organized a turkey drive for laid-off Clairton workers, but by now the ministers and their spouses, and the group's supporters, most of them from middle-class backgrounds, were becoming more radical. "We decided we had to do something more than give away turkeys," Von Dreele said.

By early 1983, the group consisted of perhaps a dozen Protestant ministers. In addition to Von Dreele and Roth, they included the Reverend John Gropp of the Christ Lutheran Church, in Duquesne; the Reverend Philip D. Long of the East Liberty Lutheran Church, in Pittsburgh; the Reverend John Yedlicka of the Lutheran Church of Our Redeemer, in McMurray; the Reverend Beth Siefert of Saint Andrew's Lutheran Church, in Carnegie; the Reverend William Rex of the Rose Crest Lutheran Church, in Monroeville, and Saint Mark's Lutheran Church, in Trafford; and the Reverend Daniel Solberg of the Lutheran Church of the Nativity, in Allison Park.

Their leader was Charles Honeywell, a tight-lipped, pallid, humorless man, the son of a Baptist preacher. Brought up in rural Michigan, he had attended Western Michigan University, from which he graduated in 1966 with a bachelor's degree and later earned a master's degree in industrial education. He had taught at Morehead State University, in Kentucky, and the State University of New York at Buffalo. After studying the confrontational tactics espoused by Saul Alinsky, the radical organizer of the

1940s, 1950s, and 1960s, he had come to Pittsburgh in 1975 as a community organizer. In 1979, he had approached Protestant clergymen in the region offering to teach what he called "leadership tactics," and he was hired. His salary—$19,986 in 1984—was paid by the Presbyterian, Episcopal, and Lutheran synods, which were anxious to expand the role of the churches in the steel communities.

Honeywell was a skilled organizer, researcher, and user of the press. He hit upon the idea of having retired church ladies do free research. They would be dispatched to a library or university archive to investigate the corporation, or whatever other institution he wanted to probe, and would return with valuable information, which he would squirrel away in the extensive files he kept in his basement. Soon he was storing data in a personal computer, and he and the ministers were connected by a computer network. They would sit in their basements or studies dashing off electronic-mail messages condemning the Pittsburgh and American power structures. There was something chilling about Honeywell. He gave the ministers and union people books and insisted that they read them. At meetings he would browbeat the ministers unmercifully in his low, usually monotone voice, sometimes reducing them to tears.

I once spent a morning with him at his home in the Mount Washington area, above downtown Pittsburgh, going over his views on why the steel industry had collapsed. He blamed (A) overproduction, (B) world markets, (C) lack of investment, (D) corporate greed, and (E) other factors. After more than an hour, I thought we were finished. "There is one more point, point F," Honeywell said. "Point 'F'?" I asked. "It may be too hot to print," he said. "Go ahead," I replied. "Drugs," Honeywell said. "Drugs?" I asked. "Exactly. Drugs." It was clear, he said, that the banks and the steel companies were associated with the Mafia and were laundering drug money from Latin America. I took no notes after that.

Almost all of the people who belonged to the Denominational Ministry Strategy were new to social protest, but they were zealous. By early 1983, there were about sixty members, including Ronnie Weisen. Weisen was starting to believe that the Tri-State Conference on Steel and the members of his own local were not aggressive enough. The demonstrations and other confrontational tactics that the religious activists were beginning to talk about—personalizing the corporation by attacking the men who led it, and also attacking other elements of the Pittsburgh power structure, such as bankers, businessmen, politicians, and clergymen—were more suited to Weisen's style.

21

REBELLION II

Ɪn February 1983, the Mellon Bank
Corporation of Pittsburgh, with two other Pittsburgh lenders, announced
that it was foreclosing on the Mesta Machine Company for failure to
make payments on a $20,048,580 mortgage. Mesta declared bankruptcy
and closed. The jobs of twelve thousand workers were eliminated. What
was particularly galling to the workers and their families was Mellon's
decision to freeze all of Mesta's accounts, which meant that Mesta was
unable to pay back wages to workers or to pay their health-insurance and
life-insurance premiums. Mellon also froze an account containing money
that Mesta had withheld from pension checks in order to pay for retirees'
health care, and this ended the program.

Mesta Machine—the company that Khrushchev had visited in 1959
in his quest to see America, the place where he had given Kenneth Jackey
his wristwatch—had been one of the leading manufacturers of steelmak-

ing machinery and other heavy machinery and equipment since 1898. Its open-hearth furnaces and manufacturing mills had employed four thousand workers as late as the 1970s. Many were members of families who had worked at Mesta for three or four generations. Together, the Homestead Works and Mesta had made the Homestead area one of the world's greatest industrial centers.

The Mesta foreclosure, following the corporation's 1982 purchase of Marathon Oil, the 1983 contract with its concessions by the union, and the continuing plant closings and layoffs, had people in Homestead and the other steel towns seething. The Mellon Bank Corporation had been a powerful part of Pittsburgh's financial community for more than a century. It had made some of the first loans that enabled Henry Clay Frick to begin his coal and coke operations in the 1880s and had been his bank for years. Now, at a time when the Monongahela Valley was being devastated, the bank had invested $5.5 billion—20 percent of its assets—overseas. Mellon's foreclosure on Mesta made the bank the perfect target for the activists.

On June 6, dozens of demonstrators appeared at the Mellon branch bank on Eighth Avenue in Homestead, diagonally across from the union hall, to urge people to withdraw their savings. It was D Day—"Disinvestment Day." Depositors withdrew roughly one hundred thousand dollars that day, and more withdrawals followed, at the Homestead branch and others. A coalition of all the activist groups took part in the campaign. Even the United Steelworkers of America asked its members to consider withdrawing their money. Union leaders had no fondness for the activists; they detested many of them. But the leaders feared that if the union did not become involved it would appear conservative and out of touch with its members.

Meanwhile, the Tri-State Conference on Steel had introduced a proposal, first advanced by Father Rice, to use the notion of eminent domain in order to seize the Mesta facilities and reopen them under the management of the workers. The old priest was extremely proud of this idea, and as he sat in his rectory in Castle Shannon discussing it one day, a drink in his hand, a twinkle came into his eye. What he liked best was the irony of using against capital a weapon that capital had so often used against workers and their communities. The notion of using eminent domain in this way was radical, but the activists believed it made sense, and so did some politicians in the steel towns, though the union leadership in Pittsburgh considered it absurd.

One day in September, about twenty unemployed steelworkers associated with the Denominational Ministry Strategy appeared at the Homestead branch of the Mellon bank, handed five-dollar bills to the tellers, and asked for rolls of pennies in return. They then said that they did not trust the bank's count of the pennies, and they began breaking open the rolls and counting the pennies one by one. Pennies began to fall on the floor. Lines lengthened. The tempers of regular customers shortened. The police arrived, and in the melee one of them hit a protestor named Joe Jurich over the head with a nightstick. Jurich was taken to the hospital and then charged with resisting arrest. At Jurich's trial, the policeman testified that his nightstick had remained sheathed, but a videotape recorded by the bank's anti-burglar system showed him hitting Jurich, and the case against Jurich was dismissed.

In October, protestors drove to the Mellon branch bank in Monessen, twenty-five miles up the Monongahela. While some stood at the tellers' windows counting pennies, a few quietly walked into the safe-deposit area, put dead fish into safe-deposit boxes that they had previously rented, locked the boxes, and left. When employees came to work the next morning, the bank reeked of rotting fish. The boxes had to be broken open, and the bank had to be cleansed of the foul smell. Over the next several weeks, dead fish were placed in safe-deposit boxes in ten more Mellon branch banks, from Monessen to Ambridge, on the Ohio River. This was war, again, on the Monongahela.

The center of protest in the Monongahela Valley was the Homestead union hall, which the local had constructed in 1966 with $220,000 in members' dues. It was on McClure Street, just above the Homestead Works and, conveniently, next to the Ancient Order of Hibernians, the Irish club, with its cheap draft beer. It was a typical union hall, somewhat shabby, not handsome by any standard, a place that smelled of cigarettes and spilled beer from years of parties. The building was constructed of brick and, naturally, beams rolled at the Homestead Works, and the front had large windows. On the wall were pictures of Franklin D. Roosevelt, Harry S. Truman, and Hubert H. Humphrey. Weisen had placed a picture of I. W. Abel in the men's room, but it soon disappeared. Over the years, some sort of substance—no one could ever figure out what it was—seemed to have oozed out of the beams and dripped down over the windows, so that the windows were always dirty, like the outside of a pot in which a roast has boiled over. Local union officials occasionally hired janitorial crews to clean the windows, but they accomplished little. Often it was impossible from inside to tell whether it was sunny or raining outside.

The hall was a frenetic place, with people coming and going, and meetings being held seemingly every day or night, often two or three at the same time. Grievance men would be talking to workers. Cheryl Bacco, Weisen's energetic secretary, would be explaining one thing or another —whom to see to file a grievance complaint, for instance, or how to apply for a pension. Michael Stout and Weisen would be putting together information on the corporation and the union, assisted by their network of spies in both organizations. Secretaries who disliked their bosses were particularly helpful to them. Stout could get the goods on just about everybody he wanted, which made him effective at winning grievance cases. He would, over a period of several years, win grievances worth two million dollars for some three thousand workers. Weisen's office—on the first floor, the third door on the right—was a somewhat disorganized place with walls festooned with protest stickers. Weisen had discovered the speaker phone and seemed to be on it more often than not, his feet on his desk, speaking in a voice that could be heard well down the hall, giving hell to some union official downtown or some supervisor in the mill, saying that he would be goddamned sorry if he continued doing what he was doing.

Always there was *1397 Rank and File,* with its attacks on the union's entrenched leadership. The newspaper criticized the practice of having local presidents, not members, vote on contracts, a relic of Philip Murray's authoritarianism. It told of how an assistant superintendent had had his office painted four times by maintenance workers until he found a color he liked. It reported on layoffs and plant closings throughout the steel industry and said that the union was doing nothing to counter them.

Crises were occurring one after the other. On December 27, 1983, two days after Christmas, Roderick announced a second major round of plant closings. The corporation would close six more facilities completely and thirty others partially. This meant the elimination of the jobs of 15,430 workers—11,000 of whom had already been "temporarily" laid off—and set a new corporation record for cutbacks. The decision had not been shared with the union and came nine months after the 1983 contract agreement that contained concessions which, many workers had assumed, would end the cycle of plant closings. Among the facilities to be closed were the Cuyahoga Works, in Cleveland; three facilities in the Monongahela Valley—a pipe mill at the National Works, in McKeesport, a beam mill at Clairton, and the steelmaking facilities at the Duquesne Works, east of Homestead; and the steelmaking facilities at the 102-year-old South Works, in Chicago, part of Federal Steel when the United States Steel Corporation was formed in 1901. Roderick said that the corporation would not close the Fairfield Works, in Alabama, where the local union had agreed to concessions three days before.

The national union, in its Pittsburgh offices, was doing almost nothing, for it had no idea how to proceed. But the activists in the Monongahela Valley were increasing their resistance. Their strategy took an important turn, one that some of them later regretted, on Easter 1984. The Presbyterian, Episcopal, and Lutheran church authorities, embarrassed by the militancy of the ministers and their supporters, had begun to attack them. They, in turn, decided to retaliate, shifting their attention away from Mellon. "We decided that if they were going to focus on our churches, we would focus on their church," said one of the DMS ministers.

The Shadyside Presbyterian Church was known as Pittsburgh's "power church," because it was attended by many wealthy and important people, among them Thomas C. Graham, the corporation's vice-chairman, and other executives. Midway through Easter Sunday services, some two dozen protestors marched into the church. Mike Bonn, president of Local 2227 at the Irwin Works, five miles up the Monongahela River from Homestead, strode to the front and stood next to the pulpit. As he accused the parishioners of ignoring the plight of the steelworkers, and of maintaining lifestyles that were "evil and against all biblical example," the bluebloods sat dumbfounded in their pews.

By now, the upheaval in Homestead and the rest of the Monongahela Valley had captured the attention of the national media. Plants were closing in steel towns, coal towns, auto towns, across America. In most cases, workers and communities made little fuss; there might be a flurry of action, speeches, even threats, by politicians and labor officials, but, in most cases, nothing substantial happened. In the Monongahela Valley it was different. A combination of factors—history and happenstance, militance going back over a hundred years, plus the existence of the maverick Homestead local—had produced what rarely happens in this country, an energetic and effective working-class insurgency. Reporters from across the country dropped into the valley like paratroopers, with pens, notebooks, tape recorders, and cameras, looking for quotes and pictures. Just about everybody came—from *The New York Times, Washington Post, Los Angeles Times, Chicago Tribune, Wall Street Journal,* and other newspapers; from magazines like *Time, Newsweek,* and *Business Week*; from network-television news programs, including *60 Minutes*; from public television, which sent Bill Moyers; and from National Public Radio. The actor David Soul, brother of the Reverend Daniel Solberg, contributed $250,000 to make a movie called *Fighting Ministers* and arrived with a production crew.

Store owners on Eighth Avenue, unemployed steelworkers and their families, and workers still on the job but apprehensive about the future were being interviewed. Some were acquiring media skills. Almost every week, it seemed, another reporter or two, sometimes more, stopped at the Homestead union hall and then went up and down Eighth Avenue for quotes. Politicians came—Jesse Jackson; Gary Hart; various congressmen; Lane Kirkland, president of the AFL-CIO. No jobs or mills were being saved, but the reporters were getting their stories and the politicians were getting their statements and pictures in the papers and on television, standing in front of another mill and lamenting its closing. "Homestead had to die before anyone began paying attention to us," Margaret Vojtko, a longtime resident, said.

Another battle now developed—the attempt to save Dorothy Six, a blast-furnace complex that was the last remaining part of the Duquesne Works, six miles up the Monongahela River from Homestead, which Frick and Carnegie had acquired in 1890. In December 1983, Roderick had said that the corporation would close the entire works. Production stopped in May 1984, and the last twelve hundred jobs at Duquesne, which only three years before had employed thirty-two hundred, were ended. Named after the wife of Leslie B. Worthington, a former corporation president, Dorothy Six, with its monstrous twenty-nine-foot hearth, had been the world's largest ironmaking facility when it went into operation in 1963.* As recently as 1983, it had set production records, and the workers had been awarded "Ironmaster" jackets, which they wore with immense pride as rewards for their achievement.

The Tri-State activists and the national union had always been enemies, but for this campaign the activists believed that they needed the support of the union, which was still scrambling to appear militant. So the two groups formed an alliance. In late 1984, Mike Locker, a New York consultant, was retained by the national union and Allegheny County to make a $150,000 study of whether the Dorothy Six furnaces could be reopened and made profitable. The corporation had not winterized the mill, so a group of workers spent several days, without pay, doing it themselves, using antifreeze paid for by the national union. When the corporation said that it planned to proceed with its plans to demolish the

---

*Corporation executives had come to regret the old practice of naming blast furnaces after wives. In the modern world, it made the corporation seem sexist, and it also lent appealing, almost human qualities to the furnaces, making it easier for protestors to organize campaigns to save them.

works and turn the area into an industrial park, Tri-State created an around-the-clock team whose members stayed in a house trailer near the main gate of the works to make sure that the corporation did not sneak people in to start the demolition.

The religious activists continued their confrontational activities. In October 1984, the Western Pennsylvania–West Virginia Lutheran Synod of America ordered the Reverend D. Douglas Roth, pastor of the Trinity Lutheran Church, in Clairton, transferred to another church. Roth refused to go, and on November 4 he locked himself inside his church, opening the doors only for Sunday services. A court order was obtained ordering him to vacate the church. He refused. At 9:30 A.M. on November 13, the Allegheny County sheriff, Eugene Coon, and a number of deputies—including two women—arrived at the church, arrested Roth, and took him to Pittsburgh. News pictures showed him being taken from his church by female law-enforcement officers, not by male officers, whose presence might have been reminiscent of the Pinkertons or the coal and iron police.

The judge who heard the case was Emil E. Narick, who in 1969, then a union lawyer, had run unsuccessfully against I. W. Abel for union president. Laws had to be enforced, he said, quoting 1 Peter 2:13: "Submit yourself to every ordinance of man for the Lord's sake." Roth, a plump, mild-looking man who somewhat resembled the comic actor Oliver Hardy, leaped up, Bible in hand. "Shame on you for misinterpreting the Scriptures," he cried. Then he quoted Matthew 6:24: "No man can serve two masters; for either he will hate the one, and love the other, or else he will hold to the one, and despise the other. Ye cannot serve God and mammon." Narick asked Roth whether he would obey the church and the court. Roth said that he would not. Narick sentenced him to ninety days for contempt of court.

On December 16, 1984, as a dozen activists demonstrated outside, three men wearing masks burst into the Shadyside Presbyterian Church, during a dinner following a Christmas pageant, and hurled balloons that were reported to be filled with dye and synthetic skunk oil—although DMS always said the balloons contained only water—at church members, including children. In the ensuing bedlam, they escaped in a station wagon. The incident created a furor. Most people could not understand how the protestors, despite what many regarded as the correctness of their cause, could interrupt a church gathering and target women and children. On December 27, with Roth still in jail, a number of people barricaded themselves inside the Trinity Lutheran Church. They stayed for nine days. Shortly after 7:30 A.M. on January 4, 1985, deputies returned and arrested seven people, among them Roth's wife, Nadine.

In January, Locker reported what Tri-State and the union had retained him to say—that the Dorothy Six blast furnaces could be restarted at a cost of $90 million and be made profitable. Under the plan, the iron it produced would be made into steel at the mill's basic oxygen shop and then be transported to a rolling mill to be made into slabs or other semifinished shapes. The slabs would, it was envisioned, be used by companies that had been using imported steel. The plant would be owned by the workers, and wages and benefits would not have to be cut, although the workforce would be limited to about three hundred, compared to the nine hundred who had formerly been employed. The corporation rejected the study. But, wary of adverse publicity, it postponed demolition of the works.

A rally attended by some nine hundred people, including Staughton Lynd, Ronnie Weisen, and a number of Duquesne workers wearing their "Ironmaster" jackets, was held on January 28 at Saint Peter's and Paul's Byzantine Catholic Church, in Duquesne. "Tonight, we want to make up your minds," said a Tri-State organizer, Jim Benn, a cold man with wire-rimmed glasses. "After this meeting, there is no neutrality." Jay Weinberg, another Tri-State organizer, said: "We kept saying you will have to stand up and determine your own destiny. People have been looking for a positive, constructive plan, and they finally have realized that we have it."

But despite their energy, their successes, and their ever-growing following, the insurgents faced difficulties. Weisen could be hard to get along with, and there was, at times, an edge to him, as though he might cold-cock you if he did not like what you were saying. He ran for union district director in 1981 and 1982 but lost each time, though by narrow margins. Feuding developed, as it had between Honest John McLuckie, Hugh O'Donnell, and other strike leaders almost a century before. People went off in different directions. There seemed no strategy, no common goal, just as there sometimes had seemed to be none among the rank-and-file activists in the 1930s.

McMills wanted to continue *1397 Rank and File* as the voice of the local's members, not of its officers. Weisen disagreed. The paper continued to attack the men who ran the mill and the corporation and the union, but it was now the voice of the Weisen administration. Some people disliked McMills's boyfriend, Greg Klink, an attorney, who was often around the union hall helping with the paper, and she turned against those who disliked him. "Everybody hated Klink," Charles McCollester said. "She got pissed."

Stout could be prickly, too, and Weisen and Stout periodically argued. Other union officials and activists attempted to curry favor with
Weisen. They did not stand up to him. "People were pissing in Ronnie's
ear," McMills said, meaning that they said what they believed he wanted
to hear. Weisen was mercurial. One moment someone would be his
friend, the next moment his enemy. Political alliances sometimes changed
from day to day or week to week, depending on his mood or his view of
events.

Weisen underwent a personal tragedy in 1982. One of his four children, Bobby, had gone swimming in the Allegheny River and, thinking
the water was deep, dived in. But he struck something—a rock, the hard
bottom closer to the surface than he thought; no one ever knew what—
and broke his neck. He lost the use of his arms, his legs, and much of his
body. Day after day he lay on his bed or sat in his wheelchair. To help
their son, the Weisens moved from the Homestead side of the river,
where they had lived for years, to a more convenient location, a small
home a few feet off Second Avenue, near the old, largely shuttered Jones
and Laughlin Works, in the Hazelwood section of Pittsburgh, where
Weisen constructed a front-porch ramp so that Bobby, in his wheelchair,
could be taken in and out of the house. He was a bright, handsome young
man, and the Weisens regretted the accident more than they ever said.

Old practices, like grievance men taking extensive lost time, gradually
returned. Weisen essentially liked people and often did not have the heart
to be strict with those who needed discipline. It is a traditional paradox
of unionism that mavericks, though energetic and combative, often have
had no leadership training; the regulars have had leadership training—
usually provided by the union—but often have no desire to confront the
entrenched leadership of the union or of the companies.

There were defections. McMills—"the brains of the outfit,"
McCollester said—was red-baited and, tiring of the game, resigned from
office in 1981. Weisen erred by not giving her his support. Weisen said
afterward, "She was a good union person. I should have leaned against
them, the people attacking her. But I didn't." Ingersoll and Weisen had
a falling-out, and Ingersoll left the scene. Some activists simply ran out of
energy. They had families and worked hard, and they could not continue
to struggle.

Some of the people associated with the Denominational Ministry
Strategy became unhappy with Honeywell. At meetings, he acted like the
leader of a cult. At demonstrations, he stayed at a safe distance and
sometimes gave hand-and-arm signals to protestors—move this way or
that, shout the slogans we rehearsed, lie down and be arrested—in the

manner of a third-base coach. Many protestors were arrested, but Honeywell was not.

Above all, the activists confronted formidable adversaries—the corporation and its hard-line chairman, David Roderick; the Pittsburgh business establishment; the Episcopal, Presbyterian, and Lutheran church establishments, which were cutting back funds to DMS; the union, which constantly attacked the Homestead local, sending auditors to go over its books four times in an attempt to find some pretext to oust Weisen and regain control of the local.

A few days before the Dorothy Six rally, on Sunday, January 20, the Denominational Ministry Strategy had held a service in a yellow school bus parked in front of the Trinity Lutheran Church, in Clairton. Roth was still in jail, and the church was shut. "A rugged industrial city," the American Guide Series—published by the Federal Writers' Project—had said of Clairton in 1940. The works, erected at the turn of the century, had 1,134 ovens and 18 coke batteries in the 1930s. In addition to its massive coke production, it was also a producer of chemicals, beginning with compounds for poison gas during World War I. For decades, it was the largest coke works in the world. It was here that striking coal miners had come in the summer of 1933 to ask steelworkers to join them in demanding unionization. An old sign welcoming people to Clairton said, "Clairton, Where Proud People Work Together for a Revitalized City." But Clairton was forlorn and abandoned, the hulk of a city, nothing more. The workforce had been reduced from six thousand to twelve hundred. On the day of the service, the temperature did not rise above zero. Clairton was being swept by cold winds that blew the snow from the ground downhill toward the works and the Monongahela River. The ground was black and frozen, hard as cement. The siege at the church had been lifted by sheriff's deputies on January 4. A bored deputy stood inside the church, peering out through the front door.

About fifty people, including half a dozen children, attended the service, huddling under layers of blankets and thick clothing on the thin, hard seats of the bus. The motor was running and the heat was on, but the bus was as cold as a coffin. Frost from the breath of the worshipers covered the insides of the windows. They sang "What a Friend We Have in Jesus" and other hymns. Then the Reverend John Gropp read a sermon written by the Reverend D. Douglas Roth in jail, condemning the corporation and the church hierarchy. It was three single-spaced pages, and it seemed, in the cold, that it took hours to read. Then everyone piled into cars, and the cars and the bus took off in a procession through the town, past the Clairton Works, and then on State Road 837 to Duquesne. They journeyed past the closed Duquesne Works, by the river, and then drove to Eighth Avenue in Homestead, past the mostly closed Homestead Works, and then over the High Level Bridge toward Pittsburgh. The plan was to demonstrate against the Catholic Church, which, the DMS activists said, was doing little or nothing for the unemployed. The protestors had fashioned tunics from white sheets and made miters and croziers. As the mock bishops ascended the steps of Saint Paul's Roman Catholic Cathedral, two churchgoers, a woman in furs and a man in a camel-hair overcoat, looked on with scorn.

At the cathedral door, Ronnie Weisen, dressed as a bishop, began reading what the protestors called their "ninety-five theses," a reference to Martin Luther: "Thou shalt not close factories. Thou shalt not cause unemployment." It was so cold that it was hard to breathe, though this did not seem to bother Weisen or the other demonstrators. He read more theses: "Thou shalt not abandon communities." Not a single person emerged from the cathedral, no altar boy, priest, or bishop. The wind blew. Was he going to read them all? The cold grew more bitter still. My hands and feet began to shake uncontrollably. Hypothermia. I clambered into Weisen's car and turned on the heater, but even after twenty minutes it was giving out no hot air. From my refuge, I could see Weisen on the steps of the cathedral, reading more theses. Photographers were taking pictures.

Finally, he stopped. He had not read all of the theses, but he had read most of them. Then he came down the steps and got into the car, still wearing his bishop's costume and carrying his crozier. It seemed to be snowing, but it was only the ferocious wind coming down Forbes Avenue, whipping up snow from the ground, and blasting straight for its target, the front of that car with the crummy heater, and me. None of this bothered Weisen. He was happy and excited. With his wonderful sense of publicity, he knew that the bishop's costumes and the ninety-five theses were something the press was going to eat up. He lay back on the seat, in his costume, cut and sewn by Betsy Von Dreele, the Reverend James Von Dreele's wife. The windows of the car were crusted with frost and snow. I could not stop my hands from shaking. He smiled. "I'll bet that goes national," he said.*

---

*It went more than that. It went international. Sometime later, I was at work back in New York, feet on the desk, riffling through some magazines. I came to a copy of the *Economist,* published in England, and there, in a story on the American steel industry, was a picture of Weisen, in his bishop's regalia, reading the ninety-five theses in front of the cathedral.

■ ■

The activists were excited. They were rallying people as the radicals one hundred years before had rallied the Homestead populace against the Pinkertons. Yet the smell of defeat was in the cold winter air. The forces arrayed against the protestors were too formidable. Moreover, there was a limit to dramatic protests. The activists had gotten press coverage, but it had given them no power. Management was demanding still more concessions while reducing crews and adding mandatory overtime. White-collar people at the Homestead Works told Michael Stout, We know we're violating the contract, but we don't have any choice. It's your ass or our ass. They're going to fire us if we don't reduce our man-hours per ton.

In February 1985, Weisen, Stout, and the other insurgents stood for reelection. Though the corporation made it clear to the union members that if they did not get rid of them the Homestead Works would be closed, the entire slate won handily. But the day after the election Stout was told by an executive: That's it. You people blew it. We're going to shut you down, and we're telling you right now.

22

"WHO WOULD HAVE THOUGHT IT?"

By the mid-1980s, a depression far worse than the Great Depression had settled upon America's steel towns. During the Great Depression, people had always had faith that one day the mills would reopen, and with the coming of World War II they did. Now it was clear that the mills would never reopen. Between 1979 and 1984, the steel companies had closed mills that had produced more than 20 percent of the nation's steel and laid off 150,000 workers, 40 percent of the industry's workforce. The steel business was, as a steelman, James Butler, had said at the turn of the century, "a merciless game." The corporation now employed ninety-one hundred workers in the Monongahela Valley, compared with twenty-eight thousand in 1979 and fifty thousand during World War II. The number of steelworkers employed in the Pittsburgh district had dropped from ninety thousand in 1980 to forty-four thousand in 1984, a reduction of more than 50 percent. Unemployment was at 25 percent, perhaps more, in Homestead and many other steel towns. Unemployment benefits were being exhausted, as were the supplemental benefits paid by the company under its contract with the union.

But hope still alternated with despair. "Homestead is doing great," Mayor Simko said. The mayor could not help himself. He was an upbeat man trying to keep people's spirits up. A rumor would arise that a mill or a works was going to be closed. Then another rumor would arise that it would be saved. Someone would come up with a plan to save a mill. Then the plan would fall apart. The corporation would say that it was going to invest and then not do it, or say that it was going to keep a mill or works open and then close it.

The despair wasn't limited to Homestead. Each steel town had its own kind of sadness. West Homestead was so broke that it was playing the state lottery. I went over to see the mayor, John Dindak, one day. He explained that municipal employees and others who wished to participate were putting two dollars a week into a kitty, and he was going down the street to Chiodo's to buy the tickets. "I'm sure we'll hit it one of these days," he said. If the town won, he was going to use the money to fix potholes. He said that he had a surefire system for picking the numbers, and he made me promise not to reveal it.

In Aliquippa, only one food store, Food City, remained on the main street, and the owner was planning to close it. The city was obtaining its police cars from Rent-a-Wreck.

Braddock was crumbling; its main street, Braddock Avenue, once as fine a street as Eighth Avenue in Homestead, was a long, bleak slum. Store after store was closed. Braddock was hit by fires, too. Houses, stores, and a beautiful old church on the hill above the largely closed Edgar Thomson Works were all burned out. One bitterly cold winter day I stopped by the Carnegie Free Library of Braddock, the first of 1,679 libraries that Andrew Carnegie had presented to 1,412 American communities—some communities received more than one library—at a cost of more than $10 million. The library had been opened in 1889, with a parade and an address by Andrew Carnegie, who dedicated it to his "fellow workmen." The corporation had maintained the library, piping gas from the Edgar Thomson Works to heat it. Then it had decided that it could no longer afford the maintenance, and in 1961 had given the library to the Braddock Board of Education. In 1971, forced to cut costs, the board had closed the library.

I looked through a window and was surprised to see a man inside. When I tapped on the window, he opened the door. His name was Roy Stell, and he had been a locomotive engineer at the Edgar Thomson Works for thirty-four years. He and some other people who were interested in local history had banded together to attempt to save the library. But they had been able only to fill a small room near the entrance with children's books and keep it open on Saturdays. He asked me whether I wanted to see the building. I said that I did.

It was like touring an abandoned castle. We would enter a room, and Stell would turn on a light, and there would be table after table covered with sheets that were in turn covered with a layer of dust and fallen plaster, and underneath all this were piles of books. We went into the "natatorium," where the pool had been empty of water for years. The diving board was still there, and in this cold, dusty, empty place Stell walked out onto the board, with the deep end thirty feet below him. "I used to swim here when I was a kid," he recalled. "Boy, those were the times." We walked upstairs, Stell turned on the light, and before us there emerged a huge auditorium with a gilted balcony. It seemed as beautiful an auditorium as the one in a far more famous structure, Carnegie Hall in New York City, which the steel master had opened in 1891. Thick curtains still hung in front of the stage. We toured the meeting room of the Tuesday-evening women's club, and the billiard room, and the two-lane bowling alley, where the pins, turned from maple, had been set by hand.

At one end of the building was the gymnasium where, before basketball became popular, Braddock boys exercised by climbing ropes and lifting the bowling-pin-shaped wooden clubs known as "Indian clubs." "Do you want to see the baths?" Stell asked. I did, so we made our way through the cold, dark halls to the basement. There were the baths and —added some years later—the showers that Carnegie had ordered built for the workers, most of whose houses had no running water, so that they could come up the hill from the Edgar Thomson Works and wash. The cost, for years, had been five cents.

Back in the children's room, Stell stood by a kerosene heater that provided the only warmth in the library. "This was quite a place years ago," he said, referring now to Braddock and the rest of the Monongahela Valley when the steel industry was thriving. "Today you walk around and you look at it, and you try to figure in your head what happened." I asked, "What do you think has happened?" Stell said, "I can't figure it out."

Another time, I stopped in to see Louis H. Washowich, mayor of

McKeesport. He was forty-four, and he had been born in McKeesport and had grown up there. "I could never in my wildest dreams think of a place I want to live outside of McKeesport," he said. But with the job losses, the atmosphere in the town was changing. This depressed him immensely, and he talked on for some two hours, sadness pouring from him. In 1940, McKeesport's population had been fifty-five thousand, he told me. Now it was thirty-one thousand. In 1982, the National Works, started by J. Pierpont Morgan, Sr., in the 1890s, employed thirty-five hundred workers. Now it had four hundred, and the corporation had recently said that it would cut the workforce again, to three hundred. Local income-tax revenues had declined by $200,000 a year. The municipal parking garages where many workers used to leave their cars had lost $150,000. Sales-tax revenues were off, and people were falling behind in their property-tax payments.

Like Homestead, McKeesport had lost much of the sense of neighborhood and of robust ethnicity that had once given it such character. Many parents, Washowich said, no longer seemed interested in what their children were doing or in what the future of their children might be. "There are large numbers of people in the valley for which this is probably the most degrading time of their lives," he said. He found it curious that Wall Street analysts applauded layoffs and plant closings as financially sensible decisions that would strengthen the corporation. He wondered what kind of people these analysts were, because their equations did not take people and communities into account. He felt that no one in government or industry was addressing these problems. "If we continue to go the way we've gone over the last twenty years," Washowich said, "I hope to hell I'm not here."

Another day I stopped at the Pizza Hut, on the border between Homestead and Duquesne, where I chatted with Betsy and Arthur Carman. Arthur Carman, a friendly, rather pudgy fellow with curly hair, had been laid off from the Duquesne Works and was now holding down two jobs, one tending bar and one at another pizza parlor. Betsy Carman, a thin brunette, was working the cash register at the Pizza Hut. It was warm and steamy there, rather pleasant, and it smelled of warm dough and cooked sausage.

I had heard about a tragedy that had struck the Carmans, and wanted to talk with them. In 1983, one of their children had drowned in an open sewer between Duquesne and Homestead. They had filed suit against the two local governments and hoped to win a substantial judgment. With their two remaining children they were living with Betsy's mother. It wasn't much of a life, Arthur said, being dependent on pizza. But what could he do? I asked how the suit was coming. He said that he was optimistic. "Hopefully, that's going to be our ticket out of here," he said. "That's a hell of a thing to say. But that's the way it is."

II

The corporation was going about the business of closing plants as if it had not been challenged by the insurgents in the Monongahela Valley. The national union leaders remained listless, still without an idea how to fight. The insurgents, though most did not acknowledge it, were powerless, and to compound their problems, they were arguing among themselves even more, sometimes splitting into factions or just giving up. Despite the national and international press coverage, they were isolated, because most of the workers and townspeople had not joined the movement. Tri-State had helped to call attention to the plight of unemployed workers. The religious protestors had caused some discomfiture to the corporation, the Mellon bank, and the hierarchies of a number of churches. The men who ran the corporation were more careful, less openly arrogant, in what they did. But despite all the protest and all the publicity, the corporation still did exactly as it pleased.

The Reverend D. Douglas Roth was eventually released from jail, after he had been defrocked. He continued to wear his clerical collar and to hold services on Sundays, small, sad affairs, first in his dining room and then in a Clairton Pentecostal church, for the two dozen people who still followed him. On May 10, 1985, the Reverend Daniel Solberg was removed as pastor of the Nativity Lutheran Church, in Allison Park, Pennsylvania. He barricaded himself inside his church, was arrested, and was jailed until September. In November, he and his wife, Ann, and three other members of the congregation were excommunicated. In February 1986, he too was defrocked by the Lutheran Synod.

In late 1986, the religious protestors hit upon a new strategy—burning skunks, squirrels, groundhogs, dogs, and other animals run over by cars, on the sidewalk in front of David C. Roderick's home in the fashionable suburb of Fox Chapel. This got into the media but produced no other results, apart from their arrest for disturbing the peace. By now, their provocative actions had eliminated almost all of the support gained in the previous three years. Leaders began to drift away, among them the Reverend John Yedlicka, Ronnie Weisen, and Mike Bonn, former president of the Irwin Works local.

Tri-State also suffered a defeat when, in January 1986, its plan to reopen the Dorothy Six furnaces at the Duquesne Works collapsed. The

New York investment house of Lazard Frères and Company, retained by the national union and Allegheny County for $100,000, said that the furnaces could not be profitably operated "under current conditions in the steel industry." The Tri-State activists and the union leaders next announced a plan to reopen two electric furnaces at the closed Jones and Laughlin Works on Pittsburgh's South Side. Despite much attention in the Pittsburgh press, this plan failed as well.

More parts of the Homestead Works were being closed, as were other mills across the country. In June 1985, the 100-inch and 160-inch mill were closed. Dating from Carnegie's time, they were the last of the great slab-and-plate operations that had given the works much of its reputation. The works now employed fewer than two thousand workers, and more layoffs were occurring each month. In May 1986, the corporation said that it was "temporarily suspending" operations at its structural and blooming mill—Number Two Structural—at the Homestead Works, idling 350 more workers. But it was clear that the mills were being closed permanently and that the corporation was just trying to blunt the impact of the announcement and to postpone paying severance benefits to the laid-off workers. By the late spring, the Homestead Works was largely empty and silent. Weeds and trees—lamb's quarter, sumac, cottonwood, and ailanthus—were growing along the railroad tracks and outside the buildings, and even inside, wherever the sun could get through. By now, forty-five hundred steelworkers remained employed in the Monongahela Valley.

On July 25, 1986, came the closing of the Homestead Works, the day that the last workers straggled out of the Amity Gate in a desolate line of rattletrap cars and pickup trucks, and began the sad journey up the hill that ended at Hess's Bar. That was the day I asked Bob Krovocheck what he was going to do, and he said, "Go down and sign up," meaning that he was going to apply for unemployment benefits. It was also the day that Bobby Schneider said, "It's a shame to see this happen to us guys. We're so young."

One day, sometime after the mill went down, a dozen or so of the last workers came to the union hall, now usually empty most of the day, to talk with me. Bob Todd was there. So were Bob Krovocheck, Bobby Schneider, Richard Holoman, Ray McGuire, Red Hrabik, and others. We sat in a circle of chairs in a large, bare room on the first floor and chatted about life in the mill—the fun as well as the work—and about why the mill had gone down.

After a while, the men got to telling stories. Bob Todd told of the great pride he had felt on his first day as a craneman. Bob Krovocheck told about an old Russian who had owned a store on Eighth Avenue during World War II. As a boy, Bob had often delivered messages in town. In the back room, the old man had box after box filled with coins. The boy had asked why he kept all the coins, and the old man had explained that he had left Russia after the 1917 Revolution with a great deal of paper money, but when he got to America it was worthless. His brother had left with just a few coins, but when he got to America they were good. The old man said that he was not going to make the same mistake twice.

Then it was time to go. I shook hands all around, the men lining up, as though in a receiving line. Toward the end of the line was Ed Buzinka, the happy man with the glasses on his head the day the mill went down. Now he looked sad and perplexed. He looked at me as we shook hands.

He asked, "Who would have thought it?"

III

The rich life that had characterized Homestead and the rest of the Monongahela Valley was disappearing. Families were breaking up. Morale and confidence were faltering. The makeup of Homestead was changing. Longtime residents were moving away. Houses were deteriorating, values were dropping, and less-affluent people were being attracted to the town. Many of the new residents were transients with no interest in the community. The Department of Housing and Urban Development began to move families into apartments and houses in Homestead under the federal government's Section Eight housing program. The program often paid above-market rents to slum landlords—$250 to $300 a month for a walk-up on Eighth Avenue, for example. "You couldn't get Section Eight housing in Upper Saint Clair or any of those well-to-do areas," said Chris Kelly, the police chief. "In Homestead, it's okay. Section Eight is killing Homestead." The deterioration began in the lower part of Homestead and moved up the hill, and when it reached the top of the hill it spilled over past the cemeteries into Munhall. "Despair is creeping up the hill," said Jennie Yuhaschek, a teacher at Steel Valley High School. "Houses are just falling apart." As the tax base fell, the town could no longer afford to maintain its sidewalks, streets, and parks. Grass grew through cracks in the asphalt and concrete, and potholes were not repaired.

A new immigration was occurring in Homestead. As Slavs had replaced English, Welsh, and Germans, and black people had replaced Slavs, now poorer people, black and white, some from Appalachia, were replacing the families who were moving away. But whereas immigrants had once come with the hope of getting ahead, the newcomers had no hope. They brought with them the problems of the poor everywhere. Many were unkempt and did not take care of their homes. They used rough language and had brought with them violent ways. In the old days, immigrants could get jobs in the mill. There were no jobs for the newcomers, at least no jobs that paid much of anything. There was domestic violence, drug-abuse, robbery, and murder. One day, Chief Kelly, on patrol, pointed out a young prostitute. "Her two brothers are prostitutes, and so is her mother," he said. He then pointed out a young man who a few years before had been a basketball player for Steel Valley High School. "You should have seen him," Chief Kelly said. "He was a great player." Now the young man did not do anything but hang out along West Street and in lower Homestead. He pointed an index finger in greeting. Chief Kelly did the same.

The stores along Eighth Avenue were closing. The building that had housed Half Brothers, a fine furniture store, was occupied by a Goodwill thrift shop. W. T. Grant closed. Autenreith's Five and Dime closed. Woolworth's closed, and the building was taken over by the state, which put a state liquor store there. Thom McAn's closed. Sol's Sporting Goods closed. The Moose Club took over the building and made it into a bingo hall. Peter Pan Paint and Hardware closed, and the building was occupied by a Saint Vincent de Paul thrift shop.

At the Goodwill store, a coat was selling for $9.95, an upholstered chair for $39, ice skates for $2. But business was not as good as had been expected. "People are not used to buying secondhand," Irene Schrecengost, the manager, said. "The workers feel degraded by shopping at Goodwill."

IV

The Homestead union, Local 1397, continued its monthly meetings even after the works closed, and at the June 1987 meeting, I saw Rich Locher, a hooker from Number Two Structural. Before the meeting began, we chatted. He was enrolled in a retraining program, studying to be a nurse. He was not happy about being a nurse, but that was the only training that was available, and he was trying to make the best of it. Though he had always thought of nursing as women's work, he was serious about his studies. Maybe he had been wrong. His wife, though still employed at the container factory, was also studying to be a nurse. Perhaps they could work together in a hospital when they finished their training. "Got to go along with the times, right?" he said, smiling.

The meeting was a tumultuous, profanity-filled affair. A thick blue cloud of cigarette smoke lay above the four hundred or more workers in the hall. At the height of the uprising, the insurgents had often gotten just a handful to attend meetings, usually fifty or so, almost never more than a hundred. Now, with people anxious to apply for unemployment, severance, and pension benefits and for retraining, and looking for something to fill their time, meetings were packed. The irony was clear. The workers had not participated in the insurgency when they should have and now, when the insurgency was past, they were participating. It was, I thought more than once, as Eugene Debs, in Atlanta Federal Penitentiary in 1920, and deeply depressed, had said: "The people can have anything they want. The trouble is they do not want anything." The subject of this meeting was retraining, and two staff members from the office of Senator John Heinz, Republican of Pennsylvania, thin men in pinstripe suits, were present to explain federal retraining programs. Making such appearances is one of the routine tasks that congressional staffers must perform, and they had not given the evening much thought. They had come to do a little public relations for Senator Heinz, a little schmoozing with the working stiffs, and then they wanted to get out of town.

The workers were in a foul mood. The retraining programs were not working. They were costing the government hundreds of millions of dollars, but they were inadequate to prepare people for new kinds of work. They were a way of extending unemployment benefits and keeping the men tranquil, and everyone knew it. The game, of course, was to pretend that the programs were useful, but the workers weren't buying this, in particular one wild-eyed man in back. It was Locher. For a few minutes he had engaged in a restrained discussion with the congressional staffers, but suddenly he seemed to lose control. "Retraining is bullshit!" he shouted.

The two men from the senator's office said they disagreed. The retraining programs might have faults, the men said, but they offered displaced workers a way to gain access to employment opportunities in the new service economy, if the workers had the patience and sense to take advantage of them. "Fuck the programs!" Locher yelled. "The programs are bullshit!" Other men joined in. "The guy is right," one cried. "Fuck the programs! The programs are bullshit!" The men in the pinstripe suits did not know what to say. It was clear that they had not been prepared for this. This wasn't part of the game. Their faces said, What the hell is going on? Who are these animals yelling at us? It having been established, to the satisfaction of the workers, that the programs were bullshit, attention turned to other matters, and the congressional staffers, with great relief, retreated from the dais and left the hall.

After the meeting I went up to Locher and said that I would like to come out and see him someday at his home. He lived in Apollo, northeast of Homestead. "Come on out," he said, and we shook on it. The men from Senator Heinz's office stopped by Chiodo's to have a couple of beers. Joe Chiodo chatted with them. They had a question about Homestead. What's that? Chiodo asked. They wanted to know, Who were those goddamned steelworkers at the union hall? What's wrong with them?

Everyone is edgy because of the mill closings and the unemployment, Chiodo said. You have to expect it.

In these months, I sometimes wandered down to Straka's, the old steelworkers' restaurant not far from the Amity Street gate, for lunch. It was a pleasant place to go, especially in cold weather, and I usually had a hot roast-beef sandwich, the special, and a bottle of Iron City. When the mill was running flat out, Straka's had kept $100,000 or more on hand to cash checks on paydays. But business had been off by 50 percent, maybe more, for years because of the closings and layoffs at the Homestead Works. "Business started to fade out, fade out, fade out, and then the bottom fell out," John Tarasevich said one day. It would have made sense for John and his wife, Millie Straka, to sell the place. But they enjoyed coming to work and chatting with the customers, many of whom were their old friends. "You think about getting out," he said. "But what are you going to do? Just close up? Where would these people go then? What would we do? You have to keep working."

On another cold, gray winter day, I was in Carol and George Couvaris's restaurant, the Sweet Shoppe, on Eighth Avenue, just off the Homestead end of the High Level Bridge. Carol Couvaris's father's business, United Candy, had produced the candy so prized in Homestead—bonbons, seafoam, fudge, ribbon candy, taffy, butterscotch, candy apples, nut brittle, caramel corn, marshmallows, chocolate rabbits at Easter, peppermint candy canes at Christmas, all hand-dipped and made from the finest ingredients. The candy represented the good life that, despite the dirt and smoke of the mill, the workers had created in Homestead.

United Candy had closed in 1974, but George and Carol Couvaris had continued to sell candy in their restaurant. Once it had represented 80 percent of their business. Now it represented 20 percent. "People can't afford to buy candy anymore," Carol Couvaris said, and it might even be necessary to close the Sweet Shoppe. George Couvaris stood by the coffeepot behind the counter and talked of how the iron and steel towns had produced weapons for the Union Army in the Civil War and

2 3

"THE BREAKUP
OF LIFE
AS WE KNEW IT"

I was at the Ancient Order of Hibernians, the Irish club, next to the union hall on McClure Street, having a beer with Wendell Brucker. I liked the club, though it had become a bit run-down. Years of spilled beer and cigarette smoke had created a sort of film that seemed to cover everything—the bar, the urinals, the toilets. But it was what it was and good enough because of that, and the boys were always friendly. Spanky O'Toole, a retired policeman, tended bar. To get into the club you had to press a buzzer and look through a glass slit in the door, and somebody came over and checked you out, and if you were okay the Spank buzzed you in, just like in Prohibition.

Brucker had been a worker for thirty-two years and had gone on unemployment benefits, $205 a week for twenty-six weeks, when he was laid off. Now he was living on his pension and he was not happy.

He said of the benefits, "Unemployment's worthwhile. But it makes you feel worthless. That's the biggest thing—feeling worthless, the loss of pride." He sat for a time. No one said anything. Then he spoke again. "We came a long way," he said, referring to himself and the other workers from the Homestead Works. "We were—how would you say it?—people nobody thought much of, and we became halfway decent people, almost middle-class people." There was silence again. Then he added, "That's right. We were almost middle-class."

When I had first come to Homestead, I had been told that steelworkers masked their feelings, that adversity meant little to men who made steel, that they regarded crying as unseemly, did not get depressed, did not commit suicide. I had been misinformed. "They don't want you to be middle-class," Brucker said. He was crying now. The rest of us did not know what to do, so we sat there and said nothing and looked away.

One cold, gray day in the spring of 1987, I spent an afternoon touring the Homestead Works with Mayor Steve Simko and Chief Kelly. We had been sitting in the borough hall, shooting the breeze, our feet on the desks, and had decided that since we had nothing better to do, we'd go down to see the mill. The chief called for a patrol car, and we went down. We spent a couple of hours there. The great steel buildings were dark and quiet, ghost buildings in a ghost works. You could yell, and after a time, from way down at the end of a building, an echo would come back. "Like the Grand Canyon," the chief said. The chief drove, and the mayor sat up front. The chief had to be careful. There were live electrical wires hanging down, beams and equipment that could tumble over at any time, huge black holes in the ground where furnaces or machines had been. We would drive to the edge of a hole, our front tires sometimes stopping just inches short of it. "Go too far and we are down a hundred ninety feet fast," the chief said. "Never find us for months," the mayor said.

We drove into a long, dark building. A line of empty ladles, two dozen or more, which had been used to transport molten iron and steel, covered one wall. Parts of the floor above had collapsed onto them. The mayor was our tour guide. "We are now in Open Hearth Five," he said. "It had eleven furnaces, each with a capacity of 283 tons of product." Then he said: "Look at that. Goddamned grass growing in the open hearth. Goddamn."

We drove on. "That's Rusin Hall," the mayor said, pointing to a gray brick building, the last remaining building from lower Homestead, the part of town below the tracks, which had been demolished early in World War II to make room for the expansion of the works. The building was sound, so it was kept. There had been many executive meetings there. "This was Fifth Avenue, right where we are now," the mayor said, referring to the old main street of lower Homestead. "You're riding on Fifth Avenue right now."

We would occasionally get out, and walk about a building, and, like soldiers picking over a battlefield, examine abandoned equipment or other items. There were shearing machines; presses; magnets, four or five feet across, used to lift steel; row after row of rolls left over from the rolling mills; a five-hundred-ton engine; lathes; huge chains for lifting forgings; batteries; open lockers; papers still on desks; a lunch bucket; dead flowers, black stems now, in a glass jar.

We drove into one of the old forge buildings. "This building houses a ten-thousand-ton press," the mayor said. "There are only two in the country like it, here and at Bethlehem, and both are down." We saw a huge steel object in the middle of the floor. "This is one of the semifinished products," he said. "That could be some kind of shaft for a powerhouse or a power station. That son of a bitch, why, it's worth half a million dollars." We saw more abandoned forgings. "There's millions of dollars of stuff just lying here," he said. We walked up to a lathe that seemed to stretch a block or more. "This is the biggest lathe in the world," he said. "It's ninety-two feet between center, with a 148-inch chuck."

We stopped for a time and sat in the car by the Monongahela River. "That's the Carrie furnaces," the mayor said, pointing to the other side of the river, where huge piles of rusting metal, several stories high, lay. "That's where our blast furnaces are. Over there is the Hot Metal Bridge." In one of the buildings that had been used to make stainless steel, we saw a sign. It said, "These people and facilities process the world's finest-quality stainless plate." The mayor said, "That ain't no bullshit, either."

We entered the mayor's old workplace, the Valley Machine Shop. "I have 130,000 square feet of work area," the mayor said. "I had 574 people working for me. My shop at night was like daylight, like Broadway. The whole mill was. There was work all over, noise all over, steam all over. You take the four-to-midnight shift, for Christ's sake. Everybody would come out of the goddamned mill and have a sandwich and a beer. Why, men would get out at eight in the morning and get a beer. You'd break up bar fights at eight o'clock in the morning. You should have been around on paydays. Oh, my, the bars. Every other Tuesday, in the old days, when they paid in cash, for Christ's sake, you'd see a bunch of women standing at the gates waiting for their husbands to come out. The wives said, 'Here's yours. You go to the saloon. I got mine. I'm going shopping with the kids.' "

We passed the thirty-inch mill, also built on what had been lower Homestead. "This is where the Club Mirador was," the mayor said, referring to Homestead's famous nightclub of the 1930s and 1940s, where people—both black and white—went to hear jazz greats like Maxine Sullivan and Earl "Fatha" Hines, and where Doc McLean and his team, born-again Democrats, celebrated their victory over Burgess Cavanaugh and his Republican administration during the Depression. "Right about here. They had a fence up between that and the mill. The wives would come down and give the husbands lunch through the fence. Over there is the pump house, the old one. We had five pump houses. We almost made the water so clean that you could drink it. But they wouldn't let us put it back into the river. Imagine that. They would pump it out of the river, clean it, make it almost good enough to drink, but they wouldn't let us put it back into the river. We had to build a water plant, a recycling plant. I think it cost us between one hundred and one hundred thirty-five million dollars, and the bastard is just sitting there."

We drove to the eastern end of the mill, the forty-eight-inch mill. It was in disarray, open to the elements, and this angered the mayor. "It makes me want to cry," he said. "I spent forty-three years in this works. I know every goddamned spot in the joint. Everybody worked here—fathers, sons, grandsons. I had my sons working here. Three generations of Simkos worked here."

We passed the building that had housed the 160-inch mill. "We made the armor plate here for World War I and World War II," the mayor said. He was wound up now. "We made some big goddamned product in this works. We made the shafting for the power plant in Hoover Dam. Right here in the Homestead Works. If you go to visit Hoover Dam, you will see 'Homestead Works' on it. The Empire State Building, the Sears Tower—we made all those big buildings. And ships—I always said we won the war with Homestead armor."

We stopped. "Here's where the office is for the slab-and-plate division," the mayor said, gesturing toward an empty building. "This is where I caught the bastard stealing the air conditioner." He pointed to another building. "This is the hundred-inch mill. It is noisy as a bastard in there. Many a fucking cold day I've been down in that goddamned place, I'll tell you. It's as cold as a son of a bitch down there, with the plate all over. Those salamander stoves, that's how you kept warm."

Cannibalizing the mill was now a way to make a few dollars for some people in the Monongahela Valley, and here and there we saw piles of rags with grease on them. Thieves would light the rags at night, and wrap them around sticks, and, like prehistoric people, use them as torches to go around the ruins and steal whatever seemed valuable, brass and copper being the most coveted items. "They're stripping copper," the chief said, exasperated. "Ten dollars of copper from a million-dollar machine." We saw a grocery cart, then another. "Christ, they've even got carts," the mayor said.

We entered the Number One Structural Mill. "Christ, we rolled steel here for the biggest buildings in the world," the mayor said. "Beams were stacked all the way up, as far as you could get them."

"It was a dangerous place," the mayor said. "We made a hard and fast rule that you weren't allowed to pile wide beams on narrow beams. 'No wide on narrow,' we'd say. Before that, somebody would hit a pile with something, and it would go down like a bunch of toothpicks, and anybody near that son of a bitch was dead. There was a guy, an instructor named Dunmore. He was from Homestead. He was instructing down where we poured steel, hot metal. He was standing on a runway up in the air, and they dropped this goddamned ladle, and the hot steel shot up and killed him, seventy feet up in the air, burned him to death."

It was traditional in steel towns for people to try to one-up each other's stories about death in the mill. The chief now said that he remembered a man who had lived at Seventeenth Avenue and West Street. The man had fallen into a ladle of molten steel and been burned to death. "That's right," the mayor said. "What they used to do is, they used to get the ingot and put it on the side of the yard." Then, after a time, the mayor said, when the death was forgotten, the ingot, with the vaporized body inside, would be reheated, rolled, and shipped.

Men melted into steel are part of the folklore of American steelmaking. Some say that the legendary Monongahela Valley steelworker Joe Magarac, a man made of steel, a man as big as a smokestack, with fingers as strong as other men's arms and arms as strong as steel rails, a man who wore size eighteen, extra-wide, triple-soled, safety-toed shoes, was, when he died, melted into steel again. But the mayor and the chief were not making up stories. They knew that this had happened. "You're just part of steel," the mayor said. "You could be a bridge," the chief said. "People could drive over you every day."

The mayor had been working for several months to find investors to purchase and reopen the Valley Machine Shop, and he was now in a confident mood. He had arranged a meeting not long before with David M. Roderick, the corporation's chairman, and Thomas C. Graham, the president. "They were both nice to me," he said. "Of course, you expect that, because they're very nice people." He expected to receive a letter of intent from the investors that very day. "We get that letter of intent today and I'm going to go in there, to U.S. Steel, and say, 'We have this. Now, how about just selling us the goddamned plant?' Which is what I think they will do."

We left the mill in the late afternoon. I did not notice it at the time, but later, when I was thinking over that day, I realized that during the tour the mayor had sometimes talked in the present tense, as though the mill were still open. But in his heart, despite his optimism, he seemed to understand that the situation was bleak. None of us said much as we drove up from the mill, crossed Eighth Avenue, and went along West Street toward the borough hall. After a time, the mayor spoke. "Everything is going to shit," he said.

I always enjoyed dropping in on the monthly pensioners' meeting at the Homestead union hall, the first Thursday of every month, before the hall closed down. Some of the men would come early to cook hotdogs and kielbasa, and soon the odors would be wafting through the hall, and the old-timers would sit in the kitchen shooting the breeze about the old days in the mill, some remembering as far back as the early years of the century. They were wonderful fellows with common sense and sharp memories. One day, I chatted with Paul Kovalalchik, who was seventy-one. He had been at the Homestead Works for forty-two years, from 1939 to 1981. His pay when he began was thirty dollars a month. During his last year, it was twenty-eight thousand dollars a year.

I asked him whether he had been worth that money. "I was worth more than that," he said. "Why?" I asked. "Because I worked on hot steel," he said. "Because I sweated. I was a line-drawer, and I wore wooden clogs to walk on hot steel, wooden clogs, like shower shoes. Your shoes used to smoke, that's how hot they were. You know, in forty-two years I never sat down to eat lunch. You'd eat on the fly. Take a bite of a sandwich, and put it down, and go to work again. Do you think that was right, not getting lunch? Do you think I was worth the money?" I said, "Yes."

Despair gripped the Homestead school district. Children knew that their families faced hard times, and they, too, were depressed. Parents no longer seemed as interested as they had been in the welfare of their children, or perhaps they were too burdened with other worries. There were more problems with students drinking and taking drugs. Fewer parents came to counseling sessions with teachers. Teachers frequently could not reach parents at home during the day. If fathers were home, they often did not answer the phone. Mothers, and sometimes mothers and fathers, were out working, often at more than one low-paying job. Sometimes parents had taken jobs that in better times only children would have taken, to earn pocket money or to save for college. A leveling was occurring. Many families who had the money to do so were leaving the district, and often their children were among the best students. Other families' incomes had dropped so dramatically, because of the layoffs and the depressed economy that the layoffs had caused, that they had fallen back in economic and social status. "Before, there were the poor and there were the rich," Jennie Yuhaschek said, meaning that there were the poor and there were the steel-mill families, who were relatively well off. "Now everybody is coming to the same level."

The exodus of families and the declining tax assessments on homes and businesses meant that the tax revenues available to Homestead and the Steel Valley Board of Education were reduced. At the same time, Homestead was attracting a poorer population who brought with them additional problems for the school system. Almost none of the students dreamed big dreams now. Some talked of computers and high technology but had no idea of what these terms meant. It was ironic that, whereas in the old days many students in the Homestead district did not consider going to college because they knew that they could go into the mill, now, with the shutting-down of the Homestead Works and the other mills, it was becoming clear that if they were to have a chance in life, they would have to graduate from high school and go on for some advanced education. But most knew that their parents could not afford to send them, and they gave up on their hopes. Often, when students spoke of continuing their education after high school, they were planning to go to a beauty school, a trade school, or a community college. Only a handful talked of going to a four-year college, and even among them, few saw themselves going far away to the nation's most prestigious universities. "The rich kids can go to college and continue to get money and be rich, but the other kids aren't able to go anywhere at all," one said.

Many students had decided to enter military service. So productive was recruiting in Homestead and the other steel towns that recruiters regarded tours there as plum assignments. "Three or five years ago, when you tried to get them to sign up, they said they were going into the mill to earn money," Sergeant Bruce Fox, an Air Force recruiter in the Homestead district, said. "It's a different story today." One day I met a Marine recruiter in Chiodo's. He had been there for a while and was loaded. "Greatest fucking place I ever saw for recruiting," the sergeant said. "Tough fucking kids. They'll make good fucking Marines."

An appearance of normalcy was maintained in the schools. The football team, the Ironmen, kept up its good record. The seniors had a formal prom at a fancy hotel in the suburbs. The boys dressed up in dinner jackets and the girls in prom dresses, and many couples went in rented limousines. But students talked of leaving the district, whatever occupation they ended up in. There was no future in Homestead, they said.

In the rich days of the mill, the school district had not used its resources well. Too many parents did not see the need for education, and too many teachers and administrators regarded themselves as custodians. They taught basic skills and kept the students from getting into trouble, but that was all. The district had not had a National Merit Scholar since 1974. Nor had much attention been paid to how money was spent. Schools bought sets of books that were not used, and school-board members went on junkets to conventions in faraway cities, and enjoyed the drinks and the good food and the sights, all expenses paid. It was a form of "get it at the mill," and no one asked questions. In the fall, when new teachers were hired, they were taken by bus to the Homestead Works and given a tour, so that they would know where the money came from.

The teachers—and, for that matter, many others in white-collar professions in the valley—had often seemed to dislike the steelworkers. The teachers had gone to college for four years, sometimes more, and here were the steelworkers, many of whom had not finished high school, some of them former students of the teachers—making more money than the teachers. Not only that, but many steelworkers bragged about not working hard and making good money doing it. They would flaunt their paychecks and say, "Not bad for four hours a day." "I used to resent terribly that I had spent four years in school, and now I was teaching, doing what I thought was most important, and here some bozo drops out of my class, doesn't even graduate, and goes into the mill, and makes twice my salary in the first year," Jennie Yuhaschek said.

At the same time, many steelworkers denigrated the teachers, saying that they did not work hard and that they often had to go to work in the mill during the summer to earn enough money to make ends meet. Only a man who wasn't a man would work at an easy job, wear a shirt and tie, and not make enough money to support his family, some steelworkers said. As for women teachers, they should be happy with whatever they got. After all, their husbands worked—or should. Now, as the mills were going down and the steelworkers were losing their jobs, some of the teachers sat in their lounge at Steel Valley High School and said, Let them lose their jobs. They have two cars and a boat, and they never finished high school. They're getting what they deserve. Jennie Yuhaschek could not understand this logic. You people are idiots, she told the other teachers. Don't you see that we're all in the same boat, that we're all going to go down together?

In the old days, the Homestead Board of Education had been highly political, filled with people from the Democratic machine who knew little about education. Now, with the increased interest in education, the board was much improved. Committed, independent people had been elected, including a new chairman, Mark Hornak, the 1974 Merit Scholar. But now funds were limited. "We used to have a bad board but a lot of money," a teacher said. "Now we have a good board but no money. If the board had the money there was ten years ago, it might be able to do something."

With the decline in revenues, substantial cuts in school services had to be made. In 1978, the high school had eighty faculty members. By 1987, it had fifty-one. Drama and music—except for the marching band, which was popular with a number of parents who had influence in the community—were eliminated. The music teacher, Tom Maches, was a talented, committed educator; he taught opera, and students and teachers walking past the music room had always enjoyed hearing the singing. Now he was terminated. "Our programs have been reduced to such a degree that there are no options, no choices," said Marie Coyne, director of the English Department at Steel Valley High School.

The staff reductions meant that the remaining teachers were forced to handle extra courses. Leslie Evans, a superb English teacher, now had five courses instead of four and ninety students instead of sixty-five, plus a study hall. The extra work was tiring. Exams and papers could not be graded and returned as promptly as before. "I go home every night with bags of work," Leslie Evans said. "Sometimes I do it, and sometimes I sit there and say, 'I can't do it.'" Some teachers were burned out and were merely putting in their time. Because of financial restrictions, no new teachers were being hired, and the district was thus deprived of new ideas, new vigor. Classes were sometimes chaotic. "We have teachers in this building who are just blowing out the year," Jennie Yuhaschek said. When they could find them, students obtained jobs to help their families. Often they were too tired at night to study. Test scores dropped. Once a number of students each year had received grades of four or five on their Advanced Placement Tests. Now many students received threes and twos, and few got fours and fives. The teachers were embarrassed, but there seemed to be nothing they could do.

In the mid-1980s, the new board, determined to improve educational standards, hired a superintendent of schools, Jerry Longo, who was from the north side, across the Allegheny River. As an outsider, he was viewed with suspicion by some people, but the board was convinced that the new superintendent had to be an outsider. "It would have been impossible for him to be a home boy," John Tichon, the assistant superintendent, said. "The professional staff would not have thought the effort was serious otherwise. They would not have allowed themselves to be led by a Steel Valley person."

Longo was a skilled, honest man with a keen sense of public relations. He had a doctorate in education, and he insisted on being called Dr. Longo, in order to show that the superintendent of the Steel Valley School District had a doctorate, and thus that the district's standards were as good as those of other districts, even the ones with more money. He began to institute reforms. He demanded that the teachers work hard and negotiated a five-year contract with their union. He obtained twenty computers—the first in the school system—through a grant from Apple Computer, one of whose vice-presidents, Bill Campbell, was among Homestead's most famous graduates, a football player who had gone on to star and coach at Columbia University. Slowly, it seemed, students and parents began to take more pride in their school system. When a Pittsburgh reporter referred in a story to "Longo," a Homestead resident called the newspaper to complain. "He is Dr. Longo," the caller said.

Numerous difficulties remained. Too many students had poor skills. Too many parents remained interested in sports, not education. The high school had only one black teacher, although the student body was 20 percent black. Few students could speak effectively in public. Reporters would come to town, and when they tried to interview students, a lot of them mumbled and hung their heads. One spring day in 1987, Longo, sitting in his office, said that the worst problem confronting students and teachers was lack of self-esteem. Homestead people, particularly those from immigrant families, had often been shy and unsure of themselves. Now despair and deterioration had caused students and teachers alike to lose whatever self-assurance they had possessed. But Longo said: "This is going to be someplace again. It's a matter of time. It's going to happen."

The Homestead borough government was dispirited and, unlike the school board, seemed incapable of confronting its difficulties. In 1961, at the height of the good years in the steel industry, the millions in taxes that the corporation had paid to Homestead made up 65 percent of the borough's budget. In the late 1970s, as production at the Homestead Works was being cut back, the corporation's taxes had fallen steadily. By

August 1986, after the closing of the works, they were only $700,000 a year, and the corporation was seeking a reduction to $353,000.

Each year in the good times, the Homestead Works had purchased $500,000 worth of water from the borough. When the works closed, this revenue was eliminated. When the corporation bought so much water, many residents did not bother to pay their water bills, and the borough did not bother to collect them. "When the people in our borough didn't pay their water bills, the borough council didn't pay much attention to it, because, hell, we were paying our water bill and still had money left over," Mayor Simko said. "Now, when that steel mill isn't there and we haven't got that money from the water, these people are so goddamned used to not paying their water bills that we can't get the money off them."

The plan to turn the Leona Theatre into apartments and shops fell through, and in January 1983 the building was purchased by the Sheetz Corporation, a retail chain. A flutter of protest arose, but not enough to save what was, after the mill and the library, the town's most treasured building. It was demolished in three days, and a twenty-four-hour gas station and convenience store went up on the site.

As revenues fell, services were reduced. Maintenance of parks and paving were neglected. In 1976, Homestead had seventeen policemen. In 1987, it had six. In 1976, there were seventeen firefighters. In 1986, there were two full-time firefighters, with the rest of the force made up of volunteers. Years before, the town had provided a summer sports program for teenagers. Perhaps three to five hundred kids would be at the Homestead athletic field, up over the hill, every afternoon. There was softball, touch football, basketball, track, Ping-Pong, checkers. "Now Homestead doesn't have a baseball team—no Little League, no Pony League, nothing," Chief Kelly said one day on patrol in his car. "What do kids do now? Stand on the corner, break bottles, and drink."

The council had never possessed real power. Power had been in the hands of the corporation, and the politicians had done little but participate in vigorous machine politics. Now the machine had fallen apart. There was no longer much patronage to dispense, with the collapse of the mill and much of the town's economy. But the council members knew no other way to operate. They had never learned how to lead when the corporation had existed. Now, with the corporation gone, town government became a sink of pettiness and purposelessness. Meetings droned on and on—the solicitor's report, the budget, reports on streets and traffic, sanitation, police, firefighting. There was a lot of windbaggery, grandstanding, squabbling, when new ideas and strong resolve were needed. Only a handful of citizens attended council meetings.

As the town was crumbling, a major subject of debate in the council was what to do about the Fantasia Health Spa, a massage parlor on Eighth Avenue. Chief Kelly had closed down the last of the Sixth Avenue whore-houses, known as Mrs. Williams's and Ernie Richie's, in 1980, when he was a young police officer. Wearing civilian clothes and a pair of big sunglasses, he had gone into one of the places and said he wanted the works. "Why, sure," the madam said. "Take off that coat." He did, but his handcuffs showed. "Oh, no, honey," she said. "None of that kinky stuff." He told her that he was a police officer, and then he closed the place down. Next he padlocked the second place, and he and other officers took everything from both places—beds, chairs, toilets, light bulbs—even though they had no warrants.

But the chief was having difficulty closing the Fantasia, a place in the tradition of the old days of the illegal sex, drinking, and gambling that had thrived in Homestead, and he was frustrated. The solicitor and some council members kept insisting that the chief was harassing the Fantasia and that if he moved against it, he had better stay within the spirit and letter of the law (although it was hard to understand why the council members were so touchy about raids on the Fantasia; the council had never seemed to be composed of strict Fourth Amendment people).

The chief had raided the Fantasia in 1982, 1985, and 1986, but each time—even the next day—it reopened. His anger mounted. "If you think the Fantasia is about massages, you're crazy," he told the council. "They're giving hand jobs in there, and worse than that." At one point, he made all the women who worked at the Fantasia attend massage school and obtain certificates to prove it. "You want to be masseuses, get trained," he said. But the Fantasia stayed open, and the chief plotted his next move.

II

To people whose roots in Homestead went far back, the decline of the town was most difficult to accept. One of them was Rich Terrick, the magistrate. He was a machine politician in the best sense of that term. He believed that politics existed to take care of people—his people. He was a Slav, and proud of it, and a Democrat, and proud of that, too—not some new-fangled Democrat but an old-time Roosevelt Democrat. He loved politics, reveled in it.

He had been born in Munhall, just across the line from Homestead, and he still lived there. But he didn't look down on Homestead people, as so many in Munhall did. He was a Homestead man, through and through. He lived across the Munhall line, that was all. He had gone to

Saint Michael's Elementary School in the 1940s, when Catholic education was still strict, before the reforms of Vatican II. At lunchtime and at the end of the day, the students left school by lining up and marching for two blocks to the beat of a drum, like little soldiers. A stern sister with a sharp stare watched over the procession, and woe—usually in the form of a whacking—to any student who misbehaved. At the end of the two blocks, everyone skedaddled home.

After graduating from Munhall High School, he served in the military, attended the University of Pittsburgh, and then went into the mill, where he worked, temporarily, as a foreman. One day supervisors told him that he was being promoted to foreman permanently. Since he had a wife and five children, it was assumed that he would eagerly accept the offer. But he wanted to get out of the mill and didn't like the way that they thought they knew what he had to do. He stepped out of the office, asked if he could borrow a secretary for a moment, had her type his resignation in triplicate, returned to the office, and handed it to his bosses.

In 1961, as a young man, he ran for justice of the peace, or magistrate, but he was recalled to the military during the Berlin Crisis and missed the election. An elderly man beat him by twenty-three votes, but then he retired suddenly. Terrick's father, the Democratic Party chief of Munhall for years, at a time when politics meant something, called Governor David Lawrence, a Democrat, and a month later Terrick was appointed. That was what politics was all about. His father, a Slav, a millworker with nine years of schooling, could call the governor, and the governor would talk to him and give his son a job. Terrick's brothers, relatives, and friends were working in the mill, making thirteen or fourteen thousand dollars a year, maybe more, and he was earning thirty-five hundred. His salary rose over the years, but so did theirs, and many continued to make more than he did. But he never regretted leaving the mill. Politics was what he did, what he cared about.

He tried to keep up the old political traditions. Each Labor Day he and his wife, Noreen, gave a huge party that spread out of their handsome brick house, on Tenth Avenue below the library, onto the lawn and into the park next door, and ended under the plane trees near the monument to the Homestead district's World War I dead. One or two hundred people came, most of them from Homestead and Munhall. Terrick and his wife spent days preparing for the event. There were mounds of food and countless kegs of beer. One year they roasted a pig and put an apple in its mouth. Another time, John Tichon, the assistant superintendent of schools, brought his guitar, and people sat in the Terricks' garage for hours and sang country-and-western songs, including every verse of "The Wabash Cannonball."

In the old days of strong party politics, the time of Terrick's father and of Doc McLean, Terrick as magistrate and party leader would have been a big man in the Homestead district, dispensing patronage and saying who would run for office. He would also have been important in Pittsburgh and Allegheny County politics, even in state politics. But nowadays he had trouble helping his people win election to the school board or the state assembly. He and his kind of politics were regarded by many people as anachronisms.

Early one summer morning, I sat with Terrick on the side porch of his home. The sun shone, the birds sang in the shrubs and trees and on the grass of the park next door, and the leaves rustled when the breeze struck them. Life had changed in the Homestead district, he said, and he missed the customs that had made the district what it was, glued it together. There was no more 6:30 mass on Saturday night, no more walking to church, no more old men in hats and starched white shirts, no more people sitting and talking on their porches in the summer, no more the rollicking fun of machine politics. The erosion of machine politics had occurred in part because in the 1960s magistrates had been barred by the state constitution from participating in politics. There had not been a good election in town in twenty years, he said. He knew that many people, such as professors of government and political science, found machine politics distasteful. But he also knew that something had been lost, and he lamented this.

"I'm talking about the basic dirty precinct politics people don't care for," Terrick said. Some of the people who lived on his street, he said, couldn't work in the mill "because they couldn't pass the physical, or weren't smart enough, or were alcoholics." He said, "My father put them to work on the borough, gave them some dignity. You can have all the pride you want, but if you don't have cash, you've got nothing. Money seems to be the measure of success in this country. We had street-sweepers in those days and somebody to haul the trash and work on water lines—that kind of menial labor. They worked and made a living if not a great wage. But my father got those people jobs. That's the way the system worked.

"Maybe there was corruption, but maybe that was also the only way the politicians could have stayed in power. Maybe that's the way it had to be done. Maybe you had to have speakeasies. Maybe you had to have money coming in every month from those operators. Maybe you had to turn your head to some of the stuff that was going on." We sat for a while longer on the cool porch. "That's probably the greatest loss," Terrick said after a time, "the suffering, the breakup of life as we knew it. I know this: The community fiber is breaking down."

III

One day I went to the union hall. It had been such a vibrant place, with the workers coming and going, the grievance men—Mike Stout, Bill Evans, Bob Todd, and the rest—sitting around with their feet on their desks dispensing advice like bigtime lawyers. The national union had not yet ordered the hall closed, but most of the life had left the place. Now just a few people were ever there—Weisen, Stout, and a handful of others. Most of the rooms were closed off to save on heating. The only time it was crowded now was when the pensioners gathered for their monthly meetings.

I was sitting in the room just off the lobby. When the mill was running, there would sometimes be twenty or more people milling around at the front of the room and dozens of others at work throughout the building. Now there was just me and a janitor, a handicapped fellow who had worked in the mill. When he got laid off, Weisen gave him a job cleaning the union hall. Except for the strokes of the janitor's broom, there was not a sound. Then Cheryl Bacco walked in. She was the secretary who had worked with the Bekich regime and then had stayed on when Weisen was elected. She had pretty much held the place together. Men often seemed astonished to see this good-looking woman there in the union hall, with her hair done, and wearing heels that clicked on the floor, and smelling of perfume. Some of the guys would stop and talk a little trash with her, but she was classy and did not run around, and they got the drift quickly and became polite.

Cheryl Bacco saw me. I was wearing a suit. "What's with the suit?" she asked. "How come you've got a suit on?" "I'm going downtown," I said. "What for?" she asked. "I've got to go to U.S. Steel, and I think maybe I'll stop at the international." She looked at the suit critically. It was a good suit, too. A nice pinstripe, not Brooks Brothers but not bad. I thought I should explain why I was wearing it. "You've got to have a suit downtown," I said. "Everybody has a suit downtown." She looked at me disapprovingly. "The suits don't care about us," she said.

2 4

RICH LOCHER IS DEAD, AND OTHER STORIES OF DESPAIR

One day, toward the end of my time in Homestead, I spent a morning walking around town. It was a marvelous May morning. The air was clear and the sky was a high, bright blue. A fresh breeze was blowing, and the sun was warm. It had rained the night before, and the town was so clean and shining that it seemed as though it had been washed and wrung and hung out to dry. The town was coming alive. The banks had just opened. The sidewalk in front of McCrory's Five and Dime and Levine's Hardware had been hosed down, even though it hadn't been necessary with the rain, and flats of plants—impatiens, geraniums, peppers, tomatoes—had been set out. The plants had been watered, and now that part of Eighth Avenue had the rich odor of wet earth. Other stores also were opening—Levine Bros. Hardware, Harry's Clothes, Revco Drugs, Katilius Furniture, the Blue Bonnet Bakery, and Capitol Cleaning, on McClure Street. The shop's dog, a Doberman named Sandy, was asleep in the side window, as it was each morning.

Larry Levine, from the hardware store, was in Michael's Restaurant having coffee. The librarian, Ann Hart, was in her office at the Carnegie Library going over the payroll. There was one patron in the library, an old man in the reading room. He would read for a while, nod off, wake with a start, read a bit more, then nod off again. Outside the library, men hammered and cut sheet metal as rock music played on their radio. They were putting new gutters and downspouts on the library. The money had come from a $78,000 grant that the library had received from the Allegheny Foundation. Below the library, on Tenth Avenue, Rich Terrick, the magistrate, and his son, Chris, were spading a patch of ground before planting tomatoes. The Terricks were one of the last families in town with a garden. Chris was going to work for the Munhall borough—work on the borough, as they say in the valley—for the summer.

Down at Chiodo's, two old men were in their usual place at the end of the bar near Eighth Avenue—so that they could see what was going on—having a glass, even though it seemed early for that. Across the street, I could see the heads of old men sitting at the window of Owl's Club 1354. Two other men, one of them Steve Pachuta—Hunkie Steve, the toughest cop in town, when he was a member of the police force—sat on a bench in front of the club, telling stories about Homestead politics in the old days. The Ancient Order of Hibernians would open at about 4:00 P.M., when Spanky O'Toole, also a former policeman, would walk down from his house on Eleventh Avenue and start getting the place ready. But the clubs always closed early these days because so few people came.

Across town, Father Bernard Costello, pastor of Saint Mary Magdalene's Roman Catholic Church, was in the kitchen of the parish house drinking tea. It was not easy these days being a pastor in Homestead. Attendance was down—sometimes there were only a few dozen people at a service—and not many young people came to church anymore. "You look out there on Sunday and you see nothing but white hair," Father Costello said. It was a particularly trying week for him. The diocese of Pittsburgh had ordered the closing of Saint Mary Magdalene's Roman Catholic School, which was ninety-nine years old. There was also talk of closing the church. Father Costello said he did not know what might happen.

The school, across from the church, had faced declining enrollments and revenues for years. In the 1960s, there had been 800 students. Now there were 164. Tuition was just $325 per student, but even this was too high for many parents. There was $73,000 in outstanding tuition payments, and the cost of running the school, $250,000 a year, could not be met. "Some people owe us as much as three thousand dollars in back tuition. I'm not going to subsidize this," Father Costello declared, though he obviously had done so for years. Father Costello was a big softy, and everybody in town knew it. He had been in Homestead for ten years and had seen the town in good times and bad. "The difference is that there is less *joie de vivre,* less enthusiasm," he said. "There is a sort of malaise over the town."

Below the town, on the flats by the river, was the mill. It had been purchased by the Park Corporation of Cleveland, an industrial-scavenging and redevelopment company. Now men were taking down what remained of the Homestead Works. I could see them, small figures way down in the mill yards, and hear the noise, faint at this distance, of their machinery. Up the hill, at the burying grounds, there was much activity. Memorial Day was approaching. Memorial Day had been conceived by the Grand Army of the Republic in 1888 to honor the fallen Union soldiers, and it had always been an important holiday throughout America, a time for decorating graves with lilacs and peonies, and for picnics and parades. Since it was moved to Monday by Congress to create a three-day weekend, Memorial Day has lost much of its significance. But it is still important in Homestead, and I suspect it always will be, as a time to pay tribute to the war dead and to the rest of the dead, as a day of redemption.

This day, men were mowing and edging in the cemeteries, and the smell of gasoline and of freshly mowed grass mingled. Already people had come up the hill to trim grass and place flowers on the graves of relatives. One man was getting a shovel out of his car. He was angry and spoke rapidly in a foreign language, and most of what he said I could not understand. But enough came through. His wife had just died. He pointed to her grave. Baskets of flowers still lay heaped on the brown earth that covered it. She should not have died, he said. She was much too young. He was not satisfied with the way the earth had been heaped on the grave, so he had gotten his shovel and come to smooth it.

I had come to the burying grounds because I wanted to see whether it was possible to find the graves of the Homestead martyrs, the men killed in the 1892 strike. Six of the slain workers were buried on the hill, but the location of their graves had been lost over the years. The last time that the graves had been identified, as far as I knew, was on that hot day, July 5, 1936, when two thousand steelworkers and their supporters had gathered in the Seventeenth Avenue playground to commemorate the strike and the workers killed, and to mark the beginning of the Committee for Industrial Organization's campaign to organize America's industrial workers. Among the speakers at the rally had been the lawyer

Michael A. Musmanno, CIO leaders, and the lieutenant governor of Pennsylvania, who said that police would be used to support union men and women, not to beat them down. People had then marched up the hill to honor the martyrs, in their graves forty-four years.

Some people I had met had gathered the plot and row numbers of a few of the graves, and a man I knew in Homestead, Randolph Harris, trudged around with me for a couple of hours, but we found nothing. A gravedigger we encountered said that much filling had gone on over the years, and that some old graves might be under thirty feet of fill. Some headstones had disappeared, and many graves had never been marked because people in the old days could not afford headstones. He apologized for the filling. It was astonishing what people had done in the old days, he said. The people who ran the cemetery today would never do anything like that, he said.

Harris and I thought we would try one more time, in the Homestead Cemetery, across the street. We thought that two of the workers, maybe three, who had been Methodists, might have been buried there. Someone who had searched before had told us to look for the Odd Fellows plot. One of the slain men, John E. Morris, had been a member of that fraternal order, so he might have been buried there. We walked around for a time but could not find the Odd Fellows plot. We asked an attendant if he could help us, and he pointed to the top of the hill, by the Civil War monument. We found the Odd Fellows plot there, and a few feet away was the grave we had been looking for, with a small granite headstone that said only this: JOHN E. MORRIS, 1868–1892.

Morris was a twenty-four-year-old worker who was shot and killed on the afternoon of the battle with the Pinkertons. It was at Morris's funeral that the Reverend John J. McIlyar of the Fourth Avenue Methodist Episcopal Church bitterly condemned Henry Clay Frick, saying: "This town is bathed in tears today, and it is all brought about by one man, who is less respected by the laboring people than any other employer in the country. There is no more sensibility in that man than in a toad." It was Morris's widow who said, "Our little home was almost paid for, and we were so happy. I was afraid John would meet with some terrible calamity, and I begged him not to go out. . . . I feel sorry for the widows of those guards and wish I could give back to them their husbands."

All Morris had gotten out of life was that small marker. The rest of the martyrs buried on the hill had received even less, it seemed. We could find none of the other graves that day or another day when I went back and searched again. It probably does not matter. I am not sure what my reason for trying to find the graves was. It was just something that seemed right to do.

I noticed one thing that day that I have not forgotten. A number of people had brought soap and buckets and rags to the burying grounds, and they were washing the headstones with the utmost care, as someone might wash a treasured possession, a glass vase or bowl, say, something that had been in the family for years. This was a custom dating from the days when the Homestead Works and the other mills were operating. They sent up thick, dark smoke that blackened the headstones, even though the cemeteries were high on the hill, far from the mills. People had to wash the headstones to keep them clean. The mills were long closed, and the smoke was gone, but people continued to wash the headstones.

II

Eighth Avenue continued to run down, and now the once-bustling street was a tatterdemalion thoroughfare made up of the few old stores that were hanging on and the Goodwill, Salvation Army, and Saint Vincent de Paul thrift shops. One of Chief Kelly's last fights had been to attempt to persuade the managers of the thrift shops to stop putting their collections of junk—worn-out toys, skates, sleds, books, kitchenware, clothes, shoes—on the sidewalk. He was not successful. But there was little market for such items. In the end, even Goodwill closed, and the windows were boarded up with plywood.

The borough building, constructed in 1909, the place where Mother Jones had been jailed and Frances Perkins had been refused permission by Burgess Cavanaugh to speak in Frick Park, was also closed. The building had not been maintained and was getting run-down. One day Chief Kelly was going down to the basement. A rotten step gave way, and he fell and wrenched his ankle. He was on crutches for several days. A half-dozen people who worked there came down with cancer, and it was thought that the building contained some carcinogen—asbestos perhaps —although this was never proven. Council meetings were moved to the old high school. The fire department was moved to a garage across the street, and the police department was moved into the old post office, which the country remodeled for the borough in exchange for the borough's agreeing to house a number of work-release prisoners in the building.

In June 1990, Saint Mary Magdalene's School closed. It was the last Roman Catholic school in Homestead. In the fall, it would have begun its one hundredth year. The students knew that they would miss their school enormously. "Everybody cares about you," Jackie Piskor said. "If you have a problem, you can go to any of the teachers, and they will help you, or to your friends, and they will help you." The students, even at their young age, knew that hard times had fastened on Homestead. They could not go across the street to play in Frick Park because they feared they would be bullied. There were often drugs being sold there, they said. Even Saint Mary Magdalene's Roman Catholic Church was locked, day and night.

Most of the students were enrolling in public schools. They said that they would especially miss their prayers. "How many times a day do you pray?" I asked. They counted the prayers, some using their fingers. "Seven," they said. The last day, the children came for half a day, and there was much crying in the halls and on the asphalt playground. A second-grade teacher, Nancy Stanich, tearfully embraced her students. Dave Lasos, a seventh grader, sat disconsolately in the hall, his head buried in his arms. Sister Marie Margaret, the principal, said "We have met our Waterloo."

The town government continued to face enormous problems. The borough's deficit increased from $30,000 in 1989 to $300,000 in 1990, and the population continued to fall. It was 4,179 in the 1990 census, down 17.9 percent from 5,092 in 1980. In 1988, the corporation sold the Homestead Works to the Park Corporation for $14 million—$2.5 million for the land and $11.5 million for the equipment and machinery. Soon, demolition crews arrived, and one by one the old mills came down. For a time, Mayor Simko continued to believe that the Valley Machine Shop would be purchased from Park and reopened, but the letter of intent that he had been expecting the day we had toured the works had not come through. The investors said that reopening the mill would not be feasible, in view of the depressed condition of the steel industry.

In 1990, Allegheny County reduced the assessed value of the mill site from $30 million to $14 million. In November, Homestead, Munhall, West Homestead, and the Steel Valley School District reached an agreement with Park to reduce the assessed value of the site from $14 million to $9.5 million. The agreement entitled Park to a refund on 1989 real estate taxes of $67,000 from the boroughs and $45,500 from the school district, which Park agreed to apply to future tax bills.

The town had become a place for small-time speculators. Wayne Laux, a man whom almost no one in Homestead knew anything about, began to buy buildings near the mill site—including the one that had housed Rufus "Sonnyman" Jackson's Skyrocket Lounge and Manhattan Music Club—and then sold them to Park. Many were demolished. Half a century after the demolition that had preceded the wartime expansion of the works, lower Homestead was again being razed.

The corporation and the union continued the missteps that had helped to bring about their downfall. In June 1990, the corporation agreed to pay $34 million in costs and penalties for the cleanup of waste water that had been illegally dumped into the Calumet River, in Indiana, by its Gary plant. In September 1990, a federal district court judge in Birmingham, Alabama, fined the corporation $4.1 million and gave prison terms to two union officials, Thermon Phillips and E. B. Rich, found guilty of conspiring with the corporation to obtain lucrative pensions for themselves in exchange for agreeing to concessions during contract negotiations in December 1983. This was the agreement that the corporation had used to persuade local unions across the country to grant similar concessions. In December 1990, the corporation agreed to pay a $3.2 million fine levied by the Occupational Safety and Health Administration for hundreds of violations the administration said had occurred at its Pennsylvania plants.

The corporation's interest in steel continued to shrink. In early 1991, its steel operations became an independent subsidiary. In May, its stock was split into two—one for energy, one for steel—and the steel stock was dropped from the Dow Jones Industrial Average and replaced by the stock of the Walt Disney Company.

By this time, the national union's membership had dropped to 490,000, one-third of the 1.4 million who had belonged in 1979. In 1991, a plan to organize white-collar workers was announced, and a woman organizer with substantial experience in the field was hired. But the effort failed.

III

The local union meetings continued until the summer of 1987, and the union hall remained open after that to assist laid-off workers. No dues had come in from Homestead since the mill had been closed, and the national union had been helping the local with its bills. But the bad blood between the national union leaders and Weisen had continued, and finally the union saw an opportunity to close the hall. In December 1986, Weisen had gone to the Soviet Union with his wife and their son Bobby for an operation on the broken vertebra in Bobby's neck. A drive to raise money for the trip had been started by Weisen's old supporters, but everyone wanted Bobby to get well, and Lynn Williams, the new president of the national union, stopped by the Weisens' home to give them a thousand dollars.

In January 1987, while Weisen was still in the Soviet Union, the national union ordered the Homestead union hall closed. Mike Stout, the grievance man, was furious, and to keep him quiet the union reluctantly allowed him to set up a local headquarters in an empty, ramshackle orange building, once a restaurant, on McClure Street, at the top of the hill. He put a sign on the door of the old hall that said: "The international has shut our union hall down and moved us to a storefront on the corner of Seventeenth Street and McClure Street (orange building). We should have the same number, but if you have any problems with TRA or SUB [Training and Relocation Allowance and Supplemental Unemployment Benefits], call me at home."

The orange building was run-down and hot and stuffy. There was no longer much spirit among the men who sat there in front of fans at desks trucked up from the old union hall. The place smelled like old hamburgers and french fries. Occasionally, unemployed workers came by for assistance, but soon they stopped coming. Not even Weisen came by much anymore. He was unemployed, like most others, and was looking for work. In June 1987 the orange building was closed. There had been eight union lodges in Homestead at the time of the 1892 strike. An Amalgamated Association lodge, the Spirit of Ninety-two, had been established in Homestead with the passage of the National Industrial Recovery Act, in June 1933. The steelworkers' union had had a local in Homestead since 1936, for more than half a century. Now there was no union in Homestead.

IV

Most of the men who lost their jobs when the mill went down accepted their fate and settled in, living on part-time work or on pensions. Many had trouble sleeping and finding things to do with the time on their hands. They dropped children or grandchildren off at school, helped around the house, worked on the lawn. After a time, their wives and children got used to having them around. Sometimes the men drove down by the works and watched the demolition crews taking it down. The men would have reunions at one of the firehouses or social clubs, but those were not much fun. One by one they stopped going, and soon no one planned reunions anymore.

"I still think about that damn place," Bob Krovocheck said. He had worked in the mill for thirty-eight years and was fifty-six years old when he lost his job. His highest pay was twenty-seven thousand dollars in 1985. He tried working as a janitor for four dollars an hour, but he was overweight and had bad knees, and the work was too demanding, so he had to quit. His wife had been seriously injured in an automobile accident on the Pennsylvania Turnpike in 1981, and he spent much of his time taking care of her. They lived on his pension of $1,100 a month, $876 after taxes and medical deductions.

Krovocheck missed the mill enormously. "I dream about it every once in a while," he said. "I miss going to work, being around the guys, the eight-hour turn, the routine. I miss the money, too. It was a good living. I wasn't living from payday to payday. It's funny. I remember that every once in a while one of us in the mill would say, 'Let's get our pension and get out of here.' But pensioneering ain't all that great, especially if you've got somebody sick you're taking care of.

"During the day, I take care of the wife, get the meals, keep the house halfway decent. It ain't like she would keep it. I do the cooking and laundry. I read quite a bit. I go up the street and have a couple of beers. I go to the store and get the groceries. I come home and make supper. I watch TV. I go to bed. I get rather depressed, especially when I drive up past where we worked, the structural mill. I'm okay, if you want to call me okay."

Richard Holoman, a craneman, had worked in the mill for thirty-two years and was fifty-one when he lost his job. His highest pay was $22,500 a year. After the mill went down, he had a job as a security guard for three months and worked for a short time cleaning an industrial garage, three and a half hours a night, for fourteen dollars a night. Then he got a job as a janitor at Saint Agnes's Roman Catholic Church, in West Mifflin. He changed light bulbs, mopped floors, cut the grass, fixed the sisters' car. It wasn't bad, as work goes. He could set his own hours, but mostly he worked 6:00 A.M. to 2:00 P.M., five days a week—good hours for an old steelworker, steady daylight.

Denny Wilcox, a roller, got a part-time job as a bank courier, twenty-five hours a week at $6.10 an hour. He received a pension of $1,100 a month. "We're not living high off the hog, but we're making it," he said. "It's hard. You start looking down on yourself. You'd think, if you put on an application that you have thirty-five years of service, an employer would know that you are dedicated. You'd think they'd grab you in a minute. But they discriminate against you because of age. They all do. I think that's why I'm not full-time now, because they discriminate because of age. They know I get a pension."

Ray McGuire, a repairman, had worked in the mill for thirty-six years and had taken only two sick days. He got a pension of $1,000 a month and caught on as an electrician, going from one shop to another, wherever he was needed. Sometimes a temporary agency found him work, or else he would hear of something himself. He worked for a while at the machine company that now occupied part of the old Mesta Machine plant. One day he had to go to the Homestead Works to pick up some tools. "I went to the exact place where I worked, and I got so nauseated I thought I was going to throw up," he said. "I thought: 'I worked here. What are you people doing to this place? What are you doing to my cranes?' And then I thought: 'Wait a minute. This wasn't my place. These weren't my cranes.' But that's the way I thought—that it was my place." He lived in Pleasant Hills, not far from Homestead, but he no longer went to Homestead at night. He was afraid of crime there, and besides, he got despondent when he went to Homestead, even when he just drove through the town. "The place looks like a morgue," he said.

Bob Todd, a craneman and grievance man, was unemployed for a year. Then he was called to the Edgar Thomson Works, where he got a job as a safety man in the slab mill, making seventeen thousand dollars a year. It was not as much as he had been making at Homestead, but it was a job. About two hundred Homestead workers were given jobs there, and another few dozen were hired by the Irvin Works.

Bill Brennan, a millwright, had worked in the mill for thirty-nine years and was sixty-four when he retired on his pension of $775 a month after deductions. He also got Social Security, and his house was paid for. His father had worked at the Homestead Works, and so had his three brothers. In 1984, when he had a heart-bypass operation, he was on sick-leave for six months. His heart was now okay, though he had to take three pills a day. When he went back into the mill after his bypass, the other millwrights carried him, hid him out, for six months—they did the heavy work that he had done and did not tell the supervisors. He would pick up a sledgehammer or a big crescent wrench, and the others would take it from him and tell him to go somewhere, get lost, and they would do the job. "I miss guys like that, good working people," he said.

Bobby Schneider, a roller, got a part-time job tending bar at the Slovak Club in Munhall. He had worked in the mill for thirty-one years and had earned $35,000 in his best year. The bartender's job wasn't much, though it got him out of the house and gave him something to do. He lived on a pension check of $1,077 a month after deductions. His wife worked as a secretary in a real-estate company. His section of the last beam rolled at the Homestead Works was still in the trunk of his car, four years after the mill went down. He had intended to shine it up and put it in the house, but he never got around to it. His two pals, Red Hrabic and Jimmie Sherlock, both lived on pensions of about $900 a month and were doing okay. The three of them met at Hess's Bar in Hunkie Hollow almost every afternoon at about four, or maybe at the Slovak Club, in Munhall, if Schneider was tending bar there.

There was much crying in Homestead. Men and women often went to wakes and funerals, for there were many deaths among the men from the works. I knew or heard of three dozen men who died or committed suicide. That's a lot of men gone, and at an early age, too. I think that many of them died because the mill closed, though I can't prove it. But it's a lot of dead guys, isn't it?

There was one man I never got out of my mind—Rich Locher, the hooker from Number Two Structural who had denounced the government's retraining programs at the meeting with the two men in the pin-stripe suits from Senator Heinz's staff. I had planned to meet with Locher, but time passed, and I was busy. One winter day, preparing for a trip to Homestead, I wrote down his telephone number, thinking I would go see him. When I got to Homestead, I ran into Mike Stout, the former grievance man. When I told him that I was going to call Locher, he said: "Don't bother. Locher is dead. He finished the retraining program but couldn't get a nursing job, so he took a gun and killed himself—shot half his head away, in his garage." Stout continued with his paperwork and did not look up. One more death was not much to him. He knew too many stories like this.

I liked Locher. He was a good man. He had a temper and often used profane language, but don't many of us? He was an excellent father and husband, and he probably deserved more out of life than to take two brief vacations at hot trailer parks in Virginia and go out to eat once a month at McDonald's or Long John Silver's, to lose his job as a craneman and not get a job as a nurse. One more thing. Locher was right about the training programs. They were bullshit.

V

Others fared better. Ron Weisen drifted away from Homestead, somewhat in the manner of Honest John McLuckie, the Homestead union leader of a century before. Weisen knew that the fight was over, and he got on with his life. He got a job operating a jackhammer on a Pittsburgh water department repair crew—working on the city, as the saying went. It was a good deal. He reported to the barn at 7:30 A.M., got his equipment, and was transported by truck to the work site. That took a half-hour or so. The men worked until 11:30 A.M., they broke for a half-hour lunch, then worked till about 3:00 P.M. The best assignments, the men said, were by the college campuses in the Oakland area, where on warm, sunny days they could see the college girls working on their tans.

About 3:00 P.M., the men started getting their tools together for the trip back to the barn. Weisen was usually home by 4:30, and if it was a nice afternoon he would sit on the porch of his house on Second Avenue, in the Hazelwood district. The old Jones and Laughlin mill, most of it closed, some already demolished, was below Second Avenue, along the Monongahela River. Weisen was big on Second Avenue. A lot of people, including many former steelworkers, would stop and reminisce about the old days, or give him the horn as they went by.

Despite Bobby Weisen's operation in the Soviet Union, he remained paralyzed. But he was a tough kid, like his father. He enrolled in community college to study computer programming, and last I heard he was doing well. Weisen ran for the Pittsburgh city council in 1988 but lost. His heart was not in it, as it had been when he was running for local president or district director, taking on the union, the company, the banks, everybody, and as it had been when he was a kid boxer, thirty years before, going crazy, lashing out furiously, without thinking, whenever he was hit. But he had not lost his interest in litigation. He supported Cheryl Bacco's lawsuit against the national union for $3,000 in severance pay, and he and Michael Stout helped bring a lawsuit against the corporation by 259 former workers at the Valley Machine Shop who charged that their jobs had been eliminated as a result of subcontracting. They were awarded $2 million in compensation, and some received as much as $55,000 apiece.

Michelle McMills went back to law school at the age of thirty-seven, fifteen years after she had dropped out to work in the mill. She continued her relationship with Greg Klink and stayed in Homestead, but she lost touch with the insurgents she had once been so close to, even though most lived just a few miles away. "I don't see hardly anybody anymore," she said. She hoped to organize a reunion sometime but never did. "I don't think that we accomplished much. We never changed the grievance procedure, and we never stopped the cheating on grievances. We never stopped the union from being so regressive. We were never able to effectively challenge the company. I don't know that we changed anything. We didn't offer a program. There was no political message. We were going to change the world, but— Well, we had a good time."

Michael Stout entered politics and ran for state representative in 1988. I knew he was serious about this when Chief Kelly and I went to a

Rotary Club meeting one Tuesday, and there was Stout in a shirt and tie, one of the new members. He also dropped "Kentucky" from his name. He was Michael Stout now.

I spent the last day of his campaign going with him to the polling places. At a firehouse, we saw the widow of Ed Buzinka, the friendly craneman I'd met on the day the mill went down, who had recently died of a heart attack. She was a small woman with a small smile. "I voted for you, Mike," she said. Most of the men from the mill and their wives did.

That evening, I went over to his campaign headquarters, which began to fill up after eight o'clock, when the polls closed and the campaign staffers at the polling places started calling in the returns. Everyone was jubilant because he was running ahead, and some people went out for beer. But late at night, returns began to come in from districts where his support was not strong, and sometime after midnight he fell behind. People began to drift away, knowing that the final tally would come in the next morning. Stout lost by fewer than a hundred votes to Chris McNally, a lawyer, a non-Homestead man from a remote part of the district.

Stout was now deeply in debt, but his friends held fund-raisers and the campaign's bills were paid. After a while, he got a job running a new printing company that opened in the old Bishop Boyle High School and later moved down to Eighth Avenue. He ran for state representative in 1990 but lost again. Weisen and Stout never saw each other much anymore, which was unfortunate, because they were both good men. But this was typical of Homestead. It was hard for people to stay together. "I haven't seen Ronnie for two years," Stout said when I bumped into him one day.

Cheryl Bacco married Terry McGartland, who owned a bar and restaurant in Wilmerding, in the Turtle Creek area. Most of Wilmerding went down when the electric companies collapsed. But the bar and restaurant continued to do well. You should have seen Cheryl at her wedding, dressed all in white, her hair black as coal. She looked like a doll.

The Reverend James Von Dreele continued to push for redevelopment of the Homestead Works site. The Reverend Philip D. Long remained pastor of the East Liberty Lutheran Church, in a run-down section of Pittsburgh, and turned to fighting drugs, crime, and urban decay. The Reverend John Gropp and his wife began working with people who were trying to improve Duquesne's schools and bring redevelopment to the town.

The Reverend Daniel Solberg, though no longer recognized as a minister by his church, was hired by Long as an assistant pastor at the East

Liberty Lutheran Church. The Lutheran Synod said nothing. The Reverend D. Douglas Roth, who had also been defrocked, held services in his home and at a Clairton Pentecostal Church for the two dozen people who still called themselves his parishioners. Then he began spending a lot of time alone, watching television. Finally, he gave up political activism. He continued to seek a pastorate, but failed. The last people heard, he was in Kansas.

The Reverend William Rex was forced to resign his two pastorates. To avoid being defrocked, he agreed to take a leave of absence from the ministry. He was penniless until he got a job at the McDonald's in Monroeville, Pennsylvania, where he worked for a year and a half and ultimately became second assistant manager. In 1988, he was given two new pastorates, at small churches near Kittanning, Pennsylvania.

Honeywell remained on the Denominational Ministry Strategies' payroll, which was made up of individual contributions. He worked with Long and Solberg at the East Liberty Lutheran Church, where he tried unsuccessfully to have the store owners in the congregation arm themselves, and where some parishioners turned to a kind of spiritualism, or, as Long called it, "Jesus-consciousness through secret and mystical rituals." He explained: "Our weekly rituals center on readings from the Holy Book, prophetic messages based on these readings, and an empty-tomb ritual that takes the form of an ancient sacrificial rite." After a time, the organization changed its name to the Confessing Synod Ministries, after the Confessing Church, founded in 1933 by Pastor Martin Niemoeller and other anti-Nazi German Protestants.

The influential people in Pittsburgh and the leaders of the corporation and the national union said that the activist ministers had achieved nothing but the blackening of the city's reputation. I did not agree. Almost everyone I met said that they had had the right beliefs but had gone too far, such as when they invaded Shadyside Presbyterian Church. At least they had taken action. Few others had. Almost all of them were good people, though I can't say the same for Honeywell. As Weisen once said, no one ever saw Honeywell in jail.*

The men and women around Tri-State Conference on Steel and an associated organization, Steel Valley Authority, continued to function.

---

* Honeywell enjoyed describing himself as a disciple of Saul Alinsky, but he often showed no understanding of Alinsky's principles. Though he seemed to be aware that Alinsky had said, "Power is not only what you have but what the enemy thinks you have," a number of other principles eluded him—among them, "Never go outside the experience of your people"; "A good tactic is one your people enjoy"; and "A good tactic that drags on too long becomes a drag."

They continued to achieve much press attention, but after a time, except for a few like Stout and Charles McCollester, they were no more radical than their old antagonist, the steelworkers' union, whose president, Lynn Williams, the activists honored in 1992 as "Man of the Year." The Tri-State activists achieved little. They never used eminent domain, despite all their talk, and saved none of the steel plants they had campaigned to save—neither Dorothy Six, nor other facilities they tried to reopen, among them electric plants in the Turtle Creek area, the 160-inch mill in Homestead, and South Side Electrics in Pittsburgh.

John Dindak, the mayor of West Homestead, who thought that he might be able to help the town out of some of its financial troubles by playing the state lottery, tended bar for a time at John Patrick's Pub, the old Buffington's. He did not need the money, of course. He just liked the opportunity to stay in touch with people. Then he got a job at the Homestead Monument Company, selling plots and headstones. You could often find him at the cemeteries, making sure that things were going smoothly. West Homestead did once win $776. The money went into the general fund. Mayor Dindak said that if the town ever won the million-dollar jackpot, the first thing he would do would be to give borough workers a pay raise. But West Homestead never won again.

Chief Kelly resigned, tired of his war with the council faction that opposed him. When he demanded back vacation pay, the council refused to pay it. He obtained a new position as chief of police in Baldwin, a larger town west of Homestead. He sued the Homestead council for $23,000 in vacation pay. He did not want to sue, just as he had not wanted to resign. He would have settled for $13,000, but the council offered only $3,000. The two sides settled out of court; the amount of the settlement was not disclosed. He and his wife, Paula, continued to live in their house in Homestead under the water tower, while talking about getting out. Finally, they moved over the hill. They found a place in Baldwin that they liked, and they purchased it. Moving from Homestead was something the chief had never thought would happen. "I loved the place," he said.

Before he left, the chief closed the Fantasia Health Spa. It was an example of superior police work. The chief had an undercover officer, a big, beefy fellow, dress up in old clothes and get into a wheelchair as if he were an invalid. Two other policemen, also in old clothes, pushed him, and up the stairs of the Fantasia they went, sweating profusely. Our friend needs a massage, they said. "Why, sure, honey," one of the girls said. She grabbed the officer's penis, as the chief told the story, and he bolted out of the wheelchair. "Honey, you're cured," she said. "I'm a police officer, and you're under arrest," he answered. The Fantasia was closed that day, and despite some threats of litigation it never reopened.

Mayor Simko decided not to stand for reelection. He was fed up with the council members' arguing all the time, hissing and striking like snakes. I ran into the mayor one night at the library and went up to say hello. I regarded him as a splendid fellow. "Mr. Mayor, I hear you're not running for reelection," I said. "Yeah, that's right," he answered. "How come?" I asked. "I don't need that shit anymore," the mayor said.

Betty Esper, who had worked as a clerk at the mill, was elected to replace Simko. She had no power, and she knew it, but she understood the difficulties that Homestead faced. "These are powerful forces we are up against," she said. "This plant wasn't built in a day. How are we supposed to make things better in a day?"

The school superintendent, Jerry Longo, had reason to be proud of what he'd accomplished in the school system. The self-esteem of students and teachers, it seemed, was rising. Graduation requirements were higher, with increased emphasis on mathematics, speaking, and writing. The system had obtained advanced computers—one terminal for every eight students, compared with one for every fifty in 1985. Students were now dreaming dreams: the number of students going on to two- and four-year colleges increased by about half. Money was found to hire a dozen or so new, energetic teachers. Students now talked of attending Carnegie-Mellon University, Syracuse University, Purdue University. "The work is harder," one student said. Another said, "A lot of teachers say get out of the Steel Valley mentality. Try to broaden yourselves." A third said, "I think the school system is trying to expose us to the world outside Steel Valley."

Still, the district's problems continued to be formidable. Test scores remained unsatisfactory. The number of students in the system increased to 2,300 in 1990, but part of the growth came about because of the closing of parochial schools and the influx of children from poor families attracted to the district because of falling real estate prices; in many cases, the poor students, and many of their parents, did not feel part of the system. Many students, often the better ones, said they had no plans to return to the Homestead district once they finished their education; there was nothing in Homestead, they said, to come back for. Longo would not lead the school district out of these problems. In 1991, he resigned and accepted the superintendency of the Quaker Valley School District in Sewickley, the wealthy suburb that had been the playground for the "Pittsburgh millionaires."

Sam Marks closed his card shop and retired. He had run the place for fifty years. One day the store next to his caught fire, and the card shop suffered extensive damage. He thought about reopening but knew it would not pay. Old Man Shupink retired and gave the jewelry store to his son, who then closed it. No one was buying much jewelry in Homestead anymore. John Tarasevich, the proprietor—with his wife, Millie Straka—of Straka's Restaurant, where the specialty was hot roast-beef sandwiches, died at the age of seventy-one. Millie kept the restaurant open, and the place continued dispensing its hearty food, but there was a void that could not be filled. George and Carol Couvaris sold their restaurant and candy store, after twenty-five years of operation, to a man who turned it into a pizza and hoagie shop. David M. Roderick retired as corporation chairman in May 1990. His compensation in his last year was $1,363,982.

I sometimes went down to the flats along the river and watched the demolition crews taking the mill down. The men had acetylene torches and a state-of-the-art metal-cutting machine. The work was difficult, for some foundations and pilings went three or four stories into the ground. Taking the mill down resembled a large root canal job. But the men went about their work with dispatch, and it was remarkable how quickly the buildings, one by one, were coming down. One sunny afternoon, I was walking with William J. Gaughan, the former white-collar worker in the mill, along a weed-covered lot on State Road 837, above the mill, and watching the men at work. Suddenly we saw a movement—a flash of color, brown and white—in the mill yard. We stopped and stared. A deer was wandering about. It entered an empty building, stayed there for a time, and then emerged. It went inside another building, then came out. We watched the deer for about twenty minutes, neither of us saying much. Then, suddenly, it turned and bounded toward a thick grove of trees on the riverbank. After it entered the grove we did not see it again.

VI

In its tragedy, Homestead became fashionable, as what might be called "working-class chic" or "working-class voyeurism" arose. For this to happen, it was necessary that the mill be closed and the workers disappear. When the Homestead Works was operating and Homestead was a dirty steel town, people from outside paid no attention to it. They had no desire to go to a dirty steel town or to hang around with steelworkers. But once Homestead was a relic, Homestead was the rage. There were study groups and committees, historical exhibits, film proposals, lectures, brown-bag lunches, dinners, economic analyses, historical surveys, oral histories, a case study of disinvestment and redevelopment plans in the Monongahela Valley done by the Harvard Business School.

Architects, city planners, historians, economists, anthropologists, sociologists, social workers, foundation experts—all these and others became involved. Michael Stout called them carpetbaggers, and he was correct. People would come to Homestead for a meeting, or to look at an old furnace or mill building, or an old office building along Eighth Avenue that might be saved. Perhaps they would stop at Chiodo's to have a beer and a sandwich, and to look at the locals and soak up some local color. "You never see anyone at Chiodo's anymore except people on committees," said Margaret Vojtko, president of the Homestead Historical Society.

There was some interest in the other steel towns of the Monongahela Valley, but most of the interest centered on Homestead. Braddock had too many blacks and was too run-down. McKeesport was far up the valley, too far from downtown Pittsburgh. Clairton was too run-down and too far up the valley. Besides, the coke works was still operating, producing its odor and grime. That left Homestead, conveniently located, with its famous mill, now coming down, and its rich history—perfect.

After the resistance movement of the early and mid-1980s died down, the influential people in Pittsburgh—the old monied families, the corporation executives, the bankers, and the factotums of all three groups, the planners—had adopted a strategy for dealing with Homestead and the other abandoned steel towns in the Monongahela Valley. They attempted to identify and build up community leaders and organizations they felt comfortable dealing with and to dampen activism by buying the rest of the people off. It was a continuation of the paternalism and authoritarianism that had existed for a century, now couched in different rhetoric. They believed that the people in the Monongahela Valley—the ordinary people and their elected leaders—had been subservient to the corporation for so long that they had no independence or creativity. Karl E. Schlachter III, a staff member of the Mon Valley Initiative, one of the new groups sanctioned by the establishment, explained this point of view to me one day. The task was to identify those persons who could be trained to be new leaders, he said. Since no existing institutions—certainly not the elected borough councils—had the necessary expertise, there was a need for new ones.

More than two dozen organizations were created to redevelop Homestead and the other communities, and to preserve their historic sites. They enjoyed substantial backing from the Pittsburgh establishment. For example, the Pittsburgh Foundation made a $450,000 grant to restore the Tindall Building, on Eighth Avenue. Carpenters, electricians, and plumbers worked for several months, and when the building was reopened the Mon Valley Initiative and the Steel Valley Heritage Task Force established offices there. The restoration meant a brightened facade on Eighth Avenue, but the rest of the Avenue remained run-down. Usually the Tindall Building was kept locked. To get in, you first rang the buzzer and identified yourself. No riffraff were allowed inside.

The National Park Service and the Department of the Interior provided $1.7 million in federal funds so that the Steel Valley Heritage Task Force could study the historical significance of the Homestead Works and the other plants in the Monongahela Valley, and develop plans for a museum and park on the site of the Homestead Works. Another $330,000 in individual and foundation grants was made available to the task force, as was $40,000 in state funds. There was talk of raising $30 to $40 million from private and government sources to build the museum and park on the site of the Homestead Works, but there seemed little chance that this would happen.

In December 1988, $1.1 million in grants from the Heinz Endowment and the Pittsburgh Foundation were made available to the Mon Valley Initiative. The Pittsburgh–Allegheny County Private Industry Council spent $95,000 in 1989 and 1990 to hire the Gallup Organization to conduct a poll of the unemployed to prove that the official figure of 3.5 percent understated unemployment in Allegheny County, a task that could have been accomplished with a little reading, a day's trip through the Monongahela Valley, and a few telephone calls. "I could run Homestead for a year on that money," Betty Esper, the mayor, said.

A master plan for Homestead and the lower Monongahela Valley was put together by the Pittsburgh establishment. The plan, they said, would clear the site of the mill and make land available for warehouses and light industry. Saying that Homestead and the rest of the Monongahela Valley was plagued by an inadequate network of roads, they proposed a highway —almost an expressway—along the Monongahela River. The planners said that this would open Homestead and the rest of the valley to development.

Homestead's fashionable status was illustrated in February and March 1988, when, as part of the Remaking Cities Conference in Pittsburgh—organized by the American Institute of Architects and the Royal Institute of British Architects and attended by about one thousand people —a group of two dozen architects from Great Britain and the United States spent four days in the lower Monongahela Valley studying how Homestead and the other towns could be reclaimed. And that wasn't all. Homestead was later visited by the main speaker at the convention, Prince Charles of Great Britain, the world's most famous architecture buff. The architects, designated as members of the Regional/Urban Design Assistance Team, set up camp in the old Bishop Boyle High School. They had a splendid time poking about Homestead and the other steel communities. They worked far into the night and left a goodly supply of empty whiskey bottles behind when they decamped.

One Saturday, they conducted a public meeting in the school's gymnasium. The building was packed with former steelworkers and other Homestead residents. From the dais, above the townspeople, the architects announced their proposals to reclaim Homestead and the other towns. For Homestead, the major plan was to use the closed mills near the High Level Bridge as exhibition halls for a flower show, perhaps to be held in 1992 to mark the one-hundredth anniversary of the Homestead strike. The Carrie furnaces should be made into a museum and the Monongahela riverbank turned into an esplanade with a landing for yachts and other pleasure craft. Streets should be extended through the site of the Homestead Works to the Monongahela River. "It is the community itself—and I do emphasize this—that must decide on its own future," one of the architects said. "It should not be left to the planners to tell you, the community, what is good for you. It is for you, the community, to decide what is good for you and what you want."

Most of the people sat silently, but not Betty Esper, Babe Fernandez, Michael Stout, and Margaret Vojtko. A flower festival? A museum? Goddamn! This was not what they wanted. They wanted jobs. Betty Esper took the microphone. "We want to make the valley come back," she said. "We haven't heard you say a thing about salvaging the mills. You say our destiny is in our hands. What do you mean by that? We have no eminent domain. I do not want to see my valley wait five or ten years."

Babe Fernandez was apoplectic. He called the architects' drawings of a revitalized Homestead "wonderful pictures" but pointed out, "You haven't mentioned anything about an industrial plan, about a machine shop. We have the best machinery, the best facilities in the world, right here in Homestead." But the town's young people were moving away, he said. "Soon we won't have anybody here but old people. We don't want a ghost town here in Homestead. We were the steel center of the world, and we want to get back that way. We want to make the valley come back!"

Stout was also furious. "The real story of this valley is not being told," he said. Then he named fifteen men who, in one year, had died of strokes or heart attacks. Another man had committed suicide by shooting himself in the head, leaving a note saying that no one would hire him. Stout said that 50 percent of the people who had lost their jobs in the steel mills were living on unemployment-insurance benefits or on welfare, or were working for the minimum wage or for under-the-table wages. "We have a national disaster here in Homestead," he said.

Margaret Vojtko, the medieval scholar and town historian, said, "When ancient Greece lost its Colossus of Rhodes, it lost its symbol." When Homestead and the rest of the mill towns of the Monongahela Valley were gone, she said, an American colossus would have been lost. What kind of country, she asked, would let this happen? The architects listened politely. Soon afterward, they left town. An hour or so later, Fernandez was still fuming. "Those architects, they're full of crap," he said. "They come to Homestead and say what Homestead should do is plant a lot of flowers and grass, make the number-one or number-two best flower garden in the country. For Christ's sake, we had a steel mill that was second to none, and they're talking about a flower garden. What the hell! We're not interested in flowers and grass. We want jobs."

Three days later, the prince made a visit to Homestead. It was a cold, snowy day, and a biting wind was blowing. His Royal Highness came to Homestead in a motorcade of scarlet Jaguars. Some residents gathered along the route, but all that could really be seen of the prince and his entourage was a whir of scarlet as they whizzed into Homestead off the High Level Bridge, made a brief stop at the old Bishop Boyle High School, and then sped up West Street and through the cemeteries to visit with students at Steel Valley High School. A handful of activist ministers had gathered along the way holding tomatoes, and Chief Kelly assumed, not without reason, that they were going to throw them at the prince— or, in the argot of the protesters, "tomato him." So the chief had the Allegheny County police arrest the Reverend James Von Dreele and the defrocked Reverend D. Douglas Roth on charges of disorderly conduct, though they had done nothing except stand on Ninth Avenue holding tomatoes. They were held for an hour and then released. Later the charges were dismissed.

The prince, escorted by George Debolt, who ran a bus company in Homestead and was one of the people who had been identified by the establishment as a leader, was in the high school about half an hour. He chatted with some students, came out, shook some hands, and then sped off toward the High Level Bridge and Pittsburgh. The prince's visit was the subject of news stories around the world, and the children and their parents enjoyed all the attention. When a group of two dozen elementary-school children had been assembled in the high school to meet the prince, Mark Hornak, the school board president, noticed how new and bright the children's clothes looked. He asked how many were wearing new clothes for the occasion. All of the children raised their hands. On March

5, the prince addressed the architects in Pittsburgh. He told them that architecture must take community values into account. The architects applauded, and the convention ended. Nothing happened with the plans for the Homestead flower show or with the proposals for Duquesne, Braddock, McKeesport, or the other steel towns.

Some good came out of Homestead's brief period of chicness, like gutters and downspouts for the Carnegie Free Library of Homestead. There were numerous reports, and this provided jobs for the report-writers. But other than that, the grant money had little effect on Homestead or the other steel towns. There never was a plan to redevelop Homestead. The goal had been to ensure there were no more protests like the ones earlier in the decade. If there was a master plan, it was death and highways. The Homestead workers were dying, and in another decade or so more would be gone. A highway through the valley would eliminate even more houses, perhaps obliterate Homestead and the other steel towns.

The Homestead Works and the rest of the Monongahela Valley were like the rest of industrial America. What ended in Homestead was not just a mill and a town but in a large way the industrial revolution in America.

It became fashionable by the early 1990s to say that the corporation and the rest of the steel industry had recovered from the massive downturn of the 1970s and 1980s. Protected by quotas against imported steel —imports also dropped because of a falling U.S. dollar—and operating with increased productivity, the American steel industry now rivaled Japan's and Germany's, the argument went. There were other bright spots. The corporation began construction of a new slab caster, which could make slabs directly from hot steel, at the Edgar Thomson Works, and continued construction of a caster at its Gary (Indiana) Works. In all, the corporation spent $2 billion in the last half of the 1980s for casters and other improved equipment; its man-hours per ton of steel production dropped to 3.6, the corporation said, down from 11 man-hours per ton of shipped steel in 1982. In 1991 USX lost $578 million on sales of $18.82 billion. By the beginning of the 1990s, the corporation said, "We [have] positioned ourselves as the premier domestic steel producer."

Industry-wide, more than $20 billion were spent in the 1980s to upgrade U.S. steel plants, and the average of man-hours to make a ton of steel fell to 5.3, the industry boasted. Managers were more efficient, reports claimed, and exports of U.S. steel had risen in twenty years from 2 percent to 8 percent of U.S. steel production.

Yet, none of this took into consideration the loss of about 125,000 jobs at the corporation and 250,000 jobs in the American steel industry in the 1980s and early 1990s and the devastation that was visited upon Homestead and the other steel towns—and upon their people—by misguided steel industry practices that went back decades.

Louis Washowich, the mayor of McKeesport, was correct: the reporters, the stock analysts, the university experts had no place in their equations for people and communities. Edward Sadlowski, the insurgent candidate defeated in his bid for the steel union presidency in 1977—and who recovered the ebulliency that made him so attractive as a steelworkers' leader at that time—was also correct: there should have been massive retraining programs and massive programs to restore the steel towns.

Nor was the industry's situation as positive as reported. In 1991, the six largest U.S. steel producers had operating losses of $27 for every ton of steel they shipped, a total of nearly $1 billion. Much investment in the U.S. industry had come from Japan and Korea, and much of the reported progress made by the industry was due to the rise of so-called mini-mills, mostly nonunion plants, with lower wages and benefits and limited product lines; between 1980 and 1990, the five largest companies had produced 60 percent of U.S. steel; because of the rise of the mini-mills, the percentage fell to 40 percent by 1990. Closings continued; the corporation in 1992 said it was closing its once-vast South Works plant in Chicago, and the number of employees at the corporation's Gary Works—the pride of Elbert H. Gary—had fallen from 28,000 in the 1970s to 8,000. By now the corporation's share of the U.S. steel market was about 10 percent.

What had happened fit the definition of a recovery, as defined by experts. But the people in Homestead and the other steel towns did not regard what had happened as a recovery. No, they knew it was not that, for they knew what the experts, in their distant offices, could not know, that what had happened in Homestead and so many other American steel towns was a cruel, crushing blow, an American disaster.

VII

It was evening, time to leave. The sky was almost black in the east, but in the west, down the Monongahela River, where the Ohio River begins, the sun was a great orange ball. It was sinking rapidly, but it reflected back up the river, so that the huge onion-shaped domes atop Saint Nicholas's Russian Orthodox Church—domes sheathed in stainless steel rolled at the Homestead Works—seemed on fire. Homestead had been on fire once, had possessed vibrancy and life, and the people of Homestead had worked hard, against formidable enemies, to make

Homestead a town. They had succeeded beyond their imaginings, for the place they had fashioned was a place like no other.

Now almost no one was on the streets, except in the asphalt playground across from the old borough hall, where a group of young men were playing basketball, and a small line of people stood waiting to purchase soft ice cream at Jack's Variety Store, the old Wilkens's Jewelry Store, where Homestead men and women once had purchased their wedding rings but which now purveyed plaster statues of saints and of Elvis Presley.

The rash of fires continued and burned out several more buildings. The DeBolt Bus Company burned. So did the old Homestead Messenger Building. So did a onetime bank, constructed in the 1890s, and the historic Tindal Building, which had been restored for $500,000. It was as though some sort of wrath was being visited upon the town.

It was an old game, what was done in Homestead—use things up, people and places, then discard them. Tobacco and cotton planters used the land in the South, then moved on when the soil was exhausted. Mining companies took the gold and silver from the West, then closed down the towns they had built. Textile companies built mills in New England to use cheap labor, then moved to Pennsylvania and New Jersey, then to the South, then abroad. Now abandonment had come to America's steel towns. The forces arrayed against the workers and the towns were too immense to be overcome. The corporation was too powerful. Its fierce anti-unionism in earlier days had beaten people down, and in a sense they never recovered. They accepted a union that was undemocratic, that controlled them just as the corporation did, and that in the end itself fell too much under the corporation's control.

Homestead had its faults. The workers and the other townspeople were suspicious of outsiders. They had allowed themselves to become dependent on the mill. They could not unite with people in other communities. "They get bogged down in petty bullshit," Randolph Harris said. The town kept black people down. Many people did not like Jews, because most of them owned businesses and could afford to move across the river to Squirrel Hill, a more attractive place—"Kike's Peak," as some Homestead people called it. But the Jews were no different from any other group. Every group stuck together and took care of its own. First the English and the Irish, then the Slavs and the Jews and the blacks. All towns discriminate and always have. Homestead did fairly well in keeping a brake on prejudices, perhaps better than most places, seeing what it was up against. The problem was, Homestead was regarded as having limited value. Homestead made iron and steel, and that was useful. The people were good enough for that. They were also good enough to go into military service and to be blown apart high in the sky or to die on battlefields in Europe or on Pacific islands most people had never heard of. But Homestead had outlived its usefulness, as its usefulness was defined, and that was that.

I got my car by the library. I drove to McClure Street and down to Eighth Avenue and then turned west. I drove past Levine's Hardware, Caspar's Appliances, McCrory's, and the Moose Club, toward which wrinkled old men and women were slowly walking for Thursday-night bingo. I had seen them there many times. They would sit for hours, covering their numbers and smoking cigarettes. I passed Amity Street, where the last workers—Bob Krovocheck, Ed Buzinka, Bob Todd, and the rest—had driven up four years before, on the day the mill went down.

I sometimes had a daydream about Homestead. In this dream, I would go back in time and stand on the hill above Homestead and watch as the years—speeded up, like the animation in one of those nickel machines that used to be in amusement arcades—went by and the great kaleidoscope of events that had happened at Homestead passed in front of me. First Indians and wild animals coming from the forest to the river to drink or to cross over to the other side; then one day a frontiersman, a long-hunter from the East, peering out at the river from the dark woods; then the imperious Braddock with his powdered hair and with pipe clay on his leggings, and a long, colorful column, the men in red, blue, and white, splashing across the ford on the bright, sunlit July day—the most brilliant sight George Washington ever saw—to be decimated on the other side by French troops and half-naked Indians. Then the pioneers with horses and oxen and wagons; then peddlers, the beginning of commerce; then, on September 17, 1871, the birth of the town, as the jobbers' excursion boat came upriver, and the brass band played, and the home sites were opened for sale. Then the construction of the Homestead Works, and the iron and steel being made, smoke and fire rising up, and the steel loaded onto barges and railroad cars for shipment across the nation and to distant lands. Then the rat-a-tat-tat of gunfire as the workers and the Pinkertons fought it out, and the thick black smoke from the burning barges, and explosions and sirens, and bodies being carted away. Then more steel—for railroad tracks, locomotives, freight cars, and passenger cars, for skyscrapers, dams, and bridges, for the great projects of twentieth-century America—and the noise of the works—the bangs, shrieks, whistles, and other piercing sounds—and the long lines of workers streaming to the works and then home as shifts changed.

How magnificent it would be, I thought, to be able to do this, to see this tableau of America being enacted in front of me in this one place. But this was a daydream. All we have is what people say, what is in old books and newspapers, that and this certainty—that once, for over a hundred years, there was the grand American town of Homestead, and it was something to see.

I turned onto the High Level Bridge. What was left of the mill was below me. With the razing, there were now many open patches in the mill, which had once been almost solid with buildings. Beyond the mill I could see the river. It was almost entirely orange, as though it too were now on fire, as the onion-shaped domes at the top of Saint Nicholas's Russian Orthodox Church had been—as Homestead had once been. Beyond the river were the low, light green hills of the far shore and then the huge black slag pile that stretched to the parkway, the pile that Chris Kelly and his friends had slid down on cardboard when they were boys and from which they had returned to their homes with shredded pants, to the distress of their parents. The Park Corporation had said that it would take several years to tear the mill down, but the demolition crews seemed to be getting on faster than that. It did not matter, because the mill and the town and what they represented—a time of American economic dominance—had been gone for a long time. All there was now was silence—and the ruins of a century of American industrialism.

I remembered meeting a salesman, Blaine Popp, who had visited Homestead often while obtaining orders in the glory times of the mill and the town. It was the day the mill went down. Popp had heard that the mill was closing and had wanted to take a last look. I met him in Chiodo's, where he was having a cold one. I asked him what he thought. He said it was strange. He had seen the mill when it was running flat out, and now, when it was down. He said the silence was as loud as the noise had been.

HOMESTEAD IS
EVERY TOWN

I have had reason in the last year to return to Homestead on several occasions. I found Homestead much as I had left it, decrepit and depressing, except that the decay and despair had increased. It was also clear in my travels that what had happened in Homestead, and was continuing to happen, was not limited to Homestead and other decaying steel towns in the Monongahela Valley. Homestead, it seems to me, is every town, meaning that it is, to some degree, the story of thousands of towns across America. It is Saginaw, Michigan, an old General Motors Corporation site, now just a shell of what it once was, where I was born and grew up; it is Ypsilanti, Michigan; Flint, Michigan; and Detroit—more auto towns, more places where I have lived and practiced journalism. It is also towns that I have visited on reporting journeys: Matewan, West Virginia; Hibbing, Minnesota; Johnstown, Pennsylvania; Lackawanna, New York; Beaumont, Texas; Morenci, Arizona—coal towns, iron towns, steel towns, auto towns, oil towns, copper towns, farm towns, ranching towns: hundreds of towns across this country that, once they yielded up the riches they were created to extract, were allowed to run down or were abandoned.

The site of the old Homestead Works was, by the summer of 1993, cleared of most of its old buildings, the buildings that, stretching several miles along the Monongahela River, had been at the center of the American iron and steel industry—of American industry itself—and had produced steel for so many of the important structures, buildings, bridges, and dams, of twentieth-century America. No new development had come to the site, although there were still hopes that it would, and haranguing continued among borough officials and between borough officials and officials of the Park Corporation, the company that had purchased the mill and the mill land from USX, the former owner, and which was clearing the property and preparing it for potential development.

The site of the old mill—a brownfield site, in the language of developers—was a vast empty space, waiting for development at a time when the American real estate market was depressed, and when vast amounts of open land—greenfield sites, in the language of developers—could easily be obtained and zoned for development. More than that, high technology industries were stagnant. In Pittsburgh, what was known as the Pittsburgh Technology Center, envisioned with extensive hoopla in the 1980s as a vast project on the north side of the Monongahela River, on the site of the old Jones & Laughlin Hazelwood plant, near the theoretically attractive site of downtown Pittsburgh, lagged. It was reported that what had been planned as a $200 million private project that was to create several thousand jobs was, by the summer of 1993, just one building, built at a cost of some $50 million in public money, and providing almost no new jobs. Nor was this unusual. Across much of the country, high technology, the hope of officials of so many old industrial towns in the 1980s, had plateaued.

Homestead seemed like an old, poor man—scruffy, holes in his pockets, holes in his shoes. There were potholes everywhere in the Homestead streets; the infrastructure was in horrible condition. Crime, including the use and sale of drugs, had increased. There were more fires in the old business district below Eighth Avenue. The police department was reduced to a half-dozen full-time officers, and the fire department was manned solely by volunteers. The ambulance service, faced with heavy debts, was hanging on, although only barely; the mayor, Betty Esper, was trying to find a place to park the town ambulance inside, out of the weather. "There aren't too many positives about Homestead," the mayor said.

The borough's housing stock continued to fall into disrepair, and housing prices stagnated or fell. Realtors, with homes that had no great appeal, sold homes to poorer whites or poorer blacks, making real estate less attractive to many whites. The Diocese of Pittsburgh closed two Homestead area churches, St. Margaret, a Hungarian church, and St. Peter and St. Paul, a Lithuanian church (some charged that it was easy to close the ethnic churches), combining the parishes with others into a new parish, St. Maximilian Kolbe Church, and announced plans to close a third church, the magnificent St. Mary Magdalene Church, unless parishioners raised $300,000 for repairs and maintenance of the massive building, so lovingly restored with money raised from Homestead people after the original church burned in the stupendous fire in the 1930s. In closing the churches, the diocese used a logic much like that USX had used in closing its mills—a logic much like that which American companies often use in closing plants and offices, a capitalist calculus that in this case held that births and baptisms in the churches did not match resignations and deaths, and thus the churches were extraneous. When a band of Homestead area Catholics protested, the diocese said that its outreach activities in the Monongahela Valley demonstrated its commitment to people of the valley, just as years before USX had pointed to its employment and retraining assistance offices, both failures, as signs that it was a benevolent employer.

Some traditions, to be sure, remained that harked to the rich, robust days. Chiodo's remained a popular place for food and drink, and the Moose still drew respectable crowds on bingo nights. Kennywood, the century-old railroad amusement park at the site of Braddock's crossing, remained popular, having decided to install metal detectors, however, as a precaution against weapons being carried into the park. On Sundays, Homestead residents, some dressed to the nines, still came to their churches, although in far smaller numbers than before. Before festive occasions, such as Easter and Christmas, Homesteaders gathered to prepare the old ethnic dishes, such as stuffed cabbage, halushky, and nut and poppy seed rolls known as kolachky. For Easter, there was added a festive bread known as paska. And on Fridays through much of the year, a visitor could go up to St. John's Cathedral, on Dickson Street, in Munhall, and enjoy, if he wanted to put on the feedbag, a lunch, made by the church ladies, of pirohy, bean and lentil soup, and, of course, the ubiquitous halushky, or portions thereof.

There were some victories. The handsome Tindall Building, hit by a fire in 1992, was rebuilt. More money was made available to the Carnegie Library of Homestead; the library's gutters and downspouts were repaired, walls cleaned, walks rebricked. Munhall and West Homestead began paving programs. Success continued in the Steel Valley School District (it was even more clear how fortunate it had been that consolidation of the three districts, Homestead, Munhall, and West Homestead, had been mandated by the state years before). The district was a far different district from the one I had first visited in the early 1980s. There seemed to be a core of excellent teachers and administrators, and in the spring of 1993, Steel Valley High School staged a well-acted, especially spirited production of "The Music Man," if the testaments of students and parents who attended can be a judge.

But the hemorrhaging could not be stanched, and there were, in the summer of 1993, "enormous feelings of uncertainty in Homestead" and other parts of the Homestead district, according to Mark Hornak, the long-time member of the school board. It seemed, but could not be proven, that there were hints of racial division, exacerbated, perhaps, by what some residents regarded as the movement of more blacks into Homestead. In March, 1993, the town, faced with a declining tax base and deteriorating infrastructure, was granted what amounted to bankruptcy status under Pennsylvania Act 47, the Municipalities Financial Recovery Act. "The borough of Homestead has experienced a substantial deterioration in its financial position as evidenced by a history of year-end deficits, accompanying increases in unpaid bills, and decreasing fund balances," the Pennsylvania state secretary of community affairs said. The state Department of Community Affairs said that Homestead faced a 1993 budget deficit of $208,000, on a projected budget of some $1.3 million. The state added that it was questionable whether the community could "continue to provide basic services to its residents."

In some ways, Homestead remained chic in its despair, although the chicness was wearing off, and, I thought, would soon be coming to an end. That is the nature of chicness. Committees continued to meet, and some money continued to be made available to those persons and organizations that the Pittsburgh authorities deemed respectable. Some of these persons did not understand that they were being used, and were displeased when they were so charged. In the summer of 1992, there was, at the Carnegie Library of Homestead, a conference to mark the 100th anniversary of the epochal 1892 Homestead strike and lockout. Yet almost no former workers from the Homestead Works participated in the commemoration, nor was the commemoration attended by many ordinary people of Homestead. Ron Weisen, the one-time Homestead steelworkers' union president, took time off from his jackhammer job with the city of Pittsburgh, went up to the library, and engaged in some guerilla theater, making insulting speeches to the union bigwigs who came out briefly for the event, inserting himself into photographs that were being taken, including some that involved Lynn Williams, president of the United Steelworkers of America. Little effort was made at the conference to learn from the past—to look at the past and attempt to see how what had happened in the 1892 strike and lockout, and in the hundred years after that, to explain the plight of Homestead; what had happened in that time to explain the situations of hundreds of other working class towns; certainly, to look at what the union had done to contribute to the downfall of Homestead and the steel industry. But then, that was to be expected. The union was helping to pay for the conference.

The planning for a highway through the Monongahela Valley continued, although no construction began. No hurry on the highway. It would come, or not come. The rundown river towns would be dead anyway; a highway would only make them more dead.

The deaths of the former mill hands continued. Michael Stout, the former Homestead grievance man, calculated in the summer of 1993 that more than seventy-five men from the Homestead Works, men in their forties, fifties, or early sixties whom Stout had known, men who seemingly should have been in the prime of their lives, had died after leaving the Homestead Works. Stout also continued his grievance work—and continued winning. One day, he put a pencil to the amount of money he had extracted from USX in grievances, and figured that the number totaled more than $10 million, a curious comment, it would seem, on USX's managerial techniques.

Since this book was published in hardcover, in 1992, unemployment in America has continued to hover at about seven percent, meaning that —because official unemployment figures always understate unemployment in America—15 to 20 percent of Americans who wanted gainful employment could not find it. Moreover, dozens of companies, in the manner of USX, announced major cuts in employment and the closings of plants and offices. IBM planned to terminate 100,000 workers, on top of another 100,000 who had already left the company. Sears, Roebuck and Co. said it planned to close more than 100 stores, plus cancel its century-old catalogue, and cut 50,000 jobs. The government planned to cut one million military jobs, a reduction expected to eliminate another 600,000 jobs in civilian manufacturing. The Department of Labor said that, normally, more than 40 percent of the workers laid off in a recession obtain their jobs back, but in the recession of the early 1990s, about 15 percent were able to get their jobs back. Moreover, it was expected that, by the end of the century, one of three U.S. workers would be contingent workers, that is, temporary workers going from one company to another as short term workers.

I realized one day, flying into Pittsburgh—I had not flown to Pittsburgh in some time—that an entire new "state of the art" airport has been built there since I began this book. Also, a new expressway has been completed between downtown Pittsburgh and the city's northern suburbs. The skyline of downtown Pittsburgh remained resplendent, especially in the morning or evening, when the sun shined on the tops of the office buildings.

All this time, in Pittsburgh and across the rest of the nation, unattractive areas, be they old industrial areas, working class communities, or inner-city black and Hispanic areas, were being written off, while new development was going to attractive suburban areas, meaning upper-class, white areas. Money was following money—the American way. It was the mentality of the frontier—extract and leave. It was an unethical way for the country to live, but no one seemed to care—not the man on the street, the city, state capital, or Washington leaders.

It occurred to me, too, at this time, that even the phrases "urban affairs" and "industrial policy" had essentially disappeared from the lexicon of Washington policy makers, university experts, newspapers, and magazines. Compassion seemed out of style—a 33-rpm album you might find in your attic. I was struck by this when I looked at a review of this book in *The New York Times* by Robert Reich, now secretary of labor in the Clinton Administration. "Why should we care about Homestead, or, for that matter, about any town or city in decline? Where exactly is the 'tragedy,' other than in the book's subtitle?" Reich asked. He went on, "Americans are always leaving some place behind: departures are in our ancestral genes. Shouldn't the objects of our concern more properly be the people who once inhabited such places, and the lives they are able to lead elsewhere? Or does rootedness matter more than we have allowed ourselves to admit?"

This, I thought, was a most curious logic. I thought that if someone had gone to Reich and said that Harvard University, that handsome and important place where Reich taught for years, should be abandoned and razed, because the facilities could be efficiently combined with those at, say, the University of Chicago, Stanford University, or the University of California at Berkeley, Reich would find clear and urgent reasons why this should not be done. Our traditions, our skills, I am sure Reich would say, must be preserved—the same logic that was expressed to me hundreds of times by Homestead steelworkers and Homestead residents. I also hoped that Reich would show more compassion for workers and members of their families than he demonstrated by these remarks. And, I suspect, rootedness does matter more than we understand—or at least Reich understands.

Yet, while one had to attempt to understand the logic of academics and technocrats, I also received many letters and telephone calls, most warm, a few not, on this book—from Homesteaders and ex-Homesteaders, from steelworkers and ex-steelworkers. These people had memories small and large of Homestead: of a grandfather who was banned for life from the steel mills for strike activity; of watching radical miners come walking into Clairton in 1933, demanding that the steel workers join their walkout, and the attack on union men by mounted state police; of playing basketball on homemade baskets in Homestead alleys until dark; of walking by the huge, turreted superintendent's house, then next to the Carnegie Library of Homestead, gone now these many years, and of being afraid to go near the house, even on Halloween; of trudging up the Carnegie Library of Homestead for books, library card in hand; of peering through the windows of the house of Doc McLean, the town's burgess, at the political meetings inside; of recollections of the town's famous brothel operator, Evelyn Marshall, a madam at age sixteen, a testament to her executive abilities; of memories of their lives in the mill, and often of their fathers' and grandfathers' lives in the mill, at a time when men and women of the town equated the steel mills with slaughterhouses; of selling the last piling rolled at Homestead, this for lock and dam number 26 on the Mississippi River—the best piling, the writer said, that Homestead ever rolled.

These people, it seemed to me, knew more about what was happening to America than those people regarded as America's leaders or its experts, for many asked why the country was allowing the closing of mills and towns to happen, why were there no policies to combat closings, to funnel new growth into areas that needed development?

What lessons remain from my time in Homestead? What lessons remain for the reader? First, there is no free lunch. Nothing is free—pencils and tools from the mill or thirteen-week vacations or repairs and investments that are not made or low-quality steel pawned off on customers. There is also the danger of the company town, and its authority, and there is the need to plan ahead, for institutions, be they companies or unions, to guard against arrogance, insularity, and inbreeding—to recognize the necessity for change. There is the need for companies to recognize the skills of their workers, and to give workers their heads, and for unions, rather than being slow and reactive, as they usually are, to be creative and vigorous, as they usually are not. To be, in a phrase, smarter than the boss. They owe that, I would argue, to their members, whose dues pay the union bosses' salaries and benefits. It must be recognized that overhiring is pernicious—that workers added without thought in good times will have to be shed in bad times. There is also the need for an early warning system, with the government assisting, to identify problems in industry, like those which occurred in the steel industry, before they occur. Finally, it is clear to me that there is a need for strong, yet democratic land-use planning, to force new development to old communities, where it is needed, and keep it out of greenfield areas, where it is not.

For many of the people who were there in the glory days of Homestead, the Homestead they knew, the Homestead that did so much for America, is nothing but a memory. But I have memories, too. I will not forget the many favors people did for me there, the many wondrous experiences I had. Surely, I will not forget the gray Saturday afternoon last winter when I received a call from a woman in southern New Jersey —south Jersey, as we say in that state. She had grown up in the Homestead area, the daughter of a white-collar man and his wife, and had lived for part of her childhood in one of the large houses for mill executives behind the library. She thanked me for writing the book and said she always looked back fondly on her days growing up in Homestead. She recalled the holidays, the proms, the trips to Eighth Avenue, to its splendid stores, on Saturdays and Sundays. As she talked, she said that she had thought of something that had not crossed her mind in years. She said she never again has had Boston cream pie like that made at Wohlfarth's bakery on the avenue.

William Serrin
Summer, 1993

NOTES

In the research for this book, I consulted some 300 books as well as hundreds of newspapers and magazine articles. Many of these are listed in the Selected Bibliography. The books I collected in the course of my research will be deposited in the Carnegie Library of Homestead.

The preponderance of the book, however, is based upon my observations and reporting; in the course of the five and a half years I worked on this book, I made more than forty trips to Homestead as well as a dozen trips as a reporter for *The New York Times* before the book was begun. Some 250 men and women who had worked in the Homestead mill or lived in Homestead or the vicinity generously allowed me to interview them. I have tried as best as I could to write accurately what I heard and saw. All characters and names in the book are real.

CHAPTER 1. THE DAY THE MILL WENT DOWN

The history of the Homestead Works and of Homestead and the discussion of the 1892 strike are from the works of Bridge, Burgoyne, Byington, Stowell, and Wolff; the *Homestead Local News* and its successor, the *Homestead Daily Messenger;* and from local materials written or assembled over the years—a number by the former town librarian, W. L. Stevens—and available in the Carnegie Library of Homestead.

CHAPTER 2. "HOMESTEAD, USA"

The information on the town's Civil War monument comes from the *Homestead Daily Messenger* and a paper prepared in September 1871 by a town historian, whose name was not recorded, and deposited in the Carnegie Library of Homestead. The information on immigration to Homestead is from both Balch and Byington. The material on the Ku Klux Klan activity is from two publications by the Historical Society of Western Pennsylvania: a pamphlet entitled "Homestead: The Story of a Steel Town, 1860–1945" (published in 1988) and "Homestead: The Story of a Steel Town" by Curtis Miner, a catalog for an exhibition, "Homestead: The Story of a Steel Town, 1890–1945," published in 1989. I also interviewed Malvin R. Goode, once a radio broadcaster in Homestead and later the first black correspondent hired by an American television network (ABC), and John Tarasevich. The information on deaths in the Homestead Works is from a corporation document. The material on the Homestead Grays is from Holway's books, Rob Ruck's *Sandlot Seasons: Sport in Black Pittsburgh* (Champaign, Ill.: University of Illinois Press, 1987), Robert W. Peterson's *Only the Ball Was White* (Englewood Cliffs, N.J.: Prentice-Hall Inc., 1970), and Donn Rogosin's *Invisible Men* (New York: Atheneum Publishers, 1983). The information on the Carnegie Library of Homestead is from Byington. Spanky O'Toole, a one-time Homestead policeman and now manager of the Homestead Ancient Order of Hibernian Club, gave me the names of the whorehouses. William "Car Wash" Brown talked to me extensively about the black community in Homestead, as did Jester Hairston.

CHAPTER 3. BEGINNINGS

The information on John Frazier is from materials, including some written by W. L. Stevens, in the Carnegie Library of Homestead. The description of Braddock's march on the forks of the Cumberland is from McCardell. Information on the Emanuel Leutze painting is from the Braddock Library Historical Association. The material on the Monongahela Valley after the Braddock fight is from the *WPA Guide to Pennsylvania,* and the material on the pioneers of the Homestead district is from monographs by Stevens. The information on the platting of Homestead and the selling of the first lots is from material prepared by Stevens and from issues of the *Homestead Daily Messenger.* For information on the Homestead district following the town's founding, I consulted numerous issues of the *Homestead Local News.*

CHAPTER 4. "WHERE IS THERE SUCH A BUSINESS!"

For the history of the acquisition of the Homestead Works by Andrew Carnegie, I consulted numerous texts, including those by Bridge, Burgoyne, Byington, and Wall. The biographical material on Carnegie is from Wall's comprehensive biography and also from Bridge, Carnegie's *Autobiography*, Livesay, and *The New York Times*; see also "Epitaph for the Steel Master" by Robert L. Heilbroner in *American Heritage,* August 1960, and Matthew Josephson's *The Robber Barons* (New York: Harcourt Brace, 1934). The information on Henry Phipps and his mare Gypsy is from Bridge. The Henry Clay Frick biographical material is from both Harvey and Wall, as well as *The New York Times*. The material on Captain William R. Jones is from Bridge, Byington, Harvey, Wall, and newspaper accounts of the era, including the *Homestead Local News.* The quotation "The Amalgamated had to go" is from Brody's *Steelworkers in America: The Non-Union Era.*

CHAPTER 5. THE MILL

The description of iron- and steelmaking at the Carrie furnaces and the Homestead Works is from numerous interviews with men who worked at these places, from standard texts on the iron and steel industry, including Fisher's *The Epic of Steel,* and from materials published over the years by the United States Steel Corporation (now USX), which include "Growing with America" (1948), "Homestead Works: United States Steel" (undated), and "Steel Making in America" (1949). Also useful was

"Elegy to the Open Hearth" by Lawrence Kuhn, *33: The Magazine of Metals Producing,* December 1969. I interviewed John Duch. The John A. Fitch material is from his most valuable work, *The Steel Workers.* The material on the men killed in the Homestead Works is from corporation records and my calculations. I interviewed William J. Gaughan several times, and I am immensely indebted to him. I also interviewed Michael Stout several times, and I am indebted to him as well. In my research, I heard no better description of a steel mill in operation than his.

Chapter 6. Rebellion I

The description of Henry Clay Frick's fence is from Burgoyne and issues of the *Homestead Local News.* For the information on the hidden issue of technology, I am indebted to research by Stephen Brier, a historian with the American Social History Project at the City University of New York. The information on the founding and character of the Amalgamated Association is based on works by Brody (*Steelworkers*), Fitch, and Robinson. The information on the footnotes in the labor contract is from Montgomery. The Andrew Carnegie *Forum* articles are quoted in Wall and are also available in major libraries. Carnegie's autobiography was first published in 1920, a year after his death. Carnegie's actions in 1867 are from Wall. The information on Frick is from both Bridge and Wall. The colloquy between William T. Roberts and John A. Potter is from Wall. Father John J. Bullion was quoted in *The New York Times.* The Rev. John J. McIlyar's sermon is quoted in Burgoyne. The material on Sheriff McCleary is from numerous texts on the fight, including Wall. The Burgoyne material is from his book. The Frick telegraph is from Wall. The information on the Pinkerton Detective Agency is from Horan.

My account of the Homestead fight and the events that followed is also drawn from the *Homestead Local News, The New York Times,* the *New York World* (which was regarded by participants in the Homestead fight as having done the best reportage), *Harper's Weekly,* and Frank Leslie's *Illustrated Weekly.* Hamlin Garland's observations on Homestead are from *McClure's Magazine,* July 1893. The Honest John McCluckie anecdote appeared in Carnegie's *Autobiography.* Hugh O'Donnell's quotation appears in Hogg. The *St. Louis Post-Dispatch* editorial appeared in that paper in August 1892 and is quoted in Wall. Carnegie's January 23, 1893, appearance in Homestead was reported in the *Homestead Local News;* his remarks were released to the press and appeared in the Pittsburgh newspapers and the *Homestead Daily Messenger.*

Chapter 7. "All Hail, King Steel"

Henry W. Oliver's journey to the Minnesota iron range is recounted in Wall. Leonidas Merritt's recollections of his conversation with Henry Clay Frick were quoted in Senate testimony. The Merritt saga is recounted in De Kruif and in Holbrook. Carnegie's dealings with John D. Rockefeller appear in Wall. Carnegie's efforts to gain control of railroad transportation are recounted in both Livesay and Wall. His conversations with Frank Thomson appear in Wall, as do his remarks to Frick. The discussion of the Carnegie board members on the efforts by Homestead workers to reorganize the Homestead works appears in Wall. The Carnegie-Frick contretemps appears in Bridge and in Wall, among others.

CHAPTER 8. "THE COMBINATION OF COMBINATIONS"

The dinner given in honor of Charles M. Schwab is recounted in Allen and in Wall, among others. J. H. Reid's remarks on Schwab appear in Senate testimony. Andrew Carnegie's new struggle against the railroads is recounted by Wall. The reaction of newspaper and magazine editorialists to the consolidation are recounted in Allen. The high jinks of the "Pittsburgh Millionaires" are described in *The Big Spenders* by Lucius Beebe (Garden City, N.Y.: Doubleday, 1966), in *The Age of the Moguls* by Stewart H. Holbrook (Garden City, N.Y.: Doubleday & Company, 1953), and in other works. Schwab's nostalgic visit to Homestead was reported in the *Homestead Local News*. The remarks of Patrick Dolan and Theodore D. Shaffer appeared in *The New York Times,* March 1901.

CHAPTER 9. THE JUDGE: A MAN OF PRINCIPLES

The installation of Judge Elbert H. Gary's electric sign is recounted in *Fortune,* June 1936, as are H. L. Mencken's remarks on Gary. The twenty-dollar gold piece story appears in Tarbell, as do J. Pierpont Morgan's question to his lawyers and Gary's reply. *Fortune*'s remarks on Gary's principles appeared in June 1936, as did the veteran steelmaker's comment. Charles M. Schwab's adventure in Monte Carlo is best recounted by John Garraty in "Charlie Schwab Breaks the Bank," *American Heritage,* April 1957. The "closed doors" episode comes from Lucius Beebe's *The Big Spenders*. The story of the construction of Gary, Indiana, is told in Tarbell and in histories of the town. Gary's statement in reply to the executive who said "If a workman raises his head, hit it" is from Brody. The Amalgamated Association situation in 1901 is reported in Brody's *Steelworkers in America,* as is the 1909–1910 strike. The "Gary dinners" are described in Tarbell. William E. Corey's adventures, including the details of his marriage, are reported in Stewart H. Holbrook's *The Age of the Moguls*. The corporation's confrontations with the government and the courts are recounted in Tarbell.

CHAPTER 10. WARS

The corporation's war production, as well as its sales and profits, are reported in Fisher's *Steel Serves the Nation: The Fifty Year Story of United States Steel,* the corporation publication celebrating the organization's fiftieth anniversary. The Chicago meatpackers' strike of 1917 is recounted in Brody's *Labor in Crisis* and in Foster's *The Great Steel Strike*. William Z. Foster's background is from his autobiography, *Organizing Steel,* as well as from his obituary in *The New York Times.* Vorse's description of Foster appears in her *A Footnote to Folly*. Elbert H. Gary's admonition to his subordinate executives is from Brody's *Labor in Crisis*. Burgess McGuire's arrest and the trial of Foster and J. L. Beaghen are also described in Brody's *Labor in Crisis*. Joe

Mayor, the Homestead worker, described his confrontation with William Munle, a plant superintendent, in testimony before the Senate committee investigating the 1919 strike. Mother Jones's speech in Homestead is recounted in her autobiography. Samuel Gompers's views of the strike appear in his autobiography, *Seventy Years of Labor and Life* (New York: E. P. Dutton, Inc., 1925). The strike is recounted in Brody's two works. Accounts of the strike can also be found in *1919: The Year Our World Began* by William K. Klingaman (New York: Thomas Dunne Books, St. Martin's, 1987) and in Robert K. Murray's *Red Scare: A Study in National Hysteria 1919–1920* (Minneapolis: University of Minnesota Press, 1955). *Fortune*'s observation on the corporation appears in that magazine in May 1936. The account of Gary's last days is from *Fortune* and *The New York Times.*

CHAPTER 11. "THE BEST SNOWBALL FIGHT I WAS EVER IN"

The description of the dedication of the Carnegie Library of Homestead is from a monograph prepared at the time and now kept in the Carnegie Library of Homestead. The Homestead worker's record of his work hours appears in the report of the Senate investigation of the 1919 strike, as does the Slav worker's account of his hours and wages. Byington comments on the men "weary from long hours of work" and on how they "wanted to show they could meet its challenge." The exchange between Senator Walsh and Judge Elbert H. Gary appears in the Senate testimony. Fitch's observation appears in *Survey Graphic.* The hauling of the lime to the creek in Hunkie Hollow is reported by Byington. Tom Girdler's comment appears in his autobiography. Byington's observations appear in her book, and O'Connor's comments appear in his. The descriptions of holidays in Homestead are from the *Homestead Local News.* The opening of the Stahl Theatre is recounted in the *Homestead Daily Messenger* and in the *Pittsburgh Press.* The recollections of Jester Hairston are from an interview. The visit of Frances Perkins, secretary of labor, to Homestead, in July 1933, is recorded in *The Roosevelt I Knew* (see also *Madam Secretary* by George Martin [Boston: Houghton Mifflin, 1976]). The *Homestead Daily Messenger* carried an account of the reaction to Miss Perkins's visit, as well as Burgess John Cavanaugh's remarks on what he described as his intelligence-gathering operation in the Monongahela Valley.

CHAPTER 12. "THE MAN NOBODY KNOWS"

The information on Elbert H. Gary's funeral and on the initial developments in the corporation following his death is from *The New York Times.* Myron C. Taylor's elevation to the chairmanship is recounted in *Fortune,* June 1936. The profile of Taylor and his efforts to reform the corporation are drawn from Bernstein, *The New York Times,* and an excellent *Fortune* series on the steel industry, published in 1936, when *Fortune* was practicing some of the finest magazine journalism ever done in America. The visit of Taylor and the other steel executives to Frances Perkins's office is recounted by Perkins. The description of William Green is from a portrait of Green by Craig Phelan, in Dubofsky and Van Tine's *Labor Leaders in America.* The reports of the mine workers' organizers are from Bernstein. The employee-representation plan at Colorado Fuel and Iron Company is described by Bernstein; that at Bethlehem Steel Corporation is described by Reutter. Charles M. Schwab's comment to Clarence W. Barron appears in Reutter. The hiring of Arthur H. Young is recounted in Bernstein.

CHAPTER 13. "TELL JOHN L. LEWIS TO STOP WINDBAGGING"

The story of Steve Bordich and other rank-and-filers planning "The Steel Workers' Declaration of Independence" is told by Powers. The description of the July 5, 1936, rally in Homestead is from Bernstein, *Fortune* (October 1936), and *The New York Times*. The profile of Michael Angelo Musmanno is from a postscript to his novel, *Black Fury*, and his obituary in *The New York Times*. Charles Scharbo's address appears in *The New York Times* and in Powers. The scene at the graves is from Bernstein, as is the description of steelworkers during the Great Depression. Rose G. Ferraro told me of Homestead children going home from school with the Mason jars of soup. *Fortune*'s description of the labor movement in the 1920s appeared in the December 1933 issue. The meeting of the "Spirit of 1892" Homestead Lodge was reported in the *Homestead Daily Messenger*, June 1933. The Amalgamated Association in the early 1930s is discussed in Bernstein and O'Connor. The discussion of the captive mines strike is from Bernstein, *Fortune*, *The New York Times*, and Sheppard. I have also, in this section, drawn from Louis Adamic's article on steel organizing in *The Nation*, June 4, 1934, and from his book, *Dynamite*. I am indebted most strongly for my interpretation of the labor-management agitation in 1933, 1934, and 1935 to the fine essay by Staughton Lynd, "The Possibility of Radicalism in the Early 1930s: The Case in Steel," which appeared in *Radical America* in November-December 1972. The piece is reprinted in *Workers' Struggles, Past and Present: A 'Radical America' Reader*, edited by James Green (Philadelphia: Temple University Press, 1983). The piece by Louis Stark, a premier U.S. labor reporter of the 1930s, appeared in *The New York Times* on June 15, 1934. William Green's address to the Amalgamated Association convention on June 15, 1934, was reported in *The New York Times*. The fact that some rank-and-file leaders were upstairs knocking back a few drinks appears in Adamic's article in *The Nation*. The agitation in 1935 is drawn from several sources, including Lynd and *The New York Times*. The American Federation of Labor's convention in October 1935 is described in numerous texts, including Bernstein. The profile of John L. Lewis is based upon my readings over the years of his work and, specifically, upon my reading of Alinsky, as well as of Dubofsky and Van Tine. David J. McDonald's observation of Lewis in Indianapolis is from McDonald's autobiography. The description of the breakfast on October 20, 1936, is from Alinsky and from Bernstein. The convention of the Amalgamated Association in April and May of 1936 is from Powers. The formation of the Steel Workers Organization Committee on June 4, 1936, is from Bernstein. The material on Philip Murray is from Bernstein and from McDonald. Lewis's radio address was published in *The New York Times*. The discussion of the John McLean and John Cavanaugh wars in Homestead is from the *Homestead Messenger*. The description of the SWOC organizing drive is from McDonald's book from a series of interviews he gave in 1970 to scholars at Pennsylvania State University and from Sweeney. The story of the meeting between Lewis and Senator Joseph F. Guffy is from *Fortune*, "It Happened in Steel," May 1937, as is the discussion of Myron C. Taylor's trip to Europe and his preparation of a statement on his view about collective bargaining. The discussion of the bargaining that led to the March 1937 agreement is from Bernstein. The description of the Memorial Day shootings (May 30, 1937) is from Bernstein and from "An Occurrence at Republic Steel" by Howard Fast in *The Aspirin Age: 1919–1941*, edited by Isabel Leighton (New York: Clarion Books, 1949).

CHAPTER 14. VICTORY VALLEY

The description of Homestead in the months before World War II is from the *Homestead Daily Messenger* and my interviews with Homestead men and women. The demolition of lower Homestead is described in booklets published by the Historical Society of Western Pennsylvania, in the *Homestead Daily Messenger,* and in Pittsburgh newspapers. The description of the corporation's production during World War II is from two corporation books, both by Fisher, *Steel in the War* and *Steel Serves the Nation.* The profile of Benjamin F. Fairless is from his book and from *The New York Times.* The information on Edward R. Stettinius is from *The New York Times.* Nelson Lichtenstein's observation on Philip Murray appears in Lichtenstein's *Labor's War at Home: The CIO in World War II* (New York: Cambridge University Press, 1982). The description of the Murray-Lewis contentions is from Alinsky and from Bernstein. The description of SWOC's first constitutional convention is from Sweeney. Murray's humiliation by Lewis is from Alinsky and from Bernstein. McDonald's recollections of SWOC are included in his book and his oral history interview. The *Fortune* description of the U.S.W.A. is from a portrait of the union that appeared in November 1946. The listing of the Homestead men killed in World War II is from a file of obituaries, carefully clipped and taped onto typing paper and made available to me by Ann Hart, the Homestead librarian. John Hart, Ann's husband, told me the story of the death of the lieutenant. Burgess McLean's trips to the train station were described to me by his son, John. Evelyn Patterson described to me her recollection of Homestead at the end of World War II. The description of life in Homestead following the war is from the *Homestead Daily Messenger,* as is the information of Murray's August 26, 1945, speech in Homestead.

CHAPTER 15. "NO LONGER A CLASS WAR"

The description of the 1946 steelworkers' strike is from *The New York Times.* Philip Murray's reaction to Walter P. Reuther is from McDonald. The description of the corporation as "the most fabulous giant yet produced" is from *Life,* November 11, 1946. The corporation's acquisition of the Homestead Works is described in the *Homestead Daily Messenger;* its acquisition of the Geneva Works was reported in *Time,* 1946. Gunnison Homes is described in the corporation publication *Steel Serves the Nation* and in *The New York Times.* The statements of George Stocking and Professor George Stigler before the House Subcommittee on the Study of Monopoly are quoted in Adams (section entitled "The Steel Industry"). Irving S. Olds's comments appeared in the corporation's history of its first fifty years. The efforts by Murray and other labor leaders to confront those they regarded as Communists appear in Cochran and in *The New York Times*. Lewis's remark, "Who gets the bird . . . ," is in Alinsky. Murray's statement that "This union will not tolerate efforts by outsiders . . ." appears in Sweeney. The information on Lee Pressman is from *The New York Times*. McDonald's statement, "They were quite honestly kangaroo courts," is from his book. I also drew, in this section, from Caute's excellent work. McDonald's recollection of Murray's speech in San Francisco is from his book. The discussion of the intellectuals leaving the union is from Brooks's biography of Clinton Golden. I interviewed Harold J. Ruttenberg. The discussion of the 1952 negotiations is from Fairless, McDonald, Sweeney, and a profile of Murray by Ronald Schatz in Dubofsky and Van Tine's "Labor Leaders in America." Murray's speech at the January 1952 convention is from John Herling, as is the conversation between McDonald and Emory Bacon. McDonald, in his autobiography, *Union Man,* provided the description of Murray leaving the San Francisco hotel.

CHAPTER 16. THE DAVE AND BEN SHOW

McDonald described in *Union Man,* his autobiography, his feelings upon being awakened to learn that Philip Murray was dead. I also consulted *The New York Times,* which reported extensively on Murray's death. Emory Bacon's thoughts about whether to welcome McDonald or to greet Murray's body are from Herling. Herling also described Murray's funeral, as did *The New York Times*. Father Charles Owens Rice discussed Murray's funeral with me. The political maneuverings in the union following Murray's death are described in Herling. McDonald's remark, "I stole four elections for Joe Germano," appeared in *The New York Times*. McDonald's selection of I. W. Abel as his secretary-treasurer is described by Herling and by McDonald in *Union Man.* My discussion of how the industry executives viewed Murray and McDonald is from my conversations with union and industry men. The May 1955 meeting of the American Iron and Steel Institute was discussed in Reutter and in *The Wall Street Journal.* The profile of McDonald is from Beachler, Herling, *Man of Steel* by Kelly and Beachler, his autobiography, and "Man of Steel," *Time,* July 20, 1959. McDonald's remark, "Where . . . would I be able to get another job," is from Herling. I also consulted *The New York Times*'s coverage of McDonald over the years. The description of the Fairless Works is from Fairless's memoir and the corporation's fifty-year history. Fairless's observation that it was not just the old-timers who "took all the risks" is from his autobiography. The tour of the steel mills by Fairless and McDonald is from *Colliers*'s "Through the Mill with Ben and Dave," Fairless, and McDonald's autobiography. The description of the Day for Dave is from *Time*'s "Man of Steel" and from *The Wall Street Journal.* William J. Hart's comment on McDonald, "We're going to give this guy everything he wants," is from Herling. The 1954 negotiations are described in McDonald and in Sweeney. The "Reuther bullshit" remark is from Herling. Lloyd McBride's remark on union lawyers is from a piece by James Warren in the *American Lawyer,* March 1982. The merger of the AFL-CIO is described in *The New York Times;* several participants have also discussed the convention with me. The Dues Protest Committee is described in Herling. For the discussion of the 1959 steel strike, I drew upon Herling, McDonald's autobiography and his interviews with Pennsylvania State researchers, and *The New York Times*. *Fortune* praised the United States Steel Corporation in January 1956. Arthur Homer's remark appears in Reutter. McDonald's view that the union "had achieved just about everything a union could provide" appears in *Union Man.*

CHAPTER 17. KHRUSHCHEV'S WRISTWATCH

The October 1952 payday is described in the *Homestead Daily Messenger* and the booklet prepared for Homestead's one hundredth anniversary. Steve Simko discussed with me his recollections of Homestead during and after World War II. Richard Holoman told me about the Works in the early 1950s. Betty Esper discussed her recollections of the mill several times with me. Numerous Homesteaders described the golden times of Homestead in the 1950s. I also drew upon issues of the *Homestead Daily Messenger* and two publications on Homestead's history: "Souvenir Program, 1880–1930, Homestead's 50th Anniversary, October 13 to 18, 1930" and "Homestead Diamond Jubilee, 1880–1955, August 21 through August 27." Anselmo "Babe" Fernandez discussed with me his recollections of the mill and the town. I chatted briefly with Steve Pachuta, and Ray McGuire told me his recollections of him. Dan Spillane, a longtime Homestead resident, chatted with me about growing up and living in Homestead and about how his father took him to see ships that contained Homestead steel. Chris Kelly told me about how the boys would ride their bicycles to Forbes Field. Rose G. Ferraro told me how the Angelus was sounded by the bells at St. Mary Magdalene's Roman Catholic Church. Betty Esper told me about her brother, Candy. The discussion of life for blacks in Homestead is from conversations with William "Car Wash" Brown, Porky Chedwick, Malvin Goode, and John Tarasevich, and from Ruck's *Sandlot Seasons,* and Holway's *Blackball Stars.* Steve Simko chatted with me several times about Homestead; I interviewed Marty Costa and Ray Hornak several times each. The discussion of corruption in the mill is based upon conversations with numerous mill workers and Homestead residents. The Muck Conlin–Doc McLean high jinks are based on accounts in the *Homestead Daily Messenger* and the *Pittsburgh Press.* John McLean's funeral and his memorial service a year later were reported in the *Homestead Daily Messenger* and the *Pittsburgh Press.* The discussion of Homestead's seventy-fifth anniversary celebration is based upon the booklet prepared by the town and on accounts in the *Homestead Daily Messenger.* The discussion of Nikita Khrushchev's visit to Homestead and West Homestead is from *The New York Times.*

CHAPTER 18. "THE CREATIVE ENERGIES OF PRIVATE ENTERPRISE"

The discussion of the corporation's press parties is from reports given me over the years and from an account in *The Washington Post* by David Ignatius. The confrontation between Roger Blough and President John F. Kennedy was reported at length in *The New York Times,* and I have also drawn upon Hoopes. Elbert H. Gary complained in Tarbell of some of Andrew Carnegie's methods. Fairless in his autobiography criticized Taylor. William H. Johnstone's and C. William Verity, Jr.'s, remarks appeared in *Fortune,* October 1966. The industry's plans for spending on new technologies is recorded in *Fortune* in the same issue. Steve Simko discussed with me several times, as did numerous others, blue-collar and white-collar workers alike, the stealing at Homestead Works. The comments of Ray Hornak, Jack Melvin, Ed Salaj, and others on whom this section is based were made in conversations with me. The Human Relations Committee is discussed in Herling, in McDonald's autobiography and his interviews with Pennsylvania State University researchers, and in Sweeney. Several Homestead workers, both white- and blue-collar, in addition to those named, discussed the safety program with me. The discussion of the extended-vacation plan is based upon David J. McDonald's comments at the time and a discussion I had with a dozen striking Homestead workers, including Jack Bair, during the 1986–1987 strike. William J. Gaughan and Marty Costa discussed Black Friday with me, as did several other former white-collar men.

CHAPTER 19. OUT OF TOUCH

The section on Edgar B. Speer is based on accounts in *The New York Times* and *33: The Magazine of Metals Producing,* a trade magazine. The Speer quotation is from the June 1969 issue of *33.* Clarence B. Randall's observations appeared in *The New York Times Magazine.* The discussion of the David J. McDonald–I. W. Abel election is drawn from Herling, McDonald, and *The New York Times.* The discussion of Abel's reign is based upon Herling's book and *The New York Times.* The *Times* editorial ran on November 26, 1964. William J. Gaughan and others told me of the movie *Where's Joe?* The passage of the experimental negotiating agreement is based upon accounts in Lynd and in *The New York Times.* The *Times* editorial is from March 31, 1973. The Lloyd McBride–Edward Sadlowski campaign is based upon accounts at the time in *The New York Times* and in *The New York Times Magazine,* and upon two pieces reappraising the McBride-Sadlowski campaign, one in the *Columbia Journalism Review* by David Ignatius and another in the magazine *Working Papers* by Ed James. I have chatted numerous times with Sadlowski and have also talked with many other men and women who participated in the McBride-Sadlowski campaign. *The New York Times* covered the 1977 contract negotiations extensively, and I have drawn from those accounts in my discussion of the negotiations. Ray Hornak and Ed Salaj discussed the Homestead Works with me. The discussion of the steel mill closings is from *The New York Times.* I sat with Ronnie Weisen in his office and was given the material from the international union in December 1986.

CHAPTER 20. THE COMBINATION COMES APART

David M. Roderick's announcement was reported in *The New York Times*; his statement, "We have no plans for shutting down our Youngstown operation," is from Lynd. Roderick's remarks to Congressman Peter Kostmayer and his statement, "I learned a long time ago not to flinch," appear in Nader and Taylor. I observed Roderick's manner and that of the Pittsburgh press corps in press conferences in Pittsburgh and again at a corporation annual meeting in Detroit. For Roderick's biography I have drawn upon my observations and readings and my discussions of him with steel industry and union executives and on the account of Roderick in Nader and Taylor. The discussion of the end of the experimental negotiating agreement is from union information sheets and from my reporting and that of other reporters at

The New York Times. My account of the rise of the insurgent movement in the Monongahela Valley is based upon my reporting for *The New York Times* and my extensive reporting on the movement for this book. For this discussion I interviewed —some, several times—Steffi Domike, Larry Evans, Leslie Evans, Charles Honeywell, Staughton Lynd, Charles McCollester, Michelle McMills, Father Charles Owen Rice, Michael "Kentucky" Stout, the Reverend James Von Dreele, Ronnie Weisen, and others. The Reverend Von Dreele also kindly provided me with numerous clippings of the insurgents' movement over the years. The section on Weisen's background is based on interviews with him and others who knew him as a youth or participated with him in the maverick movement. I also had at my disposal, in describing the maverick movement and Weisen, copies of issues of *1397 Rank and File,* the mavericks' monthly newspaper, newsletters published over the years by the Denominational Ministry Strategy, and a history of Tri-State Conference on Steel written by Mc-Collester. Numbers of workers and ex-workers and Homestead district residents also shared their recollections and views of the insurgent movement with me. The portrait of Homestead in the 1980s draws upon my observations, files in the Carnegie Library of Homestead, and conversations with numerous Homestead residents, among them Joseph Chiodo, Marty Costa, George and Carol Couvaris, Betty Esper, Ann Hart, Mark Hornak, Ray Hornak, Sam Marks, Spanky O'Toole, Rich Terrick, and Margaret Vojtko. Roderick's statement that the corporation is "committed to remaining in the steel business in the Monongahela Valley" appears in Lynd. The announcement of construction of the Leona Shops and Apartments of Homestead Village, Pennsylvania, appeared in the Homestead booklet marking the town's one hundredth anniversary. The corporation's decision not to build a Conneaut, Ohio, Works was reported in the *Pittsburgh Post-Gazette,* the *Pittsburgh Press,* and *The New York Times.* I covered important junctures in the 1982–1983 negotiations, and I have drawn upon numerous corporation and union documents provided me at the time, among them "Steel and America," a May 1986 publication of the American Iron and Steel Institute, and "USS Today," published by U.S. Steel Corporation in June 1986. I also consulted Hoerr. I spent two days in 1982 with Rich Locher and his wife and also chatted with him twice on later occasions.

CHAPTER 21. REBELLION II

The closing of Mesta Machine was discussed in the *Pittsburgh Post-Gazette,* the *Pittsburgh Press,* and *The New York Times. The Wall Street Journal* followed with an excellent two-part series on how the company encountered its misfortunes. I also drew upon two histories of the Mesta company prepared by Mesta. The discussion of the actions by the Monongahela Valley insurgents that followed is based upon my reporting, which include interviews with numerous members of the insurgent movement, readings of the insurgents' newspapers and other publications, and of pieces from the *Pittsburgh Post-Gazette* and *Pittsburgh Press.* A number of Pittsburgh reporters did splendid work on plant closings and on the Monongahela Valley insurgent movement, and I am indebted to them. The discussion of the Local 1397 union hall is based upon my observations at the time and the recollections of Cheryl Bacco, Charles McCollester, Michelle McMills, Michael Stout, the Reverend James Von Dreele, Ronnie Weisen, and others. Margaret Vojtko's comment that "Homestead had to die" was made in conversation with me. I attended the Pittsburgh press conference at which Mike Locker unveiled his study of the Dorothy Six furnace. The Reverend D. Douglas Roth's colloquy with Judge Emil E. Narick was reported in the *Pittsburgh Post-Gazette*. Weisen, Von Dreele, and others shared their recollections of the DMS protests with me, and I attended the Duquesne, Pennsylvania, rally to save Dorothy Six. I was on the yellow school bus on which the insurgents conducted their January 1985 rally and followed the caravan to the cathedral and watched as Weisen read the theses. Stout told me of the treatment of the union insurgents by company executives following the reelection of Weisen and his team in February 1985.

CHAPTER 22. "WHO WOULD HAVE THOUGHT IT?"

I toured the shuttered Carnegie Library of Braddock with Ray Stell and interviewed Louis H. Washowich, mayor of McKeesport. Betsy and Arthur Carman and I spent an afternoon together in the Pizza Hut between Homestead and Duquesne. I observed several DMS actions in this period and have relied on reportage in the *Pittsburgh Post-Gazette* and *Pittsburgh Press,* as well as interviews with numerous participants. Ed Buzinka, Bob Krovocheck, and Bobby Schneider shared their thoughts with me in interviews. Chief Chris Kelly and I toured Homestead together on three occasions and talked with him several times. I interviewed at length four teachers at Steel Valley High School: Marie Coyne, Leslie Evans, Mary Edna Ruhaba, and Jennie Yuhaschek. I interviewed the manager of the local Goodwill store, Irene Schrecengost. I attended the meeting at the Local 1397 union hall at which the two men in pinstripe suits from Senator John Heinz's staff spoke; I also interviewed Rich Locher, among numerous other ex-workers, at that meeting. Joseph Chiodo related to me his conversation at his tavern with the two Heinz staff members. I spent part of a winter morning at the Couvaris's restaurant and interviewed George Couvaris at length at a later time.

CHAPTER 23. "THE BREAKUP OF LIFE AS WE KNEW IT"

I met Wendell Brucker at the union hall when I began this project and chatted with him a number of times, including the afternoon at the Ancient Order of Hibernians. I covered the DMS in 1986 or drew upon stories in the *Pittsburgh Post-Gazette* and *Pittsburgh Press.* I attended a union press conference in Pittsburgh at which the Lazard Frères study was discussed. The information on Joe Magarac is from *Joe Magarac and His U.S.A. Citizen Papers* by Irwin Shapiro (Pittsburgh: University of Pittsburgh Press, 1979). I visited Steel Valley High School several times and conducted extensive interviews with students and with Jerry Longo (the superintendent), John Tichon (an assistant to Longo), and Ray Supak (principal of Steel Valley High School), and counselors at the school. At the invitation of coach Jack Giran, I also attended Steel Valley High School football games at their home field and traveled with the team. I went to a senior prom and a graduation ceremony at the high school. I attended a number of meetings of the Homestead borough council. Chief Kelly related to me his efforts to close the Fantasia Health Spa. I interviewed Rich Terrick at length one spring morning at his home and later attended a Labor Day party he hosted at his home for a couple hundred of his friends and associates. Cheryl Bacco chatted with me one morning at the Local 1397 union hall and later at Chiodo's.

CHAPTER 24. RICH LOCHER IS DEAD, AND OTHER STORIES OF DESPAIR

I interviewed Father Bernard Costello, the pastor of St. Mary Magdalene's Roman Catholic Church, in his parish home and interviewed students and faculty members at St. Mary Magdalene's School. I interviewed Kelly Park twice at his office at Park Corporation in West Homestead. The fines levied on the corporation were reported in *The New York Times.* The Birmingham, Alabama, case was reported in *Business Week, The New York Times,* and *The Wall Street Journal.* The corporation's stock split was reported in *The New York Times* and by Reutter. I observed the closing of Local 1397's union hall and interviewed Richard Holoman, Red Hrabic, Bob Krovocheck, Ray McGuire, Bobby Schneider, Jimmie Sherlock, Bob Todd, Denny Wilcox, and others about their lives after the mill went down. I interviewed Weisen and other members of his work team about his job with the city of Pittsburgh, and also interviewed Michelle McMills and Michael Stout about their lives after the end of the insurgency. I spent an afternoon with Stout as he campaigned on election day and spent the evening at his first happy, then sad, campaign party. Cheryl Bacco discussed with me her life after she lost her job at the local and how Weisen helped her recover her severance pay. The Reverend Von Dreele helped me in tracing what happened to the DMS ministers. I chatted with Chief Kelly several times after he left Homestead for his new job in Baldwin, and he related to me, with some glee, how he got the Fantasia. Samuel Marks told me why he closed his card shop. The discussion of how Homestead, in its agony, became fashionable is based on my observations and reporting. I attended the Saturday morning meeting at which the architects told Homesteaders they should put on a flower show at the mill site, and I also observed the visit to Homestead by Prince Charles.

I would also like to especially thank the reporters and editors who for more than a century labored at the *Homestead Daily Messenger,* which, with its predecessor, the *Homestead Local News,* was Homestead's local paper from 1891 to 1979. It is common wisdom that journalism is the first rough draft of history. This is not always true, for—as the columns of almost a century of the *Homestead Daily Messenger* demonstrate—journalism is often the only and often an accurate and surprisingly complete draft of history.

SELECTED BIBLIOGRAPHY

BOOKS

Adamic, Louis. *Dynamite*. New York: Viking, 1934.

Adams, Walter, ed. *The Structure of American Industry*. New York: Macmillan, 1977.

Alinsky, Saul. *John L. Lewis: An Unauthorized Biography*. New York: Putnam, 1949.

Allen, Frederick Lewis. *The Great Pierpont Morgan*. New York: Harper & Row, 1948.

Atkinson, Linda. *Mother Jones: The Most Dangerous Woman in America*. New York: Crown Publishers, 1978.

Auerbach, Jerold S. *Labor and Liberty: The La Follette Committee and the New Deal*. New York: Bobbs-Merrill, 1966.

Balch, Emily Greene. *Our Slavic Fellow Citizens*. New York: Charities Publication Committee, 1910.

Berglund, Abraham. *The United States Steel Corporation*. New York: Columbia University Press, 1907.

Bernstein, Irving. *Turbulent Years*. Boston: Houghton Mifflin, 1970.

Bodnar, John, Roger Simon, and Michael P. Weber. *Lives of Their Own*. Urbana, Ill.: University of Illinois Press, 1982.

Bridge, James Howard. *The Inside History of the Carnegie Steel Company*. New York: The Aldine Book Company, 1903.

Brody, David. *Labor in Crisis: The Steel Strike of 1919*. Urbana, Ill.: University of Illinois Press, 1987.

————. *Steelworkers in America: The Non-Union Era*. Cambridge: Harvard University Press, 1960.

————. *Workers in Industrial America*. New York: Oxford University Press, 1980.

Brooks, Robert R. R. *As Steel Goes, . . .* New Haven: Yale University Press, 1940.

Brooks, Thomas R. *Clint: A Biography of a Labor Intellectual*. New York: Atheneum, 1978.

Burgoyne, Arthur G. *Homestead: A Complete History of the Struggle of July, 1892*. Pittsburgh: University of Pittsburgh Press, 1979.

Butler, Joseph G. *Recollections of Men and Events*. New York, 1927.

Byington, Margaret F. *Homestead: The Households of a Mill Town*. Pittsburgh: University of Pittsburgh Press, 1974.

Carnegie, Andrew. *The Autobiography of Andrew Carnegie*. Boston: Northeastern University Press, 1986.

————. *Triumphant Democracy: Or Fifty Years' March of the Republic.* Boulder, Col.: Johnson Reprint Corporation, 1971 (reprint of 1886 edition)

Casson, Herbert. *The Romance of Steel: The Story of a Thousand Millions.* New York: A. S. Barnes, 1907.

Caute, David. *The Great Fear: The Anti-Communist Purge Under Truman and Eisenhower.* New York: Simon & Schuster, 1978.

Cochran, Bert. *Labor and Communism.* Princeton: Princeton University Press, 1977.

Commons, John R., et al. *History of Labour in the United States.* 4 vols. New York: Macmillan, 1918.

Cotter, Arundel. *The Authentic History of the United States Steel Corporation.* New York, 1921.

Crandall, Robert. *The U.S. Steel Industry in Recurrent Crisis.* Washington, D.C.: Brookings, 1981.

Davis, Horace B. *Labor and Steel.* New York: International, 1933.

De Caux, Len. *Labor Radical: From the Wobblies to the C.I.O.* Boston: Beacon Press, 1970.

De Kruif, Paul. *Seven Iron Men.* New York: Harcourt Brace, 1929.

Dickerson, Dennis C. *Out of the Crucible.* Albany, N.Y.: State University of New York Press, 1986.

Dubofsky, Melvyn, and Warren Van Tine. *John L. Lewis.* Urbana, Ill.: University of Illinois Press, 1986.

————, eds. *Labor Leaders in America.* Urbana, Ill.: University of Illinois Press, 1987.

Eggert, Gerald G. *Steelmasters and Labor Reform, 1886–1923.* Pittsburgh: University of Pittsburgh Press, 1981.

Fairless, Benjamin F. *It Could Happen Only in the U.S.: A Coal Miner's Son Describes His Remarkable Career That Led from Pigeon Run, Ohio, to the Summit of American Industry.* New York: Time Inc., 1956.

Feldman, Jacob. *The Jewish Experience in Western Pennsylvania.* Pittsburgh: The Historical Society of Western Pennsylvania, 1986.

Fisher, Douglas A. *The Epic of Steel.* New York: Harper & Row, 1963.

————. *Steel in the War.* New York: United States Steel Corporation, 1946.

————. *Steel Serves the Nation: The Fifty Year Story of United States Steel.* Pittsburgh: United States Steel Corporation, 1951.

Fitch, John A. *The Steel Workers.* New York: Russell Sage Foundation, 1911.

Foster, William Z. *The Great Steel Strike and Its Lessons.* New York: B. W. Huebsch, Inc., 1920.

————. *Organizing Steel.* New York: International Publishers, 1936.

Girdler, Tom M. *Boot Straps.* New York: Scribner's, 1943.

Golden, Clinton S., and Harold J. Ruttenberg. *The Dynamics of Industrial Democracy.* New York: Harper & Brothers, 1942.

Green, Marguerite. *The National Civic Federation and the American Labor Movement: 1900–1925.* Washington, D.C.: Catholic University of America Press, 1956.

Harvey, George. *Henry Clay Frick: The Man.* New York: Scribner's, 1928.

Hendrick, Burton J. *The Life of Andrew Carnegie.* New York: Doubleday Doran, 1932.

Herling, John. *Right to Challenge: People and Power in the Steelworkers Union.* New York: Harper & Row, 1972.

Hessen, Robert. *Steel Titan: The Life of Charles M. Schwab*. New York: Oxford University Press, 1975.

Hoerr, John. *And the Wolf Finally Came*. Pittsburgh: University of Pittsburgh Press, 1988.

Holbrook, Stewart H. *Iron Brew*. New York: Macmillan, 1939.

Holway, John. *Voices from the Great Negro Baseball Leagues*. New York: Dodd, Mead, 1975.

———— *Blackball Stars*. New York: Meckler Books, 1988.

Hoopes, Roy. *The Steel Crisis*. New York: The John Day Company, 1963.

Horan, James D. *The Pinkertons: The Detective Dynasty That Made History*. New York: Crown Publishers, 1968.

Interchurch World Movement. *Public Opinion and the Steel Strike*. Commission of Inquiry, 1921.

Jones, Mary Harris. *The Autobiography of Mother Jones*. Chicago: Charles H. Kerr, 1980.

Kelly, George, and Edwin Beachler. *Man of Steel: The Story of David J. McDonald*. New York: North American Book Co., 1954.

Livernash, E. Robert, ed. *Collective Bargaining in the Basic Steel Industry*. Washington, D.C.: Department of Labor, 1961.

Livesay, Harold C. *Andrew Carnegie and the Rise of Big Business*. Boston: Little, Brown and Company, 1975.

Lorant, Stefan. *Pittsburgh: The Story of an American City*. Garden City, N.Y.: Doubleday, 1964.

Lynd, Staughton. *The Fight Against Shutdowns: Youngstown's Steel Mill Closings*. San Pedro, Calif.: Singlejack Books, 1982.

Lynd, Staughton and Alice. *Rank and File: Personal Histories of Working Class Organizers*. Princeton: Princeton University Press, 1981.

McCardell, Lee. *Ill-Starred General: Braddock of the Coldstream Guards*. Pittsburgh: University of Pittsburgh Press, 1958.

McDonald, David J. *Union Man*. New York: E. P. Dutton & Co. Inc., 1969.

Mills, C. Wright. *The New Men of Power: America's Labor Leaders*. New York: Harcourt Brace, 1948.

Montgomery, David. *Workers' Control in America*. Cambridge, England: Cambridge University Press, 1979.

————. *The Fall of the House of Labor*. England: Cambridge University Press, 1989.

Murray, Philip. *Organized Labor and Production*. New York: Harper & Brothers, 1940.

Nader, Ralph, and William Taylor. *The Big Boys: Power and Position in American Business*. New York: Pantheon, 1986.

O'Connor, Harvey. *Steel—Dictator*. New York: The John Day Company, 1935.

Perkins, Frances. *The Roosevelt I Knew*. New York: Viking, 1946.

Perrett, Geoffrey. *America in the Twenties: A History*. New York: Simon & Schuster, 1982.

Powers, George. *The Cradle of Steel Unionism: Monongahela Valley, Pa.* East Chicago, Ind.: Figueroa Printers, Inc., 1972.

Reutter, Mark. *Sparrows Point*. New York: Summit Books, 1988.

Robinson, Jesse S. *The Amalgamated Association of Iron, Steel and Tin Workers*. Baltimore: John Hopkins, 1920.

Rowan, Richard L. *The Negro in the Steel Industry.* Philadelphia: University of Pennsylvania Press, 1968.

Rowan, Richard W. *The Pinkertons.* Boston: Little, Brown, 1931.

Schwab, Charles M. *Succeeding with What You Have.* Privately printed, 1917.

Sheppard, Muriel Earley. *Cloud by Day: A Story of Coal and Coke and People.* Uniontown, Pa.: Heritage, 1947.

Spahr, Charles B. *America's Working People.* New York: Longmans, Green & Co., 1900.

Stowell, Myron R. *Fort Frick: Or the Siege of Homestead.* Pittsburgh: Pittsburgh Printing Co., 1893.

Sweeney, Vincent D. *The United Steelworkers of America.* Pittsburgh: The United Steelworkers of America, 1956.

Tarbell, Ida M. *The Life of Elbert H. Gary.* New York: Appleton, 1926.

Taylor, Myron C. *Ten Years of Steel.* These are extensions of remarks made at the meeting of stockholders of the United States Steel Corporation in Hoboken, N.J., 1938.

Ulman, Lloyd. *The Government of the Steel Workers Union.* New York: Wiley, 1962.

Van Tine, Warren. *The Making of the Labor Bureaucrat: Union Leadership in the United States, 1870–1920.* Amherst, Mass.: University of Massachusetts Press, 1973.

Vorse, Mary Heaton. *Labor's New Millions.* New York: Boni and Liveright, 1920.

———. *Men and Steel.* New York: Boni and Liveright, 1920.

———. *A Footnote to Folly.* New York: Farrar & Rinehart, 1935.

Walker, Charles Rumford. *Steel: The Diary of a Furnace Worker.* Boston: Atlantic Monthly Press, 1922.

———. *Steeltown.* New York: Harper & Brothers, 1950.

Wall, Joseph Frazier. *Andrew Carnegie.* New York: Oxford University Press, 1970.

Ware, Norman. *The Labor Movement in the United States 1860–1895.* New York: Appleton, 1929.

Wechsler, James A. *Labor Baron.* New York: William Morrow, 1944.

Wolff, Leon. *Lockout.* New York: Harper & Row, 1964.

The WPA Guide to Pennsylvania: The Keystone State. New York, 1936.

Yellen, Samuel. *American Labor Struggles.* New York, Harcourt Brace, 1936.

MAGAZINES AND REPORTS

Adamic, Louis. "The Steel Strike Collapses." *The Nation,* July 4, 1934.

"The American Federation of Labor." *Fortune,* December 1933.

Bemis, Edward W. "The Homestead Strike." *The Journal of Political Economy,* June 1894.

"Big Steel's Men." *Life,* November 11, 1946.

Brown, Mark. "Homestead Steel Works and Carrie Furnaces," Washington: National Park Service, 1991.

Chamberlain, John. "The Steelworkers." *Fortune,* February 1944.

"The Corporation." A four-part series in *Fortune,* March, April, May, and June 1936.

"Employees as Partners." *Harper's Weekly,* March 7, 1903.

Fitch, John A. "Old Age at 40." *American Magazine,* March 1911.

———. "A Man Can Talk in Homestead." *Survey Graphic,* February 1936.

Galenson, Walter. "The Unionization of the American Steel Industry." *International Review of Social History,* 1956.

Garland, Hamlin. "Homestead and Its Perilous Trades." *McClure's Magazine,* June 1894.

Garraty, John A. "The United States Steel Corporation vs. Labor." *Labor History,* Winter 1960.

"The Great Labor Upheaval." *Fortune,* October 1936.

Hard, William, "Making Steel and Killing Men." *Everybody's Magazine,* November 1907.

Harding, Rebecca. "Life in the Iron Mills." *Atlantic Monthly,* April 1861.

Hogg, Bernard J. "Homestead Strike of 1892," unpublished Ph.D. thesis. University of Chicago, 1943.

"It Happened in Steel." *Fortune,* May 1937.

"Man of Steel." *Time,* July 20, 1959.

McDonald, Dwight. "Steelmasters: The Big Four." *The Nation,* August 29, 1936.

McDonald, John. "Steel Is Rebuilding for a New Era." *Fortune,* October 1966.

Parton, James. "Pittsburgh," *Atlantic Monthly,* January 1868.

Randall, Clarence B. "Business, Too, Has Its Ivory Towers," *The New York Times Magazine,* July 8, 1963.

Raskin, A. H. "The Mild Yet Militant Chief of the CIO." *The New York Times Magazine,* July 20, 1952.

Ruttenberg, Harold J. "The Big Morgue." *Survey Graphic,* April 1936.

"Steel Mill, Homestead, Pennsylvania," United States Defense Plant Corporation, Washington, undated.

"The Steel Rail." *Fortune,* December 1933.

"Steel: Report on the War Years." *Fortune,* May 1945.

"Through the Mill with Ben and Dave." *Colliers,* June 11, 1954.

"U.S.A." *Fortune,* November 1946.

U.S. Bureau of Labor. *Report on Conditions of Employment in the Iron and Steel Industry.* 4 vols. Washington, D.C., 1911, 1913.

U.S. Commissioner of Corporations. *Report on the Steel Industry.* 3 vols. Washington, D.C., 1911–1913.

U.S. Congress. House. Committee on the Judiciary. *Investigation of the Homestead Troubles.* 52nd Cong., 1892–1893.

U.S. Congress. House. Stanley Committee. *Hearings of the Committee on the Investigation of the United States Steel Corporation.* 8 vols. 62nd Cong., 2d sess., 1911–1912.

U.S. Congress. Senate. Committee on Labor & Education. *Investigation of Strike in the Steel Industry.* 66th Cong., 1st sess., 1919.

U.S. Immigration. *Report on Immigrants in Industries, Iron and Steel Manufacturing.* Washington, D.C., 1911.

"The U.S. Steel Story." *33: The Magazine of Metals Producing,* February 1968.

U.S. vs. U.S. Steel Corporation 223 F55 (1912). Testimony, 30 vols. Defendants' Exhibits, 9 vols., Government Exhibits, 14 vols.

INDEX